Kerr-Brown, A. PSYC 3002

Kerr-Brown, A. PSYC 3002

CULTURE AND PSYCHOLOGY

CULTURE AND PSYCHOLOGY

SIXTH EDITION

David Matsumoto

San Francisco State University and Humintell

Linda Juang

University of Potsdam

CENGAGE
Learning™

Australia • Brazil • Mexico • Singapore • United Kingdom • United States

CENGAGE
Learning®

Culture and Psychology,
Sixth Edition
David Matsumoto, Linda Juang

Product Director: Erin Joyner

Product Manager: Timothy Matray

Content Developer and Senior Content Project Manager: Tanya Nigh

Product Assistant: Kimiya Hojjat

Art Director: Vernon Boes

Manufacturing Planner: Karen Hunt

Production Service and Compositor: Lumina Datamatics Inc.

Photo and Text Researcher: Lumina Datamatics Inc.

Text and Cover Designer: Lisa Henry

Cover Image: Masterfile, alexmakatova

For product information and technology assistance, contact us at **Cengage Learning Customer & Sales Support, 1-800-354-9706.**

For permission to use material from this text or product, submit all requests online at **www.cengage.com/permissions.** Further permissions questions can be e-mailed to **permissionrequest@cengage.com.**

Library of Congress Control Number: 2015960088

ISBN: 978-1-305-64895-1

Cengage Learning
20 Channel Center Street
Boston, MA 02210
USA

Cengage Learning is a leading provider of customized learning solutions with employees residing in nearly 40 different countries and sales in more than 125 countries around the world. Find your local representative at **www.cengage.com.**

Cengage Learning products are represented in Canada by Nelson Education, Ltd.

To learn more about Cengage Learning Solutions, visit **www.cengage.com.**

Purchase any of our products at your local college store or at our preferred online store **www.cengagebrain.com.**

Printed in the United States of America
Print Number: 01   Print Year: 2016

To the memories of my mom and dad, for their wonderful teachings and the great family they gave to me.

—David Matsumoto

To Tayo and Keanu, for being my everyday reminders of our increasingly multicultural world.

—Linda Juang

ABOUT THE AUTHORS

DAVID MATSUMOTO received his B.A. from the University of Michigan in 1981 with high honors in psychology and Japanese. He subsequently earned his M.A. (1983) and Ph.D. (1986) in psychology from the University of California at Berkeley. He is currently professor of psychology and director of the Culture and Emotion Research Laboratory at San Francisco State University, where he has been working since 1989. He is also director of Humintell, LLC, a company that provides research, consultation, and training on nonverbal behavioral analysis and cross-cultural adaptation. He has studied culture, emotion, social interaction, and communication for over 30 years. His books include well-known titles such as *Culture and Psychology,* the *APA Handbook of Nonverbal Communication* (ed.), *Nonverbal Communication: Science and Applications* (ed.), the *Cambridge Dictionary of Psychology* (ed.), and *Cross-Cultural Research Methods in Psychology* (ed.). He is the recipient of many awards and honors in the field of psychology, and is the series editor for the Cambridge University Press series on *Culture and Psychology.* He is also former editor-in-chief for the *Journal of Cross-Cultural Psychology.*

LINDA JUANG is a professor of diversity and education at the University of Potsdam, Germany. She earned her B.A. in child development from the University of Minnesota and her M.A. and Ph.D. in developmental psychology from Michigan State University, and was also a postdoctoral fellow at the University of Jena in Germany for three years. Over the past 20 years, she has studied adolescent development in various family and cultural contexts. She has published and presented studies on immigration-related issues such as ethnic identity, acculturation, and adjustment of culturally diverse adolescents and youth in the United States, Germany, and China.

BRIEF CONTENTS

CONTENTS

3 Enculturation   57

7   Culture and Gender   147

8   Culture and Cognition   171

9 Culture and Emotion 202

10 Culture, Language, and Communication 226

12 Culture and Psychological Disorders   278

13 Culture and Treatment for Psychological Disorders   310

WE WOULD LIKE TO BEGIN BY FIRST THANKING YOU—past, current, and prospective future users of our book. We sincerely appreciate all of you for all the hard work and efforts you make in the classroom every day in service of the education of future generations of our world, and for the greater good that comes from those efforts. We appreciate all the kind notes, comments, questions, and messages that many of you have sent to us throughout the years. And we appreciate all of you who come to introduce yourselves at meetings and conferences. It is especially a joy to meet you in person, and we thank you from the bottom of our hearts for the reception you always give us.

We would also like to thank the reviewers of the previous edition of the book. They provided us with many valuable comments, which guided us in the current revision. We thank the reviewers especially for the many positive comments about so many parts of the book. We can only hope that our revisions have improved the book even more.

We also would like to thank the editors and production staff at Cengage. They have been professional, competent, and courteous throughout the years, and have kept us on track in the revision of this edition. We also thank Hyisung C. Hwang for her review and edit of the entire book manuscript from start to finish. Her comments and suggestions were invaluable and helped us to improve the readability and content of the material tremendously.

There are many changes that we have made that are applicable throughout the book. With regard to content, you will see that we have reorganized the structure of the book. We moved the chapter on self and identity (formerly Chapter 13) up to Chapter 5. We follow this with chapters on personality (Chapter 6) and gender (Chapter 7), followed by cognition (Chapter 8) and emotion (Chapter 9). We hope that this structural change aids readers in moving through the material in a way that presents the larger factors of influence (development, personality, gender) before discussing specific topics (emotion, cognition, language, social behavior, etc.).

Also with regard to content, we have tightened the writing throughout, and in many cases have deleted material that was superfluous to the main message of the chapter. We did this because one of the concerns we had about the book was that we were presenting too many "facts" without a coherent message in some places. This situation was partly due to the burgeoning numbers of cross-cultural studies that have been published in recent years, and our previous wish to be comprehensive and inclusive of the literature. But sometimes this lost our focus on the important messages of the chapter. Thus we decided to reduce the number of facts by removing material we deemed superfluous to the main message of each chapter so that readers can stay focused on that main message.

We have also made a number of significant changes with regard to pedagogy. In this edition, you'll notice a larger trim size for the book, which should aid in reading. We have also added text call-outs to important phrases, and now include glossary definitions in the margins when the words first appear. We have added more figures and tables in all chapters to break up the monotony of reading and to provide visual examples of the text material. We have also added substantially more cross-referencing to related topics in other chapters throughout the book.

In addition to these major changes described above, we list below the specific changes we have made in each chapter:

Chapter 1—An Introduction to Culture and Psychology

■ Simplified the writing and the message throughout, deleting sections that were not directly relevant to the main message of the chapter, and reordered some material

■ Included more call-outs to other professions as end users are not always psychology students

■ Clarified the concept of universal psychological toolkits

■ Included more call-outs to material that will be explored in the rest of the book, cross-referencing other chapters

■ Updated figures and added a few more to aid understanding; dropped old Figure 1.2, which was too complex

■ Updated the writing with two new citations

Chapter 2—Cross-Cultural Research Methods

■ Simplified the writing and the message throughout, especially concerning the types of cross-cultural research and types of cross-cultural comparisons

■ Deleted sections that were not directly relevant to the main message of the chapter

■ Reordered some material

■ Reincorporated brief discussion of the evolution of cross-cultural research

■ Included more figures and tables to organize and summarize the material, including tables organizing types of cross-cultural research and types of cross-cultural comparisons

■ Redrew Table 2.1 and split into two tables

■ Expanded on the "Exploration and Discovery" section

■ Added a new question in the "Suggestions for Further Exploration" that invites students to find their culture and compare its scores with other scores and their experiences

Chapter 3—Enculturation

■ Simplified the writing and the message throughout

■ Added more figures to aid understanding

■ Deleted Figure 3.2 (from the 5th edition) as it was unclear

■ Deleted overlapping material with former Chapter 5 on math achievement. The education section now focuses on the education system as an important source of enculturation.

■ Added content on "tiger mothering"

■ Updated the writing with 13 new citations

Chapter 4—Culture and Developmental Processes

■ Added a section on Vygotsky's sociocultural theory on cognitive development

■ Updated, deleted, and rewrote sections on attachment to reflect the newest research and theorizing about this topic

■ Included more figures and tables (such as Piaget's and Kohlberg's stages) to organize and summarize the material

■ Deleted sections that were not directly relevant to the main message of the chapter (such as section on "Other Cognitive Theories" and "Other Developmental Processes")

■ Updated the writing with four new citations

Chapter 5—Culture, Self, and Identity (formerly Chapter 13)

■ Moved the section on attributional styles to Chapter 14, as we considered it to better fit the chapter there, especially with the decision to move this chapter up in the book sequence

■ Paid attention to repositioning the theory of independent vs. interdependent self-construals within a larger perspective of theoretical views of the self and the evolution of thought concerning culture and self

■ Simplified the writing and the message throughout, reordering and restructuring as necessary

■ Included more figures and tables to organize and summarize the material

■ Updated the writing with 12 new citations

Chapter 6—Culture and Personality (formerly Chapter 10)

■ Simplified the writing and the message throughout, reordering and restructuring as necessary

■ Included one additional figure and one additional table to organize and summarize the material

■ One figure included clarified the five-factor theory (FFT); also revised the writing in this section to clarify the distinction between the five-factor model (FFM) and FFT

■ Updated the writing with nine new citations

Chapter 7—Culture and Gender (formerly Chapter 6)

■ Included a new table as suggested comparing the differences between "sex" and "gender" as described in the book

■ Moved the section on sex from Chapter 14 to this chapter

■ Consolidated the writing on jealousy that overlapped with that elsewhere

■ Updated the writing with three new citations

Chapter 8—Culture and Cognition (formerly Chapter 5)

- Provided an overall structure for the chapter in a new figure early on, focusing on attention, then sensation and perception, then higher order thinking in the first half of the chapter, and consciousness and intelligence in the second half

- Consequently, moved the section on attention up first before sensation and perception

- Consolidated and integrated info on math performance from Chapter 3; reduced the amount of facts listed in the section on math and focused on the cross-cultural elements

- Figure 5.4 (now Figure 8.8) was made larger

- Reduced the amount of coverage in the section on intelligence, focusing on cross-cultural aspects

- Updated the writing with nine new citations

Chapter 9—Culture and Emotion (formerly Chapter 8)

- Moved the initial section on the cultural regulation of emotion to later, after the presentation of basic emotions, and integrated with the section on the "Cultural Calibration of Emotions"

- Separated the discussion of cultural regulation of basic emotions, the cultural construction of subjective experience, and cultural construction of concepts, attitudes, etc. into three separate sections

- Dropped the detailed discussion of front-end calibration, and cleaned up the presentation of front- and back-end calibration throughout, simplifying the description

- Redrew original Figure 8.10 into new, simpler figure

- Added a new reflection question at the end of the chapter

- Updated the writing with 12 new citations

Chapter 10—Culture, Language, and Communication (formerly Chapter 9)

- Added two new figures and one new table to facilitate understanding, especially to elaborate on cultural differences in nonverbal behaviors

- Included new section concerning recent research on possible bilingual advantages in cognitive processing

- Updated the writing with 21 new citations

Chapter 11—Culture and Health (formerly Chapter 7)

- Added more figures to illustrate chapter concepts

- Added discussion on an emerging field of study—cultural neuroscience

- Rearranged some sections for better flow

- Deleted sections not relevant to main message of chapter

- Former Figure 7.7 has been updated into a better graphic

- Acculturation is discussed in this chapter and non-Western remedies are discussed in Chapter 13
- Updated the writing with 12 new citations

Chapter 12—Culture and Psychological Disorders

- Completely updated section to include the newest DSM V conceptualization of "cultural syndromes of distress"
- Added information on the upcoming revisions for the ICD-11
- Added more figures and tables (such as table summarizing schizophrenia, depression, and anxiety) to illustrate key chapter concepts
- Rearranged some sections for better flow
- Deleted sections not relevant to main message of chapter
- Added more detail on the CBCL
- Added links to the ICD and DSM websites where students can find more detailed information on some of the issues discussed in the chapter
- Updated the writing with six new citations

Chapter 13—Culture and Treatment for Psychological Disorders

- Added more figures to illustrate chapter concepts
- Rearranged some sections for better flow
- Updated terminology to clarify indigenous healing, traditional medicine, and complementary medicine
- Updated the writing with eight new citations

Chapter 14—Culture and Social Behavior

- Moved the material on attributions from Chapter 5 to this chapter
- Moved the material on sex to Chapter 7
- Added a brief description of the sanctions used in the Yamagishi (1986) experiment
- Tightened up and clarified the discussion of the origin of stereotypes
- Dropped the discussion concerning "Need for Cognitive Closure" in the section on acculturation
- Included a new table on the content of stereotypes from 1933, 1951, and 1969
- Also included a new table from Karlins et al.'s (1969) analysis of changes in the favorableness of stereotype ratings across time
- Also included a new table from Madon et al.'s (2001) study of stereotypes
- Increased the overall number of tables and figures throughout to be commensurate with other chapters
- Tightened the writing throughout
- Updated the references with 17 new citations

Chapter 15—Culture and Organizations

- Updated the data in Table 15.4
- Changed the title and labels in Table 15.8 to be less offensive
- Redrew Figure 15.2 to simplify its message and content
- Included new writing on "Culture Shock and Reverse Culture Shock" in section on "Overseas Assignments"
- Tightened the writing throughout
- Updated the references with 10 new citations

We are excited about the many changes and improvements that were made to the book. We are also especially excited about the interest and growth in cultural and cross-cultural psychology today around the world. We sincerely hope that this book can help to facilitate that excitement even more in all readers, and to encourage strong, critical thinking about culture and psychology in the future. As always, if you have any comments or suggestions on how we can continually improve this work, please don't hesitate to let us know.

Finally, although we are indebted to so many people who have helped us along the way in the writing of this book, any errors in the book are only ours.

David Matsumoto and Linda Juang
San Francisco, CA, and Potsdam, Germany
September, 2015

1

An Introduction to Culture and Psychology

Most of what we know about the human mind, psychological processes, and human behavior comes from scientific research conducted in the United States involving American university students enrolled in introductory psychology courses as study participants. The information researchers get from those studies form the basis of what we think we know about people, and the basis of mainstream psychology. In this book we ask this simple question: Is what we know in mainstream psychology applicable for most people of the world? Besides raising that question, this book also looks to research involving participants from other cultures for those answers.

Why is asking that question important? All we have to do is to see how rapidly the world around us is changing, and how we live, work, play, and interact with people from many different cultural backgrounds more today than ever before. Think about this: Just over a century ago in 1904,

- The average life expectancy in the United States was 47 years.
- Only 14 percent of the homes in the United States had a bathtub.
- Only 8 percent of the homes had a telephone.
- A 3-minute call from Denver to New York City cost $11.
- There were only 8,000 cars in the United States, and only 144 miles of paved roads.
- The maximum speed limit in most cities was 10 mph.
- Alabama, Mississippi, Iowa, and Tennessee were each more heavily populated than California. With a mere 1.4 million residents, California was only the 21st most-populous state in the union.
- The average wage in the United States was 22 cents an hour; the average U.S. worker made between $200 and $400 per year.
- More than 95 percent of all births in the United States took place at home.
- Ninety percent of all U.S. physicians had no college education; instead, they attended medical schools, many of which were condemned in the press and by the government as "substandard."
- Sugar cost 4 cents a pound; eggs were 14 cents a dozen; coffee cost 15 cents a pound.
- Most women washed their hair only once a month and used borax or egg yolks for shampoo.
- The five leading causes of death in the United States were pneumonia and influenza, tuberculosis, diarrhea, heart disease, and stroke.
- The population of Las Vegas was 30.
- Crossword puzzles, canned beer, and iced tea had not yet been invented.
- There was no Mother's Day or Father's Day.
- One in 10 U.S. adults could not read or write.
- Only 6 percent of Americans had graduated high school.
- Marijuana, heroin, and morphine were all available over the counter at corner drugstores. According to one pharmacist, "Heroin clears the complexion, gives buoyancy to the mind, regulates the stomach and the bowels, and is, in fact, a perfect guardian of health."
- Eighteen percent of households in the United States had at least one full-time servant or domestic help.

- There were only about 230 reported murders in the entire United States.
- And we got this list from someone else whom we have never met, without typing it ourselves, on the Internet, which did not exist, on a computer, which did not exist.

The world is changing at an amazingly rapid pace, and one of the most important ways in which it is changing is in terms of cultural diversity. This increasingly diversifying world has created a wonderful environment for personal challenge and growth, but it also brings with it an increased potential for misunderstandings, confusion, and conflict.

Cultural diversity and intercultural relations are some of our biggest challenges. Those challenges are also our biggest opportunities. If we can meet those challenges and leverage them, we can achieve a potential in diversity and intercultural relations that will result in far more than the sum of the individual components that comprise that diverse universe. This sum will result in tremendous personal growth for many individuals, as well as in positive social evolution, bringing about mutual welfare and benefit built on interpersonal and intercultural respect.

This book was written with this belief—to meet the challenge of cultural diversity and turn that challenge into opportunity. Doing so is not easy. It requires each of us to take an honest look at our own cultural background and heritage, and at their merits and limitations. Fear, rigidity, and sometimes stubborn pride come with any type of honest assessment. Yet without that assessment, we cannot meet this challenge and improve intercultural relations.

In academia, that assessment begs fundamental questions about what is taught in our colleges and universities today. To ask how cultural diversity potentially changes the nature of the truths and principles of human behavior delivered in the halls of science is to question the pillars of much of our knowledge about the world and about human behavior. From time to time, we need to shake those pillars to see just how sturdy they are. This is especially true in the social sciences and particularly in psychology—the science concerned with people's mental processes and behaviors.

▶ Psychology with a Cultural Perspective

The Goals of Psychology

Psychology as a discipline is well equipped to meet the challenge of cultural diversity. One of the ways psychology has met this challenge is by recognizing the large impact culture has on psychological processes and human behavior. In the past few decades, a new and thriving subdiscipline within psychology known as **cultural psychology** has emerged to capture this spirit. In order to get a better handle on what cultural psychology is all about, it is important first to have a good grasp of the goals of psychology.

As a discipline, the field of psychology essentially has two main goals. The first is to build a body of knowledge about people. Psychologists seek to understand behavior when it happens, explain why it happens, and even predict it before it happens. Psychologists achieve this by conducting research and creating theories of behavior based on the findings from that research.

The second goal of psychology involves allowing others to take that body of knowledge and apply it to intervene in people's lives to help improve those lives. Psychologists achieve this in many ways: as therapists, counselors, trainers, and

cultural psychology
A subdiscipline within psychology that examines the cultural foundations of psychological processes and human behavior. It includes theoretical and methodological frameworks that posit an important role for culture and its influence on mental processes behavior, and vice versa.

FIGURE 1.1
The Goals of Psychology
as a Discipline

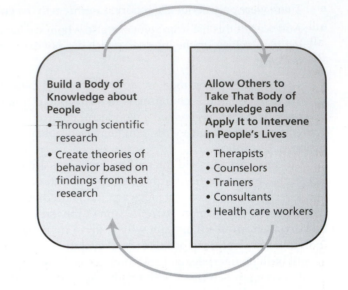

consultants. The field of psychology also achieves this goal by providing information to students and professionals in many other fields, such as nursing and health care, businesspersons, and teachers, to help them in their professions as well. Psychologists and many others work on the front lines, dealing directly with people to affect their lives in a positive fashion (Figure 1.1).

The two goals of psychology—creating a body of knowledge and applying that knowledge—are closely related. Psychologists and other professionals who are informed by psychology take what psychology as a field has collectively learned about human behavior and use that knowledge as a basis for their applications and interventions. This learning initially comes in the form of academic training in universities. But it continues well after formal education has ended, through continuing education and individual scholarship—reviewing the literature, attending conferences, and joining and participating in professional organizations. Psychologists and professionals in many other fields engage in a lifelong learning process that helps them intervene in people's lives more effectively, all influenced by research and knowledge generated in psychology. Researchers often understand the practical implications of their work, and many are well aware that the value of psychological theory and research is often judged by its practical usefulness in society (see, for example, Gergen, Gulerce, Lock, & Misra, 1996). Theories are tested for their validity not only in the halls of science but also on the streets, and they should be revised because of what happens on those streets. Real life is ground truth for psychology.

Culture and Psychology

Because knowledge generation is an important part of psychology, we need to have a good grasp of how that knowledge is generated in the first place, and that is through scientific research. As we mentioned at the beginning of this chapter, most research on human behavior reported in mainstream psychology comes from studies conducted in the United States involving American university students enrolled in introductory psychology courses as study participants. Thus, most knowledge we have in psychology is based on studies with American students.

Considering that U.S. Americans comprise only a small fraction of the world population (around 5%), some scholars have questioned the applicability of findings to all or most people around the world based so much on a single demographic (Arnett, 2008). Some have suggested that most research to date is based on WEIRDOS—Western, educated, industrialized, rich, and democratic cultures—and is severely limited because WEIRDOS aren't representative of everyone as a whole and that psychologists routinely use them to make broad, and quite likely false, claims about what drives human behavior (Henrich, Heine, & Norenzayan, 2010).

We don't take such an extreme view; we believe that there is nothing inherently wrong with such research, and the findings obtained from American samples are definitely true for those samples at the times the studies were conducted. Those findings may be replicated across multiple samples using different methods, and many findings weather tests for scientific rigor that would normally render them acceptable as a truth or principle about human behavior. And, there are a number of universal psychological processes that can certainly be tested on WEIRDOS and that are likely applicable to non-WEIRDOS. Thus, rather than raising questions specifically about WEIRDOS, we believe that psychology should question the characteristics of the people in *any* study: Is what we know about human behavior true for all people, regardless of gender, race, ethnicity, culture, class, or lifestyle (see Figure 1.2)?

Cultural psychology asks this question by conducting research with people of differing cultural backgrounds, and uses cross-cultural research as the primary research method that tests the cultural parameters of psychological knowledge. **Cross-cultural research** involves participants of differing cultural backgrounds and allows for comparisons of findings across those cultures. Cross-cultural research is a method that allows psychologists to examine how knowledge about people and their behaviors from one culture may or may not hold for people from other cultures.

As a method, cross-cultural research can be understood as a matter of *scientific philosophy*—that is, the logic underlying the methods used to conduct research and generate knowledge. This idea is based on a few assumptions. First, the results of

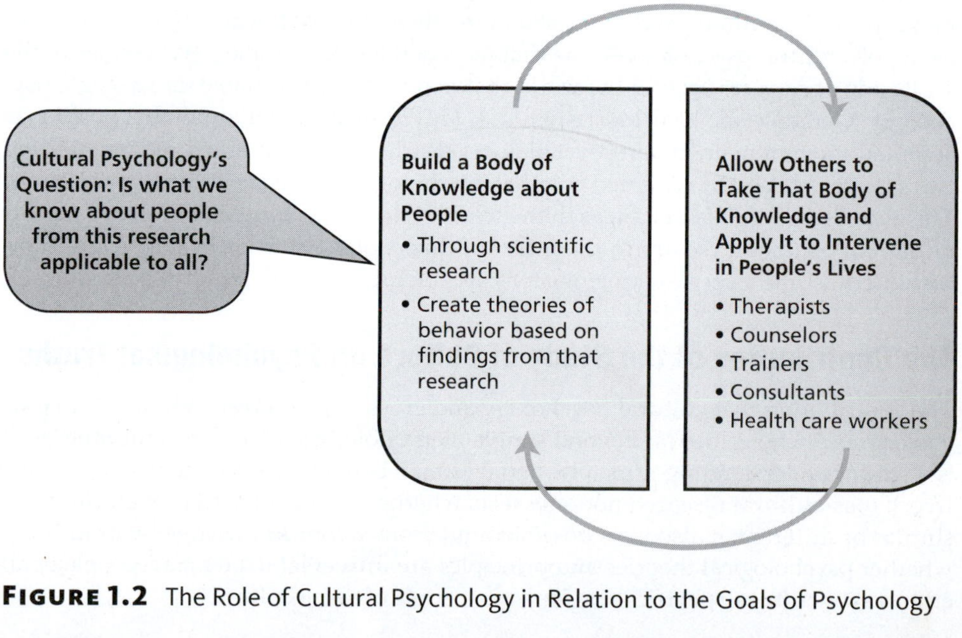

cross-cultural research A research methodology that tests the cultural parameters of psychological knowledge. Traditionally, it involves research on human behavior that compares psychological processes between two or more cultures. In this book, we also incorporate knowledge contrasting human cultures versus nonhuman animal cultures. This approach is primarily concerned with testing the possible limitations of knowledge gleaned from one culture by studying people of different cultures.

Cultural Psychology's Question: Is what we know about people from this research applicable to all?

Build a Body of Knowledge about People
- Through scientific research
- Create theories of behavior based on findings from that research

Allow Others to Take That Body of Knowledge and Apply It to Intervene in People's Lives
- Therapists
- Counselors
- Trainers
- Consultants
- Health care workers

FIGURE 1.2 The Role of Cultural Psychology in Relation to the Goals of Psychology

any psychological research are bound by our methods, and the standards of care we use when we evaluate the rigor and quality of research are also bound by the cultural frameworks within which our science occurs (Pe-Pua, 1989). Theories depend on research to confirm or disconfirm them; research involves methods designed to collect data to test theories and their hypotheses. Methods involve many parameters, one of which includes decisions about the nature of the participants in the study. Cross-cultural research involves the inclusion of people of different cultural backgrounds—a specific type of change in one of the parameters of research methods. Thus, in some sense, cross-cultural research is relatively easy to understand conceptually because it involves a change in the nature of the participant characteristics (i.e., their cultural backgrounds).

But this basic change in research methods allows us to ask profound questions about what we think we know in mainstream psychology. We need to examine whether the information we have learned, or will learn in the future, is applicable to all people of all cultures or only to some people of some cultures. Scientific philosophy suggests that we have a duty and an obligation to ask these questions about the scientific process and about the nature of the truths we have learned, or will learn, about human behavior. The knowledge that is created in psychology should be accurate and descriptive of all people, not only of people of a certain culture (or race, ethnicity, nationality, gender, or sexual orientation). The field of psychology has an obligation—to its teachers, students, practitioners, and especially all the people whose lives are touched by its knowledge—to produce accurate knowledge that reflects and applies to them. Cross-cultural research plays an important role in helping psychologists produce that accurate knowledge for all because it tests whether what is true for some is also true for others.

This is not an easy challenge for the field to embrace. In almost any contemporary resource in psychology, cultural diversity in findings and cultural differences in research are widespread and commonplace. These differences are forcing psychologists to take a good, hard look at their theories and, in many cases, to call for revisions, sometimes major, in the way we have conceptualized many aspects of behavior. As a result, many psychologists see an evolution in psychology, with culture incorporated as a necessary and important ingredient. Some authors have even argued that the move toward a cultural psychology should really be a move toward a multicultural or even polycultural psychology— one that incorporates the unique psychologies of the multitude of cultures around the world that may not be assimilable into a single psychology (Gergen et al., 1996; Morris, Chiu, & Liu, 2015). Whether or not that position is accepted, current mainstream psychology is clearly moving in this direction, finding ways to educate and be educated by other psychological approaches in other cultures. This move involves basic changes in the way psychologists understand many aspects of human behavior. We are in the midst of this evolution in knowledge right now, making this time a very exciting one for psychology.

The Contribution of the Study of Culture on Psychological Truths

universal A psychological process that is found to be true or applicable for all people of all cultures.

culture-specific A psychological process that is considered to be true for some people of some cultures but not for others.

The contribution that cultural psychology and cross-cultural research makes to psychology as a whole goes far beyond simple methodological changes in the studies. It is a way of understanding principles about human behaviors within a global perspective. Cross-cultural research not only tests whether people of different cultures are similar or different; it also tests possible limitations in our knowledge by examining whether psychological theories and principles are **universal** (true for all people of all cultures) or **culture-specific** (true for some people of some cultures).

Because cross-cultural research is a method, it is not topic-specific. Thus, cultural psychologists are interested in a broad range of phenomena related to human behavior—from perception to language, child rearing to psychopathology. What distinguishes cultural psychology from mainstream psychology, therefore, is not the topic of study but the interest in understanding cultural influences on behavior, and the testing of limitations to knowledge using cross-cultural research methods. The impact of the growth of cultural psychology and cross-cultural research on mainstream psychology has been enormous, and we introduce you to the main cross-cultural findings in various areas of psychology in the rest of this book.

The Contribution of the Study of Culture in Our Own Lives

Psychological theories are only as good as their applicability to people in their lives (Amir & Sharon, 1988; Gergen et al., 1996), and one of the main contributions of cross-cultural research to application is the process it fosters in asking questions. Practicing psychology with a cultural perspective is an exercise in critical thinking. Is what we know true for all people regardless of their cultural backgrounds? If not, under what conditions do differences occur, and why? What is it about culture that produces such differences? What factors other than culture, such as socioeconomic class, heredity, or environment, may contribute to these differences? Asking these questions, being skeptical yet inquisitive, together define the process underlying psychology from a cultural perspective. This process is even more important than the content because it can be applied to all areas of our lives, especially in this multicultural world.

The Growth of Cultural Psychology and Cross-Cultural Research

Although cross-cultural research has been conducted for over a century, cultural psychology has truly made a substantial impact on psychology in the past two decades. Much of this popularity is due to the increased awareness of the importance of culture as an influential factor on behavior and, unfortunately, to increased awareness of the frequency of intercultural conflicts within and between countries (e.g., see Christopher, Wendt, Marecek, & Goodman, 2014). The flagship journal of the International Association of Cross-Cultural Psychology, the *Journal of Cross-Cultural Psychology,* has now passed its 40th year of publishing top-level cross-cultural research. Other specialty journals also exist, such as *Cross-Cultural Research* and *Culture and Psychology.* The number of research articles incorporating people of different cultures has increased tremendously in all top-tier mainstream journals as well, such as the *Journal of Personality and Social Psychology, Developmental Psychology,* and *Psychological Science.* Theoretical models are increasingly incorporating culture, and the number of books involving culture has also increased.

Broadly speaking, an increased interest in cultural psychology is a normal and healthy development. As psychology has matured, many scientists have come to recognize that much of the research and theories once thought to be universal for all people is indeed culture-bound. The increasing importance and recognition of cultural psychology are reactions to this realization.

▶ What Is Culture?

Understanding psychology from a cultural perspective starts with a better appreciation of what is culture. Many scholars and laypersons use the words *culture, race, nationality,* and *ethnicity* interchangeably, as if they were all terms denoting the same

culture A unique meaning and information system, shared by a group and transmitted across generations, that allows the group to meet basic needs of survival, pursue happiness and well-being, and derive meaning from life.

concepts. They do not, and as we begin our study of culture and psychology, it is important to define exactly what we mean by the term **culture**.

We use the word *culture* in many different ways in everyday language and discourse. We use the concept of culture to describe and explain a broad range of activities, behaviors, events, and structures in our lives. We use culture to describe rules, norms, learning, or problem solving; refer to the origins of a group and its heritage or traditions; and define the organization of a group (Berry, Poortinga, Segall, & Dasen, 1992; Kroeber & Kluckhohn, 1952/1963). Culture can refer to general characteristics; food and clothing; housing and technology; economy and transportation; individual and family activities; community and government; welfare, religion, and science; and sex and the life cycle (Murdock, Ford, & Hudson, 1971; Barry, 1980; Berry et al., 1992). The concept of culture is used in many different ways because it touches on so many aspects of life. Culture, in its truest and broadest sense, cannot simply be swallowed in a single gulp—not in this book, not in a university course, not in any training program. Although we will attempt to bring you closer to a better understanding of what culture is and how it influences our lives, we must begin by recognizing and admitting the breadth, scope, and enormity of culture.

We should also recognize that the concept of culture has different meanings in other cultures. In Japan, culture may refer to flower arranging or tea ceremony. In France, culture might refer to art, history, or food. In the United Arab Emirates, culture may refer to traditions and religious rituals. Thus the concept of culture itself is culture-bound. Let's begin our introduction to culture by discussing where culture comes from.

Where Does Culture Come From?

Understanding the origins of any human culture helps us to appreciate cultures and cultural differences (and similarities) when we engage with them. There are four important sources of the origins of culture: group life, environment, resources, and the evolved human mind (Table 1.1).

Group Life

Humans are social animals, and have always lived in groups. We learned many hundreds of thousands of years ago that living in groups was better than living alone (just as many other animal species have). A man or woman alone has trouble surviving the attacks of animals, feeding themselves, taking care of their children, and meeting all the other tasks of living. And we all want the companionship of others.

Groups increase our chances for survival because they increase efficiency through division of labor. The division of labor allows groups to accomplish more

TABLE 1.1 Factors That Influence the Creation of Cultures

Group Life	Environments	Resources	The Evolved Human Mind
■ Division of Labor	■ Climate	■ Food	■ Basic Human Needs and Motives
■ Efficiency	■ Population Density	■ Water	■ Universal Psychological Toolkit
■ Increase Survival Probability	■ Arable Land	■ Money	
	■ Diseases		
	■ Previous Cultures		
	■ Contact with Other Cultures		

than any one person can, which is functional and adaptive for all the members of the group. Division of labor allows for accomplishing more tasks so that survival rates increase. But there's a downside to living in groups, which is that there is potential for social conflict and chaos *because people are different*. Because of those differences, groups can become inefficient, reducing the probability for survival. And if groups are uncoordinated and individuals just do their own thing without consideration of others, conflict and disorganization will occur, which lead to social chaos.

Environment

Groups live in specific environments, and the ecologies of those environments have a major impact on *how* they live. One aspect of ecology that influences cultures is climate. Some areas of the world, like New York or Seoul, South Korea, have harsh winters and miserably hot summers. Other areas of the world, like South and Southeast Asia, have hot, humid weather all year long, while other areas (like the Middle East or North Africa) have hot dry weather all year long. Some areas have relatively mild climates all year long, like San Francisco or Seattle. These ecological differences influence ways of living. Groups that live near the equator, in hot, humid, tropical areas, will exhibit a lifestyle that is very different from that of groups living in temperate or arctic zones, with seasonal changes and extremely cold weather. Those groups will have different dress styles, different ways of walking, different architecture, and different rituals and traditions, just because of the climate.

More important to culture than the absolute temperature of an area is the **deviation from temperate climate** (van de Vliert, 2009). Humans need to regulate their body temperatures and have an easier time doing so in temperate climates, which happens to be around 22°C (about 72°F). Much colder or hotter climates make life much more difficult and demanding, and these harsher climates require people to do more to adjust and adapt. Harsher climates also create greater risks of food shortage and food spoilage, stricter diets, and more health problems (infectious and parasitic diseases tend to be more frequent in hotter climates). Demanding climates require special clothing, housing, and working arrangements, special organizations for the production, transportation, trade, storage of food, and special care and cure facilities. People in hotter climates tend to organize their daily activities more around shelter, shade, and temperature changes that occur during the day. For example, part of Spanish culture is to shut down businesses in the midafternoon, during the hottest time of the day, and reopen later, pushing back the working hours. There, it is not uncommon for people to be having dinner outside at 11:00 P.M. or even midnight. People who live nearer the poles may organize their lives around available sunlight. In psychological terms, more demanding cold or hot climates arouse a chain of needs shared by all inhabitants of an area (van de Vliert, 2009).

Another ecological factor that influences culture is **population density**. This is the ratio of the number of people that live in a specific area relative to the size of that area. Some geographic areas have lots of people living in a very small space; that is, they have large population density, like New York City, Tokyo, Hong Kong, or Mexico City. Other areas have only few people in a very large area; they have low population density, like Alaska or the northern island of Hokkaido in Japan.

What's important about population density is the number of people in an area in relation to the amount of **arable land** in that area—that is the amount of land on which food can grow to sustain the people in that area. A huge number of people in a small amount of space with scarce food will create a different way of living compared to a small number of people in a huge amount of space with abundant food. Moreover, the type of food that can be produced can be linked to interesting psychological

deviation from temperate climate The degree to which the average temperature of a given region will differ from what is considered to be the relatively "easiest" temperature to live in, which is 22°C (about 72°F).

population density The number of people living within a given unit of space. In a place like a city in which a large number of people live in a relatively small space, the population density is higher than in a rural area where fewer people live in each similar amount of space.

arable land The type of land that can sustain life by food production of some sort.

and cultural differences. Within China, for example, people who live in regions with a history of farming rice are generally more interdependent on others around them, while people who live in regions with a history of farming wheat are generally more independent of others around them (Talhelm, et al., 2014).

Other ecological factors also influence culture. For instance, global changes in climate across history have affected the evolution of humans (Behrensmeyer, 2006), as has the incidence and prevalence of infectious diseases in different regions of the world (Murray & Schaller, 2010). Unless we talk about the very beginnings of human life, most human groups live in a region with a previous culture; thus, their previous culture will have had an impact on the kind of culture they have now. This is especially true for immigrants, who come to a land with an already existing culture and must deal with the process of acculturation (which we will talk about later in Chapter 14). Finally, environments differ in the amount of contact they allow with other cultures through geographical proximity and accessibility. Is the environment bounded by many other regions with many other cultures, as in Europe? Or is the environment bounded by ocean, creating an island mentality, like Japan, the United Kingdom. One could even argue that the United States has some aspects of an island mentality. All these factors are likely to influence people's attitudes, beliefs, and behaviors, and hence their culture.

Resources

Another source for the origin of cultures is resources. Resources can be natural, such as the presence or absence of water or land to farm to grow vegetables or raise animals. A land void of natural resources may encourage teamwork and community spirit among its members and interrelationships with other groups that have abundant resources in order to survive. These needs and relationships will foster certain psychological characteristics and attributes that complement teamwork, community spirit, and interdependence. In a land with abundant resources, however, a group would have less need for such values and attitudes, and these attributes would be less important in its culture.

Perhaps the major type of resource that influences cultures today is money. Money is a human cultural product; it is not a natural resource part of the land or environment. Affluence, which refers to the amount of money available to a person or group, can have a major impact on culture (van de Vliert, 2009). Abundant money can help to buffer the consequences of a lack of resources and harsh climates, which in turn have interesting psychological consequences. People and groups with more money can afford to be less in sync with others because cooperation is not as essential for survival. People and groups with less money, however, need to cooperate in order to survive.

Thus the combination of the environment (climate, population density, arable land, etc.) and resources (food, water, and affluence) are some of the most important factors that contribute to a culture. For example, in the United States, we have the most sophisticated technology and the most money any country has ever had, so we can live in a similar way almost anywhere in the country. Even then, each part of the country has a local economy that comes from the geography, climate, and resources available. It is hard to grow corn on the north slope of Alaska. There is no timber or fishing industry in Death Valley. There aren't many gold or coal mines in Florida. We all still have to make a living from what we can find around us (unless huge amounts of money are used to overcome the harsh environment, such as in Las Vegas). Harsh climates and scarce resources tend to push people toward valuing the idea of hospitality and helping one's family and neighbors. In very dissimilar places like the

Middle East and northern Greenland, we find similar emphases on hospitality and helping, which is not as much emphasized in many other places, and much of these emphases result from geography and climate. People who live in places with high population density and low resources need to cooperate in order to survive.

The Evolved Human Mind

Fortunately, people do not come to the world as complete blank slates in order to deal with the problem of adapting to their environments and surviving. Survival depends on the degree to which people can adapt to their environments and to the contexts in which they live. To do so, they come to the world with specific needs and motives and with what we call a psychological toolkit that provides them with the tools with which to adapt and survive.

Needs and Motives Humans have basic needs that are ultimately related to reproductive success (Boyer, 2000; Buss, 2001). These include physical needs—the need to eat, drink, sleep, deal with waste, and reproduce if they are to survive. They also include safety and security needs—the need for hygiene, shelter, and warmth (remember the discussion above about climate). These needs are universal to all people of all cultures.

These basic needs are associated with social motives (Hogan, 1982; Sheldon, 2004), which include the motive to achieve and the motive to affiliate with others. Over history, people must have solved a host of distinct social problems in order to adapt and thus achieve reproductive success. These social problems include negotiating complex status hierarchies, forming successful work and social groups, attracting mates, fighting off potential rivals for food and sexual partners, giving birth and raising children, and battling nature (Buss, 1988, 1991, 2001). In fact, we need to do these things in our everyday lives today as well. All individuals and groups have a universal problem of how to adapt to their environments in order to address these needs and motives, and must create solutions to these universal problems. These solutions can be very specific to each group because the contexts in which each group lives—the physical environment, social factors, and types and sizes of their families and communities—are different.

Universal Psychological Toolkits Another resource that humans bring with them to the world is what we call the **universal psychological toolkit** (Table 1.2). The universal psychological toolkit is a term we use to refer to the many abilities and aptitudes that nature and evolution endowed humans with in order to help them to address their basic needs and social motives, and ultimately to adapt and survive. These tools emerged with the evolution of the human brain, and are important parts of the human mind.

universal psychological toolkit A set of basic psychological skills and abilities that people can use to meet their needs. These include complex cognitive skills, language, emotions, and personality traits.

TABLE 1.2 Contents of the Universal Psychological Toolkit

Cognitive Abilities	Emotions	Personality Traits
▪ Language	▪ Basic Emotions	▪ Extraversion
▪ Complex Social Cognition	▪ Self-Conscious Emotions	▪ Neuroticism
▪ Memory	▪ Moral Emotions	▪ Openness
▪ Hypothetical Reasoning		▪ Agreeableness
▪ Problem Solving		▪ Conscientiousness
▪ Planning		

For example, language is one of the tools in our toolkit. Humans, unlike other animals, have the unique ability to symbolize their physical and metaphysical world (Premack, 2004), to create sounds representing those symbols (morphemes), to create rules connecting those symbols to meaning (syntax and grammar), and to put all these abilities together in sentences. Moreover, since the use of papyrus to develop paper, humans developed writing systems so we can reduce those oral expressions to words on paper. This book, in fact, is a uniquely human product.

Another tool in our toolkit involves a host of cognitive abilities that allow for complex social cognition, memory, hypothetical reasoning, problem solving, and planning. For instance, one of the most important thinking abilities that humans have unlike other animals is the ability to believe that other people are intentional agents—that is, that they have wishes, desires, and intentions to act and behave. We know that we have our own intentions. But we also know that other people have their own intentions. And we know that they know that we have intentions. That's why being in the "public eye" takes on special meaning for humans, because we know that others can make judgments about us. And that's also why the anonymity of a darkened theater or an anonymous Internet chatroom or online cyberspace allows us to do and say things we normally wouldn't in person. Thus, we have causal beliefs (which form the basis for the study of *attributions,* which we will discuss later in Chapter 14). *Morality*, a uniquely human product, is probably rooted in this unique human cognitive ability (and we will discuss this more in Chapter 4). This ability apparently turns on in humans around nine months of age (Tomasello, 1999), which is a critical time of development of many cognitive abilities (we will discuss these more in Chapter 4). That is probably why we don't just take off our clothes in the middle of the street, have sex in the middle of the park in broad daylight, or just punch those with whom we disagree. Other animals, however, seem to not care as much.

Other animals can and do view themselves as somewhat intentional agents. But one thing that differentiates humans from other animals is the fact that we have the cognitive ability to share our intentions with others. One of the major functions of language, in fact, is to allow us to communicate a **shared intentionality** (Matsumoto & Hwang, 2016; Tomasello & Herrmann, 2010). The fact that we can read each other's facial expressions of emotion, and that this is a universal ability (see Chapter 8), also contributes to our ability to create shared intentions. Shared intentionality may be at the heart of social coordination, which allows for the creation of human culture (Fiske, 2000).

Another important ability that humans have that animals do not is the ability to continually build upon improvements. When humans create something that is good, it usually evolves to a next generation, in which it is even better. This is true for computers, cars, audio music players, and unfortunately, weapons. Tomasello, Kruger, and Ratner (1993) call this the **ratchet effect**. Like a ratchet, an improvement never goes backward; it only goes forward and continues to improve on itself. The ratchet effect does not occur in other animals. Monkeys may use twigs to catch insects, but they don't improve on that tool.

Our cognitive skills also include memory, and because we have memory, we can create histories, and because we can create histories, we have traditions, customs, and heritage (Balter, 2010; Liu et al., 2005; Liu et al., 2009; Paez et al., 2008; Wang, 2006; Wang & Ross, 2007). Our cognitive skills also include the ability to think hypothetically and about the future. This allows us to plan things and to worry about the uncertainty of the future, both of which form the basis of important cultural practices.

People are also equipped with the ability to have emotions. As we will learn later in Chapter 8, emotions are rapid, information processing systems that aid humans

shared intentionality Knowledge about motivations concerning behaviors that are common among people in a group.

ratchet effect The concept that humans continually improve on improvements, that they do not go backward or revert to a previous state. Progress occurs because improvements move themselves upward, much like a ratchet.

in reacting to events that require immediate action and that have important consequences to one's welfare with minimal cognitive processing. They are part of an archaic, biologically innate system that we share with some other animals. People can have many different types of emotions, such as self-conscious emotions like pride, shame, guilt, or embarrassment, and moral emotions such as outrage or indignation.

Finally, people come equipped with personality traits. As we will learn in Chapter 6, humans around the world share a core set of traits that give them predispositions in order to adapt to their environments, solve social problems, and address their basic needs. Many cultures of the world are associated with differences in mean levels of several personality traits. Although it is possible that cultures shaped the average personalities of its members, it is also possible that groups of individuals with certain kinds of personalities and temperaments banded together in certain geographic regions because it was beneficial for their adaptation to the environment, and thus influenced culture. For example, cultures high on the dimension known as uncertainty avoidance (more below) are associated with higher means on the personality trait known as Neuroticism. It could be that uncertainty avoidant cultures produce more neurotic individuals; but it is also possible that more neurotic individuals exist in these areas in the first place because these traits are more beneficial for survival in those environments, and they help to create cultural systems that are more uncertainty avoidant.

Collectively, the universal psychological toolkits allow humans to adapt to their environments in order to meet their needs. Individuals differ in how much of these toolkits they have, or how they use them, but we all have pretty much the same toolkits. That's why anyone born anywhere in the world could be taken at birth and raised in a different culture, and they would have the basic toolkit to get along in that new culture, and the new culture would seem normal to them. They would think and act like other people in that culture. They would still have their own personal character, but it would be expressed in ways appropriate to their new culture. Thus, people come to the world pre-equipped with an evolved, naturally selected set of abilities and aptitudes that allows them to adapt, survive, and create cultures.

A Definition of Culture

A Functional Understanding of Culture   Putting the previous section all together, we know that people have needs that must be met in order to survive, and come to the world with a universal psychological toolkit to help address those needs. They live in groups, and the groups exist in different ecologies, with different resources. Thus, groups of people need to adapt their behaviors to their ecologies by maximizing the use of their available resources in order to meet their needs; the abilities and aptitudes in their psychological toolkits give them the tools to adapt. These adaptations produce behaviors, ways of living, ways of thinking, and ways of being. These ways become the contents of a group's culture. The concept of "culture," in fact, is an abstract metaphor for these ways. Culture helps explain and describe those ways.

Living in groups requires social coordination. If we are coordinated, then people are efficient in doing their part for their group to survive. And shared intentionality is at the root of social coordination. If we are not coordinated, there is social chaos, which is one of the potential downsides of living in groups. Thus we need to keep social order and be coordinated and minimize social chaos, so we can accomplish tasks efficiently and survive.

To achieve social order, coordination, and group harmony, and avoid chaos, we create rules of life, or systems of living, or ways of being. This is culture. Culture provides guidelines or roadmaps on what to do, how to think, and what to feel. Those guidelines

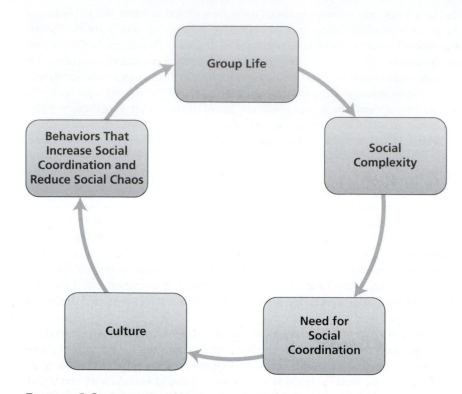

FIGURE 1.3 A Functional Understanding of Culture

are passed along from one generation to the next, so that future generations don't have to keep reinventing the wheel. That's why cultural products are always improved; they are always ratcheted up, never down. Have you ever noticed that computers and cell phones always get better, not worse? Same for raising crops, making cars, and all other cultural products. Those ways of living that groups create take advantage of our universal psychological toolkits to meet our basic human needs (Figure 1.3).

A Definition   Over the years, many scholars have attempted to define culture. Tylor (1865) defined culture as all capabilities and habits learned as members of a society. Linton (1936) referred to culture as social heredity. Kroeber and Kluckholn (1952/1963) defined culture as patterns of and for behavior acquired and transmitted by symbols, constituting the distinct achievements of human groups, including their embodiments in artifacts. Rohner (1984) defined culture as the totality of equivalent and complementary learned meanings maintained by a human population, or by identifiable segments of a population, and transmitted from one generation to the next. Jahoda (1984) argued that culture is a descriptive term that captures not only rules and meanings but also behaviors. Pelto and Pelto (1975) defined culture in terms of personality, whereas Geertz (1975) defined it as shared symbol systems transcending individuals. Berry et al. (1992) defined culture simply as the shared way of life of a group of people, and Baumeister (2005) defined culture as an information-based system that allows people to live together and satisfy their needs.

There is no one perfect or accepted definition of culture that everyone can agree upon. That's OK because culture is all encompassing. What is important, however, is that we have a working definition of culture for our use. In this book, we define human **culture** as *a unique meaning and information system, shared by a group and transmitted across generations, that allows the group to meet basic needs of survival, pursue happiness and well-being, and derive meaning from life.*

Human cultures exist first to enable us to meet basic needs of survival. Human cultures help us to meet others, to procreate and produce offspring, to put food on the table, to provide shelter from the elements, and to care for our daily biological essential needs, all of which are necessary for survival.

But human culture is so much more than that. It allows for complex social networks and relationships. It allows us to enhance the meaning of normal, daily activities. It allows us to pursue happiness, and to be creative in music, art, and drama. It allows us to seek recreation and to engage in sports and organize competition, whether in the local community Little League or the Olympic Games. It allows us to search the sea and space. It allows us to create mathematics, as well as an educational system. It allows us to go to the moon, to create a research laboratory on Antarctica, and send probes to Mars and Jupiter. Unfortunately, it also allows us to have wars, create weapons of mass destruction, and recruit and train terrorists.

Human culture does all this by creating and maintaining complex social systems, institutionalizing and improving cultural practices, creating beliefs about the world, and communicating a meaning system to other humans and subsequent generations. It is the product of the evolution of the human mind, increased brain size, and complex cognitive abilities, in response to the specific ecologies in which groups live and the resources available to them to live. Culture results from the interaction among universal biological needs and functions, universal social problems created to address those needs, and the context in which people live. Culture is a solution to the problem of individuals' adaptations to their contexts to address their social motives and biological needs. As adaptational responses to the environment, cultures help to select behaviors, attitudes, values, and opinions that may optimize the tapping of resources to meet survival needs. Out of all the myriad behaviors possible in the human repertoire, cultures help to focus people's behaviors and attention on a few limited alternatives in order to maximize their effectiveness, given their resources and their environment (Poortinga, 1990).

Is Culture a Uniquely Human Product?

If we understand culture as a solution to the problem of adapting to our contexts in order to meet basic biological and social needs, then one question that arises is whether humans are the only beings that have culture. After all, *all* living beings need to adapt to their life contexts so as to meet basic needs and survive. In fact, there are many characteristics of human cultural life that are shared with other animals. For example, consider:

- Many animals are social; that is, they work and live in groups. Fish swim in schools, wolves hunt in packs, and lions roam in prides.

- In animal societies, there are clear social networks and hierarchies. The staring game played by humans as children is used by animals to create dominance hierarchies. And like the human game, the animal that smiles or averts its gaze loses and becomes the subordinate.

- Many animals invent and use tools (Whiten, Horner, & De Waal, 2005). Perhaps the most famous initial example of this is monkeys who use twigs to get insects to eat. Japanese monkeys at Koshima Island washed sweet potatoes and bathed in the sea (Matsuzawa, 2001).

- Many animals communicate with each other. Bees communicate via a complex dance concerning the source of flowers. Ants leave trails to communicate their paths to themselves and others. Relatives of monkeys who wash sweet potatoes at Koshima Island themselves began to wash sweet potatoes.

The list goes on and on. Thus it is clear that animals have at least a rudimentary form of culture consisting of social customs (McGrew, 2004) as we defined it above (responses and solutions to the problem of adapting to context in order to meet basic needs for survival) (Boesch, 2003). So the answer to the question—Is culture a uniquely human product?—appears to be *no* (see also de Waal, 2013).

Yet human cultures are different from other animal cultures, and understanding how we are different serves as an important basis to understanding how all humans are universally similar in important ways. Addressing the uniqueness of human culture begs the question of what unique skills humans have that other animals don't.

There are several characteristics of human social and cultural life that differentiates human culture from those of animals. Human cultures are cumulative; knowledge, tools, technology, and know-how accumulate over time and continue to improve (recall our discussion above about ratcheting) (Dean, Kendal, Schapiro, Thierry, & Laland, 2012). Recent research has demonstrated that humans have specialized socio-cognitive skills, which include teaching through verbal instructions, imitation, and prosociality, that allow them to reach higher-level solutions when solving problems. Other animals do not possess these skills, which prevents them from achieving a cumulative culture that rachets up (Dean, et al., 2012).

Cumulative culture allows human cultures to differ from animal cultures on *complexity, differentiation,* and *institutionalization.* For example, not only do humans make tools. We make tools to make tools. We automate the process of making tools and mass distribute tools around the world for global consumption. Because humans have complex social cognition, language, shared intentionality, and ratcheting, human social and cultural life is much more complex than that of other animals. We are members of multiple groups, each having its own purpose, hierarchy, and networking system. Much of human cumulative culture is based on uniquely human cognitive skills, such as teaching and learning through verbal instruction, imitation, and prosociality (Dean et al., 2012). Humans have evolved to have unique human cultures, and human cultures ensure a great diversity in life. Increased diversity, in fact, greatly aids in survival, and humans appear to be doing a good job at surviving.

The Difference between "Society" and "Culture"

Although these terms are often used interchangeably, we distinguish between "society" and "culture." *Society* is "a system of interrelationships among people." It refers to the structure of relationships that exist among individuals. In human societies, individuals have multiple relationships with multiple groups, and the groups themselves have interrelationships with other groups. Thus human societies are complex. Nonhuman animals are also social and have societies.

Culture, however, refers to the meanings and information that are associated with those social networks. "Family," for example, is a social group that exists in both the human and nonhuman animal world. But human cultures give the concept of family its own unique meaning, and individuals draw specific information from these meanings. Moreover, different human cultures assign different meanings to this social group. Thus, while many societies have a structural system of interrelationships, the meanings associated with those systems are cultural. For example, "older brother" is a part of many families and thus of many societies. The meaning of "older brother," however, is different in different cultures. In some cultures there is little difference between older or younger brothers or sisters. In other cultures, the older brother is a relatively more exalted position within the family, associated with certain duties and obligations that do not exist with other siblings.

Groups That Have Cultures

Given our definition of culture and what influences it, the next question that arises is, which human groups have culture? Certainly there are many groups of individuals that have culture, and here we discuss only a few (see Table 1.3).

Culture and Nationality

Nationality refers to a person's country of origin, and countries have their own cultures. This is because countries are associated with each of the factors that influence culture. For example, countries are defined by specific boundaries that describe their ecology—geography, climate, and natural resources. Countries also have their own unique sociocultural history, language, government, and economic base, all of which affect culture. Countries also have differences in mean levels of aggregate personality traits, which can affect culture.

Of course, this is a generalization, and although countries can certainly have a dominant culture, they can also have many subcultures. The concept of "country" is a geopolitical demarcation that may include many different cultures. There are vast cultural differences, for instance, within countries in the Middle East and North Africa. This is true within nearly all countries as well, including the United States, with the differences between the East and West Coasts, the South, the Midwest, Alaska, and Hawaii. Thus, we need to engage in a study of culture and psychology by first acknowledging the multicultural reality that exists around the world, both between and within countries.

Culture and Language

As we will discuss in Chapter 9, a cultural group defines meaningful things in its world by encoding its world in words, and by incorporating unique aspects of language (syntax, grammar, pragmatics). Thus different language groups typically have different cultures. Even if the language is the same, different dialects of a language often denote slightly different cultures. English, for example, is the primary language of England, parts of Canada, the United States, Australia, and New Zealand. But there are differences in the use of English in each of these countries, and they denote interesting differences in their cultures. Even within each of these countries, there are

TABLE 1.3 Contrasting Groups That Have Cultures from Social Constructs That Are Not Culture

Groups That Have Cultures	Constructs That Are Not Culture
▪ Countries/Nations	▪ Race
▪ Language	▪ Personality
▪ Ethnicity	▪ Popular Culture
▪ Gender	
▪ Disabilities	
▪ Sexual Orientations	

different dialects and regional differences in the language that denote differences in local and regional cultures. In the United States, for instance, English is vastly different between the West Coast, Hawaii, the deep South, and the northeast.

Culture and Ethnicity

The word *ethnicity* is derived from the Greek *ethnos*, meaning people of a nation or tribe, and is usually used to denote one's racial, national, or cultural origins. In the United States, ethnic groups include African Americans, Asians and Pacific Islanders, Hispanics and Latinos, and Native Americans. Ethnicity is generally used in reference to groups characterized by a common nationality, geographic origin, culture, or language (Betancourt & Lopez, 1993). Understanding the relationship between ethnicity and culture can be tricky. To the extent that ethnicity refers to national origins, it may denote aspects of culture. But psychologists and laypersons often equate ethnicity with race, and as we will discuss below, this is problematic. Most importantly, ethnicity as a label has no explanatory value; although information about ethnic differences on a broad range of psychological phenomena can be useful, such information by itself does not explain the nature of the relationship between ethnicity and psychology. Exactly what variables related to ethnicity account for psychological differences among groups of individuals? The use of ethnicity (or race) as a categorical descriptor does little to address this important concern. Put simply, just knowing the ethnicity or race of a person does little to explain psychological outcomes in cognition, emotion, motivation, or health (Phinney, 1996). Given these limitations, psychologists need to go beyond the use of ethnic labels to explain individual and group differences.

Phinney (1996) has outlined three key aspects of ethnicity that deserve further attention: cultural norms and values; the strength, salience, and meaning of ethnic identity; and attitudes associated with minority status. We agree with the emphasis on culture as an underlying determinant of psychological functioning. Culture makes ethnic group differences meaningful.

Culture and Gender

Sex refers to the biological differences between men and women, the most obvious being the anatomical differences in their reproductive systems. Accordingly, the term *sex roles* is used to describe the behaviors and patterns of activities men and women engage in that are directly related to their biological differences and the process of reproduction (such as breast-feeding). *Gender* refers to the behaviors or patterns of activities that a society or culture deems appropriate for men and women. These behavior patterns may or may not be related to sex and sex roles, although they oftentimes are. *Gender role* refers to the degree to which a person adopts the gender-specific and appropriate behaviors ascribed by his or her culture.

Describing and understanding psychological gender differences requires us to go beyond the biological differences between men and women. Gender differences arise because of differences in the psychological cultures transmitted to men and women. Gender differences are thus cultural differences. Of course, men and women also belong to a larger culture such as a national culture, and their gender cultures may coexist within the larger culture. This is yet another example of how culture can be understood on multiple levels of analysis, as the definition of culture presented earlier in the chapter suggests.

Culture and Disability

Persons with disabilities share some type of physical impairment in their senses, limbs, or other parts of their bodies. Although the lay public has generally viewed the main distinction of persons with disabilities as the physical impairments they have, a growing body of work has found important sociopsychological characteristics of disability as well (e.g., De Clerck, 2010). Persons with disabilities share the same feelings, ways of thinking, and motivations as everyone else. Beyond that, however, they also share some unique ways of thinking and feeling that may be specific to their disability. To the extent that they share certain unique psychological attitudes, opinions, beliefs, behaviors, norms, and values, they share a unique culture.

A number of authors have begun to describe the culture of disability (Conyers, 2003; Eddey & Robey, 2005). These works highlight the unique psychological and sociocultural characteristics of disabled individuals, refocusing our attention on a broader picture of the person in understanding the psychological characteristics of persons with disabilities. Seen in this light, psychological studies involving participants with disabilities can be viewed as yet another example of cross-cultural studies, as they involve comparisons not only of the presence or absence of impairment, but of more important conditions of culture.

Culture and Sexual Orientation

People form different sexual relationships with others, and the persons with whom they form such relationships constitute their sexual orientation. We often view these relationships as the sole or major defining characteristic of a person's sexual orientation. Yet one of the most important aspects of any sexual orientation—whether straight or gay, mono or bi—is the particular psychological outlook and characteristics that are shared by and unique to each orientation.

These distinctive psychological characteristics may be cultural. Understanding shared psychological attributes among people sharing the same sexual orientation as cultural (e.g., gay culture) has become well accepted in the social sciences (Herdt & Howe, 2007).

The common thread in this section is that people are often grouped on the basis of shared characteristics that are visible or otherwise easily identifiable (race, ethnicity, nationality, sex, disability, or sexual orientation). Although there may or may not be objective bases underlying these classifications or groupings, we cannot forget that they are important social constructs and categories. We use these groupings as mental categories, as Hirschfield (1996) has suggested with race. Problems occur, however, when we consider these mental categories as endpoints in and of themselves, instead of as gatekeepers to important sociopsychological—that is, cultural—differences (and similarities) among the categories. Thus, it is crucial to recognize that one of the most important features of each of these social categories is its underlying culture—that unique set of shared attributes that influences its members' mental processes and behaviors.

Contrasting Culture, Race, Personality, and Popular Culture

Culture and Race

Race is not culture, and the terms should not be used interchangeably. There is considerable controversy surrounding what race is (Anderson & Nickerson, 2005). Many contemporary scholars suggest that there are three major races—Caucasoid, Mongoloid, and Negroid— but past studies of the origins of race have proposed as many as 37 different races (Yee, Fairchild, Weizmann, & Wyatt, 1993). Although laypersons typically use skin color, hair, and other physical characteristics to define race, most physical anthropologists use population gene frequencies. Regardless of which biological or physical characteristics one uses to define race, the very concept of race is much less clear-cut than previously believed (Lewontin, Rose, & Kamin, 1984).

Some authors have suggested that the distinctions among races are arbitrary and dubious at best (Zuckerman, 1990). Even studies of genetic systems, including blood groups, serum proteins, and enzymes, have shown considerably more within-group than between-group variation, suggesting that racially defined groups are actually more similar than different.

There is also controversy about the origins of race. Prevalent theories posit a common ancestor originating in Africa 200,000 years ago, whose descendants then migrated to other parts of the world. Evidence for these theories comes from physical anthropology and archaeology. Other theories and apparently conflicting sets of evidence, however, suggest that humans may have existed in multiple regions of the world as far back as two million years ago and that intermixing among regions occurred (Wolpoff & Caspari, 1997).

Many psychologists today agree that race is more of a social construction than a biological essential. People have a natural propensity to create categories, especially those dealing with human characteristics (Hirschfield, 1996). Because easily identifiable physical characteristics are often used in this category formation process, "race" becomes central to these folk theories and thus gains cognitive and social meaning and importance. And although race as a biological construct may be questionable, race as a *social* construct is real (Smedley & Smedley, 2005).

Interesting issues arise when race is understood as a social construction. Category boundaries among the socially constructed races are ambiguous and vary with social context (Davis, 1991; Eberhardt & Randall, 1997; Omi & Winant, 1994). And people of different cultures differ in their definitions of race. In some cultures, race is a continuum along a dimensional scale, not a category (Davis, 1991). Many Brazilians believe that race is not heritable and varies according to economic or geographic mobility (Degler, 1971, reported in Eberhardt & Randall, 1997). In some countries, socioeconomic mobility is associated with changes in perceptions of physical properties such as skin color and hair texture (Eberhardt & Randall, 1997).

Our view is that "racial" differences are of little scientific or practical use without a clear understanding of the underlying causes of the similarities and differences observed (Betancourt & Lopez, 1993; Helms, Jernigan, & Mascher, 2005; Zuckerman, 1990). These causes will necessarily involve culture, as we defined in this book, because culture is a functional concept that determines what is psychologically meaningful and important for different races. Culture is what gives race its meaning.

Culture and Personality

Culture is not personality, and just because individuals exist in a culture and are representatives of a culture, they should not be equated with the culture. Culture is a macro, social, group-level construct; it is the social psychological frame within which individuals reside, much like the structure of our houses and homes. *Personality* refers to the unique constellation of traits, attributes, qualities, and characteristics of individuals within those frames; it refers to the individual differences that exist among individuals within groups.

Individuals have their own mental representations of culture, and these differing representations may be an aspect of their personality. But individual-level mental representations of culture are not culture on the macro-social level, a point we will come back to in the next chapter on research methods. Culture, as we have defined it, involves a meaning and information system that is shared among individuals and transmitted across generations. Personality and individual differences are not necessarily shared. Culture is relatively stable across individuals, whereas personality is vastly different.

Culture versus Popular Culture

From time to time, it is fashionable to refer to fads that come and go as "culture." This is also referred to as "popular culture" by the mass media and in everyday conversation. *Popular culture* refers to trends in music, art, and other expressions that become popular among a group of people.

Certainly popular culture and culture as we have defined it share some similarities—perhaps most importantly, the sharing of an expression and its value by a group of people. But there are also important differences. For one, popular culture does not necessarily involve sharing a wide range of psychological attributes across various psychological domains. Culture as defined here involves a system of rules that cuts across attitudes, values, opinions, beliefs, norms, and behaviors. Popular culture does not involve a way of life.

A second important difference concerns cultural transmission across generations. Popular culture refers to values or expressions that come and go as fads or trends within a few years. Culture is relatively stable over time and even across generations (despite its dynamic quality and potential for change).

Thus, although culture and popular culture have some similarities, there are important differences. The cross-cultural literature in psychology and the culture described in this book is the culture defined in this chapter, not popular culture (although the psychology of popular culture is a topic well deserving of consideration).

▶ The Contents of Culture

As culture is a meaning and information system, it is an abstraction that we use to refer to many aspects of our ways of living. The contents of culture can be divided roughly into two major categories—the objective elements of culture and the subjective elements of culture (Kroeber & Kluckholn, 1952/1963; Triandis, 1972).

Objective Elements

The objective elements of culture involve objective, explicit elements that are physical. These would include architecture, clothes, foods, art, eating utensils, and the like. In today's world, advertising, texts, architecture, art, mass media, television, music, the Internet, Facebook, and Twitter are all physical, tangible, and important artifacts of culture (Lamoreaux & Morling, 2012; Morling & Lamoreaux, 2008). A recent study analyzed millions of digitized books—about 4% of all books ever printed—to investigate cultural trends over time (Michel et al., 2011) and demonstrated changes in vocabularies, grammar, collective memory, the adoption of technology, the pursuit of fame, censorship, and historical epidemiology. The objective elements of culture are much of the focus of archaeology or physical anthropology.

Subjective Elements

The subjective elements of culture include all those parts of a culture that do not survive people as physical artifacts. They include psychological processes such as attitudes, values, beliefs, as well as behaviors. Cultural psychologists are generally much more interested in the subjective elements of culture because they tap into psychological processes and behaviors (see Figure 1.4).

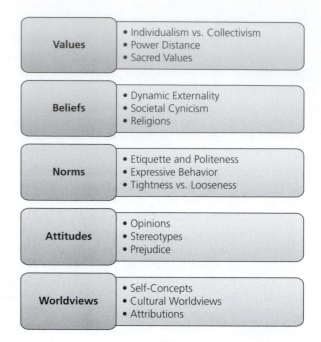

FIGURE 1.4
The Subjective Elements of Culture

Values

values A trans-situational goals that serve as a guiding principle in the life of a person or group (e.g., kindness, creativity). Values motivate and justify behavior and serve as standards for judging people, actions, and events.

Values are guiding principles that refer to desirable goals that motivate behavior. They define the moral, political, social, economic, esthetic, or spiritual ethics of a person or group of people. Values can exist on two levels—personal values and cultural values. Personal values represent transitional desirable goals that serve as guiding principles in people's lives. Cultural values are shared, abstract ideas about what a social collectivity views as good, right, and desirable.

Scientists have suggested several ways in which cultures differ from one another on their values. The most well-known approach to understanding cultural values comes from work by Geert Hofstede. He studied work-related values around the world, and to date has reported data from 72 countries involving the responses of more than 117,000 employees of a multinational business organization, spanning over 20 different languages and seven occupational levels to his 63 work-related values items (Hofstede, 2001). Hofstede suggests that there are five value dimensions that differentiate cultures:

- **Individualism versus Collectivism.** This dimension refers to the degree to which cultures will encourage, on one hand, the tendency for people to look after themselves and their immediate family only, or, on the other hand, for people to belong to ingroups that are supposed to look after its members in exchange for loyalty.

- **Power Distance.** This dimension refers to the degree to which cultures will encourage less powerful members of groups to accept that power is distributed unequally.

- **Uncertainty Avoidance.** This dimension refers to the degree to which people feel threatened by the unknown or ambiguous situations, and have developed beliefs, institutions, or rituals to avoid them.

- **Masculinity versus Femininity.** This dimension is characterized on one pole by success, money, and things, and on the other pole by caring for others and quality of life. It refers to the distribution of emotional roles between males and females.

■ **Long- versus Short-Term Orientation.** This dimension refers to the degree to which cultures encourage delayed gratification of material, social, and emotional needs among its members.

Another approach to understanding cultural values comes from Shalom Schwartz, who has identified seven cultural values that are universal (all descriptions taken from Schwartz & Ros, 1995, pp. 96–97).

■ **Embeddedness.** The degree to which cultures will emphasize the maintenance of the status quo, propriety, and restraint of actions or inclinations that might disrupt the solidarity of the group or the traditional order. It fosters social order, respect for tradition, family security, and self-discipline.

■ **Hierarchy.** The degree to which cultures emphasize the legitimacy of hierarchical allocation of fixed roles and resources such as social power, authority, humility, or wealth.

■ **Mastery.** The degree to which cultures emphasize getting ahead through active self-assertion or by changing and mastering the natural and social environment. It fosters ambition, success, daring, and competence.

■ **Intellectual Autonomy.** The degree to which cultures emphasize promoting and protecting the independent ideas and rights of the individual to pursue his/her own intellectual directions. It fosters curiosity, broadmindedness, and creativity.

■ **Affective Autonomy.** The degree to which cultures emphasize the promotion and protection of people's independent pursuit of positive experiences. It fosters pleasure and an exciting or varied life.

■ **Egalitarianism.** The degree to which cultures emphasize transcending selfish interests in favor of the voluntary promotion of the welfare of others. It fosters equality, social justice, freedom, responsibility, and honesty.

■ **Harmony.** The degree to which cultures emphasize fitting in with the environment. It fosters unity with nature, protecting the environment, and a world of beauty.

Of these approaches to values, individualism versus collectivism has by far received the greatest attention in cross-cultural research. It has been used to both predict and explain many differences across cultures, especially in many aspects of thinking and emotions (Oyserman & Lee, 2008; Schimmack, Oishi, & Diener, 2005; Triandis, 2001). Much of the work cited and described later in this book use this dimension to understand cultural differences.

The Hofstede and Schwartz cultural values are not mutually exclusive of each other, and they shouldn't be because they are merely different ways of examining cultural value systems. For example, Hofstede's individualism is positively correlated with Schwartz's affective and intellectual autonomy and egalitarianism (Schwartz, 2004). Power distance is positively correlated with long-term orientation, embeddedness, and hierarchy (Schwartz, 2004). And individualism, affective and intellectual autonomy, and egalitarianism tend to be negatively correlated with power distance, long-term orientation, embeddedness, and hierarchy.

Some cultural values are non-negotiable. These are called **sacred values** (Atran & Axelrod, 2007; Ginges, Atran, Medin, & Shikaki, 2007) and they differ from normal values because they incorporate moral beliefs that drive action in ways dissociated

sacred values Values considered to be nonnegotiable. They differ from normal values because they incorporate moral beliefs that drive action in ways dissociated from prospects for success. Across the world, people believe that devotion to core values (such as the welfare of their family and country or their commitment to religion, honor, and justice) is, or ought to be, absolute and inviolable. Such values outweigh other values, particularly economic ones.

from prospects for success. Across the world, people believe that devotion to core values (such as the welfare of their family and country or their commitment to religion, honor, and justice) is, or ought to be, absolute and inviolable. Such values outweigh other values, particularly economic ones. We have all learned some things we regard as moral values, some of which may be a part of religion. Most of us believe there is something morally wrong with letting down your team members. Most Americans believe you shouldn't cheat on your wife or husband even if they don't have particular religious beliefs. Some cultures permit a man to have more than one wife or a woman to have more than one husband. Some cultures believe that a family has honor that depends on the chastity of the women of the family and it is more important than the life of the woman.

Differences in values (and beliefs; see below) lead to different characterizations of cultures. Over the years, many characterizations have been proposed such as shame or guilt cultures (Piers & Singer, 1971), honor cultures (Cohen, Nisbett, Bowdle, & Schwarz, 1996; Vandello, Cohen, Grandon, & Franiuk, 2009), face and dignity cultures (Kim, Cohen, & Au, 2010; Ting-Toomey, 1994), high or low context cultures (Hall, 1966, 1973; Matsumoto et al., 2009), and power or hierarchical cultures (Matsumoto, 2007a; Torelli & Shavitt, 2010).

Beliefs

beliefs A proposition that is regarded as true. People of different cultures have different beliefs.

social axioms General beliefs and premises about oneself, the social and physical environment, and the spiritual world. They are assertions about the relationship between two or more entities or concepts; people endorse and use them to guide their behavior in daily living, such as "belief in a religion helps one understand the meaning of life."

A **belief** is a proposition that is regarded as true, and different cultures foster different belief systems. Cultural beliefs are known as **social axioms** (Bond et al., 2004; Leung et al., 2002). These are general beliefs and premises about oneself, the social and physical environment, and the spiritual world. They are assertions about the relationship between two or more entities or concepts; people endorse and use them to guide their behavior in daily living, such as "belief in a religion helps one understand the meaning of life." Leung et al. (2002) demonstrated the universal existence of five types of social axioms on the individual level in 41 cultural groups. Bond et al. (2004) then conducted cultural-level analyses on these data, and demonstrated that two social axiom dimensions existed on the cultural level:

- **Dynamic Externality.** This dimension represents an outward-oriented, simplistic grappling with external forces that are construed to include fate and a supreme being. It is the culture-level reflection of the belief structures that form part of a psychological constellation that aids citizens to mobilize psychologically to confront environmental difficulties. "Belief in a religion helps one understand the meaning of life" and "good deeds will be rewarded, and bad deeds will be punished" are examples of beliefs that comprise this dimension. Cultures high on this dimension tend to be more collectivistic, conservative, hierarchical; have high unemployment levels, less freedom, and fewer human-rights activities; and have aspirations for security, material resources, and a longer life. There is a strong sense of spirituality in this dimension.

- **Societal Cynicism.** This dimension represents a predominantly cognitive apprehension or pessimism of the world confronting people. "Caring about societal affairs only brings trouble upon oneself" and "kind-hearted people usually suffer losses" are examples of beliefs of this dimension. Cultures high on this dimension believe that the world produces malignant outcomes, that they are surrounded by inevitable negative outcomes, and that individuals are suppressed by powerful others and subjected to the depredations of willful and selfish individuals, groups, and institutions.

Religions are organized systems of beliefs, and are important to many people and cultures (Saroglou & Cohen, 2011). They tie together many attitudes, values, beliefs, worldviews, and norms. They provide guidelines for living. Religions are all similar in the sense that they serve a specific need—to help people manage themselves and their behaviors with others in order to avoid social chaos and provide social coordination. But they all do so in different ways. In some cultures like in the United States, religions can be considered somewhat separate from one's daily life practices. It's compartmentalized, like going to church on Sunday. In other cultures, religions are more infused with daily life, and it is impossible to think of daily practices without their religious meanings and connotations. In some cultures like the United States, there is a clear separation between religions and government. In other cultures, religions are so infused in the culture that it is impossible to think of culture, state, and religion separately. These differences are neither good nor bad; they are just the way things have evolved in different regions of the world.

religion Organized systems of beliefs that tie together many attitudes, values, beliefs, worldviews, and norms. They provide guidelines for living.

Norms

Norms are generally accepted standards of behavior for any cultural group. Norms dictate the behavior that members of any culture have defined as the most appropriate in any given situation. All cultures give guidelines about how people are expected to behave through norms. For instance, in some cultures, people wear little or no clothing, while in others people normally cover almost all of their bodies. Recent research has uncovered norms for describing the behaviors of people of other cultures (Shteynberg, Gelfand, & Kim, 2009), as well as norms for controlling one's expressive behavior when emotional (Matsumoto et al., 2009; Matsumoto et al., 2008).

norms A generally accepted standard of behavior within a cultural or sub-cultural group.

Norms and others kinds of social conventions are a normal aspect of our everyday lives. They can arise as the unintended consequence of people's efforts to coordinate with each other locally on small scales, and even global norms can emerge from these small-scale, local interactions even though people have no idea about the larger population or that they are coordinating on a larger, global scale (Centola & Baronchelli, 2015). Thus, large institutions or organizations are not necessary for the development of norms.

Normal behavior is related to social rituals in different cultures. Rituals are culturally prescribed conduct or any kind of established procedure or routine. These might include religious rituals, a bride's walking down the aisle with her father in American weddings, and having a cup of coffee in the morning. Rituals are important because they reinforce cultural meaning systems.

Some rituals are related to politeness, and many cultures reify norms of politeness in shared behavioral patterns called "etiquette." This is a code of behavior that describes expectations for social behavior according to contemporary cultural and conventional norms within a cultural group. Etiquette is a big part of many cultures, although cultures often differ in what is polite, and what kinds of behaviors are deemed polite, and thus appropriate and "good." They are considered signs of maturity and sanity within each culture. People who don't follow social rules are considered strange in some way. Politeness is culture specific so that what is polite behavior in one culture is often different in another. For example, in some cultures, it is considered good manners and a sign of respect to avoid looking directly at another person. In the American culture, however, people are taught to "look others in the eye" as a form a respect. In the Middle East and North Africa, showing the soles of one's feet is insulting; Americans who cross their legs in a meeting may be unwittingly communicating this insult to their interacting partners.

tightness versus looseness A dimension of cultural variability that refers to the variability within a culture of its members to norms. Tight cultures have less variability and are more homogeneous with respect to norms; loose cultures have more variability and are more heterogeneous.

An important dimension of cultural variability with respect to norms involves a concept known as **tightness versus looseness** (Pelto, 1968). Tightness–looseness has two key components: The strength of social norms, or how clear and pervasive norms are within societies, and the strength of sanctioning, or how much tolerance there is for deviance from norms within societies. Pelto (1968) was the first to coin this term, arguing that traditional societies varied in their expression of and adherence to social norms. In his work, the Pueblo Indians, Hutterites, and the Japanese were examples of tight societies, in which norms were expressed very clearly and unambiguously, and in which severe sanctions were imposed on those who deviated from norms. By contrast, he identified the Skolt Lapps of northern Finland and the Thais as loose societies, in which norms were expressed through a wide variety of alternative channels, and in which there was a general lack of formality, order, and discipline and a high tolerance for deviant behavior.

Recent research involving surveys of 6,823 people in 33 modern nation or cultures has demonstrated the importance of tightness-looseness (Gelfand et al., 2011). This dimension appears to be part of a loosely integrated system that incorporates ecological and historical components, such as population density, resource availability, history of conflict, and disease) with the strength of everyday recurring situations in facilitating mental processes and behaviors. (Note that that ecological and historical components mentioned in this model and documented in this research are exactly those environmental factors we discussed earlier in this chapter as part of the foundational building blocks of culture.) The tightest cultures in this study—that is, cultures with the strongest social norms and sanctions for social transgressions—were Pakistan, Malaysia, Singapore, and South Korea; the loosest cultures were Ukraine, Estonia, Hungary, and Israel.

attitudes Evaluations of objects occurring in ongoing thoughts about the objects, or stored in memory.

cultural worldviews Culturally specific belief systems about the world. They contain attitudes, beliefs, opinions, and values about the world. People have worldviews because of evolved, complex cognition; thus, having a worldview is a universal psychological process. The specific content of worldviews, however, is specific to and different for each culture.

Attitudes

Attitudes are evaluations of things occurring in ongoing thoughts about those things, or stored in memory. Cultures facilitate attitudes concerning actions and behaviors, which produces cultural filters, which we will discuss in Chapter 14; these serve as the basis of stereotypes and prejudice. Cultures also foster attitudes that are not tied to specific kinds of actions, such as believing that democracy is the best form of government. In many other cultures, especially in the past, people believed that most people aren't capable of understanding government, and that countries are best ruled by kings who are very religious or spiritually advanced.

Worldviews

Cultures also differ importantly in **cultural worldviews**. These are culturally specific belief systems about the world; they contain attitudes, beliefs, opinions, and values about the world. They are assumptions people have about their physical and social realities (Koltko-Rivera, 2004). For example, American culture fosters a worldview centering on personal control—that you are in control of your life, destiny, and happiness. Many other cultures do not foster this worldview; instead, one's life may be in the hands of God, fate, or the supernatural.

self-concept The cognitive representations of who one is, that is, the ideas or images that one has about oneself, especially in relation to others, and how and why one behaves. The sum of one's idea about one's self, including physical, mental, historical, and relational aspects, as well as capacities to learn and perform. Self-concept is usually considered central to personal identity and change over time. It is usually considered partially conscious and partially unconscious or inferred in a given situation.

An important aspect of our worldviews is how we think about our self—what we know of as our **self-concept** (which we will discuss more in Chapter 5). In the United States, we tend to think that we are responsible for our choices, and that we are independent individuals. In other cultures, however, people see themselves as fundamentally connected with others, and do not consider themselves as unique, separate individuals. In some cultures, it is assumed that fate makes choice inevitable, or that everybody depends on everyone else. In these cultures, all choices are group choices and everyone expects to share both the benefits and the failures of everyone's choices.

People have worldviews because of evolved, complex cognition; thus, having a worldview is a universal psychological process. The content of worldviews, however, is specific and different to each culture. Also, it's important to remember that behaviors and cultural worldviews are not necessarily related to each other; people of different cultures may have a belief about something that may not correspond with what their actual behaviors are (Matsumoto, 2006b); what people say is not always what they do. This distinction also needs to be taken into account when understanding the relationship between culture and psychology: cultural differences in worldviews may or may not be associated with cultural differences in behaviors.

▶ How Does Culture Influence Human Behaviors and Mental Processes?

How can we understand the relationship between culture and human behaviors and mental processes? We believe that culture influences psychological processes—behaviors and mental processes—through the process outlined in Figure 1.5. Cultures exert their influences on individuals primarily through situational contexts because cultures give social contexts important meanings, and it is these meanings that drive behavior. (Recall the discussion of the cultural dimension of tightness vs. looseness above, and the important of situational contexts there.) We learn cultural meanings and information associated with specific situational contexts. Newborns have no culture (although they may very well have biological and temperamental dispositions to learning certain cultural tendencies; see Chapters 3 and 4). Individuals begin the process of learning about their culture, and more specifically, the rules and norms of appropriate behavior in specific situations and contexts, through a process known as **enculturation**, which we will discuss in Chapter 3. The enculturation process gradually shapes and molds individuals' psychological characteristics, including how individuals perceive their worlds, think about the reasons underlying their and other people's action, have and express emotions, and interact with others in specific contexts. As children grow older, they learn specific behaviors and patterns of activities appropriate and inappropriate for their culture in specific situational contexts.

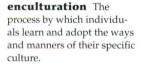

enculturation The process by which individuals learn and adopt the ways and manners of their specific culture.

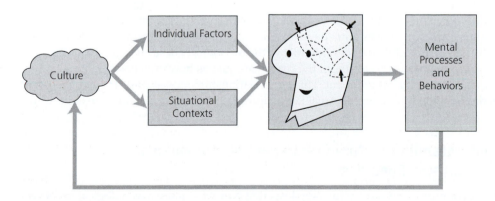

FIGURE 1.5 How Culture Influences Behavior

Scientists agree that many psychological processes—attitudes, values, beliefs, personality, cognition—are inherently constructed by culture, that is, that they are so intertwined and infused with cultural influences that it doesn't make sense to understand them outside of a cultural context. This makes sense, especially since attitudes, values, and beliefs are all based in language, and language is culturally constructed.

At the same time, much of our behaviors and mental processes are influenced by individual factors, which include personality, biological factors, and human nature. No one can deny that people come to the world with an amazing degree of individual differences in personality, temperament, reactivity, and sensitivity. These factors all influence how one perceives and evaluates the world, and behaves in that world.

Thus mental processes and behaviors are the product of the interaction between two major forces—one of which is culture, the other of which is the all the factors individuals brings with them to the world. In some contexts, behavior may be mostly influenced by individual factors; in other contexts, behaviors may be more highly influenced by cultural factors.

Figure 1.5 provides a very simplistic view of how culture influences mental processes and behaviors. Surely culture is associated with the individual factors, and the individual factors also engage in a complex interplay with situational contexts. Mental processes and behaviors feedback and affect culture, and all of these processes exist within a larger environment with a specific ecology, climate, history, and organizations. Understanding the influence of culture, therefore, requires us to adopt a relatively sophisticated way of understanding and explaining human behavior, one that acknowledges and incorporates other great factors that push and pull behaviors.

Another important point to remember is that the system described above and in Figure 1.5 is not static or unidirectional. It is dynamic and interrelated; it feeds back on and reinforces itself. Cultures change over time as the behaviors of its members change, and the environments within which groups exist change. Technological changes bring about changes in ways of living that in turn change culture. Even changes in the ecology, such as changes in climate, can bring about changes in ways of living, which will bring about changes in culture. Changes in affluence of a region, culture, or even individuals bring about changes in ways of living, and thus changes in culture. Look at countries and cultures such as Japan, South Korea, Singapore, China, or Barbados for major changes in culture because of affluence. Cultural changes produce changes in the people, in terms of their attitudes, values, opinions, beliefs, and their behaviors (Allen et al., 2007; Matsumoto, Kudoh, & Takeuchi, 1996). Communication technology (such as cellular phones, the Internet, e-mail, social media), for instance, brings with it its own brand of communication culture, in which rules regarding interactions and interpersonal engagement change rather rapidly. The widespread use of computers has brought with it the ability to work independently, loosening the reliance on others to get work accomplished and the need to interact with coworkers. These changes also affect the factors that influence culture in the first place, just as how our lifestyles today affect our ecologies and environment. Thus, the relationship between culture and behaviors is definitely not a one-way street; it is a reciprocal, dynamic, and complex relationship.

Understanding Culture in Perspective: Universals and Culture-Specifics

The evolution of human culture suggests that there are many psychological processes in which all humans engage. For example, because humans have the unique ability to recognize that others are intentional agents, we can draw inferences about the reasons underlying other people's behavior. These are called **attributions**, and the process of making attributions may be something that is universal to all humans (we'll discuss this more in Chapter 14).

> **attributions** Beliefs about the underlying causes of behavior.

But because all human cultures exist in their own specific, unique environment, there are differences among them. Thus, while making attributions may be something universal to all humans, people of different cultures may differ in the *way* they make them. That is, there are cultural differences in attributional styles among different human cultures.

This approach provides us with a relatively nuanced way of understanding the relationship between culture and psychology. With this approach, we can understand how, at one level comparing human cultures with nonhuman animal cultures, the same psychological process may be universal to all humans. At another level, comparing human cultures among themselves, the same psychological process may be done differently. This is true for attributions, emotions, cognition, and motivation. One of the goals of this book is to highlight the universal *and* culture-specific aspects of these psychological processes. (See Lonner, 1980; Norenzayan & Heine, 2005, for more discussion on universal psychological processes.)

Etics and Emics

Cultural psychologists have a vocabulary for talking about universal and culture-specific psychological processes. **Etics** refer to those processes that are consistent across different cultures; that is, etics refer to universal psychological processes. **Emics** refer to those processes that are different across cultures; emics, therefore, refer to culture-specific processes. These terms originated in the study of language (Pike, 1954), with *phonetics* referring to aspects of language and verbal behaviors that are common across cultures, and *phonemes* referring to aspects of language that are specific to a particular culture and language. Berry (1969) was one of the first to use these linguistic concepts to describe universal versus culturally relative aspects of behavior.

> **etics** Aspects of life that appear to be consistent across different cultures; universal or pancultural truths or principles.
>
> **emics** Aspects of life that appear to differ across cultures; truths or principles that are culture-specific.

Each culture has had a different combination of geography, climate, resources, previous culture, and contact with other cultures. Although we're all born with the same toolkits, our cultures help us use those toolkits in different ways. So we can all make sounds, but cultures teach us how to shape those sounds into words and how to arrange those words into the different languages we humans speak. We all have emotions, but cultures tell us what to become emotional about, and what to do about it when we are emotional. We all have a sense of morality, but cultures differ on what is right and wrong, good and bad. Thus culture influences how we communicate, think, make decisions, plan for the future, and solve problems. It dictates about politeness and etiquette. It defines religion and taboos. Because cultures exist in different regions of the world, they all "do" these things differently. That's why we see cultural differences in these (emics).

But while people of different cultures are often different in what they do, they are very similar in why they do them. All humans share the same basic needs and abilities, and it's important to understand the reasons why people of different cultures do things the way they do them. If we just look at the surface, they may seem strange. But if we get to know how and why they developed as a part of the culture, they will make sense. We all have a need for respect and a need to belong. We all want to find someone to share our life with, and we all are worried about our social image to others, and about feeling good about ourselves. People all around the world in different cultures are trying to accomplish many of the same things (etics); they are just going about doing them in very different ways (emics).

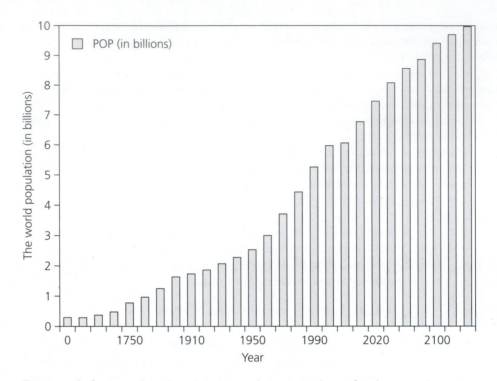

FIGURE 1.6 Growth in the Human Population—Evidence for the Success of Human Cultures

Basically, people around the world are very similar in their basic needs to get along, find a mate, achieve goals, and carry out the basic functions of living. Cultures find ways to allow people to address those needs. Because cultures exist in different regions of the world, with different histories, they often find different ways to address those same needs.

- Sometimes culture is like a multiplier, enhancing certain behaviors.
- Sometimes culture is like a creator, producing new behaviors not seen elsewhere.
- Sometimes culture is an enabler, facilitating and encouraging behaviors, and sometimes culture is a suppresser, discouraging behaviors.

Above that, different people in every culture find their own ways, producing many individual differences within cultures.

An important thing to remember about all cultures is that they have all worked until now. To support this, all one has to look at are world population statistics, because the purpose of culture is to help people survive. If cultures hadn't worked people would not have survived. Cultures have long histories of having worked for many generations in the past, and it is apparent that cultures are very successful in doing what they are supposed to do: help people survive (Figure 1.6).

THE GOAL OF THIS BOOK

After all is said and done, what do we intend that you gain from this book? In challenging the traditional, we do not mean to disregard its importance or the importance of the work that produced that knowledge. Instead, we seek to raise questions about the traditional, mainstream knowledge of human behavior. We want to know whether what we know of organizations, development, personality, emotion, communication, and many other aspects of human behavior is applicable to people of all cultural backgrounds. We want to challenge the traditional by seeking out answers to these questions in the cross-cultural literature. And if the research suggests that people are different from what is typically believed, we want to find better ways to understand those differences than are available today. We want to impart the flavor of the evolution in science and knowledge that is now occurring.

We offer this book to you as a way to understand, appreciate, respect, and feel cultural diversity and its influence on human behavior. In this book, there is no right and wrong, or good and bad. In learning about others—in meeting the challenge of cultural diversity—our biggest challenge is always within ourselves.

EXPLORATION AND DISCOVERY

Why Does This Matter to Me?

1. How does the definition of culture in this chapter differ from the definition of culture you may have had before reading it? What implications do you think those differences may have in your life? In psychology? In research? Did you equate culture with race or ethnicity previously?

2. What are some of the values, beliefs, norms, and worldviews that are important to you? Do you have any sacred values? What about the values, beliefs, norms, and worldviews of your friends? Classmates? Acquaintances in the community?

3. How do you identify yourself in terms of race? Ethnicity? Sexual orientation? What cultural characteristics do these have for you?

4. What kinds of cultural differences have you encountered in your daily life? At your workplace?

5. From your experiences, how do you think people of different cultures are similar?

Suggestions for Further Exploration

1. If you could design a study on anything about human behavior to show how it is the same across cultures, what would that be?

2. Likewise, if you could design a study on anything about human behavior to show how it is different across cultures, what would that be?

3. How would you design a study to show how culture can be beneficial to people? Likewise, how would you design a study to show how culture can be hurtful to people?

2 Cross-Cultural Research Methods

CHAPTER CONTENTS

One of the points we tried to make in Chapter 1 was that most findings in psychology are limited to the parameters of the research that generated them, and that cultural psychology examines the boundaries of that knowledge by altering one of those methodological parameters—the cultural background of the participants in the studies. Including participants from different cultural backgrounds is conceptually pretty easy—just add people from different cultures to an experiment. But doing so raises many important questions that need to be dealt with in order for such studies to be meaningful. This chapter introduces you to those special issues that are associated with cross-cultural research. We do so not only because is it important to be able to read cross-cultural research and understand its contributions to knowledge; you also need to be able to evaluate it on its own merits. As active consumers of research in your everyday and academic lives, you need to review cross-cultural research with a critical but fair and open mind, accessing the literature directly and evaluating it with established criteria for quality. And you should be able to evaluate the research that we present in this book. We begin by discussing the different types of studies that exist in cultural psychology.

▶ Types of Cross-Cultural Research

Over the last century cross-cultural research has progressed through different stages, with different types of studies prominent at different times (Bond, 2004b; Matsumoto & Yoo, 2006). Very loosely, the first stage involved initial tests of cultural differences and the discovery of fascinating cultural differences. A second stage involved the search for meaningful dimensions of cultural variability that can possibly explain those differences. The dimension known as individualism versus collectivism emerged during this stage, as did others. A third stage of research involved the conceptual application of those meaningful dimensions in cross-cultural studies. The fourth stage of research, in which the field is currently in, involves empirically applying those dimensions and other possible cultural explanations of behavior experimentally (i.e., not just conceptually) in order to scientifically document their effects.

Below we describe the three main types of studies in use today by cultural psychologists: method validation studies, indigenous cultural studies, and cross-cultural comparisons (Figure 2.1).

Method Validation Studies

All researchers are concerned with issues concerning **validity** and **reliability** of measurement. Validity refers to whether or not a scale, test, or measure accurately measures what it is supposed to measure. Reliability refers to whether the scale, test, or measure does so consistently. These concepts are extremely important to all researchers, cross-cultural or not.

When conducting a cross-cultural study, researchers cannot simply take a scale or measure that was developed and validated in one culture and use it in another. This is because even if that scale was validated in one culture, there is no reason to assume that it is equally valid in any other culture. It would have to be equivalently valid in all the cultures it was to be used; else, data derived from its measurement would not be comparable across cultures. (We will have a lot more to say about the concept of equivalence later.)

Cross-cultural researchers thus are concerned with equivalence in validity of their measures, scales, and tests. And importantly, just translating a measure does not

validity The degree to which a finding, measurement, or statistic is accurate, or represents what it is supposed to.

reliability The degree to which a finding, measurement, or statistic is consistent.

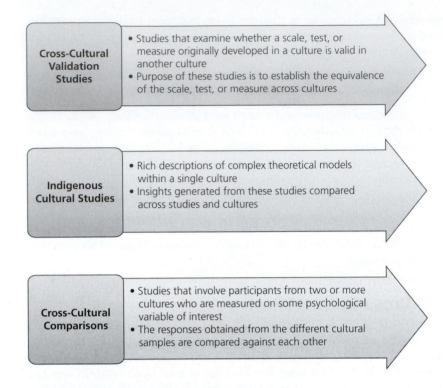

FIGURE 2.1 Types of Cross-Cultural Research

ensure measurement equivalence; there is a need to conduct studies to test the reliability and validity of measures in different cultures in order to be sure they can be used in the various cultures, thereby ensuring the cross-cultural measurement equivalence of the measure used. **Cross-cultural validation studies** do so. They examine whether a measure of a psychological construct that was originally generated in a single culture is applicable, meaningful, and most importantly psychometrically equivalent (that is, equally reliable and valid) in another culture. These studies do not test a specific hypothesis about cultural differences; rather, they test the equivalence of psychological measures and tests for use in other cross-cultural comparative research, and they are important to conduct before cross-cultural comparisons.

Indigenous Cultural Studies

Another type of cross-cultural study conducted is **indigenous cultural studies**. These are characterized by rich descriptions of complex theoretical models of a single culture that predict and explain cultural differences. A basic philosophy underlying this approach is that psychological processes and behaviors can only be understood within the cultural milieu within which it occurs. Thus understanding mental processes and behaviors requires an in-depth analysis of the cultural systems that produce and support those processes and behaviors, linking them to each other. Mesquita (Mesquita, 2001; Mesquita & Karasawa, 2002), for instance, described how cultural systems produce different concepts of the self, which in turn produce different types of specific concerns. According to her framework, individualistic cultures encourage the development of independent senses of self that encourage a focus on personal concerns and the view that the emotions signal internal, subjective feelings. Collectivistic

cross-cultural validation study A study that examines whether a measure of a psychological construct that was originally generated in a single culture is applicable, meaningful, and thus equivalent in another culture.

indigenous cultural studies Studies that use rich, complex, and in-depth descriptions of cultures and cultural differences to predict and test for differences in a psychological variable.

cultures, contrastingly, encourage the development of interdependent senses of self that encourage a focus on one's social worth and the worth of one's ingroup and the notion that emotions reflect something about interpersonal relationships.

Because indigenous cultural studies involve in-depth analyses of only a single culture, they are not cross-cultural per se. But the insights generated from these studies are compared to insights from similar studies in other cultures, allowing for cross-cultural comparisons after the fact. This type of research has its roots in anthropology, such as in the works of Margaret Mead or Ruth Benedict. Early cross-cultural psychologists such as John Berry and Beatrice Whiting made use of such methods. More recently, this methodology has been used to explain cultural differences in a number of psychological processes including morality (Shweder, 1993), attributional style (Nisbett, Peng, Choi, & Norenzayan, 2001), eye movements when viewing scenes (Masuda & Nisbett, 2001), the nature of unspoken thoughts (Kim, 2002), the need for high self-esteem (Heine, Lehman, Markus, & Kitayama, 1999), and many others. We will be discussing much of this research throughout the book.

Cross-Cultural Comparisons

The third type of cross-cultural study is perhaps the most prevalent in psychology, and these are known as **cross-cultural comparisons**. These are studies that involve participants from two or more cultures and that measure those participants' responses on a psychological variable of interest. The responses obtained from the different cultural samples are compared against each other, allowing for a direct cross-cultural comparison within that study. This comparison allows for conclusions to be drawn about cross-cultural similarities or differences on the variable of interest. Cross-cultural comparisons serve as the backbone of cross-cultural research.

> **cross-cultural comparisons** A study that compares two or more cultures on some psychological variable of interest, often with the hypothesis that one culture will have significantly higher scores on the variable than the other(s).

▶ Types of Cross-Cultural Comparisons

Exploratory versus Hypothesis Testing

There are four important ways to characterize cross-cultural comparisons (Table 2.1). The first involves the distinction between **exploratory versus hypothesis-testing studies**. Exploratory studies are designed to *examine the existence of cross-cultural similarities and differences*. Researchers tend to stay "close to the data" in exploratory studies. Hypothesis-testing studies are designed to *examine why cultural differences may exist*. Thus these studies make larger inferential jumps by testing theories of cross-cultural similarities and differences.

The methodological strengths and weaknesses of exploratory and hypothesis-testing studies mirror each other. The main strength of exploratory studies is their broad scope for identifying cross-cultural similarities and differences, which is particularly important in under-researched domains of cross-cultural psychology. The main weakness of such studies, however, is their limited capability to address the causes of the observed differences. The focused search of similarities and differences in hypothesis-testing studies leads to more substantial contribution to theory development and explicit attempts to deal with rival explanations, but is less likely to discover interesting differences outside of the realm of the tested theory. Also, inferences from hypothesis-testing studies are especially vulnerable to problems related to cross-cultural biases and inequivalence (more below).

> **exploratory studies** Studies designed to examine the existence of cross-cultural similarities or differences. These are generally simple, quasi-experimental designs comparing two or more cultures on a psychological variable.

> **hypothesis-testing studies** Studies designed to test why cultural differences exist. They go beyond simple quasi-experimental designs by either including context variables or by using experiments.

TABLE 2.1 Types of Cross-Cultural Comparisons

Exploratory vs. Hypothesis Testing	Presence or Absence of Contextual Factors	Structure vs. Level Oriented	Individual vs. Ecological (Cultural) Level
■ Exploratory studies examine whether or not cultural similarities or differences exist ■ Hypothesis-testing studies examine why cultural differences exist	■ Context factors are any variables that can explain, partly or fully, cross-cultural differences when they are observed in a study	■ Structure-oriented studies compare constructs, their measurements, or their relationships with other constructs across cultures ■ Level-oriented studies compare mean levels of scores between cultures	■ Individual-level studies are those where data from individuals are the unit of analysis ■ Ecological-level studies analyze data with country or culture as the unit of analysis

Presence or Absence of Contextual Factors

contextual factors
Any variable that can explain, partly or fully, observed cross-cultural differences. These may involve characteristics of the participants (such as socioeconomic status, education, and age) or their cultures (such as economic development and religious institutions).

A second way to differentiate cross-cultural studies from each other refers to the presence or absence of **contextual factors** in the design. Contextual factors involve any variable that can explain, partly or fully, cross-cultural differences when they are observed in a study (Poortinga, van de Vijver, Joe, & van de Koppel, 1987). Including such factors in a study and testing them will enhance the study's validity and help rule out the influence of biases and inequivalence because an evaluation of their influence can help to confirm or disconfirm their role in accounting for the cultural differences observed. Contextual factors may involve background characteristics of the participants (such as socioeconomic status, education, personality, and age) or their cultures (such as economic development and religious institutions). For example, administering a measure of response styles can help to evaluate the extent to which cross-cultural differences on extroversion are influenced by these styles. Hypothesis-testing studies generally need to include contextual variables.

Structure versus Level Oriented

structure-oriented studies Studies that examine whether constructs are conceptualized the same way across cultures, the relationship of a construct to other constructs, or the measurement of a construct.

level-oriented studies
Studies that examine cultural differences in mean levels of variables.

A third way to differentiate cross-cultural studies concerns the distinction between **structure-** and **level-oriented studies**. Structure-oriented studies involve comparisons of constructs (e.g., is depression conceptualized in the same way across cultures?), their structures (can depression be assessed in the same way in different cultures?), or their relationships with other constructs (is depression and anxiety positively related to each other in all cultures?). Level-oriented studies involve the comparisons of mean levels of scores between cultures (do individuals from different cultures show the same level of depression?). Structure-oriented studies focus on relationships among variables and attempt to identify similarities and differences in these relations across cultures. Level-oriented studies ask whether people of different cultures have different amounts of different variables.

Individual versus Ecological (Cultural) Level

ecological (cultural) level studies A study in which countries or cultures, not individuals, are the unit of analysis.

A fourth way to differentiate cross-cultural comparisons concerns individual versus ecological (cultural) levels of analysis, which are differentiated by the unit of analysis. Individual-level studies are the typical type of study in psychology, in which individual participants provide data and those individual participants' data are the unit of analysis. **Ecological- or cultural-level studies** use countries or cultures as the unit of analysis. Data may be obtained from individuals in different cultures, but they are often summarized or averaged for each culture and those averages are used as data points for each culture. Or country data are obtained from other sources (such as population statistics, average temperature or rainfall).

Concretely, a data file with individual-level data will have *individual* data in rows, and variables in columns, which are comprised of each individuals' response to each variable. A data file with ecological-level data will have data for *cultures* in rows, and variables in columns. If the data in an ecological-level study originally came from individuals, the data would be comprised of each culture's mean score on the variables (i.e., individual participants' data are averaged). Tables 2.2 and 2.3 give examples of how data are set up in individual- and ecological-level studies. Note the differences in what data are included and where they come from.

Ecological-level studies are an important type of cross-cultural comparison because they allow researchers to examine relationships between psychological variables with ecological-level variables like climate, population density, or gross national product. Thus researchers can begin to link psychological variables with ecological-level variables.

The most-well-known ecological-level study of culture is Hofstede's seminal work. In his original work, Hofstede (1980) reported data from 40 countries, and soon thereafter from an additional 13 (Hofstede, 1984). Most recently, he has reported data from 72 countries involving the responses of more than 117,000 employees of a multinational business organization, spanning over 20 languages and seven occupational levels to his 63 work-related values items (Hofstede, 2001). Respondents completed a 160-item questionnaire; 63 were related to work values. Hofstede conducted ecological-level analyses on the country means of the 63 items

TABLE 2.2 Example of Data from an Individual-Level Study

Level of Analysis	Self-Esteem	Academic Performance	Personality	Gender
Participant 1	Participant 1's score on Self-esteem	Participant 1's score on Academic Performance	Participant 1's score on Personality	Participant 1's Gender
Participant 1	Participant 2's score on Self-esteem	Participant 2's score on Academic Performance	Participant 2's score on Personality	Participant 2's Gender
Participant 3	Participant 3's score on Self-esteem	Participant 3's score on Academic Performance	Participant 3's score on Personality	Participant 3's Gender

TABLE 2.3 Example of Data from an Ecological-Level Study

Level of Analysis	Self-Esteem	Academic Performance	Climate	Population Density
Country 1	Country 1's mean on Self-esteem	Country 1's mean on Academic Performance	Country 1's score on Climate	Country 1's score on Population Density
Country 2	Country 2's mean on Self-esteem	Country 2's mean on Academic Performance	Country 2's score on Climate	Country 2's score on Population Density
Country 3	Country 3's mean on Self-esteem	Country 3's mean on Academic Performance	Country 3's score on Climate	Country 3's score on Population Density

and generated three dimensions that he suggested could describe the cultures of the countries sampled. Hofstede split one of the dimensions into two, based on theoretical reasoning and the fact that controlling for country-level gross national product produced a different set of scores. This resulted in his well-known set of four dimensions, introduced in Chapter 1: individualism versus collectivism, power distance, uncertainty avoidance, and masculinity versus femininity. Later Hofstede incorporated a fifth dimension called "long versus short-term orientation" (Hofstede, 2001; Hofstede & Bond, 1984), which was derived from Bond's work on Asian values (Connection, 1987).

To give you a flavor of the nature of ecological-level data, we reproduce for you the scores of each of the countries and regions in Hofstede's (2001) data set in Appendix A. Other ecological sets of cultural data exist, such as Schwartz's value orientations (Schwartz, 2004), and Leung and Bond and colleagues' social axioms (Bond et al., 2004), both of which were introduced in Chapter 1. Ecological-level data also have been published for many other psychological constructs, such as personality traits (McCrae, Terracciano, Khoury, Nansubuga, Knezevic, Djunc Jocic et al., 2005; discussed more fully in Chapter 10) and emotional display rules (Matsumoto et al., 2008).

In recent years, individual- and cultural-level data have been combined in what are known as **multi-level studies**. These are studies that use data from both individual and ecological levels, and incorporate the use of sophisticated statistical techniques that examine the relationship of data at one level to data at another. For example, multi-level studies can examine how individual differences in performance on a cognitive task (level 1) may be related to personality traits of those individuals (level 2) and how those personality traits may be related to cultural values or other ecological variables (level 3). Cross-cultural comparisons in the future will increasingly involve this type of multi-level approach.

multi-level studies
Studies that involve data collection at multiple levels of analysis, such as the individual level, context, community, and national culture.

▶ Designing Cross-Cultural Comparative Research

As we mentioned at the beginning of the chapter, cross-cultural comparisons raise many important methodological issues that influence the meaningfulness of the research. In the following sections, we discuss the issues most relevant to understanding the complexity of valid and reliable cross-cultural comparative research today.

Getting the Right Research Question

By far the most important part of any study, cross-cultural or not, is knowing what research questions to ask in the first place. Because cultural differences are relatively easy to obtain, researchers should remember that the purpose of conducting research is to contribute to a body of knowledge and not just to "find some cool differences." The "research literature" is the field's institutional memory and repository of that knowledge. Thus, any consideration of research designs starts first with a comprehensive and functional knowledge of that literature so that one understands what gaps in knowledge exist and what research questions should be addressed in order to contribute to that knowledge. Sometimes researchers focus on designing the methodology of a study or using new statistics without considering adequately what research question should be addressed in the first place. Sophisticated statistical techniques and elegant research designs cannot "salvage" studies that are neither novel nor insightful.

Understanding why any study is to be conducted in the first place leads to questions about how to conduct it, which is a discussion about research methodology. Questions related to the taxonomy described earlier apply here. Is the study exploratory or hypothesis testing? Should it include context variables? Is it structure oriented or level oriented? What is the level of analysis? Of course, no one study can do everything, and it's usually better to do something of limited scope very well than to try to conduct a study that addresses too much not so well at all.

With regard to cross-cultural studies, the field has gone much beyond the need for exclusively exploratory studies—that is, studies designed to merely document differences between two or more cultures on any psychological variable. Indeed, it is fairly easy to document differences on something, provided the cultures being compared are different enough. Instead, one of the major challenges that faces cross-cultural researchers today concerns how to isolate the *source* of such differences, and identify the active cultural (vs. noncultural) ingredients that produced those differences. It is in the empirical documentation of those active cultural ingredients that cross-cultural research designs need to pay close attention to. In doing so, researchers need to pay attention to a number of theoretical and empirical issues (see Matsumoto & Yoo, 2006, for a more complete discussion).

One of the major challenges that faces cross-cultural researchers today concerns how to isolate the source of such differences, and identify the active cultural (vs. noncultural) ingredients that produced those differences.

For example, is the source of the differences to be explained cultural or not? Examining this question forces researchers to have a definition of what culture is and to find ways of objectively measuring it. Once the active cultural ingredients that produce differences are identified, there is a level of analysis issue. Cultural variables exist on the group and individual levels. And studies themselves can be on the individual or cultural level, or involve a combination of the two in varying degrees with multiple levels. Different variables at different levels of analysis bring with them different theoretical and methodological implications, and require different interpretations of the research literature. When individual-level cultural variables are incorporated in a study, researchers need to distinguish between them and noncultural variables such as personality. A variable is not "cultural" just because a researcher says so; there needs to be a well-thought-out rationale based on theory and data that supports the identification and distinction of such variables.

Another question that researchers must deal with in designing studies concerns their theoretical model of how things work. A commonly held view that culture "produces" differences in a top-down fashion is a theoretical bias held by many. How do we know that to be true, and more importantly, how does one demonstrate that empirically? It may very well be that individual-level psychological processes and behaviors produce culture in a bottom-up fashion. Or that both top-down and bottom-up processes occur simultaneously. Regardless of how one believes things are put together, it behooves researchers to adopt research design strategies that are commensurate with their beliefs and models.

Designs That Establish Linkages between Culture and Psychological Variables

As mentioned above, an exploratory study that merely documents differences between cultures on some psychological variable cannot say anything about whether the source of the differences is cultural or not. Thus most researchers realize that it's important to empirically establish linkages between the contents of culture and the psychological variables of interest in hypothesis-testing studies. This has led to the emergence of a class of studies called **linkage studies** that attempt to do just that. There are two types of linkage studies conducted in the field today: unpackaging studies and experiments.

linkage studies Studies that attempt to measure an aspect of culture theoretically hypothesized to produce cultural differences and then empirically link that measured aspect of culture with the dependent variable of interest.

Unpackaging Studies

unpackaging studies
Studies that unpackage the contents of the global, unspecific concept of culture into specific, measurable psychological constructs and examine their contribution to cultural differences.

Unpackaging studies are cross-cultural comparisons that include the measurement of a variable (contextual factor) that assesses a cultural factor considered to produce the differences on the target variable being compared across cultures. The underlying thought to these studies is that cultures are like onions, for which layer after layer needs to be peeled off until nothing is left. Poortinga, van de Vijver, Joe, and van de Koppel (1987) expressed the view this way:

> "In our approach culture is a summary label, a catchword for all kinds of behavior differences between cultural groups, but within itself, of virtually no explanatory value. Ascribing intergroup differences in behavior, e.g., in test performance, to culture does not shed much light on the nature of these differences. It is one of the main tasks of cross-cultural psychology to peel off cross-cultural differences, i.e., to explain these differences in terms of specific antecedent variables, until in the end they have disappeared and with them the variable culture. In our approach culture is taken as a concept without a core. From a methodological point of view, culture can be considered as an immense set of often loosely interrelated independent variables." (p. 22; see also Segall, 1984; Strodtbeck, 1964)

context variables
Variables that operationalize aspects of culture that researchers believe produce differences in psychological variables. These variables are actually measured in unpackaging studies.

In unpackaging studies, "culture" as an unspecified variable is replaced by more specific variables in order to explain observed differences. These variables are called **context variables**. (That is why whether or not studies involve context variables is one of the major ways to differentiate cross-cultural comparisons; see Table 2.1.) When measured, researchers then examine the degree to which they statistically account for the differences in the comparison. If the context variables statistically account for differences, then the researchers are empirically justified in claiming that that specific aspect of culture—that is, that context variable—was related to the differences observed. If they do not, then researchers know that that specific context variable did not produce the observed differences. In either case, researchers are empirically justified in making claims about specific variables that account for cultural differences in the variables of interest.

individual-level measures of culture
Measures that assess psychological dimensions related to meaningful dimensions of cultural variability and that are completed by individuals. They are often used as context variables to ensure that samples in different cultures actually harbor the cultural characteristics thought to differentiate them.

Individual-Level Measures of Culture   There are many different types of context variables that can and have been used over the past few years. One of the more common types has been **individual-level measures of culture**. These are measures that assess a variable on the individual level that is thought to be a product of culture. To date, a number of different types of such measures have been used. By far, the most common dimension of culture operationalized on the individual level is individualism versus collectivism (IC).

As mentioned in Chapter 1 and above in this chapter, this dimension was first coined by Hofstede (2001). Thereafter, Harry Triandis, a noted cross-cultural scientist, championed the cause for this dimension and argued that the IC framework organizes and explains many different types of cultural differences (Triandis, 1994, 1995). Triandis then took the lead in developing a number of ways to measure IC on the individual level in order to use it as a context variable in hypothesis-testing research (e.g., Hui, 1984, 1988; Triandis, Leung, Villareal, & Clack, 1985; Triandis et al., 1986, 1988; Triandis, McCusker, & Hui, 1990). These researchers viewed individual-level IC as a syndrome that includes values, beliefs, attitudes, and behaviors (see also, Triandis, 1996); they treated the various psychological domains of subjective culture as an entire collective rather than as separate aspects of culture. Their multiple-method approach included ratings of the social content of the self, perceptions of homogeneity of ingroups and outgroups, attitude and value ratings, and perceptions of social behavior as a function of social distance. Participants were classified as either individualist or collectivist on the basis of their scores on each method. On the individual level, Triandis referred to individualism and collectivism as **idiocentrism** and **allocentrism**, respectively (Triandis et al., 1986).

Triandis and colleagues (Singelis, Triandis, Bhawuk, & Gelfand, 1995) further refined their measurement system by including items assessing a revised concept of individualism and collectivism they called "horizontal and vertical individualism and collectivism," representing yet further advances in the conceptual understanding of IC. In horizontal collectivism, individuals see themselves as members of ingroups in which all members are equal. In vertical collectivism, individuals see themselves as members of ingroups that are characterized by hierarchical or status relationships. In horizontal individualism, individuals are autonomous and equal. In vertical individualism, individuals are autonomous but unequal.

Matsumoto, Weissman, Preston, Brown, and Kupperbusch (1997) also developed an individual-level measure of IC that assesses context-specific IC tendencies in interpersonal situations—the IC Interpersonal Assessment Inventory (ICIAI). Matsumoto et al. (2002) used it in an unpacking study examining American and Japanese cultural differences in judgments of emotion. They showed that Americans and Japanese differed in how strongly they perceived facial expressions of emotion. More importantly, they also demonstrated that these differences were linked with differences in individual-level IC, and that this linkage empirically accounted for the cultural differences in judgment of faces. Thus, the inclusion of the ICIAI and the empirical linkage of it with the target variable (judgments of faces) provided empirical justification in claiming that IC accounted for cultural differences in those judgments, exemplifying the utility of an unpacking study.

A meta-analysis of 83 studies examining group differences on individual-level measures of IC reported that European Americans were more individualistic and less collectivistic than others in general (Oyserman, Coon, & Kemmelmeier, 2002). But contrary to common stereotypes, European Americans were not more individualistic than African Americans or Latinos, nor were they less collectivistic than Japanese or Koreans. These findings challenged researchers' notions about how IC may be the source of cultural differences and spurred the way to the search for other kinds of context variables.

Self-Construal Scales

Spurred on by the IC framework, Markus and Kitayama (1991b) proposed that individualistic and collectivistic cultures differed in the kinds of self-concepts they fostered, with individualistic cultures encouraging the development of independent self-construals, and collectivistic cultures encouraging the development of interdependent self-construals (we will discuss these more fully in Chapter 5). This theoretical advance led to the development of scales measuring independence and interdependence on the individual level, most notably the Self-Construal Scale (Singelis, 1994). Using this scale, cultural differences in self-esteem and embarassability were empirically linked to individual differences on these types of self-construals, again exemplifying the utility of unpacking studies (Singelis, Bond, Sharkey, & Lai, 1999).

Personality

Although personality is clearly not culture (remember our discussion in Chapter 1), it has been used as a context variable in many cross-cultural studies because it is

idiocentrism Refers to individualism on the individual level. On the cultural level, individualism refers to a how a culture functions. Idiocentrism refers to how individuals may act in accordance with individualistic cultural frameworks.

allocentrism Refers to collectivism on the individual-level. On the cultural level, collectivism refers to a how a culture functions. Allocentrism refers to how individuals may act in accordance with collectivistic cultural frameworks.

associated with many psychological processes, and because there are differences in aggregate personality traits across cultures. The United States, Australia, and New Zealand, for example, are noted for their relatively high degrees of extraversion, while France, Italy, and the French Swiss are associated with high levels of neuroticism (we will discuss this more in Chapter 6). Thus, cultural differences may be explained by different levels of personality traits in each culture.

For instance, Matsumoto (2006a) measured emotion regulation—the ability that individuals have to modify and channel their emotions—in the United States and Japan, and demonstrated the existence of cultural differences in emotion regulation. He also measured several personality traits and demonstrated that the personality traits known as extraversion, neuroticism, and conscientiousness were linked to emotion regulation and accounted for the cultural differences in it. Thus, what were apparent "cultural" differences on a variable could be explained by differences in aggregate levels of personality between the two cultures studied.

Cultural Practices

Another important type of context variable that is important in linkage studies is those that assess cultural practices such as child-rearing, the nature of interpersonal relationships, or cultural worldviews. Heine and Renshaw (2002), for instance, showed that Americans and Japanese were different in their liking of others, and that differences in liking were linked to different cultural practices. Americans liked others they thought were similar to them or shared their own views. For Japanese, liking was related to familiarity and interdependence with others.

Experiments

experiments Studies in which researchers create conditions to establish cause–effect relationships. Participants are generally assigned randomly to participate in the conditions, and researchers then compare results across conditions.

The second major type of linkage study is **experiments**, in which researchers create conditions to establish cause–effect relationships. Participants are generally assigned randomly to participate in the conditions, and researchers then compare results across conditions. These studies are different from cross-cultural comparisons because in cross-cultural comparisons, researchers cannot create the cultural groups, nor can they randomly assign participants to those groups. (Cross-cultural comparisons are examples of what are known as quasi-experimental designs.) Experiments differ because researchers create the conditions and assign participants to those conditions.

There are different types of experiments conducted in cross-cultural research today. Here we cover two types: priming studies and behavioral studies.

Priming Studies

Priming studies involve experimentally manipulating the mindsets of participants and measuring the resulting changes in behavior. These are interesting because researchers manipulate mindsets supposedly related to culture in order to see if participants behave differently as a function of the primed mindset. If they do, researchers then infer that the primed cultural mindset *caused* the observed differences in behavior, thereby providing a link between a cultural product (the mindset) and a psychological process (the behavior).

One of the first studies that primed cultural contents of the mind was by Trafimow, Triandis, and Goto (1991). In that study, American and Chinese participants were primed to think in either a private or collective, group-oriented way. Participants primed in the private way read instructions that stated:

> For the next two minutes, you will not need to write anything. Please think of what makes you different from your family and friends.

Participants primed in the collective, group-oriented way were primed with these instructions:

> For the next two minutes, you will not need to write anything. Please think of what you have in common with your family and friends. What do they expect you to do?

Then all participants were asked to complete a self-attitude instrument that involved their completing a series of incomplete questions that started "I am _____." Their responses were then coded according to whether they were individually oriented or group oriented. As expected, Americans as a whole produced more individually oriented responses than the Chinese, while the Chinese produced more group-oriented responses. But the results also showed that the priming worked. Individuals who were primed privately—that is, to think about how they were *different* from others—produced more individually oriented responses, regardless of whether they were American or Chinese. Likewise, individuals who were primed collectively—that is, to think about how they were similar to others—produced more group-oriented responses, regardless of whether they were American or Chinese (Figure 2.2).

Behavioral Studies   Perhaps the most stringent experiments involve manipulations of actual environments and the observation of changes in behaviors as a function of these environments. For example, it is commonly thought that members of collectivistic cultures cooperate more with each other because cooperation is necessary for groups to function effectively and because of the group-oriented nature of

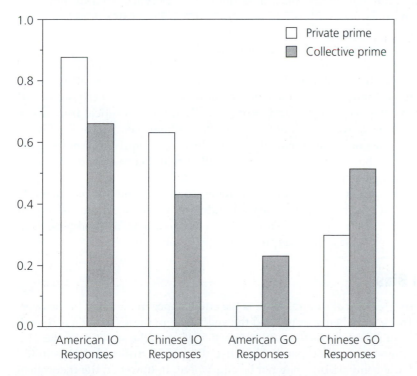

FIGURE 2.2 Amount of Individually Oriented (IO) and Group-Oriented (GO)

Source: Responses for Americans and Chinese in Trafimow et al. (1991).

collectivism. Two classic studies on cooperative behavior elucidate the importance of experiments in identifying what about cultures contributes to such differences. In the first study, Yamagishi (1986) used a questionnaire to categorize Japanese participants who were high trusters and low trusters; all of the participants then participated in an experiment in which they could cooperate with others by giving money to them, either with a sanctioning system that provided for punishments or without such a system. The conditions, therefore, were the presence or absence of the sanctioning system. High trusters did indeed cooperate more than low trusters without the sanctioning system; when the sanctioning system was in effect, however, low trusters cooperated more than did the high trusters.

Yamagishi (1988) then replicated this study in the United States and compared American and Japanese responses. He found the same results for Americans as he did for the Japanese; when there was no sanctioning system, high-trusting Americans cooperated more than low-trusting Americans. When there was a sanctioning system, the findings reversed. Moreover, there were no differences between the Americans and the Japanese when the sanctioning system was in effect. This suggested, therefore, that the greater cooperation observed in Japanese culture exists because of the sanctioning system within which individuals exist; when Americans were placed in that same type of system, they behaved in the same ways.

▶ Bias and Equivalence

bias Differences that do not have exactly the same meaning within and across cultures; a lack of equivalence.

equivalence A state or condition of similarity in conceptual meaning and empirical method between cultures that allows comparisons to be meaningful; a lack of bias.

In conducting and evaluating cross-cultural research, no concepts are more important than equivalence and bias. **Bias** refers to differences that do not have exactly the same meaning within and across cultures. **Equivalence** is a state or condition of similarity in conceptual meaning and empirical method between cultures that allows comparisons to be meaningful. These constructs go hand in hand; bias refers to a state of nonequivalence, and equivalence refers to a state of no bias.

In a strict sense, the greater the bias in any aspect of a cross-cultural study, the less meaning the comparison has. Bias (or lack of equivalence), in a cross-cultural study, is akin to comparing apples and oranges. Only if the theoretical framework and hypotheses have equivalent meaning in the cultures being compared—and if the methods of data collection, management, and analysis have equivalent meaning— will the results from that comparison be meaningful. Apples in one culture should be compared only to apples in another.

conceptual bias The degree to which a theory or set of hypotheses being compared across cultures are equivalent—that is, whether they have the same meaning and relevance in all the cultures being compared.

Thus it's important for cross-cultural researchers to understand the many aspects of their studies that may be culturally biased and work to establish equivalence in them. Below we discuss five major areas of bias: **conceptual bias**, method bias, measurement bias, response bias, and interpretational bias (Table 2.4).

Conceptual Bias

A major concern of cross-cultural research is the equivalence in meaning of the overall theoretical framework being tested and the specific hypotheses being addressed. If these are not equivalent across the cultures participating in the study, then the data obtained from them are not comparable because they mean different things in the first place, and any comparisons may not be equivalent. If, however, the theoretical framework and hypotheses are equivalent across the participating cultures, the study may be meaningful and relevant.

TABLE 2.4 Questions Raised by Five Types of Bias

Conceptual Bias	Method Bias	Measurement Bias	Response Bias	Interpretational Bias
■ Does the theoretical framework and hypotheses being tested mean the same thing in the cultures being tested?	■ Sampling bias: are the samples in the cultures tested appropriate representatives of their culture and equivalent to each other? ■ Linguistic bias: are the research protocols semantically equivalent across the languages used in the study? ■ Procedural bias: do the procedures by which data are collected mean the same in all cultures tested?	■ Are the specific measures, tests, or instruments used to collect data in different cultures equally valid and reliable across those cultures?	■ Do people of the different cultures tested use scales differently or have a bias when responding?	■ Are statistically significant findings practically meaningful? ■ Are the interpretations made about the findings and conclusions drawn biased in some way? ■ Are interpretations about cultural sources of differences justified by data?

For example, people trained to do research in the United States or Europe may be bound by a sense of "logical determinism" and "rationality" that is characteristic of their educational systems. In addition, because we are so used to drawing two-dimensional theories of behavior on paper, that medium affects the way we think about people and psychology (more about this in Chapter 8). People of other cultures who have not been exposed to such an educational system or who are not used to reducing their thoughts about the world onto paper may not think in the same way. If this is the case, then a question arises as to whether a theory created within a Western European or American cultural framework is meaningful in the same way to people who do not share that culture. If the theory is not meaningful in the same way, then it is not equivalent.

Past debates concerning cross-cultural studies of intelligence also highlight issues concerning conceptual equivalence. Intelligence typically is thought to consist of verbal and analytical critical-thinking skills and tests such as the Wechsler Adult Intelligence Scale (WAIS) have been widely used to assess IQ. Different cultures, however, may have a different conception of what constitutes intelligence. For example, a culture may consider nobility of character and sincerity to be markers of intelligence. Another culture may consider the ability to have smooth, conflict-free interpersonal relationships a marker for intelligence. Comparisons of WAIS data from these cultures may not be a meaningful cross-cultural comparison of intelligence.

Method Bias

Sampling Bias

There are two issues with regard to sampling bias, which refers to whether cross-cultural samples can be compared. One concerns whether the samples are appropriate representatives of their culture. Most cross-cultural studies are, in fact, not just cross-cultural; they are cross-city, and more specifically, cross-university studies. A "cross-cultural comparison" between Americans and Mexicans may, for instance, involve data collected in Seattle and Mexico City. Are the participants in Seattle representative of American culture? Would they provide the same responses as participants from Beverly Hills, the Bronx, or Wichita? Would the participants in Mexico City provide the same results as those in San Luis Portosi, Guadalajara, or the Yucatan Peninsula? The answer is "we don't know," and it is important for cross-cultural researchers, and consumers of that research (you) to recognize that sound cross-cultural comparisons would entail the collection of data from multiple sites within the same cultural group, either in the same study or across studies, to demonstrate the replicability of a finding across different samples within the same culture.

A second question concerning sampling bias concerns whether the samples are equivalent on noncultural demographic variables, such as age, sex, religion, socio-economic status, work, and other characteristics. For example, imagine comparing data from a sample of 50 Americans from Los Angeles with 50 individuals from Bombay, India. Clearly, the Americans and the Indians come from entirely different backgrounds—different socioeconomic classes, different educational levels, different social experiences, different forms of technology, different religious backgrounds, and so on. Are they really comparable to each other? To deal with this issue, researchers need to find ways of controlling these noncultural demographic factors when comparing data across cultures. They do this in one of two ways: experimentally controlling them by holding them constant in the selection of participants (e.g., conducting studies in which only females of a certain age can participate in the study in all cultures) or statistically controlling them when analyzing data.

A problem arises in cross-cultural research in that some noncultural demographic characteristics are inextricably intertwined with culture such that researchers cannot hold them constant across samples in a comparison. For example, there are differences in the meaning and practice of religions across cultures that often make them bound to culture. Holding religion constant across cultures does not address the issue because being Catholic in the United States does not mean the same thing as being Catholic in Japan or Malaysia. Randomly sampling without regard to religion will result in samples that differ not only on culture but also on religion (to the extent that one can separate the influences of the two). Thus presumed cultural differences often reflect religious differences across samples as well. The same is often true for socioeconomic status (SES), as there are vast differences in SES across cultural samples from around the world.

Linguistic Bias

One arena in which potential bias in cross-cultural research becomes quickly apparent is in language. Cross-cultural research is unique because it often involves collecting data in multiple languages, and researchers need to establish the linguistic equivalence of the research protocols. **Linguistic bias** refers to whether the research protocols—items on questionnaires, instructions, etc.—used in a cross-cultural study are semantically equivalent across the various languages included in the study.

There are generally two procedures used to establish linguistic equivalence. One is known as **back translation** (Brislin, 1970). Back translation involves taking the research protocol in one language, translating it to the other language, and having someone else translate it back to the original. If the back-translated version is the same as the original, they are generally considered equivalent. If it is not, the procedure is repeated until the back-translated version is the same as the original. The concept underlying this procedure is that the end product should be a semantic equivalent to the original language. The original language is **decentered** through this process (Brislin, 1970, 1993), with any culture-specific concepts of the original language eliminated or translated equivalently into the target language. That is, culture-specific meanings and connotations are gradually eliminated from the research protocols so that what remains is something that is the closest semantic equivalent in each language. Because they are linguistic equivalents, successfully back-translated protocols are comparable in a cross-cultural study.

linguistic bias The semantic equivalence between protocols (instruments, instructions, questionnaires, etc.) used in a cross-cultural comparison study.

back translation A technique of translating research protocols that involves taking the protocol as it was developed in one language, translating it into the target language, and having someone else translate it back to the original. If the back-translated version is the same as the original, they are generally considered equivalent. If it is not, the procedure is repeated until the back-translated version is the same as the original.

decenter The concept underlying the procedure of back translation that involves eliminating any culture-specific concepts of the original language or translating them equivalently into the target language.

A second approach to establishing language equivalence is the committee approach, in which several bilingual informants collectively translate a research protocol into a target language. They debate the various forms, words, and phrases that can be used in the target language, comparing them with their understanding of the language of the original protocol. The result of this process reflects a translation that is the shared consensus of a linguistically equivalent protocol across languages and cultures.

Researchers may combine the two approaches. A protocol may be initially translated and back-translated. Then the translation and back-translation can be used as an initial platform from which a translation committee works on the protocol, modifying the translation in ways they deem most appropriate, using the back-translation as a guideline.

Procedural Bias

The issue of bias and equivalence also applies to the procedures used to collect data in different cultures. For instance, in many universities across the United States, students enrolled in introductory psychology classes are strongly encouraged to participate as research subjects in partial fulfillment of class requirements. American students generally expect to participate in research as part of their academic experience, and many American students are "research-wise."

Customs differ in other countries. In some countries, professors simply collect data from their students or require them to participate at a research laboratory. In some countries, students may consider it a privilege rather than a chore or course requirement to participate in an international study. Thus, expectations about and experience with research participation may differ.

All the decisions researchers make in any other type of study are made in cross-cultural studies as well. But those decisions can mean different things in different countries. Laboratory or field, day or night, questionnaire or observation—all these decisions may have different meanings in different cultures. Cross-cultural researchers need to confront these differences in their work and establish procedures, environments, and settings that are equivalent across the cultures being compared. By the same token, consumers need to be aware of these possible differences when evaluating cross-cultural research.

Measurement Bias

Measurement bias refers to the degree to which measures used to collect data in different cultures are equally valid and reliable. As mentioned above, validity refers to whether a measure accurately measures what it is supposed to measure; reliability refers to how consistently a measure measures what it is supposed to measure.

One of the most important lessons to learn about cross-cultural research methods is that linguistic equivalence alone does not guarantee measurement equivalence. This is because even if the words being used in the two languages are the same, there is no guarantee that those words have exactly the same meanings, with the same nuances, in the two cultures. A successful translation gives the researcher protocols that are the closest linguistic equivalents in two or more languages; but, they still may not be exactly the same. In translating the English word *anger*, for example, we might indeed find an equivalent word in Cantonese or Spanish. But would it have the same connotations, strength, and interpretation in those languages as it does in English? It is very difficult to find exact translation equivalents of most words. Thus, cross-cultural researchers need to be concerned with measurement equivalence in addition to linguistic equivalence.

measurement bias
The degree to which measures used to collect data in different cultures are equally valid and reliable.

Measurement equivalence starts on the conceptual level. Different cultures may conceptually define a construct differently and/or measure it differently. Just because something has the same name in two or more cultures does not mean that it has the same meaning (Wittgenstein, 1953, cited in Poortinga, 1989) or that it can be measured in the same way. If a concept means different things to people of different cultures, or if it is measured in different ways in different cultures, then comparisons are less meaningful. Cross-cultural researchers need to be keenly aware of the issue of equivalence with regard to their conceptual definitions and empirical **operationalization** of the variables (the way researchers conceptually define a variable and measure it) in their study. Another way to think about measurement equivalence is on the statistical level—that is, in terms of **psychometric equivalence**. Psychometric equivalence can be ascertained in several different ways. One of the most important ways, especially when using questionnaires to collect data (which is used in many cross-cultural studies), is to determine whether the questionnaires in the different languages have the same structure. For example, researchers often use a technique called **factor analysis** to examine the structure of a questionnaire. Factor analysis creates groups of the items on a questionnaire based on how the responses to them are related to each other. The groups, called factors, are thought to represent different mental constructs in the minds of the participants responding to the items. Scores are then computed to represent each of these mental constructs.

When using questionnaires across cultures, one concern that arises is whether the same groups of items, or factors, would emerge in the different cultures. If so, then the measure is said to have **structural equivalence**. If not, the measure is structurally nonequivalent (biased), which suggests that people of different cultural groups have different mental constructs operating when responding to the same questionnaire. Thus, their responses may not be comparable to each other.

Another way in which psychometric equivalence can be ascertained is by examining the **internal reliability** of the measures across cultures. Internal reliability can be assessed by examining whether the items on a questionnaire are all related to each other. If they are measuring the same mental construct, then items should be related to each other; that is, they should have high internal reliability. If the items are working in the same way across cultures, then they should have high internal reliability in each of the cultures being tested.

Response Bias

Cross-cultural researchers also need to be aware of the fact that different cultures can promote different types of response biases. A **response bias** is a systematic tendency to respond in a certain way to items or scales. If response biases exist, then it is difficult to compare data between cultures because it is not clear whether differences refer to "true" differences in what is being measured or are merely differences in how people respond using scales.

There are several different types of response biases. **Socially desirable responding**, for instance, is the tendency to give answers that make oneself look good (Paulhus, 1984), and it may be that people of certain cultures have greater concerns that lead them to respond in socially desirable ways than people of other cultures. There are two facets of socially desirable responding, which include *self-deceptive enhancement*—seeing oneself in a positive light—and *impression management*. Lalwani, Shavitt, and Johnson (2006) demonstrated that European American university students score higher on self-deceptive enhancement than both Korean Americans and students

---

operationalization The ways researchers conceptually define a variable and measure it.

psychometric equivalence The degree to which different measures used in a cross-cultural comparison study are statistically equivalent in the cultures being compared—that is, whether the measures are equally valid and reliable in all cultures studied.

factor analysis A statistical technique that allows researchers to group items on a questionnaire. The theoretical model underlying factor analysis is that groups of items on a questionnaire are answered in similar ways because they are assessing the same, single underlying psychological construct (or trait). By interpreting the groupings underlying the items, therefore, researchers make inferences about the underlying traits that are being measured.

structural equivalence The degree to which a measure used in a cross-cultural study produces the same factor analysis results in the different countries being compared.

internal reliability The degree to which different items in a questionnaire are related to each other, and give consistent responses.

response bias A systematic tendency to respond in certain ways to items or scales.

socially desirable responding Tendencies to give answers on questionnaires that make oneself look good.

from Singapore, but the latter score higher on impression management than do European Americans (Figure 2.3).

Lalwani et al. (2006) also demonstrated that individuals with more individualistic cultural orientations engaged in more self-deceptive enhancement,

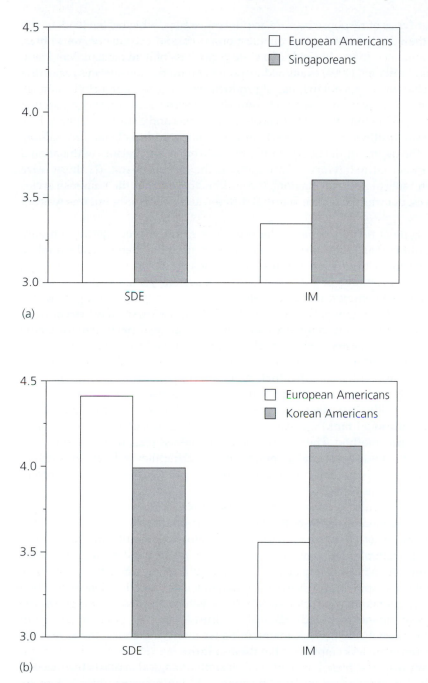

(a)

(b)

FIGURE 2.3 Socially Desirable Responding

(a) Comparison of European Americans and Singaporeans, (b) Comparison of European Americans and Korean Americans. SDE = self-deceptive enhancement; IM = impression management.

Source: Adapted from Lalwani et al., 2006.

while individuals with more collectivistic orientations engaged in more impression management. Relatedly, Matsumoto (2006b) showed that differences between Americans and Japanese university students' individualistic versus collectivistic cultural orientations disappeared once socially desirable responding was statistically controlled.

acquiescence bias The tendency to agree rather than disagree with items on questionnaires.

extreme response bias The tendency to use the ends of a scale regardless of item content.

Two other types of response bias are **acquiescence bias**, which is the tendency to agree rather than disagree with items on questionnaires, and **extreme response bias**, which is the tendency to use the ends of a scale regardless of item content. Van Herk, Poortinga, and Verhallen (2004) examined responses on marketing surveys regarding household behaviors (e.g., cooking, use of products, shaving, washing clothes) in six European countries. They reported that countries near the Mediterranean (Greece, Italy, and Spain) exhibited more of both acquiescence bias and extreme response bias than countries in northwestern Europe (France, Germany, and the United Kingdom). Interestingly, the degree of the two response biases were not correlated with national differences in actual behaviors with regard to the issues raised. (If there were differences in rates of actual behaviors, it could be argued that the response styles were not biases, but were reflective of actual differences in behaviors, but this was not the case.)

reference group effect The idea that people make implicit social comparisons with others when making ratings on scales. That is, people's ratings will be influenced by the implicit comparisons they make between themselves and others, and these influences may make comparing responses across cultures difficult.

Another type of response bias is the **reference group effect** (Heine, Lehman, Peng, & Greenholz, 2002). This idea is based on the notion that people make implicit social comparisons with others when making ratings on scales, rather than relying on direct inferences about a private, personal value system (Peng, Nisbett, & Wong, 1997). That is, when completing rating scales, people will *implicitly* compare themselves to others in their group. For example, Japanese individuals may appear to be fairly individualistic on questionnaires, even more so than Americans. But Heine et al. (2002) argue that this may be because the Japanese implicitly compare themselves to their own groups, who are actually fairly collectivistic, when making such ratings, and thus inflate their ratings of individualism. Likewise, Americans may inflate their ratings of collectivism because they implicitly compare themselves to others, who are actually fairly individualistic. Peng et al. (1997) examined four different value survey methods: the traditional ranking, rating, attitude scaling procedures, and a behavioral scenario rating method. The only method that yielded reasonable validity estimates was what is known as a behavioral scenario rating method, which involves rating of behaviors through observations or vignettes, and which is the most uncommon of all the measures tested.

What aspects of culture account for response biases? Johnson, Kulesa, Cho, and Shavitt (2004) examined these biases in 19 countries around the world and correlated indices of the biases with each country's score on Hofstede's cultural dimensions. (This study is an example of an ecological-level study.) On one hand, extreme response bias occurred more in cultures that encourage masculinity, power, and status. They suggested that this response style achieves clarity, precision, and decisiveness in one's explicit verbal statements, characteristics that are valued in these cultures. On the other hand, respondents from individualistic cultures were less likely to engage in acquiescence bias, probably because maintaining harmony and conveying agreeableness and conveying deference are less emphasized in these cultures.

In the past, response biases were viewed as methodological artifacts that needed to be controlled in order to get to "true" responses. Today, however, there is a growing view of them as an important part of cultural influence on data. Regardless of how researchers choose to view this issue, their effects should be acknowledged and incorporated when analyzing data and interpreting findings.

Interpretational Bias

Analyzing Data

In testing cultural differences on target variables of interest, researchers often use inferential statistics such as chi-square or analysis of variance (ANOVA) and engage in what is known as null hypothesis significance testing. These statistics compare the differences observed between the groups to the differences one would normally expect on the basis of chance alone and then compute the probability that the results would have been obtained solely by chance. If the probability of obtaining the findings they did is very low (less than five percent), then researchers infer that the findings did not occur because of chance—that is, that the findings reflect actual differences between the cultural groups from which their samples were drawn. This "proof by negation of the opposite" is at the heart of the logic underlying hypothesis testing and statistical inference.

In the past, researchers were quick to take "statistically significant" results and interpret them as if they were "practically meaningful to all or most members of the groups being compared." That is, researchers (and consumers of research) often assume that most people of those groups differ in ways corresponding to the mean values. Thus, if a statistically significant difference is found between Americans and Chinese, for instance, on emotional expressivity such that Americans had statistically significantly higher scores than the Chinese, people often conclude that all Americans are more expressive than all Chinese.

But the fact that the differences between group means are statistically significant does not by itself give an indication of the degree of practical meaningfulness of the difference between the groups. Group means may be statistically different even though there is considerable overlap among the scores of individuals comprising the two groups. The tendency to make glossy, broad-sweeping statements based on "statistically significant" results is a mistake in interpretation that is fueled by the field's fascination and concern with statistical significance and perhaps stereotypes.

Fortunately, statistical procedures are available that help to determine the degree to which differences in mean values reflect meaningful differences among individuals. The general class of statistics is called "effect size statistics"; when used in a cross-cultural setting, they are known as "cultural effect size statistics" (Matsumoto, Grissom, & Dinnel, 2001). There are a number of different types of such statistics that can help researchers and readers get an idea of the degree to which the between-group cultural differences actually reflect differences among the individuals tested, helping to break the hold of stereotypic interpretations based on group difference findings.

Dealing with Nonequivalent Data

Despite the best attempts to establish equivalence in theory, hypothesis, method, and data management, cross-cultural research is often inextricably, inherently, and inevitably nonequivalent. It is nearly impossible to create any cross-cultural study that means exactly the same thing to all participating cultures, both conceptually and empirically. What cross-cultural researchers often end up with are best approximations of the closest equivalents in terms of theory and method in a study. Thus, researchers are often faced with the question of how to deal with nonequivalent data. Poortinga (1989) outlined four different ways in which the problem of nonequivalence of cross-cultural data can be handled:

1. *Preclude comparison.* The most conservative thing a researcher could do is not make the comparison in the first place, concluding that it would be meaningless.

2. *Reduce the nonequivalence in the data.* Many researchers take steps to identify equivalent and nonequivalent parts of their methods and then refocus their comparisons solely on the equivalent parts. For example, if a researcher used a 20-item scale to measure anxiety in two cultures and found evidence for non-equivalence on the scale, he or she might then examine each of the 20 items for equivalence and rescore the test using only the items that are shown to be equivalent. Comparisons would then be based on the rescored items.

3. *Interpret the nonequivalence.* A third strategy is for the researcher to interpret the nonequivalence as an important piece of information concerning cultural differences.

4. *Ignore the nonequivalence.* Unfortunately, what many cross-cultural researchers end up doing is simply ignoring the problem, clinging to beliefs concerning scale invariance across cultures despite a lack of evidence to support those beliefs.

How researchers handle the interpretation of their data given nonequivalence depends on their experience, biases and the nature of the data and the findings. Because of the lack of equivalence in much cross-cultural research, researchers are often faced with many gray areas in interpreting their findings. Culture itself is a complex phenomenon, neither black nor white but replete with gray. It is the objective and experienced researcher who can deal with these gray areas, creating sound, valid, and reliable interpretations that are justified by the data. And it is the astute consumer of that research who can sit back and evaluate those interpretations relative to the data in their own minds and not be unduly swayed by the arguments of the researchers.

Interpreting Findings

Culture can bias the ways researchers interpret their findings. Most researchers inevitably interpret the data they obtain through their own cultural filters, and these biases can affect their interpretations to varying degrees. For example, for years American–Japanese cultural differences in emotionality were interpreted by researchers as indicative of Japanese suppression of emotion (Matsumoto & Ekman, 1989). Later studies, however, provided evidence that it may not be so much that the Japanese suppress, but that Americans exaggerate their emotional responses (Matsumoto, Kasri, & Kooken, 1999). Thus, our own interpretations of the data were biased in implicitly considering the American data as the "true" responses and non-American data as somehow different.

In hypothesis-testing cross-cultural studies, cultural groups are often treated as independent variables in research designs and data analysis, making these studies a form of quasi-experiment. Data from such studies are basically correlational, and inferences drawn from them can only be correlational inferences. For example, if a researcher compared data from the United States and Hong Kong on social judgments and found that Americans had significantly higher scores on a person perception task, any interpretations of these data would be limited to the association between cultural membership (American or Hong Kong Chinese) and the scores. Cause–effect inferences (for example, being American *causes* one to have higher person-perception scores) are unwarranted. For such causal statements to be justified, the researcher would have had to: (1) create the conditions of the experiment (the cultural groups) and (2) randomly assign people to each of the conditions. These experimental conditions cannot apply in any study in which one of the main variables is cultural group. It makes no more sense to assume a causal relationship between cultural membership and a variable of interest than it does to assume such a relationship on the basis of sex, hair color, or height.

A related type of mistaken interpretation is to suggest specific reasons why cultural differences occurred even though the specific reasons were never measured in the study. Matsumoto and Yoo (2006) call these **cultural attribution fallacies**, which occur when researchers claim that between-group differences are cultural when they really have no empirical justification to do so. This can occur easily in exploratory studies (with quasi-experimental designs) that only document differences between cultures, because researchers often interpret the source of the differences to some cultural factors even though those cultural factors were never measured in the study or linked to the variables of interest. For instance, a researcher might take the significant American–Hong Kong differences found in the previous example and suggest that these differences occurred because of differences between individualism and collectivism in the two cultures. Unless the researchers actually measured individualism and collectivism in their study, found that the two cultures differed on this dimension, and showed that it accounted for the cultural-group differences on social judgments, the interpretation that this construct (IC) is responsible for the group differences is unwarranted. Linkage studies address this problem.

cultural attribution fallacies A mistaken interpretation in cross-cultural comparison studies. Cultural attribution fallacies occur when researchers infer that something cultural produced the differences they observed in their study, despite the fact that they may not be empirically justified in doing so because they did not actually measure those cultural factors.

CONCLUSION

As we mentioned earlier, cross-cultural research is easy in concept—just test people from different cultural backgrounds. But in reality cross-cultural research is difficult because going across cultures raises many important issues. There are many threats to the validity of any cross-cultural study, including threats to theoretical frameworks (construct bias), methods of data collection (method bias), measurement (measurement bias), responses (response bias), and analyzing data and interpreting findings (interpretational bias). Even when cultures are compared correctly, there is the additional problem of how we can link the differences to meaningful aspects of culture.

Despite all the inherent difficulties, cross-cultural research offers a number of exciting and interesting opportunities not available with traditional research approaches. Through cross-cultural research, we can test the limits and boundaries of our knowledge about human behavior. We can push the envelope of our understanding of people in ways that are impossible with traditional research approaches. The cross-cultural enterprise itself offers a process by which scientists and laypersons from disparate cultures can come together and work toward common goals, thereby improving human relations across what otherwise may seem a considerable chasm. The findings from cross-cultural research offer scientists, scholars, and the public ways to further our understanding of human diversity that can serve as the basis for renewed personal and professional relationships, and can help to focus public and social policy. Methodologically, cross-cultural studies offer researchers a way to deal with empirical problems related to the conduct of research, such as confounding variables present in traditional research approaches.

The process of evaluating the merits of studies and then accumulating information across the studies you trust is integral to learning about a field. We have tried to provide a solid basis for developing and practicing these skills. The material presented in this chapter is just the tip of the iceberg. Many excellent resources, other than those cited throughout this chapter, explain cross-cultural research issues in greater detail for specialists (see Matsumoto & van de Vijver, 2011). And there are many things researchers can do before and after collecting data to ensure their studies reduce bias and establish equivalence.

It is this cumulative process that we went through in selecting studies from the various areas of cross-cultural research to present to you in this book. But do not take our word for it; please evaluate that research for yourself. It is a skill that takes practice in order to do well, but like many skills, it can be honed. Hopefully the issues we have discussed above can serve as a platform by which you can conduct your own evaluations of cross-cultural research. As you read and evaluate the studies presented in this book and elsewhere, we hope you will find that while cross-cultural research has its own problems and limitations, it has advantages and potentialities that far outweigh the difficulties.

EXPLORATION AND DISCOVERY

Why Does This Matter to Me?

1. When someone makes claims concerning the nature of human behavior and mental processes, how do you know to believe those claims? Adopting a scientific point of view requires a good deal of healthy skepticism about the validity of those claims. Evaluating the validity of such claims requires asking about the data that informs such claims. What kinds of questions would you ask?

2. Have you ever participated in a research study? What was it like? How did your participation affect how you thought scientific knowledge was created?

3. And if you were in a cross-cultural study what culture would you represent? Your national culture? The culture of students enrolled in psychology courses? The culture of your ethnic origins?

Suggestions for Further Exploration

1. Find a cross-cultural study in your library or through any reference source for primary research articles. Try evaluating it using each of the issues raised in this chapter. What differences and similarities do you think exist between that cross-cultural study and the same study conducted within a single culture?

2. If you could design a cross-cultural study on anything about human behavior, what would it be? What hypotheses would you have?

3. In a study, how would you isolate the specific aspect of culture that produces differences in a cross-cultural study?

4. For those who speak more than one language—have you ever considered whether the words spoken in both languages actually mean exactly the same thing or not? If not, what implications do you think such differences have for cross-cultural research in different languages?

5. Find your country in the Appendix and check out its scores on the five cultural dimensions. How do those scores compare to scores from other countries in the Appendix? How do those comparisons compare to your experiences with people from other cultures?

APPENDIX A **Listing of Countries and Regions and Their Scores on the Five Hofstede Cultural Dimensions** (From Hofstede, 2001; Reproduced by Permission of Geert Hofstede)

EXHIBIT A2.1 Index Scores for Countries and Regions from the IBM Set

Country	Index				
	Power Distance	**Uncertainty Avoidance**	**Individualism Collectivism**	**Masculinity/ Feminity**	**Long-/Short- Orientation**
Argentina	49	86	46	56	
Australia	36	51	90	61	31
Austria	11	70	55	79	31
Belgium	65	94	75	54	38
Brazil	69	76	38	49	65
Canada	39	48	80	52	23
Chile	63	86	23	28	
Colombia	67	80	13	64	
Costa Rica	35	86	15	21	
Denmark	18	23	74	16	46
Ecuador	78	67	8	63	
Finland	33	59	63	26	41
France	68	86	71	43	39
Germany	35	65	67	66	31
Great Britain	35	35	89	66	25
Greece	60	112	35	57	
Guatemala	95	101	6	37	
Hong Kong	68	29	25	57	96
India	77	40	48	56	61
Indonesia	78	48	14	46	
Iran	58	59	41	43	
Ireland	28	35	70	68	43
Israel	13	81	54	47	
Italy	50	75	76	70	34
Jamaica	45	13	39	68	
Japan	54	92	46	95	80
Korea (South)	60	85	18	39	75
Malaysia	104	36	26	50	
Mexico	81	82	30	69	
Netherlands	38	53	80	14	44
New Zealand	22	49	79	58	30
Norway	31	50	69	8	44
Pakistan	55	70	14	50	0
Panama	95	86	11	44	

EXHIBIT A2.1 (*Continued*)

Country	Power Distance	Uncertainty Avoidance	Individualism Collectivism	Masculinity/ Feminity	Long-/Short- Orientation
Peru	64	87	16	42	
Philippines	94	44	32	64	19
Portugal	63	104	27	31	30
Salvador	66	94	19	40	
Singapore	74	8	20	48	48
South Africa	49	49	65	63	
Spain	57	86	51	42	19
Sweden	31	29	71	5	33
Switzerland	34	58	68	70	40
Taiwan	58	69	17	45	87
Thailand	64	64	20	34	56
Turkey	66	85	37	45	
United States	40	46	91	62	29
Uruguay	61	100	36	38	
Venezuela	81	76	12	73	
Yugoslavia	76	88	27	21	
Regions:					
Arab countries	80	68	38	53	
East Africa	64	52	27	41	25
West Africa	77	54	20	46	16

Source: From *Culture's Consequences: Comparing Values, Behaviors, Institutions and Organizations across Nations* (2nd ed.) by G. H. Hofstede, 2001. p. 500. Copyright © 2001 by Geert Hofstede. Reprinted with permission by Geert Hofstede B.V.

Enculturation

3

CHAPTER CONTENTS

When the study of culture and psychology uncovers cultural differences among people, some natural questions come to mind: How did these differences arise in the first place? What happens during development that makes people of different cultures different? What are the relative influences of parents, families, extended families, schools, and other social institutions? Are people born with inherent, biological predispositions to behavioral and cultural differences, or are such differences due entirely to environment and upbringing? This chapter examines how the process of enculturation works. That is, how do people come to acquire their cultures? Research in this area has focused on parenting, peer groups, and institutions such as the educational system, each of which will be discussed here. First, we discuss how humans are different from other animals in their ability to acquire culture. Then we define and compare two important terms in this area of study: enculturation and socialization.

▶ Humans Engage in Cultural Learning

In Chapter 1, we learned that one of the most important thinking abilities that humans have that other animals do not is the ability to share intentions with one another. In other words, humans can get into another person's mind, see things from that person's point of view, understand the intentions of that person, and recognize that the person understands our own intentions too. This unique ability of humans to engage in shared intentionality allows us to engage in "cultural learning"—that is, learning not only *from* others but *through* others (Tomasello, Kruger, & Ratner, 1993).

Tomasello at the Max Planck University in Leipzig, Germany, studied how humans are unique from other animals in this aspect of cultural learning (Tomasello & Herrmann, 2010). In one study, he compared two types of great apes (chimpanzees and orangutans) to two-year old human children. In many ways, the great apes and children looked very similar in terms of how they thought about space, quantities, and causality. But there was one big difference. The children were much more sophisticated than the great apes in the ways they thought about the social world. Children understood intentionality, social learning, and social communication on a much deeper and complex level than the great apes. Tomasello proposed that this facility with social learning and communication provides the foundation for cooperation with other humans; this fundamental ability to cooperate is the basis for participating successfully in a cultural group. Because humans are intrinsically able to learn from one another and collaborate together as a group on a much more complex and larger scale than all other animals, only humans are capable of creating and transmitting a culture that is more sophisticated and differentiated than any other animal. From the moment they are born, children are ready to learn culture.

▶ Enculturation and Socialization

Childhood in any society is a dynamic period of life. One aspect of childhood that is constant across cultures is the expectation that people should hopefully emerge from this period with a wish to become competent, productive adults later in life. Cultures differ, however, in exactly what they mean by "competent" and "productive." Despite similarities in the overall goals of development, cultures exhibit a tremendous degree of variability in its content.

Each culture has an understanding of the adult competencies needed for adequate functioning (Kagitcibasi, 1996b; Ogbu, 1981), but these competencies differ by culture and environment. For example, children who need a formal education to succeed in their culture are likely to be exposed to these values early in childhood. These children are likely to receive books and instruction at a young age. Children in another culture may be required to do spinning and weaving as part of their adult livelihood. These children are likely to receive exposure to those crafts at an early age.

By the time we are adults, we have learned many cultural rules of behavior and have practiced those rules so much that they are second nature to us. Much of our behavior as adults is influenced by these learned patterns and rules, and we are so well practiced at them that we engage in these behaviors automatically and unconsciously.

Still, at some time in our lives, we must have learned those rules and patterns of behavior. Culture, in its truest and broadest sense, involves so many different aspects of life that it is impossible to simply sit somewhere and read a book and learn about, let alone thoroughly master, a culture. Culture must be learned through a prolonged process, over a considerable period of time, with much practice. This learning involves all aspects of the learning processes that psychologists have identified over the years, including classical conditioning, operant conditioning, and social learning. As we grow from babies into adults and learn about culture, we make mistakes along the way, but people, groups, and institutions are always around to help us, and in some cases force us, to correct those mistakes.

Socialization is the process by which we learn and internalize the rules and patterns of the society in which we live. This process, which occurs over a long time, involves learning and mastering societal norms, attitudes, values, and belief systems. The process of socialization starts early, from the very first day of life.

Closely related to the process of socialization is the process called **enculturation**. This is the process by which youngsters learn and adopt the ways and manners of their specific culture. There is very little difference, in fact, between the two terms. *Socialization* generally refers to the actual *process and mechanisms* by which people learn the rules of society—what is said to whom and in which contexts. *Enculturation* generally refers to the *products* of the socialization process—the subjective, underlying, psychological aspects of culture that become internalized through development (see Figure 3.1). The similarities and differences between the terms *socialization* and *enculturation* are thus related to the similarities and differences between the terms *society* and *culture*.

socialization The process by which we learn and internalize the rules and patterns of behavior that are affected by culture. This process, which occurs over a long time, involves learning and mastering societal and cultural norms, attitudes, values, and belief systems.

enculturation The process by which individuals learn and adopt the ways and manners of their specific culture.

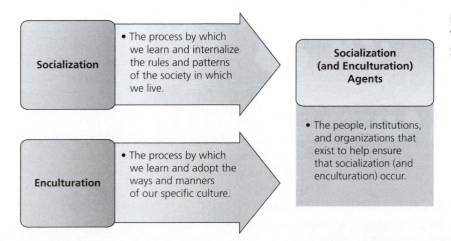

FIGURE 3.1
We Learn Culture Through Socialization and Enculturation

Socialization
• The process by which we learn and internalize the rules and patterns of the society in which we live.

Enculturation
• The process by which we learn and adopt the ways and manners of our specific culture.

Socialization (and Enculturation) Agents
• The people, institutions, and organizations that exist to help ensure that socialization (and enculturation) occur.

Socialization (and enculturation) agents are the people, institutions, and organizations that exist to help ensure that socialization (or enculturation) occurs. One of the most important of these agents is parents, who help instill cultural mores and values in their children, reinforcing those mores and values when they are learned and practiced well and correcting mistakes in that learning.

Parents, however, are not the only **socialization agents**. Siblings, extended families, and peers are important socialization and enculturation agents for many people. Organizations such as school, church, and social groups such as Boy or Girl Scouts also become important agents of these processes. In fact, as you learn more about the socialization process, you will find that culture is enforced and reinforced by so many people and institutions that it is no wonder we all emerge from the process as masters of our own culture.

Bronfenbrenner's ecological systems theory provides a useful framework for organizing the many dimensions of enculturation (Bronfenbrenner, 1979; Bronfenbrenner & Morris, 1998). In Bronfenbrenner's view, human development is a dynamic, interactive process between individuals and various ecologies that range from the proximal, immediate environment to the more distal. These environments include the *microsystem* (the immediate surroundings, such as the family, school, peer group, with which children directly interact), the *mesosystem* (the linkages between microsystems, such as between school and family), the *exosystem* (the context that indirectly affects children, such as parent's workplace), the *macrosystem* (culture, religion, society), and the *chronosystem* (the influence of time and history on the other systems). See Figure 3.2.

socialization and enculturation agents
The people, institutions, and organizations that exist to help ensure that socialization and enculturation occurs.

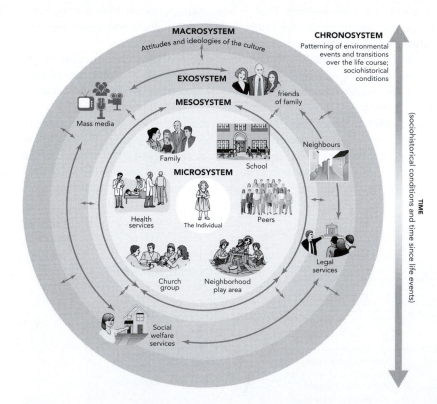

FIGURE 3.2 Bronfenbrenner's Ecological Systems Theory of Human Development
Source: Santrock, J. W. (2007). *Child Development. Eleventh edition.* NY: McGraw-Hill Companies, Inc. Reprinted with permission.

Bronfenbrenner argued that to understand how a child develops, we must consider the experience of the child within each of these systems. In other words, context matters. Who you are today is a result of interactions with the people in your family, classmates in school, friends and neighbors in your community, policies and institutions of the country (or countries) that you were raised in, and the particular point in history in which you are living. In Bronfenbrenner's view, studying children in relation to their particular contexts, on multiple levels, is key to understanding development.

An important tenet of ecological systems theory is that children are not simply passive recipients of the enculturation and socialization processes. That is, children do not simply absorb cultural information from their families, peer groups, and educational institutions. Rather, children also contribute to their own development by interacting with and influencing the people, groups, and institutions around them. Thus, children are active producers and architects of their own culture and development.

Another useful framework to understand enculturation is Super and Harkness's notion of a *developmental niche* (Super & Harkness, 1986, 1994, 2002). The developmental niche focuses on how the broader macrosystem structures the child's immediate microsystems. The developmental niche includes three major components: the physical and social setting, the customs of child care and child rearing, and the psychology of the caregivers. The developing child is influenced by all three components, or more precisely by their interaction. In their niche, children are influenced by the various socialization agents and institutions around them, ensuring their enculturation. At the same time, the child also brings his or her temperamental disposition, motivations, and cognitions to the interaction. In the following sections, we will review research that focuses on several important contexts of enculturation.

▶ Culture, Parenting, and Families

The most important microsystem to a child's development is the family (Bronfenbrenner, 1979), and parents are one of the most important socialization agents (Collins, Steinberg, Maccoby, Hetherington, & Bornstein, 2000). Margaret Mead, the famous anthropologist, proposed that by observing parents, we are observing the essence of a culture. By examining the way that parents interact with their children, we can see how cultural rules and values are reinforced and passed on from generation to generation (Mead, 1975). As such, a study of parenting within a cultural context gives us a good idea of what is important to that culture (Bornstein, 2012).

Whiting and Whiting's Six Cultures Study

One of the most in-depth and well-known studies of parenting, children, and culture was conducted by Beatrice and John Whiting in their Six Cultures Study (Whiting & Whiting, 1975). In this ambitious cross-cultural project led by the Whitings, anthropologists collected field data in Mexico, India, Kenya, the United States, Okinawa, and the Philippines. The major focus of the project was to systematically examine child rearing and children's behavior in these varied cultural contexts. Based on in-depth, naturalistic observations and interviews, the researchers documented how the natural environment shaped how households were structured, which in turn shaped how parents raised their children to fit into that particular society. A child who grew up in a society of hunters and gatherers versus a society of urban dwellers had very different experiences regarding whom the child spent time with, what activities the child was exposed to, and what behaviors and personality traits were valued, emphasized, and encouraged. Importantly, by observing parenting and child development across different cultures, the Whitings could show how a child's behavior and personality is, in fact, intimately connected to characteristics of the broader ecology.

Another major finding of the Six Cultures Study was that women's work roles contributed to children's social behaviors. In cultures where women contributed greatly to the subsistence base of the family—such as in sub-Saharan Africa where women were the major food providers—the children learned to share in family responsibilities and scored low on dependence (e.g., seeking comfort and support, seeking help and information, seeking approval, praise or attention). In contrast, in cultures in which women were not expected to substantially contribute to the subsistence base of the family—such as for high-caste families in Khalapur, India—the children scored high on dependence (Whiting & Edwards, 1988). The Six Cultures Study clearly demonstrated that variations in the natural and cultural environment were linked to variations in child-rearing patterns and this, in turn, was linked to children's behaviors and personalities.

Diversity in Parenting as a Function of Economics

The Six Cultures Study brought attention to how the broader ecological context is tied to child rearing and, ultimately, to children's development. Another important context to consider is the economic conditions under which child rearing takes place. Parenting and child rearing often occur in very different economic conditions in different countries and cultures, and even within one culture, such as the United States. These diverse conditions produce socialization processes that vary widely from culture to culture.

If a society has a high rate of infant mortality, parenting efforts may concentrate on meeting basic physical needs. Parents may have little choice but to disregard other developmental demands. Sometimes the response to harsh and stressful conditions is parenting behavior that we might consider positive. In the Sudan, for example, the mother traditionally spends the first 40 days after delivery entirely with her baby. She rests while her relatives tend to her, and she focuses all her energy on her baby (Cederblad, 1988). In other cultures, the response to harsh and stressful conditions is parenting behavior that some might consider negative. For example, the anthropologist Scheper-Huges (1992) described an impoverished community in northeast Brazil, where, if the infant is weak, mothers show little responsiveness and affection, and sometimes even neglect to the point of death, to the infant. Some of these mothers think of their infants as temporary "visitors" to their home. Scheper-Hughes writes that in this community, "mother love grows slowly, tentatively, fearfully." These mothers are adapting to the harsh environment in which they must raise their children.

LeVine (1977, 1997) has theorized that the caregiving environment reflects a set of goals that are ordered in importance. First is physical health and survival. Next is the promotion of behaviors that will lead to self-sufficiency. Last are behaviors that promote other cultural values, such as prestige. Families with adequate resources are fortunate in that they can turn their attention to meeting the second two goals. In other families with fewer resources, the primary goal of survival is all-important and often overrides the other goals in the amount of parental effort exerted.

Parenting Goals and Beliefs

If the basic goals of physical health and survival are taken care of, parents can focus on other goals, such as instilling cultural values important to that culture. Parenting goals provide the motivation and framework for what parents think is the best way to raise their children.

An example of how parenting goals may lead to variation in parenting behaviors across cultures is seen by contrasting middle-class mothers in Berlin, Germany, with middle-class mothers in New Delhi, India (Keller, Borke, Chaudjhary, Lamm, & Kleis, 2010). In Germany, an important goal of parenting is to raise children who are autonomous. During infancy, parents recognize and emphasize that their child is a separate person with unique thoughts, wishes, desires, and needs. In India, an important goal of parenting is to raise children who are autonomous, but also closely interdependent with other people, especially the family. During infancy, parents emphasize physical contact, emotional closeness, and indulgence. Keller et al.'s study found that these different parenting goals translated into differences in how Berlin and Delhi mothers talked and played with their infants. When the mothers were videotaped engaging in free-play with their three-month-olds, Berlin mothers emphasized autonomy by talking about the infant's intentions, thoughts, emotions, and needs. They were also more likely than Delhi mothers to focus their infants' attention to objects and engage in face-to-face interactions. In contrast, Delhi mothers emphasized relatedness by talking to their infant about other people, the social context, social regulations, and how the child was acting together with someone else (mostly the mother) more so than Berlin mothers. Thus, differences in cultural values and goals concerning autonomy and relatedness were evident in mothers' conversational and play styles with their infants.

Parents' beliefs concerning their roles as caregivers also influence their behaviors. Many parents in the United States believe that they play a very active, goal-directed role in the development of their children (Coll, 1990; Goodnow, 1988). Traditional parents in Turkey, however, believe that their children "grow up" rather than are "brought up" (Kagitcibasi, 1996b). This range of parenting beliefs is reflected in how parents interact with their children, such as whether parents share cultural knowledge primarily through verbalization and direct instruction or by expecting their child to learn primarily through observation and imitation.

Current research has emphasized the importance of examining such **parental ethnotheories**, or parental cultural belief systems (Harkness & Super, 2006). Harkness and Super argue that parental ethnotheories serve as a basis for guiding parenting practices that structure children's daily lives. Harkness and Super identify ethnotheories by conducting in-depth interviews with parents and asking them to keep a daily diary of what they do with their children. One study using these methods compared the ethnotheories of middle-class American and Dutch parents (Harkness & Super, 2006). The researchers found that American parents hold an ethnotheory about the importance of spending *special time* with their children, whereas Dutch parents hold an ethnotheory of spending *family time* with their children. American parents talked extensively about creating time alone with their child in an activity (usually outside the home) that was focused primarily on attending to the needs of that particular child. Dutch parents talked extensively about the importance of spending time together as a family, such as sitting down for dinner every night. In contrast to the American parents, they did not believe it was necessary to create a special time for each individual child. By studying parental ethnotheories we see how parents' cultural belief systems motivate and shape what parents think is the "right" way to parent their children.

parental ethnotheories Parental cultural belief systems.

Global Parenting Styles

authoritarian parent
A style of parenting in which the parent expects unquestioned obedience and views the child as needing to be controlled.

permissive parents A style of parenting in which parents allow children to regulate their own lives and provide few firm guidelines.

authoritative parent
A style of parenting that is viewed as firm, fair, and reasonable. This style is seen as promoting psychologically healthy, competent, independent children who are cooperative and at ease in social situations.

uninvolved parents A style of parenting in which parents are often too absorbed in their own lives to respond appropriately to their children and may seem indifferent to them.

Parenting styles are another important dimension of caregiving. Baumrind (1971) identified three general patterns of parenting based on two key dimensions: warmth/ responsiveness and control. **Authoritarian parents** expect unquestioned obedience and view the child as needing to be controlled. They have also been described as being low on warmth and responsiveness toward their children. **Permissive parents** are warm and responsive to their children; however, they allow their children to regulate their own lives and provide few firm guidelines (low control). **Authoritative parents** are sensitive to the child's maturity and are firm, fair, and reasonable. They exhibit higher levels of control, providing clear guidelines for their children combined with a high degree of warmth and affection.

Maccoby and Martin (1983) identified a fourth type of parenting style, called uninvolved. **Uninvolved parents** are often too absorbed in their own lives to respond appropriately to their children and may seem indifferent to them. They do not seem committed to caregiving, beyond the minimum effort required to meet the physical needs of their child. An extreme form of this type of parenting is neglect. Parenting styles are important because they set the tone for the family context (see Figure 3.3).

Which of the four parenting styles is optimal for a child's development? In general, research on American and European children indicates that children benefit from the authoritative parenting style. Compared to children of other parenting styles, children of authoritative parents demonstrate better school performance, more positive mood, self-reliance, self-confidence, higher emotional and social skills, and

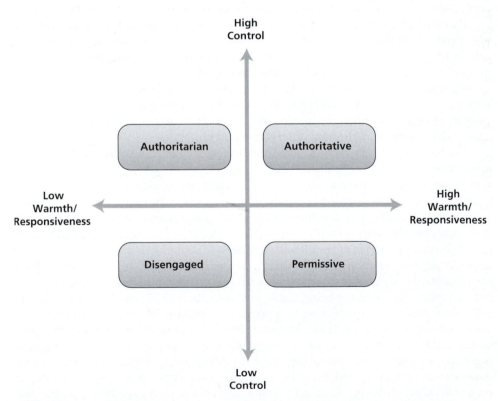

FIGURE 3.3 Four Parenting Styles Based on Two Dimensions: Warmth/ Responsiveness and Control

secure attachment to caregivers (Baumrind, 1967, 1971; Denham, Renwick, & Holt, 1997; Karavasilis, Doyle, & Markiewicz, 2003; Kerr, Stattin, & Özdemir, 2012). This style appears to promote psychologically healthy, competent, independent children who are cooperative and at ease in social situations. Children of authoritarian parents, in contrast, are found to be more anxious and withdrawn, lacking spontaneity and intellectual curiosity. Children of permissive parents tend to be immature; they have difficulty controlling their impulses and acting independently. Children of uninvolved parents fare the worst, being noncompliant and demanding.

However, because Baumrind's parenting styles were originally based on observations of a European American sample, others have argued that the benefits of authoritative parenting may depend on the particular ethnic or cultural group (Steinberg, Lamborn, Dornbusch, & Darling, 1992). For example, a study comparing several thousand U.S. adolescents from four ethnic groups (European American, African American, Asian American, and Hispanic American) found that authoritative parenting predicted higher school achievement for European American, African American, and Hispanic American adolescents, but not for Asian Americans (Steinberg et al., 1992). This finding led the researchers to argue that authoritative parenting may not consistently predict positive outcomes for all ethnic groups.

In the last decade, findings have expanded to include studies in other countries using the classifications of parenting derived from Baumrind's original research. A study of almost 3,000 Arab adolescents from eight Arab societies revealed that authoritative parenting was associated with greater family connectedness and better adolescent mental health (Dwairy, Achoui, Abouseire, & Farah, 2006). Studies in China, Taiwan, and Hong Kong found that authoritative parenting was related positively, and authoritarian parenting negatively, to children's adjustment within the school and family (Chen, 2014; Chen, Dong, & Zhou, 1997; Pong, Johnston, & Chen, 2010). These findings are inconsistent with Steinberg et al.'s (1992) assertion that the positive effects of authoritative parenting may be less pronounced for children of diverse cultural backgrounds. Evidence is accumulating that the authoritative style is linked to positive development for children of many different backgrounds.

Nonetheless, to address the critique that Baumrind's parenting styles may not adequately capture parenting in other cultures, researchers have focused on identifying parenting styles indigent to a culture. Using Baumrind's classifications, Chinese parents have been often described as authoritarian. However, for Chinese parents, the significance and meaning of this parenting style may originate from a set of cultural beliefs that may differ greatly from the European American cultural belief system (Chao, 1994, 2001). Based on Confucian philosophy, Chinese parenting may be distinguished by the concept of *chiao shun*, or "training," in child rearing. Training emphasizes very close parental supervision in order to promote children's obedience, discipline, and adherence to family obligation. To a European-American parent, this type of parenting may look over-controlling and authoritarian. To a Chinese parent, this type of parenting is culturally appropriate, reflecting love and concern for their children. Chao argued that this training aspect, which is not considered in Baumrind's styles of parenting, may be more useful in understanding Chinese-heritage children's development.

Instigated in large part by Chao's work on Chinese parenting, researchers have hypothesized that authoritarian parenting may actually encourage *positive* child adjustment in collectivistic cultures. However, a review of studies applying Baumrind's parenting styles typology in cross-cultural studies concluded that, in general, authoritarian parenting is associated with negative psychological adjustment in cultures as diverse as Egypt, China, India, and Turkey (Sorkhabi, 2005). In other words, there is evidence that when children and adolescents of collectivistic as well as individualistic cultures perceive parents as lacking warmth and exerting unilateral control (aspects of authoritarian parenting), this is seen as undesirable and hostile. This negative perception of authoritarian parents also predicts less family harmony and more family conflict. Authoritative parenting, in contrast, is consistently associated with positive outcomes (e.g., getting good grades, regarded positively by peers, being self-reliant) and has not been associated with negative outcomes across cultures such as Hong Kong, China, and Pakistan.

More recently, discussions of parenting and culture have been hot topics in the U.S. and Chinese popular media. The term "tiger mother" has emerged to describe Asian parenting (Chua, 2011). According to Chua, tiger mothers are highly demanding and drive their children to high levels of academic success while Western parents are much less demanding and more concerned about their children's social and emotional development, such as fostering high self-esteem. This very public discussion has sparked scholars to examine this notion of tiger mothering more closely. Some studies appear to support aspects of tiger mothering. For instance, Fu and Markus (2014) found that Asian American high-school students reported that their mothers did indeed pressure them more than European American high-school students. Importantly, however, while this pressure was related to lower perceived support for European American students, for Asian American students this pressure was a source of motivation that did not relate to more strained relationships with mothers. Other scholars, however, have found that although tiger mothering (defined by researchers as harsh, highly demanding, and emotionally unsupportive) exists among Asian heritage families, it is not common. Tiger mothering is also linked to poorer child outcomes, both academically and socioemotionally. And finally, there is much more variation in Asian-heritage parenting beyond the stereotypical depictions of being strict, controlling, and demanding. Adolescents of Asian-heritage parents in the U.S. and China also report that their mothers are supportive, loving, openly communicative, and warm (Juang, Qin, Park, 2013; Kim, Wang, Orozco-Lapray, Shen, & Murtuza, 2013; Way et al., 2013). Discussions, debates, and studies of parenting across cultures will persist as researchers continue to search for what style of parenting is optimal in raising healthy and competent children in their particular cultural context.

Parenting Behaviors and Strategies

Over the past several decades, a considerable amount of cross-cultural research has examined variations in parenting behaviors and how these variations contribute to different aspects of child development. One of the most representative cultural differences in parenting behaviors concerns sleeping arrangements. Americans are one cultural group that holds beliefs about sleeping arrangements that differ from the majority of the world. To begin, one of the single greatest concerns of American parents is getting their baby to sleep through the night, and to do so in a room separate from that of the parents. Traditionally, Americans shun co-sleeping arrangements, with the underlying assumption that sleeping alone will help develop independence. In the United States, prominent pediatricians and medical doctors have proposed that co-sleeping fosters children's unhealthy dependence on parents. They argued that, developmentally, it is better for babies to sleep alone to promote independence and autonomy (Ferber, 1985). To date, however, there is no evidence that sleeping alone actually does so (McKenna & McDade, 2005). Some sleep experts have revised their stance on co-sleeping by no longer explicitly opposing it (e.g., Ferber, 2006). Still, many American parents do not co-sleep with their babies. To help babies learn to fall asleep alone, "security objects," such as a special blanket or toy, and bedtime rituals, are often used.

Most other cultures do not share this notion of promoting independence in children by learning to sleep alone, and comfort objects or bedtime rituals are not common in other cultures. In Japanese families, infants and young children sleep next to their parents on mattresses, or on futons on the floor, or all together in the adult bed (Fukumizu, Kaga, Kohyama, & Hayes, 2005). In China, it is common for school-age children to sleep in the same bed or room as their parents (Li, Jin, Yan, Wu, Jiang, & Shen, 2009). Mayan mothers allow their children to sleep with them for several years because of a commitment to forming a very close bond with their children. When a new baby comes along, older children move to a bed in the same room or share a bed with another member of the family (Morelli, Oppenheim, Rogoff, & Goldsmith, 1992). Again, these practices foster behaviors and values that are consistent with the developmental goals of the culture.

Differences in infant sleeping arrangements can also be seen within cultures. A national U.S. survey conducted from 1993 and 2000 revealed an overall increase in parents reporting their infant "usually" slept in bed with them, from 5.5% to 12.8%. But there was great variation across ethnic groups: African American caregivers reported the highest percentage of co-sleeping (27.9%), followed by Asian Americans (20.9%), and lastly, European American caregivers (7.2%) (Willinger, Hoffman, Kessler, & Corwin, 2003). It is important to note, too, that differences in sleeping arrangements are also based on economic as well as cultural reasons. In this national study, households making less than $20,000 a year were more likely to report co-sleeping (Willinger et al., 2003). And in eastern Kentucky, families who had large houses were more likely to have their children sleep in another room (Abbott, 1992). Nonetheless, even when economic status was controlled for in this study in eastern Kentucky, locally born mothers were more likely to have their babies sleep with them compared to mothers who were born in another state, suggesting that there were indeed cultural (as well as economic) reasons that led to different sleeping arrangements. Overall, the literature on sleeping arrangements across cultures illustrates how parental behaviors may vary depending on each culture's developmental goals.

In addition to sleeping arrangements, cross-cultural research has also shown differences in how parents structure the home environment for their children. One of the most widely used measures of the home environment is the Home Observation and Measurement of the Environment Inventory (HOME Inventory) (Bradley, Caldwell, & Corwyn, 2003). To administer the HOME Inventory, a researcher visits a family in their home for about one hour. During this hour, the researcher makes observations of parent–child interactions and also asks the parents a number of questions concerning how they interact with their child.

In a summary of cross-cultural studies that have used the HOME Inventory, Bradley and Corwyn (2005) described three general areas in which cultures vary: warmth and responsiveness, discipline, and stimulation/teaching. For instance, warmth and responsiveness are conveyed differently across cultures. In the United States, one way parents show responsiveness is through physical affection. The Yoruba of Nigeria, however, show responsiveness not by physical affection primarily, but through their tone of voice or praising their child. In many Western industrialized societies, responsiveness is also measured by how often the parent engages in spontaneous conversations with their child. In India, however, where children are expected to respect their elders, it is considered disrespectful to speak without permission. Thus, the type of home environment parents create will depend on the broader cultural belief systems.

Cross-cultural research has not only demonstrated cultural differences in parenting behaviors; it has documented cultural similarities as well. As children grow older, both European American and Chinese American mothers place more emphasis on manners, school-related skills, and emotional adjustment when their children are six to eight years old than when they were three to five (Kelley & Tseng, 1992). In China, Mexico, India, and the United States, when parents allowed their adolescents greater behavioral autonomy (such as choosing own clothes and friends), adolescents reported greater perceptions of parental support and higher motivation to do well in school (Supple, Ghazarian, Peterson, & Bush, 2009). Across 12 different nations or ethnic groups from Africa, Australia, Asia, the Balkans, Europe, the Middle East, North America, and South America, there was one thing in common that parents did that made their children feel loved: providing a valuable commodity (McNeely & Barber, 2010). What varied by culture was what was considered a valuable commodity. In some cultures, it was emotional support and time, for others it was moral guidance and advice, and for still others it was material resources.

In sum, research suggests both differences and similarities across cultures in parenting and child rearing. All of the studies have shown that parenting beliefs and practices tend to be congruent with developmental goals dictated by culture; that is, cultural differences in specific values, beliefs, attitudes, and behaviors necessary for survival are associated with different developmental goals so that developing members of a society can carry on culture-relevant work related to survival. It seems that all people are similar in that their developmental processes are designed to meet cultural goals; people differ, however, in the specific nature of those goals and how to get there.

All people are similar in that their developmental processes are designed to meet cultural goals; people differ, however, in the specific nature of those goals and how to get there.

A Domain-Specific Approach to Parenting

One exciting development in the parenting literature is a proposal that outlines a domain-specific approach to understanding parent socialization. This approach counters the global parenting styles (Baumrind, 1971) reviewed earlier. One major criticism of global parenting styles is that it ignores the fact that parents tend to act and respond differently depending on the particular child, the situation, and the context (Turiel, 1998). Thus, scholars have proposed a domain-specific approach that focuses on parenting behaviors rather than general styles to better understand the socialization process (Grusec & Davidov, 2010).

The domain approach emphasizes the complexity of the socialization process by distinguishing between distinct types or domains of parent–child socialization. One domain is protection. Especially in the first years of life, children depend on their parents to protect them from harm. When children are distressed, an appropriate parenting behavior is to respond sensitively and offer comfort. In doing so, children learn to develop a sense of security and, eventually, learn how to regulate their own distress. Another domain is control. In order to function in society, children must learn how to live by culturally defined rules. This means that children must sometimes suppress their own personal desires that violate these rules. An appropriate parenting behavior would be to modify children's misbehavior using suitable levels of control or discipline. In doing so, children eventually internalize cultural rules and no longer rely entirely on their parents' control. So depending on the particular situation—whether the child is distressed or whether the child is misbehaving—a different type of parenting behavior will be required. From this perspective, appropriate parenting behaviors should correspond to the relevant domain of socialization. If, for instance, your child was pushed by another child and started crying, but you misinterpreted your child's crying as fussiness and responded with discipline and control, your parenting response, according to Grusec and Davidov (2010), would probably not be very effective.

In addition to protection and control, other domains are reciprocity (learning how to cooperate), guided learning (learning specific skills), and group participation (learning to participate in social groups and cultural practices). Grusec and Davidov (2010, pg. 692) emphasized that these five domains of socialization are universal (e.g., in every culture, children need to be protected and disciplined), but that there are cultural variations:

> First, there can be variation in the degree to which a given domain of interaction is frequently engaged in or emphasized in different cultures. For example, guided learning is more widespread in cultures that rely heavily on formal schooling, whereas other cultures may utilize group participation processes to a greater extent (observational learning, intent community participation; Odden & Rochat, 2004; Rogoff et al., 2007). Second, culture can influence the nature of successful rearing in a given domain of interaction: Certain practices that are successful in one cultural context may appear to be less so in another culture, probably because of different meanings attached to those practices or different goals of socialization emphasized by each cultural group. High levels of rigid control, for example, seem to be more detrimental in Western cultures than in Asian cultures because, in the former, they tend to be associated with parental rejection and lack of warmth, whereas in the latter, they reflect parental care and a desire to instill the important values of hard work, self-discipline, and obedience. (Chao & Tseng, 2002)

Despite cultural differences in what parents do, how often they do them, and what specific behaviors mean, the important thing for parents in all cultures is that parenting practices must be appropriate for the domain in which the child is functioning. This domain-specific approach is a promising new framework that will help researchers pinpoint what specific parenting practices promote what specific child outcomes in what specific context or culture.

Siblings

The longest relationship that many of us will have is with our siblings. Siblings play an important role in the socialization of children (Dunn, 1988; Teti, 2002; Whiting & Whiting, 1975). However, research on family socialization has focused predominantly on parents and, for a long time, neglected the role of siblings (McHale, Crouter, & Whiteman, 2003). This is unfortunate, as siblings are an integral part of the social contexts of children's lives in almost every culture. In five of the cultures of Whiting and Whiting's Six Cultures Study (1975), other caretakers (which included mostly siblings) were observed to be present an equal or greater amount of time with the young child compared with the mother. In only one culture, the United States, were siblings less likely to be present with the young child than the mother.

The definition of who is considered a sibling may differ across cultures (Economic and Social Research Council, 2005). In many cultures, siblings refer to family members who are biologically related. In other cultures, siblings refer to people who are biologically *and* nonbiologically related. Changing family structures in many countries are also redefining who is a sibling. Because of the high rates of divorce, separation, remarriage, and creation of step-families in industrialized countries, children can now have full siblings (sharing both biological parents), half siblings (sharing one parent), and stepsiblings (sharing no biological parent).

Siblings can fulfill many roles; they can be tutors, buddies, playmates, or care-takers (Parke, 2004). In many cultures, it is common practice for older siblings to act as caretakers for younger siblings, and in some cultures, siblings are the primary caretakers of young children (but not infants) (Weisner & Gallimore, 1977). An auto-biographical account by Lijembe (1967), a Western Kenyan, described his role as a caretaker for his younger sister:

> Because there was no older sister in the family, and my mother had to go off to work in the *shamba* [gardens] every day, it wasn't long before I obliged, though still a very young child myself, to become the day-to-day "nurse" for my baby sister. For my mother to make me succeed in this function, she had to train me—to give me instructions and to see how well I carried them out . . . . As her *shamba* work increased, so did my nursing duties . . . before moving off to the *shamba*, she would give me instructions: Do not leave the home unguarded, she would tell me . . . . (as quoted in Weisner & Gallimore, 1977, p. 171)

In his account, Lijembe tells of the many important caretaking duties he was respon-sible for: he plays with his younger sister, bathes her, feeds her, and toilet trains her. Clearly, studies of caretaking in different cultures would be incomplete if they focused solely on the mother and father and ignored the role of siblings.

Another example of siblings as highly involved caregivers can be seen among the Kwara'ae in the Solomon Islands. In this culture, the responsibilities involved in care-giving are viewed as a training ground for siblings to become mutually dependent on one another in adulthood. For example, one sibling may be designated to go to school while the others combine their resources to support that sibling. In turn, this sibling will support the family financially once he has finishing his schooling and found a job (Watson-Gegeo, 1992). Thus, many of the culture's values, such as family interde-pendence, are transferred through siblings (Zukow-Goldring, 1995).

Through our interactions with our siblings we learn skills important to all cul-tures, such as perspective-taking, social understanding, and conflict negotiation (Parke, 2004; Whiting & Whiting, 1975). Our sibling relationships provide a context to learn prosocial and antisocial behaviors such as empathy and aggression (Ostrov, Crick, & Staffacher, 2006; Tucker, Updegraff, McHale, & Crouter, 1999). Importantly, what children learn with siblings (the good and bad) can transfer into relationships with other children (Parke, 2004; Stauffacher & DeHart, 2006; Teti, 2002).

One study of adolescents in the United States examined how older siblings influ-enced younger siblings' perspectives on gender (McHale, Updegraff, Helms-Erikson, & Crouter, 2001). These researchers followed a group of sibling pairs over one year. They found that younger siblings tended to model their older siblings in terms of their gender-role attitudes, gendered personality traits, and gender-stereotyped leisure activities. Gender-role attitudes referred to how traditional their attitudes toward women were; gendered personality traits referred to stereotypical traits such as "kind" and "active"; and gender-stereotyped activities referred to activities such as sports and craftwork. Interestingly, the study showed that it was the older siblings', and not parents', gendered attitudes, personality, and activities that were a better pre-dictor of younger siblings' attitudes, personality, and activities.

Another study of Dutch adolescents examined how older siblings' delinquent behaviors related to younger siblings' delinquent behaviors including getting into trouble with the law and using alcohol and cigarettes (Buist, 2010). The study showed that if older siblings engaged in delinquent behaviors, their younger siblings were also more likely to do so, and especially if they were of the same sex (brother-brother or sister-sister sibling pairs). The researcher followed the siblings over a two-year period and could also show that changes in older siblings' delinquency (e.g., engaging in increasing rates of delinquency) were related to similar changes in younger siblings' delinquency. Because most siblings live in the same household throughout childhood and adolescence, there are many opportunities for observing, modeling, and imitating one other. This repeated and prolonged exposure and interaction means that older siblings can be influential role models— for both positive and negative behaviors—to their younger siblings. Taken together, these findings speak to the important role that siblings play in children's lives in areas such as gender identity and delinquency. More research is needed to explore the ways in which siblings contribute to other areas of children's development across cultures.

Extended and Multigenerational Families

Extended families include members other than parents and children, such as aunts, uncles, cousins, or grandparents. Multigenerational families include grandparents in addition to both parents and children or just children (e.g., a grandmother raising her grandchild). In many cultures, such as in India (Chaudhary, 2004), extended- and multigenerational-family child rearing is an integral and important part of the enculturation process. The extended family is an important means of transmitting cultural heritage from generation to generation. Extended family members can also provide a buffer to stresses of everyday living. In these cultures, it is not only parents, but a whole network of relatives, who provide the major context of enculturation for children.

In the United States, multigenerational households have been steadily increasing in the last decade (Pew Research Center, 2010). In 2008, 53 percent of African American, 52 percent of Latino, and 44 percent of Asian and Pacific-Islander children lived in multigenerational families, compared with 35 percent of European American families (Pew Research Center, 2010). As such, ethnic minority families in the United States are more likely to include a broader array of family members. Of course, not all ethnic minority families are extended or multigenerational, and caregiving between nuclear and extended families may differ. For instance, African American extended families tend to emphasize cooperation and moral and religious values more than African American nuclear families do (Tolson & Wilson, 1990).

Although extended and multigenerational families are important contexts of socialization for children in the United States and other cultures, one major difference is that living with extended and multigenerational families in the United States is often seen as a consequence of poor economics rather than a desirable state of affairs. Indeed, the steadily increasing percentage of multigenerational households in the United States has been partly attributed to the financial crisis in 2008 (Pew Research Center, 2010). Limited resources are a reality, with one out of five children (20%) living in poverty (U.S. Census Bureau, 2013). Compounding this picture is the reality that ethnicity also confounds social class: 16% of white, 10% of Asian, 33% of Latino, and 38% of black children live in poverty (U.S. Census Bureau, 2013).

A significant number of these children are born to single mothers, and here the extended and multigenerational family plays an important role in the child-rearing process, especially in the case of teenage parents. The presence of the maternal grandmother in these families has been found to cancel out some of the negative child outcomes associated with teen mothering (Baydar & Brooks-Gunn, 1998; Garcia-Coll, 1990; Leadbeater & Way, 2001). The grandmother often serves as a valuable source of information about child development. She also tends to be more responsive and less punitive with the child than the teen mother is. The grandmother in these three-generation households plays a very important role as teacher and role model to her daughter and can provide favorable, positive social interaction for her grandchild.

Extended and multigenerational families differ in their composition from one culture to another but have in common a sharing of resources, emotional support, and caregiving (Crozier & Davies, 2006). The experiences of a child growing up in these situations can be quite different from those of a child in a nuclear family. Future research needs to focus on family members other than parents and siblings to more accurately and comprehensively describe socialization in the family context.

Summary

In a child's life, family is one of the most important and influential sources of enculturation, especially in the early years. Families, however, come in many forms. Much of the research across cultures thus far has focused primarily on how parents' goals, beliefs, styles, and practices relate to their child's development. Other family members, such as siblings, cousins, aunts, uncles, grandparents, and in-laws also play an essential role in children's lives. Moving forward, it will be important to consider a more diverse family constellation than has been studied up until now. Moreover, researchers will need to continue to study family constellations not in isolation, but within the broader economic, social, and historical settings in which families and children are embedded. Doing so will provide a better picture of how families contribute to a child's development, in a certain place and time.

▶ Culture And Peers

Peers are another powerful source of enculturation. Humans, especially, are highly attuned to learning from their peers. A fascinating study asked the question: Do chimpanzees, orangutans, and two-year-old human children differ in how influential peers are to solving a problem (Haun, Rekers, & Tomasello, 2014)? To test this, the researchers first gave all three groups a task to solve. The task was to drop a ball into a set of boxes that had three different holes. Dropping the ball into only one of the holes would release a highly desirable reward—peanuts for the great apes and chocolate chips for the human children. Once the three groups figured out which hole released the food by dropping the ball themselves, they then watched similar peers (either other chimpanzees, orangutans, or human children) drop the ball into a different hole that also released food. The three groups were then given the chance to go back to the set of boxes and to drop balls in again. The results clearly showed that only human children were likely to switch by dropping the ball into the hole their peers did. The great apes stuck with their original solution. In other words, human children were more likely to conform to their peers' behavior compared to the great apes. Moreover, human children were even more likely to conform if the peer was present in the same room. For the great apes, the presence of a peer did not influence their behavior. Importantly, it is the ability of humans to so easily conform and desire to conform to peers that facilities the learning of norms and behaviors of specific social and cultural groups.

By comparing human children with great apes, Tomasello and others have offered valuable insight to how humans are fine-tuned to respond to peers, more so than other species. Across cultures, however, the extent to which peers contribute to child development may differ. It may depend on how rapidly the culture is changing. Mead (1978) described three types of cultures with differing levels of peer influence on the socialization of its young people. In **postfigurative cultures**, in which cultural

postfigurative culture A culture in which change is slow and socialization occurs primarily by elders transferring their knowledge to their children. Elders hold the knowledge necessary for becoming a successful and competent adult.

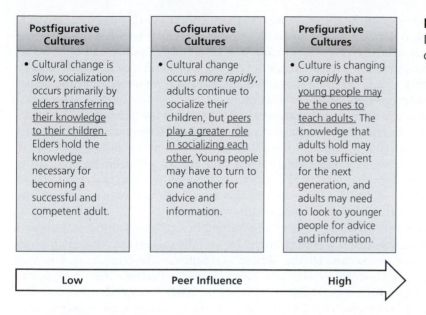

Postfigurative Cultures	Cofigurative Cultures	Prefigurative Cultures
• Cultural change is *slow*, socialization occurs primarily by <u>elders transferring their knowledge to their children.</u> Elders hold the knowledge necessary for becoming a successful and competent adult.	• Cultural change occurs *more rapidly*, adults continue to socialize their children, but <u>peers play a greater role in socializing each other.</u> Young people may have to turn to one another for advice and information.	• Culture is changing *so rapidly* that <u>young people may be the ones to teach adults.</u> The knowledge that adults hold may not be sufficient for the next generation, and adults may need to look to younger people for advice and information.

Low   Peer Influence   High

FIGURE 3.4
Differing Levels of Peer Influence on Socialization

change is slow, socialization occurs primarily by elders transferring their knowledge to their children. In this case, elders hold the knowledge necessary for becoming a successful and competent adult. In **cofigurative cultures**, in which cultural change occurs more rapidly, adults continue to socialize their children, but peers play a greater role in socializing each other. Young people may have to turn to one another for advice and information. In **prefigurative cultures**, the culture is changing so rapidly that young people may be the ones to teach adults. The knowledge that adults hold may not be sufficient for the next generation, and adults may need to look to younger people for advice and information (see Figure 3.4).

Exposure to Peer Groups

Cultures vary in the exposure that children have to their peer groups. In industrialized countries, children spend a significant amount of time with same-aged peers. For instance, American teenagers spend much more time per week (18 hours) with their peers outside of school compared with Japanese (12) and Taiwanese (8) teenagers (Fuligni & Stevenson, 1995). The nature and strength of peers as socializing agents in these industrialized cultures will differ from other cultures. For instance, children growing up in solitary farm settlements will have limited options to interact with a wide range of potential playmates. Or, children growing up in a hunting and gathering society may be socialized by multiple-age peers instead of the same-age groups that are characteristic of countries with formal education, where age-stratified schooling is the norm (Krappmann, 1996). Thus, depending on the culture, the extent to which children interact with their peers may be quite significant.

Peers and Bullying

Today, bullying by peers is recognized internationally as a serious public health and safety issue. Olweus, a research professor of psychology in Norway, conducted the first large-scale scientific study of bullying in the 1980s. His research has led an anti-bullying movement in countries around the world to acknowledge peer bullying as a serious problem in schools and develop interventions to combat bullying.

cofigurative culture A culture in which change occurs rapidly. Both adults and peers socialize young people. Young people may have to turn to one another for advice and information in this type of culture.

prefigurative culture A culture that is changing so rapidly that young people may be the ones to teach adults cultural knowledge.

Olweus (1993) outlined three criteria to define bullying: (1) *intentional* physical or psychological harm, (2) that is based on a power imbalance between the bully and victim, and (3) which is *repeated* over time. The imbalance of power can refer to differences in age, physical size, having or not having a disability, or being of majority versus minority status. Based on this definition, bullying can include hitting, name-calling, spreading rumors, and social exclusion.

Using Olweus's definition, researchers have found that the rate of bullying varies across cultures. In one cross-national comparison, 41% of elementary school children from Italy, 27% from England, 20% from Portugal, 18% from Spain, 11% from Japan, and 9% from Norway reported being bullied (Smith et al., 1999). Before concluding that children in Italy are much more likely to become bullies than children in Japan or Norway, however, we have to recognize that cross-national comparisons may be problematic if cultures define bullying in different ways.

To address this problem, Smith has explored how the definition and expression of bullying may differ across cultures. He and his colleagues studied children (8-year-olds) and adolescents (14-year-olds) in 14 countries—Austria, China, England, France, Germany, Greece, Iceland, Italy, Japan, Norway, Portugal, Slovenia, Spain, and Thailand (Smith, Cowie, Olafsson, & Liefooghe, 2002). To identify what was considered bullying, 25 stick-figure pictures of different situations were shown to children and adolescents in each country (see Figure 3.5). They then had to decide which actions were considered bullying. Twenty-three pictures depicted various forms of aggressive or exclusionary behavior that might be considered bullying (such as

FIGURE 3.5 Examples of Stick-Figure Cartoons in Smith et al.'s (2002) Cross-National Study of Bullying in 14 Countries

Source: Smith, P.K., Cowie, H., Olafsson, R. F., Liefooghe, A. P. D., Almeida, A. Araki, H., del Barrio, C., Costabile, A., Dekleva, B., Houndoumadi, A., Kim, K., Olaffson, R.P., Ortega, R., Pain, J., Pateraki, L., Schafer, M., Singer, M., Smorti, A., Toda, Y., Tomasson, H., & Wenxin, Z. (2002). Definitions of bullying: A comparison of terms used, and age and gender differences, in a fourteen-country international comparison. *Child Development, 73*(4), 1119–1133.

excluding a child from playing a game) and two pictures illustrated prosocial behaviors (such as offering a pencil to another child who forgot to bring one).

Across all countries, there were few gender differences in what was considered bullying. In other words, girls and boys defined bullying in very similar ways. Another similarity across countries was a general age difference in what was considered bullying: at age 8, children distinguished between aggressive and nonaggressive behaviors, but at 14, adolescents distinguished between different kinds of aggression: physical aggression, verbal aggression, and social exclusion. There were also some cultural differences. In England, bullying was commonly seen as occurring between two individuals, happening usually on the playground. In contrast, in Japan bullying was commonly seen as an entire class excluding an individual, happening usually within the classroom. Other studies in Asian countries have also found that social exclusion, rather than physical or verbal aggression, is the main form of bullying. In Korea, for instance, a distinction is made between *wang-ta,* referring to exclusion by classmates, and *jun-ta,* referring to exclusion by the entire school (Koo, Kwak, & Smith, 2008). In contrast to countries such as England and the United States, in Korea, girls are more likely to be bullies than boys, and physical aggression is a relatively rare form of bullying (Koo, Kwak, & Smith, 2008).

Although some progress has been made in studying culturally specific ways of bullying, future research will also need to focus on new ways of bullying. For countries that have wide access to technologies such as cell phones, computers, and the Internet, different forms of peer bullying are emerging such as cyberbullying. **Cyberbullying** is defined as bullying through electronic means, for example, using the Internet, social media, or through text messaging. In the past decade, studies on cyberbullying around the world have increased sharply (Barlett, Gentile, Anderson, Suzuki, Sakamoto, Yamaoka, & Katsura, 2014; Cassidy, Faucher, & Jackson, 2013; Huang & Chou, 2010; Smith, Mahdavi, Carvalho, Fisher, Russell, & Tippett, 2008). Some of these studies indicated that children who are cyberbullied are less likely to tell someone about being bullied than children who are bullied in person. Further, unlike traditional bullying, children report being more likely to experience cyberbullying outside, not inside, of school. Thus, new technologies have created new contexts for social interactions. Children now have greater opportunities to interact more frequently with a larger, more diverse set of peers, and for a much longer period of time throughout the day. Future research needs to keep up with rapidly changing technologies to better understand how new mediums of social interaction are changing the way we are socialized by our peers.

cyberbullying Bullying through electronic means, for example, using the Internet, social media, or sending text messages.

Summary

From a very young age, we learn from our peers. We want to be like them and do what they do. Our readiness to learn from our peers means that enculturation is driven to a large extent also by the peer group, and not just family. What is important to remember, however, is that peer influence is not always one way. We select which peers to spend time with, and over time, we influence each other. We learn our culture from peers, but they also learn from us.

Peers are a large part of one important setting—the education system. Because children in many parts of the world spend most of their time in school more so than any other context (Eccles & Roeser, 2011), what happens in the school has been subject of intense research focus. In the next section we look at various aspects of the educational system as a major agent of enculturation.

► Culture and the Educational System

The single most important formalized mechanism of instruction in many societies and cultures today is the educational system. Many of us think of a country's educational system solely as an institution that teaches thinking skills and knowledge. But a society's educational system is probably the most important institution that teaches and reinforces its cultural values. In this last part of the chapter, we review key enculturation agents within an educational context to show how education and culture are tightly linked (see Figure 3.6).

School Systems

Educational systems in which children take part play an important role in imparting cultural values. First of all, the content of what is taught in the schools reflects a priori choices by that culture or society regarding what it believes is important to learn. Different cultures believe different topics to be important for later success in that society. By teaching a certain type of content, the educational system reinforces a particular view of cognition and intelligence.

Another important factor to consider is the environmental setting in which education occurs. Many industrialized societies have a formal educational system, with identifiable areas and structures (schools) and identifiable education agents (teachers) to "do" education. In other cultures, formalized education may take place in small groups led by elders of the community. In yet other cultures, formalized education may be a family task (e.g., the mother tutoring her own children in cognitive and other skills necessary for members of their community). Regardless of the environmental setting, the vehicle by which education occurs reinforces certain types of cultural values in its recipients.

The organization, planning, and implementation of lesson plans are other important cultural socializers. Some cultures encourage a didactic model of teaching, in which an expert teacher gives information to students, who are expected to listen and learn. Other cultures view teachers as leaders through a lesson plan, providing the overall structure and framework by which students discover principles and concepts. Some cultures view the imparting of praise as an important process. Other cultures focus on mistakes made by students in the learning process. Some cultures have special classes and mechanisms to deal with many different types of students—for example, students with learning disabilities, physical handicaps, and special gifts or talents. Other cultures tend to downplay such differences among their students, treating them all as equals.

Once in school, children spend the majority of their waking hours away from their parents. The socialization process that began in the primary relationship with the parents continues with teachers and peers in the classroom and school. School

Education
School System
Parental and Familial Values
Attitutdes and Appraisals of Students
Teaching Practices
School Environment

Important Agents
of Enculturation
That Teach and
Reinforce Cultural Values

FIGURE 3.6 An Example of Enculturation Within the Context of Education

institutionalizes cultural values and attitudes and is a significant contributor not only to the intellectual development of the child but, just as important, to the child's social and emotional development.

To highlight the role of the educational system as an enculturation agent, one need only recognize that not all cultures of the world rely solely on an institutionalized school setting to teach math. For example, important math skills are taught to Micronesian islanders in the Puluwat culture through navigation, and to coastal Ghanaians by marketing fish (Acioly & Schliemann, 1986; Gladwin, 1970; Gladwin & Gladwin, 1971; see also the discussion of everyday cognition in Chapter 4).

Regardless of the way education occurs, the choices a society and culture make concerning its structure, organization, planning, and implementation all encourage and reinforce a certain view of culture. We are not always cognizant of our own cultural view because we are in the middle of it. To see our own biases and choices, we need to observe education in other cultures and compare what is done elsewhere to what we do. Through such comparisons, the differences and the similarities often become clear.

Parental and Familial Values

Cultural differences in parenting beliefs about education have an impact on children's educational experiences (Chao, 2000; Russell, Crockett, & Chao, 2010). For example, Japanese and Chinese parents are more likely to consider all children as equal, with no differences between them. American parents are more likely to recognize differences and find reasons to treat their children as unique. American parents are also more likely to consider innate ability more important than effort; for Japanese and Chinese parents, however, effort is far more important than ability (Stevenson & Zusho, 2002). These cultural differences among the three countries have enormous implications for education.

American parents tend to be more easily satisfied at lower levels of competence than either Japanese or Chinese parents. Also, when problems arise, Americans are more likely to attribute the cause of the problem to something they cannot do anything about (such as ability). These cultural differences in attribution of causality are directly related to cultural differences in self-construals, discussed in Chapter 5.

Believing that ability is more important than effort has yet another side to it—a belief that each child is limited in his or her abilities. In a series of intriguing studies, Dweck (2008) has found that children who believe that ability, rather than effort, determines intelligence tend to give up faster when faced with a difficult or challenging problem. They also prefer easier tasks to more difficult ones. Once this belief that ability determines intelligence becomes a cultural institution, it dictates how the educational system should respond. The resulting emphasis in the case of the American system is to seek unique, innate differences among the students, to generate separate special classes for these unique groups of students, and generally to individualize the process of education. As a result, more time is spent on individualized instruction and less on whole-group instruction.

Research has documented other interesting effects of parental and familial values related to achievement and academic success. Chao's (1996) cross-cultural study examined maternal beliefs regarding school success between Chinese and European American mothers of preschoolers. She found that Chinese mothers of preschoolers placed a very high value on education, believed they needed to engage in much time, effort, and sacrifice in order for their children to succeed, believed in the importance of direct intervention approaches to their children's schooling, and believed that they play a major role in their children's school success. European American mothers of preschoolers in her study also valued education and emphasized reading in the home as important to school success. However, European American mothers also believed in a less directive approach in instruction, showed greater concern for building their children's social skills and self-esteem, and were concerned about "burnout" if they pushed their child to excel academically. American parents' early emphasis on self-esteem, coupled with satisfaction at lower levels of academic performance (Stevenson & Zusho, 2002), may partly explain why American adolescents report far higher beliefs in their mathematical competencies than Hong Kong Chinese adolescents, and yet consistently score lower on math achievement (Liu, 2009). Taken together, these findings suggest the importance of parental cultural values in understanding academic success.

Attitudes and Appraisals of Students

A number of studies have examined cultural differences between Asian or Asian American children and European Americans. Pang (1991), for example, studied the relationships among test anxiety, self-concept, and student perceptions of parental support in Asian American and European American middle-school students. This study found that Asian American students exhibited a stronger desire to please parents, greater parental pressure, but also higher levels of parental support, than did the European American students. Yan and Gaier (1994) looked at causal attributions for college success and failure in Asian and American college undergraduate and graduate students; they found that American students attributed academic achievement more often to ability than did Asian international students. American students also believed that effort was more important for success than lack of effort was for failure, whereas Asian international students considered effort equally important for success or failure. These results are consonant with similar tendencies in parental attitudes described earlier, and with attributional biases discussed in Chapter 14.

Cross-national differences have been found in other samples as well. Studies comparing American, German, Russian, and Japanese children's beliefs about school performance showed that American children had the highest levels of personal agency and control expectancy, but the lowest belief-performance correlations (Little, Oettingen, Stetsenko, & Baltes, 1995; Little et al., 2003). That is, American children believed they had the most control over their academic outcomes, but this degree of perceived control was actually unrelated to their actual performance.

Together, these findings suggest that students around the world approach their academic work with quite different worldviews, attitudes, and attributional styles; that these differences are related to parental variations found in other research; that they relate to how children do in school; and that the entire process is intimately related to culture.

Teaching Practices and School Environment

Researchers have found that what happens in the classroom can vary greatly across cultures. Japanese and Chinese school children spend more days per year in school, more hours per day in school, a greater proportion of time in school devoted to purely academic subjects, and a greater proportion of time devoted to math (Takahashi & Takeuchi, 2006). In addition, Japanese and Chinese teachers spend a greater proportion of time working with the whole class than do American teachers. As a result, American students spend less time working under the supervision and guidance of a teacher.

During class, American teachers tend to use praise to reward correct responses. Teachers in Japan, however, tend to focus on incorrect answers, using them as examples to lead into discussion of the computational process and math concepts. Teachers in Taiwan tend to use a process more congruent with the Japanese approach. These teaching differences speak to the cultural emphasis in the United States on rewarding uniqueness and individualism and the emphasis in Japan and China on finding ways to engage in group process and sharing responsibility for mistakes with members of the group. Praise, while nice, often precludes such discussion.

Finally, cross-cultural differences in the school environment have also been found. In Japan, principals of eighth-graders reported far fewer behaviors threatening a safe and orderly learning environment (e.g., intimidation or verbal abuse occurring between students and classroom disturbances) than in the United States (National Center for Education Statistics, 2009; Trends in the International Mathematics and Science Study, 2007) (see Figure 3.7).

Interestingly, although Japanese principals reported far fewer disturbances, they were much more likely than U.S. principals to see these disturbances as serious problems (see Figure 3.8). Taken together, these studies highlight important differences in

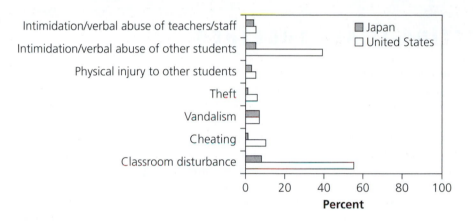

FIGURE 3.7 Percentage of Eighth-Grade Students Whose Principals Reported That Behavior Threatening a Safe and Orderly Environment Occurs at Least Weekly

Source: Trends in the International Mathematics and Science Study, 2007; National Center for Education Statistics, 2009.

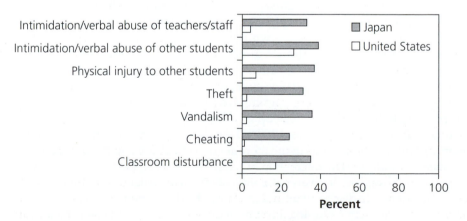

FIGURE 3.8 Percentage of Eighth-Grade Students Whose Principals Reported That Behavior Threatening a Safe and Orderly Environment Is a Serious Problem

Source: International Association for the Evaluation of Educational Achievement (IEA), Trends in Mathematics and Science Study (TIMSS), 2007.

the classroom in terms of teaching style, expectations, and actual behaviors contribute to children's academic achievement.

Summary

Research highlights the role of the educational system as an important enculturation agent in any society. Parents' and children's attitudes, educational practices and curricula, teacher behaviors, and all other associated factors are important transmitters of culture. They impart important cultural knowledge to the students as members of a culture or society, and thus play a major role in the socialization and enculturation of children in many societies of the world. Differences in these institutions not only reflect but reinforce cultural differences in values, beliefs, attitudes, norms, and behaviors and help transmit this important cultural information from one generation to the next. The school-age period of life is indeed a critical time in any culture, when culture is strongly reinforced in children by society as a whole.

PUTTING IT ALL TOGETHER

The information presented so far speaks to just a few of the many ways in which enculturation occurs around the world. Differences in parenting styles and child rearing provide learning platforms for children that allow them to achieve developmental goals fostered by their particular cultures. Each culture's way of raising children—through parenting behaviors, sleeping arrangements, educational systems, and other concrete mechanisms—represents that culture's way of ensuring that its values and norms are transmitted to those children. In all cultures, these practices are ritualized so that this transmission of information can occur generation after generation. Learning cultural values is as much a part of the process of socialization as it is an outcome of socialization.

Early cross-cultural work in development (e.g., Caudill & Frost, 1974; Caudill & Weinstein, 1969) focused primarily on the role of culture in "driving" parenting behaviors that resulted in changes in the infant and young child. This model suggests that culture unidirectionally provides the structure and environment for parents, particularly mothers, to affect their children in culturally appropriate ways: culture → parent → infant. Others (e.g., Shand & Kosawa, 1985) have focused on biology, proposing a developmental model that starts with the effects of genes, biology, and heredity on infant temperament, which then affects a parent's behaviors, which in turn produce cultural differences: genes → infant → parent → culture.

Contemporary theories of child development incorporate elements of both, recognizing that communities, caregivers, and children are dynamic, interactive partners—all contributing to how children develop (Bronfenbrenner, 1979; Grusec & Davidov, 2010; Lerner, 2006; Super & Harkness, 2002). This view suggests that children's active processing of information results in the reproduction of culture and the production of new elements of culture. The interaction of language between parent and child provides the platform on which divergent points of view construct new realities. These theories also attempt to discover cultural meanings held in common between parents and children, rather than assuming a common understanding "imposed" by an outside culture.

Future research on the enculturation process will hopefully bridge the gaps among all of these various components, assessing the interplay among children's characteristics (such as temperament, see Chapter 4), parenting styles, institutions, and psychological culture in the milieu. Although we have focused primarily on children in this chapter, it is important to remember that enculturation occurs throughout our entire lives. On an individual level, we are continually learning and being socialized into new roles and contexts as we grow older. On a cultural level, cultures are also changing, creating new contexts for enculturation. We must continually adapt to ongoing technological innovations and social changes in norms, attitudes, and behaviors in each culture. Enculturation, therefore, is a lifelong process. Ideally, future research will include longitudinal studies that will enable researchers to examine the interactions among various components of the enculturation process, in the same individuals, in different contexts, across time.

EXPLORATION AND DISCOVERY

Why Does This Matter to Me?

1. What are some life values that are important to you (e.g., treat others with respect, work hard to succeed in life)? How did you come to hold those values? Who did you learn them from?

2. For those of you who grew up in a different country than your parents/caregivers, in what ways do you differ from them in terms of life values, behaviors, and/or worldviews? In what ways are you similar to them? How has their cultural upbringing influenced the way they have parented you?

3. You are now studying in a college/university. Think about different experiences in your life that made this possible. Why did you decide to continue onto higher education? What role did your parents, peers, and teachers play in your decision to continue onto higher education?

Suggestions for Further Exploration

1. Interview your parents/caregivers and ask them what lessons in life they thought were important to teach you. Ask them what they did to pass on these lessons to you. Afterward, reflect on whether it easy or difficult for them to describe how they taught you these life lessons. You might find that it is difficult to describe how socialization/enculturation occurs because we are all so deeply immersed in the process.

2. Find someone from a different culture and ask about the sleeping arrangements for babies in his or her culture. Are the sleeping arrangements similar or different from what is practiced in your culture? If they are different, what are the reasons behind this difference?

3. Imagine you are an education researcher interested in understanding why some children do better in school than others. The theoretical framework you adopt for your study is Bronfenbrenner's ecological systems perspective. According to this perspective, you must consider children's development on several levels—the microsystem, mesosystem, exosystem, and macrosystem. Within each of these four systems, what are key factors you would focus on to find out why some children do better in school than others?

4 Culture and Developmental Processes

Are people born with inherent, biological predispositions to behavioral and cultural differences, or are such differences due entirely to environment and upbringing? What psychological differences are there in childhood and development when people are raised in different cultures? This chapter examines the main question of what kind of developmental differences exists across cultures during infancy and childhood, and beyond. A considerable amount of cross-cultural research has been conducted on topics such as temperament, attachment, and cognitive and moral development; in this chapter, we review that literature. The information presented complements that in the previous chapter (Chapter 3); together they provide an in-depth view of the role of culture on developmental processes.

First, we define what "development" is. Human development is how people change over time on many different levels—biological, physical, cognitive, emotional, and social. Development, however, is more than just change. Development refers to changes that show greater complexity, organization, and competencies. Dyeing your hair from brown to purple is an example of change. Accruing greater perception, balance, and spatial skills as a young child that enable you to go from crawling to walking, is an example of development.

One important issue in understanding human development is whether developmental pathways are universal or culture specific. Earlier theories of human development, for example, assumed a "universal child." In-depth observational studies conducted by Arnold Gesell in the 1930s and 1940s established a normative timetable for motor development milestones among infants (when do babies start grasping, rolling over, sitting, crawling, walking). The timing of these milestones was assumed to be the same for children all over the world. Cross-cultural studies have shown, however, that the timing also depends on culture (Cole, 2006). Contemporary theorists of human development recognize there are universal developmental pathways (e.g., all children undergo puberty) as well as culture-specific developmental pathways (e.g., the experience, meaning, and implications for undergoing puberty vary across cultures). In this chapter, we will discuss what aspects of temperament, attachment, and cognitive and moral development appear to be universal, and what aspects appear to be culture specific.

Another important issue for understanding human development is to explain what drives development. In other words, how do we become the people that we are? Is it because of nature (our genetic and biological predispositions) or nurture (the environment in which we grew up in)? Contemporary theorists of human development agree that development is not primarily driven by nature *or* nurture, but of nature's close *interaction* with nurture—the two cannot be separated. Thus, development is the result of the interaction between the characteristics that children are born with (such as temperament), and children's relations to their unique environment—the people, settings, institutions, and culture in which they grow up (Bronfenbrenner, 1979; Lerner, 2006). This **developmental contextualism** perspective proposes that the multiple levels of a developing child—ranging from the inner biological, psychological, social relational, and sociocultural—are inextricably intertwined and function as an integrated system. Developmental contextualism stresses that it is the *relation* between these changing multiple levels that constitutes human development. This contemporary view of development is complex, dynamic, and counters traditional views of development where either nature or nurture was emphasized to a greater degree than the other.

developmental contextualism A contemporary theoretical perspective that proposes that the multiple levels of a developing child—ranging from the inner biological, psychological, social relational, and sociocultural—are inextricably intertwined and function as an integrated system. Developmental contextualism stresses that it is the *relation* between these changing multiple levels that constitutes human development.

▶ Culture and Temperament

temperament Qualities of responsiveness to the environment that exist from birth and evoke different reactions from people in the baby's world. Temperament is generally considered to be a biologically based style of interacting with the world.

As discussed in Chapter 3, the process of socialization starts early, from the very first day of life. The biological temperament and predispositions we bring with us into the world at birth are an integral part of the socialization process. In other words, the characteristics we are born with determine, to some extent, how our caregivers react and interact with us, initiating the lifelong process of socialization. We begin this review by examining the possibility that children of different cultures are born with different biological predispositions to learn certain cultural practices— that is, the issue of **temperament**.

What Is Temperament?

easy temperament A type of temperament that is defined by a very regular, adaptable, mildly intense style of behavior that is positive and responsive.

difficult temperament A type of temperament that is characterized by an intense, irregular, withdrawing style that is generally marked by negative moods.

slow-to-warm-up A type of temperament in which infants need time to make transitions in activity and experiences. Though they may withdraw initially or respond negatively, given time and support they will adapt and react positively.

Any parent can tell you that no two babies are alike. It is not simply that they look different but that they differ from the very beginning in temperament. Each baby has its own way of being in the world—easygoing or fussy, active or quiet. These qualities of responsiveness to the environment evoke different reactions from people in the baby's world. Temperament is a biologically based style of interacting with the world that exists from birth. Although it is biologically based, it does not mean that temperament is fixed at birth or impervious to experience. Instead, temperament reflects an interaction between a child's predispositions and experiences in life. And, while temperament is relatively stable, it can be modified over time (Fox, Henderson, Rubin, Calkins, & Schmidt, 2001; Rothbart & Bates, 2006).

Thomas and Chess (1977), pioneers in the study of temperament, described three major categories: easy, difficult, and slow-to-warm-up. **Easy temperament** is defined by a very regular, adaptable, mildly intense style of behavior that is positive and responsive. **Difficult temperament** is an intense, irregular, withdrawing style, generally marked by negative moods. **Slow-to-warm-up** children need time to make transitions in activity and experiences (see Figures 4.1, 4.2, and 4.3). Though they may withdraw initially or respond negatively, given time and support they will adapt and react positively. A child's temperamental style is believed to provide a foundation for later personality (see Chapter 6).

The Goodness of Fit between Temperament and Culture

goodness of fit How well a child's temperament fits into the expectations and values of the parents, environment, and culture.

Thomas and Chess (1977) developed an important concept in temperament research— the notion of **goodness of fit**. Goodness of fit refers to how well the child's temperament matches the expectations and values of the parent, environment, and culture. If there is a mismatch, more negative child outcomes are expected. Conversely, if there is a good match, better child outcomes are expected.

Research on Masai infants in Kenya has corroborated the importance of the goodness of fit between an infant's temperament and his or her environment. Based on Thomas and Chess's (1977) temperament classifications, DeVries (1984, 1989) identified difficult and easy Masai infants and followed them for several years. What was considered a "difficult" temperament by Western standards actually became a protective factor against malnutrition during a time of drought. Those infants who were classified as difficult had a greater chance of survival compared with their easy counterparts. DeVries explained this surprising finding by suggesting that the difficult infants, who were very active and fussy, demanded and consequently received more feeding and caring from their mothers. Thus, a particular type of temperament may

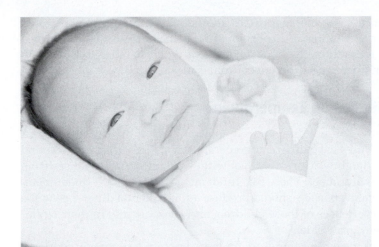

FIGURE 4.1
Easy Temperament Is Defined by a Very Regular, Adaptable, Mildly Intense Style of Behavior That Is Positive and Responsive

Source: Supri Suharjoto/Shutterstock.com

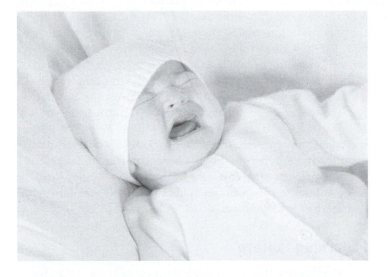

FIGURE 4.2
A Difficult Temperament Is an Intense, Irregular, Withdrawing Style, Generally Marked by Negative Moods

Source: Shanta Giddens/Shutterstock.com

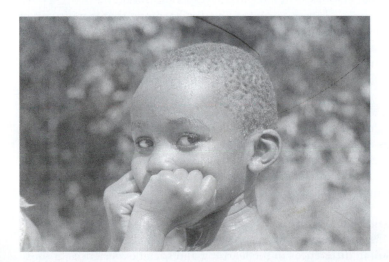

FIGURE 4.3
Slow-to-Warm-Up Infants Need Time to Make Transitions in Activity and Experiences

Source: Steffen Foerster Photography/Shutterstock.com

be adaptive in one culture and maladaptive in another. His findings demonstrated that the way we interpret an infant's dispositions and behaviors must be considered in relation to the specific culture; the same dispositions and behaviors may have different meanings when placed in a different cultural context.

Cross-Cultural Studies on Temperament

The implications of cross-cultural differences in temperament, if they exist, are large. If children of other cultures have different temperaments at birth, they will respond to the environment differently. Moreover, they will evoke different responses from caregivers and their environment. These two fundamental differences—in temperament and environmental response—should produce a fundamental difference in the learning and social experiences of those children, and consequently in their worldview and culture as they grow older.

In general, most of the earlier literature on temperament has compared North American or Western European infants to Asian infants, with the conclusion that Asian infants seem to have a predisposition to be less irritable compared to North American or Western European infants. Freedman (1974) found that Chinese American babies were calmer and more placid than European American babies or African American babies. When a cloth was placed on their faces covering their noses, the Chinese American babies lay quietly and breathed through their mouths. The other babies turned their heads or tried to pull the cloth off with their hands. In other studies, Chinese, Japanese, and Hmong infants were significantly less active, less irritable, and less vocal than European American infants (Caudill & Frost, 1974; Kagan, Snidman, Arcus, & Reznick, 1994; Muret-Wagstaff & Moore, 1989). It is important to note that there is variation among Asian countries as well. A study comparing newborns from China and Japan demonstrated that Chinese newborns were more irritable compared to Japanese newborns (Loo, Ohgi, Zhu, Akiyama, Howard, & Chen, 2005). Taken together, studies of newborns show that very early on in life, temperamental differences are evident across cultures.

Temperament and Learning Culture

The quiet temperament and placidity that are notable in infants from Asian backgrounds may be further stabilized in later infancy and childhood by the response of caregivers. For instance, Chinese parents value the harmony that is maintained through emotional restraint and emphasize and reinforce quiet behaviors (Bond & Wang, 1983; Chen, Wang, & Desouza, 2006). Differences in infant temperament may make it easier for parents of different cultures to engage in parenting styles and behaviors that teach and reinforce their particular cultural practices. Temperament, therefore, may serve as a baseline biological predisposition of the infant that allows this type of learning to occur.

The cultural differences that we find concerning temperament, evident very early in life, give us a clue to what kinds of personalities and behaviors are valued in a culture as an adult. For instance, in Japan, nonreactivity (which is related to not expressing emotionality) is more valued than in Western cultures, where higher levels of reactivity (expression of emotionality) are more acceptable. The differences in temperament we see in the first few days of life may be a reflection of what each culture values concerning appropriate ways of acting and being. A child's temperament and the environmental response to his or her temperamental style will most likely result in differences in the learning and social experiences of those children, and consequently in their behaviors, personalities, and worldviews as they become adults.

Dimensions of Temperament: A Focus on Behavioral Inhibition

Current research on temperament has included a wider range of samples beyond North American and Asian countries, including infants from Poland, Russia, Israel, Spain (Gartstein Slobodskaya, Żylicz, Gosztyła, & Nakagawa, 2010), Australia, South Korea, and Italy (Rubin et al., 2006). Current research has also focused on specific temperamental dimensions (as opposed to general temperamental styles such as Thomas and Chess's approach). At least six temperament dimensions have been identified: activity level (gross motor activity such as moving arms and legs and squirming), smiling and laughter (being sociable), fear (showing distress in novel situations, also known as behavioral inhibition), distress to limitations (levels of distress when an infant's goal is blocked), soothability (how easy it is to soothe an infant when distressed), and duration of orienting (how long an infant pays attention to an object when no other stimulations are introduced) (Rothbart, 1981; Rothbart, Sheese, & Conradt, 2009). Of these six dimensions, the one that has received the most attention cross-culturally is behavioral inhibition.

Behavioral inhibition refers to when a child shows signs of wariness, discomfort, or distress when confronted with novel, challenging, or unfamiliar situations (Kagan, Snidman, Kahn, & Towsley, 2007). Kagan and colleagues have studied this aspect of temperament longitudinally, by testing infants early in life, at 4 months of age, and following them to young adulthood. To study behavioral inhibition, the infants sat in a chair (like a car seat) and various stimuli were introduced—an interesting mobile, a noise, or a scent. The researchers found that infants who reacted more negatively to new stimuli by becoming very agitated—balling up their fists, squirming around, crying—were more likely to become anxious and worrisome young adults compared to those who remained calm and relaxed when exposed to the same stimuli. The researchers were able to show that even as infants, children display variations in temperamental characteristics such as behavioral inhibition, and these characteristics may be early indicators of underlying personalities later in life.

A child who displays behavioral inhibition in novel social situations is considered "shy." This temperamental aspect has received much attention because it has been clearly linked to children's adjustment and social competence. In some cultures, such as in North America, shyness is not a desirable trait. Shy children are considered socially immature and are less liked by their peers in North America than assertive children (Chen, Rubin, & Sun, 1992). Shyness in North America has also been linked to greater anxiety, loneliness, and a more negative and stressful family environment in childhood (Rubin, Chen, McDougall, Bower, & McKinnon, 1995; Volbrecht & Goldsmith, 2010).

In other cultures, however, shyness is a highly desirable trait. Shy children in China are considered mature, well behaved, and understanding (Chen et al., 1992). They also tend to have high self-esteem and do well in school (Chen et al., 1992; Chen et al., 2006; Chen, Rubin, Li, & Li, 1999). In fact, in sharp contrast to children in North America, shy children in China are more socially accepted by their peers than assertive children (Chen et al., 1992). Thus, the same temperamental disposition will be discouraged and provoke negative responses from parents and peers in one culture, while in another, it will be encouraged and positively reinforced. If a child's temperament matches what is valued in that cultural context (an example of "goodness of fit") then more positive developmental outcomes are expected. If a child's temperament

behavioral inhibition An aspect of temperament where a child shows signs of wariness, discomfort, or distress when confronted with novel, challenging, or unfamiliar situations. Also known as fearfulness or shyness.

does not match what is valued in that cultural context (a "poor fit") then negative developmental outcomes are expected (Rubin et al., 2006). Culture provides the meaning and consequences related to particular temperamental traits.

Interestingly, cultures and communities may change in terms of which temperamental traits are desirable. Chen and colleagues' most recent study of urban and rural Chinese children demonstrated how cultural ideals concerning shyness are changing in the context of globalization (Chen, Wang, & Wang, 2009). In their study of almost 1,000 school-aged children, they found that shyness was associated with leadership, social competence, and academic achievement—but only for children living in rural areas in China. In urban areas, shyness was associated with more depression and more social and school problems for children—similar to what has been found in North American studies. The authors noted that China has undergone many significant changes (social and economic) in the last several decades such that competition, individual freedom, and self-expression are increasingly emphasized. Subsequently, characteristics such as assertiveness are increasingly valued and deemed necessary to be successful—at least in urban areas. This is a rather startling change in just 30 years.

Sources behind Temperamental Differences

The research reviewed thus far shows cross-cultural differences in which temperamental styles may be more common in a culture and how temperamental styles are related to children's adjustment. Why does temperament differ across cultures? From a developmental contextualism perspective, differences in temperament reflect differences in genetics and in reproductive histories as well as environmental and cultural pressures over generations that may have helped to produce minor biological differences in infants through a functionally adaptive process. Saco-Pollitt (1989), for instance, investigated how altitude may relate to newborn behaviors. She compared Peruvian infants who were raised in high-altitude (in the Andes) and low-altitude (Lima) environments. She reported that in comparison with low-altitude infants, those raised in the Andes were less attentive, less responsive, and less active, and had a more difficult time quieting themselves. The harsh environment of living in the high Andes may have contributed to these differences. Another study of Nepalese infants, who by Western standards were undernourished, found that they were actually more alert and had better motor performance compared with a sample of U.S. infants (Walsh Escarce, 1989). The researcher hypothesized that these findings may reflect an adaptation on the part of the Nepalese infant to years of poverty. She also noted that the cultural practice of daily massaging the infant, along with special rituals surrounding the baby, may have contributed to their higher alertness and motor performance.

In addition to environmental pressures, the cultural experiences of the mother during pregnancy, including diet and other culture-related practices, may contribute to a prenatal environment that modifies an infant's biological composition. The fetal environment is one context in which significant stimulation occurs. Chisholm (1983) argued that cross-cultural differences between Navajo and European American infants (Navajo infants were less irritable than European American infants) can partly be attributed to the prenatal environment. Mothers with higher blood pressures during the second and third trimesters had infants who were more irritable—and Navajo mothers, on average, reported lower blood pressure than the European American mothers. This connection between maternal blood pressure and infant irritability has also been found in Malaysian, Chinese, and Aboriginal and white Australian infants (Chisholm, 1981; Chisholm, Woodson, & da Costa Woodson, 1978). A more recent study on the prenatal environment found that mothers who reported high anxiety during pregnancy were more likely to have newborns who spent less time in quiet and active alert and showed poorer motor performance compared to newborns whose mothers reported low anxiety (Field et al., 2003). Although the prenatal environment has been linked to aspects of infant temperament, there are still very few studies that examine this link and even fewer that examine this link cross-culturally. Subsequently, the nature and consequences of prenatal stimulation, and possible variations across cultures, are still largely unknown (Talge, Neal, & Glover, 2007).

Whatever the causal mechanism, temperamental differences that are evident from birth contribute to the personality differences we observe in adults of different cultures (see Chapter 6). Therefore, it is important to understand the magnitude of their contributions as building blocks in the development of adult members in cultures around the world. Future research in this area should focus on the cultural practices and actual behaviors of people of different cultural groups, and examine the relationship between these practices and behaviors with infant temperament.

Temperamental differences that are evident from birth contribute to the personality differences we observe in adults of different cultures.

In sum, cross-cultural research suggests that there are group differences across cultures in infants' and children's temperaments. These differences are the result of the complex interplay between multiple factors such as what temperamental styles are valued in each culture, specific environmental demands (such as living in poverty or in a high-altitude environment), and physiological aspects of the mother (for example, higher blood pressure). Some aspects of temperament appear to be universal. Studies of behavioral inhibition find infants from around the world who exhibit a higher level of fear or discomfort when confronted with a novel stimulation. However, the developmental consequences associated with this aspect of temperament vary by the specific culture. Future research should continue to examine the interaction between children's temperament and the caregiving environment into which they are born to better understand the process of how children eventually learn to internalize the values, attitudes, and behaviors appropriate to their culture.

▶ Culture and Attachment

Traditional View of Attachment: Bowlby and Ainsworth

Attachment refers to the special bond that develops between the infant and his or her primary caregivers and provides the infant with emotional security. Once attached, babies are distressed by separation from their caregiver (separation distress or anxiety). There is evidence that seven- to nine-month-old infants in many different cultures show distress when they are separated from their primary caregiver (Grossman & Grossman, 1990). Many psychologists believe that the quality of attachment with caregivers during childhood has lifelong effects on our relationships with loved ones later.

attachment The special bond that develops between the infant and his or her primary caregiver and provides the infant with emotional security. The quality of attachment has lifelong effects on our relationships with loved ones.

Bowlby's (1969) evolutionary theory of attachment proposed that infants have a preprogrammed, biological basis for becoming attached to their caregivers. This innate behavioral repertoire includes smiling and cooing to elicit physical attachment behaviors on the part of the caregiver. He argued that the attachment relationship between caregiver and child functioned as a survival strategy: Infants had a greater chance of survival if they remained close to the caregiver for comfort and protection.

Attachment as a survival strategy is illustrated in a study in Nigeria of Hausa infants and their caregivers (Marvin, VanDevender, Iwanaga, LeVine, & LeVine, 1977). The researchers reported that the attachment relationship protected infants from the dangers of their environment, which included open fires, tools, and utensils that were easily accessible. Infants explored their environment, but only when they were in close proximity to an attachment figure. Similarly, among the Dogon of Mali, infants were always kept in close proximity with the mother (being held most of the time) and infants did not roam freely, thus avoiding dangers such as open fires, snakes, and animal droppings (True, Pisani, & Oumar, 2001).

Based on Bowlby's attachment theory, Ainsworth's (1967, 1977) study of mothers and infants in Uganda led to the tripartite classification system of attachment relationships. Based on her careful observations of 26 mother–infant pairs over a span of one year, she described three attachment styles: **secure**, **ambivalent**, and **avoidant**. The latter two attachment styles she labeled as "insecurely attached." The secure style described infants who became distressed when their mother left but were easily comforted by her when she returned. The ambivalent style described infants who also experienced distress when their mother left but when she returned they sent mixed signals—they wanted to be comforted by her yet, at the same time, appeared to have a difficult time letting her soothe them. The avoidant style described infants who did not seem to be distressed when their mother left and when she returned these infants actively avoided reuniting with their mother and instead focused their attention elsewhere. Ainsworth later replicated her results in a sample of U.S. (from Baltimore, Maryland) mothers and their infants. In her samples, she found that approximately 57% of mothers and infants were classified as securely attached, 25% as ambivalent, and 18% as avoidant (Ainsworth, 1967; 1977).

Studies from other cultures have found a similar distribution of attachment classifications; others have found considerable differences. And some attachment styles are not reported in certain cultures. For example, no avoidant infants were found in True et al.'s (2001) study of the Dogon of Mali. Mali mothers kept their infants close to them throughout the day and practiced constant, responsive nursing (nursing on demand when the infant is hungry or distressed). This type of caregiving, True et al. argued, "prevents" avoidant attachment to the mother. These findings highlight the importance of understanding the attachment system in the context of parenting practices specific to each culture.

Cross-Cultural Studies and a Contemporary View on Attachment

Since Ainsworth's early studies, hundreds of studies of attachment have been conducted in cultures all over the world. To measure attachment, the Strange Situation, developed by Ainsworth, has been the most widely used. In the Strange Situation, infants are brought into a research lab and separated from their mothers for a brief period of time. During this brief separation a stranger comes into the room to interact with the infant. The separation and interaction with the stranger is thought to trigger the attachment system in the infant. The quality of attachment is derived partly from an assessment of the infant's reaction to the separation, to the stranger, and subsequent reunion with the mother.

Although this method has been used extensively across cultures, the cross-cultural validity of this method and the meaning of the attachment classifications themselves have been questioned for some time. One main issue is that the meaning of the separation may differ across cultures (Takahashi, 1990). Japanese infants are rarely separated from their mothers, and the separation during the Strange Situation may represent a highly unusual situation that may imply something different for Japanese infants and their mothers than for U.S. infants and their mothers.

More recently, Otto and colleagues (2013) have argued that the attempt to standardize a test such as the Strange Situation cuts out key cultural features that are necessary for interpreting attachment behaviors. Using modified Strange Situation

secure attachment A style of attachment in which infants are described as warm and responsive to their caregiver.

ambivalent attachment A style of attachment in which children are uncertain in their response to their mothers, going back and forth between seeking and shunning her attention. These mothers have been characterized as insensitive and less involved.

avoidant attachment A style of attachment in which children shun their mothers, who are suspected of being intrusive and overstimulating.

procedures that are conducted not in a lab but in a natural environment such as the home, these researchers showed that the interpretation of reactions and interactions with strangers—one of the key ways to measure attachment—heavily depended on the developmental goals of the culture. Studies of infants' reactions to strangers in Cameroon versus Germany, for instance, showed very different patterns of behavior. In Cameroon, young children are cared for by multiple caregivers and children are actively socialized to be comfortable with strangers. In the modified Strange Situation, when a stranger picks up the baby and the baby is uncomfortable, the mother may not intervene but allow it some time to get used to the stranger. In contrast, German children are usually primarily cared for by the mother, so strangers look to the mother as an important point of reference on how to handle the baby, and wait for cues from both the mother and infant on whether and how to approach (Otto, Potinius, & Keller, 2013). Otto and colleagues argued that observing scripted parent–child interactions in a research lab that is void of the cultural context gives an inaccurate picture of the quality of attachment relationships.

In addition to criticisms leveled at the traditional measurement of attachment, cross-cultural researchers have questioned how secure attachment is developed. In other words, what must caregivers do to promote secure attachment? Mothers of securely attached infants are described as sensitive, warm, and more positive in their emotional expression. Mothers of avoidant children are suspected of being intrusive and overstimulating. Mothers of ambivalent children have been characterized as being insensitive and uninvolved. Thus, according to Ainsworth, a major determinant of attachment security is having a caregiver who is sensitive and responsive to the child's needs. In a review of 65 studies of attachment, however, caregiver sensitivity was related only modestly to security of attachment (De Wolff & van IJzendoorn, 1997). And studies with other cultures found an even weaker connection between parent sensitivity and security of attachment (van IJzendoorn & Sagi, 1999).

One possible reason for why maternal sensitivity has not been consistently linked to secure attachment is that sensitivity may mean different things and be expressed in different ways across cultures. One study contrasted U.S. caregivers' with Japanese caregivers' sensitive responsiveness (Rothbaum, Weisz, Pott, Miyake, & Morelli, 2000). In the United States, parents tend to wait for their child to express and communicate a need and then respond to that need. In other words, sensitive parenting in the United States allows the child to express his or her individual needs to the parent so that the parent can appropriately address those needs. In contrast, in Japan, parents tend to anticipate their child's needs instead of waiting for their child to communicate a need. This can be done by being aware of situations that may cause distress to a child and anticipating ways to minimize the stress.

Rothbaum and colleagues argued that researchers need to pay more attention to how different cultures conceptualize and demonstrate sensitive parenting to better understand what type of parenting leads to secure attachment. Further, parenting behaviors that, from a Western perspective, may seem to promote insecure attachment, may, in fact, do the opposite in other cultures. For example, Ainsworth suggested that parenting that is "intrusive," namely, directive and controlling, leads to an insecure attachment. However, this type of parenting may have an entirely different meaning in non-Western cultures (Chao, 1996). What Westerners may see as inappropriate and "intrusive," parents in other parts of the world may see as appropriate and "guiding" (Keller, 2013; Otto et al., 2013).

Indeed, even the idea of maternal sensitivity that Ainsworth described as necessary for secure attachment is based on the idea that infants are unique, separate, and autonomous persons who participate in a somewhat equal interaction with their caregiver, a cultural framework that is not shared by other cultures (Keller, 2013). Cultures

Three Cultural Models of Attachment

Psychological Autonomy	Hierarchical Relatedness	Hybrid
• There are strong emotional bonds between infants and one or few caregivers. Infants are conceptualized as autonomous, unique individuals.	• Infants in this cultural environment have a sense of security not based on a specific caregiver or relationship, but security within a network of community members.	• This cultural model emphasizes unique attachment relationships with one or few caregivers and at the same time, view the social community as another integral part of the network of attachment.

FIGURE 4.4 The Form and Organization of Attachment Relationships between Infants and Their Caregivers May Differ Depending on Cultural Models Such as These Three Proposed by Keller (2013)

vary in conceptions of the self (see Chapter 5), which will shape how the self is perceived in relation to others, and subsequently, of attachment relationships. Thus, children in some cultures will have developed a different kind of "relational security" that is not defined by a close, emotional bond with one or few specific caregivers, but by a deep trust in a strong network of general, communal support (Keller 2013).

Contemporary scholars of attachment such as Keller are leading the call for a radical new approach to theorizing about attachment, one that grounds attachment in specific cultures, communities, and contexts. To demonstrate, Keller (2013) proposed three cultural models that set the stage for different attachment relationships: psychological autonomy, hierarchical relatedness, and hybrid (see Figure 4.4). The psychological autonomy model is the foundation for Bowlby and Ainsworth's theories of attachment. In this cultural model, infants are conceptualized as autonomous, unique individuals. Caregiving that promotes a strong emotional bond between infants and one or few caregivers is adaptive. In the hierarchical relatedness cultural model, infants are part of a network of attachment relationships that are hierarchical, where caregivers use a more directive approach in raising their children. The primary relationship for infants is not with one or few caregivers, but with the entire social community. Infants in this cultural environment have a sense of security not based on a specific caregiver or relationship, but security derived from being a part of a network of community members. The network is reliable and available, not just the parent. In the hybrid cultural model there is a blend of both, emphasizing autonomous relatedness. This type of model may emphasize both unique attachment relationships with one or few caregivers and, at the same time, view the social community as another integral part of the network of attachment.

Keller argued that other adaptive attachment conceptualizations may be derived from other cultural models. The task for the next generation of attachment researchers is to systematically study different cultural models and infant caregiver–community relationships that are adaptive for that particular culture. It is increasingly clear that the traditional view of attachment, as a primary relationship between mother and child, is just one of several possible models of attachment that is adaptive for a particular cultural context. The form and organization of attachment relationships between infants and their caregivers may differ depending on cultural models such as these three proposed by Keller (2013).

In sum, the traditional view of attachment proposed by Bowlby and Ainsworth privileged the mother–infant relationship as necessary, primary, and unique for positive child development. The vast literature concerning attachment in different cultures has shifted slowly away from the notion that attachment between infants and one primary caregiver (usually the mother) is a universal phenomenon. The contemporary view of attachment argues that relationship security in the form of a strong bond between infants and a community of caregivers can also be developmentally adaptive. Further, attachment scholars have moved away from using the evaluative terms "secure" and "insecure," replaced by terms such as "adaptive" and "maladaptive" (Crittenden, 2000; Keller, 2013). "Adaptive" attachments, then, would refer to relationships or a network of relationships that promote the maximum level of safety for the child within a specific cultural context. Researchers could then define an "optimal" relationship between the infant and the caregiver or community of caregivers as one that may be achieved in different ways, under different circumstances, in different cultures.

▶ Temperament and Attachment: A Summary

Much still needs to be done to understand the attachment patterns in other cultures and the relationship among cultural milieu, infant temperament, and infant–caregiver relationships. Notions about what type of relationship in the early years of life is necessary and optimal to ensure survival in different cultures and communities are still being discovered. The attachment literature is finally acknowledging how the predominant theory of attachment laid down by Bowlby and Ainsworth is very much culturally bound.

The information presented so far concerning temperament and attachment relationships reveals just a few of the many ways in which enculturation occurs around the world. Children may be born with differences in biological predispositions or temperament that may make it easier for them to engage in the cultural learning that occurs throughout socialization and enculturation. Differences in attachment provide learning platforms for children that allow them to achieve developmental goals fostered by their particular cultures. Thus, the temperamental characteristics with which you were born, your caregivers' responses to your temperamental style, and the resultant attachment relationship you develop with your caregiver or community together play important roles in how you come to acquire your culture. There is a close interaction between a child's temperament, attachment relationship with his or her caregiver or community, and broader environment (e.g., cultural expectations of desirable temperament and attachment relationships) that contribute to a child's development.

We turn now to examine culture's role in two major developmental processes: cognitive and moral development. These topics are of great interest to developmental psychologists, both mainstream and cross-cultural.

▶ Cognitive Development

Piaget's Theory

Cognitive development is a specialty in psychology that studies how thinking skills and processes develop over time. In other words, psychologists interested in cognitive development focus on how children perceive and come to understand the world around them. Theories of cognitive development have traditionally focused on the

cognitive development A specialty in psychology that studies how thinking skills develop over time. The major theory of cognitive development is that of Piaget.

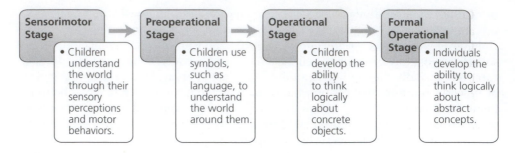

FIGURE 4.5 Piaget's Four Stages of Cognitive Development

period from infancy to adolescence. The theory that has dominated the field of cross-cultural studies of cognition is Piaget's stage theory of cognitive development.

Piaget based his theories on detailed, intensive observations of his own three children as well as other children. He found that children tended to solve problems quite differently at different ages. What was more interesting to Piaget was not why children solved problems correctly, but why children of similar ages tended to make the same mistake in solving problems incorrectly. To explain these differences, Piaget (1952) proposed that children progress through four stages as they grow from infancy into adolescence (see Figure 4.5).

Piaget's four stages of cognitive development are as follows.

1. **Sensorimotor stage.** This stage typically lasts from birth to about two years of age. In this stage, children understand the world through their sensory perceptions and motor behaviors. In other words, children understand by perceiving and doing. The most important achievement of this stage is the capability to use mental symbols to represent objects and events. The acquisition of object permanence—that is, knowing that objects exist even when they cannot be seen—illustrates this achievement. Early in this stage, children appear to assume that when a toy or other object is hidden (e.g., when a ball rolls under a sofa), it ceases to exist. Later in this stage, children will search under the sofa for the lost ball, demonstrating that they have come to understand that objects exist continuously.

   Other cognitive developments that also depend on the development of mental representation typical of this stage include deferred imitation and language acquisition. These developments have important implications for later cognitive development and enculturation. Imitation is an important cognitive component of observational learning, and language skills are necessary to ensure proper communication of verbal socialization processes.

conservation An awareness that physical quantities remain the same even when they change shape or appearance.

centration The tendency to focus on a single aspect of a problem.

irreversibility The inability to imagine "undoing" a process.

egocentrism The inability to step into another's shoes and understand the other person's point of view.

animism The belief that all things, including inanimate objects, are alive.

2. **Preoperational stage.** This stage lasts from about two to six or seven years of age. Piaget described children's thinking at this stage in terms of five characteristics: conservation, centration, irreversibility, egocentrism, and animism. **Conservation** is the awareness (or in this stage, the lack of awareness) that physical quantities remain the same even when they change shape or appearance. **Centration** is the tendency to focus on a single aspect of a problem. **Irreversibility** is the inability to imagine "undoing" a process. **Egocentrism** is the inability to step into another's shoes and understand the other person's point of view. **Animism** is the belief that all things, including inanimate objects, are alive. For example, children in the preoperational stage may regard a book lying on its side as "tired" or "needing a rest," or they may think that the moon is following them. Children at this stage do not yet think in a logical and systematic manner.

3. **Concrete operations stage.** This stage lasts from about six or seven years until about eleven years of age. During this stage, children acquire new thinking skills to work with actual objects and events. They are able to imagine undoing an action, and they can focus on more than one feature of a problem. Children also begin to understand that there are points of view different from their own. This new awareness helps children master the principle of conservation. A child in the concrete operations stage will understand that six apples are always six apples, regardless of how they are grouped or spaced and that the amount of clay does not change as a lump is molded into different shapes. This ability is not present in the preoperational stage. However, instead of thinking a problem through, children in this stage tend to rely on trial-and-error strategies.

4. **Formal operations stage.** This stage extends from around 11 years of age through adulthood. During this stage, individuals develop the ability to think logically about abstract concepts, such as peace, freedom, and justice. Individuals also become more systematic and thoughtful in their approach to problem solving.

The transition from one stage to another is often gradual, as children develop new abilities alongside earlier ways of thinking. Thus, the behavior of some children may represent a "blend" of two stages when they are in a period of transition from one to the other. Piaget hypothesized that two primary mechanisms are responsible for movement from one stage to the next: assimilation and accommodation. **Assimilation** is the process of fitting new ideas into a preexisting understanding of the world. **Accommodation** refers to the process of changing one's understanding of the world to accommodate ideas that conflict with existing concepts.

Piaget believed that the stages were universal, and that progression through these stages was invariant in order. According to Piaget, knowledge is constructed through the interactions between the biological maturation of the child and his or her actions and experiences with the physical and social environment. Because there are similarities across cultures in how individuals mature physically and in how they act on the physical world (for example, in every culture individuals ask questions, exchange information, and work together), the stages are thought to be universal. The richness of Piaget's theory has prompted a multitude of studies of cognitive development in cultures all over the world.

assimilation The process of fitting new ideas into a preexisting understanding of the world.

accommodation The process of changing one's understanding of the world to accommodate ideas that conflict with existing concepts.

Piaget's Theory in Cross-Cultural Perspective

Cross-cultural research on Piaget's theory has focused on four central questions. The findings to date show an interesting blend of cultural similarities and differences in various aspects of cognitive development that parallel Piaget's stages.

- Do Piaget's stages occur in the same order in different cultures? Studies that have addressed this question have demonstrated that Piaget's stages occur in the same fixed order in other cultures. For instance, a study of Zinacantec children from Mexico and children from Los Angeles, California, in the United States, showed similar movement from the preoperational to concrete operational stages (Maynard & Greenfield, 2003). We do not find cultures in which four-year-olds typically lack an awareness of object permanency or five-year-olds who understand the principle of conservation. Thus, we know that children from very different cultures do indeed learn groups of Piagetian tasks in a similar order. One thing that is less clear, however, is what defines a stage in Piaget's cognitive theory. Evidence accumulated across cultures suggest that children's thinking does not undergo abrupt, qualitative general shifts in thinking that is applied across all situations, but a rather gradual accumulation of many, many skills across many situations, changing incrementally, over time (Mishra, 2014).

- Are the ages that Piaget associated with each stage of development the same in all cultures? Studies have found surprising cultural variations in the ages at which children in different societies typically reach the third and fourth Piagetian stages. In some cases, the difference may be as much as five or six years. However, research also shows that children may have the potential to solve tasks sooner than their answers would indicate. For example, a child in the concrete operations stage will typically give the first answer that comes to mind during a test. If the child comes from a culture in which he or she has had practice performing the task in question, this answer is likely to be correct. However, a child who has never thought about the concept before may well utter the wrong answer and only later realize the mistake. When researchers checked for this possibility by repeating tests a second time at the end of testing sessions, they found that many children corrected their previous answers on the second attempt (Dasen, Lavallee, & Retschitzki, 1979; Dasen, Ngini, & Lavallee, 1979). Thus, it is important to remember that performance on a task may not reveal actual cognitive competence or ability.

- Are there cultural variations within, rather than between, Piaget's stages? There is considerable cultural variation in the order in which children acquire specific skills *within* Piaget's stages. In a comparative study of tribal children (the Inuit of Canada, the Baoul of Africa, and the Aranda of Australia), half of all Inuit children tested solved a spatial task at the age of seven years, half of the Aranda solved it at nine years, and the Baoul did not reach the halfway point until the age of 12 (Dasen, 1975). On a test of the conservation of liquids, however, the order changed dramatically: half of the Baoul children solved the problem when they were eight years old, the Inuit at nine years, and the Aranda at 12 years. Why did the ages at which these children could perform the same task vary so much? The Inuit and Aranda children live in nomadic societies, in which children need to learn spatial skills early because their families are constantly moving. The Baoul children live in a settled society, where they seldom travel but often fetch water and store grain. The skills these children used in their everyday lives seem to have affected the order in which they were able to solve Piagetian tasks within the concrete operations stage.

- Do non-Western cultures regard scientific reasoning as the ultimate developmental end point? Piaget's theory assumes that the scientific reasoning associated with formal operations is the universal end point of cognitive development—that the thinking most valued in Swiss and other Western societies (formal operations) is the yardstick by which all cultures should be judged. Because Piaget considered scientific reasoning to be the ultimate human achievement, his stage theory is designed to trace the steps by which people arrive at scientific thinking. This perspective has been widely accepted within North American psychology, and generally by the North American public, at least until recently.

Many cultures around the world do not share the conviction that abstract, hypothetical thought processes are the ultimate or desired end point in the cognitive development process. Many cultures, for example, consider cognitive development to be more relational—involving the thinking skills and processes needed to engage successfully in interpersonal contexts. What North Americans refer to as "common sense," rather than cognitive development per se, is considered a much more desired outcome in many cultures.

Piaget's Theory: Summary and Discussion

Cross-cultural studies of Piaget's stage of formal operations have found that in some cultures, very few people are able to complete fourth-stage Piagetian tasks. Does this mean that entire cultures are suspended at a lower stage of cognitive development? To answer this question, we must first ask whether Piagetian tasks are a culturally appropriate way of measuring an advanced stage of cognitive development. In fact, those tasks may not be meaningful in other cultures. Besides the issue of cultural appropriateness, there is also the issue of what is being tested. Tests of formal operations may tell us whether people can solve a narrow range of scientific problems, but they do not tell us whether people in different cultures develop advanced cognitive skills in areas other than those selected by Piaget.

We can say with certainty, however, that people who have not attended high school or college in a Westernized school system perform very poorly on tests of formal operations (Cole, 2006). These findings again raise the question of the degree to which Piagetian tasks depend on previous knowledge and cultural values rather than on cognitive skills. It is also important to remember the wide range of differences in cognitive development within a given culture. These within-culture differences make it extremely difficult to draw valid conclusions or inferences about differences in cognitive development between cultures. For example, not only do members of non-Western cultures have difficulty with tests of formal operations, but many adults in North American society also have such difficulties. Scientific reasoning does not appear to be as common in Western societies as Piaget thought, and it is frequently limited to special activities. Individuals who apply scientific logic to a problem on the job may reason quite differently in other situations.

Because large numbers of people are unable to complete Piagetian tasks of formal operations, it has not been possible to demonstrate the universality of the fourth stage of Piaget's theory of cognitive development. Even Piaget himself (1972) came to the conclusion that the fourth stage is highly dependent on whether one was raised in a particular context, such as a culture that incorporates formal schooling. Alternatively, it is possible that most adults do possess the ability to complete Piagetian tasks but lack either motivation or knowledge of how to demonstrate such ability. To demonstrate success on a task purporting to measure some aspect of cognitive ability or intelligence, it is crucial that the test-taker and the test-maker agree on what is being assessed. Cultural differences in the desired endpoint of cognitive development, as well as in definitions of intelligence (see Chapter 8), contribute to this dilemma.

Despite critiques of the universality of Piaget's stages of cognitive development, his theory is valuable in terms of several concepts that are still important for cross-cultural work in cognitive development today (Maynard, 2008):

- Cognitive development is an *ongoing, adaptive process* whereby children learn to solve problems that allow them to adapt to their environment. When their environment changes, children must also adapt and change.

- Children *actively participate in their development* by testing, exploring, and interacting with their environment.

- Cognitive development occurs within the *context of important socialization agents such as parents and peers*. Parents and peers contribute to children's cognitive development through discussions and interactions that support and challenge children's thinking.

Vygotsky's Sociocultural Theory of Cognitive Development

Vygotsky's (1978) sociocultural theory of cognitive development is an important alternative to Piaget's theory. Vygotsky was a Russian psychologist who proposed a theory of cognitive development that contemporary cultural psychologists have embraced. In contrast to earlier cross-cultural studies of cognition that compared how people of different cultures completed standard Piagetian tasks, cultural psychologists adopting Vygotsky's theory attempt to uncover how children in different cultures are socialized in "everyday cognition"—the knowledge, abilities, and skills to carry out everyday tasks such as shopping for groceries, caring for sheep, weaving a basket, or behaving in a classroom. In Vygotsky's view, cognitive development is inseparable from culture. A culture's symbols and generational knowledge (e.g., language and knowledge passed on from generation to generation) structure cognition. Unlike Piaget he did not emphasize stages of development, but rather the close interactions between a child and his or her social environment as well as cultural symbols that stimulated development. Say you were asked to solve a math problem, such as $100 - 33 = ?$. If you successfully solved the problem, Vygotsky would say that your success is not an individual accomplishment but rather an inherently social, cultural, and historical one. In other words, in order to solve this math problem you relied on the cultural and historical knowledge passed on from previous generations (such as math rules and solutions that have been passed down in your culture), along with the guidance of "more knowledgeable others" such as teachers. Cognition, then, is not an individual task that occurs and develops inside a person's head, but rather, is an inherently social and cultural process that develops within a relationship.

zone of proximal development The gap between the actual developmental level of a child versus the potential developmental level that the child is capable of, with some assistance by more knowledgeable others (such as parent, teacher, or more experienced peers)

Concepts such as scaffolding, and **zone of proximal development** are central to Vygotsky's ideas of cognitive development. The zone of proximal development refers to the gap between the actual developmental level of a child versus the potential developmental level that the child is capable of with some assistance by more knowledgeable others (such as parent, teacher, or more experienced peers). In other words, the actual developmental level is what the child can do individually, while the potential developmental level is what the child can do with a little help from others. This help from others is the scaffolding that pushes the child to the next level of thinking (see Figure 4.6). In Vygotsky's view, understanding both of these processes is key to understanding the development of cognition and how it unfolds.

Building on Vygotsky's theory, Rogoff (2003) investigated everyday cognition, or cognition in the context of daily activities within the cultural community. Some examples of everyday cognition she has studied are how children learn to make

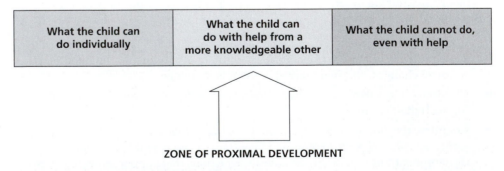

ZONE OF PROXIMAL DEVELOPMENT

FIGURE 4.6 In Vygotsky's Sociocultural View, Cognitive Development Occurs Through Our Close Interactions with Others

complicated weaving patterns, calculate change in the market, or narrate lengthy stories (Rogoff & Chavajay, 1995; Rogoff, Baker-Sennett, Lacasa, & Goldsmith, 1995). In everyday cognition children become more sophisticated in their thinking by participating in tasks alongside more knowledgeable others. In line with Vygotsky's view, Rogoff studied the actual activities and institutions (such as the home or school) in which children's thinking takes place. Cognition, therefore, is understood within a particular social, cultural, and historical context. The Vygotskyian perspective that cognitive development is inherently a social process, and that it should be studied as an integral part of a culture's everyday activities (and not solely by testing people with unfamiliar tasks), inspires contemporary psychologists interested in understanding cognitive development across many diverse cultures (Rogoff, 2003; see also Chapter 8 for other discussion on everyday cognition).

▶ Moral Reasoning

Another area of development crucial to our becoming functional adults in society and culture concerns moral judgments and reasoning. As they grow, children develop increasingly complex ways of understanding their world. These cognitive changes also bring about changes in their understanding of moral judgments. Why something is good or bad changes from the young child's interpretation of reward and punishment conditions to principles of right and wrong.

Morality and culture share a very close relationship. Moral principles and ethics provide guidelines for people's behaviors with regard to what is appropriate and what is not. These guidelines are products of a specific culture and society, handed down from one generation to the next. Morality is thus heavily influenced by the underlying, subjective, and implicit culture in which it is embedded. Morality also serves as the basis of laws, which are formalized guidelines for appropriate and inappropriate behavior. In this way, culture also affects the laws of a society. For these and other reasons, morality occupies a special place in our understanding of culture and cultural differences.

What Is Moral?

Before we begin our discussion on how moral reasoning develops, we first address a more basic question—what is considered moral? What is considered right or wrong? Do children distinguish between what is moral and what is not? To find out, Turiel and his colleagues studied whether children distinguished between moral and non-moral issues by presenting children with questions such as "Is it ok to wear pajamas to school?," "Is it ok to call someone's grandfather by his first name?." "Is it ok for someone to push his little brother off the swing?." Based on children's responses, Turiel and his colleagues (Nucci & Turiel, 1978; Turiel, 1983; Turiel, Killen, & Helwig, 1987) outlined three types of rules that children as young as three years old can differentiate: moral, conventional, and personal. Moral rules are rules that apply to everyone, cannot be changed, and are based on values such as the safety and well-being of all humans. Conventional rules apply to certain groups, are changeable, and are based on agreed-upon norms by a group of people. Personal rules apply to individuals, are changeable, and are based on the preferences of a specific person. Cross-cultural studies show that children all over the world do indeed distinguish between moral and nonmoral issues. There are similarities across cultures, such as deeming hitting an innocent child or stealing from someone as immoral. But there are also differences.

Hindu children in India consider it immoral for a widow to eat fish or wear bright jewelry after her husband's death (Shweder, Mahapatra, & Miller, 1987) and Korean children consider it immoral to not give up a seat for an elderly person on the bus (Song, Smetana, & Kim, 1987). Children in the United States probably would not view these as moral transgressions. As with virtually all aspects of development, there are both similarities and differences across cultures concerning what is considered moral.

How do children's views of morality develop? To answer this question we now turn to the work of Kohlberg.

Kohlberg's Theory of Morality

Our knowledge of the development of moral reasoning skills, at least in the United States, has been heavily influenced by the work of a psychologist named Kohlberg. His model of moral reasoning and judgment is based in large part on Piaget's model of cognitive development. Inspired by Piaget's theory suggesting that cognitive development proceeds in a predictable, invariant sequence, Kohlberg wondered if this was true of moral development as well. To find out, he presented participants in his study with hypothetical dilemmas and asked them to respond to the dilemma. He was interested not only in the content of their response, but more importantly, the reasoning behind their responses. The most famous of Kohlberg's dilemmas is the story of Heinz:

> A woman was near death from a special kind of cancer. There was one drug that the doctors thought might save her. It was a form of radium that a druggist in the same town had recently discovered. The drug was expensive to make, but the druggist was charging ten times what the drug cost him to produce. He paid $200 for the radium and charged $2,000 for a small dose of the drug. The sick woman's husband, Heinz, went to everyone he knew to borrow the money, but he could only get together about $1,000, which is half of what it cost. He told the druggist that his wife was dying and asked him to sell it cheaper or let him pay later. But the druggist said: "No, I discovered the drug and I'm going to make money from it." So Heinz got desperate and broke into the man's store to steal the drug for his wife.

> Should Heinz have broken into the store to steal the drug for his wife? Why or why not?

Based on participant responses to dilemmas such as this one, Kohlberg proposed a stage theory of moral development (see Figure 4.7).

Kohlberg's theory of moral development (1976, 1984) proposes three general stages of development of moral reasoning skills. (Kohlberg further divided each

FIGURE 4.7 Kohlberg's Theory of Moral Development

of these three general stages into two stages, for a total of six substages of moral development).

1. **Preconventional morality** involves compliance with rules to avoid punishment and gain rewards. A person operating at this level of morality would condemn stealing as bad because the thief might get caught and be thrown in jail or otherwise punished. The focus of the justification is on the punishment (or reward) associated with the action.

2. **Conventional morality** involves conformity to rules that are defined by others' approval or society's rules. A person operating at this level of morality would judge stealing as wrong because it is against the law and others in society generally disapprove of it.

3. **Postconventional morality** involves moral reasoning on the basis of individual principles and conscience. A person operating at this level of morality would judge stealing within the context either of societal or community needs or of his or her own personal moral beliefs and values, which supersede perceived societal and community needs.

Gilligan (1982) challenged Kohlberg's theory by suggesting that its stages are biased toward the particular way in which males as opposed to females view relationships. She argued that male moral reasoning is based on abstract justice, whereas female moral reasoning is based on obligations and responsibilities. These two types of moral reasoning have been called "morality of justice" versus "morality of caring." Despite the fervor of the debate, however, reviews of the research seem to indicate few gender differences in moral reasoning (Walker, 1984, 2006). It appears that variations between males and females in moral reasoning can be explained by other variables, such as education, occupation, or types of issues under consideration. Cross-cultural research may shed more light on this issue.

Cross-Cultural Studies of Moral Reasoning

The universality or cultural specificity of moral principles and reasoning has been an area of interest for anthropologists and psychologists alike. A number of anthropological ethnographies have examined the moral principles and domains of different cultures (see review by Shweder et al., 1987; Schweder, Goodnow, Hatano, LeVine, Markus, & Miller, 2006). Many of these works have complemented and challenged traditional American views of morality, and for good reason.

The findings from a number of cross-cultural studies have suggested that some aspects of Kohlberg's theory of morality are universal. Snarey (1985), for example, reviewed 45 studies involving participants in 27 countries and concluded that Kohlberg's first two stages could be regarded as universal. A more recent review revisited this claim. Gibbs, Basinger, Grime, and Snarey (2007) extensively reviewed 75 cross-cultural studies involving participants in 23 countries. In line with Snarey's (1985) review, Gibbs et al. also concluded that there is evidence that Kohlberg's first two stages may be universal.

While there seems to be solid evidence for the first two stages of Kohlberg's theory, a number of cross-cultural studies on moral reasoning have raised questions about the universal generalizability of Kohlberg's highest stage (postconventional). One of the underlying assumptions of Kohlberg's theory is that moral reasoning on the basis of individual principles and conscience, regardless of societal laws or cultural customs, represents the highest level of moral reasoning. This assumption is grounded in Western philosophical thought and in the cultural milieu in which

preconventional morality The first stage of Kohlberg's theory of moral development, emphasizing compliance with rules to avoid punishment and gain rewards.

conventional morality The second stage of Kohlberg's theory of moral development, emphasizing conformity to rules that are defined by others' approval or society's rules.

postconventional morality The third stage of Kohlberg's theory of moral development, emphasizing moral reasoning on the basis of individual principles and conscience.

Kohlberg developed his theory, which had its roots in studies involving American males in the Midwestern United States in the 1950s and 1960s. Although democratic notions of individualism and unique, personal conscience may have been appropriate to describe his samples at that time and place, those same notions may not represent universal moral principles applicable to all people of all cultures.

In fact, researchers have criticized Kohlberg's theory for harboring such cultural biases. Cross-cultural studies have shown that people from different cultures do reason differently about moral dilemmas. Miller and Bersoff (1992) compared the responses to a moral judgment task by respondents in India and the United States. The Indian participants, both children and adults, considered not helping someone a moral transgression more than did the American participants, regardless of the life-threatening nature of the situation or whether the person in need was related. These researchers interpreted the cultural differences as having to do with values of affiliation and justice, suggesting that Indians are taught a broader sense of social responsibility—individual responsibility to help a needy person.

Another study suggested that Chinese and Icelandic children differ in a way similar to the differences between Indians and Americans concerning moral judgments (Keller, Edelstein, Schmid, Fang, & Fang, 1998). Chinese children emphasized altruism and relationships when reasoning about moral dilemmas, whereas Icelandic children emphasized contractual and self-interest considerations. The issue of interpersonal responsiveness that Miller and Bersoff (1992) and Keller et al. (1998) raised was related to Gilligan's (1982) claims of gender bias in U.S. studies. It is entirely possible that Gilligan's findings were influenced by cultural as well as gender differences.

In sum, Kohlberg's theory, as well as the methods for scoring moral stages according to verbal reasoning, may not recognize higher levels of morality as defined in other cultures. Should different cultures define those higher levels of morality along different dimensions, those differences would imply profound differences in people's judgments of moral and ethical appropriateness. Fundamental differences in the bases underlying morality and ethics across cultures are not at all impossible, given that they feed and are fed by subjective culture. Above all, those fundamental differences in morality as a function of culture form the basis for the possibility of major intercultural conflicts.

Three Ethics Approach to Moral Reasoning

Since Kohlberg's time, other scholars have proposed different models to describe moral development for a broader range of cultures. Jensen (2008, 2011) has outlined a different approach to moral development that synthesizes several theories. She argues that several key concepts of morality are missing from Kohlberg's theory—concepts related to religion, spirituality, and divinity and an emphasis on community and interdependence. These concepts are central to the moral belief systems in the majority of cultures around the world. Based on Jensen's own work (1991) and the work by Shweder (1990; Shweder, Much, Mahapatra, & Park, 1997), the three ethics of morality are: the ethics of autonomy, community, and divinity (see Figure 4.8).

The **ethic of autonomy** emphasizes individual rights and justice, in line with the type of moral reasoning highlighted in Kohlberg's theory. For someone primarily operating from this viewpoint, individual choices and freedoms are important to the extent that they do not harm others and others' choices and freedoms. Notions of equality and respect for all individuals are highlighted.

The **ethic of community**, in contrast, emphasizes interpersonal relationships and community. What is right is not what is right for each individual necessarily, but for important social groups such as the family, community, or nation. In this ethic,

ethic of autonomy Moral reasoning that emphasizes individual rights and justice. Individual choices and freedoms are important to the extent that they do not harm others and others' choices and freedoms.

ethic of community Moral reasoning that emphasizes interpersonal relationships and community. One's duties, obligations, and roles within the group are highlighted.

Ethic of Autonomy	• Emphasizes individual rights and justice. Individual choices and freedoms are important to the extent that they do not harm others and others' choices and freedoms.
Ethic of Community	• Emphasizes interpersonal relationships and community. Moral understanding relies heavily on considering one's duties, obligations, and roles within the group.
Ethic of Divinity	• Emphasizes the centrality of religious beliefs and spirituality. Moral understanding is based on self in relation to divine or natural law.

FIGURE 4.8 Three Ethics Approach to Morality (Jensen, 2011). Cultures Differ on Which Ethics are Prioritized and Reinforced

moral understanding relies heavily on considering one's duties, obligations, and roles within the group. For instance, in China, the concept *oijen,* which connotes love and filial piety, contributes to the way Chinese individuals view morality (Ma, 1997). In response to Kohlberg's moral dilemmas, Chinese individuals tend to emphasize the importance of filial piety—respecting and honoring parents and fulfilling their wishes—when judging what is right or wrong. Thus, in Chinese culture people may be more likely to base their moral reasoning on the ethic of community rather than, for instance, the ethic of autonomy.

Finally, the **ethic of divinity** emphasizes the centrality of religious beliefs and spirituality in moral reasoning. For instance, Algerians' responses to Kohlberg's moral dilemmas are based on the belief that God is the creator and supreme authority of the universe (Bouhmama, 1984). In another example, fundamental Baptists in the United States consider divorce morally wrong based on their beliefs concerning the relationship between God, the church, and human relationships (Jensen, 1997).

Although the three ethics differ from one another in their understanding of why something is wrong or right, one ethic is not considered more morally advanced than the others. Jensen (2008, 2011) cites evidence that all three ethics show up in diverse cultures around the world. The three ethics approach expands Western notions of morality to encompass other, equally valid, worldviews on morality.

ethic of divinity Moral reasoning that emphasizes the centrality of religious beliefs and spirituality.

CONCLUSION

There are two key issues concerning human development: whether developmental pathways are universal or culture specific, and how development occurs. The studies have shown that there are some universals in development: in all cultures children exhibit several patterns of temperamental styles, form attachment relationships to their caregivers and communities, think about the world differently as they get older, and increasingly view morality based on obligations to significant others and the broader community. Studies also have shown that there are many cultural variations in development and, in some cases, have challenged researchers to reconsider what aspects of development are universal versus culturally bound. Further, from a developmental contextualism perspective, cross-cultural studies on temperament and attachment have demonstrated how the characteristics and dispositions that children are born with interact with multiple levels of their environment—ranging from relationships with caregivers within the family to expectations of sociocultural systems—to influence children's development and adjustment.

The developmental research presented in this chapter provides a view of how culture influences a number of developmental psychological processes. Still, much work remains to be done. In particular, cross-cultural developmental work has focused largely on infants and children, but mainstream psychology has come to recognize the importance of developmental processes throughout the entire life span, including early, middle, and late adolescence; young, middle, and older adulthood; and old age.

The developmental differences discussed in this chapter all speak to how a sense of culture develops in each of us. All people are born into their specific cultures with their own unique set of characteristics and predispositions. In turn, each culture exerts its influence in its own special and unique ways, and, in combination with each unique cultural member, produces specific tendencies, trends, and differences in their members when compared to others. When we are in the middle of a culture, as we all are, we cannot easily see how culture itself develops in us. Only when we look outside ourselves and examine the developmental and socialization processes of other cultures are we able to see what we are ourselves. Only then can we come to appreciate that those differences and similarities are our culture, or at least manifestations of our culture. While cultures produce differences in development that we observe in our research, these differences simultaneously contribute to the development of culture.

EXPLORATION AND DISCOVERY

Why Does This Matter to Me?

1. In your culture, is shyness (behavioral inhibition) a positive or negative trait? If it is positive, why is it considered positive? If it is negative, why is it considered negative? As a child, were you shy? If yes, how did your culture's view of shyness shape your experiences?

2. Would you wear your pajamas to school? Would you cheat on your final exam for this course? Would you steal your classmate's computer?

If you grew up in a different culture, do you think your answers to these questions would remain the same? How did you develop your beliefs about what is morally right or wrong versus what is a social convention?

3. Think about the three ethics approach to moral reasoning. Which of the three approaches do you adopt when thinking about moral issues? Does it depend on the particular issue?

Suggestions for Further Exploration

1. Piaget describes two ways that we learn: through assimilation and accommodation. Give an example of each process. For instance, think about a new piece of information that you have learned. Did you use assimilation or accommodation to process this information? Or both?

2. Present Kohlberg's Heinz dilemma to several people. How did they respond to the dilemma? In their responses, could you see evidence of the three broad stages of Kohlberg's moral reasoning—preconventional, conventional, and postconventional?

3. The research reviewed in this chapter shows the difficulty of measuring such a complex phenomenon as attachment. The Strange Situation, the most widely used measure of attachment, has been criticized as being too "artificial." Some researchers have advocated for methods that may be more contextually valid, such as observing preschoolers' separation and reunion behaviors toward their parents when they are dropped off and picked up from preschool. Can you think of other ways to observe attachment behavior that may be more "natural"?

Culture, Self, and Identity

5

CHAPTER CONTENTS

One important aspect of our psychological composition is our sense of self. As we have seen in Chapters 3 and 4, culture plays a large role in our development and maturation as individuals in any society. One of the major outcomes of this process of enculturation is our sense of "self" and a related concept known as "identity." Our sense of self and identity frames much of the ways we perceive others and interact with the world around us, and is intimately tied into many of the mental processes and behaviors that we will discuss throughout the remainder of the book.

In this chapter, we begin our exploration of the relationship between culture, self, and identity, first focusing on the notion of the self. Below we define the self, explore where it comes from, and examine how the notion of the self may differ across cultures. The concept of self is an important first step to exploring mental processes and behaviors because it organizes information about oneself. As we will discuss more fully below, the concept of self is intimately related to our concepts of others. In fact, we cannot create a sense of self without being able to discriminate ourselves from others. It is in recognizing that we are part of a social group, living with others, that we first differentiate what our own sense of self is.

A topic related to self is that of identity. We will define and discuss identity, and an increasingly important topic around the world today: multicultural identities. A central topic in this area will be cultural code frame switching. We will also explore how labels such "American" convey implicit assumptions about who is an American.

Related to the topic of self is the concept of self-esteem, and its relative, self-enhancement. We will review the many cross-cultural studies on self-esteem that have had important implications for our understanding of self. We will examine a theoretical framework that suggests that self-enhancement is a universal process, but that people of different cultures do it in different ways.

▶ Culture and Self

Defining Self

One of the most powerful and pervasive concepts in psychology is the self-concept. Other terms that denote this same concept are self-image, self-construal, self-appraisal, or just self. We define **self-concept** as *the cognitive representations of who one is, that is, the ideas or images that one has about oneself, especially in relation to others, and how and why one behaves.* Self is a psychological construct that people create in order to help themselves understand themselves and their world better. We may not consciously think about our selves very much, yet how we understand our sense of self is intimately tied to how we understand the world around us and our relationships with others in that world. Whether conscious or not, our concept of self is an integral part of our lives.

Think about some descriptions of yourself. You may believe you are an optimist or a pessimist, extroverted or introverted. We use labels such as these as shorthand descriptions to characterize ourselves. Suppose someone tells you he or she is "sociable." An array of underlying meanings is attached to this one-word description. Descriptive labels such as this usually imply that (1) we have this attribute within us, just as we possess other attributes such as abilities, attitudes, perceived rights, or interests; (2) our past actions, feelings, or thoughts have close connections with this attribute; and (3) our future actions, plans, feelings, or thoughts will be controlled or guided by this attribute and can be predicted more or less accurately by it. In short, if someone describes him or herself as "sociable," we know that his or her concept

self-concept The cognitive representations of who one is, that is, the ideas or images that one has about oneself, especially in relation to others, and how and why one behaves. The sum of one's idea about one's self, including physical, mental, historical, and relational aspects, as well as capacities to learn and perform. Self-concept is usually considered central to personal identity and change over time. It is usually considered partially conscious and partially unconscious or inferred in a given situation.

of self is rooted in rich and contextualized beliefs about actions, thoughts, feelings, motives, and plans. The concept of self as "sociable" may be central to one's self-definition, enjoying a special status as a salient identity (Stryker, 1986) or self-schema (Markus, 1977).

A sense of self is critically important to organizing, and in many cases determining, our thoughts, feelings, and actions, and how we view the world, ourselves, and others in that world. This includes our relationships with other people, places, things, and events. Our sense of self is at the core of our being, unconsciously and automatically influencing our thoughts, actions, and feelings. Each individual carries and uses these perceived internal attributes to guide his or her thoughts and actions in different social situations.

Where Does the Self-Concept Originate?

Let's consider where the concept of self originates and why humans have a sense of self. The concept of self is an important product of human cultures. You might remember that in Chapter 1, we made a distinction between cultural practices and cultural worldviews. *Cultural practices*, on one hand, refer to the discrete, observable, objective, and behavioral aspects of human activities in which people engage related to culture. For example, parent–child sleeping arrangements are an example of a cultural practice, as would be the specific ways in which people of a culture manage their emotional expressions in a social context. Cultural practices refer to the *doing* of culture.

Cultural worldviews, on the other hand, are belief systems about one's self and culture. They are cognitive generalizations about how oneself and one's culture is or should be, regardless of whether those generalized images are true or not (i.e., regardless of whether or not they are rooted in actual cultural practices or behaviors).

Cultural worldviews are products of several uniquely human abilities. As you might recall from Chapter 1, humans are unique in that we have the cognitive ability to know that (1) the self exists and is an intentional agent, (2) that other selves exist and they are also intentional agents, and (3) that others make judgments about oneself as an intentional agent. While clearly other animals also have a sense of self (perhaps a more rudimentary one), humans are unique in that we know that we have intentions, that others know that we have intentions, and that others can judge our intentions. Humans also have cognitive skills that allow for long-term memory and hypothetical thinking about the future. Humans uniquely use symbolic and verbal language and create narratives of their lives and cultures. These verbal descriptions can be oral or written and are social constructions of reality expressed in consensual ideologies about one's culture. One of these descriptions is the self, which is a cognitively constructed perception of reality. The concept of self is part of one's cultural worldviews because how one sees oneself in relation to the rest of the world is an integral part of one's culture. Like cultural worldviews, the concept of self is also a cognitive generalization about one's nature or composition (whether that belief is grounded in reality or behaviors or not).

The concept of self is functional and useful. Having a sense of self aids in addressing needs for affiliation and uniqueness, and explains the importance of understanding values as guiding principles within a specific culture (Schwartz, 2004; Schwartz & Bardi, 2001). Concepts of self are social constructions "that consist of viewing oneself as living up to specific contingencies of value . . . that are derived from the culture at large but are integrated into a unique individualized worldview by each person" (Pyszczynski, Greenberg, Solomon, Arndt, & Schimel, 2004).

The concept of self is part of one's cultural worldviews because how one sees oneself in relation to the rest of the world is an integral part of one's culture.

The Dynamic and Multifaceted Nature of the Concept of Self

The topics of self and self-concept have been important areas of study in psychology for years. Decades ago, psychologists recognized that the self-concept does not just reflect on-going thoughts and behaviors at the moment. Instead it organizes those thoughts and behaviors in the past and mediates and regulates those thoughts and behaviors in the future (Markus & Wurf, 1987); thus self-concepts are *dynamic*, not static.

Related to the dynamic nature of the concept of self is the fact that scientists have recognized early on that people don't have a unitary or single self-concept, but that self-concepts are multifaceted and context-specific. That is, there are multiple aspects to people's self-concepts. For example, a widely used scale of self-concept in the past was the Tennessee Self-Concept Scale (TSCS). It produced different scores for the physical, moral, personal, family, social, and academic aspects of one's self. Higgins (1987) distinguished between "ideal" selves (selves we want to be) and "ought" selves (selves we should be). Thus self-concepts assume that people have and embrace multiple and different aspects of oneself that are context-dependent (Linville & Carlston, 1994; see Figure 5.1). These multiple domains of the self can be expressed in multiple, different ways in different contexts (see Figure 5.2 for a hypothetical example of how the self may be expressed for "Eva").

Early Research on Cultural Differences in Self-Concepts: The Independent versus Interdependent Self-Construal Theory

Cross-cultural research on self-concepts received a major boost over two decades ago with a theory about cultural differences in self-construals—the theory of independent and interdependent self-construals (Markus & Kitayama, 1991b). This theory suggested that, given that self-concepts are rooted in cultural worldviews, and given that cultural worldviews differ across cultures, it follows that the concept of self also differs in different cultures. These differences in self-concepts occur because different cultures are associated with different systems of rules of living and exist

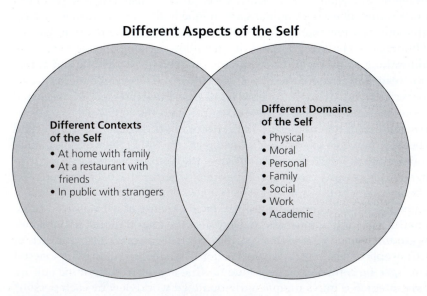

Different Aspects of the Self

Different Contexts of the Self
- At home with family
- At a restaurant with friends
- In public with strangers

Different Domains of the Self
- Physical
- Moral
- Personal
- Family
- Social
- Work
- Academic

FIGURE 5.1 Different Aspects of the Self

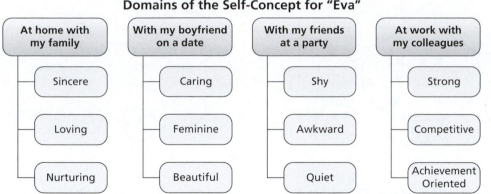

Example of Multiple Contexts and Multiple Domains of the Self-Concept for "Eva"

At home with my family	With my boyfriend on a date	With my friends at a party	At work with my colleagues
Sincere	Caring	Shy	Strong
Loving	Feminine	Awkward	Competitive
Nurturing	Beautiful	Quiet	Achievement Oriented

FIGURE 5.2 Example of Multiple Contexts and Multiple Domains of the Self-Concept for "Eva"

within different social and economic environments and natural habitats. The varied demands that cultures place on individual members mean that individuals integrate, synthesize, and coordinate their worlds in a variety of ways, producing differences in self-concepts.

Markus and Kitayama (1991b) used these ideas to describe two fundamentally different senses of self, contrasting the Western or individualistic construal of self as an independent, separate entity against a composite construal of self more common in non-Western, collectivistic cultures, in which the individual is viewed as inherently connected or interdependent with others and inseparable from a social context. They argued that in the United States, standing out and asserting yourself is a virtue. Successful people in the United States routinely credit their success to self-confidence, trusting their instincts, and the ability to make decisions and stick by them. In many individualistic cultures like the United States, there is a strong belief in the separateness of individuals. The normative task in these cultures is to maintain the independence of the individual as a separate, self-contained entity.

American culture, for example, encourages its members to be unique, expressive, realize, and actualize the inner self, and promote our personal goals. These are the tasks the culture provides for its members. These cultural tasks have been designed and selected throughout history to encourage the independence of each individual. With this set of cultural tasks, our sense of self-worth or self-esteem takes on a particular form. When individuals successfully carry out these cultural tasks, they feel satisfied with themselves, and self-esteem increases accordingly (which is why we cover the topic of self-esteem in this chapter below). Under this **independent construal of self**, individuals focus on personal, internal attributes—individual ability, intelligence, personality traits, goals, or preferences—expressing them in public and verifying and confirming them in private through social comparison.

This independent construal of self is illustrated graphically in Figure 5.3a. The self is a bounded entity, clearly separated from relevant others. Note that there is no overlap between the self and others. Furthermore, the most salient self-relevant information (indicated by bold Xs) relates to attributes thought to be stable, constant, and intrinsic to the self, such as abilities, goals, attitudes, and perceived rights.

In contrast to the independent self, Markus and Kitayama (1991b) suggested that many non-Western, collectivistic cultures neither assume nor value overt separateness.

independent construal of self A sense of self that views the self as a bounded entity, clearly separated from relevant others.

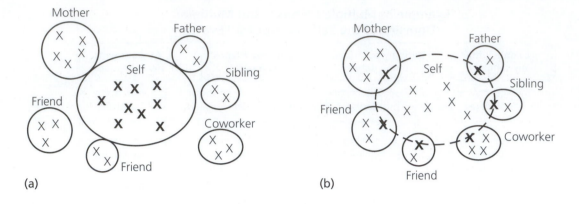

FIGURE 5.3 (a) Independent Construal of Self (b) Interdependent Construal of Self

Source: Markus, H., and S. Kitayama (1991). Culture and the Self: Implications for Cognition, Emotion, and Motivation, *Psychological Review, 98*, pp. 224–253. Copyright © 1991 by the American Psychological Association. Reprinted by permission of the authors.

Instead, these cultures emphasize what may be called the "fundamental connectedness of human beings." The primary normative task is to fit in and maintain the interdependence among individuals. Individuals in these cultures are socialized to adjust themselves to an attendant relationship or a group to which they belong, to read one another's minds, to be sympathetic, to occupy and play their assigned roles, and to engage in appropriate actions. These cultural tasks have been designed and selected throughout history to encourage the interdependence of the self with others.

In the interdependent construal of the self, self-worth, satisfaction, and self-esteem can have very different characteristics from those of the independent self. The self-esteem of those with interdependent construals of the self may depend primarily on whether they can fit in and be part of a relevant ongoing relationship. Under this construal of self, individuals focus on their interdependent status with other people and strive to meet or even create duties, obligations, and social responsibilities. The most salient aspect of conscious experience is intersubjective, rooted in finely tuned interpersonal relationships.

interdependent construal of self A sense of self that views the self as unbounded, flexible, and contingent on context. This sense of self is based on a principle of the fundamental connectedness among people.

The **interdependent construal of self** is illustrated graphically in Figure 5.3b. The self is unbounded, flexible, and contingent on context. Note the substantial overlap between the self and relevant others. The most salient aspects of the self (shown by bold Xs) are defined in relationships—that is, those features of the self related to and inseparable from specific social contexts. This does not mean that those with interdependent selves do not have any knowledge of their internal attributes, such as personality traits, abilities, and attitudes. They clearly do. However, these internal attributes are relatively less salient in consciousness and thus are unlikely to be the primary concerns in thinking, feeling, and acting.

Markus and Kitayama (1991b) suggested that two idioms summed up differences in the nature of independence versus interdependence. An idiom in the United States, "The squeaky wheel gets the grease," highlights how sticking out and being independent is valued and "good." An idiom in Japan goes, "The nail that sticks up shall get pounded down," suggesting that independence will be met with strong opposition from the cultural system.

The independent versus interdependent self-construal framework was used to explain many cross-country differences in psychological processes, especially between the United States and Asian countries, based on the assumption that Asian countries were collectivistic (Markus & Kitayama, 1991b). One of these processes was self-perception. For example, with an independent construal of self, one's internal attributes such as abilities or personality traits are the most salient self-relevant information. These internal attributes should be relatively less salient for those with interdependent selves, who are more likely to think about the self in particular social relationships (e.g., "me" with family members, "me" with my boyfriend) or in specific contexts ("me" in school, "me" at work). In cultures that foster an interdependent self-construal, therefore, internal attributes are not the most salient self-relevant information; instead, information concerning one's social roles and relationships with others are more salient and important.

Several studies were cited to support these ideas (Bond & Tak-Sing, 1983; Shweder & Bourne, 1984). In these studies, subjects wrote down as many of their own characteristics as possible. Participants typically generated several types of responses. One response type was the abstract, personality-trait description of the self, such as "I am sociable." Another response type was the situation-specific self- description, such as "I am usually sociable with my close friends." Consistent with the theory of independent and interdependent selves, Americans tended to generate a greater number of abstract traits than did Asians. These data were interpreted that people with an independent construal of self view their own internal attributes, such as abilities or personality traits, as the most salient self-relevant information. Internal attributes are relatively less salient for those with interdependent selves, who are more likely to think about the self in particular social relationships or contexts.

To demonstrate the power of cultural self-construals, Kim and Markus (1999) devised a clever experiment in which airport travelers were offered a pen as a token of appreciation for completing a survey. The pens were all identical except for their color, and the ratio of unique to majority pens was either 1:4 or 2:3. East Asian participants chose more majority pens than European Americans. The authors argued that Western culture values uniqueness, and thus people from the West have an internalized preference for uniqueness and demonstrated this preference by choosing unique pens. East Asian cultures, they argued, don't value uniqueness, and thus East Asian individuals do not have such an internalized preference.

Recent Developments in Our Understanding of Cultural Differences in Self-Concepts

The theory of independent versus interdependent self-construals was very important to an understanding of the relationship between culture and psychology for several reasons. For one, it allowed scientists to organize and understand disparate and sometimes contradictory findings across different cultures in cross-cultural research, such as the research on self-perception mentioned above. Also, the theory provided scientists with a possible variable that might "explain" why those differences occurred, that is, differences in the concept of self. For these important reasons the independent versus interdependent self-construal theory stimulated much cross-cultural research, which is an important function of any theory in any field. That new research has led to important discoveries that allow us today to go beyond the notion of independent vs. interdependent selves. Some of that new research involved direct tests of the theory that challenged it and facilitated the field's continuing evolution in knowledge about cultural differences in self-concepts, which we describe below.

New research has led to important discoveries that allow us today to go beyond the notion of independent vs. interdependent selves.

An Empirical Assessment of the Independent versus Interdependent Self-Construal Theory

One assumption that the theory of independent versus interdependent self-constru-als made was that American culture is individualistic and Asian cultures like Japan, are collectivistic, or more specifically, that *people* in the United States are more indi-vidualistic and less collectivistic than *people* in cultures such as Japan. As mentioned in Chapters 1 and 2, the recent years have seen a large increase in the number of instruments that have been developed to actually measure individualism and col-lectivism. When these studies have actually compared scores between Americans and Asians, including Japanese, however, they often did *not* find that Americans are more individualistic and Japanese are more collectivistic. For instance, Matsumoto, Kudoh, and Takeuchi (1996) administered an individualism–collectivism scale to Japanese university students and, based on their scores classified the participants as either individualists or collectivists. They reported that over 70% of the Japanese respondents were actually classified as individualists (Figure 5.4). Kleinknecht and colleagues (Kleinknecht, Dinnel, Kleinknecht, Hiruma, & Harada, 1997) assessed American and Japanese students and found that there were no cultural differences on independent self-construals. There were differences on interdependent self-con-struals; but the Americans were *more* interdependent than the Japanese (Figure 5.5). Similar large-scale studies of cultural dimensions have found similar results (House, Hanges, Javidan, Dorfman, & Gupta, 2003).

Oyserman and colleagues (2002) summarized this area of research convincingly by conducting a meta-analysis involving 83 studies in which individualism and col-lectivism were actually measured, and in which North Americans (Americans and Canadians) were compared against people from other countries and other ethnic groups within the U.S. European Americans were, in general, more individualis-tic and less collectivistic than, for instance, Chinese, Taiwanese, Indians, and Asian Americans. However, European Americans were not more individualistic than Afri-can Americans or Latinos, and not less collectivistic than Japanese or Koreans. These findings questioned assumptions about culture underlying many cross-cultural

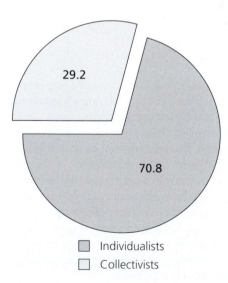

FIGURE 5.4

Percentage of Individualists and Collectivists among Japanese University Students

Source: Matsumoto, D., T. Kudoh, and S. Takeuchi (1996). Changing patterns of individualism and collectivism in the United States and Japan. *Culture and Psychology, 2,* 77–107.

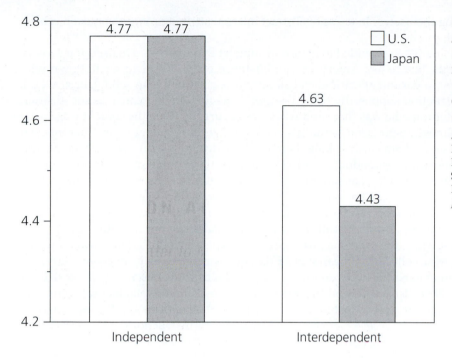

FIGURE 5.5
American and Japanese Students Do Not Differ in Independent Self-Construals but Differ in Interdependent Self-Construals Opposite to What Theory Might Predict

Source: Kleinknecht, R. A., D. Dinnel, E. E. Kleinknecht, N. Hiruma, and N. Harada (1997). Cultural Factors in Social Anxiety: A Comparison of Social Phobia Symptoms and Taijin Kyofusho. *Journal of Anxiety Disorders, 11,* 157–177.

comparisons in the literature, including the theory of independent versus interdependent self-construals.

Numerous reports after Oyserman and colleagues' (2002) meta-analysis have corroborated their findings. For example, Li (2003) utilized ethnographic, qualitative, and quantitative methodologies to explore differences between Anglo-Canadians and mainland Chinese in their self-construals and self-other boundaries, and reported findings contrary to that predicted by the theory of independent versus interdependent self-construals. DeAndrea and colleagues (DeAndrea, Shaw, & Levine, 2010) analyzed self-expressions in realistic, naturalistic communications on Facebook and found no differences among African, Asian, and European Americans in their proportion of independent and interdependent self-expressions. Levine and colleagues (2003) conducted a meta-analysis of studies that measured self-construals in different countries and concluded that "the evidence for predicted cultural differences is weak, inconsistent, or non-existent" (p. 210).

Another issue to consider is the degree to which previous findings may have been limited by the research methodologies used to test for those differences in the first place. Take, for instance, the research on cultural differences on self-perception described above. Those findings did not necessarily mean that Americans have more knowledge about themselves than Asians do, or vice versa. Because the most salient information about self in some cultures is context-specific, individuals in such cultures may find it difficult or unnatural to state anything in abstract, non-contextual terms. The studies described earlier suggested that Asians found it difficult to describe themselves in terms of abstract internal attributes; that is, they find it artificial and unnatural to make abstract statements such as "I am sociable" without specifying a relevant context. Whether a person is sociable or not depends on the specific situation. If this interpretation is correct, then Asians should be comfortable describing themselves in terms of abstract internal attributes once a context has been specified.

Cousins (1989) provided evidence to support this analysis. He used the Twenty Statements Test to ask American and Japanese respondents to write down who they were in various specific social situations (e.g., at home, in school, or at work). This instruction supposedly helped respondents to picture a concrete social situation, including who was there and what was occurring. Once the context was specified, Japanese respondents actually generated a *greater* number of abstract internal attributes (e.g., I am hardworking, I am trustworthy, I am lazy) than did the Americans. American respondents tended to qualify their descriptions (I am more or less sociable at work, I am sometimes optimistic at home), as if to say "This is how I am at work, but don't assume that this is the way I am everywhere." With this more contextualized task, the Americans may have felt awkward providing self-descriptions because their self-definitions typically are not qualified by specific situations. Thus, the previous differences were specific to the certain way in which the data were collected in the first place (i.e., in a noncontextualized, general task).

Another experiment reexamining the pen choice study described earlier (Kim & Markus, 1999) also challenged the independent versus interdependent self-construal framework (Yamagishi, Hashimoto, & Schug, 2008). American and Japanese participants were asked to select a pen but under different instructions. The Default condition mirrored the original Kim and Markus (1999) study. In the Initial Selection condition, participants were told they were the first person to choose a pen; that is, others would be choosing later. In the Final Selection condition, participants were told they were the last to choose a pen; that is no one else would be choosing later. The results from the Default condition replicated the Kim and Markus (1999) results, with more Americans choosing a unique pen. In the Initial Selection condition, however, the American rates for choosing the unique pen dropped to the level of the Japanese. In the Final Selection condition, the Japanese rates for choosing the unique pen increased to the level of the Americans. The authors argued that strategies related to incentive structures, rather than cultural self-construals, influenced unique pen choice. That is, all participants had a preference to choose the unique pen, but did so (or not) based on how people have learned to behave depending on the rewards and incentives in a situation.

A further extension of the pen study demonstrated that within Japan, the choice of a unique color pen was highest among people from metropolitan areas and lowest from rural, nonurban areas (Yamagishi, Hashimoto, Li, & Schug, 2012). Once again these authors argued that the "unique choice of pen" was not as much a product of a cultural self-construal as it is product of a situational constraint. Other studies have demonstrated that choice plays an important role as a form of agency in other presumably collectivistic cultures such as India (Miller & Das, 2011).

Revisiting Possible Cultural Differences in Self-Construals: A Multifaceted, Contextualized, Dynamic View of Self

The concept of independent versus interdependent selves is similar to other dualities of self and human nature proposed throughout the history of psychology, not only in mainstream American psychology but also in other cultures (e.g., Doi, 1973; Heelas and Lock, 1981; Kim & Berry, 1993; Singelis, 2000). Sampson (1988), for instance, referred to the sense of self in mainstream approaches as *self-contained individualism*, contrasting it with what he termed *ensembled individualism*, in which the boundary between self and others is less sharply drawn, and others are part of oneself.

The recent work reviewed above, however, is consistent with the notion that independent and interdependent self-construals are not mutually exclusive dichotomies, but instead coexist simultaneously within individuals. Many have echoed this sentiment. Guisinger and Blatt (1994) suggested that mainstream American psychology has traditionally emphasized self-development, stressing autonomy, independence, and identity over the development of interpersonal relatedness. They suggested, however, that evolutionary pressures of natural selection have fostered two basic developmental approaches—one involving self-definition as described in mainstream psychology, the other focusing on the development of interpersonal relatedness. They cited evidence from observational research as well as social biology to support their claims that cooperation, altruism, and reciprocation are aspects of self-development equally as important as autonomy and individual definition. Moreover, they suggested that these dual developmental processes are not mutually exclusive. Rather, they are fundamentally and basically intertwined, with the development of a mature sense of self in one aspect depending, in part, on the development of a mature self in the other.

Niedenthal and Beike (1997) carried these concepts a step further, proposing the existence of both interrelated and isolated self-concepts. Whereas previous theories of self distinguished different types of self on the level of personality, motivation, and culture, their view focused on the level of cognitive representation. Specifically, they suggested that "some concepts derive their meaning through mental links to concepts of other people, whereas other concepts of self have an intrinsic or cognitively isolated characterization" (p. 108). Like Guisinger and Blatt (1994), they suggested that these concepts exist not as dichotomies but rather as interrelated dualities. Niedenthal and Beike (1997) suggested that individuals represent the self with a variety of more or less interrelated structures at the same time, and that one person can have separate interrelated and isolated self-concepts in the same domain. Kagitcibasi (1996a, 1996b) also proposed an integrative synthesis of the self that is both individuated and, at the same time, relational.

Even prior to the theory of independent and interdependent self-construals, Triandis (1989) proposed the existence of three types of selves—the private, public, and collective self—that coexist in everyone. Triandis suggested that individuals sampled different self-construals depending on the specific context in which they were. People in individualistic settings may sample their private self more than their public or collective self, whereas people in collectivistic settings may sample their collective self more than their private or public self. This characterization is consistent with that of other writers who have suggested the existence of other, multiple types of self-construals, such as the independent, relational, and collective selves (Cross & Morris, 2003; Cross, Morris, & Gore, 2002; Greenwald & Pratkanis, 1984; Kosmitzki, 1996; Oyserman, 1993; Oyserman, Gant, & Ager, 1995).

Recent cross-cultural research has shown that multiple self-construals exist in people of different cultures (Kashima & Hardie, 2000; Y. Kashima, Yamaguchi, Kim, & Choi, 1995; Uleman, Rhee, Bardoliwalla, Semin, & Toyama, 2000), and even to different degrees within cultures depending on area (Y. Kashima, Kokubo, Kashima, Boxall, Yamaguchi, & Macrae, 2004). Moreover, the cultural values of people of different cultures vary depending on the specific context in which they live (Matsumoto, Weissman, Preston, Brown, & Kupperbusch, 1997; Rhee, Uleman, & Lee, 1996). People switch from one mode to the other depending on context (Bhawuk & Brislin, 1992), and different behaviors can be elicited in the same individuals if different self-construals are primed (Gardner, Gabriel, & Lee, 1999; Kemmelmeier & Cheng, 2004; Trafimow, Silverman, Fan, & Law, 1997; Trafimow, Triandis, & Goto, 1991; Verkuyten & Pouliasi, 2002; Ybarra & Trafimow, 1988). (Recall the priming experiment that was

Independent and interdependent self-construals are not mutually exclusive dichotomies, but instead coexist simultaneously within individuals.

described in Chapter 2.) Individuals can clearly balance both the need to belong with the need to be different (Brewer, 2004; Hornsey & Jetten, 2004).

Thus the notion that cultures are associated with a single sense of self, or even *primarily* with one sense of self, is not commensurate with the literature and may be a false dichotomy based on the erroneous assumption that cultures are homogeneous, externally distinctive, and geographically located, all of which were not true in the past and are increasingly less true in today's world (Hermans & Kempen, 1998). It very well may be that the theory of independent versus interdependent self-construals, or *any* theory that suggests people fall into one of two supposedly mutually exclusive categories, is itself culture-bound, that is, a product of Western education and thinking.

To be sure, given that self-concepts are rooted in cultural worldviews and that cultural worldviews differ across cultures, it is very likely that there be differences in self-construals across cultures. But what exactly is the nature of this difference? The evidence to date points to the notion that people around the world may have multifaceted, contextualized, dynamic self-concepts, that the relative weighting of the various facets differ across cultures, and that the meanings derived from those relative differences may be different. What may be those multiple facets? Harb and Smith (2008) proposed a six-dimension view of self-construals, including the personal self, relational horizontal and relational vertical selves, collective horizontal and collective vertical selves, and humanity-bound self. Hardin and colleagues (Hardin, 2006; Hardin, Leong, & Bhagwat, 2004) also proposed a six-dimension view of self-construals: autonomy, individualism, behavioral consistency, primacy of self, esteem for group, and relational interdependence. Other perspectives are sure to emerge in the future as well. The field seems to have come full circle back to the notion of multiple selves across cultures, and future research will hopefully shed more light on the multifaceted, contextualized, and dynamic nature of the self. Future research will also need to examine more culture-specific self-construals. Recent research, for instance, has demonstrated that a simpatico self-construal accounts for differences in social behaviors between Latinos and non-Latinos (Holloway, Waldrip, & Ickes, 2009). Future research will also need to uncover the fascinating question of how the brain parses different senses of self neuropsychologically (see, e.g., Zhu, Zhang, Fan, & Han, 2007; Ng, Han, Mao, & Lai, 2010).

▶ Culture, Self-Esteem, and Self-Enhancement

What Is Self-Esteem, and Where Does It Come From?

self-esteem The cognitive and affective evaluations we make about ourselves.

Self-esteem refers to the cognitive and affective evaluations we make about ourselves. For example, how would you rate yourself on the following questions?

1. I am pretty satisfied with myself.
2. I have a number of good qualities.
3. I am able to do things as well as anyone else.

The questions above are adapted from the Rosenberg Self-Esteem Scale (Rosenberg, 1965), one of many widely used tests of self-esteem. These tests measure overall self-worth by assessing both positive and negative feelings about oneself. People who score higher on these scales are thought to have higher self-esteem than those who do not. Higher scores refer to greater positive regard or feelings about oneself.

One way of understanding the origin of self-esteem is through cultural world-views, which are ideological belief systems about the world. As we discussed earlier in this chapter, the concept of self is a cognitive generalization about who one believes one is and is an important part of one's cultural worldviews. Self-esteem refers to how we *evaluate ourselves* within our cultural worldview. **Self-enhancement** refers to the ways by which we bolster our self-esteem.

One popular theory about the origin of self-esteem is **terror management theory** (Becker, 1971, 1973). This theory suggests that because humans have unique cognitive abilities, we are aware of the fact that we will die eventually and are terrified of that inevitable death. Thus we create psychological phenomena as a buffer against the ter-ror of dying (Greenberg, Solomon, & Pyszcynski, 1997). We fabricate and give meaning to our lives in order to raise our human existence above nature so that meaning can be drawn from life (Becker, 1971). This meaning is not physical in nature nor does it actually exist as an objective element (Triandis, 1972) of culture. Rather the meanings afforded in cultural worldviews and the worth we place on ourselves arise because humans must balance a propensity for life with an awareness of the inevitability of death.

> From this perspective, then, each individual human's name and identity, family and social identifications, goals and aspirations, occupation and title, are humanly created adornments draped over an animal that, in the cosmic scheme of things, may be no more significant or enduring than any individual potato, pineapple, or porcupine. But it is this elaborate drapery that provides us with the fortitude to carry on despite the uniquely human awareness of our mortal fate. (Pyszczynski et al., 2004, p. 436)

Self-esteem, therefore, is "a culturally based construction that consists of viewing oneself as living up to specific contingencies of value . . . that are derived from the culture at large but are integrated into a unique individualized worldview by each person" (Pyszcynski et al., 2004, p. 437). In this theory, cultural worldviews are fabri-cated and given meaning by people's minds (Becker, 1971). One of the goals of these cultural worldviews is to raise human existence above nature so that meaning can be drawn from life, resulting in self-esteem.

Despite popular myths about the importance of self-esteem, research has demon-strated that self-esteem is not often correlated with objective standards of competence or performance (Baumeister, Campbell, Krueger, & Vohs, 2003; Pyszcynski et al., 2004; Rodriguez, Wigfield, & Eccles, 2003). The lack of association between self-esteem and actual competence probably occurs because people create feelings of unique-ness about themselves regardless of objective reality. As a part of one's self concept, cultural worldviews are subject to the same need for uniqueness. That's one reason why people often report what their cultures are like with pride, saying that's what makes their cultures unique, even though in many instances people of different cul-tures report the same content (e.g., "the emphasis in my culture is in the importance of family"). And in all our travels around the world, we have never met a person who proudly boasts that their culture is second rate! Ideological cultural worldviews and self-esteem serve as a psychological defense against the anxieties of living and pro-vide humans with the ability to achieve a sense of value (Salzman, 2001).

Is Self-Enhancement Universal or Culture-Specific?

A very active debate concerning the question of whether self-enhancement is universal or culture-specific has been occurring for over a decade. Early cross-cultural research on self-esteem reported that members of individualistic cultures, such as Americans and Canadians, had higher self-esteem scores than members of collectivistic cultures,

self-enhancement A collection of psychological processes by which indi-viduals maintain or enhance their self-esteem.

terror management theory The theory that suggests that, because hu-mans have unique cognitive abilities, they are the only animals that are aware of the fact that we will die eventu-ally, and we are afraid, terri-fied in fact, of that inevitable death. Because inevitable death is terrifying to us, we create psychological phe-nomena as a buffer against the terror of dying.

self-effacement The tendency to downplay one's virtues.

such as Asians (Heine, Lehman, Markus, & Kitayama, 1999). In fact, early studies suggested that not only did collectivistic Asians not self-enhance, but that they engaged in more of the opposite tendency, that is to self-efface. **Self-effacement** refers to the tendency to downplay one's virtues. Some researchers have suggested that Asians not only are more self-effacing; they are more critical about themselves and are more attuned to negative than positive self-evaluations, in both private and public settings (Kitayama, Matsumoto, Markus, & Norasakkunkit, 1997; Leung, 1996).

better than average effect (also known as the false uniqueness effect) The tendency for individuals to underestimate the commonality of desirable traits and to overestimate their uniqueness.

One reason why some have argued for cultural differences in self-enhancement is the **better than average effect** (also known as the false uniqueness effect). American adults typically consider themselves to be more intelligent and more attractive than average (Wylie, 1979). This effect appears to be stronger for males than for females in the United States (Joseph, Markus, & Tafarodi, 1992). In a national survey of American students, Myers (1987) found that 70% of the students thought they were above average in leadership ability; with respect to the ability to get along with others, 0% thought they were below average, while 60% thought they were in the top 10%.

These types of studies showed that there is a tendency to view oneself and one's abilities and traits more positively in comparison to others, at least in the United States. Early studies of the false uniqueness effect in countries and cultures outside the United States, however, did not find these biases. For example, when Japanese students were asked to rate themselves in comparison to others on a number of abilities and traits, they claimed that about 50% of students would be better than they are (see Figure 5.6; Markus & Kitayama, 1991a; Markus, Mullally, & Kitayama, 1997). In other words, the better than average effect was nonexistent in this sample.

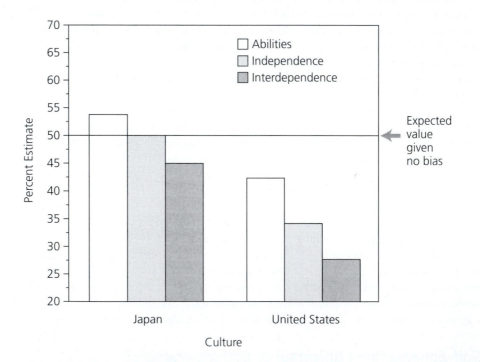

FIGURE 5.6 Estimates of the Percentage of People Who Are Better Than Oneself in Three Categories of Behavior

Source: Markus, H. R., and S. Kitayama, (1991). Cultural Variation in Self-Concept. In G. R. Goethals & J. Strauss (Eds.), *Multidisciplinary Perspectives on the Self.* (pp. 18–48). New York: Springer-Verlag. Reprinted with kind permission from Springer Science BusinessMedia B.V.

Because of the contradictory findings on the false uniqueness effect in supposedly collectivistic cultures, some scholars have argued that self-enhancement is a product of individualistic cultures and does not exist in collectivistic cultures, or is relatively lower, and that is why members of individualistic cultures score higher on self-esteem tests (Falk, Heine, Yuki, & Takemura, 2009; Heine & Hamamura, 2007). But a host of new research over the past two decades has challenged this position, suggesting that people of all cultures self-enhance, but they just do so in different ways. For example, it could be the case that individualism fosters a certain type of self-esteem—one that is often measured in psychological research—whereas collectivism fosters a different type of self-esteem. Tafarodi and Swann (1996) tested this "cultural trade-off" hypothesis in a study of Chinese and American college students. They hypothesized that highly collectivistic cultures promote the development of global self-esteem, which is reflected in generalized self-liking, while at the same time challenging the development of another dimension of self-esteem, reflected in generalized self-competence. Individualistic cultures, they hypothesized, foster the opposite tendencies. They found that the Chinese were lower in ratings of self-competence but higher in self-liking than the Americans. These findings supported the notion that self-esteem may have multiple facets, and that different cultural milieus either support or challenge the development of different facets.

Although self-enhancement may not occur in other cultures when people are asked to focus on their own individual traits and attributes, when people are asked about relational and community-related traits, however, self-enhancement does indeed take place (Kurman, 2001). Sedikides, Gaertner, and Toguchi (2003) showed that Americans self-enhanced on individualistic attributes, while Japanese self-enhanced on collectivistic attributes. A subsequent meta-analysis of cross-cultural studies on self-esteem and self-enhancement conducted to date provided more evidence that both Westerners and Easterners self-enhanced, but they did so in different ways (Sedikides, Gaertner, & Vevea, 2005).

This notion also receives support from a number of studies examining the question in different ways. For example, studies using the Implicit Attitudes Test, where self-esteem is measured implicitly instead of explicitly using rating scales, have shown that there are no differences between Americans' and East Asians' self-esteem (Boucher, Peng, Shi, & Wang, 2009; Brown & Kobayashi, 2002; Kobayashi & Brown, 2003; Kobayashi & Greenwald, 2003). Other studies have demonstrated that self-esteem functions similarly across cultures—that is, it is correlated with the same variables, such as perceived stress, depression, life satisfaction, and subjective well-being—regardless of mean differences in absolute levels of self-esteem (Brown, Cai, Oakes, & Deng, 2009; Gaertner, Sedikides, & Chang, 2008). And recent studies have shown that in cultures thought to not self-enhance directly and explicitly, members can enhance their selves through a process known as **mutual self-enhancement**, in which self-enhancement is achieved through the giving and receiving of compliments between partners in close relationships (Dalsky, Gohm, Noguchi, & Shiomura, 2008). For example, a host bringing out dinner may say that she's not a good cook, or the food is too salty, to which her close friends may reply that she's an excellent cook and her food is delicious. And, while people of some Asian cultures like to say that they don't boast, they often boast about the fact that they don't boast.

mutual self-enhancement Self-enhancement that is achieved through the giving and receiving of compliments between partners in close relationships.

Another related line of research is that on distinctiveness. Despite the notion that the motive to maintain one's identity as distinct is stronger in individualistic cultures, a recent study involving data from 4,751 respondents in 21 cultures showed that the motivation for distinctiveness was not weaker but in fact stronger in collectivistic cultures than in individualistic cultures (Becker et al., 2012).

Another recent interesting study reported scores on the Number Series test from participants from 33 countries and nine regions of the world (Stankov & Lee, 2014). The Number Series test involves the presentation of a series a numbers in a sequence where participants need to figure out the next number in the sequence. For example, participants were given the following sequence of numbers and were asked to insert the next number in the sequence:

4, 12, 8, 7, 12, 8, 10, 12, 8, 13, 12, _____

In this example the correct answer is 8. After doing five such items participants also rated their confidence on this task on a scale from 0–100%. There were large differences across the world regions on the actual accuracy rates on the task; but there was relatively *little* difference across the world regions on the confidence ratings. The bias to be overconfident, therefore, was relatively larger in world regions with less accuracy (see Figure 5.7).

Thus self-enhancement appears to be a universal motive, but people of different cultures find different ways to enhance their selves. Enhancement may occur on different traits, explicitly or implicitly, or in different contexts. This is known as **tactical self-enhancement** (Sedikides, Gaertner, & Toguchi, 2003). In this view, cultures incentivize different ways of motivating and expressing self-enhancement (Yamaguchi, Lin, Morio, & Okumura, 2008). People around the world may access the same potential sources in determining their self-esteem, such as controlling one's life, doing one's duty, benefiting others, and achieving social status, but different cultures facilitate more or less importance to some factors over others (Becker, et al., 2014; see also Hepper, Sedikides, & Cai, 2013). Cross-cultural findings on the applicability of terror management theory (Heine, Harihara, & Niiya, 2002) also suggest that self-enhancement is a universal psychological process, and that individuals will universally work to bolster their self-esteem.

tactical self-enhancement The idea that people of different cultures all self-enhance, but they choose to do it in different ways (i.e., tactically).

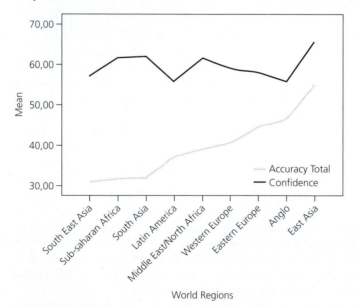

FIGURE 5.7 Average Accuracy and Confidence Scores on the Number Series Test in Nine World Regions

Source: Stankov, L., & Lee, J. (2014). Overconfidence across World Regions. *Journal of Cross-Cultural Psychology, 45*, 821–837.

▶ Culture and Identity

Types of Identities

Identity refers to the way individuals understand themselves and are recognized by others. Psychologists generally differentiate three large types of identity. One is **personal identity**, which refers to the qualities and attributes that distinguish oneself from others. This type of identity is closely akin to the concept of the self described above. **Collective identities** refer to our recognition that we belong to social categories, such as occupation, religion, or culture. **Relational identities** refer to our qualities of ourselves in relation to others.

Identities are creations of the human mind and are important because they fulfill a universal need to belong to social groups. Collective identities in particular occur because humans have a universal need for affiliation (as we discussed in Chapter 1). Creating a collective identity addresses our need for affiliation and helps us create meaningful and lasting relationships. The fundamental need to affiliate with others leads to the secondary need to belong to social groups. These relationships, in turn, help us reproduce, ensuring survival; they also help us to live longer, healthier, and happier lives. Multiple studies, in fact, have shown that individuals accepted into social groups have better physical and psychological consequences; those rejected by social groups have more negative consequences (Baumeister, Ciarocco, & Twenge, 2005). Ostracized and isolated individuals exhibit a wide range of distress (see also Chapter 11).

We create many different types of collective identities, including gender identity and occupational identity. Some identities that are most relevant to our discussion here are **cultural, ethnic, and racial identities**, which refer to our recognizing that we belong to specific cultures, ethnicities, and races. (Recall our discussion of the difference between culture, ethnicity, and race in Chapter 1.) We also have national identities, which refer to our recognition that we belong to a specific nation or country. Identity can also be distinguished by language group in a region; in Montreal, for example, individuals are often identified as Anglophones, Francophones, or Allophones.

Although the existence of identities is universal, the specific content of any individual's or group's identity is culturally determined. How one identifies with a particular identity is influenced heavily by the meanings and associations attributed by his or her culture to various groups. Identity is strongly shaped by narratives (Hammack, 2008), and narratives are stories that are infused with cultural meaning. U.S. Americans, for instance, are accustomed to identifying themselves with ethnic or racial categories (e.g., Hispanic/Latino, African American, Asian American). But these categories themselves are products of American culture's history of immigration and the meanings attributed to that history. Because this history and cultural meaning is unique to the United States, individuals in many other countries and cultures don't identify themselves with these same social groups.

Identity Is Fluid

Identity is not fixed. It is fluid and changes in different contexts and cultures. Identity is always constructed in relation to whom you're talking and where you are. If you're outside the United States and talking with someone from another country, for example, you might identify yourself as an American. If you're in New York, however,

personal identity
A form of identity characterized by the qualities and attributes that distinguish oneself from others.

collective identity
A form of identity that refers to our recognition that we belong to social categories, such as occupation, religion, or culture.

relational identity
A form of identity that refers to our qualities of ourselves in relation to others.

cultural identity This refers to individuals' psychological membership in a distinct culture.

ethnic identity
Individuals' psychological membership in a distinct ethnic group.

racial identity
Individuals' psychological membership in a distinct racial group.

and you're originally from California, you might identify yourself as a Californian. But if you're talking with another American about ethnicity or race, you might identify yourself as Hispanic, African, or Asian American. If you were born and raised in Hawaii, like one of us (D.M.) was, and you meet another person from Hawaii, one of the first questions to be asked is what high school one graduated from, because one's high school affiliation has important cultural meaning there.

Many individuals of immigrant ethnic groups in the United States have a surprising realization when visiting the country of their ethnic origins. While growing up in the United States, individuals of many groups such as Korean Americans, Japanese Americans, and Filipino Americans identify themselves as such. But when they visit Korea, Japan, or the Philippines, they have the sometimes shocking revelation that others view them as just "Americans." Thus, how people of other cultures view us is not necessarily the same as how we view ourselves.

In fact, what exactly is the category of "American," and who identifies themselves as being American? Of course, anyone born and raised in the United States is technically an American in nationality, as well as those who are naturalized citizens. Yet research provides strong evidence for an implicit assumption that being "American" equals being "white." Devos and Banaji (2005) conducted six studies with African, Asian, and white Americans in which they showed that, although all participants expressed strong principles of egalitarianism—a founding value in American culture—both African and Asian Americans were less associated with the category "American" than were whites. This nonattribution of being American to non-whites occurred for both white and Asian American participants but not for the African Americans. In fact, African and Asian Americans were explicitly reported to be even more American than white Americans, but implicitly the opposite pattern was found.

identity denial When an individual is not recognized as a member of a group to which he or she identifies.

Having one's ethnic identity acknowledged is meaningful, and sometimes one is not recognized as a member of a group to which he or she identifies. This is known as **identity denial**. Cheryan and Monin (2005) showed that Asian Americans experience identity denial more frequently than other ethnic groups in the United States, and in reaction to this, they tend to demonstrate knowledge of American culture and greater participation in American cultural practices (e.g., watching TV, listening to music, having American friends). Two studies involving U.S. Asians and Latinos demonstrated that individuals whose ethnic identities were not acknowledged by others felt more negative emotions and evaluated their partners more negatively than individuals whose ethnic identities were appropriately acknowledged (Flores & Huo, 2012). Almost all of the participants (91%) reported having some sort of ethnic identity neglect in their every daily lives.

Multicultural Identities

As culture is a psychological construct—a shared system of rules—it is conceivable that people have not just a single cultural identity, but in some circumstances, two or more such identities. These multicultural identities are becoming increasingly commonplace in today's world, with borders between cultural groups becoming less rigid, increased communication and interaction among people of different cultural groups, and more intercultural marriages.

If culture is defined as a psychological construct, the existence of multicultural identities suggests the existence of multiple psychocultural systems of representations in the minds of multicultural individuals. In fact, there is a growing literature on this important topic, all of which document the existence of such multiple psychological systems in multicultural individuals. Oyserman (1993), for example, conducted four studies testing Arab and Jewish Israeli students in Israel. Although social, collectivistic types of identities had long been considered central to many cultures of that region, Oyserman suggested that these cultures would include considerable individualistic aspects as well, given the history of the region and the influence of the British. In her studies, participants completed a battery of tests, including assessments of individualism, collectivism, public and private self-focus, and intergroup conflicts. Across all four studies, both Arab and Jewish Israelis used both individualistic and collectivistic worldviews in organizing perceptions of self and others. Other studies have also demonstrated the existence of multiple identities (Oyserman, Gant, & Ager, 1995).

The research we review in Chapter 10 is also relevant here. As we will learn there, bicultural individuals have multiple cultural systems in their minds and access one or the other depending on the context in which they are in. This is known as **cultural frame switching** (see code frame switching in Glossary of Chapter 10; Benet-Martinez, Leu, Lee, & Morris, 2002; Hong, Morris, Chiu, & Benet-Martinez, 2000). This refers to the fact that people who speak multiple languages will switch between one cultural meaning system and another when switching languages, because language is a culture's symbolic representation of the world. Thus, when speaking languages, multilingual people will be switching cultural frameworks in their minds.

Studies have documented a **cultural reaffirmation effect** among multicultural individuals living in multicultural societies. For example, Kosmitzki (1996) examined monocultural and bicultural Germans and Americans, who made trait attribute ratings of themselves, their native cultural group, and their adoptive cultural group. The bicultural individuals endorsed even more traditional values associated with their native culture than did native monocultural individuals in those native cultures.

This curious finding is well supported in other studies. For example, Matsumoto, Weissman, and colleagues (1997) compared ratings of collectivistic tendencies in interpersonal interactions of Japanese Americans with those of Japanese nationals in Japan. They found that the Japanese Americans were more collectivistic than the Japanese nationals in the native culture. Sociological studies involving immigrants to the United States, including China, Japan, Korea, and the Philippines, also suggest that the immigrant groups in the United States from other Asia-Pacific countries appear to be more traditional than the native cultures from which they came (for example, Takaki, 1998). Anecdotally, strong cultural traditions, customs, heritage, and language seem to continue among Chinese American immigrant populations throughout the United States.

What may account for such findings? We speculate that when immigrant groups arrive in the United States, they bring with them the culture of their native group at that time. As they are immersed within a multicultural society, the stress of multicultural life in a different world contributes to the cultural reaffirmation effect. The immigrant group thus *crystallizes* its culture—the one they brought with them at the time—and it is this culture that is communicated across generations of immigrant groups. As time passes, the home culture itself may undergo change, but the immigrant group continues to transmit the original cultural system they brought with them previously. After some time, if you compare the immigrant group with the native cultural group, you will find that the immigrant group actually conforms more to the original cultural stereotype than does the native group, because the immigrant culture has crystallized while the native culture has changed. At the same time, the immigrant group clings to the only culture it knows in order to deal with the uncertainties of living in a new place and time. Thus, while individual members of immigrant groups often grow up with multicultural identities, the identity of their native culture is often one of long-standing tradition and heritage.

cultural frame switching The process by which bicultural (or multicultural) individuals switch between one cultural meaning system and another depending on context.

cultural reaffirmation effect The amplified endorsement of home cultural values by bicultural individuals.

CONCLUSION

Self and identity are important psychological phenomena that organize how we understand ourselves and the world around us. They are universal products of our cultures, and exist uniquely in humans because humans have unique cognitive skills and abilities to create them in the first place. At the same time, different cultures facilitate the creation of different senses of self and identity. Moreover, cultural identity, self-concepts, and self-esteem are all related to each other. Individuals with clearer cultural identities generally have clearer self-concepts, higher self-esteem, and higher well-being (Usborne & Taylor, 2010). These culturally-based self-construals and identities organize the various specific mental processes and behaviors we will learn about in the remainder of the book.

EXPLORATION AND DISCOVERY

Why Does This Matter to Me?

1. How do you view yourself? Do you see yourself as more independent or interdependent? Does that self-view apply across different contexts, or is it different in different contexts? And how does that self-view influence your interactions with others, especially with those from a different culture?

2. What things do you do to enhance your sense of self? Do you think that the ways in which you enhance your self is similar or different to people around you from different backgrounds? Why?

3. List the types of collective identities you may have. Do you notice how you change how you identify yourself depending on the context you're in and with whom you're interacting?

Suggestions for Further Exploration

1. Conduct a simple replication of the better-than-average effect by surveying your classmates about how they rate themselves with regard to others on some characteristic. If possible do the same survey with professors. Can you manipulate the instructions so that the effect occurs or not?

2. How many different identities does a person have? Conduct a survey examining this question, and investigate the roles and behaviors associated with the various identities a person has. Then have people rate which identities and roles are most important and examine cultural differences in the identities and their relative importance.

3. If you know of bilingual or bicultural individuals, ask them to do the tasks described above twice, once in each language and see what differences occur, if any. If you see a difference, how can you link those differences to code frame switching?

Culture and Personality

6

CHAPTER CONTENTS

A topic closely related to self and identity, which we covered in the last chapter, is personality. Like the topics of self and identity, personality is also one of the most important and widely studied areas in cultural psychology. Indeed, the search for the underlying bases of individual differences, which serve as the backbone of understanding personality, shares a close conceptual and empirical connection with culture in any cultural milieu, and it's important to get a good grasp of the difference between culture and personality because, as we mentioned in Chapter 1, they are not the same.

We begin this chapter by first defining personality, discussing briefly the major perspectives that have been used to study it, and the measurement of personality across cultures. Then we review cross-cultural research on a view of personality known as the five-factor model (FFM), which suggests that five personality dimensions are universal to all humans. We discuss two theories that account for that universality in personality structure and research that goes beyond the FFM. We also discuss indigenous and culture-specific approaches to personality and some of the research that has been conducted in this area. Although culture-specific aspects of personality and universal notions of personality may seem contradictory, we present a way of understanding their mutual coexistence and conceptualizing and studying their duality.

▶ Defining Personality

Definitions

personality A set of relatively enduring behavioral and cognitive characteristics, traits, or predispositions that people take with them to different situations, contexts, and interactions with others, and that contribute to differences among individuals.

Personality is a broad concept that refers to many aspects of an individual's unique characteristics, and is generally considered to be a set of *relatively enduring behavioral and cognitive characteristics, traits, or predispositions that people take with them to different situations, contexts, and interactions with others, and that contribute to differences among individuals*. Personality consists of the qualities that make a person a distinctive individual. It is the aggregate of behavioral and mental characteristics that are distinctive of an individual. Personality is generally believed to be relatively stable across time and consistent across contexts, situations, and interactions (Allport, 1936; Funder, 2001).

Over the years, scientists have identified and studied many specific aspects of personality within this broad definition, and that it's helpful to understand the broad concept of personality along multiple levels of analysis. In this chapter, we broadly define personality along two levels of analysis that allow us to understand potentially disparate approaches to the study and understanding of personality across cultures. One level includes what are known as dispositional traits, or just traits for short. A **trait** is a characteristic or quality distinguishing a person. It refers to a consistent pattern of behavior, feelings, and thoughts that a person would usually display in relevant circumstances. For example, if we describe someone as "outgoing," that would generally refer to a specific pattern of behavior in which this person is likely to engage when with others. A person who is outgoing will likely strike up conversations, meet comfortably with strangers, and be expressive with their thoughts and emotions. A person who is "shy" would not. The trait approach in psychology has a long and rich history, dating to the work of Allport (1936). Theories and research on this area of personality are known as *trait psychology*.

trait A characteristic or quality distinguishing a person. It refers to a consistent pattern of behavior that a person would usually display in relevant circumstances.

Another level of personality can be broadly construed as identity, which includes our perceived roles in life, aggregate role and life experiences, narratives, values, and motives (Markus & Kitayama, 1998; Wood & Roberts, 2006). This aspect of identity is slightly different than the identity we discussed in the last chapter, which referred more to the ways by which individuals identify themselves with the groups of which they are members. The identity discussed in this chapter refers to that aspect of our personalities that are created by performing repeated roles—thoughts, feelings, and behaviors that occur in real life across single role experiences—producing a history that comprises aggregate role experiences. These experiences, in turn, form the basis of other important aspects of personality, including narratives, values, and general motives (Roberts, 2006).

Perspectives

There are three major perspectives that inform our understanding of personality across cultures (see Table 6.1). Some of the earliest contributions to our understanding of the relationship between personality and culture came from anthropologists who were interested in psychology in what is known as *psychological anthropology*. Through mostly ethnographic fieldwork, anthropologists such as Margaret Mead, Edward Sapir, Weston Labarre, Ruth Benedict, Ralph Linton, Cora DuBois, and Abraham Kardiner developed theories about culture and personality that served as a basis for cross-cultural comparisons of personalities (see review in Piker, 1998). Many of these works formed the basis for the notion of "national character," which is still popular today. A **national character** refers to the perception that each culture has a modal personality type, and that most persons in that culture share aspects of it. Although many cultural and psychological anthropologists recognize the important contributions of biologically innate factors to personality and psychology, the main thrust of the psychological anthropology is its view of personality as culturally specific, formed by the unique forces each culture deals with in its milieu. The psychological anthropological view of personality attributes more importance to the learning of psychological mechanisms and personality in the environment through cultural practices than to biological or evolutionary factors. In this view the foundations of personality development are set in early childhood according to each culture's unique cultural traits.

Whereas psychological anthropology made major contributions to the study of culture and personality in the first half of the twentieth century, the second half was dominated by *cross-cultural perspectives*, which focused on traits (see review by Church & Lonner, 1998). This approach generally viewed personality as something discrete and separate from culture, and as a dependent variable in research. Thus, two or more cultures are treated as independent variables, and they are compared on some personality traits or dimensions. In contrast to the psychological anthropological

national character
The perception that each culture has a modal personality type, and that most persons in that culture share aspects of it.

TABLE 6.1 Major Perspectives in the Study of Personality across Cultures

Psychological Anthropology	Cross-Cultural Perspectives	Cultural Indigenous Perspectives
■ Based mostly on ethnographic fieldwork by anthropologists, this perspective forms the basis of the notion of a "national character," which refers to the perception that each culture has a modal personality type and that most persons in that culture share aspects of it.	■ This perspective views personality as something discrete and separate from culture, and as an etic or universal phenomenon that is equivalently relevant and meaningful across cultures (which allows for comparisons to be made).	■ This perspective views personality as constellations of traits and characteristics found only in a specific culture; personality and culture are not separate entities, but are mutually constituted with each other.

approach, the cross-cultural approach tended to see personality as an etic or universal phenomenon that is equivalently relevant and meaningful in the cultures being compared. The cross-cultural perspective also asked the question: To the extent that personality does exhibit universal aspects, how did they originate?

The cross-cultural perspective to personality has also been concerned with the discovery of culture-specific personality traits. Cross-cultural psychologists describe culture-specific **indigenous personalities** as constellations of personality traits and characteristics found only in a specific culture (for more information, see reviews by Ho, 1998; Diaz-Loving, 1998). These types of studies, though psychological in nature, are heavily influenced in approach and understanding by the anthropological view of culture and personality.

indigenous personalities Conceptualizations of personality developed in a particular culture that are specific and relevant only to that culture.

Work on indigenous personalities has led to what is known as the *cultural indigenous perspective* to personality (e.g., Shweder, 1979a, 1979b, 1980, 1991; Markus & Kitayama, 1998). This approach sees culture and personality not as separate entities, but as a mutually constituted system in which each creates and maintains the other.

> The cultural perspective assumes that psychological processes, in this case the nature of functioning of personality, are not just influenced by culture but are thoroughly culturally constituted. In turn, the cultural perspective assumes that personalities behaving in concert create the culture. Culture and personality are most productively analyzed together as a dynamic of mutual constitution . . .; one cannot be reduced to the other. . . A cultural psychological approach does not automatically assume that all behavior can be explained with the same set of categories and dimensions and first asks whether a given dimension, concept, or category is meaningful and how it is used in a given cultural context. (Markus & Kitayama, 1998, p. 66)

The cultural indigenous perspective has been heavily influenced by the cultural anthropologists, as well as by the cross-cultural work on indigenous psychologies (see Kim, 2001) and personalities. On its face, it is somewhat antithetical to the cross-cultural search for universals and rejects the possibility of biological and genetic mechanisms underlying universality. Instead, it suggests that just as no two cultures are alike, the personalities that comprise those cultures should be fundamentally different because of the mutual constitution of culture and personality within each cultural milieu.

Today, the cross-cultural and cultural indigenous perspectives are the dominant perspectives with regard to understanding personality across cultures. The cross-cultural perspective, rooted in the study of traits, suggests that personality organization and dimensions are universal (and somewhat biologically innate, as we will see below). The cultural indigenous perspective, rooted in culture-specific perspectives of personality as identities, suggests that personalities are dependent on the cultures in which they exist, and rejects notions of universality. How to make sense of this all is perhaps the greatest challenge facing this area of cultural psychology today. Below we review the major research evidence for both perspectives, and describe an integrated perspective that suggests that the universal and indigenous approaches are not necessarily mutually exclusive to each other. This later analysis will make use of an understanding of different levels of personality.

Measuring Personality across Cultures

Before delving into what we know in this area, we need to contend with one of the most serious issues in all cross-cultural research on personality: whether personality can be measured reliably and validly across different cultures. If methods of assessing personality are not reliable or valid across cultures, then the results of research using these methods cannot be trusted to give accurate portrayals of personality similarities or differences across cultures.

This issue is directly related to the differences in perspectives discussed immediately above. The etic, universal perspective to personality (which underlies cross-cultural perspectives), assumes that there are aspects of personality that exist across cultures, that they can be measured in similar ways across cultures, and that the results of those measurements can be compared across cultures. The emic, indigenous perspective, however, suggests that because aspects of personality are likely to be culture-specific, it is difficult if not impossible to create measures of personality that have the same meaning (and validity) across cultures. Thus, when considering the measurement of personality across cultures, we need to first consider the aspect of personality that is being measured and the theoretical perspective of the researcher measuring it.

If one assumes that there are aspects of personality that can be measured and compared across cultures, then important questions arise concerning its measurement. Most personality measures used in cross-cultural research were originally developed in a single language and culture and validated in that language and culture. The psychometric evidence typically used to demonstrate a measure's reliability and validity in a single culture involves examination of internal, test–retest, and parallel forms reliabilities, convergent and predictive validities, and replicability of the factor structures that comprise the various scales of the test. To obtain all these types of psychometric evidence for the reliability and validity of a test, researchers typically conduct multiple studies addressing each of these specific concerns. The best measures of personality—as well as all other psychological constructs—have this degree of psychometric evidence backing them.

A common practice in many of the early cross-cultural studies on personality was to take a personality scale that had been developed in one country or culture—most often the United States—and simply translate it and use it in another culture. In effect, the researchers merely assumed that the personality dimension measured by that scale was equivalent between the two cultures, and that the method of measuring that dimension was psychometrically valid and reliable. Thus, many studies imposed an assumed etic construct upon the cultures studied (Church & Lonner, 1998). Realistically, however, one cannot safely conclude that the personality dimensions represented by an imposed etic are equivalently and meaningfully represented in all cultures included in a study.

As we discussed in Chapter 2, just the fact that personality scales have been translated and used in cross-cultural research is not sufficient evidence that the personality domains they measure are indeed equivalent in those cultures. In fact, when this type of research is conducted, one of the researchers' primary concerns is whether the personality scales used in the study can validly and reliably measure meaningful dimensions of personality in all the cultures studied. As discussed in Chapter 2, the equivalence of a measure in terms of its meaning to all cultures concerned, as well as its psychometric validity and reliability, is of prime concern in cross-cultural research if the results are to be considered valid, meaningful, and useful.

The cross-cultural validation of personality measures requires psychometric evidence from all cultures in which the test is to be used. In the strictest sense, therefore, researchers interested in cross-cultural studies on personality should select instruments that have been demonstrated to have acceptable psychometric properties in cultures of interest. This is a far cry from merely selecting a test that seems to be interesting and translating it for use in another culture. At the very least, equivalence of its psychometric properties should be established empirically, not assumed or ignored (Matsumoto & Van de Vijver, 2011).

Data addressing the psychometric evidence necessary to validate a test in a target culture would provide the safest avenue by which such equivalence can be demonstrated. If such data exist, they can be used to support contentions concerning psychometric equivalence. Even if those data do not offer a high degree of support (reliability coefficients are lower, or factor structures are not exactly equivalent), that does not necessarily mean that the test as a whole is not equivalent. There are multiple alternative explanations of why such data may not be as strong in the target culture as in the culture in which the test was originally developed. Paunonen and Ashton (1998) described 10 such possible interpretations, ranging from poor test translation and response style issues to different analytic methods. Thus, if a test is examined in another culture for its psychometric properties and the data are not as strong as they were in the original culture, each of these possibilities should be examined before concluding that the test is not psychometrically valid or reliable. In some cases, the problem may be minor and fixable; in others, not.

Fortunately, many recent studies in this area have been sensitive to this issue, and researchers have taken steps to ensure some degree of psychometric equivalence across cultures in their measures of personality. Tests assessing traits have a long history in cross-cultural research, and researchers have addressed issues of cross-cultural equivalence and validity of their measures for years. The NEO Personality Inventory-Revised (NEO-PI-R), for example, and its subsequent NEO PI3, which was used in many of the studies described below on traits, has undergone extensive cross-cultural reliability, validity, and equivalence testing (Costa & McCrae, 1992; McCrae, Costa, & Martin, 2005). Similar findings have been obtained using other tests of traits, such as the California Psychological Inventory, the Comrey Personality Scales, the 16 Personality Factors Questionnaire, the Pavlovian Temperament Survey, the Personality Research Form, and the Nonverbal Personality Questionnaire (Paunonen & Ashton, 1998). Studies demonstrating the relationship between traits and adjustment, and the possible biological sources of traits (reviewed below), also lend support to the cross-cultural validity of the measures. Thus, the research findings we report below concerning traits and other personality dimensions have used measures that appear to be equivalent and valid across cultures (although not without at least some controversy; see Church, Alvarez, Mai, French, & Katigbak, 2011).

▶ Cross-Cultural Studies on Personality Traits: The Five-Factor Model and Five-Factor Theory

Evidence for the Five-Factor Model

In the past two decades, trait approaches to personality have become extremely important in understanding the relationship between culture and personality, and it is the dominant view today, especially within the cross-cultural perspective. That work culminated in what is known today as the five-factor model (FFM) of personality, which we now describe.

The FFM is a conceptual model built around five distinct and basic personality dimensions that appear to be universal for all humans. The five dimensions are neuroticism, extraversion, openness to experience, agreeableness, and conscientiousness. The FFM was conceived after researchers noticed the similarities in the personality dimensions that had emerged across many studies, both within and between cultures. Most notably, support for the FFM arose out of factor analyses of trait adjectives from the English lexicon that were descriptive of self and others (Juni, 1996). The factors that emerged from these types of analyses were similar to dimensions found in the analysis of questionnaire scales operationalizing personality. Further inquiry across cultures, using both factor analysis of descriptive trait adjectives in different languages and personality dimensions measured by different personality questionnaires, lent further credence to the FFM.

Many early (e.g., Eysenck's, 1983) and contemporary studies have provided support for the cross-cultural validity of the FFM, spanning different countries and cultures in Europe, East and South Asia, North America, Africa, and Australia. One of the leading researchers on personality and culture in the tradition of the FFM is Robert R. McCrae, who published self-report data for 26 countries in 2001 (McCrae, 2001). In 2002, the database was expanded to 36 cultures (Allik & McCrae, 2004; McCrae, 2002). In later studies in this line of work, McCrae and his colleagues in 51 cultures of the world replicated the FFM in all cultures studied (McCrae, Terracciano, Khoury et al., 2005; McCrae, Terracciano, Leibovich et al., 2005). These studies provided convincing and substantial evidence to support the claim that the FFM—consisting of neuroticism, extraversion, openness, agreeableness, and conscientiousness—represented a universal taxonomy of personality that is applicable to all humans.

These studies provided convincing and substantial evidence to support the claim that the FFM—consisting of neuroticism, extraversion, openness, agreeableness, and conscientiousness—represented a universal taxonomy of personality that is applicable to all humans.

One of the most widely used measures of the FFM in previous research was the Revised NEO Personality Inventory (NEO PI-R) (Costa & McCrae, 1992), which evolved to the NEO PI-3 (McCrae, Costa, & Martin, 2005). It is a 240-item instrument in which respondents rate the degree to which they agree or disagree that the item is characteristic of them. These instruments have been used in many studies across many different cultures. It produces scores on the five major personality traits, as well as six subscores for each major trait (Table 6.2).

Two of the most important traits for describing behavioral differences are extraversion and neuroticism. The former refers to the degree to which an individual experiences positive emotions, and is outgoing, expressive, and sociable or shy, introverted, and avoids contact; the latter refers to the degree of emotional stability in an individual. McCrae, Terracciano, Khoury et al. (2005) graphed the cultural groups they studied along these two dimensions in order to create a useful visual aid in distinguishing among the cultures in terms of their personality (Figure 6.1). This graph provides some ideas about the mean levels of these two personality traits of individuals in these cultural groups. Americans, New Zealanders, and Australians, for instance, tended to be high on extraversion and in the middle of the scale for neuroticism. The French, Italians, and Maltese tended to be high on neuroticism and in the middle of the scale for extraversion.

One of the concerns with findings generated with scales like the NEO PI-R is that the findings may reflect bias on the part of the respondent to answer in a socially desirable way (see Chapter 2 to review response biases). These concerns are especially important to note in cross-cultural work. McCrae, Terracciano, Leibovich, and colleagues (2005), therefore, conducted a follow-up study in which they asked samples of adults and college students in 50 cultural groups to rate someone they know well on the NEO PI-R. The questionnaire was modified so that the ratings were done in the third person. The same five-factor model emerged, indicating that the previous results were not dependent on who made ratings of a target person. In another interesting study, Allik and McCrae (2004) showed that the personality traits were *not* related to geographic location (defined as distance from the equator or mean temperature);

TABLE 6.2 Traits Associated with the Five-Factor Model

Major Trait	Subtrait
Neuroticism	Anxiety
	Angry hostility
	Depression
	Self-consciousness
	Impulsiveness
	Vulnerability
Extraversion	Warmth
	Gregariousness
	Assertiveness
	Activity
	Excitement seeking
	Positive emotions
Openness	Fantasy
	Aesthetics
	Feelings
	Actions
	Ideas
	Values
Agreeableness	Trust
	Straightforwardness
	Altruism
	Compliance
	Modesty
	Tender-mindedness
Conscientiousness	Competence
	Order
	Dutifulness
	Achievement striving
	Self-discipline
	Deliberation

and, geographically or historically close cultures had more similar personality profiles. The results to date provide strong evidence that the FFM is a universal model of personality structure.

Do Perceptions of National Character Correspond to Aggregate Personality Traits?

The works described above have been important because they measured the actual personality traits of large numbers of individuals in a wide range of cultures. Thus, they are reliable data on what the actual personality structures of individuals in these cultures are like. These data also allow us to compare those actual personality profiles with our *perceptions* of national character. As described above, national character refers to perceptions of the average personality of people of different cultures. Perceptions of national character are, in fact, stereotypes about average personalities of people of different cultures.

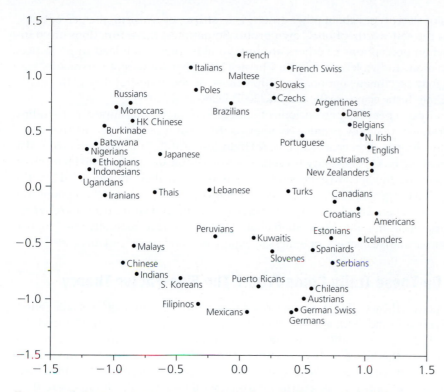

FIGURE 6.1 Graphic Display of Cultures from McCrae et al. (2005)
The vertical axis refers to neuroticism, while the horizontal axis refers to extroversion.
HK Chinese = Hong Kong Chinese; N. Irish = Northern Irish; S. Koreans = South Koreans.

Source: McCrae, R. R., Terracciano, A., Leibovich, N. B., Schmidt, V., Shakespeare-Finch, J., Neubauer, A., et al., "Personality profiles of cultures: Aggregate personality traits," *Journal of Personality and Social Psychology,* 89, pp. 407–425, 2005, Copyright © American Psychological Association. Reprinted by permission.

But are they accurate? Terraciano et al. (2005) asked approximately 4,000 respondents in 49 cultures to describe the "typical member" of a culture using 30 bipolar scales with two or three trait adjectives on the poles of each scale. There was relatively high agreement about the national character perceptions of the various cultures; that is, most people within each of the cultures agreed on their perceptions. But, their perceptions were *not* correlated with the actual personality trait levels of the individuals of those very same cultures. In other words, perceptions of national character were not associated with the actual, aggregate personality levels of individuals of those cultures.

One of the limitations of that study, however, was that different measures were used to assess personality and national character. Two subsequent studies corrected for this limitation, and found some degree of similarity between the two ratings, but with considerable dissimilarity as well (Allik, Mottus, & Realo, 2010; Realo et al., 2009). These findings suggested that perceptions of national character may actually be unfounded stereotypes of the personalities of members of those cultures to some degree.

If perceptions of national character are inaccurate, why do we have them? Terraciano and colleagues (2005) suggested that one of the functions of these unfounded stereotypes is the maintenance of a national identity. That is, one of the functions of stereotypes about other groups is to affirm, or reaffirm, the perceptions, and often the self-worth, of one's own group. Sometimes, these functions are dangerous; when perceptions of others are unfavorable, they often lead to prejudice, discrimination, and violence (see also Chapter 14). Other sources of personality stereotypes may be climate, national wealth, values, or social desirability (Allik et al., 2010; McCrae, Terracciano, Realo, & Allik, 2007; Realo et al., 2009).

Not only are people's perceptions of national character inaccurate, but studies have also shown that how people see others is different from how people see themselves (Allik, Mottus, Borkenau, Kupens, & Hrebickova, 2010). This research involved a reanalysis of the NEO Personality Inventory across 29 cultures. People see themselves as more neurotic and open to experience compared to how they are perceived by others; others have a generally higher opinion of one's conscientiousness than people do of themselves. There are also fairly consistent cross-cultural similarities in *perceived* gender differences in traits (Lockenhoff et al., 2014); women are generally rated higher on neuroticism, agreeableness, openness to experience, and conscientiousness.

Where Do These Traits Come From? The Five-Factor Theory

The five-factory theory (FFT) was developed to explain the source of the traits found to be universal in the FFM, and it's important to distinguish between FFT and the FFM. The FFM of personality is a model of the number of traits that are universal to all people in their personality structure. The FFT of personality is a theoretical framework about the *source* of those traits. One is not entirely dependent on the other; the model of the traits may be entirely correct, while the theory about where they come from entirely wrong. Alternatively, research may show that there are more than five universal traits, while the theory that explains them is correct. Here we discuss the FFT, which attempts to account for where the universal personality traits come from. The core components of the FFT are basic tendencies, characteristic adaptations, and the self-concept, which is a subcomponent of characteristic adaptations (McCrae & Costa, 1999).

The traits correspond to the Basic Tendencies; they refer to internal dispositions to respond to the environment in certain, predictable ways. The FFT suggests that personality traits that underlie basic tendencies are biologically based. Several sources of evidence support this idea. As described earlier, the same personality traits have been found in all cultures studied, and using different research methods (McCrae, Terracciano, Khoury, Nansubuga, Knezevic, Djuric Jocic et al., 2005; McCrae et al., 2005). Parent–child relationships have little lasting effect on personality traits (Rowe, 1994); and traits are generally stable across the adult life span (McCrae & Costa, 2003), although there are some developmental changes (Roberts, Walton, & Viechtbauer, 2006). Studies of twins demonstrate that the personalities of identical twins reared apart are much more similar than those of fraternal twins reared together (Bouchard & Loehlin, 2001; Bouchard, Lykken, & McGue, 1994). The FFM can predict variations in behavior among individuals in longitudinal studies (Borkenau & Ostendorf, 1998), and some evidence suggests that the FFM may apply to nonhuman primates as well (King & Figueredo, 1997). Recent studies have demonstrated culture-level associations between national levels of neuroticism and specific genes related to serotonin transportation (Minkov, Blagoev, & Bond, 2015). Thus there is considerably strong evidence for the idea that personality traits (like those measured in the FFM) are biologically based; these are referred to in FFT as basic tendencies (see Figure 6.2).

The FFT suggests that the universal personality traits representing basic tendencies are expressed in characteristic ways; these characteristic ways can be

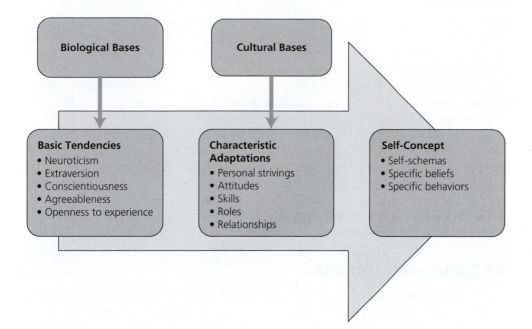

FIGURE 6.2 Graphical Representation of the Five-Factor Theory (FFT)

largely influenced by the culture in which one exists, and here is where culture has important influences on personality development and expression. *Characteristic adaptations* include habits, attitudes, skills, roles, and relationships. They are characteristic because they reflect the psychological core personality trait dispositions of the individual; they are also *adaptations* because they help the individual fit into the ever-changing social environment (McCrae & Costa, 1999). Culture can substantially influence these characteristic adaptations through the resources, social structures, and social systems available in a specific environment to help achieve goals. Culture can influence values about the various personality traits. Culture defines context and provides differential meaning to the components of context, including who is involved, what is happening, where it is occurring, and the like. Culture, therefore, plays a substantial role in producing the specific behavioral manifestations—the specific actions—that individuals will engage in to achieve what may be universal affective goals. Culture is "undeniably relevant in the development of characteristics and adaptations that guide the expression of personality in thoughts, feelings, and behaviors" (McCrae et al., 1998), and the characteristic adaptations vary greatly across cultures. The basic tendencies representing the universal personality traits, however, are not culturally variable, and a universal personality structure is the mechanism by which such goals are achieved through a balance and interaction with culture.

The characteristic adaptations help to produce a self-concept, as well as specific behaviors. For example, a person low in depression, a facet of neuroticism (basic tendency), may develop a low self-esteem, irrational perfectionistic beliefs, and pessimistic or cynical attitudes about the world (Characteristic Adaptations and Self-Concept). He or she may thus feel guilty about work or dissatisfied with his or her life (behavior). A person high on gregariousness, which is part of extraversion (basic tendency), may be outgoing, friendly, and talkative (characteristic adaptations). This person is likely to have numerous friendships and be a member of various social clubs (behaviors).

One of the most contentious parts of the FFT is its suggestion that the origin of the personality traits is at least partially biologically determined. An alternative perspective suggests a role of culture or environment in the shaping of the personality traits underlying basic tendencies of behavior (Allik & McCrae, 2002; Roberts, Caspi, & Moffitt, 2003; Roberts & Helson, 1997; Roberts, Helson, & Klohnen, 2002). There is little debate that culture can influence the characteristic adaptations and self-concepts associated with underlying personality traits (Heine & Buchtel, 2009). Debate continues concerning the origins of the traits, and future research in this area will undoubtedly need to explore many possibilities.

As mentioned above, we need to be clear about the difference between the FFM, which is a model of the universal personality traits, and FFT, which is a theory about the source of those traits. It is entirely possible that the FFM will be amended in the future to allow for the possibility of other traits, but for the theory underlying them to be the same. Or it could be that the FFM will turn out to be reliable but that the theory accounting for the source is entirely wrong. The number of traits that are universal and where they come from are two distinct issues we need to keep separate in our minds.

An Evolutionary Approach

Other theories exist to explain the universality of the FFM. One (MacDonald, 1998) is based in an evolutionary approach and overlaps conceptually with the FFT. This approach posits universality both of human interests and of the neurophysiological mechanisms underlying trait variation. Personality structure is viewed as a universal psychological mechanism, a product of natural selection that serves both social and nonsocial functions in problem solving and environmental adaptation. Based on this theory, one would expect to find similar systems in animals that serve similar adaptive functions, and one would expect personality systems to be organized within the brain as discrete neurophysiological systems. One of the key questions about the FFM that an evolutionary perspective brings, for example, concerns why socially undesirable traits like neuroticism have been preserved through evolution (Penke, Denissen, & Miller, 2007).

In the evolutionary view, traits such as conscientiousness (which refers to the degree of organization, persistence, control, and motivation in goal-directed behavior), neuroticism (tendency to experience negative emotions, vulnerability to stress, emotional stability), and the other components of the FFM are considered to reflect stable variations in systems that serve critical adaptive functions. Conscientiousness, for example, may help individuals to monitor the environment for dangers and impending punishments, and to persevere in tasks that are not intrinsically rewarding (MacDonald, 1998). Neuroticism may be adaptive because it helps mobilize behavioral resources by moderating arousal in situations requiring approach or avoidance. These ideas are somewhat akin to the notion of basic tendencies in FFT.

According to MacDonald (1991, 1998), an evolutionary approach suggests a hierarchical model in which "behavior related to personality occurs at several levels based ultimately on the motivating aspects of evolved personality systems" (p. 130). In this model, humans possess evolved motive dispositions—needs, if you will (for example, intimacy, safety; recall our discussion of needs in Chapter 1). These needs are serviced by a universal set of personality dispositions that help individuals achieve their affective goals by managing personal and environmental resources. This resource management leads to concerns, projects, and tasks, which in turn lead to specific actions or behaviors through which the individual achieves the goals specified by the evolved motive dispositions (see Figure 6.3).

Note that this model—and the assumptions about universality of the FFM made by McCrae, Costa and others (e.g., McCrae & Costa, 1997)—does not minimize the

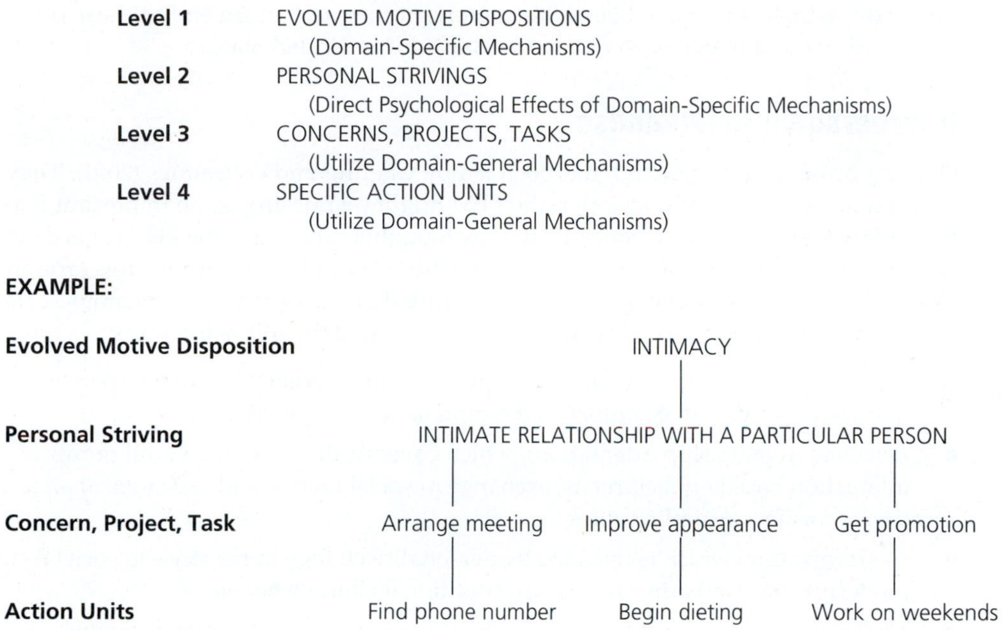

Level 1	EVOLVED MOTIVE DISPOSITIONS
	(Domain-Specific Mechanisms)
Level 2	PERSONAL STRIVINGS
	(Direct Psychological Effects of Domain-Specific Mechanisms)
Level 3	CONCERNS, PROJECTS, TASKS
	(Utilize Domain-General Mechanisms)
Level 4	SPECIFIC ACTION UNITS
	(Utilize Domain-General Mechanisms)

EXAMPLE:

Evolved Motive Disposition — INTIMACY

Personal Striving — INTIMATE RELATIONSHIP WITH A PARTICULAR PERSON

Concern, Project, Task — Arrange meeting | Improve appearance | Get promotion

Action Units — Find phone number | Begin dieting | Work on weekends

FIGURE 6.3 Hierarchical Model of Motivation Showing Relationships between Domain-Specific and Domain-General Mechanisms

Source: Republished with permission of Taylor & Francis Group LLC—Books, from *Goal concepts in personality and social psychology,* Pervin, L (Ed.), 1989. Permission conveyed through Copyright Clearance Center, Inc.

importance of cultural and individual variability. Culture can substantially influence personality through the resources, social structures, and social systems available in a specific environment to help achieve goals. Culture can therefore influence mean levels of personality and values about the various personality traits. As stated earlier, culture is "undeniably relevant in the development of characteristics and adaptations that guide the expression of personality in thoughts, feelings, and behaviors" (McCrae et al., 1998). Culture defines context and provides differential meaning to the components of context, including who is involved, what is happening, where it is occurring, and the like. Culture, therefore, plays a substantial role in producing the specific behavioral manifestations—the specific actions—that individuals will engage in to achieve what may be universal affective goals. An underlying, universal personality structure, which is relatively culturally invariant, however, is considered to be the structure by which such goals are achieved through a balance and interaction with culture.

▶ Cross-Cultural Studies on Other Dimensions of Personality

Research documenting the robustness of the FFM of personality traits around the world has clearly made a major contribution to our understanding of personality organization and culture. As mentioned above, the FFM does not necessarily imply that the five universal traits—neuroticism, extraversion, conscientiousness, agreeableness, and openness to experience—are the *only* traits that exist. Important new lines of research have uncovered several other personality traits that also may be universal, which we review below. It's important to note that several of these other lines of research initiated with researchers outside the United States.

Interpersonal Relatedness

One important line of research has been led by Cheung and colleagues (2001). They began their work with the idea that the FFM might be missing some important features of personality in Asia. Specifically, they thought that none of the FFM traits dealt well with relationships, which are central in China (as well as many cultures around the world). Thus, they developed what they initially considered an indigenous scale designed to measure personality in China that included the following traits:

- Harmony, which refers to one's inner peace of mind, contentment, interpersonal harmony, avoidance of conflict, and maintenance of equilibrium;

- *Ren Qing* (relationship orientation), which covers adherence to cultural norms of interaction based on reciprocity, exchange of social favors, and exchange of affection according to implicit rules;

- Modernization, which is reflected by personality change in response to societal modernization and attitudes toward traditional Chinese beliefs;

- Thrift versus extravagance, which highlights the traditional virtue of saving rather than wasting and carefulness in spending, in contrast to the willingness to spend money for hedonistic purposes;

- *Ah-Q* mentality (defensiveness), which is based on a character in a popular Chinese novel in which the defense mechanisms of the Chinese people, including self-protective rationalization, externalization of blame, and belittling of others' achievements, are satirized;

- Face, which depicts the pattern of orientations in an international and hierarchical connection and social behaviors to enhance one's face and to avoid losing one's face (Cheung, Leung, Zhang, Sun, Gan, Song et al., 2001) (p. 408).

Cheung and colleagues named these dimensions "interpersonal relatedness." Although they originally found support for the existence of this dimension in their studies of mainland and Hong Kong Chinese, they have also documented the existence of the interpersonal relatedness dimension in samples from Singapore, Hawaii, the Midwestern United States, and with Chinese and European Americans (Cheung, Cheung, Leung, Ward, & Leong, 2003; Cheung et al., 2001; Lin & Church, 2004).

Filipino Personality Structure

Another major line of research comes from studies on the personality structures of Filipinos headed by Church and colleagues. In early research, they identified as many traits as they could that existed in the Filipino language and asked Filipino students to rate them, just as they would on any personality test. Early studies using the same statistical techniques that have been used to test the FFM demonstrated that seven, not five, dimensions were necessary to describe the Filipino personality adequately (Church, Katigbak, & Reyes, 1998; Church, Reyes, Katigbak, & Grimm, 1997). The two additional traits were tempermentalness and self-assurance. Similar types of findings were found previously with Spanish-speaking samples in Europe as well (Benet-Martinez & Waller, 1995, 1997).

In one of their later studies, Church and colleagues (Katigbak, Church, Guanzon-Lapena, Carlota, & del Pilar, 2002) used two Filipino indigenous personality scales encompassing a total of 463 trait adjectives, and a Filipino version of the NEO PI-R to measure the FFM, and asked 511 college students in the Philippines to complete these measures. Analyses indicated that there was considerable overlap in the personality dimensions that emerged from the Filipino scales and the FFM measured by the NEO PI-R. Still, several indigenous factors emerged, including *pagkamadaldal* (social curiosity), *pagkamapagsapalaran* (risk-taking), and religiosity. These latter traits were especially important in predicting behaviors such as smoking, drinking, gambling, praying, tolerance of homosexuality, and tolerance of premarital and extramarital relations, above and beyond what could be predicted by the FFM.

Dominance

In the mid-twentieth century, European psychologists suggested the existence of an "authoritarian personality," and developed scales to measure it (Adorno, Frenkel-Brunswik, & Levinson, 1950). This dimension is related to the concept of dominance, and refers to the fact that people differ in their dependence on authority and hierarchical status differences among interactants. Hofstede, Bond, and Luk (1993) analyzed data from 1,300 individuals in Denmark and the Netherlands, and found six personality dimensions. Five of these were related to the FFM; the sixth, however, was not. The researchers labeled this "authoritarianism," which is related to dominance.

Dominance is a trait that emerges in studies of the personalities of animals. King and Figueredo (1997), for instance, presented 43 trait adjectives with representative items from the FFM to zoo trainers who work with chimpanzees in 12 zoos. The trainers were asked to describe the chimpanzees in terms of the adjectives provided. The results showed no differences between the zoos, and the interrater reliability was high. Factor analysis of the ratings produced six factors, five of which corresponded to the FFM; the sixth corresponded to dominance. The same findings have been reported in studies of orangutans and chimpanzees (Pederson, King, & Landau, 2005; Weiss, King, & Enns, 2002; Weiss, King, & Figueredo, 2000), and suggest that dominance is an inherited trait among animals.

Recent work involving a theory known as social dominance theory has highlighted the potential importance of social dominance as a stable personality trait across cultures (Pratto, Sidanius, Stallworth, & Malle, 1994). This theory concerns the maintenance and stability of social hierarchies, and suggests that cultural ideologies, values, attitudes, and worldviews provide the justification for intergroup behaviors such as discrimination and prejudice. A scale used to measure individual-level tendencies to endorse these ideologies is the social dominance orientation scale, which has been widely used across cultures to assess this aspect of dominance (Pratto et al., 2000; Sidanius, Henry, Pratto, & Levin, 2004).

To date, attempts to find other universal traits mostly do not contradict the FFM, but instead add to it. A question that remains unresolved concerns exactly what other dimensions, if any, reliably exist across cultures. The findings reported above are promising in terms of an answer to this question, but certainly much more research is necessary across a wider range of cultures to gauge its comparability with the FFM. Other indigenous approaches to studying traits have also been developed in countries such as India, Korea, Russia, and Greece (Allik et al., 2009; Cheung, Cheung, Wada, & Zhang, 2003; Saucier, Georgiades, Tsaousis, & Goldberg, 2005). At the same time, there is some evidence involving respondents from illiterate, indigenous societies that suggests that the FFM may not be applicable in such societies (Gurven, von Rueden, Massenkoff, & Kaplan, 2012). Certainly future research will hopefully shed more light on this important topic in the future.

Internal versus External Locus of Control

Aside from cross-cultural research on traits, there has also been a considerable amount of cross-cultural research examining other dimensions of personality that do not fall cleanly within the trait perspective but are noteworthy in their own right. One of these concerns the personality concept of **locus of control**. This concept was developed by Rotter (1954, 1966), who suggested that people differ in how much control they believe they have over their behavior and their relationship with their environment and with others. According to this schema, locus of control can be perceived as either internal or external to the individual. People with an internal locus of control see their behavior and relationships with others as dependent on their own behavior. Believing that your grades are mostly dependent on how much effort you put into study is an example of internal locus of control. People with an external locus of control see their behavior and relationships with the environment and others as contingent on forces outside themselves and beyond their control. If you believe your grades are mostly dependent on luck, the teacher's benevolence, or the ease of the tests, you would be demonstrating an external locus of control.

Research examining locus of control has shown both similarities and differences across cultures. In general, European Americans have higher internal locus of control scores than East Asians, Swedes, Zambians, Zimbabweans, African Americans, Filipinos, and Brazilians (for example, Hamid, 1994; Lee and Dengerink, 1992; Munro, 1979; Dyal, 1984; Paguio, Robinson, Skeen, & Deal, 1987). These findings have often been interpreted as reflecting the mainstream American culture's focus on individuality, separateness, and uniqueness, in contrast to a more balanced view of interdependence among individuals and between individuals and natural and supernatural forces found in many other cultures (recall Chapter 5, for a related discussion of self-construals). People of non-mainstream American cultures may be more likely to see the causes of events and behaviors in sources that are external to themselves, such as fate, luck, supernatural forces, or relationships with others. Americans, however, prefer to take more personal responsibility for events and situations, and view themselves as having more personal control over such events. These examples of internal versus external locus of control are also related to cultural differences in attributional styles, which we will discuss in Chapter 14.

Although cultural differences in internal versus external locus of control are interesting and provocative, they still leave some gaps to be filled. For example, they do not account for phenomena such as self-serving bias or defensive attributions, in which Americans tend to place the responsibility for negative events on others, not themselves (recall discussion in Chapter 5 on self-enhancement). Also, some researchers have suggested that locus of control is really a multifaceted construct spanning many different domains—academic achievement, work, interpersonal relationships, and so on—and that separate assessments of each of these domains are necessary to make meaningful comparisons on this construct. Smith, Dugan, and Trompenaars (1997) examined locus of control across 14 countries, and found some cross-national differences in locus of control, but larger differences by gender and status across countries. Moreover, the *meaning* of internal versus external locus of control may be different across cultures. For example, external locus of control is generally related to greater depression and anxiety; these relationships, however, are stronger in individualistic cultures than in collectivistic cultures (Cheng, Cheung, Chio, & Chan, 2013). Thus, the search for cross-cultural differences in internal versus external locus of control may obscure more important differences based on other social constructs. Future research needs to address all these concerns to further elucidate the nature of cultural influences on locus of control.

locus of control
People's attributions of control over their behaviors and relationships as internal or external to themselves. People with an internal locus of control see their behavior and relationships with others as dependent on their own behavior. People with an external locus of control see their behavior and relationships as contingent on forces outside themselves and beyond their control.

Direct, Indirect, Proxy, and Collective Control

Yamaguchi (2001) has offered another interesting way of understanding control across cultures. He distinguished between direct, indirect, proxy, and collective control. In **direct control**, the self acts as an agent, and individuals feel themselves to be more self-efficacious when their agency is made explicit, leading to greater feelings of autonomy and efficacy. Direct control may be the preferred mode of behavior in cultural contexts that promote independence or autonomy, such as in the United States.

Other cultural contexts, however, may encourage different modes of control, primarily because of their focus on interpersonal harmony. For instance, in **indirect control**, one's agency is hidden or downplayed; people pretend as if they are not acting as an agent even though in reality they are doing so. Yamaguchi (2001) tells of an example in which a Japanese *rakugo* (comic master) was annoyed at his disciple's loud singing. Instead of directly telling him to stop, he instead praised him with a loud voice. Although at first it sounded as if the comic master was praising the disciple, in reality he was telling him to be quiet; thus, the disciple stopped singing.

Proxy control refers to control by someone else for the benefit of oneself. This is a form of control that can be used when personal control—either direct or indirect—is not available or inappropriate. These are third-party interventions, when intermediaries are called in to regulate or intervene in interpersonal relationships or conflicts between parties with potential or actual conflicts of interest. This type of control is essential for survival for those in weaker positions and thus unable to change their environments by themselves.

Finally, in **collective control**, one attempts to control the environment as a member of a group, and the group serves as the agent of control. In this situation, individuals need to worry about interpersonal harmony less because the group shares the goal of control.

Yamaguchi (2001) suggested that direct, personal control may be the strategy of choice in cultures that value autonomy and independence, such as the United States. In cultures that value the maintenance of interpersonal harmony, however, indirect, proxy, and collective control strategies may be more prevalent (Figure 6.4). Much like the concept of tactical self-enhancement (recall the discussion in Chapter 5), all people

direct control A type of control in which the self acts as an agent, and individuals feel themselves to be more self-efficacious when their agency is made explicit, leading to greater feelings of autonomy and efficacy. Direct control may be the preferred mode of behavior in cultural contexts that promote independence or autonomy, such as in the United States.

indirect control A type of control in which one's agency is hidden or downplayed; people pretend as if they are not acting as an agent even though they are doing so in reality.

proxy control Refers to control by someone else for the benefit of oneself. This is a form of control that can be used when personal control—either direct or indirect—is not available or inappropriate. These are third-party interventions.

collective control A type of control in which one attempts to control the environment as a member of a group, and the group serves as the agent of control.

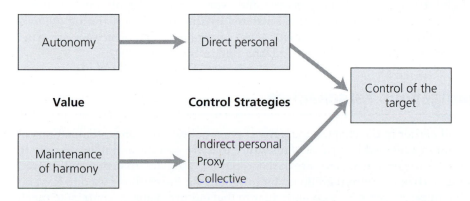

FIGURE 6.4 The Relationships between Cultural Values and Preferred Control Strategies

Source: Yamaguchi, S. (2001). Culture and Control Orientations. In D. Matsumoto (Ed.), The handbook of *culture and psychology* (pp. 223–243). New York: Oxford University Press. (www.oup .com). By permission of Oxford University Press.

around the world probably have similar needs in controlling their environment, but do so differently depending on cultural norms for appropriateness about how to do so.

Autonomy

Another personality construct that has received considerable research attention is that of autonomy, which has often been discussed within a theory known as *self-determination theory* (Deci & Ryan, 1985; Ryan & Deci, 2000). This theory states that people from all cultures share basic psychological needs for autonomy, competence, and relatedness, but that the specific ways in which these needs are met and expressed differ according to context and culture. Meeting these needs, in whatever form or by whatever means, should be related to greater well-being of people in all cultures.

Of these claims, the one concerning autonomy has been controversial. Conceptualizations of cultures that focus on individualism versus collectivism, and particularly those rooted in Markus and Kitayama's (1991b) framework of independent versus interdependent self-construals (Chapter 5), suggest that people of collectivistic cultures are not autonomous. Deci and Ryan suggest, however, that there is a large distinction among autonomy, individualism, independence, and separateness. According to self-determination theory, people are autonomous when *their behavior is experienced as willingly enacted and when they fully endorse the actions in which they are engaged or the values expressed by them* (Chirkov, Ryan, Kim, & Kaplan, 2003). Thus, people are autonomous whenever they act in accord with their interests, values, or desires. The opposite of autonomy in this perspective is not dependence, but heteronomy, in which one's actions are perceived as controlled by someone else or are otherwise alien to oneself. Thus, one can be either autonomously independent or dependent; they are separate constructs.

These ideas have received support in several studies involving participants from South Korea, Turkey, Russia, Canada, Brazil, and the United States (Chirkov et al., 2003; Chirkov, Ryan, & Willness, 2005). In all cultures tested to date, studies have shown that individuals tend to internalize different cultural practices, whatever those practices may be, and that despite those different practices, the relative autonomy of an individual's motivations to engage in those practices predicts well-being. Autonomy, therefore, appears to be a universal psychological need and phenomenon, although the way in which it is practiced and expressed is different in different cultures (Kagitcibasi, 1996). This idea is bolstered by findings demonstrating the universality of self-efficacy—an optimistic sense of personal competence—a construct related to autonomy (Scholz, Hutierrez Dona, Sud, & Schwarzer, 2002).

▶ Indigenous Personalities

As stated earlier in the chapter, indigenous personalities are conceptualizations of personality developed in a particular culture that are specific and relevant only to that culture. In general, not only are the concepts of personality rooted in and derived from the particular cultural group under question, but the methods used to test and examine those concepts are also particular to that culture. Thus, in contrast to much of the research described so far on universal traits, in which standardized personality measures are used to assess personality dimensions, studies of indigenous personalities often use their own, nonstandardized methods.

Indigenous conceptions of personality are important because they give us a glimpse of how each culture believes it is important to carve up their psychological world. By identifying indigenous concepts, each culture pays tribute to a specific way of understanding their world, which is an important part of each cultural worldview. By giving these concepts names, each culture is then allowed to talk about them, thereby ensuring each indigenous concept's special place in their culture.

Over the years, many scientists have been interested in indigenous conceptions of personality, and have described many different personality constructs considered to exist only in specific cultures. Early work in this area produced findings of many other personality constructs thought to be culture-specific, including the personality of Arabs (Beit-Hallahmi, 1972), North Alaskan Eskimos (Hippler, 1974), the Japanese (Sakamoto & Miura, 1976), the Fulam of Nigeria (Lott & Hart, 1977), the Irulas of Palamalai (Narayanan & Ganesan, 1978), Samoans (Holmes, Tallman, & Jantz, 1978), South African Indians (Heaven & Rajab, 1983), and the Ibo of Nigeria (Akin-Ogundeji, 1988).

Indigenous perspectives have also allowed the field to uncover ways different cultures conceptualize personality structure. Berry, Poortinga, Segall, and Dasen (1992) examined three indigenous personality concepts, each of which was fundamentally different from American or Western concepts. The African model of personality, for example, views personality as consisting of three layers, each representing a different aspect of the person. The first layer, found at the core of the person and personality, embodies a spiritual principle; the second layer involves a psychological vitality principle; the third layer involves a physiological vitality principle. The body forms the outer framework that houses all these layers of the person. In addition, family lineage and community affect different core aspects of the African personality (Sow, 1980; see also Vontress, 1991).

Doi (1973) postulated *amae* as a core concept of the Japanese personality. The root of this word means "sweet," and loosely translated, *amae* refers to the passive, childlike dependence of one person on another, and is rooted in mother–child relationships. According to Doi, all Japanese relationships can be characterized by *amae*, which serves as a fundamental building block of Japanese culture and personality. This fundamental interrelationship between higher- and lower-status people in Japan serves as a major component not only of individual psychology but of interpersonal relationships, and it does so in ways that are difficult to grasp from a North American individualistic point of view.

Along with different conceptualizations of personality, different cultures have specific, important concepts that are crucial to understanding individuals in their culture. These include the Korean concept of *cheong* (human affection; Choi, Kim, & Choi, 1993); the Indian concept of *hishkama karma* (detachment; Sinha, 1993); the Chinese concept *ren qing* (relationship orientation; Cheung, Leung, Fan, Song, Zhang, & Zhang, 1996); the Mexican concept *simpatia* (harmony, avoidance of conflict; Triandis, Marin, Lisansky, & Betancourt, 1984; Holloway, Waldrip, & Ickes, 2009); and the Filipino concepts of *pagkikipagkapwa* (shared identity), *pakikiramdam* (sensitivity, empathy), and *pakikisama* (going along with others; Enriquez, 1992) (all cited in Church, 2000, p. 654).

Much of the work on indigenous personality has provided fuel for those who subscribe to the view that culture and personality are mutually constituted. In this view, it makes no sense to consider personality as a universal construct (like traits); instead, it makes more sense to understand each culture's personalities as they exist and have developed within that culture. This viewpoint rejects the notion of a universal organization to personality that may have genetic, biological, and evolutionary components. Its proponents (Markus & Kitayama, 1998; Shweder & Bourne, 1984) argue that the research supporting universality and its possible biological substrates may be contaminated by the methods used. These methods, the argument goes, have been developed in American or European research laboratories by American or European researchers; because of this cultural bias, the studies support findings such as the FFM as a default by-product of the methods used to test it. Indigenous approaches, it is claimed, are immune from such bias because their methods are centered around concepts and practices that are local to the culture being studied (see, however, the replication of the FFM using nontraditional methods of assessing taxonomies of trait adjectives in multiple languages; De Raad, Perugini, Hrebickova, & Szarota, 1998).

▶ Integrating Universal and Culture-Specific Understandings of Personality

There is a middle ground that integrates both universal and culture-specific understandings and empirical findings on personality.

We believe there is a middle ground that integrates both universal and culture-specific understandings and empirical findings on personality. This middle ground starts with our understanding of personality as a multidimensional construct. If, as we have done at the beginning of this chapter, we broadly conceptualize two different aspects of personality, one involving traits and the other involving identities, then we can consider that they come from different sources and are influenced differently by biology and culture. On one hand, it appears that traits are more enduring aspects of a person's personality, referring to underlying dispositions for thoughts, feelings, and actions. These appear to be at least somewhat rooted in biology and genetics; thus individuals are born with a set of genetic predispositions for certain aspects of their personalities. Because these are biologically based genetic predispositions, they are relatively less impervious to cultural and environmental influences (although the exact degree of potential influence is an interesting question if one considers the possible influence of culture on biological processes across evolution).

On the other hand, identities, which is a loose term that refers to perceived roles in life, aggregate role and life experiences, narratives, values, motives, and the conceptualization and understanding of oneself, should be less influenced by biology and more influenced by culture because these are in large part *cultural constructions* of the meaning and value of one's thoughts, feelings, and actions. As such, they are more likely to be "mutually constituted" in development, arising out of an interaction between the individual and the environment. During these interactions, culturally determined meanings of right and wrong, good and bad, appropriate and inappropriate help to guide the construction of meaning, and thus the creation of identities, roles, and motives. It is no wonder, therefore, that this aspect of personality is less influenced by biology and more heavily influenced by culture.

This integrative perspective allows us to move beyond questioning whether personality is universal or culture-specific, as if they are mutually exclusive, dichotomous categories. A better and more fruitful approach might be to consider how some aspects of personality are influenced relatively more by biology and how some other aspects are influenced relatively more by culture. It is entirely possible that some aspects of personality (e.g., traits) may be organized in a universal fashion, either because of biological or genetic factors or because of culture-constant learning and responses to the environment.

The fact that some aspects of personality may be organized universally, however, does not necessarily argue against the possibility that other aspects of personality may be culturally unique. It may be these culturally unique aspects that give personality its own special flavor in each specific cultural milieu, and allow researchers the possibility of studying aspects of personality that they might not observe in other cultures. This is, in fact, the major premise underlying FFT that we discussed earlier. Thus, a more beneficial way of understanding the relationship between culture and personality may be to see indigenous and universal aspects of personality as two sides of the same coin, rather than as mutually exclusive. If we come to understand the relationship between culture and personality (and biology, for that matter) in ways that allow for the coexistence of universality and indigenization, then we can tackle the problem of exactly how to conceptualize and study this coexistence.

In terms of research findings, evidence for indigenous conceptions of personality is not necessarily antithetical to the existence of universal personality traits such as the FFM described earlier in this chapter. Both the FFM and indigenous personality concepts are empirical findings based on scientifically valid research. As we suggest here the validity of one set of data do not necessarily argue against the validity of the other; the two may exist simultaneously. Trait approaches such as the FFM probably refer more to the universal aspects of personality that are true of all people regardless of culture (underlying dispositional traits and action tendencies), while indigenous aspects of personality refer to those aspects of personality that are culture-specific, especially concerning their understandings and conceptualizations of personality. Both are likely accurate.

Recent research that directly examines competing hypotheses from a universal trait perspective as opposed to a cultural, indigenous perspective of personality also sheds light on how both types of personalities exist and are differentially influenced by biology and culture. The universal trait view of personality suggests that traits exist in all cultures, and influence behavior in multiple contexts, because traits are inherent to people regardless of context. The indigenous view of personality, however, suggests that traits would not be endorsed or even existing in all cultures, and that even if they did, they would not influence behaviors across different contexts. Two studies, however, have shown that traits are endorsed even implicitly across cultures, cross-context consistency in traits exist across cultures, and this consistency is related to adjustment similarly across cultures, demonstrating support for the universal trait view of personality (Church et al., 2008; Church et al., 2006). At the same time, cultural differences in *self-perceptions* of traitedness existed, which supported indigenous, culture-specific perspectives. It makes sense that self-perceptions were more culturally variable, because these are more influenced by cultural meaning and construction. Perceptions of traits are different than the actual traits themselves.

The integrative perspective we suggest here proposes two separate but not mutually exclusive possibilities about the sources of personality: (1) the existence of biologically innate and evolutionarily adaptive factors that create genetic predispositions to certain types of personality traits and (2) the possibility of culture-constant learning principles and processes (MacDonald, 1998; McCrae, 2000). Dispositional traits that humans bring with them into the world may be modified and adapted throughout development and the life span via interactions with the environment. Over time, dipping into this resource pool in order to adapt to various situational contexts may serve as the impetus for changes to the pool itself, which may account for changes in consistency and mean levels of the dispositional traits observed in previous studies (Roberts & DelVecchio, 2000; Roberts, Walton, & Viechtbauer, 2006).

CONCLUSION

In this chapter, we have discussed the major approaches to understanding and studying the relationship between culture and personality, and have examined many different types of studies on this topic. We began by defining personality and briefly describing major approaches to the topic. We described research on the FFM, which suggests that there is universality in personality organization around a small set of basic personality traits. Additional studies in this area have suggested that there may be additional personality traits that are universal; future research is necessary to test this idea more fully. We also discussed the FFT, a theory about where the universal personality traits come from. FFT suggests that the underlying traits reflect biologically based, inherited dispositions for behavior. But, how these traits are expressed may be culturally variable, as each person develops characteristic adaptations to address each of the traits.

In addition, we discussed interesting cross-cultural research on control and autonomy. These studies are important because they inform us about personality organization from a different perspective. The evidence to date suggests that autonomy is a universal personality construct, and that all individuals of all cultures are autonomous. How we exert control over the environment in managing that autonomy, however, may differ in different contexts. That is, how we exert our personalities may be tactical.

Research on indigenous approaches to personality has demonstrated culturally specific aspects of personality that cannot be accounted for by the FFM. These two seemingly disparate sets of findings suggest a conflict in our understanding of the relationship between culture and personality. We presented above, however, an integrative theoretical perspective that suggests that these two seemingly opposing viewpoints need not be seen as mutually exclusive; rather, it may be more beneficial to view them as different, coexisting aspects of personality. The challenge for future research is to capture this coexistence, examining the relative degree of contribution of biological and cultural factors in the development and organization of personality. Future theories and studies will likely benefit from a blending of universal, etic approaches with indigenous, emic approaches (Cheung, van de Vijver, & Leong, 2011).

EXPLORATION AND DISCOVERY

Why Does This Matter to Me?

1. Have you ever taken a personality test? Did you think the results were applicable to you or not? Why or why not? Do you think that such a test would be applicable in another cultural context?

2. What makes you unique? And how important is it to you to have that unique aspect of yourself? Do you think people of other cultures consider uniqueness and important aspect of themselves?

3. When there is an obstacle to your goal, how do you prefer to deal with it? Head on? Go around it? People of other cultures may prefer a different way of dealing with such obstacles. How will you manage when you have to work with others with vastly different perspectives on how to deal with problems?

Suggestions for Further Exploration

1. How predictive of actual behavior do you think personality tests are? How would you conduct a study that examines this question? How would you do it across cultures?

2. Do you believe animals have personalities? How would you study that and document those personalities?

3. Are indigenous personalities really indigenous? For example, the Japanese culture includes the concept of *amae* described above. Do you think that *amae* also exists in other cultures, at least in terms of behaviors or mental processes? How would you go about showing that?

Culture and Gender

7

Culture influences the behaviors associated with being male or female, and events around the world have brought international attention to gender issues. From the role of women in Muslim culture to global concern over female circumcision in Africa and Asia—gender roles, ideals, and expectations are heated topics widely discussed today. An example of a controversial cultural practice that is rooted in perceptions of gender and gender roles is female circumcision. It has been described as part of a female initiation ceremony and an important rite of passage marking the transition from childhood to adulthood (Lightfoot-Klein, 1989). Behind this practice lie many strongly held beliefs about women and their roles. Those who defend the practice argue that it is a requirement for marriage and emphasize the importance of upholding tradition; those who condemn it emphasize the pain, suffering, and health risks involved. To understand this controversy, recognizing how this practice came to be in the cultures in which they originated may be beneficial, as is examining how our own cultural filters shape the way we view issues related to gender. If you find this practice abhorrent, why? If not, why? How did you come to develop those beliefs?

The parallels between the impact of gender and culture on psychology are interesting. Beginning 40 or 50 years ago, what is commonly known as the women's movement in the United States led American academic communities to evaluate the treatment and presentation of women in textbooks and research. They found that most research was conducted using men as participants, and most information presented about "people" in academic textbooks and university courses was based on information gathered from men. This gender bias also affected what scholars considered important to study, the relative status of different studies and topics, and the probability and outlet for publication. Psychologists became increasingly aware of the possibility that men and women may differ psychologically, calling into question previous research findings and the theories based on them. Scholars, researchers, teachers, and students alike began to question whether knowledge based primarily on men was accurate for people in general.

One consequence of this growing awareness among researchers and scholars was a conscious effort to include women as research participants to ensure that research findings would be applicable to women as well as men. At the same time, an increasing number of women became researchers and scholars, bringing different perspectives to the field, its theories, and its findings. Today, psychology enjoys more balanced contributions by both men and women, and this combination of different perspectives and concerns makes for a dynamism that is rich, interesting, and important for the field.

As a result, we have come a long way toward improving our knowledge about all people in the social sciences. Although questioning the imbalance of research on men and women was difficult, many behavioral and social scientists have responded well to this inequity in our knowledge and practice. Today, studies of gender differences are commonplace in social science research and textbooks routinely incorporate sex and gender differences when imparting knowledge about people.

We are witnessing the same type of questioning regarding culture. Just as knowledge about women and women's concerns was missing from research and scholarship 30 years ago, so too was knowledge about cultural similarities and differences and cultural diversity. Much of this gap still exists today. Many of the same questions are still being raised concerning whether what we are learning in classes and in our laboratories is indeed true for people of all cultures and ethnicities. The answer so far has been "not necessarily." To address this gap, many researchers have made a conscious effort to study behaviors across cultures to learn what is similar across cultures and what is different. Academic institutions have also made a conscious effort to recruit and train people of diverse cultural backgrounds so that they too can contribute to the research, teaching, and scholarship in psychology.

These changes are evidence of a continuing evolution in the field similar to what has happened in relation to gender. As the United States and the entire world become increasingly diverse, the need for mainstream psychology to incorporate, explain, and describe that diversity increases. The field has become aware of this need only in the past decade or two (although cross-cultural research has a much longer history). Theories, research, and teaching are becoming more culturally sensitive and this increasing awareness is bound to bring with it another evolution in the face and content of psychology. For this reason, it is an exciting time in both mainstream and cultural psychology as the gap between them narrows.

In this chapter, we will examine how culture influences behavior related to sex and gender. First, we will discuss some terminology and definitions concerning sex and gender that will help us understand what we are talking about and how to focus on cultural influences. Then we will discuss cross-cultural research on gender differences on a broad range of psychological processes. Then we will discuss gender stereotypes, gender roles, and self-concepts, all of which suggest the existence of universality in stereotypes related to gender and its role around the world. We will next discuss some theoretical notions of how psychologists believe gender differences come to exist, and why cultures seem to differ in these differences. We will also discuss how changing cultures and clashes between cultures bring differences in gender roles to the forefront in the daily lives of many people today. Throughout this discussion, we will see that the issues surrounding gender and gender differences, both pancultural and culture-specific, are complex as well as interesting.

▶ Sex and Gender

Sex generally refers to the physical characteristics and differences between men and women, and the term **sex roles** is used to describe the behaviors that men and women may engage in that are directly related to their biological differences and the process of reproduction. An example of a sex role for females is breastfeeding, a behavior that only women can engage in (Brislin, 1993). The term **sexual identity** is used to describe the degree of awareness and recognition of sex and sex roles an individual may have. Male sexual identity typically includes "his awareness that he has the potential to impregnate women and knows the necessary behaviors. Female sexual identity includes the woman's awareness of her reproductive potential and her knowledge about behaviors that lead to pregnancy" (p. 287).

In contrast, **gender** refers to the behaviors that a culture deems appropriate for men and women. These behaviors may or may not be related to sex and sex roles, although they often are. **Gender role** refers to the degree to which a person adopts the gender-specific behaviors ascribed by his or her culture. For example, traditional gender roles suggest that males are aggressive and unemotional (with the exception of anger) and that the male should leave the home every day to make a living and be the principal wage earner. Traditional gender roles for females suggest that women are nurturant, caring, and emotional and that they should stay at home and take care of the children. **Gender identity** refers to the degree to which a person has awareness or recognition that he or she adopts a particular gender role. **Gender stereotypes** refer to the psychological or behavioral characteristics typically associated with men and women (see Table 7.1 for summary of the differences between sex and gender).

sex The biological and physiological differences between men and women, the most obvious being the anatomical differences in their reproductive systems.

sex roles The behaviors and patterns of activities men and women may engage in that are directly related to their biological differences and the process of reproduction.

sexual identity The degree of awareness and recognition by an individual of his or her sex and sex roles.

gender The behaviors or patterns of activities a society or culture deems appropriate for men and women. These behavioral patterns may or may not be related to sex and sex roles, although they often are.

gender role The degree to which a person adopts the gender-specific behaviors ascribed by his or her culture.

gender identity The degree to which a person has awareness of or recognition that he or she has adopted a particular gender role.

gender stereotype The psychological or behavioral characteristics typically associated with men and women.

TABLE 7.1 Differences between "Sex" and "Gender"

	Sex	Gender
Definition	Refers to physical characteristics and differences between men and women	Refers to the behaviors that a culture deems appropriate for men and women
Roles	Refers to the behaviors that men and women may engage in that are directly related to their biological differences and the process of reproduction	Refers to the degree to which a person adopts the gender-specific behaviors ascribed by his or her culture
Identity	Degree of awareness and recognition of sex and sex roles an individuals may have	Degree of awareness or recognition that a person adopts a particular gender role

Not everyone can be pigeonholed into stereotypes according to sex or gender roles, as there are considerable individual differences across people with regard to these roles. In addition, gender role stereotypes interact with other forms of group membership. Separating the biological facts of sex from the behavioral aspects of gender is the first step in understanding the differences between males and females. Culture has a large influence on gender differences.

▶ Gender Differences across Cultures

Research on sex and gender differences within the United States has demonstrated how men and women are different, or not, on a variety of psychological and behavioral outcomes. But do the same differences occur in other cultures? If so, to what degree? In this section, we describe major findings in the field that have documented how the nature and size of sex differences differ across cultures.

Masculinity and Femininity

In Chapter 1, we discussed research by Hofstede who studied work-related attitudes across 50 countries. As you might remember, Hofstede (1980) conducted a large-scale survey of work-related values in a major multinational corporation. Based on the data obtained, he originally generated four dimensions of differentiation among the cultures in his sample. One of these dimensions was called "Masculinity v. Femininity." This dimension referred to the degree to which a culture will foster, encourage, or maintain differences between males and females. In Hofstede's research, Japan, Austria, Venezuela, and Italy had the highest masculinity versus femininity scores, while Denmark, the Netherlands, Norway, and Sweden had the lowest scores.

Hofstede (2001) identified key differences between masculine and feminine cultures in terms of sexuality (Table 7.2). For instance, cultures high on masculinity tended to have moralistic attitudes about sex, double standards about sex (i.e., women should be virgins at marriage but not men), and norms encouraging passive roles of women. Cultures low on masculinity tended to have matter-of-fact attitudes about sex, a single standard concerning sex for men and women, and norms that encouraged an active role for women in society.

Masculine and feminine cultures also differed in their attitudes about religion. Masculine cultures tended to be more traditional, focusing on religion and God or

TABLE 7.2 Key Differences between Low and High Masculinity Societies Concerning Sexuality and Religion

Low Masculinity	High Masculinity
In Sexual Behavior	
Matter-of-fact attitudes about sex.	Moralistic attitudes about sex.
AIDS prevention campaigns very outspoken.	AIDS prevention campaigns restricted by taboos.
Single standard for women and men.	Double standard: Women should be chaste at marriage yet men needn't.
Norm of active role of woman.	Norm of passive role of woman.
Sexual attraction unrelated to career success.	Men become more attractive by career success, women less.
In uncertainty-accepting cultures, few teenage pregnancies.	In uncertainty-accepting cultures, frequent teenage pregnancies.
Young people more influenced by parents.	Young people more influenced by peers.
Other-oriented sex.	Ego-oriented sex.
Women enjoy first sex.	Women feel exploited by first sex.
Unwanted intimacies not major issue.	Sexual harassment major issue.
Homosexuality is a fact of life.	Homosexuality is a taboo and a threat.
Weak distinction between sex and love.	Sharp distinction between sex and love.
Sex and violence in media taboo.	Sex and violence in media frequent.
Lovers should be educated, social.	Lovers should be successful, attractive.
Happy lovers overbenefit from the other.	Happy lovers get equitable mutual deal.
Interaction with other sex more intimate.	Interaction with other sex less intimate.
Sex is a way of relating to someone.	Sex is a way of performing.
In Religion	
"Tender" religions and religious currents.	"Tough" religions and religious currents.
Secularization in Christian countries.	Maintenance of traditional Christianity.
Religion not so important in life.	Religion most important in life.
Religion focuses on fellow human beings.	Religion focuses on God or gods.
Children socialized toward responsibility and politeness.	Children socialized toward religious faith.
Exemplarism and mysticism.	Traditionalism, theism, and conversionism.
Dominant religions stress complementarity of the sexes.	Dominant religions stress male prerogative.
Men and women can be priests.	Only men can be priests.
Sex is for procreation and recreation.	Sex is primarily for procreation.
Positive or neutral attitude toward sexual pleasure.	Negative attitude toward sexual pleasure.
Sexuality as one area of human motivation.	Sexuality as primordial area of human motivation.

Source: From G. H. Hofstede, *Culture's Consequences: Comparing Values, Behaviors, Institutions and Organizations across Nations* (2nd ed.), 2001. p. 330. Copyright © 2001 by Geert Hofstede. Reprinted with permission by Geert Hofstede B. V.

gods. Feminine cultures tended to be less traditional, emphasized the importance of religion in life less, and focused on fellow humans.

Hofstede's study was important because his findings highlighted that cultures will arrive at different ways of dealing with differences between men and women. The behaviors men and women engage in produce different psychological outcomes that have direct ramifications for actual life behaviors. Cultures vary in how they act on these gender differences, with some cultures fostering and encouraging large differences between the genders and other cultures minimizing those differences. At the same time, close inspection of the contents of Table 6.2 and Hofstede's (1980) original data suggest that Masculinity in this dimension may also be interpreted as "Materialism."

Differences in masculinity and femininity are related to sexist ideologies. These are doctrines, myths, or beliefs about differences between men and women, and in particular about their sex or gender roles. They are pervasive in any society and culture, and have long been considered as myths that help to legitimatize the creation and maintenance of gender inequality. One recent study involving 82,905 participants from 57 societies provided the first evidence that sexist ideologies not only can create gender inequality within societies, legitimatizing the status quo, but also enhances its severity (Brandt, 2011). In this study, sexist ideologies were measured at one time in the survey, and gender equality was measured at the same and a later time (two, three, or five years later, depending on the country). Higher sexism predicted higher gender equality at the later time, even when controlling for the amount of gender equality at the first time. Sexism was more prevalent in countries that were less developed and had more gender inequality to begin with. Interestingly, there were no gender differences, which indicated that both men and women endorsed the effects of sexist ideologies across the countries.

Cognitive Differences

It is common folklore that males are better at mathematical and spatial reasoning tasks, whereas females are better at verbal comprehension tasks. An analysis of the scores for males and females on standardized tests in elementary school, college entrance examinations, or graduate school entrance examinations shows some degree of support for these notions, although the difference between males and females have narrowed in recent years. Years ago, Maccoby and Jacklin (1974) concluded in their review of the literature that males tend to do better on spatial tasks.

But early on, Berry (1966) pointed out that such differences do not appear to exist among males and females of the Inuit culture in Canada. Berry suggested that the gender difference did not exist because "spatial abilities are highly adaptive for both males and females in Inuit society, and both boys and girls have ample training and experience that promote the acquisition of spatial ability" (Berry et al., 1992, p. 65). Following up on the possibility of cultural differences on this gender difference, Berry (1976) and his colleagues conducted a study in which a block design task was given to males and females in 17 different cultures. A stimulus card depicting a geometric representation of a set of blocks was presented and the task was to manipulate an actual set of blocks to emulate the design provided. In a number of cultures, males indeed did better than females on the task; however, in other cultures, females did better than males. Berry et al. (1992) suggested that male superiority on the task were found in cultures that were tight (that is, relatively homogeneous), sedentary, and agriculturally based but that female superiority was found in cultures that were loose, nomadic, and based on hunting and gathering (recall our discussion in Chapter 1 on the cultural dimension tightness versus looseness). In these latter cultures, the roles ascribed to males and females are relatively flexible, with more members performing a variety of tasks related to the survival of the group.

Thus, some cultures foster male superiority in these types of tasks, but others foster female superiority, and still others foster no differences. Although some suggestions have been made as to the nature and causes of these various gender differences, research has yet to pinpoint exactly what factors influence which types of differences, and why.

Conformity and Obedience

One common stereotype is that females are more conforming and obedient than males. In actuality, the degree to which this difference occurs varies from culture to culture. In Berry's (1976) study described above, the researchers obtained an index of the degree to which each person conformed in the 17 cultures included in the sample. Across all cultures, clear variations emerged; as with gender differences in spatial reasoning, these variations appeared to be related to the cultural concept of tightness versus looseness. Cultures that were tighter appeared to foster greater gender differences on conformity, with females more conformist than males. Tight cultures may require a greater degree of conformity to traditional gender roles on the part of both males and females. In contrast, cultures that were looser fostered less gender differences on conformity, and in some of these cultures, males were found to be more conforming than females. Thus cross-cultural differences exist in both the degree and the direction of this difference.

Aggressiveness

Another common gender stereotype is that males are more aggressive than females. There is support for this stereotype in all cultures for which documentation exists (Block, 1983; Brislin, 1993). Males account for a disproportionate amount of violent crime in both industrialized and nonindustrialized societies. The focus in research on this topic has been adolescent males. Several researchers have searched for the biological correlates of aggression. In particular, Berry and his colleagues (1992) have questioned whether increased levels of the hormone testosterone during male adolescence may account for or contribute to increased aggression in males. Increased testosterone levels have been associated with dominance hierarchies in some nonhuman primates, but the human analog is less clear. On the basis of the evidence available, it appears that hormones may contribute in some degree to aggressiveness, but culture and the environment can certainly act to encourage or discourage its emergence (Berry et al., 1992).

A study examining physical aggression between partners shed some light on this topic. In this study (Archer, 2006), male and female participants' aggression toward their partners was examined in 52 countries. Both males and females committed acts of aggression toward their partners in developed, Westernized nations; but this did not generalize to all nations. The magnitude of the sex difference in physical aggression was related to levels of gender empowerment and individualism in each of the countries. Cultures that were more individualistic and that empowered women more had less female victimization and more male victimization. Archer argued that these findings are best explained by social role theory (Eagley, 1987), which states that sex differences in social behavior result from the division of labor between men and women with regard to homemaker or worker outside the home. These roles, it was argued, produce expectancies that lead to different patterns of behavior in men and women, and these expectancies are transmitted across generations as social norms and traditions; that is, they are a part of culture. Expectancies associated with the male role include the use of direct aggression to resolve problems; expectancies associated with female roles include communal responses to resolve problems.

Studies of sex differences in development across cultures support these ideas. Barry, Josephson, Lauer, and Marshall (1976), for instance, examined the degree to which cultures foster aggressive tendencies in the socialization of children. They found a sex difference in the average amount of teaching about aggressiveness across 150 different cultures. Inspection of their data, however, revealed that this average difference was produced by a disproportionate number of high-scoring cultures in which teaching aggression actually occurs. In fact, a large majority of societies did not show a sex difference in teaching aggression.

Some cultures are known for their aggressive tendencies. Among these is the Yanomami culture of Venezuela and Brazil (e.g., Sponsel, 1998), often referred to in anthropological circles as the "fierce people." Yet even with regard to these supposedly aggressive groups, more recent research and discussion have begun to call into question the potential bias in anthropological and comparative methods that may see only part of the culture (Sponsel, 1998).

Another study (Glick et al., 2004) also shed interesting light on this topic. In this study, 8,360 participants from 16 cultures responded to a questionnaire that assessed hostile and benevolent attitudes toward men. When people harbor both types of attitudes toward men at high degrees, they were labeled ambivalent. Ambivalent attitudes toward men were related with the degree of gender inequality in a country; that is, the more people in a country saw men as both hostile and benevolent, the greater the degree of gender inequality in the country. These findings suggested that gender inequality in a country may start with how the people view the role of men. (Women were rated more positively than men in all cultures.)

Neither biology nor sex differences in teaching aggressive acts can account for gender differences in aggression observed across cultures. Some researchers (Berry et al., 1992; Segall, Dasen, Berry, & Poortinga, 1990) suggest that male aggression may be a compensatory mechanism to offset the conflict produced by a young male's identification with a care provider and his initiation into adulthood as a male. In this model, aggressiveness is viewed as "gender marking" behavior.

Personality

In Chapter 6, we discussed how recent cross-cultural studies have documented the universal existence of a five-factor model of personality (McCrae & Costa, 1999). This theory suggests that five personality traits—neuroticism, extraversion, agreeableness, openness to experience, and conscientiousness—exist universally and can describe most human dispositions for behavior. In one study examining gender differences in personality traits around the world, Costa and colleagues (Costa, Terracciano, & McCrae, 2001) analyzed data obtained from 23,031 respondents in 26 cultures, and tested for gender differences on the five universal personality traits and their subfacets (each of the five personality traits are associated with six subfacets). Women universally reported higher scores on neuroticism, agreeableness, warmth, and openness to feelings, while men scored higher on assertiveness and openness to ideas. Interestingly, the differences between men and women were the largest in Europe and the United States, which typically promote more individualistic and egalitarian values. Also as we mentioned in Chapter 6, there are also fairly consistent cross-cultural similarities in *perceived* gender differences in traits (Lockenhoff et al., 2014); women are generally rated slightly higher on neuroticism, agreeableness, openness to experience, and conscientiousness.

Sex and Sexuality

Sex is necessary for human reproduction, and is a biological necessity for survival of the species. Yet it is associated with much psychological and cultural meaning, especially before marriage. Many cultures of the world share some degree of normative attitudes toward sex, including a taboo on incest and a condemnation of adultery (Brown, 1991). Thus, there appears to be some degree of similarity in some types of norms regarding sex around the world.

But there are cultural differences in the degree of importance placed on values concerning chastity, especially for women. Many traditional, conservative cultures of the world view chastity as a virtue among nonmarried women. Other cultures are more open and explicit about sex, approving and even encouraging multiple sexual partners before marriage. This is, in fact, one of the areas of contention between capitalistic societies found in the United States and Western Europe with those of predominantly Muslim countries in North Africa, the Middle East, and South and Southeast Asia as changing values, attitudes, and behaviors concerning sex are often attributed to the influence of countries like the United States (more in our discussion below in the section on Changing Cultures, Changing Gender Roles).

There are cultural differences in the degree of importance placed on values concerning chastity, especially for women.

Studies bear out many cultural differences in attitudes and values about sex, especially regarding premarital sex and homosexuality. A 37-country study by Buss (1989), for instance, reported that people from many non-Western countries, such as China, India, Indonesia, Iran, and Taiwan, and Palestinian Arabs valued chastity very highly in a potential mate, whereas people in Western European countries such as Sweden, Norway, Finland, the Netherlands, West Germany, and France attached little importance to prior sexual experience. Homosexuality is generally more accepted in cultures that are industrialized, capitalistic, and affluent (Inglehart, 1998). Cultures also differ in how open they are about expressing sexuality in public, for example, displaying advertising for condoms (Jones, Forrest, Goldman, Henshaw, Lincoln et al., 1985).

Widmer, Treas, and Newcomb (1998) surveyed 33,590 respondents in 24 countries on their attitudes toward premarital sex, teen sex, extramarital sex, and homosexuality. They found a widespread acceptance of premarital sex across the samples. Teen sex and extramarital sex, however, were not as accepted. Attitudes about homosexuality varied greatly across cultures. Widmer and colleagues then grouped the countries into those that had similar responses. One group was called the "Teen Permissives"; it included East and West Germany, Austria, Sweden, and Slovenia. A second group was called "Sexual Conservatives"; it included the United States, Ireland, Northern Ireland, and Poland. A third group was called "Homosexual Permissives"; it included the Netherlands, Norway, Czech Republic, Canada, and Spain. And the fourth group was called "Moderates"; it included Australia, Great Britain, Hungary, Italy, Bulgaria, Russia, New Zealand, and Israel. Japan and the Philippines did not merge with any of the groups and had their own unique attitudes toward sex.

Cultures also associated with attitudes concerning sex within marriage. Cultures with fewer resources and higher stress—especially insensitive or inconsistent parenting, physically harsh environments, or economic hardships—are associated with more insecure romantic attachments and higher fertility rates (Schmitt, Alcalay, Allensworth, Allik, Ault, & Austers, 2004). There may be an evolutionary explanation for these findings: stressful environments may cause insecure attachments, which may be linked to short-term mating strategies—to reproduce early and often. This link may be seen today; as cultures become more affluent, birth rates tend to decline.

Not surprisingly, cultural differences in attitudes related to sex are also related to cultural differences in attitudes related to sexual orientation. Many traditional cultures view homosexuality as a curse or worse. These kinds of attitudes exist in some quarters of relatively egalitarian cultures like the United States as well. In some cultures, open homosexuals may be beaten, publicly humiliated, and shamed, and even persecuted by the state. Attitudes concerning sex and sexuality are often linked with cultural values of honor and transgressions; that is, premarital sex or homosexuality can be seen as an injury to one's own or one's family's honor and as a disgrace, with sometimes deadly consequences. Interestingly, people across cultures appear to be able to categorize men in terms of their sexual orientation (as gay or straight) at better than chance rates (Rule, Ishii, Ambady, Rosen, & Hallett, 2011).

Culture affects the practice of circumcision for males and female genital mutilation (FGM) for females. The latter is a procedure that involves partial or complete removal of female genitalia or other injury to the female genital organs for nontherapeutic reasons (World Health Organization, 1997). FGM is still practiced in some African, Middle Eastern, Asian, South American, and Pacific cultures. It can be carried out in settings as wide ranging as sterile, operating rooms in hospitals to home with no anesthesia, antiseptics, antibiotics, or analgesics (Barstow, 1999). In many cultures in which FGM is practiced, it has ties with attitudes concerning virtuousness, chastity, and honor for women. It is also considered a way to promote marital fidelity, control women's sex drives, and even to enhance fertility among women (Whitehorn, Ayonrinde, & Main-gay, 2002). These kinds of attitudes were used in part to justify the enforcement of passive gender roles on women, much like the practice of foot binding in China.

The practice of FGM is associated with many complex issues. On the one hand, there appears to be no apparent health benefit to the practice, and studies have demonstrated many health problems associated with it including death, infertility, or urinary tract infection. As a result, many in affluent and more egalitarian cultures view the practice as barbaric and outdated. On the other hand, the practice is tied with honor and virtue and for many women in many cultures, not having FGM would prevent a woman from finding a husband or to live life as a social outcast. For instance, a study of Egyptian female student nurses found that approximately 60% favored circumcising their own daughters and thought it beneficial (Dandash, Refaat, & Eyada, 2001). The clash of cultures through immigration and improved communications technology brings these issues to the forefront for many in the world today.

Jealousy

In Chapter 14, we will discuss universal differences between men and women in their preferences for mates and in the process of mate poaching—attempting to steal other's mates. These differences are typically explained using an evolutionary model that suggests that males look for younger, chaste mates to bear offspring, while females look for mates that can provide resources for offspring in the long term.

One important construct related to these concepts is fidelity of a mate. When extramarital sex occurs, do people of different cultures differ in their responses? Apparently not; jealousy appears to be a universal reaction to the infidelity of one's mate. There are interesting gender differences in the sources of infidelity. Sexual infidelity occurs when a partner has sex or engages in sex-related behaviors with others. Emotional infidelity refers to the formation of an emotional bond with other people. Men appear to become jealous with sexual infidelity, that is, when they experience a loss of sexual exclusivity in their mates. Women appear to become jealous when they experience emotional infidelity, that is, a loss of emotional involvement in their mates. This pattern has been found in a wide variety of cultures (Buss, Shackelford, Kirkpatrick, Choe, Lim, & Hasegawa, 1999; Fernandez, Sierra, Zubeidat, & Vera-Villarroel, 2006). Buss and Schmitt (1993) suggest that these universal gender differences are predictable on the basis of biological sex differences and evolutionary needs. Violations of emotional involvement for women threaten the care of offspring; violations of sexual exclusivity for men threaten their ability to reproduce and produce offspring.

Division of Labor

While there are many similarities between men and women both physically and psychologically, there are differences as well. These sex differences include the fact that men are generally physically bigger and stronger than women, and women but not men carry a child, give birth, and breastfeed. These types of sex differences lead to some differences in sex roles. Men's larger size, on one hand, probably enabled them to take on the primary role of making and maintaining shelter, hunting for or producing food, and warding off enemies and rivals for food, mates, and other resources. Women, on the other hand, took on the primary role of caring for infants and newborns. Biological differences between men and women, therefore, are probably the platform by which decisions concerning a division of labor were made in our evolutionary history. One of the biggest differences between men and women worldwide concerns their division of labor in the house.

Georgas and colleagues' (Georgas, Berry, van de Vijver, Kagitcibasi, & Poortinga, 2006) study of families highlighted this issue. They assessed families in 30 countries around the world concerning a number of issues related to family functioning. One issue they assessed concerned division of labor related to household chores (housework). In all countries surveyed, there was a very large gap between the amount of work men and women did. Women took up the brunt of the housework in all societies surveyed (Figure 7.1). This was true even among societies in which women made up a large and increasing proportion of income earners. Hochschild and Machung (1989) called this housework after coming home from work the "second shift" for women. These differences were, in fact, some of the most robust and consistent findings in Georgas and colleagues' study. Thus the division of labor in the house and home appears to be quite universal. What is also apparent from the data in Figure 7.1 is that some cultures have larger differences in the division of labor between men and women than others.

In all countries surveyed, there was a very large gap between the amount of work men and women did. Women took up the brunt of the housework in all societies surveyed.

Or take another piece of data from Georgas et al.'s (2006) study. They identified three types of roles mothers and fathers played in families: expressive, focused on maintaining a pleasant environment and providing emotional support for one another; financial, including contributing to and managing finances; and childcare. In near all cultures surveyed, fathers were primarily concerned with finances first, then expressive issues next, and childcare last. The concerns of mothers, however, differed according to culture. Mothers were most concerned with childcare, but only in less affluent cultures. In more affluent cultures, mothers appeared to be equally concerned with all three family roles (Figure 7.2).

Similar findings were also reported by Wood and Eagly's (2002) review of the literature, who reported strong evidence of the universality of sex-typed division of labor. Men were primarily concerned with the provision of resources, while women

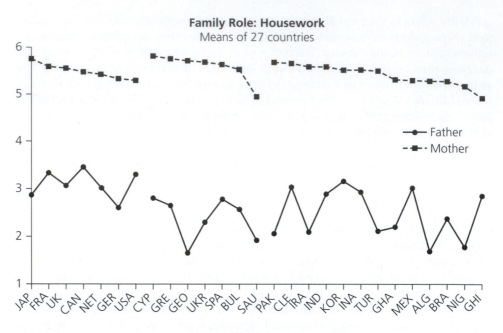

FIGURE 7.1 Findings Regarding Division of Housework between Men and Women across 27 Countries, Reported by Georgas et al. (2006)

Source: Reprinted by permission of James Georgas.

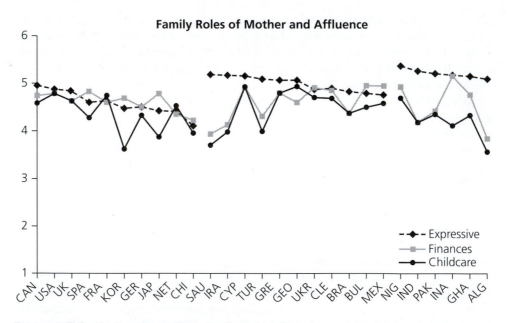

FIGURE 7.2 Findings Regarding Family Roles of Mothers across 27 Countries

The countries are listed on the bottom in three groups of affluence; the richest on the left, moderate affluence in the middle, and least affluent on the right.

Source: Figure 8.3 from Georgas, J., Berry, J. W., van de Vijver, F., Kagitcibasi, C., & Poortinga, Y. H. (2006). *Families across Cultures: A 30 Nation Psychological Study* (New York: Cambridge University Press). Reprinted with permission of Cambridge University Press.

were primarily focused on childcare. The relative difference in the division of labor between men and women, however, differed depending on whether the society was industrialized and the degree to which the society as a whole was dependent on gathering for survival. Women contributed to the provision of resources more in societies that were predominantly dependent on gathering or were more greatly industrialized. Mothers predominated in the care of infants and substantially shared in the care of young children with other family members and the community. Fathers contributed to childcare more than to infant care, but their contributions were almost universally less than those of mothers.

In Table 7.3, Wood and Eagly (2002) listed the average percentage of male participation in activities from 185 societies. As shown in the left half of table, the activities that were performed exclusively or predominantly by men included hunting large aquatic fauna, smelting ores, metalworking, lumbering, and clearing land. The far right columns in table display the activities that were performed mainly by women, and these included preparation of vegetal foods, cooking, and water fetching. "Swing activities" were activities that were performed by men in some societies, by women in others, and interchangeably by both in others. Swing activities included bodily mutilation, crop planting, harvesting, crop tending, and burden carrying. Although few activities were assigned exclusively to one sex or the other when considered across cultures, the division of labor is evident in that, within societies, most activities were performed primarily by one sex. Wood and Eagly (2002) argued that physical differences between the sexes interacted with the resources and characteristics of the environment so that different societies produced different solutions to the needs of survival. While sex differences existed in virtually all societies, the exact nature of those differences varied across societies. They called this model a **biosocial model** of sex differences.

biosocial model A model that suggests that biological differences between the sexes interact with the environment to produce culture-specific sex roles that are adaptations to the environment.

Summary

While different sex roles exist in all societies of the world, cultures differ in the specific type and degree of differentiation they encourage between the sexes. Differences in sex roles raise interesting questions about the gender stereotypes that arise because of sex role differentiation. Gender, gender roles, gender role ideologies, and gender stereotypes are culturally specific psychological constructs that differ across cultures.

How does culture influence gender? The process of learning gender roles begins very early in life. The importance of gender in organizing our expectations and thinking is illustrated in the first question that we ask when a baby is born: "Is it a boy or a girl?" In American culture, we tend to give boys and girls different types of toys to play with and dress infants according to gender (although that trend may be changing in recent years). If you look back to your baby pictures, you may find that you were often dressed in either blue or pink. About 30 years ago, one U.S. study reported that 90% of the infants observed at a shopping mall were dressed in gendered colors and/or styles (Shakin, Shakin, & Sternglanz, 1985). By the age of three, children begin to accurately label people by sex (Fagot, Leinbach, & Hagen, 1986). Gender role socialization continues throughout life from various sources—expectations from parents, modeling of gender roles by peers, and images of males and females in the social and mass media, to name a few—that contribute to our ideas on what it means to be male or female.

In terms of the definitions presented earlier, a newborn has sex but no gender. Gender is a construct that exists in society and develops in children as they are socialized in their environments. As children grow older, they learn specific behaviors and

TABLE 7.3 Average Percentage of Male Participation in Activities in Societies from the Standard Cross-Cultural Sample

Predominantly Masculine Activities	Index (%)	Quasi-Masculine Activities	Index (%)	Swing Activities	Index (%)	Quasi-Feminine Activities	Index (%)
Hunting large aquatic fauna	100	Butchering	92.3	Generation of fire	62.3	Fuel gathering	27.2
Smelting of ores	100	Collection of wild honey	91.7	Bodily mutilation	60.8	Preparation of drinks	22.2
Metalworking	99.8	Land clearance	90.5	Preparation of skins	54.6	Gathering of wild vegetal foods	19.7
Lumbering	99.4	Fishing	86.7	Gathering small land fauna	54.5	Dairy production	14.3
Hunting in large land fauna	99.3	Tending large animals	82.4	Crop planting	54.4	Spinning	13.6
Work in wood	98.8	House building	77.4	Manufacture of leather products	53.2	Laundering	13
Fowling	98.3	Soil preparation	73.1	Harvesting	45	Water fetching	8.6
Making musical instruments	97.6	Netmaking	71.2	Crop tending	44.6	Cooking	8.3
Trapping	97.5	Making rope and cordage	69.9	Milking	43.8	Preparation of vegetal food	5.7
Boatbuilding	96.6			Basketmaking	42.5		
Stoneworking	95.9			Burden carrying	39.3		
Work in bone, horn, shell	94.6			Matmaking	37.6		
Mining and quarrying	93.7			Care of small animals	35.9		
Bonesetting	92.7			Preservation of meat or fish	32.9		
				Loom weaving	32.5		
				Gathering small aquatic fauna	31.1		
				Manufacture of clothing	22.4		
				Potterymaking	21.1		

Note: Reprinted with permission. Each index represents the average percentage of male participation in each activity, as calculated by Murdock and Provost (1973) from 185 societies of the Standard Cross-Cultural Sample (Murdock and White, 1969). Each index was calculated for a given activity such that each society received a weight indicating whether the activity was exclusively male (1.0), predominantly male (0.8), equally performed by both sexes (0.5), predominantly female (0.2), or exclusively female (0). The weights were summed across societies in which the activity was performed and then divided by the number of societies. Murdock and Provost identified the four clusters of activities on the basis of this index and the variability in the index across geographic regions. The swing activities were more variable than the quasi-masculine or quasi-feminine activities, which were more variable than the strictly masculine ones.

Source: Data are from Tables 1–5 of G. P. Murdock and C. Provost, "*Factors in the Division of Labor by Sex: A Cross-Cultural Analysis,*" 1973, *Ethnology,* 12, pp. 207–210. Copyright 1973 by the University of Pittsburgh Press.

patterns of activities deemed appropriate and inappropriate for their sex, and they either adopt or reject those gender roles. Sandra Bem (1981), a prominent theorist on gender, argued that gender is one of the fundamental ways we organize information and understand experiences about the world. For instance, we learn what behaviors, attitudes, objects, and conventions are associated with being "male" and what are associated with being "female," and apply these gender schemas to understand the people around us as well as ourselves.

Ensuring that reproduction occurs fulfills men's and women's sex roles. But what happens before and after that depends on a host of variables. One of these variables is culture. The biological fact and necessity of reproduction, along with other biological and physiological differences between men and women, lead to behavioral differences between men and women. In earlier days, these behavioral differences were reinforced by a necessary division of labor. Someone had to look after children while someone else had to find food for the family; no one person could have done it all. Thus, the existence of reproductive differences led to a division of labor advantageous to the family as a unit. These differences, in turn, likely produced differences in a variety of psychological traits and characteristics such as aggressiveness, nurturance, and achievement.

Survival requires that societies balance a number of factors, including natural resources, affluence, and population density. These external factors help to frame and mold specific behaviors that may affect the division of labor between men and women originally necessitated by biological differences. These differential behaviors that occur because of differences in external, environmental factors lead to patterns of behaviors across time that are associated with men and women. This pattern of behaviors across time is culture. In turn, it feeds back reciprocally onto the pattern of behaviors, reinforcing those behaviors, beliefs, attitudes, and values. Thus, as different cultures must deal with different external factors, it is only natural that gender differences vary by culture. One culture may foster considerable equality between women and men and relatively few differences in their cultural practices and psychological characteristics. Another culture may foster considerable disparity between the sexes, their cultural practices related to reproduction, and psychological characteristics associated with sex roles. Some cultures may foster differences between the sexes in one direction (e.g., males as primary decision makers, females compliant and obedient); another culture may foster differences in the opposite direction. This type of biosocial explanatory model may account for the range of differences obtained in previous cross-cultural research on psychological constructs.

▶ Culture, Gender Roles, and Gender Stereotypes

Culture and Gender Stereotypes

Universality in sex differences in the division of labor described above suggests that gender roles and gender stereotypes may also be universal. We are all familiar with "traditional" gender stereotypes—that males should be independent, self-reliant, strong, and emotionally detached, while women should be dependent, reliant, weak, nurturant, and emotional. To what degree is this an American or Western cultural phenomenon? Several programs of research have examined this interesting question over the years, and have shown that many gender-related stereotypes are, in fact, universally held across cultures.

The best-known study of gender stereotypes across cultures was conducted by Williams and Best (1982), who sampled people in 30 countries, 52–120 respondents per country, for a total of almost 3,000 individuals. The study used a questionnaire known as the Adjective Check List (ACL), which is a list of 300 adjectives. Respondents in each country were asked to decide whether each adjective was considered more descriptive of a male or of a female. Whether the subjects agreed with the assignment of an adjective to males or females was irrelevant; instead they were asked to report the characteristics generally associated with males and females in their culture. The researchers tallied the data from all individuals. Looking at responses within each culture, Williams and Best (1982) established the criterion that if more than two-thirds of a sample from a country agreed on a particular term for either males or females, there was a consensus within that culture on that general characteristic. Then looking at responses across the cultures, the researchers decided that if two-thirds of the cultures reached a consensus on the characteristic, there was cross-cultural consensus on that characteristic as describing males or females. The results indicated a high degree of pancultural agreement across all the countries studied in the characteristics associated with men and women. Table 7.4 lists the 100 items of the pancultural adjective checklist reported by Williams and Best (1994).

The degree of consensus these adjectives received in describing males and females is amazing. Berry and colleagues (1992) suggested "this degree of consensus is so large that it may be appropriate to suggest that the researchers have found

TABLE 7.4 The 100 Items of the Pancultural Adjective Checklist

Male-Associated		Female-Associated	
Active	Loud	Affected	Modest
Adventurous	Obnoxious	Affectionate	Nervous
Aggressive	Opinionated	Appreciative	Patient
Arrogant	Opportunistic	Cautious	Pleasant
Autocratic	Pleasure-seeking	Changeable	Prudish
Bossy	Precise	Charming	Self-pitying
Capable	Progressive	Complaining	Sensitive
Conceited	Rational	Confused	Sexy
Confident	Realistic	Curious	Shy
Courageous	Reckless	Dependent	Softhearted
Cruel	Resourceful	Dreamy	Sophisticated
Cynical	Rigid	Emotional	Submissive
Determined	Robust	Excitable	Suggestible
Disorderly	Serious	Fault-finding	Superstitious
Enterprising	Sharp-witted	Fearful	Talkative
Greedy	Show-off	Fickle	Timid
Hardheaded	Steady	Foolish	Touchy
Humorous	Stern	Forgiving	Unambitious
Indifferent	Stingy	Frivolous	Understanding
Individualistic	Stolid	Fussy	Unintelligent
Initiative	Tough	Gentle	Unstable
Varied interests	Unfriendly	Imaginative	Warm
Inventive	Unscrupulous	Kind	Weak
Lazy	Witty	Mild	Worrying

Source: Lonner, Walter J., Malpass, and Roy S., *Psychology and Culture*, 1st Edition, Copyright © 1994, p. 193. Reprinted by permission of Pearson Education, Inc., Upper Saddle River, NJ

a psychological universal when it comes to gender stereotypes" (p. 60). In addition, the possibility of a universally accepted set of gender stereotypes may make sense given the universality in division of labor independently demonstrated by other studies (described above).

Williams and Best (1982) conducted a second type of analysis on their data in order to summarize their major findings. They scored the adjectives in each country in terms of favorability, strength, and activity to examine how the adjectives were distributed according to affective or emotional meaning. They found surprising congruence in these analyses: the characteristics associated with men were stronger and more active than those associated with women across all countries. On favorability, however, cultural differences emerged: Some countries (such as Japan and South Africa) rated male characteristics as more favorable than female, whereas other countries (e.g., Italy and Peru) rated female characteristics as more favorable.

How can we interpret these results? It could be that a division of labor for males and females according to reproductive processes produced differences in behaviors that, in turn, produced differences in psychological characteristics. These psychological characteristics may have had some evolutionary and adaptive advantages for males and females to fulfill their roles as prescribed by the division of labor. Men and women in most cultures may have become set in these ways, accounting for universal consensus on these descriptors. At the same time, men and women may have adopted particular mindsets about cultural differences because of perceived social inequality or social forces and indirect communication via mass media and the like. Some researchers claimed that the persistence of gender stereotypes across culture cannot be attributed to sociocultural factors and can only be explained by sociobiological models (Lueptow, Garovich, & Lueptow, 1995). Or these findings could all be a function of the way the research was conducted, using university students as participants, which would tend to make the entire sample more homogeneous than if people were sampled randomly from each culture.

Although it is difficult to disentangle these factors, it is important to note that Williams and Best also collected and analyzed data concerning gender stereotypes from young children and found a considerable degree of agreement between the findings for children and those for university students (Williams & Best, 1990). These results argued against (but did not entirely eliminate) the notion that the original findings were due to homogeneity among university students.

Williams and colleagues extended their earlier work on gender stereotypes in important ways. Williams, Satterwhite, and Best (1999), for example, took the ACL data from 25 countries in their previous work and rescored them in terms of five personality dimensions known as the big five, or five factor model of personality. As you may remember from our discussion in Chapter 6, these terms refer to the five personality traits or dimensions that are considered universal or consistent around the world. Males were perceived to have significantly higher scores than females on all traits except agreeableness; females, however, were perceived to have significantly higher scores than males on this personality dimension. They also correlated the sex differences with culture scores from two large value surveys (Hofstede, 1980; Schwartz, 1994), some demographic variables, and gender ideology scores from a previous study (Williams & Best, 1990). Differences in gender stereotypes were larger in countries that were conservative and hierarchical, with a lower level of socioeconomic development, a relatively low degree of Christian affiliation, and a relatively low proportion of women attending university. Countries that valued harmony and egalitarianism, had less traditional sex-role orientations, and viewed male stereotypes as less favorable than female stereotypes were associated with less gender stereotype differences on the five factors.

In summary, this set of studies informs us that gender stereotypes around the world are rather stable and are related to interesting and important psychological characteristics. Men are generally viewed as active, strong, critical, and adult like, with psychological needs such as dominance, autonomy, aggression, exhibition, achievement, and endurance. Men are also associated more with the personality traits of conscientiousness, extroversion, and openness. Women are generally viewed as passive, weak, nurturing, and adaptive, with psychological needs such as abasement, deference, succorance, nurturance, affiliation, and heterosexuality. They are also associated with higher scores on the personality traits of agreeableness and neuroticism. As described earlier, the degree of stability of these findings across a wide range of countries and cultures provides a strong base of evidence for some pancultural universality in psychological attribution.

Still many questions remain unanswered in this important area of psychology. How congruent are people's behaviors with their stereotypes, and does this congruence differ across cultures and countries? Are stereotypes related to important psychological constructs or behaviors that affect everyday lives? How do we come to develop such stereotypes—what are the factors that produce them, and their boundaries?

Culture, Gender Role Ideology, and Self-Concept

gender role ideology Judgments about what gender roles in a particular culture ought to be.

Another important topic that has been studied across cultures is **gender role ideology**—judgments about what males and females ought to be like or ought to do. To examine this topic, Williams and Best (1990) asked participants in 14 countries to complete the ACL (the list of adjectives they used in the previous research described above) in relation to what they believe they are and what they would like to be. Participants also completed a sex role ideology scale that generated scores between two polar opposites labeled "traditional" and "egalitarian." The traditional scores tended to describe gender roles that were consistent with the traditional or universal norms found in their earlier research; egalitarian scores reflected a tendency toward less differentiation between males and females on the various psychological characteristics. The most egalitarian scores were found in the Netherlands, Germany, and Finland; the most traditional ideologies were found in Nigeria, Pakistan, and India. Women tended to have more egalitarian views than men. Gender differences within each country were relatively small compared to cross-country differences, which were considerable. In particular, countries with relatively high socioeconomic development, a high proportion of Protestant Christians, a low proportion of Muslims, a high percentage of women employed outside the home, a high proportion of women enrolled in universities, and a greater degree of individualism were associated with more egalitarian scores. These findings make sense, as greater affluence and individualistic tendencies tend to produce a culture that allows women increased access to jobs and education, thus blending traditional gender roles.

Williams and Best (1990) also examined gender differences in self-concepts (recall our discussion of this topic in Chapter 5). The same students in the same 14 countries rated each of the 300 adjectives of the ACL according to whether it was descriptive of themselves or their ideal self. Responses were scored according to masculinity/femininity as well as in terms of favorability, strength, and activity. When scored according to masculinity/femininity both self and ideal-self ratings for men were more masculine than were the women's ratings, and vice versa, across all countries. However, both men and women in all countries rated their ideal self as more masculine than their actual self. In effect, they were saying that they wanted to have more of the traits traditionally associated with males.

Gender role ideologies have also been studied in younger populations by Gibbons and her colleagues (De Silva, Stiles, & Gibbons, 1992; Gibbons, Bradford, & Stiles, 1989; Gibbons, Stiles, Schnellman, & Morales-Hidalgo, 1990; Stiles, Gibbons, & Schnellman, 1990). These researchers conducted several cross-cultural studies involving almost 700 adolescents ranging in age from 11 to 17 years from Spain, Guatemala, and Sri Lanka. In their surveys, adolescents were asked to draw and describe characteristics of the ideal man or woman. Interestingly, the most important quality in these countries for both boys and girls was being "kind and honest," a characteristic that was not gender-specific. Some gender differences emerged, however, with being good-looking more often mentioned as an ideal for women and being employed in a job as more of an ideal for men.

Gibbons conducted another study on adolescents' attitudes toward gender roles that involved 265 international students, ages 11 to 17, who attended school in the Netherlands. Students completed an Attitude Towards Women Scale for Adolescents (Galambos, Petersen, Richards, & Gitelson, 1985) that included 12 statements such as "Boys are better than girls" and "Girls should have the same freedom as boys." The adolescents were asked to report their level of agreement with these statements. Girls were less traditional than boys, and adolescents from wealthier and more individualistic countries were less traditional than adolescents from poorer and more collectivist countries (Gibbons, Stiles, & Shkodriani, 1991).

Gibbons's study of Sri Lankan adolescents (De Silva et al., 1992) indicated that gender role ideologies may be changing as societies undergo change. She found that more than half the girls in her study depicted the ideal woman as being employed outside the home even though the traditional role of a Sri Lankan woman was that of a homemaker. Mule and Barthel (1992) described social change in Egypt, where there was an increase in women's participation in the workforce and, to some extent, political life. Furthermore, globalization and exposure to Western culture have presented this traditionally Islamic country with alternative gender ideologies. Subsequently, gender role ideologies may undergo modification or redefinition in these countries as Eastern and Western influences continue to combine.

Maintaining, not modifying, traditional gender roles in the face of modernization is also likely. For instance, a study of Palestinian women and their families found that one's level of education, participation in political activities, and employment were *not* major factors predicting more egalitarian family roles (Huntington, Fronk, & Chadwick, 2001). The authors were surprised by this finding and argued that cultural values defined by Islamic beliefs and practices are resisting the forces of modernity. In other words, Islamic teachings on women, the family, and relationships between men and women may be a powerful influence in maintaining traditional family functioning, and especially traditional ideas of women's roles in family and society. These findings highlighted the important role of religion in understanding how gender role ideologies are defined and preserved in different cultures.

Ethnicity and Gender Roles

Research within cultures also points to important differences in gender roles, especially among different ethnic groups. Some research, for instance, has suggested that the gender identities of African Americans are more androgynous than those of European Americans. **Androgyny** refers to a gender identity that involves endorsement of both male and female characteristics. Harris (1996), for example, administered the Bem Sex Role Inventory, a scale that is widely used to measure gender identity, to African and European American males and females, and found that both African

androgyny A gender identity that involves endorsement of both male and female characteristics.

American males and females were more androgynous than European American males and females. In addition, he found that African American males and females have an equal propensity to endorse typically masculine traits, whereas European American males regard more masculine traits as self-descriptive than European American females do. Other studies conducted in the United States (Frome & Eccles, 1996), Israel (Orr & Ben-Eliahu, 1993), and Hong Kong (Lau, 1989) have found that adolescent girls who adopt an androgynous identity have higher levels of self-acceptance than either feminine or masculine girls. For boys, however, a masculine, not androgynous, identity is associated with the highest level of self-acceptance.

Many Asian American families have carried on traditional gender roles associated with males and females from their original culture. Asian females are often expected to bear the brunt of domestic duties, to raise children, and to be "good" daughters-in-law. Asian American males are often raised to remain aloof, unemotional, and authoritative, especially concerning familial issues (D. Sue, 1998). Some studies, however, have suggested a loosening of these rigid, traditional gender roles for Asian American males and females. Although Asian American males may still appear as the figurative head of the family in public, in reality, much decision making power within the family in private is held by the Asian American female head of the household (Huang & Ying, 1989).

machismo A concept related to Mexican American gender role differentiation that is characterized by many traditional expectations of the male gender role, such as being unemotional, strong, authoritative, and aggressive.

The traditional role of the Mexican American female was to provide for the children and take care of the home (Comas-Diaz, 1992). Likewise, Mexican American males were traditionally expected to fill the role of provider for the family. These differences are related to the concept of **machismo**, which incorporates many traditional expectations of the male gender role, such as being unemotional, strong, authoritative, and aggressive. However, research has shown that these gender differences for Mexican American males and females are also on the decrease. Mexican American women are increasingly sharing in decision making in the family, as well as taking on a more direct role as provider through work outside the home (Espin, 1993). Although adolescent Mexican American males are generally still given more freedom outside the home than are females, gender differences may be decreasing in the contemporary Mexican American family. This is likely to continue as increasing numbers of Latina women are employed and an emerging Latina feminist movement takes hold (Espin, 1997). It is important to note, however, that this movement continues to place high value on the traditional role of wife and mother, yet offers a wider interpretation of roles acceptable for Latinas.

Gender role differentiation for Native Americans seems to depend heavily on the patriarchal or matriarchal nature of the tribal culture of origin. In patriarchal tribes, women assume primary responsibility for the welfare of the children and extended family members. But males of the Mescalero Apache tribe often take responsibility for children when they are with their families (Glover, 2001). As with other ethnic groups, the passage of time, increased interaction with people of other cultures and with mainstream American culture, and the movement toward urban living seems to have effected changes in these traditional values and expectations for Native American males and females.

▶ Changing Cultures, Changing Gender Roles

The 191 members of the United Nations have committed to creating sustainable human development and to recognizing equal rights and opportunities for men and women that are critical for social and economic progress. Tragically, one of the obstacles to this progress concerns violence against women, which is a concrete manifestation of inequality between males and females. A few years ago, the World Health Organization (WHO) reported the results of a study involving over 24,000 interviews with women from 15 sites in 10 countries (Garcia-Moreno, Heise, Jansen, Ellsberg, & Watts, 2005). In 13 of the 15 sites, between 35% and 76% of the women had reported being physically or sexually assaulted by someone else since the age of 15. In all settings but one, the majority of the violence was perpetrated by a current or previous partner, not a stranger. Overall, 15% to 71% of the women who ever had a partner had been physically or sexually assaulted. In most settings, almost half of the respondents reported that the violence was currently ongoing (see Figure 7.3). There was substantial variation both within and between countries, and findings indicated that women in industrialized countries may find it easier to leave abusive relationships.

These kinds of findings make it strikingly clear that despite desires for equality, inequality still persists quite strongly around the world, and with often negative consequences. This, coupled with the fact that cultures are always in flux, and that cultures clash because of increased contact of peoples of different worldviews, brings many of the issues discussed in this chapter to the forefront of numerous people's lives. In many cases, they represent an interesting and complex interplay between culture, psychology,

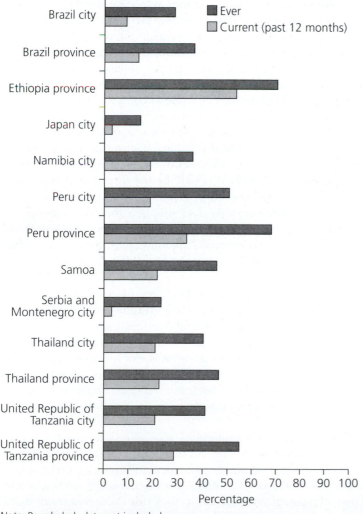

FIGURE 7.3

Percentage of Ever-Partnered Women Reporting Physical or Sexual Violence, or Both, by an Intimate Partner, by Site

Source: Garcia-Moreno, C., Heise, L., Jansen, H. A. F. M., Ellsberg, M., & Watts, C. (2005). Violence against women. *Science*, 310, 1282–1283.

Note: Bangladesh data not included.

and law (Shweder, Minow, & Markus, 2002). In Europe, for instance, debates occur concerning hymenoplasty, a surgical procedure that replaces a woman's hymen. Because the hymen usually breaks in the first act of intercourse, its restoration allows women who have had sex to appear as if they are virgins. This is particularly important for some women in some cultures, such as traditional Muslim culture, which values virginity in marriage partners. Many young Muslim women (as are many women around the world) are caught between the freedoms that American or European societies and cultures offer and the deep-rooted traditions of their families for generations, and many seek certificates of virginity to provide proof to family and prospective marriage partners.

In many cultures, the preference for one sex over the other is also very apparent and strong. In many Muslim and Asian cultures, for example, boys are prized and girls are not. Thus the differential treatment of boys and girls happens immediately at birth. In Afghanistan, some families even go as far as to dress up their girls to masquerade as boys and send them off to school. The reasons for this include economic need, social pressure to have sons, and in some cases a superstition that doing so can lead to the birth of a real boy. This also occurs because of the pervading thought in some cultures that girls should not receive an education, only boys.

These aspects of clashing cultures exist in the United States as well. For instance, among the most pressing issues and concerns facing the United States today are gender differences across different ethnicities and the continuing struggle for gender equity across all cultural and ethnic groups. Just as people in different cultures in faraway lands may have different gender roles and expectations, people of different ethnic backgrounds in the United States can have different gender role expectations as well. Many of these gender differences across ethnic lines are rooted in the cultures people of these ethnicities brought with them when they came to the United States. Gender differences in the United States today, along with this melting pot effect, produce a uniquely "American" influence and reflect gender issues in a uniquely American way.

How is one to deal with the social isolation, physical beating, and even murder of young women that would be justified in another culture because of perceived dishonor brought about by premarital sex? What should be the response of communities and societies toward female genital mutilation, especially when condoned by the operators and recipients? How can democracies deal with acts that they condemn in their laws while at the same time being open and embracing of cultural differences? These are tough questions that all of us have to face in today's pluralistic world. While finding answers is difficult, at the very least we should be able to have meaningful, objective discussions of these issues.

Clearly, as we have mentioned throughout this book, culture is not a static entity; it is dynamic and ever changing. Cultural changes are brought about by many factors, especially economic. Witness the great cultural changes that are occurring in many countries of the world since the end of World War II. Japan, for instance, was decimated at the end of that war; yet, today it stands as one of the world's economic powers. Such changes bring with them a major shift in the culture of the society, and we are witness to such shifts in Japan today (Matsumoto, 2002a). Similar changes are occurring or have occurred in many other cultures as well, including South Korea, China, or Singapore.

Much of the cultural changes that are brought by economics give rise to tensions between tradition and progress, conservatism and liberalism. Images capture these tensions: watching young women in Japan dressed in traditional Japanese *kimono* as they observe a centuries-old tradition of coming-of-age (*seijin-shiki*), as they talk on their cell phones and instant message with friends, as they ride the fastest trains in the world, produce a stark contrast between tradition and progress. Similarly, young adults in the Middle East may, on one hand, condemn the United States yet, on the other, be willing to obtain a visa and immigrate to the United States.

Changing and clashing cultures bring about many confrontations between gender differences across culture. Changing culture around the world, for example, that is associated with increased economic power, affluence, and individualism is associated with changing gender roles. More women work outside the home, are more economically independent, and have a greater say at home and at work. Yet there are social consequences of such cultural changes; in such cultures, divorce rates increase (Matsumoto, 2002a; Yodanis, 2005); the amount and type of health-related problems for women increase, such as rising incidence of cardiovascular problems, alcoholism, and rates of smoking (Allamani, Voller, Kubicka, & Bloomfield, 2000). Changes in culture, therefore, have both positive and negative consequences, and full consideration should be given before weighing in on the pros and cons of such changes.

CONCLUSION

Sex refers to the biological and physiological differences between males and females. *Sex roles* are behaviors expected of males and females in relation to their biological differences and reproduction. *Gender* refers to the psychological and behavioral traits and characteristics cultures carve out using sex differences as a base. *Gender roles* refer to the degree to which a person adopts the gender-specific behaviors ascribed by his or her culture. Gender and its permutations—roles, identities, stereotypes, and the like—share an important link with culture.

Gender roles are different for males and females in all cultures. Some stereotypic notions about gender differences seem to be universal across cultures such as aggressiveness, strength, and lack of emotionality for males and weakness, submissiveness, and emotionality for females. Other research, however, has shown that the degree, and in some case the direction, of these differences varies across cultures. That is, not every culture will necessarily harbor the same gender differences in the same way as other cultures. Further research is needed to gain a better understanding of culture-constant and culture-specific aspects of gender differences.

Examining gender differences in the United States is especially challenging because of the cultural and ethnic diversity within this single country and the influence of interactions with mainstream American culture. Each ethnic group has its own cultural preferences for gender differentiation, but some blending of the old with the new, the traditional with the modern, appears to be taking place. Without evidence to the contrary, it is probably best to consider this blending as an addition of cultural repertoires concerning gender differences rather than a subtraction from the old ways.

As we meet people from different cultural backgrounds, we may encounter gender roles that are different from our own. Often we feel strongly and negatively about these differences. But despite our own personal outlook, we must exercise considerable care and caution in imposing our preferences on others. In most cases, people of other cultures feel just as strongly about their own way of living. Many people of many other cultures, men and women, still harbor many of the traditional values of their ancestral culture, and conflicts arise because some—men and women alike—look down on these traditional ways, criticize them, and attempt to force change. Many women in many cultures want to marry early, stay home, and take care of the family; many men want to adopt the traditional male roles as well. These tendencies are alive in many different people within the most egalitarian cultures and societies. Respecting these differences is different from attempting to change them because they are not consonant with our own individual or cultural preferences. Nonetheless, this is a delicate balancing act for all of us because there is a fine line between cultural relativity (a desired state of comprehension) and the unacceptable justification of oppression.

Future research will need to tackle the important questions posed by our understanding of cultural and gender differences, elucidating on the mechanisms and factors that help produce and maintain those differences in individual cultures, and then across cultures. In addition, future research will need to explore the relationship between differences in actual behaviors and psychological constructs and gender-related stereotypes, investigating whether these are two different psychological systems of the mind or whether they are linked in ways that are not yet apparent. Research to date is rather silent on the mechanisms that produce gender and cultural differences, and the interrelationship among different psychological processes. The important point to remember is that different cultures may arrive at different outcomes through the same process. Men and women will have gender specific roles in any society or culture. All cultures encourage particular behavioral differences between the genders and help to define the roles, duties, and responsibilities deemed appropriate for males and females.

EXPLORATION AND DISCOVERY

Why Does This Matter to Me?

1. Have you encountered a gender role or behavior that was culturally different than yours? How did you feel? What did you think? What were the origins of that gender role?

2. Do you think gender roles are produced by gender stereotypes, or vice versa?

3. How do some of the findings from the studies reviewed in this chapter relate to your preconceived notions about gender roles?

4. How do you perceive your national culture with respect to Hofstede's masculinity versus femininity dimension?

5. As a parent, what kind of gender role and identity would you want your children to adopt? Why?

Suggestions for Further Exploration

1. Consider a hypothetical research study that you might like to conduct that would investigate gender differences of a particular behavior or psychological phenomenon. How would you conduct the study cross-culturally?

2. What do you think are the origins of some of the universal aspects of gender differences described in the chapter? How would you study them?

3. Consider the ways women have been portrayed in recent television shows and movies that you have watched. Do you think that portrayals of women and men are changing in the media or not? Design a study that would test your ideas.

InfoTrac College Edition

Use InfoTrac College Edition to search for additional readings on topics of interest to you. For more information on topics in this chapter, use the following as search terms:

culture and sex roles
culture and gender identity
ethnicity and gender

Culture and Cognition

8

CHAPTER CONTENTS

Just as atoms and molecules serve as the building blocks of matter, some psychological processes serve as the building blocks of other psychological constructs. In this chapter, we examine the nature of those psychological building blocks under the name of *cognition*.

The term **cognition** denotes all the mental processes we use to transform sensory input into knowledge. Some of the first cognitive processes to consider are **attention**, **sensation**, and **perception**. Attention refers to the focusing of our limited capacities of consciousness on a particular set of stimuli, more of whose features are noted and processed in more depth than is true of nonfocal stimuli. Sensation refers to the feelings that result from excitation of the sensory receptors (touch, taste, smell, sight, hearing). Perception refers to our initial interpretations of the sensations.

Once stimuli are perceived, individuals engage in higher-order mental processes such as thinking and reasoning, language, memory, problem solving, and decision making. Cross-cultural research on these basic cognitive processes highlights important cultural similarities and differences in each of these ways people think. There appears to be universality in cognitive processes such as hindsight bias and regrets over inaction as opposed to action. At the same time, there are interesting cultural differences in perception and attention, categorization, some memory tasks, math performance, problem solving, and factors that enhance creativity. The universal aspects of cognition point to important ways in which people are similar the world over. The differences, however, are also fascinating. Where do these differences come from? What is the *source* of these observed differences between countries?

In the first part of this chapter, we review cross-cultural research across a broad spectrum of basic cognitive processes as outlined in Figure 8.1. We begin with attention, as it is important to understand possible cultural differences in what we attend to in the first place. We then discuss culture and perception, discussing research that has examined cultural similarities and differences in how we perceive stimuli. We then move to culture and thinking processes such as categorization, memory, math, problem solving, creativity, and counterfactual thinking. We will also introduce an important concept known as dialectical thinking. In the second part of this chapter, we continue our broad overview of culture and cognition by discussing the important

cognition A term denoting all mental processes we use to transform sensory input into knowledge.

attention The focusing of our limited capacities of consciousness on a particular set of stimuli, more of whose features are noted and processed in more depth than is true of nonfocal stimuli.

sensation The feelings that result from excitation of the sensory receptors such as touch, taste, smell, sight, or hearing.

perception The process of gathering information about the world through our senses; our initial interpretations of sensations.

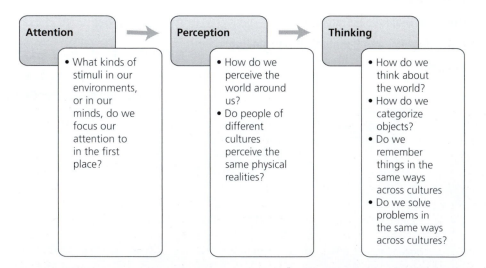

FIGURE 8.1 An Outline of Basic Cognitive Processes and the Issues Raised in Each

topics of consciousness and intelligence and what recent cross-cultural research has to say about these topics. But first we discuss the relationship between culture and cognition.

▶ Culture as Cognition

It's interesting to note that many psychologists view culture itself as cognition. That is, culture is generally viewed as a set of mental representations about the world. Hofstede (1980) called culture "mental programming." He likened culture to computer software; just as different software exists to do different things with the same hardware (computer equipment), different cultural "programs" exist that enable individuals to engage in different behaviors, even given the same hardware (physical anatomy).

The view of culture as cognition has a long history in psychology. Many previous definitions of culture, for instance, defined culture as the norms, opinions, beliefs, values, and worldviews shared by a group of individuals and transmitted across generations (Berry, Poortinga, Segall, & Dasen, 1992; recall also our review and discussion in Chapter 1). Norms, opinions, beliefs, values, and worldviews are all cognitive products and as such, one can view the contents of culture as being essentially cognitive.

More contemporary definitions of culture, like that adopted in this book, are also cognitive. In Chapter 1, we defined human culture as *a unique meaning and information system, shared by a group and transmitted across generations, that allows the group to meet basic needs of survival, pursue happiness and well-being, and derive meaning from life.* This definition of culture also views culture as a knowledge system—one from which individuals create and derive knowledge about how to live. This knowledge system is shared, imperfectly, by a group of individuals, and this knowledge is manifested in concrete objects, behaviors, and other physical elements of culture. This knowledge system—culture—was created by groups to solve complex problems of living and social life, enabling them to survive more functionally and effectively.

This view of culture is cognitive because humans have certain mental skills that other animals do not, and these skills allow humans to have the kinds of cultures that we do. As we discussed in Chapter 1, humans reap the fruits of major cognitive advances that allow the creation of human cultures. These cognitive advances include the evolution of language and the ability to know that others can make judgments about oneself as an intentional agent—that is, as a person who has motives, desires, and intentions, and the ability to share intentions with each other. These skills do not exist in other animals (or at least not to the same degree), and they allow for human cultures to be created in the first place. Thus human cultures have a very strong cognitive component. They are knowledge representations that include specific meanings and information, translated into norms, opinions, attitudes, values, and beliefs. These in turn are manifest in overt behaviors and the physical elements of culture.

Many psychologists also believe that culture is represented in the human mind, that people's mental models of culture influence their ways of thinking, feeling, and behaving, and that those mental models can be accessed. This way of thinking about culture underlies frameworks like that of cultural self-construals, which we discussed in Chapter 5. This way of thinking also underlies research that involves a technique known as **priming**, which is a method used to determine if one stimulus affects another. Many studies, for example, have primed individuals on individualism or collectivism and have found that different mental primes produce different kinds of behaviors (Oyserman & Lee, 2008). These kinds of studies are often used as

priming A method used to determine if one stimulus affects another.

"proof" of the impact of culture on psychological processes (recall our discussion of experiments that primed culture in Chapter 2).

But while the view that culture is cognition is pervasive and influential in psychology, one must pause to consider how much of this view is rooted in the biases of psychologists to view everything as existing in between people's ears. Other scholars, especially in disciplines such as sociology and anthropology, would not agree that culture is cognition and can be located in the human mind. It is possible that culture itself is comprised of collective rules, norms, and institutions that are larger than any one individual, and that individuals have mental representations of culture, but those representations are not culture itself. Thus, it is important to examine one's own biases in approaching an understanding of culture and cognition.

▶ Culture and Attention

Attention is an important topic to consider first because it helps us understand what kind of stimuli in our environment we pay attention to. Recent research has demonstrated how culture may influence attention. Much of this research comes from studies by Masuda and colleagues. In one of their first studies, Masuda and Nisbett (2001) asked American and Japanese university students to view an animated version of the scene in Figure 8.2 twice for 20 seconds each. Immediately after viewing the scene, they were asked to recall as many objects in the scene as possible. The researchers categorized the responses into whether the object recalled was a focal, main object of the picture, or a background object. There were no differences between the Americans and Japanese in recalling the focal, main objects of the scene; the Japanese, however, remembered more of the background objects.

In a second task, Masuda and Nisbett (2001) then showed respondents new stimuli and asked them if they had seen them before in the original fish scene. The new stimuli were created so that some objects were in the original and some were not. The researchers also varied the background so that some stimuli included the old

FIGURE 8.2 Shot of Animated Swimming Fish Scene

Source: Reprinted from Masuda and Nisbett (2001), with permission.

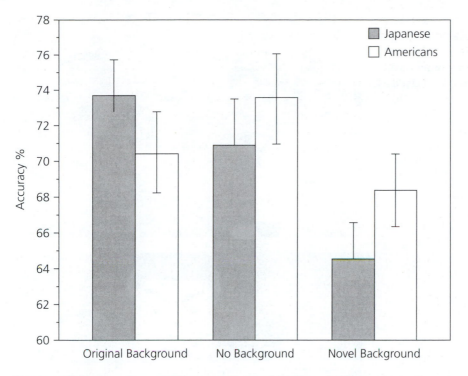

FIGURE 8.3 American and Japanese Recognition Rate Differences as a Function of Background

Source: From "Attending holistically versus analytically: Comparing the context sensitivity of Japanese and Americans," *Journal of Personality and Social Psychology,* 81, pp. 922–934, 2001, Copyright © American Psychological Association. Reprinted with permission.

background, some the new, and some no background at all. The Japanese were much more influenced by the changes in the background; when the Japanese saw new or no backgrounds, their rates of recognition were significantly worse than when they saw the original backgrounds. Background did not affect the Americans (Figure 8.3).

In a later study, Masuda and colleagues (Masuda, Ellsworth, Mesquita, Leu, Tanida, & Van de Veerdonk, 2008) showed American and Japanese observers pictures of groups of individuals in which a focal individual was expressing an emotion that was either congruent or incongruent with the rest of the group (Figure 8.4). The observers judged what emotion the focal individual was expressing. Americans often reported the emotion that the focal individual was expressing while the Japanese more often reported the emotion that the group was expressing, even if it was incongruent with the emotion expressed by the focal individual. Masuda and colleagues argued again that the Japanese were susceptible to the group's expressions because they paid more attention to them, while the Americans paid less attention to the group and focused more on the individual.

Nisbett and colleagues have suggested that these differences may have occurred because of differences in environment: Japanese environments may be more ambiguous and contain more elements than American scenes. To examine whether differences in this characteristic of the environments may have played a part in the perceptual differences observed above, Miyamoto, Nisbett, and Masuda (2006) showed Americans pictures from a Japanese environment, and showed Japanese individuals pictures from an American environment. After being shown these scenes,

FIGURE 8.4

An Example of the Cartoon Images Used in Studies 1 and 2. A Caucasian Figure (top panel) or an Asian Figure (bottom panel) Was Used as the Central Figure

Source: Masuda, T., Ellsworth, P. C., Mesquita, B., Leu, J., Tanida, S., & Van de Veerdonk, E. (2008). Placing the face in context: Cultural differences in the perception of facial emotion. *Journal of Personality and Social Psychology*, 94(3), 365–381.

respondents were shown pairs of culturally neutral scenes in which they had to note the differences between them. Both Americans and Japanese detected a larger number of contextual changes in the scenes after they saw pictures from a Japanese environment, suggesting that the environment facilitated the cultural differences in perception and attention.

This line of research has led to the interesting idea that people of different cultures differ on whether they facilitate **holistic** versus **analytic perception** (Nisbett & Miyamoto, 2005). On one hand, people in Western cultures may tend to engage in context-independent and analytic perceptual processes by focusing on a salient object (or person) independently from the context in which it is embedded. On the other hand, people in East Asian cultures may tend to engage in context-dependent and holistic perceptual processes by attending to the relationship between the object and the context in which the object is located.

The holistic versus analytic difference in cognition has become an important distinction, one that we will return to again later in this chapter. Current research is examining the boundaries of this framework. Hsiao and Cottrell (2009) examined whether holistic processing can also be observed in expert-level processing of Chinese characters, which share many properties with faces. Non-Chinese readers (novices) perceived these characters more holistically than Chinese readers (experts).

holistic perception
Context dependent perceptual processes that focus on the relationships between objects and their contexts.

analytic perception
Context-independent perceptual processes that focuses on a salient object independently from the context in which it is embedded.

Chinese readers had a better awareness of the components of characters, which were not clearly separable to novices. This finding suggested that holistic processing is not a marker of general visual expertise; rather, it depends on the features of the stimuli and the tasks typically performed on them. East Asians also tend to produce more information rich cultural products (e.g., academic conference posters, web pages) and are faster in dealing with the information than do North Americans, supposedly highlighting differences between holistic and analytic processing tendencies (Wang, Masuda, Ito, & Rashid, 2012).

▶ Culture and Perception

Perception and Physical Reality

Once stimuli are attended to, they are perceived. It's important to realize first that, regardless of culture, our perceptions of the world do not necessarily match the physical realities of the world, or of our senses. For instance, all humans have a **blind spot** in each eye—a spot with no sensory receptors, where the optic nerve goes through the layer of receptor cells on its way back toward the brain. But if you close one eye, you probably won't experience a hole in the world. There is no blind spot in our conscious perception, even though we have no receptors receiving light from one area of the eye. With the help of microeye movements called **microsaccades**, our brains fill it in so it looks as if we see everything. It is only when something comes at us out of this spot that we get some idea that something is wrong with our vision in this particular location.

Or fill three bowls with water—one with hot water, one with ice water, and one with lukewarm water. If you put your hand in the hot water for a few seconds and then in the lukewarm water, the lukewarm water will feel cold. If you wait a few minutes, then put your hand in the ice water and then the lukewarm water, the lukewarm water will feel warm. The lukewarm water will not have changed its temperature; rather, it is our perception of the water that has changed (compare Segall, 1979).

Once we begin to question our own senses, we want to know their limits. Do our experiences and beliefs about the world influence what we perceive? Do other people perceive things the same as we do? If others do not see things as we do, what aspects of their experiences and backgrounds might explain those differences? How does culture influence this process? These questions were addressed initially by research on the cultural influences on perception.

blind spot A spot in our visual field where the optic nerve goes through the layer of receptor cells on its way back toward the brain, creating a lack of sensory receptors in the eye at that location.

microsaccades Micro eye movements that help our brains fill in scenes so it looks as if we see everything.

Cultural Influences on Visual Perception

Optical Illusions

Much of what we know about cultural influences on perception comes from cross-cultural research on visual perception. Much of this work began with studies on optical illusions by Segall, Campbell, and Hersokovits (1963, 1966). **Optical illusions** are perceptions that involve an apparent discrepancy between how an object looks and what it actually is. They are often based on inappropriate assumptions about the stimulus characteristics of the object being perceived.

One of the best-known optical illusions is the Mueller-Lyer illusion (see Figure 8.5). Individuals viewing these two figures typically judge the line with the arrowheads pointing in as longer than the other line—even though the lines are actually the same length. Another well-known illusion is the horizontal-vertical illusion

optical illusions Perceptions that involve an apparent discrepancy between how an object looks and what it actually is.

FIGURE 8.5
The Mueller–Lyer Illusion

Which line is longer? To most people, the top line appears longer than the bottom line. The lines are actually identical in length.

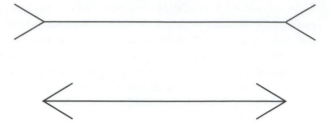

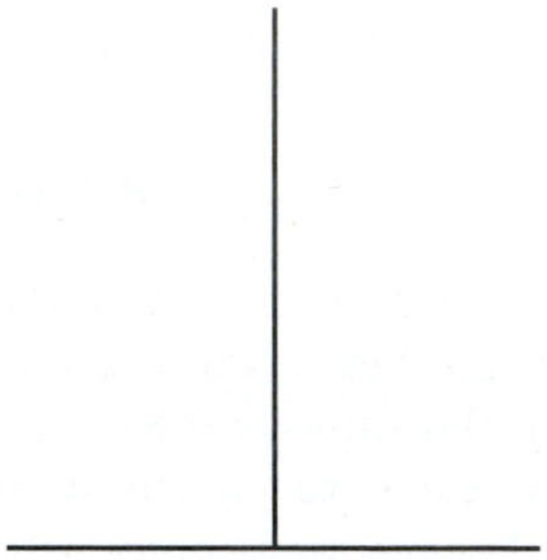

FIGURE 8.6
The Horizontal–Vertical Illusion

Which line is longer? To most people, the vertical line appears longer than the horizontal line, although both lines are the same length.

FIGURE 8.7
The Ponzo Illusion

Which horizontal line is longer? To most people, the upper line appears longer, although both lines are the same length.

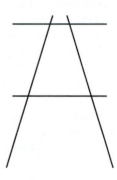

carpentered world theory A theory of perception that suggests that people (at least most Americans) are used to seeing things that are rectangular in shape, and thus unconsciously expect things to have square corners.

front-horizontal foreshortening theory A theory of perception that suggests that we interpret vertical lines as horizontal lines extending into the distance. Because we interpret the vertical line in the horizontal–vertical illusion as extending away from us, we see it as longer.

(see Figure 8.6). When participants are asked to judge which line is longer, they typically respond that the vertical line is longer—when, again, they are the same length. A third well-known example is the Ponzo illusion (see Figure 8.7). When participants view this image, they typically report that the horizontal line closer to the origin of the diagonals is longer than the one away from the origin. Of course, they are the same length.

Several important theories have been developed to explain why optical illusions occur. One of these is the **carpentered world theory**, which suggests that people in urbanized, industrialized societies are used to seeing things that are rectangular in shape and unconsciously come to expect things to have squared corners (because much of their world is carpentered, such as houses, buildings, etc.). If we see a house from an angle and the light reflected off it does not form a right angle on the eye, we still perceive it as a house with square corners. In the Mueller–Lyer illusion, we tend to see the figures as having square corners that project toward or away from us. We know that things that look the same size to our eyes but are at different distances are actually different in size.

The **front-horizontal foreshortening theory** suggests that we interpret vertical lines as horizontal lines extending into the distance. In the horizontal–vertical illusion, we interpret the vertical line as extending away from us, and we know that a line of set length that is farther away from us must be longer.

These two theories share some common characteristics. Both assume that the way we see the world is developed over time through our experiences. What we see is a combination of the way the object reflects light to our eyes and our learning about how to see things in general. Although learning helps us see well most of the time, it is the very thing that causes us to misjudge optical illusions. The second idea these theories share is that we live in a three-dimensional world that is projected onto our eyes in two dimensions. Our eyes are nearly flat, and light striking the eye in two places right next to each other may be coming from very different distances. Thus, we need to interpret distance and depth from cues other than where the light falls on the eye.

A number of cross-cultural studies challenge our traditional notions about optical illusions, as would be expected if experience contributes to our perceptions. As early as 1905, W. H. R. Rivers compared the responses to the Mueller–Lyer and horizontal–vertical illusions using groups in England, rural India, and New Guinea. He found that the English saw the lines in the Mueller–Lyer illusion as being more different in length than did the two other groups. He also reported that the Indians and New Guineans were more fooled by the horizontal–vertical illusion than were the English. These results surprised Rivers and many others from Europe and the United States. They believed that the people of India and New Guinea were more primitive and would therefore be more readily fooled by the illusions than the more educated and "civilized" people of England. The results showed that the effect of the illusion differed by culture, but that something other than education was involved. The researchers concluded that culture must have some effect on the way the world is "seen." How this difference in perception comes about has been a source of curiosity ever since.

Both the carpentered world theory and the front-horizontal foreshortening theory can explain Rivers's results. Whereas the English people in Rivers's study were used to seeing rectangular shapes, people in India and New Guinea were more accustomed to rounded and irregular environments. In the Mueller–Lyer illusion, therefore, English people would tend to see the figures as squared corners projecting toward or away from them, but Indians and New Guineans would have less tendency to make the same perceptual mistake. The front-horizontal foreshortening theory can also account for the cultural differences obtained in Rivers's study. With fewer buildings to block long-distance vistas in India or New Guinea, the Indians and New Guineans had learned to rely more on depth cues than did the English. As a result, they were more likely to see the horizontal–vertical figure as three-dimensional and therefore to misjudge the line lengths.

A third theory has been offered to explain cultural differences in visual perception. The **symbolizing three dimensions in two** theory suggests that people in Western cultures focus more on representations on paper than do people in other cultures and spend more time learning to interpret pictures. Thus, people in New Guinea and India are less likely to be fooled by the Mueller–Lyer illusion because it is more "foreign" to them. They are more fooled by the horizontal–vertical illusion, however, because it is more representative of their lifestyle (although in this example it is unclear whether the differentiation between the cultures is Western versus non-Western or industrialized versus nonindustrialized).

To ensure that Rivers's findings held for cultures in general, Segall and colleagues (1963, 1966) compared people from three industrialized groups to people from 14 nonindustrialized groups on the Mueller–Lyer and the horizontal–vertical illusions.

symbolizing three dimensions in two
A theory of perception that suggests that people in Western cultures focus more on representations on paper than do people in other cultures, and in particular spend more time learning to interpret pictures.

The Mueller–Lyer illusion was stronger for the industrialized groups, whereas the effect of the vertical–horizontal illusion was stronger for the nonindustrialized groups. Rivers's findings were supported.

Segall and colleagues (1963, 1966), however, reported some evidence that did not fit with any of the three theories—namely, that the effects of the illusions declined and nearly disappeared with older participants. Based on the theories, we might expect the effects of the illusions to increase with age because older people have had more time to learn about their environments than younger people.

Wagner (1977) used different versions of the Ponzo illusion and compared the performance of people in both rural and urban environments, some of whom had continued their education and some of whom had not. One version of the Ponzo illusion looked like Figure 8.7; another showed the same configuration of lines embedded in a complete picture. Wagner found that with the simple line drawing, the effect of the illusion declined with age for all groups. With the illusion embedded in a picture, however, he found that the effect of the illusion increased with age, but only for urban people and people who continued their schooling. This study provided more direct evidence of the effects of urban environments and schooling on the Ponzo illusion.

There is also a physical theory that must be considered. Pollack and Silvar (1967) showed that the effects of the Mueller–Lyer illusion are related to the ability to detect contours, and this ability declines with age. They also noted that as people age and are more exposed to sunlight, less light enters the eye, and this may affect people's ability to perceive the lines in the illusion. In addition, they showed that retinal pigmentation is related to contour-detecting ability. Non-European people have more retinal pigmentation, and so are less able to detect contours. Thus, Pollack and Silvar (1967) suggested that the cultural differences could be explained by racial differences in retinal pigmentation (but recall our discussion of the difficulties of defining race in Chapter 1).

To test whether the racial or the environmental learning theory was more correct, Stewart (1973) noted that both race and environment need to be compared without being mixed together, as was done in the study by Segall and his colleagues. Stewart first tested the effects of the Mueller–Lyer illusion on black and white children living in one American town (Evanston, Illinois). There were no differences between the two racial groups. She then compared groups of elementary school children in Zambia in environments that ranged from very urban and carpentered to very rural and uncarpentered, and indicated that the effects of the illusion depended on the degree to which the children lived in a carpentered environment. She also reported that the effect declined with age, suggesting that both learning and physiology played roles in the observed cultural differences.

Hudson (1960) conducted an interesting study that highlighted cultural differences in perception. He had an artist draw pictures, similar to those in the Thematic Apperception Test (TAT), that psychologists thought would evoke deep emotions in Bantu tribe members. They were surprised to find that the Bantu often saw the pictures in a very different way than anticipated; in particular, they often did not use relative size as a cue to depth. In Figure 8.8, for example, most Americans would see the hunter preparing to throw his spear at the gazelle in the foreground, while an elephant stands on a hill in the background. Many of the Bantu, however, thought the hunter in a similar picture was preparing to stab the baby elephant. In another picture, an orator, who we would see as waving his arms dramatically with a factory in the background, was seen as warming his hands over the tiny chimneys of the factory. Hudson (1960) concluded that these differences in depth perception were related to both education and exposure to European cultures. Bantu people who had been

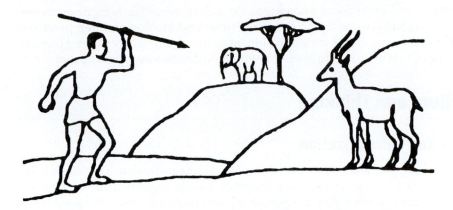

FIGURE 8.8 Hudson's (1960) Picture of Depth Perception

What is the hunter's target? Americans and Europeans would say it is the gazelle in the foreground. The Bantu in Hudson's research, however, said it was the elephant.

educated in European schools, or who had more experience with European culture, saw things as Europeans did. Bantu people who had no education and little exposure to Western culture saw the pictures differently.

Later work by McGurk and Jahoda (1975) documented that children of different cultures, ranging in age from 4 to 10 years old, also saw things differently. For example, they found that Scottish children were more accurate than Ghanaian children in depicting spatial relationships in pictures in which a woman and child stood in different positions relative to one another.

A more recent study, however, argued against these types of cultural influences on perception. This study compared the reactions of the Himba, a seminomadic people who live in a remote region of northwestern Namibia and have little contact with the manufactured products that are so prevalent in daily life in developed societies, with those of Americans (Biederman, Yue, & Davidoff, 2009). The researchers used a match-to-sample task, in which various shapes were presented and the participants had to match the presented shape to one of two alternatives provided. The shapes used included those that were common to urban environments and those that occurred in nature. There were no differences between the Himba and the Americans, and the authors argued that humans might have a genetic predisposition for perceiving irregular, artifactual shapes, independent of culture.

Important questions exist about the generalizability of these findings above and beyond the sorts of tasks used in the previous studies. For example, in most research on visual perception and optical illusions, the stimuli are presented in two dimensions—either on a piece of paper or projected on a screen. Cultural differences in depth perception may certainly exist using these types of stimuli (as shown in the studies described here, as well as in drawing and other artwork). But to what extent do such effects actually exist in the three-dimensional world? Would Bantu tribespeople see the hunter ready to stab the elephant, and not the gazelle, if the same scene were portrayed out in the open space of their actual environment?

Motivation may be a factor as well. That is, people of different cultures may be differently motivated to perceive certain types of objects, or to perceive them in certain ways. In one study that demonstrated this effect (Broota & Ganguli, 1975), Hindu, Muslim, and American children in India perceived faces associated with either a reward or a punishment in a pretraining session. In the testing session, the participants viewed these and other faces, and judged their characteristics. Significant differences were found between the groups: The Hindu and Muslim children perceived more of the faces associated with punishment than reward, whereas the American children perceived more faces associated with reward rather than punishment.

▶ Culture and Thinking

Culture and Categorization

categorization The process by which objects are grouped or classified together based on their perceived similarities.

One of the most basic mental processes is known as **categorization**. This refers to the manner in which people group things together. This is important because it helps people keep track of what they are perceiving and thinking about. We perceive so many different stimuli, and it is too difficult to track each and every one. By creating categories and placing stimuli in those categories, we can process information more efficiently. Creating mental categories helps us sort out all the complex stimuli that we are exposed to every day. It helps us create rules and guidelines for behavior and to make decisions. Verbal language is based on categorization and concept formation; words are symbols for objects in our physical environment.

People categorize on the basis of similarities and attach labels (words) to groups of objects perceived so that they have something in common. In so doing, people create categories of objects that share certain characteristics. People often decide whether something belongs in a certain group by comparing it to the most common or representative member of that category. For instance, a beanbag chair, a straight-backed dining room chair, and a seat in a theater differ in appearance from one another, but all belong to the basic category *chair.* All these things can be grouped together under the label *chair* because all share a common function. When we say "That thing is a chair," we mean that the item can and should be used as something for people to sit on (Rosch, 1978).

The process of categorization is universal to all humans, and some categories appear to be universal across cultures. Facial expressions that signal basic emotions—happiness, sadness, anger, fear, surprise, and disgust—are placed in the same categories across cultures (see Chapter 9). Likewise, there is widespread agreement across cultures about which colors are primary and which are secondary (Lindsey & Brown, 2009; see also Chapter 10). The way people select and remember colors appears to be largely independent of both culture and language. Regardless of whether people speak a language that has dozens of words for colors or one that distinguishes colors only in terms of whether they are bright or dark, individuals universally group colors around the same primary hues. They also remember primary colors with greater ease when asked to compare and recall colors in an experimental setting. Stereotypes are a type of category, and stereotyping is probably a universal psychological process (Chapter 14). And there is universality in how people across cultures categorize shapes in terms of the best examples of basic forms (perfect circles, equilateral triangles, and squares) rather than forming categories for irregular geometrical shapes. These cross-cultural parallels suggest that physiological factors influence the way humans categorize certain basic stimuli. That is, humans seem to be predisposed to prefer certain shapes, colors, and facial expressions.

There are also interesting cultural differences. For example, although all cultures may have a category for furniture, the prototype or "best model" of a chair is likely to differ across cultures because the materials used to construct furniture differ across cultures. One common way to study cultural differences in categorization involves the use of sorting tasks. When presented with pictures that could be grouped in terms of function, shape, or color, young children in Western cultures tend to group by color. As they grow older, however, they group by shape and then by function (Bruner, Oliver, & Greenfield, 1966). Western adults were inclined to put all the tools in one group and all the animals in another, rather than grouping all the red things or all the round things together. It had been assumed that this trend was a function of basic human maturation. But given similar sorting tasks, adult Africans showed a strong tendency to group objects by color rather than function (Greenfield, Reich, & Oliver, 1966; Suchman, 1966), suggesting that something other than simple maturation must be responsible for the category shifts.

East Asians may categorize differently altogether. In an early study by Chiu (1972), Chinese and American children were presented with sets of three objects and were asked to select two of the objects that should go together. The American children grouped objects according to shared features, whereas the Chinese children grouped objects according to shared contextual or functional relationships. For instance, when presented with a man, woman, and child, the Americans grouped the man and woman together because they were both adults, while the Chinese grouped the woman and child together because of their perceived relationship. Ji, Zhang, and Nisbett (2004) conducted similar tests with Americans and bilingual Chinese (mainland and Taiwan) participants, having them group sets of three words in either English or Chinese. The bilingual Chinese categorized objects in more relational ways than did Americans, regardless of whether they were tested in English or Chinese, suggesting that the cultural differences in categorization styles were not affected by language.

Culture and Memory

There may be some constants about memory across cultures that suggest some universal aspects to it. For example, memory abilities tend to decrease as people get older (or at least people become more selective about what they remember!), and one study showed that such memory decreases with age were consistent across cultures (Crook, Youngjohn, Larrabee, & Salama, 1992). Another aspect of memory that studies have found to be universal is in the effect known as **hindsight bias**, which refers to the process in which individuals adjust their memory for something after they find out the true outcome. For example, when someone is asked to guess the number of beads in a jar, they may say 350. When they find out later that the actual number is 647, people will often remember their original estimate to be 450, or some number *closer* to the true outcome. Choi and Nisbett (2000) found that Koreans exhibited more hindsight bias than Americans, but Heine and Lehman (1996) reported no differences between Japanese and Canadians. A more recent study involving participants from Asia, Australia, Europe, and North America also found no cultural differences in hindsight bias (Pohl, Bender, & Lachmann, 2002), providing evidence for its similarity across cultures.

But there are also interesting cultural differences. Some have claimed that individuals from nonliterate societies develop better memory skills because they do not have the ability to write things down to remember them (Bartlett, 1932). Is it true that our memories are not as good when we habitually use lists as aids in remembering? Ross and Millson (1970) suspected that reliance on an oral tradition might make people better at remembering. They compared the ability of American and Ghanaian college students to remember stories that were read aloud. In general the Ghanaian students were better than the Americans at remembering the stories. But Cole, Gay, Glick, and Sharp (1971) reported that nonliterate African participants did not perform

hindsight bias The process in which individuals adjust their memory for something after they find out the true outcome.

better when they were tested with lists of words instead of with stories. These findings suggest that cultural differences in memory as a function of oral tradition may be limited to *meaningful material.*

serial position effect The finding that people tend to remember something better if it is either the first or the last item in a list.

One of the best-known aspects of memory is the **serial position effect**. This effect suggests that we remember things better if they are either the first (primacy effect) or last (recency effect) item in a list of things to remember. Early cross-cultural comparisons challenged the universality of this effect. Cole and Scribner (1974), for instance, found no relation between serial position and the likelihood of being remembered in studying the memory of Kpelle tribespeople in Liberia. Wagner (1980) hypothesized that the primacy effect depends on rehearsal—the silent repetition of things you are trying to remember—and that this memory strategy is related to schooling. Wagner compared groups of Moroccan children who had and had not gone to school and found that the primacy effect was much stronger in the children who had been to school. This makes sense; in a classroom setting, children are expected to memorize letters, multiplication tables, and other basic facts. Participants who have been to school have had more practice in memorizing than have unschooled individuals. They are also able to apply these skills in test situations that resemble their school experience. A study by Scribner (1974) with educated and uneducated Africans supported this idea. Educated Africans were able to recall lists of words to a degree similar to that of American participants, whereas uneducated Africans remembered fewer words. It is not clear whether culture or schooling or both contribute to the observed differences.

The studies reviewed above, however, tested memory for self-unrelated materials. What about memory for things that are relevant to oneself? Liu and colleagues (Liu, Goldstein-Hawes, Hilton, Huang, Gastardo- Conaco, Dresler-Hawke et al., 2005; Liu, Paez, Slawuta Cabecinhas, Technio, Kokdemir et al., 2009) asked respondents in 24 cultures about the "most important events in world history" and the "most influential person in world history in the last 1,000 years." There was large cross-cultural consensus, with events focused on the recent past, centered around politics and dominated by world wars, with the most influential person being Hitler. Recency effects were pervasive, with events and figures from the past 100 years accounting for 72% of nominated events and 78% of nominated individuals. The results indicated that collective remembering of the past is dynamically interlinked to political issues of the present for all cultures surveyed.

Cultural differences in memories of the recent past also affect responses to current day events. Despite the fact that the 2011 Japanese earthquake and tsunami generally elicited worldwide empathy, Yang and colleagues (Yang, Liu, Fang, & Hong, 2014) reported that Chinese participants consistently showed less empathy toward that disaster than did Americans. Moreover, those cultural differences in empathy were attributed to Chinese participants' tendencies to consider the event as retribution for Japan's acts in World War II.

episodic memory The recollection of specific events that took place at a particular time and place in the past.

There are also interesting cultural differences in **episodic memory**, which refers to the recollection of specific events that took place at a particular time and place in the past. Across several studies, European and European American adults and children often exhibited greater episodic memories in the recollection of autobiographic events than Asian and Asian Americans (Wang, 2001, 2004; Wang & Ross, 2005). In one study, for example, European Canadian and Chinese 8-, 11-, and 14-year-old children recalled early childhood memories of events that occurred before they went to school. Across all age groups, Canadian children produced more episodic memories than those cultural differences were *not* accounted for by general cognitive or memory capacity differences between the groups, language artifacts or narrative style, different norms of expression, different life experiences, or influences of the test context. Instead, the differences may have occurred because of differences in cultural differences in self-construals, emotion knowledge, and interpersonal processes. For example, memories of specific episodes are often distinct personal experiences that help individuals distinguish themselves from others, and individuals with an independent self-construal may be more motivated to attend to or encode such memories. Memories of generic activities (e.g., going to church every Sunday) often imply social conventions and interactions with others, and individuals with interdependent self-construals may be more motivated to attend to and remember such events. Consistent with this framework, when Chinese individuals are primed independently, they performed more poorly in a memory recognition test related to the concept of "mothers" (Sui, Zhu, & Chiu, 2007).

Culture and Math

Math, like other symbolic languages, is unique to human cultures, and the ability to do math is a universal human psychological process. The representation of numbers along a mental number line appears to universally go from smaller to larger, left to right in both humans and even animals with very little experiences with numbers as symbols (Rugani, Vallortigara, Priftis, & Regolin, 2015). Math and culture have a very special relationship because, as Stigler and Baranes (1988) put it, math skills "are not logically constructed on the basis of abstract cognitive structures, but rather are forged out of a combination of previously acquired (or inherited) knowledge and skills, and new cultural input" (p. 258). Culture is not only a stimulator of math, but is itself represented in math, and how a society teaches and learns it.

There are cross-national differences in overall math abilities and achievements. The International Association for the Evaluation of Educational Achievement conducts worldwide testing in mathematics and science. Beginning in 1995, they have surveyed 4th and 8th graders every four years. In every survey there has been a substantial range in performance between the highest and lowest performing countries. In their survey in 2011, the highest performing countries in math were Singapore, Korea, and Hong Kong in 4th grade, and Korea, Singapore, and Taiwan at 8th grade. In science the highest performing countries in 4th grade were Korea and Singapore; in 8th grade it was Singapore, Taiwan, Korea, and Japan.

Although differences across countries exist in math and science performance, the *source* of these differences is not clear. The mapping of numbers onto space may be a universal intuition, and the initial intuition of numbers is logarithmic (Dehaene, Izard, Spelke, & Pica, 2008), but there are interesting cultural differences in numbering systems, which may contribute to national differences in math abilities. In many languages, for example, the number system is a base 10 system, with unique words for the numbers 1 through 10. Eleven is often counted 10-1, twelve is 10-2, twenty is 2-10, etc. In English, however, numbers 1 through 19 are unique, and an additive system similar to other languages starts at 20. Historically Western math was influenced by Roman numerals, which has no zero, and modern math systems were acquired by acculturation with the Middle East. Other languages have different base systems (see our related discussion in Chapter 10 on the relationship between language and thought). Research has shown that students from cultures that use a base 10 system make fewer errors than others in counting and understand some basic math concepts related to counting and numbers better (Miller, Kelly, & Zhou, 2005; Miura, Okamoto, Vladovic-Stetic, Kim, & Han, 1999).

One study took these ideas further and tested whether American children could more accurately recognize fractions if the language to represent fractions was made more transparent—to mirror the way fractions are represented in the Korean language (Paik & Mix, 2003). In one experiment, American first- and second-graders were tested on how well they recognized pictures of fractions (e.g., a circle divided into four equal parts with one part shaded to represent one-fourth). The researchers reported that children were much more likely to correctly identify the fraction when transparent language was used, for instance, by using the terms "of four, one part" (as in the Korean language) or "one of four parts," rather than when less transparent language was used (e.g., "one-fourth"). Paik and Mix (2003) argued that using more transparent language when children are beginning to learn fractions could facilitate children's math learning in this area. Nonetheless, they also concluded that language differences in numerical systems could not fully explain why there are wide cross-national differences in math achievement.

One interesting cross-cultural phenomenon concerns the gender gap in mathematics achievement. This gap exists in some cultures but not others. Else-Quest, Hyde, and Linn (2010) provided evidence for a **gender stratification hypothesis** that suggests that gender differences are related to cultural variations in opportunity structures for girls and women. They meta-analyzed two major data sets representing 493,495 students in 69 nations, and found that gender equity in school enrollment, women's share of research jobs, and women's parliamentary representation were the most powerful predictors of cross-national variability in gender gaps in math.

gender stratification hypothesis The idea that gender differences are related to cultural variations in opportunity structures for girls and women.

Studies of an area known as **everyday cognition** indicate that, even without formal educational systems, members of all cultures learn math skills (Schliemann & Carraher, 2001). Kpelle rice farmers, for instance, estimate amounts of rice as part of their work, and are better than Americans at volume estimation. Farmers in some areas of Brazil use a nonstandard system of measures and formulas to calculate areas of land. Illiterate individuals in India can use the movements of sun, moon, and stars to tell time accurately. Knotted string devices known as *khipu* were used for bureaucratic counting devices in the Inke Empire in ancient Peru, and were used to keep census and tribe data (Urton & Brezine, 2005). Geometry, a topic we typically associate with middle- or high-school math classes, may in fact be a core intuition found in all humans. Even isolated indigenous groups of individuals living in the Amazon use geometric concepts to locate hidden objects (Dehaene, Izard, Pica, & Spelke, 2006). Findings from studies on everyday cognition have provided fairly clear evidence that math abilities are universal to all humans.

everyday cognition An area of study that examines cognitive skills and abilities that are used in everyday functioning that appear to develop without formal education, but from performing daily tasks of living and working.

Culture and Problem Solving

Problem solving refers to the process by which we attempt to discover ways of achieving goals that do not seem readily attainable. Psychologists have tried to isolate the process of problem solving by asking people from different cultures to solve unfamiliar problems in artificial settings. One such experiment (Cole et al., 1971) presented American and Liberian participants with an apparatus containing various buttons, panels, and slots. After basic instruction in how to work the apparatus, participants were to figure out how to open the device and obtain a prize. The solution involved combining two different procedures—first pressing the correct button to release a marble, and then inserting the marble into the appropriate slot to open a panel. Americans under the age of 10 were generally unable to obtain the prize, but older Americans combined the two steps with ease. Unlike older the Americans, Liberians of all ages and educational backgrounds experienced great difficulty solving the problem; less than a third of the adults were successful.

problem solving The process by which we attempt to discover ways of achieving goals that do not seem readily attainable.

This experiment, however, may have been biased in favor of the Americans. Remember the first time you ever worked on a computer, or looked under the hood of a car? Cole and his colleagues repeated their experiment with materials familiar to people in Liberia, using a locked box and keys instead of the mechanical contraption. In the new version of the two-step problem, the Liberian participants had to remember which key opened the lock on the box and which matchbox container housed the correct key. Under these conditions, a great majority of Liberians solved the problem easily.

The success of the Liberians in solving a two-step problem with a familiar set of materials raises the question of whether the experiment tested their ability to think logically or tested their previous knowledge and experience with locks and keys. In an attempt to clarify this issue, the researchers designed a third experiment, combining elements from both the first and second tests. Liberian and American participants were again presented with a locked box, but the key that opened the box had to be obtained from the apparatus used in the first experiment. To the surprise of the researchers, the third test produced results similar to the first experiment. While Americans solved the problem with ease, most Liberians were not able to retrieve the key to open the box.

Cole and his colleagues concluded that the Liberians' ability to reason logically to solve problems depended on context. When presented with problems using materials and concepts already familiar to them, Liberians drew logical conclusions effortlessly. When the test situation was alien to them, however, they had difficulty knowing where to begin. In some cases, the problem went beyond confusion; uneducated Liberians appeared visibly frightened by the tests involving the strange apparatus and were reluctant to manipulate it. Although adult Americans did very well in these experiments in comparison to the Liberians, how might average Americans react if placed in a similar experimental situation that required the Americans to use wholly unfamiliar concepts and technology—for example, tracking animals by means of footprints and smells?

Another type of problem that has been studied cross-culturally involves syllogisms (for example: All children like candy. Mary is a child. Does Mary like candy?). As with other cultural differences in cognition and thought, the ability to provide the correct answer to verbal problems was found to be closely associated with school attendance. Individuals from traditional societies who were illiterate were generally unable to provide answers to syllogisms containing unfamiliar information. Individuals from the same culture and even from the same village who had received a single year of schooling could respond correctly.

Various explanations have been proposed to account for the difficulty of uneducated people to complete word problems. It may be that illiterate people think differently from those who are educated. According to this hypothesis, logical reasoning is essentially artificial; it is a skill that must be learned in a Westernized school setting. Some studies lend support to this interpretation. Tulviste (1978) asked schoolchildren in Estonia ages 8 to 15 to solve verbal problems and explain their answers. Although the children were able to solve most of the problems correctly, they explained their answers by citing the logical premises of the problem only in areas in which they did not have firsthand knowledge. Elsewhere, their answers were justified with appeals to common sense or statements about their personal observations.

Scribner (1979) questioned whether illiterate participants were truly incapable of thinking logically and looked more closely into the reasons uneducated people failed to give correct responses to verbal problems. When uneducated peasants were asked to explain illogical answers to syllogism problems, they consistently cited evidence that was known to them personally or stated that they did not know anything about the subject, ignoring the premises given to them. For example, in response to the word problem "All children like candy; Mary is a child; does Mary like candy?" participants might have shrugged their shoulders and commented, "How would I know whether Mary likes candy? I don't even know the child!" or "Maybe she doesn't like candy; I've known children who didn't." These individuals appeared to have been unable or unwilling to apply concepts of scientific thinking to verbal problems. But this was not because they lack the capacity to reason logically; rather, they did not understand the hypothetical nature of verbal problems or view them with the same degree of importance. People who have been to school have had the experience of answering questions posed by an authority figure who already knows the correct answers. Uneducated people, however, may have difficulty understanding the notion that questions need not be requests for information.

Culture and Creativity

Another aspect of cognition that has received attention in the literature is creativity. Creativity is an interesting area of study because it highlights a universal and unique human process. Creativity is what enables humans and only humans to create art and symphonies, explore space and the sea, and design machines to improve life. Unfortunately creativity also is what enables humans and only humans to create and improve on weapons of mass destruction and other terrible deeds.

Research on creativity in the United States suggests that it depends on divergent thinking rather than on the convergent thinking that is typically assessed in measures of intelligence. Creative individuals have been shown to have a high capacity for hard work, a willingness to take risks, and a high tolerance for ambiguity and disorder (Sternberg & Lubart, 1995, 1999). These same characteristics appear to be true of creative individuals in other cultures as well. For example, Khaleefa, Erdos, and Ashria (1996) highlighted these characteristics in their study of creativity in a conformist culture (Sudan); Simonton (1996) documented them in his study of creative individuals in Japanese history; and Satoh (1996) described their implementation in kindergarten programs in Japan to foster the development of creativity in children in that culture. All of these examples are consistent with Sternberg and Lubart's (1995, 1999) studies of the processes that creative individuals go through, particularly in overcoming obstacles presented to them by conformist-centered organizations.

Some important differences have been noted, however, in the specific ways in which creativity can be fostered in different cultures. Shane, Venkataraman, and MacMillan (1995), for example, studied innovative strategies among a sample of 1,228 individuals from 30 countries who were employees of four different work organizations. The authors characterized the countries in terms of Hofstede's dimensions of individualism, power distance, and uncertainty avoidance (see Chapter 1 for a review). They found that countries high on uncertainty avoidance preferred creative individuals to work through organizational norms, rules, and procedures. Countries higher on power distance preferred creative individuals to gain support from those in authority before action is taken, or to build a broad base of support among members for new ideas. Collectivistic countries preferred creative people to seek cross-functional support for their efforts.

Thus, although creative individuals may share some common core characteristics across cultures, they need to adapt their abilities to the specific cultural milieu within which they function, particularly in the implementation and adoption of their creative ideas (Csikszentmihalyi, 1999). Creativity requires people to "get outside of their own box" or framework; another area of cultural difference would be the degree to which this ability is fostered. These effects also exist on the group level. Individualistic groups have been shown to be more creative than collectivistic groups (Goncalo & Staw, 2006), and cultures that have histories of greater prevalence of disease-causing pathogens are also associated with less creativity, as assessed by different measures of innovation (Murray, 2014).

Intercultural experiences may promote growth and creativity. Maddux and Galinsky (2009) showed that time spent living abroad (but not time spent traveling abroad) was positively related with creativity, that priming foreign living experiences temporarily enhanced creative tendencies for participants who had previously lived abroad, and that the degree to which individuals had adapted to different cultures while living abroad mediated the link between foreign living experience and creativity. Subsequent research demonstrated that it was the specific multicultural learning experiences—learning how and why people of different cultures do what they do—that facilitated improvements in creativity (Maddux, Adam, & Galinsky, 2010).

Culture and Dialectical Thinking

Dialectical thinking can be broadly defined as the tendency to accept what seem to be contradictions in thought or beliefs. This is in contrast to **positive logical determinism** that characterizes much of American and Western European thinking. Dialectical thinking tries to find the way in which both sides of an apparent contradiction are correct, tolerates the contradiction, and tries to find mutual middle ground. Logical deterministic thinking tends to see contradictions as mutually exclusive categories, as either-or, yes-no, one-or-the-other types of categories.

Cross-cultural research of the past decade has produced interesting cultural differences in dialectical thinking, demonstrating that East Asians tend to prefer dialectical thinking, whereas Americans tend to prefer logical deterministic thinking. Peng and Nisbett (1999), for instance, conducted an interesting series of studies to demonstrate these differences. In one, American and Chinese graduate students were presented with the following two vignettes:

> Mother–Daughter Conflict:
>
> Mary, Phoebe, and Julie all have daughters. Each mother has held a set of values that has guided her efforts to raise her daughter. Now the daughters have grown up, and each of them is rejecting many of her mother's values. How did it happen, and what should they do?
>
> School–Fun Conflict:
>
> Kent, James, and Matt are college juniors. They are feeling very frustrated about their three years of routine tests, paper assignments, and grades. They complain that going through this process has taken its toll, undermining the fun of learning. How did it happen, and what should they do?

The participants were asked to write what they thought about both conflicts, including what they thought were the sources of the differences and what the persons in the vignettes should do. The researchers then categorized the participants' responses as either dialectical or not. A dialectical response was defined as one that "(a) addressed the issues from both sides and (b) attempted to reconcile the contradictions," for example, a response such as "both the mothers and the daughters have failed to understand each other" (p. 746). Nondialectical responses generally found exclusive fault with one side or the other, such as "mothers have to recognize daughters' rights to their own values" (p. 746). There were strong cultural differences in the

dialectical thinking
The tendency to accept what seem to be contradictions in thought or beliefs.

positive logical determinism A tendency to see contradictions as mutually exclusive categories, as either-or, yes-no, one-or-the-other types of categories.

FIGURE 8.9 Comparison of American and Chinese Responses to the Conflicting Situations in Peng and Nisbett (1999)

Source: From K. Peng and R. Nisbett. "Culture, dialectics, and reasoning about contradiction," *American Psychologist, 54,* pp. 741–754, 1999, Copyright © *American Psychological* Association. Reprinted with permission.

responses (Figure 8.9), with the Americans responses being much more nondialectical, and the Chinese responses as more dialectical.

Recent research in many areas of psychology, typically comparing East Asians with U.S. Americans, have shown that dialectical thinkers show greater expectation of change when trying to explain or predict events and greater tolerance of contradiction. These effects have been demonstrated in studies on self, emotional experience, psychological well-being, attitudes and evaluations, social categorization and perception, and judgment and decision making (Spencer-Rodgers, Williams, & Peng, 2010). For example, while it is typical to find that positive and negative feelings are negatively correlated in Western cultures, research on East Asian cultures has shown that they are either not correlated or even positively correlated with each other (Bagozzi, Wong, & Yi, 1999). These kinds of findings in many different domains of psychology have allowed researchers to expand on the concept of dialectical thinking to the construct of **naïve dialectivism** (Peng, Spencer-Rodgers, & Zhong, 2006), which is a constellation of lay beliefs about the nature of the world (rather than a cognitive style as suggested by dialectical thinking). Naïve dialecticism is characterized by the doctrine of the mean, or the belief that the truth is always somewhere in the middle. Contrarily, Western lay theories are dominated by the idea that something cannot be both truth and false at the same time, and the belief that all propositions must be either true or false (Peng & Nisbett, 1999).

Dialectical thinking is not a concept that is exclusive to East Asians. It was a central aspect of the work of the German philosopher Hegel, as well as prominent in the work of writers influential to modern psychology such as Freud and Piaget. Perhaps the zeitgeist of cognitive styles and lay theories may evolve over time, as do many other aspects of culture.

naïve dialectivism A constellation of lay beliefs about the nature of the world (rather than a cognitive style as suggested by dialectical thinking). Naïve dialecticism is characterized by the doctrine of the mean, or the belief that the truth is always somewhere in the middle.

Culture, Regrets, and Counterfactual Thinking

Counterfactual thinking can be defined as hypothetical beliefs about the past that could have occurred in order to avoid or change a negative outcome. For example, if you got a bad grade on a test, an example of counterfactual thinking would be "If I had only studied harder." These types of counterfactual thoughts often are related to feelings of regret (Gilovich, Medvec, & Kahneman, 1998).

Counterfactual thinking can be broadly classified into two types: actions and inactions. On one hand, "If I had only studied harder," "If I had only been a better parent," and "If I had only trained harder," are examples of counterfactual thinking related to inaction. On the other hand, "If I hadn't said what I said," "If I didn't eat that last piece of cake," and "If I weren't driving so fast," are examples of counterfactual thinking of actions.

Research in the United States has shown that regrets related to thoughts of inaction are more prevalent than regrets related to action (Gilovich & Medvec, 1995). Interestingly, this same trend has been found in other cultures as well. In a study of Americans, Chinese, Japanese, and Russians, all participants in all cultures experienced more regret over inaction than action (Gilovich, Wang, Regan, & Nishina, 2003). Moreover, the degree to which they experienced regret over inaction than over action was comparable across all cultures and to previous data involving just Americans. Another study also demonstrated cultural similarity in the nature of counterfactual thinking, although cultural differences did emerge in specific domains (schoolwork, family) (Chen, Chiu, Roese, Tam, & Lau, 2006). Thus, the emotion of regret, and the potential causes of it, appears to be universal.

counterfactual thinking Hypothetical beliefs about the past that could have occurred in order to avoid or change a negative outcome.

Summary

How can we understand why cultural differences in basic cognitive processes occur? Some researchers believe that the source of those differences can be found in systemic cultural differences in individualism versus collectivism and rooted in differences in ancient philosophies in Greece and China, the former promoting autonomy and independence, the latter promoting relations and interdependent collectivism (Nisbett, 2003; Nisbett, Peng, Choi, & Norenzayan, 2001). According to this framework, these ancient cultural systems produce differences in ways of perceiving and thinking about the world, with the Westerners characterized by analytic ways of thinking, whereas the East Asians are characterized by holistic thinking. These differences in holistic versus analytic thinking, in turn, influence a variety of cognitive processes, including attention, categorization, attributions, and reasoning (Table 8.1).

Nisbett and colleagues have suggested that the various differences in cognition that have been documented can be organized and explained by a **social orientation hypothesis** (Varnum, Grossman, Kitayama, & Nisbett, 2010). According to this hypothesis, cultures differ in independent versus interdependent social orientation patterns (according to their independent versus interdependent self-construals; see Chapter 5). These social orientations, in turn, influence and affect the ways members of those cultures attend to and think about their worlds. On one hand, independent social orientations emphasize self-direction, autonomy, and self-expression, which fosters a tendency to focus on a single dimension or aspect when categorizing objects or evaluating arguments. On the other hand, interdependent social orientations emphasize harmony, relatedness, and connection, which in turn fosters a broad attention to context and relationships in visual attention, categorization, and explaining social behavior.

social orientation hypothesis The hypothesis that cultural differences in individualism versus collectivism are associated with differences in social orientation patterns that affect the ways individuals attend to and think about their worlds.

TABLE 8.1 Analytic versus Holistic Cognitive Patterns

Domain	Analytic Cognition	Holistic Cognition
Attention	Field independent	Field dependent
	Narrow	Broad
	Focus on salient objects with intent to manipulate them	Focus on relationship of elements, background
Categorization	Taxonomic, focus on a single dimension or shared property	Thematic, focus on functional relationship or overall similarity
Attribution	Dispositional	Situational
	Traits and attributes of individuals determine events	External forces, context, and situations determine events
Reasoning	Analytic	Dialectical
	Use of formal logic Trends continue	Middle Way philosophy Trend reversals are likely

Source: Varnum, M., Grossman, I., Kitayama, S., & Nisbett, R. E. "The origin of cultural differences in cognition: The social orientation hypothesis." *Current Directions in Psychological Science*, 19(1), pp. 9–13, Copyright © 2010 by Sage Publications. Reprinted by Permission of SAGE Publications.

This theoretical hypothesis is interesting. Yet there are still many other potential factors for the cultural differences uncovered to date that have not been examined, including differences in educational systems and practices, linguistic, and genetic differences. In the educational systems of many East Asian countries today that do well on math and science tests, for example, there is much more emphasis on rote memorization and passive learning in a didactic environment. In a nutshell, the teachers lecture, and the students listen and memorize everything. This is in contrast to the typical European or American educational style, in which students are much more active learners, and discussion is promoted. It may very well be that, after 12 or 16 years of such educational practices, East Asian students, who are generally the participants in cross-cultural research, remember more things and think differently about things than do their American counterparts.

Another way to think about cultural differences in cognition is through the perspective of culture *as* cognition, as discussed earlier in this chapter. This perspective suggests that one's performance on cognitive tasks depends on the type of cultural "mind set" that one is in at the time of engagement with the task. Across eight studies examining attention involving Koreans, Korean Americans, Hong Kong Chinese, European-, Hispanic- and Asian-heritage Americans, and Norwegians, Oyserman and colleagues (2009) demonstrated that performance on cognitive tasks were dependent on the cues in the moment for all groups studied. When contrast and separation was made salient in the minds of the participants through priming, participants attended to single targets or main points. When assimilation and connection were primed, participants focused on multiple points and integration.

Thus, the differences observed in research may be attributed to educational practices or contextual factors and not necessarily to cultural ideologies rooted in ancient philosophies. The differences may be rooted in other sources as well, such as the amount and type of technology used in the countries today, or the type of animated video games played. Future research will need to explore exactly what are the sources of the observed differences. Some of the sources may be cultural, others not.

▶ Culture and Consciousness

Culture and Dreams

There are considerable cultural differences in the content of dreams. Punamaeki and Joustie (1998), for example, examined how culture, violence, and personal factors affected dream content among Palestinian children living in a violent environment (Gaza), Palestinian children living in a peaceful area, and Finnish children living in a peaceful area. Participants recorded the dreams they recalled every morning for seven days, and researchers coded their contents. The dreams of the Palestinian children from Gaza incorporated more external scenes of anxiety, whereas the Finnish children's dreams had more "inner" anxiety scenes. Themes present in these children's everyday lives affected the dreams considerably as well. Cultural differences in dream content were also reported by Levine (1991) in her study of Irish, Israeli, and Bedouin children, and by Kane (1994) in her study of Anglo American, Mexican American, and African American women.

There are also differences in the role of dreams in different cultures. In many cultures, dreams are an important part of the cultural system, involving an organized, conventional set of signs. Tedlock (1992) reported that dream sharing and interpretation was a common practice among Mayan Indians in Central America, regardless of the role or position of the person in the culture, and was important in the teaching of cultural folk wisdom. Desjarlais (1991) examined dream usage among the Yolmo Sherpa of Nepal. Here, too, dreams constituted a local system of knowledge that helped in the assessment and communication of personal and social distress and conflict, and hence were an important vehicle for social understanding.

Culture and Time

People of different cultures perceive and experience time differently, even though time should be objectively the same for everyone. Differences in time orientation and perspective are often a source of confusion and irritation for visitors to a new culture. Many visitors from cultures in which time is respected and punctuality is cherished have difficulty adjusting to U.S. public transportation systems, which may not always be on time as scheduled. Visitors from other cultures, however, in which time is not so much of the essence and queuing is commonplace, seem less affected by such deviations from schedule, viewing them as trivial and to be expected.

Hall (1973) was one of the first to suggest that cultures differ in their time perspective and orientation. He analyzed differences among people of different cultures in their use of time and how these differences manifested themselves in actual behavioral practices within such contexts as business. Cultural differences in time orientation can be especially agonizing in intercultural negotiation situations (see Chapter 15).

Perhaps the largest-scale cross-cultural study on time perception is that of Hofstede (2001). As we discussed in Chapters 1 and 2, Hofstede suggested that long-versus short-term orientation was a cultural dimension that differentiates among cultures. People in long-term cultures delay gratification of material, social, and emotional needs, and think more about the future. Members of short-term cultures think and act more in the immediate present and the bottom line. Hofstede surveyed long-versus short-term orientation across 36 countries of the world by asking their members to respond to a survey about their perceptions of time. He then characterized each of the countries in terms of their time orientations (Table 8.2).

TABLE 8.2 Results from Hofstede's (2001) Study on Time Orientation across Cultures

Short-Term Oriented	In the Middle	Long-Term Oriented
Ghana	Portugal	Norway
Nigeria	Australia	Denmark
Sierra Leone	Austria	Hungary
Philippines	Germany	Thailand
Spain	Poland	Czech Republic
Canada	Sweden	India
Botswana	Italy	Brazil
Malawi	Belgium	South Korea
Zambia	France	Japan
Zimbabwe	Switzerland	Taiwan
United States	Finland	Hong Kong
New Zealand	Netherlands	China

Cultural differences in time orientation may be related to interesting and important aspects of our behaviors. Levine and colleagues have conducted an interesting set of studies on this topic (Levine & Bartlett, 1984; Levine, Lynch, Miyake, & Lucia, 1989; Levine & Norenzayan, 1999). In one of them (Levine & Norenzayan, 1999), experimenters measured how fast people walked a 60-foot distance in downtown areas of major cities, the speed of a transaction at the post office, and the accuracy of clocks in 31 countries. Pace of life was fastest in Switzerland, Ireland, Germany, Japan, and Italy, and slowest in Mexico, Indonesia, Brazil, El Salvador, and Syria. Pace of life was correlated with several ecological and cultural variables. Hotter cities were slower than cooler ones, cultures with vibrant and active economies were faster, and people in individualistic cultures were faster. People in faster places tended to have worse health but greater happiness.

In recent years, a number of other studies have reported cultural differences in the use and understanding of time (Boroditsky, Fuhrman, & McCormick, 2011; Boroditsky & Gaby, 2010; Fuhrman & Boroditsky, 2010). For instance, most cultures of the world represent time spatially from left to right or right to left, or from front to back or back to front, with respect to the body. Boroditsky and Gaby (2010) demonstrated that individuals in Pormpuraaw, a remote Australian Aboriginal community, represented time from east to west regardless of one's body orientation. That is, time flows from left to right when one is facing south, from right to left when one is facing north, toward the body when one is facing east, and away from the body when one is facing west. Arabic speakers tend conceptualize the future as behind and the past as ahead despite the fact that the future is ahead and the past is behind in the Arabic language (as it is in many languages) (De la Fuente, Santiago, Roman, Dumitrache, & Casasanto, 2014). European Canadians attach more monetary value to an event in the future than to identical events in the past, whereas Chinese and Chinese Canadians place more monetary value to a past event (Guo, Ji, Spina, & Zhang, 2012). Thus conceptions of even such fundamental domains as time can differ dramatically across cultures.

Culture and Pain

Cross-cultural psychologists and anthropologists alike have long been interested in the relationship between culture and pain, mainly because of anecdotal reports and observations of considerable differences in pain management and tolerance in different cultures. Almost 40 years ago, scientists began to formally recognize the influence of culture and attitudinal factors on the response to pain (Wolff & Langley, 1968). Today, we know that culture influences the experience and perception of pain in several ways, including: (1) the cultural construction of pain sensation, (2) the language associated with pain expression, and (3) the structure of pain's causes and cures (Pugh, 1991). There is also a growing literature documenting the important implications and ramifications of cultural differences in the perception and management of pain, such as in doctor-patient interactions (Streltzer, 1997).

Although most cross-cultural research on pain has involved older children and adults, researchers are now recognizing that cultural differences in pain experiences, such as pain response, may occur quite early in life. For example, in a comparison of Chinese and non-Chinese Canadian two-month-old infants, Chinese babies showed greater (more intense) response to pain as measured by facial expression and crying (Rosmus, Halifax, Johnston, Chan-Yip, & Yang, 2000).

One hypothesis concerning cultural differences in pain experience has to do with the effect of language on perception and cognition. The Sapir–Whorf hypothesis (discussed in Chapter 10) suggests that the structure of language, which is highly dependent on culture, affects our perceptions and cognitions of the world around us—including our pain experiences. Because the structure, content, and process of language differ across cultures, so does the experience of pain (Fabrega, 1989).

Another related topic is that of cultural display rules (discussed in Chapter 9). Just as people of different cultures have different rules for the appropriate expression of emotion, they may have similar rules governing the expression, perception, and feeling of pain. As the strength of people's emotional expressions are correlated with the intensity of their emotional experiences, the rules governing the expression of pain will ultimately affect people's subjective experiences of pain. For example, a study of Indian and American college students showed that Indians were less accepting of overt pain expression and also had a higher level of pain tolerance than Americans (Nayak, Shiflett, Eshun, & Levine, 2000). Furthermore, level of pain tolerance and acceptance of overt pain expression were linked: The less acceptable overt pain expression was, the greater was the tolerance of pain.

The tolerance of pain may also be rooted in cultural values. Sargent (1984) interviewed females of reproductive age and 18 indigenous midwives in the Bariba culture of Benin, West Africa. In this culture, stoicism in the face of pain was idealized, and the "appropriate" response to pain was considered intrinsic to Bariban identity. Features such as the tolerance of pain through circumcision or clitoridectomy signaled courage and honor and were considered crucial values within the culture. In a qualitative study of Finnish women and their experiences of childbirth, participants described labor pain as something natural that they should accept. One mother said, "It is God's will for women to feel pain when giving birth" (as reported in Callister, Vehvilainen-Julkunen, & Lauri, 2001, p. 30). Asians appear to be less sensitive to internal physiological cues compared to European Americans (Ma-Kellums, Blascovich, & McCall, 2012).

► Culture and Intelligence

Traditional Definitions of Intelligence and Its Measurement

The English word *intelligence* is derived from the Latin word *intelligentia*, coined 2,000 years ago by the Roman orator Cicero. In contemporary American psychology, intelligence has generally been considered a conglomeration of numerous intellectual abilities centering around verbal and analytic tasks. Piaget (described in Chapter 4) viewed intelligence as a reflection of cognitive development through a series of stages, with the highest stage corresponding to abstract reasoning and principles. Spearman (1927) and Thurstone (1938) developed factor theories of intelligence, viewing it as a general concept comprised of many subcomponents, or factors, including verbal or spatial comprehension, word fluency, perceptual speed, and others. Guilford (1985) built on factor theories to describe intelligence using three dimensions—operation, content, and product—each of which had separate components. Through various combinations of these three dimensions, Guilford suggested that intelligence is composed of more than 150 separate factors.

Spearman (1927) also proposed, along with the multiple factors of intelligence, a "general" intelligence representing overall mental ability. This factor, called g, is typically measured through a process of combining and summarizing the various scores of a multiple-factor intelligence test. Aside from pure knowledge, the ability to reason logically and deductively about hypothetical and abstract issues and events is generally considered a part of intelligence. This definition of intelligence has dominated its measurement and, consequently, the research in this area.

Modern intelligence tests were first developed in the early 1900s when they provided a way to distinguish children in need of special education from those whose schoolwork suffered for other reasons. In the years that followed, intelligence tests came into widespread use in public schools and other government programs. But not everyone benefited from the new tests of intelligence. Because such tests relied at least in part on verbal performance and cultural knowledge, immigrants who spoke English poorly and came from different cultural backgrounds were at a disadvantage. For example, when tests of intelligence were administered to immigrants at Ellis Island beginning in 1913, more than three-quarters of the Italian, Hungarian, and Jewish immigrants tested as mentally defective. Such low scores for certain immigrant groups provoked a storm of controversy. Some people defended the scientific nature of the new tests, charging that southern European immigrants were not fit to enter the country. Others responded that intelligence tests were biased and did not accurately measure the mental ability of people from different cultures.

Today, numerous studies have documented differences in intelligence across a wide range of cultural and ethnic groups within the United States and around the world. For example, the average scores of some minority groups in the United States are 12 to 15 percentage points lower than the average for European Americans. This does not mean that all the individuals in these groups test poorly—high-scoring individuals can also be found in all ethnic groups—it simply means that larger percentages of some ethnic groups score relatively lower than others. These types of differences have raised large debates about the source of those differences, and a nature versus nurture controversy.

The Nature versus Nurture Controversy

The nature side of the debate argues that differences in IQ scores between different societies and ethnic groups are mainly hereditary or innate. Much of the evidence for this position originated with the studies of Arthur Jensen (1968, 1969, 1971, 1973, 1977, 1980, 1981, 1983, 1984), who found that African Americans typically scored lower on IQ tests than European Americans. Twin studies also provided evidence for the nature hypothesis. The most important of these studies compared identical twins who grew up in separate homes to fraternal twins raised together (Bouchard & McGue, 1981). If test scores are determined by heredity, identical twins raised apart should have very similar scores. But if environment is primary, the scores of the fraternal twins raised together should be more similar. These twin studies revealed that the scores of identical twins raised in different environments were significantly more alike than those of fraternal twins raised together. Jensen (1971) concluded that the correlation between twins on IQ was .824, which he interpreted as constituting an upper limit on the heritability of IQ. Environmental factors, however, were normally distributed and IQ was not correlated with those factors. Jensen concluded that environmental factors could not have been systematically related to the intelligence levels of twin pairs.

The nurture (and thus cultural) side of the debate argues that ethnic and societal differences in IQ occur because of nonbiological factors such as environment, history, and learning. For example, some scholars have suggested that members of certain ethnic groups in the United States score lower because most subcultures in this country are economically deprived (Blau, 1981; Wolf, 1965). Advocates of this position have turned to studies showing that IQ scores are strongly related to social class. The average IQ score of poor whites, for instance, is 10 to 20 percentage points lower than the average score of members of the middle class. The effect of environment over race can be seen most clearly in studies showing that poor whites tested in Southern states scored lower than blacks who lived in Northern states.

Scarr and Weinberg (1976) also offered evidence for an environmental basis of intelligence. They showed that black and interracial children adopted by white families scored above the IQ and school achievement means for whites. Such a finding argued against biological predetermination and in favor of cultural and environmental factors. Greenfield (1997) argued that intelligence tests can be understood in terms of symbolic culture and therefore have little translatability (reliability or validity) when used with people of different cultural backgrounds— whether ethnic minorities within one country or across countries. Such arguments have been proffered for decades now, and have led to the development of a number of "culture-free" or "culture-fair" tests of intelligence, such as the Cattell Culture Fair Intelligence Test.

One theory that has received considerable research attention recently concerns the construct known as **stereotype threat**—"the threat that others' judgments or their own actions will negatively stereotype them in the domain" (Steele, 1998, p. 613). Steele posited that societal stereotypes about a group—for instance, concerning academic or intellectual performance—can influence the performance of individuals from that group. In an interesting set of experiments with black and white college students at Stanford University, Steele and Aronson (1995) reported that when black students were asked to record their race on a demographic questionnaire before taking a standardized test, they performed significantly worse as compared with black students who were not primed to think about their race before taking the test. Furthermore, they also found that when the exam was presented as a measure of intellectual ability, black students performed worse than white students. However, when

stereotype threat The threat that others' judgments or one's own actions will negatively stereotype one in a domain (such as academic achievement).

the same test was presented as unrelated to intellectual ability, the detrimental effects of the stereotype threat disappeared.

Today there is widespread agreement that at least 40 percent of intelligence can be attributed to heredity (Henderson, 1982; Jencks, Smith, Acland, Bane, Cohen, Gintis, Heyns, & Michaelson, 1972; Plomin, 1990). At the same time, there appears to be an equally large and strong literature base suggesting that IQ is at least malleable to cultural and environmental factors, and that previous findings indicating racial or ethnic differences in IQ are equivocal because of problems of validity in the tests used to measure intelligence in different cultural groups. What we do know is that intelligence tests are a good predictor of the verbal skills necessary for success in a culture associated with the formalized educational systems of modern industrial societies and increasingly adopted as a model throughout the world. However, such tests may not measure motivation, creativity, talent, or social skills, all of which are important factors in achievement.

It is also possible that group differences in intelligence are the result of different measures of intelligence. That is, if intelligence is at least partially a cultural construct, then it would be impossible to construct a test that is indeed "culture-fair" or "culture-free" because any such test would, by definition, have to include specific items that are generated within a specific cultural milieu; that is, intelligence cannot be understood outside a cultural framework (Sternberg, 2004). Even culture-free tests and items would have the underlying bias of culture—a "culture of no culture." In fact, some studies have shown that such tests do suffer from the very biases they were designed to address. Nenty (1986), for example, administering the Cattell Culture Fair Intelligence Test to Americans, Indians, and Nigerians in order to test the validity of the scale, found that 27 of the 46 items administered were culturally biased, thus rendering scores for the three cultures incomparable to one another. Recent data from twin studies have indicated counterintuitively that the contribution of genetic heritability is larger in studies with culturally "loaded" tests compared to culturally "reduced" tests, suggesting that general intelligence reflects more societal than cognitive demands (Kan, Wicherts, Dolan, & van der Maas, 2013).

Expanding the Concept of Intelligence across Cultures

It is possible that group differences in intelligence occurs because of cultural differences in beliefs about what intelligence is (recall our discussion in Chapter 2 on conceptual equivalence). For example, many languages have no word that corresponds to our idea of intelligence. The closest Mandarin equivalent, for instance, is a Chinese character that means "good brain and talented." Chinese often associate this concept with traits such as imitation, effort, and social responsibility (Keats, 1982). The Baganda of East Africa use the word *obugezi* to refer to a combination of mental and social skills that make a person steady, cautious, and friendly (Wober, 1974). The Djerma-Songhai in West Africa use the term *akkal*, which has an even broader meaning—a combination of intelligence, know-how, and social skills (Bissilat, Laya, Pierre, & Pidoux, 1967). The Baoule, uses the term *n'glouele*, which describes children who are not only mentally alert but also willing to volunteer their services without being asked (Dasen, Dembele, Ettien, Kabran, Kamagate, Koffi, & N'Guessean, 1985).

Because of the enormous differences in the ways cultures define intelligence, it may be difficult to make valid comparisons from one society to another. That is, different cultures value different traits and have divergent views concerning which traits are useful in predicting future important behaviors (also culturally defined). People in different cultures not only disagree about what constitutes intelligence but also about the proper way to demonstrate those abilities. In mainstream North American society, individuals are typically rewarded for displaying knowledge and skills. This same behavior may be considered improper, arrogant, or rude in societies that stress personal relationships, cooperation, and modesty.

These differences are important to cross-cultural studies of intelligence because successful performance on a task of intelligence may require behavior that is considered immodest and arrogant in Culture A (and therefore only reluctantly displayed by members of Culture A) but desirable in Culture B (and therefore readily displayed by members of Culture B). Clearly, such different attitudes toward the same behavior could lead researchers to draw inaccurate conclusions about differences in intelligence between Culture A and Culture B.

Another reason it is difficult to compare intelligence cross-culturally is that tests of intelligence often rely on knowledge that is specific to a particular culture; investigators based in that culture may not even know what to test for in a different culture. For example, one U.S. intelligence test contains the following question: "How does a violin resemble a piano?" Clearly, this question assumes prior knowledge about violins and pianos—quite a reasonable expectation for middle-class Americans, but not for people from cultures that use different musical instruments.

The Impact of Cross-Cultural Research on the Concept of Intelligence in Mainstream American Psychology

One of the most important contributions of cross-cultural psychology has been in expanding our theoretical understanding of intelligence in mainstream American psychology. Until very recently, for example, creativity was not considered a part of intelligence; now, however, psychologists are increasingly considering this important human ability as a type of intelligence. Other aspects of intelligence are also coming to the forefront. Gardner (1983) has suggested that there are seven different types of intelligence: logical mathematical, linguistic, musical, spatial, bodily kinesthetic, interpersonal, and intrapersonal. According to this scheme, not only do the core components of each of these seven types of intelligence differ, but so do some sample end states (such as mathematician versus dancer). His theory of multiple intelligences has broadened our understanding of intelligence to include areas other than "book smarts."

Sternberg (1986) has proposed a theory of intelligence based on three separate "subtheories": contextual, experiential, and componential intelligence. Contextual intelligence refers to an individual's ability to adapt to the environment, solving problems in specific situations. Experiential intelligence refers to the ability to formulate new ideas and combine unrelated facts. Componential intelligence refers to the ability to think abstractly, process information, and determine what needs to be done. Sternberg's theory focuses more on the processes that underlie thought than on specific thought outcomes. Because this definition of intelligence focuses on process rather than outcome, it has the potential for application across cultures.

While most views of intelligence focus on individuals, recent work has suggested the existence of **collective intelligence** of groups of people (Woolley, Chabris, Pentland, Hashmi, & Malone, 2010). Interestingly, collective intelligence was not strongly correlated with the average or maximum intelligence of the group members, but with the average social sensitivity of group members, the equality in distribution of conversational turn-taking, and the proportion of females in the group.

collective intelligence
The general ability of a group to perform a wide variety of tasks.

Perhaps the field is coming to realize that intelligence in its broadest sense may be more aptly defined as "the skills and abilities necessary to effectively accomplish cultural goals." If one's culture's goals involve successfully pursuing a professional occupation with a good salary in order to support yourself and your family, that culture will foster a view of intelligence that incorporates cognitive and emotional skills and abilities that allow for pursuing such an occupation. If one's culture's goals, however, focus more on the development and maintenance of successful interpersonal relationships, working with nature, or hunting and gathering, intelligence will more aptly be viewed as the skills and abilities related to such activities. On one level, therefore, people of all cultures share a similar view of intelligence—a catchall concept that summarizes the skills and abilities necessary to live effectively in one's culture. At the same time, however, cultural differences naturally exist because of differences in how cultures define goals and the skills and abilities needed to achieve those goals. Future research will need to delve into these dual processes, searching for commonalities as well as differences across cultures and exploring what contextual variables affect intelligence-related behaviors, and why.

CONCLUSION

In this chapter, we have broadly reviewed how culture influences the basic cognitive processes of attention, perception, thinking, consciousness, and intelligence. We have seen how there are many universals as well as culture-specific aspects of cognition. These findings have important implications for our understanding of the relationship between culture and psychological processes. The issues discussed in this chapter serve as the basis for understanding findings from many cross-cultural studies to be discussed in subsequent chapters. Perception, cognition, and consciousness are at the core of many psychological constructs and cultural differences in these processes exemplify the various levels of psychology that culture influences. As consciousness reflects our subjective experience of the world, we take for granted that our consciousness is shared by others. Research in this area, however, has shown that there may be large cultural, as well as individual, differences in consciousness.

These differences are also important for intercultural interactions and applied settings. If people from different cultural backgrounds can view such things as optical illusions differently, it is no wonder they perceive so much of the rest of the world differently as well. When this information is coupled with information concerning other basic psychological processes such as attribution, emotion, and personality, the effect of culture on mental processes and behaviors is amazing.

EXPLORATION AND DISCOVERY

Why Does This Matter to Me?

1. What do you think about intelligence? Is it influenced by one's genes, environment, or both? If environment plays some role, what kind of environmental conditions facilitate intelligence, and what kinds hinder it?

2. Different cultures encourage vastly different ways of thinking about time and punctuality. Have you ever experienced a time conflict with someone from a different culture? What did you do about it?

3. Different cultures produce different ways of expressing pain. How do you express pain? How do you think people of other cultures do so? Can you think of some instances where your way of expressing and thinking about pain may be a disadvantage?

Suggestions for Further Exploration

1. Take the figure of the fish (Figure 5.5) and show it to people from different cultures for ten seconds, and then ask them to recall as many things in the picture as possible. Would you replicate the findings of the studies described in the text?

2. What kinds of things or events in your life do you remember? How do those memories differ from those around you? Of people from different cultures? How do you think those differences in memories affect your daily lives and interactions? Construct a simple experiment testing memory differences across cultures. Why do these differences exist?

3. Ever notice how people see the world differently? How do people come to have their views of the world? Their perceptions? Take any of the figures in the section on optical illusions and conduct your own cross-cultural experiment. Or better yet, design your own illusions or find others not discussed in this book and try them.

4. How would you respond to the mother–daughter conflict, or school-fun conflict described in the section on dialectical thinking above? Try writing out your responses to these vignettes and discuss them with your classmates. How much dialectical thinking did you exhibit? Why?

9 Culture and Emotion

CHAPTER CONTENTS

► **The Evolution of Human Emotion**

Emotions as Evolved Information-Processing Systems

Life without emotion is impossible to imagine. We treasure our feelings—the joy we feel at a ball game, the pleasure of the touch of a loved one, the fun we have with our friends on a night out, seeing a movie, or visiting a nightclub. Even our negative emotions are important: the sadness when away from our loved ones, the death of a family member, the anger when violated, the fear that overcomes us in a scary or unknown situation, and the guilt or shame toward others when our sins are made public. Emotions color our life experiences. They inform us of who we are, what our relationships with others are like, and how to behave. Emotions give meaning to events. Without emotions, those events would be mere facts.

But what are emotions? Most people don't distinguish between emotions and feelings, but many researchers do. Feelings (also known as subjective experience, or **affect**) are a part of emotion, but not emotion itself. Emotion involves much more than feelings. **Emotions** are transient, biopsychosocial reactions to events that have consequences for our welfare, and that potentially require an immediate behavioral response. Emotions include feelings, but also physiological reactions, expressive behaviors, behavioral intentions, and cognitive changes.

Emotions are rapid information processing systems that evolved to help us act with minimal conscious thinking or deliberation (Tooby & Cosmides, 2008). For instance, think about the last time you drank spoiled milk or ate something rotten. Doing so has some pretty negative consequences for our welfare. The emotion of disgust helps us immediately take action by vomiting to get them out of our system, and to not to eat or drink them in the first place in the future. This response is incredibly adaptive because it aids in our survival and allows us to take action immediately and quickly without thinking too much. This aspect of emotion helped us in our evolutionary history, as there were many instances in which immediate action without much thought was necessary to survive, such as encountering wild animals or hostile neighbors. In these instances, taking the time to think deliberately about what to do might have cost one one's life; thus emotions evolved to help us make rapid decisions with minimal cognition.

Emotions are elicited as we scan our environments. We evaluate the events that we perceive to see if they have consequences to our welfare and requires immediate response. If such an event does not occur, we continue to scan our environments, constantly searching for and evaluating such events. If and when such an event is perceived, it triggers an emotion so that we can react and adapt quickly and efficiently (Figure 9.1). When emotions are triggered, they recruit a coordinated system of components; they inform us about our relationship to the triggering event, and prepare us to deal with it in some way. The system of components includes subjective experience (feelings); expressive behavior such as facial expressions or verbal utterances; physiological reactions such as increased heart rate or faster breathing; action tendencies such as moving toward or away from an object; and cognition—specific patterns of thinking. "Emotion" is a metaphor for these reactions.

Emotions are quick; they last only a few seconds or minutes. They are different from moods, which last longer—for hours or days. Emotions are functional; when they occur, they tell us something important about our relationship to the event that elicited it, they help prepare our bodies for action, and they communicate our states and intentions to others (e.g., watch out when the boss is angry). All humans in all cultures have emotions, and for the most part we all have mainly the same types of emotions. Thus emotion is a human universal.

affect Feelings, or subjective experience.

emotions Transient, neurophysiological reactions to events that have consequences for our welfare, and require an immediate behavioral response. They include feelings, but also physiological reactions, expressive behaviors, behavioral intentions, and cognitive changes.

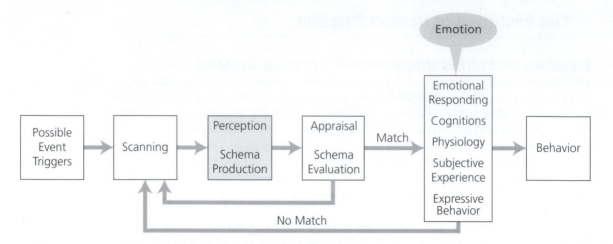

FIGURE 9.1 A Model of Emotion Elicitation

Different Categories of Emotion

basic emotions A small set of emotion categories, or families of emotions, that are considered to be universal to all humans, biologically based and genetically coded, and evolutionarily based. Humans come into the world with programs for these basic emotions; social and cultural learning then influences how they are used in life.

Not all emotions are the same. As we will learn below, humans share a small set of emotions, known as **basic emotions** (Ekman, 1999; Izard, 2007), with other nonhuman primates. Basic emotions are triggered by a biologically innate system in our brains. They evolved originally to help us adapt to our natural and social environments in order to live. From an evolutionary standpoint, it's very difficult to consider how survival could have occurred *without* basic emotions helping us adapt our behaviors quickly and reliably.

Humans have many shades of the basic emotions. As we discussed in Chapter 1, the evolution of the human brain brought with it improvements in many cognitive capacities, including memory, language, and problem solving skills. These cognitive enhancements allowed for the evolution of human culture and facilitated the emergence of uniquely human emotions that go beyond the basic emotions that we share with other animals. These cognitive abilities allow us to make many fine distinctions among the basic emotions in terms of intensity and complexity. For example, anger is a basic emotion. But humans don't just get angry; we are sometimes irritated, aggravated, agitated, annoyed, grouchy, grumpy, frustrated, hostile, exasperated, mad, enraged, or furious. Not only do humans have fear, as do animals, but humans also become anxious, nervous, tense, uneasy, worried, alarmed, shocked, frightened, horrified, terrorized, or mortified. Humans also can feign emotion—expressing it when they do not feel it, or expressing an emotion different from the one they are feeling. Thus the universe of human emotions is invariably much more complex than the set of basic emotions we share with animals.

self-conscious emotions Emotions that focus on the self, such as shame, guilt, pride, or embarrassment. They are important in studies of culture because humans universally have a unique knowledge of self that is different from that of other animals, thus giving rise to self-conscious emotions.

Humans clearly have many other emotions beyond the basic emotions as well. For instance, because humans uniquely have cognitive representations of self and others as intentional agents, humans have emotions that are associated with these self-reflective processes. These are called **self-conscious emotions**, and include emotions such as shame, guilt, pride, and embarrassment. Because humans uniquely have cognitive representations of self and others as intentional agents, humans exclusively have the construct of morality, in which moral emotions such as contempt and disgust play a particularly important role (Haidt, 2001; Rozin, Lowery, Imada, & Haidt, 1999). Disgust is especially interesting; while nonhuman primates share with humans a biologically based version of disgust that helps them to avoid or expel nasty objects (e.g., through vomiting), probably only humans have the interpersonal version of disgust, in which we can be disgusted at others as people (i.e., a moral version of disgust). No wonder that contempt and disgust have been shown to be particularly explosive and devastating emotions when seen in marital interactions (Gottman, 1994; Gottman & Levenson, 2002), and even in terrorist acts (Matsumoto, Frank, & Hwang, 2015; Matsumoto, Hwang, & Frank, 2013, 2014). Shame, pride, guilt, jealousy, regret, nostalgia, loneliness, and many others are all universal emotions (e.g., see Breugelmans, Zeelenberg, Gilovich, Huang, & Shani, 2014; Hepper et al., 2014; Lykes & Kemmelmeier, 2013).

Below we first describe in more detail the category of emotions known as basic emotions. These emotions are biologically based; thus it is important to know what base of emotions exist biologically so that we can understand how cultures influence and regulate these biologically based emotions.

▶ The Biological Bases of Emotion—Basic Emotions

The Original Universality Studies

The concept of basic emotions is rooted in research examining the universality of emotional expressions. Although philosophers argued for centuries about whether or not facial expressions of emotion are universal, contemporary cross-cultural research on facial expressions of emotion stems from the writing of Charles Darwin. Many people are familiar with Darwin's theory of evolution, outlined in *The Origin of Species* (1859). Darwin proposed that humans had evolved from other, more primitive animals, such as apes and chimpanzees, and that our behaviors exist today because they were naturally selected through a process of evolutionary adaptation. In a subsequent volume, *The Expression of Emotion in Man and Animals* (1872), Darwin suggested that facial expressions of emotion, like other expressive behaviors, are biologically innate and evolutionarily adaptive. Humans, Darwin argued, express emotions in their faces in exactly the same ways around the world, regardless of race or culture. Moreover, those facial expressions can also be seen across species, such as in nonhuman primates. According to Darwin, facial expressions of emotion have both communicative and adaptive value. They ensure the survival of the species by providing both internal information to the individual about well-being and person–environment relationships, and social information for others in the community.

During the first half of the twentieth century, several studies were conducted to test Darwin's ideas (e.g., Triandis & Lambert, 1958; Vinacke, 1949; Vinacke & Fong, 1955). Unfortunately, many of them had methodological problems that made drawing conclusions based on them difficult (see Ekman, Friesen, & Ellsworth, 1972, for a review). At the same time, prominent anthropologists such as Margaret Mead and Ray Birdwhistell argued that facial expressions of emotion were not universal; instead, they suggested that facial expressions of emotion had to be learned, much like a language (Ekman, Friesen, & Ellsworth, 1972), and that just as different cultures had different languages, they also had different facial expressions of emotion.

It was not until the 1960s, when psychologists Sylvan Tomkins (Tomkins & McCarter, 1964), Paul Ekman, and Wallace Friesen (Ekman, 1972) and Carroll Izard (1971) independently conducted the first set of methodologically sound studies that this debate was laid to rest. Spurred by the earlier work of Tomkins (1962, 1963), these researchers conducted a series of studies now called the **universality studies**. Four

universality studies
A series of studies that demonstrated the pancultural universality of facial expressions of emotion.

different types of studies were originally included in the series. In the first, photographs of facial expressions of emotion thought to portray universally recognizable emotions were shown to observers in different countries, who had to label each expression. If the expressions were universal, judges in all cultures would agree on what emotion was being portrayed; if the expressions were culturally specific, the observers from different cultures should disagree. There was high level of agreement across all observers in all cultures in the interpretation of six emotions: anger, disgust, fear, happiness, sadness, and surprise.

One problem with these studies was that all the cultures included in the research were literate, industrialized, and relatively modern. It was possible, therefore, that the observers in those cultures could have learned how to interpret the facial expressions in the photographs. The fact that these cultures shared mass media—television, movies, magazines—reinforced this possibility. The research was limited, therefore, because of shared visual input across the cultures studied.

Two studies involving two preliterate tribes of New Guinea addressed these concerns (Ekman, Sorenson, & Friesen, 1969). Participants were asked to select a story that best described a facial expression. The data were very similar to those obtained in literate, industrialized societies. These judgments of posed expressions by preliterate cultures constituted a second source of evidence in support of universality.

Then different tribe members were asked to show on their faces what they would look like if they experienced the different emotions. Photographs of these expressions were brought back to the United States and shown to American observers, none of whom had ever seen the tribe members from New Guinea. When asked to label the emotions shown on the tribe members' faces, the data were again similar to those found in previous studies. Judgments of expressions posed by preliterate tribes thus constituted a third source of evidence for universality (Figure 9.2).

Nevertheless, a question remained as to whether people actually spontaneously display those expressions on their faces when they experience emotion. To address this question, in a fourth study (Friesen, 1972), Americans and Japanese participants were asked to view highly stressful stimuli as their facial reactions were videotaped without their awareness. Analysis of the video records indicated that Americans and Japanese did indeed show exactly the same types of facial expressions at the same points in time, and these expressions corresponded to the same expressions that were considered universal in the judgment research. Data from spontaneous facial expressions of emotion, therefore, constituted the fourth line of evidence in the original set of universality studies (Figure 9.3). Collectively, these studies comprised what is commonly known in the field as the original universality studies that provided the initial evidence for the universality of anger, disgust, fear, happiness, sadness, and surprise.

Subsequent Research after the Original Universality Studies

Since the original universality research above, there have been almost 200 studies that have documented the universal perception or production of the same facial expressions of emotion (Matsumoto, Keltner, Shiota, Frank, & O'Sullivan, 2008; Hwang & Matsumoto, 2016). These studies have demonstrated that the facial expressions postulated by Darwin and later by Tomkins are produced when emotion is aroused and there is no reason to modify the expression because of social circumstances. Moreover, the range of cultures across those studies is impressive. Matsumoto and Willingham's (2006) study of Olympic athletes, for instance, involved 84 athletes from 35 countries. Collectively these studies demonstrate that the facial expressions actually do occur when emotion is aroused in people of different cultures.

Enjoyment   Sadness

Anger   Disgust

FIGURE 9.2
Examples of Emotional Expressions of Members of a Preliterate Culture
Source: Paul Ekman.

FIGURE 9.3
Example of American and Japanese Faces from Ekman (1972)
Source: Paul Ekman.

Other evidence for universality comes from the developmental literature. The same facial musculature that exists in adult humans exists in newborn infants, and is fully functional at birth (Ekman & Oster, 1979). Infants have a rich and varied repertoire of facial expressions, including those that signal not only emotional states, but also interest and attention (Oster, 2005). There is widespread consensus that distaste, the infant precursor of adult disgust, and crying, the universal signal of sadness or distress, occur in neonates (Oster, 2005). Other than these, infants in the first year of life display relatively undifferentiated facial expressions of negative emotions, which later transform into more differentiated, discrete expressions (Camras, Oster, Campos, & Bakeman, 2003; Oster, 2005). Discrete expressions of anger and sadness have been reported in the early part of the second year of life (Hyson & Izard, 1985; Shiller, Izard, & Hembree, 1986). By the time they reach preschool age, children display discrete expressions of the other emotions as well (Casey, 1993).

One compelling line of evidence that suggests that facial expressions of emotion are genetically encoded and not socially learned are studies of congenially blind individuals (Charlesworth & Kreutzer, 1973; Dumas, 1932; Eibl-Eibesfeldt, 1973; Freedman, 1964; Fulcher, 1942; Galati, Scherer, & Ricci-Bitti, 1997; Goodenough, 1932; Ortega, Iglesias, Fernandez, & Corraliza, 1983; Thompson, 1941). In one of our experiments, we compared the spontaneously produced facial expressions of emotion between blind and sighted athletes competing at the 2004 Athens Olympic and Paralympic Games, immediately at the end of a match for a medal (Matsumoto & Willingham, 2009) (Figure 9.4). There was an almost perfect correspondence between the facial behaviors produced between the blind and sighted athletes. As many of the blind athletes were congenitally blind—blind from birth— they could not have possibly learned to produce them by watching others do so. They had to come to the world with an inborn ability to produce those expressions.

Another line of evidence for universality and the genetic encoding of facial expressions of emotion comes from studies of nonhuman primates. For years, ethologists (Chevalier-Skolnikoff, 1973; Geen, 1992; Hauser, 1993; Snowdon, 2003; Van Hoof, 1972) have noted the morphological similarities between human expressions of emotion and nonhuman primate expressions displayed in similar contexts. The evolution

Blind athlete   Sighted athlete

FIGURE 9.4 Comparison of Blind and Sighted Athletes Who Just Lost a Match for a Medal. Photos Copyright © Bob Willingham (Reprinted with Permission)
Source: Bob Willingham.

of the smile and laugh, for instance, occurs along two different evolutionary tracts across early mammals, monkeys, apes, chimpanzees, and humans (Van Hoof, 1972). Among nonhuman primates, facial displays described as grimaces are akin to the human emotions of fear and surprise, while the tense-mouth display was similar to anger (Redican, 1982); these two combined to form the often-identified threat display. Nonhuman primates also show a play face that is similar to the happy face of humans, and a pout similar to that of the human sad face. Both infant rhesus macaques and infant chimpanzees show different facial expressions in reaction to sweet and bitter tastes, but chimps' facial expressions are more similar to human facial expressions than to that of the macaques (Ueno, Ueno, & Tomonaga, 2004). However, even some of the smaller apes, such as siamangs (*Symphalangus syndactylus*), noted for their limited facial expression repertoire, have distinguishable facial expressions accompanying sexuality, agonistic behavior, grooming, and play (Liebal, Pika, & Tomasello, 2004). For some emotional states, a species less closely related to humans than chimpanzees, bonobos, may have more emotions in common with humans (de Waal, 2002).

Other Sources of Evidence for the Universality of Basic Emotions and Their Possible Biological Bases

Universality in Emotion Recognition

One important aspect of basic emotions is that not only are they universally expressed, but that they are also universally recognized. Some of the original universality studies of emotion were judgment studies, in which observers of different cultures viewed facial stimuli and judged the emotions portrayed in them. The earliest studies by Tomkins, Ekman, and Izard demonstrated the existence of six universal expressions—anger, disgust, fear, happiness, sadness, and surprise—in literate and preliterate cultures (Ekman, 1972, 1973; Ekman & Friesen, 1971; Ekman, Sorenson, & Friesen, 1969; Izard, 1971; Tomkins & McCarter, 1964).

Since the original studies, at least 27 studies examining judgments of facial expressions have replicated the finding of universal recognition of basic emotion in the face (Matsumoto, 2001). In addition, a meta-analysis of 168 datasets examining judgments of emotion in the face and other nonverbal stimuli indicated universal emotion recognition well above chance levels (Elfenbein & Ambady, 2002). It would be very difficult to obtain such robust and consistent findings if expressions were not universally recognized. Even when low-intensity expressions are judged across cultures (Ekman, Friesen, O'Sullivan, Chan, Diacoyanni-Tarlatzis, I., Heider, K. et al., 1987; Matsumoto, Consolacion, Yamada, Suzuki, Franklin, Paul, S. et al., 2002), there is strong agreement across cultures as to the emotion in the expression.

Research from the past two decades has also demonstrated the universal recognition of a seventh basic emotion—contempt (Ekman & Friesen, 1986; Ekman & Heider, 1988; Matsumoto, 1992; Matsumoto & Ekman, 2004). Figure 9.5 shows examples of the seven facial expressions of emotion for which research has provided solid evidence for universal recognition.

Universality in Physiological Responses to Emotion

Another part of the emotion response package is physiological reactions. For years there has been debate concerning whether different emotions are associated with different, specific, and unique physiological profiles of responding. Early research in this area was inconclusive. The first definitive evidence for this came from a study that used the universal facial expressions as markers to signal when to examine

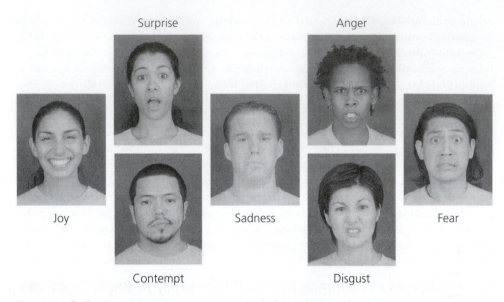

Surprise　　　　　　　Anger

Joy　　　　　　　Sadness　　　　　　　Fear

Contempt　　　　　　　Disgust

FIGURE 9.5 The Seven Basic Emotions and Their Universal Expressions
Source: David Matsumoto, Ph.D.

physiological reactions. In this study, Ekman, Levenson, and Friesen (1983) demonstrated that each of the universal emotions, when signaled by the universal expressions, had a distinct and discrete physiological signature in the autonomic nervous system. Subsequent research has replicated these findings, and has shown how there are specific patterns in central nervous system activity (the brain) as well (Davidson, 2003; Ekman, Davidson, & Friesen, 1990; Levenson, Carstensen, Friesen, & Ekman, 1991; Levenson & Ekman, 2002; Levenson, Ekman, & Friesen, 1990; Mauss, Levenson, McCarter, Wilhelm, & Gross, 2005). These findings have also been replicated in cross-cultural samples, including Chinese and European Americans (Tsai and Levenson, 1997), and the Minangkabau of West Sumatra, Indonesia (Levenson, Ekman, Heider, & Friesen, 1992). The data indicate that emotions help individuals to respond to emotional stimuli by preparing the body to engage in activity. Fear prepares us to flee, while anger prepares us to fight.

Universality in Subjective Emotional Experience

Another component of the emotion package is subjective experience. The most prominent study to examine subjective experiences across cultures is the work by Scherer and his colleagues (Scherer & Wallbott, 1994). They asked respondents to rate their subjective feelings, physiological sensations, motor behaviors, and expressions when they felt anger, disgust, fear, joy, sadness, shame, and guilt. For all response domains, the seven emotions differed significantly and strongly among each other. Geographical and sociocultural factors were much smaller than the differences among the emotions. Thus, the researchers concluded that there are strong and consistent differences between the reaction patterns for the seven emotions, and that these are independent of the country studied. In other words, there were many more similarities in the responses across the cultures than there were differences, providing evidence for universal, psychobiological emotional patterning in subjective response.

Universality in the Coherence among Emotion Response Systems

Not only has the evidence shown that there is universality in the various responses of emotion—antecedent events, appraisals, expressive behavior, subjective experience, and physiology—but that there is also coherence among them. **Emotion response system coherence** refers to the idea that the various response components—face, voice, physiology—are related to each other in a meaningful way.

There are many studies that demonstrate coherence among emotion response systems (reviewed in Matsumoto et al., 2007). Matsumoto et al. (2007), for example, reanalyzed the data from the Scherer studies described above, and examined the relationships among the self-reported expressive behaviors, emotional experiences, and physiological sensations. There were moderately sized correlations between these three systems of responses across the respondents in all 27 countries analyzed. There were also consistent correlations between verbal and nonverbal expressions, as well as between emotion intensity and physiological sensations, all of which suggest coherence in an underlying neurophysiological reality. Moreover, this coherence was true cross-culturally.

Universality in Emotion Antecedents

A central aspect of emotion is the events that trigger them in the first place. **Emotion antecedents** are the events or situations that trigger or elicit an emotion. For example, losing a loved one may be an antecedent of sadness; getting an "A" in a class in which you wanted to do well may elicit happiness or joy. In the scientific literature, emotion antecedents are also known as emotion *elicitors* or *triggers.*

A considerable number of studies has supported the universality of emotion antecedents (Boucher & Brandt, 1981; Brandt & Boucher, 1985). The most prominent work to study emotion antecedents across a wide range of cultures has been that of Scherer and his colleagues, who conducted studies using questionnaires designed to assess the quality and nature of emotional experiences in many different cultures. Their largest study involved approximately 3,000 participants in 37 countries on five continents (Scherer, 1997a, 1997b; Scherer & Wallbott, 1994). Respondents wrote about the situations that brought about the last time they felt anger, disgust, fear, joy, sadness, shame, and guilt. Trained coders then systematically sorted the situations described by participants into general categories such as good news and bad news, temporary and permanent separation, and success and failure in achievement situations. No culture-specific antecedent category was necessary to code the data, indicating that all categories of events generally occurred in all cultures to produce each of the seven emotions studied. In addition, there were many similarities across cultures in the relative frequency with which each of the antecedent events elicited emotions. For example, the most frequent elicitors of happiness across cultures were "relationships with friends," "temporary meetings with friends," and "achievement situations." The most frequent elicitors of anger were "relationships" and "injustice." The most frequent elicitors of sadness were "relationships" and "death." These findings supported the view that emotion antecedents are universal across cultures.

Universality in Emotion Appraisal Processes

Just as central as the event that triggers an emotion are the cognitive processes that occur to evaluate it in order to know whether to trigger an emotion in the first place. This process is known as appraisal, which can be loosely defined as the process by which people evaluate the events, situations, or occurrences that lead to their having emotions. The largest cross-cultural study on emotion appraisal processes is Scherer and colleagues' study described above. There, respondents not only described the events that brought about their emotions (the antecedents described above); they were

emotion response system coherence The idea that the various response components of an emotion—facial expressions, voice, physiological reactions, movements, etc.—are related to each other in a coordinated fashion that prepares individuals to do something vis-à-vis the emotion aroused.

emotion antecedents The events or situations that elicit or trigger an emotion.

TABLE 9.1 Underlying Appraisals That Elicit Emotions

Emotion	Universal Underlying Psychological Theme
Happiness	Goal attainment or accomplishment
Anger	Goal obstruction
Sadness	Loss of loved one or object
Disgust	Contamination
Fear	Threat to physical or psychological well-being
Surprise	New or novel objects
Contempt	Moral superiority

also asked about how they appraised or evaluated those events. For example, the respondents were asked to rate whether the antecedent helped them achieve their goals or blocked their goals; were expected or not; or were fair or unfair. The findings indicated that emotion appraisal processes were more similar than different across cultures.

Moreover, there was a very high degree of cross-cultural similarity in emotion appraisal processes, and this cross-cultural agreement in appraisal has been replicated by other researchers as well (Mauro, Sato, & Tucker, 1992; Roseman, Dhawan, Rettek, Nadidu, & Thapa, 1995). These findings support the idea that the basic emotions appear to be appraised in the same way universally. Table 9.1 summarizes the universal psychological content of emotion appraisals for each of the universal emotions.

Summary

Research on basic emotions has indicated that these emotions are universal psychological phenomena that are based in the evolution of the species. Humans are born with a core set of basic emotions that are biologically innate and genetically encoded. They allow us to appraise events and situations in reliable and predictable ways, thus revealing the same types of underlying psychological elicitors across cultures: loss brings about sadness in all cultures; threat brings about fear. When emotions are elicited, they trigger a host of responses, and these responses are part of a universal emotion package. They are associated with unique physiological signatures in both the central and autonomic nervous systems, which are part of a coordinated response system that prepares individuals to fight, flee, or jump for joy. They are expressed universally in all humans via facial expressions, regardless of race, culture, sex, ethnicity, or national origin. As such, humans can also universally recognize emotions in others, and this has important social meaning. Overall, these universal processes allow us to adapt, respond, and cope with problems that occur in our social lives and environments, aiding us to live, work, and function more effectively, regardless of the culture in which we are embedded.

▶ Cultural Influences on Emotion

Revisiting how human cultures have evolved may help in understanding how cultures influence emotions. Human social life is complex. Individuals are members of multiple groups, with multiple social roles, norms, and expectations, and people move rapidly in and out of the multiple groups of which they are members. This creates the enormous potential for social chaos, which can easily occur if individuals are not coordinated well and relationships not organized systematically. The potential for chaos is also great because of the very large amount of individual differences that exist in any society. One of the crucial functions of culture is to provide the coordination and organization necessary to maintain order, minimize chaos, and maximize group efficiency. Doing so allows individuals and groups to negotiate the complexity of human social life. Culture does this by providing an information system to its members, which is shared by a group and transmitted across generations, and which allows the group to meet basic needs of survival, pursue happiness and well-being, and derive meaning from life. Recall that we had defined culture as a meaning and information system, transmitted across generations (Chapter 1).

In order to maintain social order, cultures create rules, guidelines, values, and norms concerning the regulation of emotion. These governing codes of conduct serve as the primary motivators of behavior (Tomkins, 1962, 1963) and regulate important social functions (Keltner & Haidt, 1999). For instance, cultural values concerning interpersonal relationships and emotions help to create and enforce norms concerning emotion regulation and behavioral expectations. Norms concerning emotion regulation in all cultures help to maintain social order by ensuring the engagement of culturally appropriate behavior mediated by culturally appropriate emotional responding (Figure 9.6) (Matsumoto et al., 2008).

The cultural regulation of emotion occurs in several ways, which we explain below. First, cultures regulate our biologically based basic emotions. Second, cultures help to construct unique emotional experiences that go beyond the basic emotions. Third, cultures help to construct unique concepts, meanings, attitudes, values, and beliefs about emotion. We begin our discussion with how cultures regulate basic emotions.

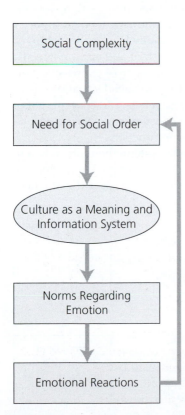

FIGURE 9.6
The Role of Culture in Regulating Emotions to Achieve Social Order

▶ Cultural Regulation of Basic Emotions

Cultures influence the biologically based basic emotion system in order to regulate emotions and ensure social coordination. There are two ways in which this occurs (Figure 9.7). One way is by regulating what people become emotional about in the first place. We call this the "front-end calibration" of the emotion system to culturally available events. In our development, we learn to have emotions to events in our lives, many of which are specific to our cultures (producing cultural differences), and to ourselves (producing individual differences). Although the core emotion system that produces basic emotions is biologically based, it as a flexible system that is adaptable to many different contexts and events, allowing humans to learn to have many different emotional reactions that color life and serve as a motivational basis for behavior. That's why we get angry not only to events in our natural environment; we also get angry to computer crashes, road rage, and flight delays, all of which are not part of our evolutionary history and which we had to learn.

The second way that culture influences emotion is by regulating emotional expressions and behaviors after emotions are elicited. We call this the "back-end calibration" of emotion responses. This process occurs in the form of cultural norms known as **cultural display rules** (more below). That is, once emotions are elicited, individuals learn to modulate, or not, their emotional reactions—including expressions—according to learned rules and norms of what is appropriate in any given circumstance. Some situations require expression management; others don't.

The basic emotion system is like the core computer processor inside the most elemental chip found in computers. Individuals and groups certainly use their computers in ways that are both similar and different; they all are based, however, on the same core processing system. Human cultures, as meaning and information systems, elaborate the use and meaning of the basic emotion system, allowing for a multiplicity of uses. Cultures, like computers, can effectively work on many levels; astonishingly, they can calibrate the emotion system to allow culture-constant and culture-specific events to be encoded with emotional meaning; regulate the type of expressive, verbal, and motor behaviors people should show depending on social situations; give culture-constant and specific meaning to attitudes, values, beliefs, and concepts about emotion; and provide the motivational basis for culture-constant and specific normative behaviors with regard to interpersonal and intergroup functions.

Cultural calibration of the biologically based emotion system, therefore, refers to front-end cultural influences on the core emotion system (regulating what we become emotional about in the first place), while display rules refer to back-end influences

cultural display rules
Culturally prescribed rules that govern how universal emotions can be expressed. These rules center on the appropriateness of displaying emotion, depending on social circumstances. Learned by people early in their lives, they dictate how the universal emotional expressions should be modified according to the social situation. By adulthood, these rules are quite automatic, having been very well practiced.

FIGURE 9.7
Cultural Influences on the Core Emotion System

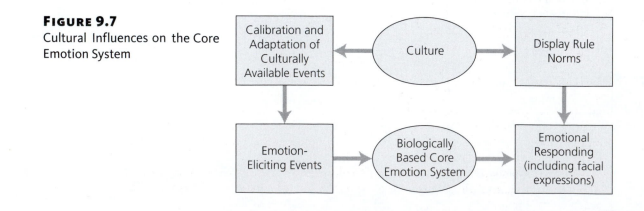

(how we express our emotions and what behaviors are appropriate once we are emotional). The cultural calibration of the evolved, biologically innate emotion and expression system allows for the regulation of culturally appropriate emotional responses to culturally available events, and allows for culturally appropriate behavioral responding. This facilitates social coordination and prevents social chaos, allowing human cultures to live and flourish.

More about Cultural Display Rules

Despite the fact that facial expressions of emotion are universal, sometimes we may have difficulties interpreting the expressions of people from a different cultural background. We may also wonder whether our own expressions are being interpreted in the way we intend. Although we see emotional expressions that are similar to ours in people from very diverse backgrounds, more often than not, we see many differences as well.

The concept of **cultural display rules** can account for the discrepancy (Ekman & Friesen, 1969). These are rules governing how universal emotions can be expressed. These rules center on the appropriateness of displaying each of the emotions in particular social circumstances. These rules are learned early, and they dictate how the universal emotional expressions should be modified according to the social situation. By adulthood, these rules are automatic, having been very well practiced.

There are multiple ways in which display rules can act to modify expressions. People can

1. express *less* than actually felt (deamplification),
2. express *more* than actually felt (amplification),
3. show nothing (neutralization),
4. show the emotion but with another emotion to comment on it (qualification),
5. Mask or conceal feelings by showing something else (masking), and
6. Show an emotion when they really don't feel it (simulation).

The existence of cultural display rules were supported by Friesen's (1972) study of spontaneous expressions of Americans and Japanese described above (one of the original universality studies). In that study, American and Japanese participants were asked to view highly stressful films while their facial reactions were videotaped. That experiment actually had multiple conditions. In the first condition (described previously), participants viewed the stimuli by themselves. In a subsequent condition, an older, higher-status experimenter came into the room and asked the participants to watch the films again, with the experimenter observing them. Their facial reactions were again videotaped. The Americans in general continued to show negative feelings—disgust, fear, sadness, and anger. The Japanese, however, invariably smiled in these instances. These findings showed how universal, biologically innate emotional expressions can interact with culturally defined rules of display to produce appropriate emotional expressions. In the first condition, when display rules did not operate, the Americans and the Japanese exhibited the same expressions. In the second condition, display rules were operative, forcing the Japanese to smile in order not to offend the experimenter, despite their obvious negative feelings. These findings were especially impressive because the participants in the second condition that produced differences were the same individuals as in the first condition that produced similarities.

To further research on display rules, Matsumoto and colleagues (Matsumoto, Takeuchi, Andayani, Kouznetsova, & Krupp, 1998; Matsumoto, Yoo, Hirayama, &

Petrova, 2005) created the Display Rule Assessment Inventory (DRAI), in which participants choose a behavioral response when they experience different emotions in different social situations. The behavioral responses were based on the six response alternatives described above. After initial research documenting the reliability and validity of the instrument, collaborators in over 30 countries administered the DRAI in order to map display rules around the world. Despite the larger potential range of scores, most countries' means on overall expression endorsement fell around the midpoint, and there was relatively small variation around this mean, suggesting a universal norm for expression regulation. Individuals of all cultures endorsed expressions toward in-groups more than toward out-groups, indicating another universal effect. Collectivistic cultures were associated with a display rule norm of less expressivity overall than individualistic cultures, suggesting that overall expressive regulation for all emotions is central to the preservation of social order in these cultures (Figure 9.8). Individualism was also positively associated with higher expressivity norms in general, and for positive emotions in particular. Individualistic cultures were also positively associated with endorsement of expressions of all emotions toward in-groups, but negatively correlated with all negative emotions and positively correlated with happiness

Graphical Representation of the Relationship between Individualism-Collectivism and Overall Expressivity Endorsement

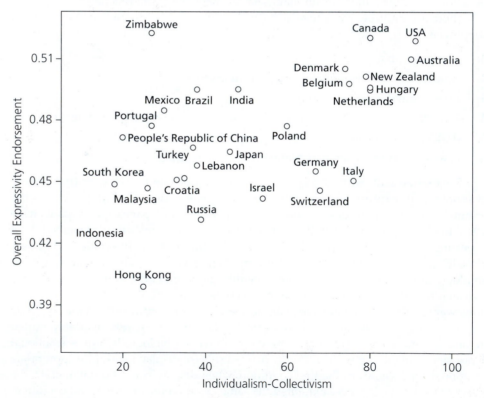

FIGURE 9.8 Relationship between Individualism–Collectivism and Display Rules Endorsing Expressivity. Reprinted with permission from Matsumoto et al. (2008)

Source: David Matsumoto, Seung Hee Yoo, Johnny Fontaine et al. "Mapping Expressive Differences around the World: The Relationship between Emotional Display Rules and Individualism Versus Collectivism," *Journal of Cross-Cultural Psychology,* 20(1), p. 66, Copyright © 2008 by Sage Publications. Reprinted by Permission of SAGE Publications.

and surprise toward outgroups. Cumulatively, these findings suggest a fairly nuanced view of the relationship between culture and expression endorsement that varies as a function of emotion, interactant, and overall expressivity endorsement levels.

Thus, although humans universally have the same base of emotional expressions, culture exerts considerable influence over when and how to use them via culturally learned display rules. Facial expressions of emotion are under the dual influence of universal, biologically innate factors and culturally specific, learned display rules (see Figure 9.9). When an emotion is triggered, a message is sent to the facial affect program (Ekman, 1972), which stores the prototypic facial configuration information for each of the universal emotions. This prototypic configuration is what constitutes the universal aspect of emotional expression, and it is biologically innate. At the same time, a message is sent to the area of the brain storing learned cultural display rules. The resulting expression represents the joint influence of both factors. When display

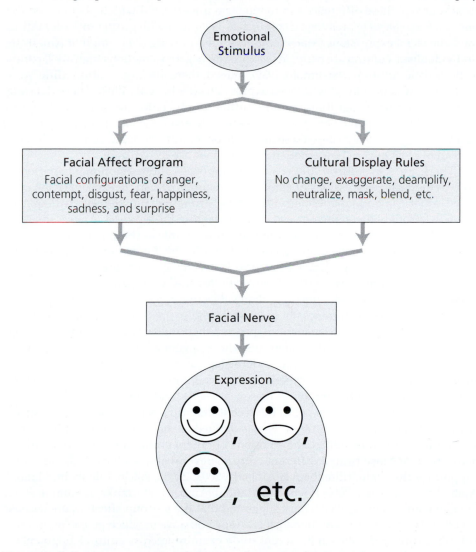

FIGURE 9.9 The Neurocultural Theory of Emotional Expression

Source: Adapted from P. Ekman, Universals and Cultural Differences in Facial Expressions of Emotion, in J. Cole (ed.), *Nebraska Symposium of Motivation*, 1971, vol. 19 (Lincoln: University of Nebraska Press, 1972).

rules do not modify an expression, the universal facial expression of emotion will be displayed. Depending on social circumstances, however, display rules may act to neutralize, amplify, deamplify, qualify, or mask the universal expression. This mechanism explains how and why people can differ in their emotional expressions despite the fact that we all share the same expression base.

Cultural Calibration of How Emotional Expressions Are Perceived

If cultures calibrate the production of facial expressions of emotion through cultural display rules, it makes sense that cultures may also calibrate how individuals perceive emotions in others. Research supports this idea. For instance, Americans are better at recognizing anger, disgust, fear, and sadness than Japanese, but accuracy rates do not differ for happiness or surprise (Matsumoto, 1992). Some research suggests the cultural source of these differences. Individualism is associated with higher recognition rates for some facial expressions (Schimmack, 1996), and with greater intensity ratings for some facial expressions (Matsumoto, 1989), supporting the claim that Americans (individualistic culture) are better at recognizing negative emotions than are Japanese (collectivistic culture) (Matsumoto, 1989). Indeed, there are large cultural differences in absolute recognition rates of facial expressions (Biehl et al., 1997). These data suggest that emotion recognition rates are influenced by culturally learned decoding rules about how to perceive expressions, especially given the fact that all posers were Caucasian. Like display rules, these are probably culturally dependent rules learned early in life that govern how emotional expressions are recognized.

There are also cultural differences in inferences about emotional experiences underlying facial expressions of emotion. Matsumoto, Kasri, & Kooken (1999) compared American and Japanese ratings of how strongly expressions were displayed and how strongly the expresser was actually feeling the emotion. Americans rated external display more intensely than did the Japanese; the Japanese, however, rated internal experience more intensely than did the Americans. Within-culture analyses indicated no significant differences between the two ratings for the Japanese. Significant differences were found, however, for the Americans, who consistently rated external display more intensely than subjective experience. Although previous American–Japanese differences in judgments and expressions were interpreted to have occurred because the Japanese suppressed their intensity ratings, these findings indicated that in fact it was the Americans who exaggerated their external display ratings relative to subjective experience, not the Japanese who suppressed. Not only are such findings wake-up calls to experienced cross-cultural researchers; they also force us to consider how culture produces these tendencies, and why.

ingroup advantage
The hypothesis that individuals can recognize emotions expressed by members of their own culture relatively better than of those from a different culture.

An interesting development in the recent literature is the notion of an **ingroup advantage** in emotion recognition. This is defined as the ability of individuals from a certain culture to recognize the emotions of others of the same culture relatively better than of those from a different culture. Several studies have provided some support for this claim (Elfenbein & Ambady, 2002, 2003a, 2003b; Elfenbein, Mandal, Ambady, & Harizuka, 2002; Elfenbein, Mandal, Ambady, Harizuka, & Kumar, 2004). Elfenbein and Ambady (2002) have suggested that the ingroup effect occurs because of cultural differences in emotion dialects—specific ways in which people of different cultures express emotions. But a recent study examining cross-cultural judgments of spontaneously produced facial expressions did not provide support for the hypothesis (Matsumoto, Olide, & Willingham, 2009). Thus, the ingroup advantage in judging emotions may be limited to when people pose emotions voluntarily, but not when it happens spontaneously.

▶ The Cultural Construction of Emotional Experience

As mentioned earlier, a second way in which cultures regulate emotions is by their facilitation of the construction of unique emotional experiences that go beyond the basic emotions. Humans have very complex emotional worlds, and have many emotions *other than* the seven basic emotions described above. Cultures influence these emotions to a very large degree. A large program of research has shown that cultures help to construct and mold emotional experiences in different ways. People in collectivistic cultures, for example, tend to report experiencing **socially engaging emotions**, such as friendliness, respect, sympathy, guilt, and shame, more than **socially disengaging emotions** such as pride, self-esteem, sulkiness, or frustration; members of individualistic cultures, however, tend to experience more socially disengaging emotions than engaging emotions (Kitayama, Mesquita, & Karasawa, 2006). Relatedly, pleasantness in emotional experience is correlated with interdependent concerns among Japanese, whereas that is not the case for Americans (Mesquita & Karasawa, 2002).

There are also interesting cultural differences in a construct known as **emotional complexity**—the co-occurrence of both pleasant and unpleasant emotions. Early research on this construct showed that this co-occurrence is more prevalent in East Asian than in Western cultures (Bagozzi, Wong, & Yi, 1999; Schimmack, Oishi, & Diener, 2002). European Americans who tend to experience positive emotions more frequently or intensely also tend to experience negative emotions less frequently or intensely. East Asians, however, are more likely to experience the co-occurrence of positive and negative emotions. These cultural differences have been linked to **dialectical thinking** (see Chapter 8) (Spencer-Rodgers, Peng, & Wang, 2010).

These findings suggest that many emotional experiences, especially those different than the basic emotions, are culturally constructed; that is, these experiences are a set of "socially shared scripts" composed of physiological, behavioral, and subjective components (Kitayama & Markus, 1994; Kitayama, Markus, & Matsumoto, 1995). These scripts develop as individuals are enculturated, and they are inextricably linked to the culture in which they are produced and with which they interact. Emotion, therefore, reflects the cultural environment in which individuals develop and live, and are as integral a part of culture as morality and ethics are.

In this view, culture constructs emotional experience. Cultures have different realities and core cultural ideals that lead to different customs, norms, practices, and institutions. These lead to different individual realities, which are comprised of recurrent episodes in local environments. These recurrent episodes, in turn, produce habitual emotional tendencies—specific ways of feelings, which give way to behaviors. The process is cyclical, as behaviors feed back and reinforce the core cultural ideas, the customs and norms, the individual realities, and the habitual emotional tendencies (Kitayama & Markus, 1994; Kitayama, Markus, & Matsumoto, 1995). This model of the "cultural construction of emotion" is summarized in Figure 9.10.

socially engaging emotions Emotions that occur as a result of themes derived from social interdependence and relationships with others.

socially disengaging emotions Emotions that occur as a result of themes grounded in independence and autonomy of the self, and its separateness from others.

emotional complexity The idea that positive and negative emotions can co-occur and be experienced simultaneously.

dialectical thinking The tendency to accept what seem to be contradictions in thought or beliefs.

▶ The Cultural Construction of Concepts, Attitudes, Values, and Beliefs about Emotion

Concepts of Emotion

A third way in which cultures regulate emotions is by their construction of unique concepts, meanings, attitudes, values, and beliefs about emotion. Throughout this

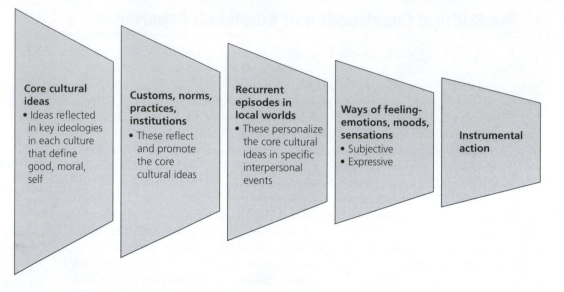

FIGURE 9.10 The Cultural Shaping of Emotion

Source: Adapted from Kitayama, Shinobu, and Hazel Rose Markus (eds). From *Emotion and Culture: Empirical Studies of Mutual Influence,* p. 342, 1994. Published by the American Psychological Association. Reprinted with permission.

chapter, we have been discussing emotion as if it means the same thing to all people. But does it? In the United States, we place a premium on feelings. We all recognize that each of us is unique and that we have our own individual feelings about the things, events, situations, and people around us. We consciously try to be aware of our feelings, to be "in touch" with them, as we say. To be in touch with our feelings and to understand the world around us emotionally is to be a mature adult in our society.

We value feelings and emotions throughout the life span. We cherish our feelings as adults, and we actively try to recognize the feelings of our children and of other young people around us. It is not uncommon for parents to ask their young children how they feel about their swimming lessons, their piano lessons, their teachers at school, or the broccoli on their plates. Parents often give considerable weight to the feelings of their children in making decisions that affect them. "If Johnny doesn't want to do it, we shouldn't make him do it" is a common sentiment among parents in the United States. Indeed, children's emotions are afforded almost the same status as the emotions of adults and the older generations.

Much therapeutic work in psychology centers around human emotions. The goal of individual psychotherapy systems is often to get people to become more aware of their feelings and emotions and to accept them. Much psychotherapeutic work is focused on helping individuals freely express the feelings and emotions they may have bottled up inside. In group therapy, the emphasis is on communicating feelings toward others in the group and listening to and accepting the expressions of feelings by others. This emphasis is also prevalent in workgroups. Industrial and organizational interventions are common, and much time, effort, and energy are spent establishing better lines of communication among employees and recognizing the feelings and emotions of individuals.

How American society values and structures people's feelings and emotions is directly related to the values fostered by American culture. In the United States, individualism has been a cornerstone of the dominant culture, and part of that individualism means that we recognize and value the unique aspects of each and every person. Diversity of feelings and emotions is part of this package; in fact, it may be the most important part in identifying individuals because emotions themselves are highly personalized and individual. Children are valued as separate entities, and their feelings are valued.

The way American culture understands and defines emotion may not be the same in other cultures. First of all, not all cultures have a word for *emotion*. Levy (1973, 1983) reports that Tahitians do not have a word for emotion; nor, according to Lutz (1980, as reported in Russell, 1991; Lutz, 1983), do the Ifaluks of Micronesia. The fact that some cultures do not even have a word that corresponds to our word *emotion* is important; clearly, in these cultures, the concept of emotion is different from ours. Perhaps it is not as important to these cultures as it is to ours. Or perhaps what we know as emotion is labeled differently, in an untranslatable way, and refers to something other than internal, subjective feelings. In this case, too, their concept of emotion would be quite different from ours.

But most cultures of the world do have a word or concept for what we call emotion. Brandt and Boucher (1986) examined the concepts of depression in different cultures, whose languages included Indonesian, Japanese, Korean, Malaysian, Spanish, and Sinhalese. Each of the languages had a word for emotion, suggesting the cross-cultural existence of this concept. But even if a culture has a word for emotion, that culture's word may have different connotations, and thus different meanings, than our English word. For example, Matsuyama, Hama, Kawamura, and Mine (1978) analyzed emotional words from the Japanese language, which included some words that are typically considered emotions (e.g., *angry, sad*) but also some words that Americans would not consider to be emotions (e.g., *considerate, lucky*). Samoans do not have a word for emotion but do have a word (*lagona*) that refers to feelings and sensations (Gerber, 1975, as reported in Russell, 1991).

In summary, not all cultures of the world have a word or concept for what we label *emotion* in English, and even among those that do, it may not mean the same thing as the English word. What we call emotion here may not mean the same thing elsewhere.

Categories of Emotion

Many English words have no equivalent in another culture, and emotion words in other languages may have no exact English equivalent. The German language, for example, contains the word *Schadenfreude*, which refers to pleasure derived from another's misfortunes. There is no exact English translation for this word. The Japanese language contains words such as *itoshii* (longing for an absent loved one), *ijirashii* (a feeling associated with seeing someone praiseworthy overcoming an obstacle), and *amae* (dependence), which also have no exact English translation. Some African languages have a word that covers what English suggests are two emotions: anger and sadness (Leff, 1973). The Ifaluk word *song* can be described sometimes as anger and sometimes as sadness (Lutz, 1980). Some English words have no equivalents in other languages; the English words *terror, horror, dread, apprehension,* and *timidity* are all referred to by the single word *gurakadj* in Gidjingali, an Australian aboriginal language (Hiatt, 1978). This aboriginal word also refers to the English concepts of shame and fear. Frustration may be a word with no exact equivalent in Arabic languages (Russell, 1991).

But just because a culture does not have a word for something that we consider an emotion certainly does not mean that people of that culture do not have those feelings. The fact that there is no exact equivalent in some Arabic languages for our word *frustration* does not mean that people of these cultures never feel frustrated. Similarly, just because our English language does not have a translation equivalent for the German word *Schadenfreude* does not mean that people in the United States do not sometimes derive pleasure from someone else's misfortunes. (Just watch an episode of *America's Funniest Videos*.)

The fact that some emotion words exist in some cultures but not others probably does say something important about how different cultures slice up their worlds using language. Different cultures and languages may **hypercognize** emotions, in which many variations of emotions are identified and words are created for these variations; or they can be **hypocognized**, in which relatively fewer variations of emotions exist (Levy, 1973). The fact that German culture, for example, contains the word *Schadenfreude* must mean that that feeling state or situation was important enough to be given a word that referred to it. The types of words that different cultures use to identify and label the emotion worlds of their members give us yet another clue about the way different cultures structure and mold the emotional experiences of their people.

The Location of Emotion

To Americans, emotions are located inside oneself. To Samoans (Gerber, 1975), Pintupi aborigines (Myers, 1979), and Solomon Islanders (White, 1980), emotions are statements about relationships among people or between people and events. The African Fulani concept *semteende,* which is commonly translated as shame or embarrassment, refers more to a situation than to a feeling; that is, if the situation is appropriate to *semteende,* then someone is feeling it, regardless of what any one individual actually feels (Riesman, 1977).

Even cultures that locate emotions within the body differ in the exact location. In the United States, emotions are associated with the heart. For the Japanese, emotions are in the *hara*—the gut or abdomen. The Chewong of Malay group feelings and thoughts in the liver (Howell, 1981); Tahitians locate emotions as arising from the intestines (Levy, 1973). The closest Ifaluk word to the English word *emotion* is *niferash,* which translates as "our insides" (Lutz, 1982).

That different cultures locate emotions in different places informs us that emotions are understood differently and have different meanings for different peoples. Locating emotions in the heart is convenient and important for American culture, as it speaks to the importance of feelings as something unique to oneself, that no one else can share. By identifying emotion with the heart, Americans identify it with the most important biological organ necessary for survival. The fact that other cultures identify and locate emotions outside the body, such as in social relationships with others, speaks to the importance of relationships in those cultures, in contrast to the individualism of American culture.

Attitudes, Values, and Beliefs about Emotion

Cultures construct attitudes, values, and beliefs about emotion; thus there are many cultural differences on these aspects of emotion. As discussed in Chapter 1, for instance, one well-known approach to studying cultural values around the world has been that of Shalom Schwartz. He has identified seven values that are universal. One of these is known as affective autonomy, which refers to the degree to which cultures emphasize the promotion and protection of people's independent pursuit of positive

---

hypercognition
Relatively greater amounts and forms of knowledge, awareness, and thought about something that go beyond the usual. This term was coined by Levy to refer to cultures that create (hypercognize) many words to differentiate many different emotional states.

hypocognition
Relatively fewer amounts and forms of knowledge, awareness, and thought about something compared to the usual. This term was coined by Levy to refer to cultures that lack (hypocognize) words to differentiate emotional states.

experiences. Affective autonomy fosters pleasure and an exciting or varied life. In Schwartz's work, France, Switzerland, Canada, Denmark, and Austria valued this dimension the most, whereas Egypt, Cameroon, Senegal, Yemen, and Ghana valued it the least.

Another cultural value is uncertainty avoidance, which refers to the degree to which people feel threatened by the unknown or ambiguous situations, and have developed beliefs, institutions, or rituals to avoid them (Hofstede, 2001). Basically it refers to a society's tolerance of uncertainty and ambiguity, which is associated with anxiety and stress. Greece, Portugal, Guatemala, Uruguay, and Belgium ranked the highest on this value; Singapore, Jamaica, Denmark, Sweden, and Hong Kong ranked the lowest.

Because values about emotions are cultural constructions, they are more culturally based and variable, and different cultures facilitate different values about emotion. Cultural values about emotion are about how people want to feel—ideal affect—and this is different than how people actually feel—actual affect (Tsai, 2007; Tsai, Knutson, & Fung, 2006). For example, European and Asian Americans tend to value more high arousal positive affect such as excitement more than do Hong Kong Chinese, who tend to value more low arousal positive affect such as being calm. But the cultural construction of values about emotion does not necessarily correspond to the emotions people actually have; temperament and personality traits, not cultural values, predict actual affect better than cultural values, whereas cultural values predict ideal affect better (Tsai et al., 2006).

Cultures also facilitate the construction of beliefs about emotions. Members of collectivistic cultures tend to associate emotions with assessments of social worth, others. Members of individualistic cultures tend to believe that emotions are individual evaluations of the environment, and reflect something about the self and not necessarily social relationships (Mesquita, 2001).

Summary

In this section, we have discussed how cultures construct concepts, attitudes, values, and beliefs about emotion. It makes sense that culture more heavily influences these aspects of emotion as they are based in language and higher-order cognitive processes than the physiological and expressive aspects of the basic emotions discussed earlier. Also, many of the culturally constructed emotions are emotions *other than* the basic emotions; these more complex emotions may require more cognitive abilities than do basic emotions. Because higher-order cognitive abilities co-evolved with human cultures, it is no wonder that emotion-related processes that depend on those cognitive abilities are more heavily related to culture.

CONCLUSION

In this chapter, we have reviewed the evidence for the universality and biological innateness of a set of basic emotions. They are elicited by the same psychological themes around the world, and when elicited, trigger a coordinated set of responses that include expressive behavior, physiology, cognitions, and action potential. They have important meaning not only to oneself but to others. Because they are universally expressed, emotions are also universally recognized.

But cultures also exert profound influences on emotions. Cultures regulate basic emotions by influencing what we become emotional about in the first place (front end calibration), and what we should do about our emotions once we have them (back end calibration). Cultures achieve front end calibration by regulating the relative frequencies by which antecedent events bring forth emotions, the types of events that trigger the basic emotions, and the specific dimensions by which emotions are appraised. Cultures achieve back end calibration by regulating expressive behavior via cultural display rules. Cultures can also influence how we judge emotions in others via cultural decoding rules. Cultures also facilitate the construction of culturally unique emotional experiences and culturally specific emotion-related concepts and meanings of emotion, along with attitudes, values, and beliefs about emotion.

The coexistence of universal and culture-specific aspects of emotion has been a source of debate for many years. But as we discussed in this chapter, we believe that these are not necessarily mutually exclusive positions. Emotions are universal; some universal emotions are based in biology and rooted in genetics (the basic emotions). Other emotions are constructed using higher-order cognitive processes moderated by culture. Because they are moderated by culture, cultures differ in the relative frequency and importance of different emotions, and have different attitudes, values, and beliefs of emotion. Some cultures hypercognize emotions so that they have many words for emotional states; others hypocognize emotions so that there are relatively fewer words. A large part of understanding the relative contribution of biology and culture to emotions requires one to make clear exactly what emotions one is talking about (e.g., anger, fear, pride, jealousy, or respect), and what aspect of emotions (e.g., physiological reactions, expressive behavior, subjective experience, values). Some aspects of some emotions are more clearly biologically based; other aspects of other emotions are clearly more culturally constructed. Scientists in this area of psychology will need to continue to take up the greater challenge of how biology interacts with culture to produce the individual and group psychologies we see around the world (see Matsumoto & Hwang, 2012, for a more detailed discussion of this issue).

If nothing else, at least our recognition of emotions as a universal process can help bring people together, regardless of culture, race, ethnicity, or gender. As we continue our study of human feelings and emotions across cultures, perhaps it is most important to recognize how these boundaries mold our emotions. Although we all have emotions, they mean different things to different people and are experienced, expressed, and perceived in different ways. One of our first tasks in learning about emotions across cultures is to recognize and respect those differences. But an equally important task is to recognize our similarities as well.

EXPLORATION AND DISCOVERY

Why Does This Matter to Me?

1. Do you ever have emotional episodes in which you later regret what you said or did? Why did they occur? Can you think of the description of the process of emotion elicitation described in this chapter and identify the "point of no return?" How do you think you can improve the way you handle your emotions?

2. Have you ever noticed how people from different cultures express themselves? Was it the same or different from what you expected? Why? Can the concept of universality and cultural display rules described in this chapter help explain some of your experiences?

3. How do you express yourself? Do you think your way of expressing yourself and your emotions is adaptive in your culture? Would it be adaptive in other cultures? Why or why not?

4. Have you worked with or counseled people from different cultures? Have you ever notice how different, or not, their emotional displays are from what you expect? Why do you think these differences exist? How are those differences possibly rooted in culture? What does that same about your own emotional expressivity? Where do you think that came from?

Suggestions for Further Exploration

1. In this chapter, we have learned how emotions are expressed universally in our faces. Do you think emotions can be recognized through vocal cues? How would you design a study to test your ideas?

2. How many words for emotions can you think of? Do you think other cultures have the same number of words? More? Less? Do you think that the emotion vocabularies are organized the same ways across cultures? Or differently? How would you test these ideas?

3. A colleague of yours claims that animals have emotions just as humans do. How would you test that?

10 Culture, Language, and Communication

CHAPTER CONTENTS

▶ The Co-Evolution of Language and Human Culture

The evolution of human cultures coincided with the evolution of the ability for verbal language in humans, and for this reason, language is a universal psychological ability in humans. All individuals have the capacity to develop language, and the vast majority of people all over the world indeed do so. Humans have an innate ability to acquire language, and although the exact mechanisms are not well understood, language acquisition occurs in all individuals. Thus, all human societies have language, and language forms the basis for the creation and maintenance of human cultures.

Human cultures are constructed from an understanding of shared intentionality, and language facilitates the creation of shared intentionality. Humans are intentional agents, having the ability to infer intentions in and share intentions with others. Language aids in our ability to communicate intentions, and our beliefs about the intentions of others, to each other quickly and efficiently. These abilities come together to help humans form human cultures.

As we defined in Chapter 1, human cultures are unique meaning and informational systems communicated across generations. This definition makes it clear that considering and understanding human cultures is impossible without acknowledging the contribution that language makes to it. Human cultures exist precisely because of the ability to have language. Language helps us to create large social networks, larger than those found in nonhuman primates; to navigate those social networks quickly and efficiently; and to solve complex social coordination problems when they occur. Language is an incredibly important ability that allows us to do all of these tasks and activities. With the advent of language in humans, we are able to create meaning about the world around us in terms of symbols. A country's flag, for instance, is typically a powerful symbol with meaning, as is the Bible or Koran. These cultural meanings are facilitated by language.

A recent set of studies highlighted the importance of language as one of the basic foundations of culture. Data from 5 million books across over 200 years indicated that sensory metaphors (i.e., phrases that relate to the senses in metaphoric ways, such as "a cold person") are used more frequently than their semantic equivalents (e.g., an "unfriendly person"). Experimental evidence demonstrated that sensory metaphors are more memorable because they relate more to the senses—which all people of all cultures have—and have more associative cues. All together, these studies suggest a way by which the five senses play a role in shaping culture through language (Akpinar & Berger, 2015).

While the ability to have language is universal to humans, each culture creates its own unique language. Language differences reflect important differences between cultures, and they also help to reinforce culture. In the next section, we begin to explore how languages are different across cultures.

▶ Cultural Influences on Verbal Language

The Structure of Language

Identifying the basic structure and features of language is useful in order to examine the relationship between culture and language. There are five critical features of all languages:

1. The **lexicon**, or vocabulary, refers to the words contained in a language. For example, the words *tree, eat, how,* and *slowly* are each part of the English lexicon.

lexicon The words contained in a language, the vocabulary.

syntax and grammar
The system of rules governing word forms and how words should be strung together to form meaningful utterances.

phonology The system of rules governing how words should sound (pronunciation, "accent") in a given language.

semantics What words mean.

pragmatics The system of rules governing how language is used and understood in given social contexts.

phonemes The smallest and most basic units of sound in a language.

morphemes The smallest and most basic units of meaning in a language.

2. The **syntax and grammar** of a language refer to the system of rules governing word forms and how words should be strung together to form meaningful utterances. For example, English has a grammatical rule that says we add "s" to the end of many words to indicate plurality (*cat* becomes *cats*). English also has a syntactic rule that we generally place adjectives before nouns, not after (e.g., *small dog*, not *dog small*).

3. **Phonology** refers to the system of rules governing how words should sound (pronunciation) in a given language. For instance, in English, we don't pronounce *new* the same as sew.

4. **Semantics** refers to what words mean. For example, *table* refers to a physical object that has four legs and a flat horizontal surface.

5. **Pragmatics** refers to the system of rules governing how language is used and understood in given social contexts. For example, the statement "It is cold" could be interpreted as a request to close a window or as a statement of fact about the temperature. How it's interpreted depends on the social and environmental context.

There are two other useful concepts to understand the structure of language. **Phonemes** are the smallest and most basic units of sound in a language, and every culture creates its own set of phonemes that are required to vocalize words. Phonemes form the base of a language hierarchy in which language gains in complexity as sounds gain meaning, which in turn produces words, which are strung together in phrases and finally sentences. For example, while English speakers can easily hear and speak the difference between l and r, these sounds are not differentiated in Japanese; thus these sounds give Japanese speakers of English trouble. The *th* sound in English (as in the word *through*) is also difficult for many. The same is true the other way as well; there are some sounds in other languages that English speakers find very difficult to understand or produce. Around the world, geographically close languages share significantly more phonemes than geographically distant language pairs, regardless of whether or not the languages are in fact closely related (Creanza et al., 2015).

Morphemes are the smallest and most basic units of meaning in a language. For example, the prefix "un" is a combination of phonemes that has a specific meaning in English. Most English speakers come to learn to differentiate words such as *cooperative* versus *uncooperative*, *known* versus *unknown*, or *decided* versus *undecided*. Each culture has its own set of morphemes in its language.

Culture and Language Acquisition

All humans have the universal ability to acquire language. Although the precise mechanisms by which language acquisition occurs are still unknown, it appears that all human infants are born with the ability to make the same range of sounds; thus, human infants produce the same range of phonemes across cultures. Through interactions with others, infants' sound production is then shaped and reinforced so that certain sounds are encouraged while certain other sounds are discouraged. These elemental sounds become associated with meanings (morphemes), and gradually are combined into words (lexicons) and sentences. The ability to create almost an infinite number of meaningful expressions from a finite set of elemental sounds is one of the characteristics that differentiates humans from nonhuman animals (Fitch & Hauser, 2004).

Culture, therefore, influences language acquisition from a very early stage, helping to shape the phonemes and morphemes of a language and the creation of words.

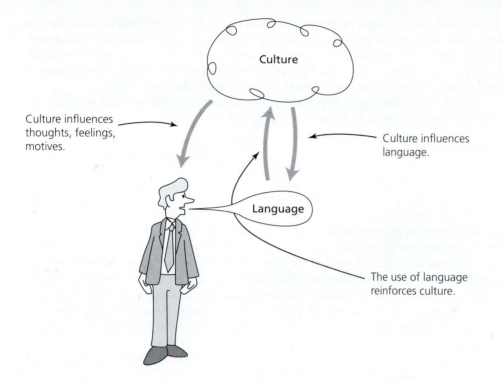

FIGURE 10.1 The Reciprocal Relation between Culture and Language

Culture provides the rules by which words are said (phonology) and strung together to form meaningful statements (syntax and grammar). Culture also provides the rules by which meaning is derived from words and statements (semantics), and the rules by which language is used in different social contexts (pragmatics). The influence of culture on language is pervasive.

Environmental factors are also important to consider. Recent research, for instance, has shown that climactic variables such as aridity (dryness) have negative effects on vocal cord movement. Some complex tone patterns are less likely to evolve in and exist in arid climates (Everett et al., 2015). Recall from our discussion in Chapter 1 that culture is a response to adapting to the environment.

Through the use of language, an individual is transformed into an agent of the culture. The feelings, associations, connotations, and nuances of language both influence and are influenced by the culture. Over time, an individual embodies the essence of culture via language, and in using the language, he or she reinforces that language's concepts of culture (see Figure 10.1). By this token, we would hypothesize that students of language may learn a language better if part of their training involves learning about the culture from which the language originates, compared to language instruction by itself. This is a viewpoint that is slowly gaining popularity in second language acquisition education.

Language Differences across Cultures

Before we discuss language differences across cultures, it's important to recognize that there are important similarities across languages as well. For example, a recent analysis of 10 languages diverse in origin and culture revealed that the words of natural human languages possess a universal positivity bias (Dodds et al., 2015). The languages studied were English, Spanish, French, German, Brazilian Portuguese, Korean, Chinese (Simplified), Russian, Indonesian, and Arabic. Approximately 5 million happiness ratings were obtained on the words. Ratings in each of the languages clearly demonstrated more positivity than negativity in the words.

But of course languages differ in many ways across cultures. Here we focus on two: cultural differences in lexicons and pragmatics.

Culture and Lexicons

One way in which cultures influence the language lexicon is in what is known as self-other referents, that is, what we call ourselves and others. In American English, for example, we generally use one of two words, and their derivatives, to describe ourselves when talking to others: *I* and *we*. We use these words irrespective of whom we are talking to or what we are talking about. If we are talking to a university professor, we use the word *I* to refer to ourselves. If we are talking to our parents, we use the same word *I*. And we use the same word *I* when referring to ourselves with friends, family, neighbors, acquaintances, bosses, or subordinates. Likewise, we generally use a single word in English to refer to another person or group of people: *you*. In conversation with our parents, bosses, friends, lovers, strangers, children, and just about anyone, we use *you* or one of its derivatives to refer to the other person or persons.

Many languages in the world, however, have much more elaborate systems of reference that depend on the nature of the relationship between people. The Japanese language, for instance, has translation equivalents of the English words *I*, *we*, and *you*, but these words are used much less frequently in Japanese than in English. In Japanese, what you call yourself and others is dependent on the relationship between you and the other person. Often, the decision about what is appropriate to call yourself and another person depends on the status differences between the two people. For example, if you are of a higher status than the other person, in Japan you would refer to yourself by position or role rather than by the English equivalent of *I*. Teachers use the word *teacher* to refer to themselves when talking to students. Doctors may use the term *doctor*, and parents use the word *mother* or *father* when speaking to their children.

In the Japanese language, if you are of a lower status than the person to whom you are speaking, you refer to yourself using one of several pronoun equivalents of *I*, such as *watashi, watakushi, boku*, or *ore*. The use of these different terms for *I* depends on your sex (women do not use *boku* or *ore*), degree of politeness, and degree of familiarity with the other person. When speaking to someone of higher status, for example, people generally use *watashi* to refer to themselves. When speaking to friends or colleagues, men usually refer to themselves as *boku or ore*.

Likewise, if you are speaking to someone of higher status, you generally refer to that person by role or title. When speaking to your teachers, you refer to them as *teacher*, even when addressing them directly. You would call your boss by his or her title, such as *section chief* or *president*. You would not use a personal pronoun such as our English "you" in addressing a person of higher status. When speaking to a person of lower status, you would generally use a personal pronoun or the person's actual name. As with personal pronouns for *I*, the Japanese language contains several pronouns for you—among them, *anata, omae,* and *kimi*. Again, the appropriate use of each depends on the relationship; generally, *omae* and *kimi* are used when speaking to someone of lower status or to someone very familiar and intimate. Indeed, the Japanese language system of self- and other-referents is very complicated, especially when compared to American English (see Figure 10.2).

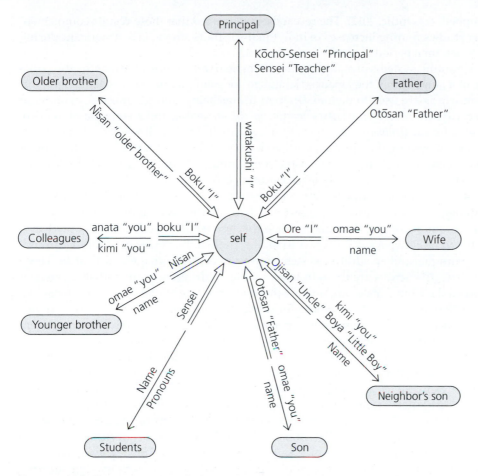

FIGURE 10.2 Japanese Words for Self and Other

Source: Suzuki, T. (1973). *Words in context*. Tokyo: Kodansha International. Copyright © 1973. Reprinted with permission.

This complex system of self-other referents occurs in many other languages as well, including Korean and Spanish, and reflects important cultural differences. In these cultures, language, mannerisms, and other aspects of behavior must be modified according to the relationship and context under which the communication is occurring. The most important dimensions along which behavior and language are differentiated are often status and group orientation. All aspects of behavior differ depend on whether one person is higher or lower in status than the other person in the conversation. Behavior and language differ depending on whether the other person is a member of your ingroup or not, and the choice of appropriate self- and other-referents in these languages reflect important aspects of those cultures. For this reason, it is generally easy to identify the status relationship between individuals in how they use the self-other referent system (and other observable aspects of their communication, such as nonverbal behaviors discussed below).

Recent studies have documented interesting changes in the use of pronouns even within the United States. One analysis of 766,513 American books published between 1960 and 2008 showed that the use of first person plural pronouns (*we, us*) decreased 10% while the use of first person singular pronouns (*I, me*) increased 42% (Twenge,

Campbell, & Gentile, 2012). The researchers suggested that these results complement other studies finding increases in individualistic traits among U.S. Americans during this same time period.

Counting systems provide another example of how culture influences the structure of a language. In the Japanese language, for example, as in many languages, different words are used to denote different things being counted. Round, cylindrical objects are counted by the suffix *hon* (*ippon, nihon, sanbon*, and so on); flat objects are counted by *mai* (*ichimai, nimai, sanmai*, and so on). In English, however, all objects are simply counted by the number, with no such prefix or suffix to denote the type of object being counted. For some reason, some cultures found it important to describe their physical world differently when counting objects in that world.

As we mentioned in Chapter 8 when discussing cross-national differences in math performance, many languages base their number system on a base 10 system, with unique words for the numbers one through ten. Eleven is often counted 10-1, twelve is 10-2, twenty is 2-10, and so on. In English, however, numbers 1 through 19 are unique, and an additive system similar to other languages starts at 20. These linguistic differences are thought to contribute to differences in math achievement between the United States and many other countries (see Stigler & Baranes, 1988).

Different cultures have words for things that do not exist in English, and vice versa. These are very interesting, especially if we understand language as a system that is created by cultures to slice up, partition, and represent their environments. If a word exists in a language that does not exist in others, then that concept was important enough in that culture to have justified having its own word to refer to it. One popular example used to illustrate this is the German word *Schadenfreude*, which is loosely translated as something like "joy in another person's misfortunes" (we discussed this word in Chapter 9). In English, there is no direct translation of this word; thus it must have been "important enough" in German culture for that concept to have its own word so that people can talk about it. Some believe that when a word exists in one culture but not another, the concept itself doesn't occur in other cultures, but we don't believe that to be true. Certainly many people who speak English experience joy in other people's misery (as depicted on TV shows such as *America's Funniest Videos*). Thus, it's not the concept that does or does not exist; it's that the word that represents the concept may or may not exist across cultures. (This is related to the terms **hypocognition** and **hypercognition** covered in Chapter 9.)

Culture and Pragmatics

Culture affects not only the language lexicons, but also pragmatics—that is, the rules governing how language is used and understood in different social contexts. In many languages, it is common to drop first- and second-person pronouns (*I/we* and *you*) from sentences; this occurs more frequently in collectivistic cultures, and it is thought that meaning can be inferred from the context in such cultures much more than in individualistic cultures (Kashima & Kashima, 1998), which require very direct statements (can you imagine having a conversation in English *without using I, we, or you?*).

There are cultural variations in how people of different cultures speak to others and use language depending on their relationship and context (Gudykunst & Nishida, 1986; Gudykunst, Yoon, & Nishida, 1987), as well as in how people of different cultures apologize (Barnlund & Yoshioka, 1990); give personal narratives (Minami & McCabe, 1995), compliments (Barnlund & Araki, 1985), and criticisms (Nomura & Barnlund, 1983); self-disclose (Chen, 1995); express sympathy (Koopmann-Holm & Tsai, 2014); or say "thank you" (Lee, Park, Imai, & Dolan, 2012; Park & Lee, 2012). For example,

hypocognition Relatively fewer amounts and forms of knowledge, awareness, and thought about something compared to the usual. This term was coined by Levy to refer to cultures that lack (hypocognize) words to differentiate emotional states.

hypercognition Relatively greater amounts and forms of knowledge, awareness, and thought about something that go beyond the usual. This term was coined by Levy to refer to cultures that create (hypercognize) many words to differentiate many different emotional states.

Americans tend to be relatively more positive about statements that include "thank you" and judge the writer to be more credible than Koreans or Japanese (Park & Lee, 2012). Even within the United States, people who live in states that value honor more than others are more likely to name their children with a component of their father or grandfather's names than with a female ancestor (Brown, Carvallo, & Imura, 2014). And there are ethnic differences among European, African, and Asian Americans in the type of information provided, self-descriptions, and psychological attributes in their Facebook pages (DeAndrea, Shaw, & Levine, 2010)

Many of these cultural differences in pragmatics can be summarized in terms of communication style. Some languages are very direct while others are very indirect. Some languages are very succinct and precise; others very elaborate and extended. Some cultures are very contextual, that is, important meanings are conveyed in the context within which language occurs, or in the way in which it is delivered, relative to the actual content of the speech. Consequently, some cultures are **high-context cultures** with high-context languages, whiles others are **low-context** (Hall, 1966, 1973). Some languages have specific forms for **honorific speech**, which are specific language forms that denote status differences among interactants, conferring higher status to others while at the same time acknowledging one's lower status when appropriate, and vice versa.

high-context cultures Cultures that promote communication in which many messages are conveyed indirectly in context rather than directly in verbal language.

low-context cultures Cultures that promote direct communication in which messages are conveyed primarily and directly in verbal languages and the effects of context are minimized.

honorific speech Speech styles in certain languages that denote status differences among interactants.

Language and Thought: The Sapir–Whorf Hypothesis

One of the most important and long-standing debates in studies of language and behavior involves the relationship between language and thought processes. This relationship is particularly important to the cross-cultural study of language because each culture is associated with a given language as a vehicle for its expression. How does culture influence language? And how does language influence culture?

The **Sapir–Whorf hypothesis**, also referred to as *linguistic relativity*, suggests that speakers of different languages think differently and that they do so because of the differences in their languages. Because different cultures typically have different languages, the Sapir–Whorf hypothesis is especially important for understanding cultural differences (and similarities) in thought and behavior as a function of language.

The Sapir–Whorf hypothesis is important to verify, because if correct, it suggests that people of different cultures think differently, just by the very nature, structure, and function of their language. Their thought processes, their associations, their ways of interpreting the world—even the same events we perceive—may be different because they speak a different language and this language has helped shape their thought patterns. This hypothesis also suggests that people who speak more than one language may actually have different thought patterns when speaking different languages, a topic to which we will return below when we discuss bilingualism.

Sapir–Whorf hypothesis The proposition that speakers of different languages think differently, and that they do so because of the differences in their languages. Also referred to as linguistic relativity.

Many studies have examined language-cognition issues since Edward Sapir and Benjamin Whorf first proposed their hypothesis in the 1950s. In one of the earliest language studies, Carroll and Casagrande (1958) compared Navajo and English speakers. They examined the relationship between the system of shape classification in the Navajo language and the amount of attention children pay to shape when classifying objects. Similar to the Japanese language described earlier in this chapter, the Navajo language has the interesting grammatical feature that certain verbs of handling (for example, "to pick up," "to drop") require special linguistic forms depending on what kind of object is being handled. A total of 11 such linguistic forms describe different shapes—round spherical objects, round thin objects, long flexible things, and so forth. Noting how much more complex this linguistic feature is in

Navajo than in English, Carroll and Casagrande (1958) suggested that such linguistic features might play a role in influencing cognitive processes. In their experiment, they compared Navajo- and English-dominant children to see how often they used shape, form, or type of material to categorize objects. The Navajo-dominant children were significantly more likely to categorize by shape than were the English-dominant children. In the same study, Carroll and Casagrande (1958) also reported that the performance of low-income African American English-speaking children was similar to that of European American children. This finding was particularly important because the African American children, unlike the European Americans, were not accustomed to blocks and form-board toys. This study provided early support for the idea that the language we speak influences the kind of thoughts we have, and later studies provided more support (e.g., Bloom, 1981; Garro, 1986; Gordon, 2004; Hoosain, 1986, 1991; Kay & Kempton, 1984; Lin & Schwanenflugel, 1995; Lucy, 1992; Santa & Baker, 1975).

At the same time, other studies challenged the Sapir–Whorf hypothesis. For instance, Berlin and Kay (1969) tested the claim that "The continuous gradation of color that exists in nature is represented in language by a series of discrete categories. ... There is nothing inherent either in the spectrum or the human perception of it which would compel its division in this way. The specific method of division is part of the structure of English" (p. 4). To test this claim, Berlin and Kay (1969) undertook a study of the distribution of color terms in 20 languages. They asked international university students in the United States to list the "basic" color terms in each of their native languages. They then asked these students to identify from an array of glass color chips the most typical or best examples of a basic color term the researchers specified. Berlin and Kay (1969) found a limited number of basic color terms in any language. They also reported that the color chips chosen as best examples of these basic terms tended to fall in clusters they termed *focal points*. In languages that had a basic term for bluish colors, the best example of the color was found to be the same "focal blue" for speakers of all the languages. These findings suggested that people in different cultures perceive colors in much the same way despite differences in their languages.

Berlin and Kay's findings were later confirmed by a series of experiments conducted by Rosch. In her experiments, Rosch (e.g., 1973) set out to test just how culturally universal these focal points were. She compared two languages that differed markedly in the number of basic color terms: English, with multiple color terms, and Dani, which has only two color terms. Dani is the language spoken by a Stone Age tribe living in the highlands of Irian Jaya, Indonesian New Guinea (coincidentally, this was one of the preliterate tribes in which the originality of facial expressions of emotion was tested, as described in Chapter 9). One color term, *mili*, was found to include both "dark" and "cold" colors (e.g., black, green, and blue), while the second color term, *mola*, included both "light" and "warm" colors (e.g., white, red, and yellow). Rosch also explored the relationship between language and memory. She argued that if the Whorfian position were correct, Dani's lack of a rich color lexicon would inhibit Dani speakers' ability to discriminate and remember colors. As it happened, Dani speakers did not confuse color categories any more than did speakers of English (Heider & Oliver, 1972). Nor did Dani speakers perform differently from English speakers on memory tasks.

Berlin and Kay (1969) also examined 78 languages and found that 11 basic color terms form a universal hierarchy. Some languages, such as English and German, use all 11 terms; others, such as Dani (New Guinea), use as few as two. Further, they noticed an evolutionary order in which languages encoded these universal categories.

For example, if a language had three color terms, those three terms describe black, white, and red. This hierarchy of color names in human language is as follows:

1. All languages contain terms for white and black.

2. If a language contains three terms, it also contains a term for red.

3. If a language contains four terms, it also contains a term for either green or yellow (but not both).

4. If a language contains five terms, it contains terms for both green and yellow.

5. If a language contains six terms, it also contains a term for blue.

6. If a language contains seven terms, it also contains a term for brown.

7. If a language contains eight or more terms, it also contains a term for purple, pink, orange, gray, or some combination of these.

Other studies have challenged the Sapir–Whorf hypothesis and the idea of linguistic relativity (e.g., Au, 1983; Liu, 1985; Takano, 1989). In a review concerning the Sapir–Whorf hypothesis, Pinker (1995) concluded that many of the earlier studies claiming linguistic relativity were severely flawed. He then pointed to the fact that we can think *without* words and language, suggesting that language does not necessarily determine our thoughts. He cited evidence of deaf children who clearly think while lacking a language, but soon invent one; of isolated adults who grew up without language but still could engage in abstract thinking; how babies, who have no words, can still do very simple forms of arithmetic (Wynn, 1992); and how thought is not just made up of words and language, but is also visual and nonverbal.

So what's the bottom line? Perhaps the best way to make sense of this area of study comes from an analysis of the Sapir–Whorf hypothesis published by Fishman years ago (1960). Many studies of the Sapir–Whorf hypothesis read as if it were only one hypothesis. Actually, there are several different Sapir–Whorf hypotheses. Fishman published a comprehensive breakdown of the most important ways the Sapir–Whorf hypothesis has been discussed (see Table 10.1). In his description, these different approaches are ordered in increasing levels of complexity. Two factors determine the level at which a given version of the hypothesis might fall. The first factor relates to the particular aspect of language that is of interest—for example, the lexicon or the grammar. The second factor relates to the cognitive behavior of the speakers of a given language—for example, cultural themes or nonlinguistic data such as a decision-making task. Of the four levels, Level 1 is the least complex; Level 4 is the most complex. Levels 3 and 4 are actually closer to Whorf's original ideas in that they concern the grammar or syntax of language as opposed to its lexicon.

In reviewing the literature on the Sapir–Whorf hypothesis, keeping in mind exactly which level of the hypothesis is being tested is important. Few studies test the Sapir–Whorf hypothesis at Fishman's Level 3 or 4. A considerable amount of research

TABLE 10.1 Fishman's Sapir–Whorf Hypothesis Schema

Data of Language Characteristics	Data of Cognitive Behavior	
	Linguistic Data	Nonlinguistic Data
Lexical/Semantic	Level 1*	Level 2
Grammatical	Level 3	Level 4**

*Least sophisticated.
**Most sophisticated.

compares lexical differences and linguistic behavior (Fishman's Level 1) or nonlinguistic behavior (Fishman's Level 2). Most of this research is at Level 2, comparing lexical differences with nonlinguistic behaviors. When such comparisons have shown differences, language is assumed to have caused these differences.

Viewed according to Fishman's classifications, the best-studied area is lexical differences between languages, which provides some of the weaker support for the hypothesis. This makes sense, because the lexicon seems to be only minimally related to thought processes, which may account for some skepticism about the Sapir–Whorf hypothesis. A less-studied area, however—that of syntactic and grammatical differences between languages—provides some evidence for the claim that language influences cognition. Perhaps stronger evidence will be found in future studies of how the pragmatic systems of different languages influence speakers' thought processes.

▶ Cultural Influences on Nonverbal Communication

nonverbal behaviors
All the dynamic behaviors, other than words, that convey messages, including facial expressions; movements and gestures of hands, arms, and legs; posture; vocal characteristics such as pitch, rate, intonation, and silence; interpersonal space; touching behaviors; and gaze and visual attention.

Verbal language is not the only component of communication; it involves **nonverbal behaviors** as well, which are all of the behaviors that occur during communication that do *not* include verbal language. These include facial expressions, nonverbal vocal cues (tone of voice, pitch, intonation, pauses, silence), gestures, body postures, interpersonal distance, touching behaviors, gaze and visual attention, and the like. In short, all our nonverbal behaviors form important channels of communication as well (see Figure 10.3).

There is an interesting paradox with regards to communication. Research has shown that the bulk of messages that occur in communication are conveyed

FIGURE 10.3 These American Servicemen Were Taken Captive When North Korea Seized the U.S. Ship *Pueblo* in 1968. Can you find the nonverbal behavior displayed by some of these men, sending a message that their captors were unaware of? (Look at the Position of Their Fingers.)

Source: Bettmann/Corbis

nonverbally; thus the nonverbal channels are actually more important in understanding meaning and especially the emotional states of the speakers (Friedman, 1978). Yet research has also demonstrated that most people consciously attend to the verbal language, not the nonverbal behaviors, when interacting with and judging others (Ekman, Friesen, O'Sullivan, & Scherer, 1980; O'Sullivan, Ekman, Friesen, & Scherer, 1985). For this reason, it may be important to be more attentive to the nonverbal cues that occur in communication.

In the previous chapter, we discussed at length how cultures influence facial expressions of emotion via display rules, which is one of the most important channels of nonverbal behavior. Here we'll discuss how cultures influence other nonverbal behaviors.

Culture and Gestures

Gestures are primarily hand movements that are used to illustrate speech or to convey verbal meaning. **Speech illustrators** are movements that are directly tied to speech, and serve to illustrate or highlight what is being said. Cultures differ in both the amount and type of these various illustrative gestures. Some cultures, such as Latin and Middle Eastern cultures, strongly encourage the use of large, illustrative gestures when speaking; they are highly expressive in their gesticulation (some people say you speak Italian with your hands). Others, such as East Asian cultures, discourage the use of such gestures, especially when in public; they are relatively less expressive in their gesticulation. Cultural differences exist in not only the overall frequency of usage, amplitude, and duration, but also in forms. When counting, for example, Germans use the thumb for one, while Canadians and Americans use the index finger (Pika, Nicoladis, & Marentette, 2009).

> **speech illustrators** Nonverbal behaviors, often gestures, that accompany speech and are used to illustrate or highlight speech.

The other purpose of gestures is to convey verbal meaning without words. These are known as *emblematic gestures*, or **emblems**. Every culture develops its own emblem vocabulary in gestures, which are tied to words or phrases. Emblematic gestures, therefore, are culture specific (and some are gender-specific within cultures). This is true not only of national cultures, but also of organizational cultures (e.g., the military, sports teams). Unlike illustrative gestures, emblematic gestures can stand on their own without speech and convey verbal meaning, such as the American A-OK sign, the peace sign (two fingers up, palm facing outward), or OK (thumb up, hand in fist). Emblems are an important part of any cultural language because they allow for communication across distances when voices cannot be readily heard; and they allow for communication when speech is not allowed or wise.

> **emblems** Nonverbal gestures that carry meaning, like a phrase or sentence.

The study of culture and gestures has its roots in the work of David Efron (Boas, Efron, & Foley, 1936; Efron, 1941), who examined the gestures of Sicilian and Lithuanian Jewish immigrants in New York City. Efron found that there were distinct gestures among traditional Jews and Italians, but that the gestures disappeared as people were more assimilated into the larger American culture. Differences in emblematic gestures have been documented all around the world (Ekman, 1976; Friesen, Ekman, & Wallbott, 1979; Morris, Collett, Marsh, & O'Shaughnessy, 1980). Because emblems are culture-specific, their meanings across cultures are often different and sometimes offensive. The American A-OK sign, for example, is an obscene gesture in many cultures of Europe, having sexual implications. Placing both hands at the side of one's head and pointing upward with the forefingers signals that one is angry in some cultures; in others, however, it refers to the devil; and in others it means that one wants sex. The inverted peace sign—two fingers up in a fist pointed inward toward oneself—is an insult in England and Australia. See Figure 10.4 for examples of some other culture-specific emblems.

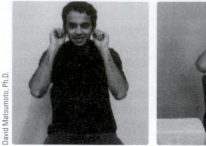

Apology in Nepal   "Too hot to touch" in China   "Oh my eye! (You liar!)"
                                                                    in Iran

FIGURE 10.4 Examples of Culturally Unique Emblems

The first two pictures above show examples of emblems with different meanings in two cultures. In Nepal the ears are grabbed as a realization that one has offended the ears of another person by saying something impolite or otherwise offensive. In China the earlobe is grabbed after touching something hot as the earlobe is the coolest part of the skin and it is believed it will relieve the pain in the burned finger. This has evolved into an emblem that means too hot in general. The third picture shows an example of a unique emblem. When you want to say you are lying you act as if you have been struck in the eye and say "Oh my eye." The meaning is that when someone tells you a lie it is like being struck in the eye.

Culture and Gaze

Gaze is a powerful nonverbal behavior most likely because of its evolutionary roots in animals. Gaze is associated with dominance, power, or aggression in both humans and animals (Fehr & Exline, 1987), as well as affiliation and nurturance (Argyle & Cook, 1976). The power of gaze is exemplified in "the staring game," in which two individuals stare at each other until one breaks off the stare or smiles; the individual that does so is the loser. Interestingly, such staring games are also done in animal societies, and establish dominance hierarchies.

Cultures create rules concerning gazing and visual attention because both aggression and affiliation are behavioral tendencies that are important for group stability and maintenance. Cultures differ in these rules. Arabs, for example, gaze much longer and more directly at their partners than do Americans (Hall, 1963; Watson & Graves, 1966). Watson (1970) classified 30 countries as either a "contact" culture (those that facilitated physical touch or contact during interaction) or a "noncontact" culture, and found that contact cultures engaged in more gazing and had more direct orientations when interacting with others, less interpersonal distance, and more touching. Even when people are thinking, their gaze follows culturally determined norms (McCarthy, Lee, Itakura, & Muir, 2006). Within the United States, ethnic groups differ in gaze and visual behavior (Exline, Jones, & Maciorowski, 1977; LaFrance & Mayo, 1976).

Gaze is often used as a nonverbal sign of respect. But because different cultures produce different rules concerning gaze, respect is conveyed differently with gaze. In the United States, individuals are taught to "look the other person in the eye," or to "look at me when you're talking." In the United States, looking directly at the individual to whom one is talking is a sign of respect. In other cultures, however, gazing directly can be a sign of disrespect, and looking away or even looking down is a sign of respect. Thus, it is easy to understand how Americans may judge people of other cultures as disrespectful or insincere, whereas individuals from other cultures may judge Americans to be aggressive or arrogant.

Stereotypes about gaze also underlie judgments of deception and credibility. Around the world, a commonly held belief is that when people are not looking one straight in the eye, they are likely to be lying (The Global Deception Research Team, 2006). Not only is that probably not true (there is little or no empirical support for this myth), but the cultural differences mentioned immediately above compound the situation even more, allowing Americans to believe that foreigners are lying when in fact they might simply be acting deferentially.

Culture and Voice

The voice is another important channel of nonverbal behavior, and conveys many different messages. Of course, words are communicated through speech and the voice, but the voice also contains many characteristics that go well beyond speech in communicating messages. These characteristics are called **paralinguistic cues** and include the tone of voice, intonation, pitch, speech rate, use of silence, and volume.

paralinguistic cues Aspects of the voice that convey information, such as tone, intonation, pitch, speech rate, use of silence.

Some specific emotional states were conveyed through the voice across cultures (Beier & Zautra, 1972; Matsumoto & Kishimoto, 1983; McCluskey & Albas, 1981; Sauter & Eimer, 2010; Sauter, Eisner, Ekman, & Scott, 2010; Scherer, 1986; Simon-Thomas, Keltner, Sauter, Sinicropi-Yao, & Abramson, 2009). Anger, for instance, produces a harsh edge to the voice; the voice gets louder, and speech rates increase. Disgust produces yuck sounds, while fear produces higher pitch and sudden inhalations. Sadness produces softer voices and decreased speech rates.

The voice and verbal style are also used to illustrate and amplify speech, and cultures differ in how they facilitate this usage. Expressive cultures use louder voices with high speech rates, whereas less expressive cultures use softer voices with lower speech rates. Additionally, pronunciations of some languages require the production of different sounds and rhythms to the voice that may be associated with different emotions (e.g., the guttural quality of some Germanic languages, the up and down rhythms of Mandarin). While they sound normal in the cultures in which these vocal cues originate, in other cultures, it's easy to have negative reactions to these because they sound different and are associated with aversive emotions.

Culture, Interpersonal Space, and Touch

The use of space in interpersonal interactions is another important nonverbal behavior and is called **proxemics**. There are four different levels of interpersonal space use depending on social relationship type: intimate, personal, social, and public (Hall, 1966, 1973; see Figure 10.5). Interpersonal distance helps to regulate intimacy by controlling sensory exposures because the possibility of sensory stimulation (smells, sights, touch) is enhanced at closer distances. For this reason, it makes good sense that cultures regulate the use of space, as such regulation is necessary for social coordination; violations of space bring about aversive reactions (Sussman & Rosenfeld, 1978). In the United States, Hall suggested that intimate distances are less than 18 inches (46 cm), personal distances are 18 inches to 4 feet (1.2m), social distance is 4-12 feet (3.66 m), and public distances are greater than 12 feet.

proxemics The use of space in interpersonal relationships.

People of all cultures appear to use space according to the four major distinctions above, but they differ in the spaces they attribute to them. Arab males, for example, tend to sit closer to each other than American males, with more direct, confrontational types of body orientations (Watson & Graves, 1966). They also use greater eye contact and speak in louder voices. Arabs, at least in the past, learned to interact with others at distances close enough to feel the other person's breath (Hall, 1963, 1966). Latin Americans tend to interact more closely than do students of European backgrounds (Forston & Larson, 1968), and Indonesians tend to sit closer than Australians (Noesjirwan, 1977, 1978). Italians interact more closely than either Germans

FIGURE 10.5
Hall's Distinctions of Interpersonal
Space

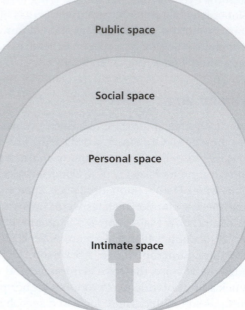

or Americans (Shuter, 1977), and Colombians interact at closer distances than do Costa Ricans (Shuter, 1976). When interacting with someone from their same culture, Japanese sat the farthest away, Venezuelans the closest, with Americans in the middle (Sussman & Rosenfeld, 1982); interestingly, in the same study, foreigners who spoke in English adopted the American conversational distance compared to when speaking with others from their home country in their native language. Cultural differences in the use of space even occur when individuals set dolls to interact with each other (Little, 1968).

A logical extension of interpersonal space is touch, as touch requires close physical contact. Touch is another powerful nonverbal behavior and is known as **haptics**. Just as cultures regulate space, they also regulate touch. As mentioned above, Watson (1970) classified 30 countries as either a "contact" culture (those that facilitated physical touch or contact during interaction) or a "noncontact" culture. Violations of the cultural rules regarding touch are likely to be interpreted in the same way as those of space, producing aversive consequences.

haptics The use of touch in interpersonal interactions.

▶ Intracultural and Intercultural Communication

Communication is a complex and intricate process that involves the exchange of messages between interactants, both verbally and nonverbally. In order to understand the complexity of the communication process, we need to build a vocabulary of its elemental units.

messages The meanings that encoders intend to convey and decoders interpret.

encoding The process by which people select, consciously or unconsciously, a particular modality and method by which to create and send a message to someone else.

- **Messages** are the information and meanings that are exchanged when two or more people communicate. These may be knowledge, ideas, concepts, thoughts, or emotions.

- **Encoding** refers to the process by which people select messages—consciously or unconsciously—imbed messages in signals, and send those message-laden signals to others.

■ **Signals** are observable behaviors that do not necessarily have inherent meaning, but carry messages that are encoded during communication. That is, these are the specific verbal language and nonverbal behaviors that are encoded when a message is sent.

■ **Channels** refer to the specific sensory modalities by which signals are sent and messages are retrieved, such as sight or sound. The most widely used channels of communication are visual—seeing facial expressions, body postures, gestures, and the like—and auditory—hearing words, tone of voice, and so on. However, all the other senses are used in communication, including touch, smell, and taste.

■ **Decoding** refers to the process by which a person receives signals from an encoder and translates those signals into meaningful messages.

The process of communication can be described as one in which a sender encodes a message into a set of signals. These signals are conveyed through a variety of channels. The receiver decodes the signals to interpret the message. Once a message is interpreted, the decoder then becomes the encoder, relaying back his or her own messages via the same process. The original encoder then becomes the decoder. This complex process of exchange, with switching roles and encoding and decoding of messages, constitutes the process of communication. It is akin to playing catch with messages (Matsumoto, 2007b). And humans do this amazingly quickly.

Cultural Influences on Encoding and Decoding

As we learned earlier in this chapter, culture influences the verbal language that we speak and the nonverbal behaviors we produce when we speak (and even when we don't speak). At the same time, people of all cultures learn rules from early childhood that aid in deciphering the cultural codes inherent in speech and nonverbal behavior. These decoding rules develop in conjunction with display or encoding rules and are a natural part of the development of communication skills.

Cultural decoding rules involve ethnocentrism, cultural filters, emotions, value judgments, stereotypes and expectations, and social cognitions. As we grow, we learn how to perceive signals and interpret messages; that is, we learn cultural rules of decoding what is appropriate, what is not, what is good and what is bad. Because we share a set of encoding and decoding rules with people of our culture, we develop a set of expectations about communication. These expectations are often based on implicit stereotypes we hold about how communication "ought to be." These rules and expectations form a basis of tacit understanding that need not be spoken each time we, as adult members of the same culture, communicate with one another.

Emotional reactions are associated with those expectations, ranging from acceptance and pleasure when expectations are met, to outrage, hostility, and frustration when expectations are violated. Our emotions, in turn, are intimately tied to value judgments and attributions, which we often make without a second thought. These judgments seem only natural because they are rooted in our upbringing; they are the only types of judgments we have learned to make. Emotions and values serve as guidelines in helping us form opinions about others and ourselves.

Thus, decoding rules, and their associated emotions and value judgments, form the basis of the "filters" that we use in seeing the world. As we become more enculturated, we add more layers to those filters. These filters are like lenses that allow us to perceive the world in a certain way. By the time we are adults, we share the same filters with others in our cultural group. They become part of our self, inseparable and invisible, and are a normal part of our psychological composition because of the

signals The specific words and behaviors that are sent during communication that convey messages.

channels The specific sensory modalities by which signals are sent and messages are retrieved.

decoding The process by which a person receives signals from an encoder and translates these signals into meaningful messages.

Cultural decoding rules These are rules that people of all cultures learn from early childhood about how to decode or decipher speech and behavior. They form the basis for the cultural filters we have in interpreting the world, and are associated with implicit (and sometimes explicit) judgments of appropriateness, goodness, socialization, or right-wrong.

way we have been enculturated. A large part of the enculturation process, in fact, can be thought of as learning one's cultural filters. These are the lenses by which people decode and interpret the world around them.

The Process of Intracultural and Intercultural Communication

intracultural communication
Communication that occurs among people of the same cultural background.

Intracultural communication refers to communication among people of the same cultural background (also known as interpersonal communication). Intracultural communication works because, as we mentioned above, interactants implicitly share the same ground rules about encoding and decoding. It's as if we all learn to wrap our thoughts into gift boxes; messages sent and received are familiar because they generally share the same type of wrapping and box. When people communicate within the boundaries of accepted ground rules, they can focus on the content of the messages that are being exchanged. They encode and decode messages using the same cultural codes. When we communicate within the shared boundaries of culture, we make an implicit judgment that the other person is a member of our culture or is engaging in socially appropriate behavior. We may consider the individual to have been socialized "well" into our culture, and we make value judgments about the process and the person's ability to engage in that accepted process.

intercultural communication
The exchange of knowledge, ideas, thoughts, concepts, and emotions among people of different cultural backgrounds.

Intercultural communication refers to communication between people of different cultural backgrounds. When we examine intercultural communication in micromomentary detail, we find much the same process as with intracultural communication. But in intercultural communication, interactants do not necessarily share the same ground rules; that is, they don't use the same gift boxes or wrapping. Thus focusing on the content of the messages that are being exchanged becomes more difficult, as people may be encoding and decoding messages using different cultural codes. If this happens, communication does not proceed smoothly and misunderstandings occur, and people may make implicit judgments that the other person does not know how to act appropriately, is rude, or not "good."

Cultural differences in nonverbal behavior make intercultural interactions and communications more difficult than intracultural communication. There are a number of potential obstacles to effective intercultural communication (Barna, 1996), including the following:

1. *Assumptions of similarities*. People may naively assume that others are the same, or at least similar enough to make communication easy.

2. *Language differences*. When people are trying to communicate in a language in which they are not entirely fluent, people often think that a word, phrase, or sentence has one and only one meaning—the meaning they intend to convey—when in fact what they are saying may have a different meaning in a different cultural perspective. To assume similarity in meaning is to ignore all the other possible sources of signals and messages discussed in the previous two chapters, including nonverbal expressions, tone of voice, body orientation, and many other behaviors.

3. *Nonverbal misinterpretations*. Misunderstandings in relation to the interpretation of nonverbal behaviors can easily lead to conflicts or confrontations that break down the communication process.

4. *Preconceptions and stereotypes*. Overreliance on stereotypes can prevent us from viewing others and their communications objectively, and from searching for cues that may help us interpret their communications in the way they were intended.

5. *Tendency to evaluate*. Different cultural values may generate negative evaluations of others, especially when communication is not as smooth as one would expect.

6. *High anxiety or tension.* Intercultural communication episodes are often associated with greater anxiety and stress than are more familiar intracultural communication situations. Too much anxiety and stress can lead to dysfunctional thought processes and behaviors. Stress and anxiety can exaggerate all of the other stumbling blocks, making it more likely that people will cling to rigid interpretations, hold onto stereotypes despite objective evidence to the contrary, and make negative evaluations of others.

7. *Uncertainty and ambiguity.* Intercultural communication is likely to be marred by uncertainty and ambiguity, not only because of questions concerning the verbal messages, but also because of cultural differences in the nonverbal behavior associated with the verbal messages. These are likely to lead to aversive reactions that increase the potential for misunderstanding, miscommunication, and misattributions about intent or character, which disrupts social coordination and increases the potential for conflict. It's easier for people from expressive cultures to judge those from reserved cultures as being untrustworthy, inscrutable, sly, or shifty. At the same time, it's easier for people from reserved cultures to judge those from expressive cultures as arrogant, loud, rude, immature, or vulgar. Many of these aversive reactions occur unconsciously and automatically because they are rooted in cultural filters for interpreting the appropriateness of behavior that are developed from early childhood through the process of enculturation.

Intercultural communication is often more uncertain and ambiguous because of differences in the ground rules of the interaction. This uncertainty is inherent in both verbal and nonverbal behaviors and in both encoding and decoding: how to package messages into signals that will be interpreted according to one's intentions, and how to open packages according to the sender's original intentions. Intercultural interactants often engage with each other in a verbal language that is not a native language for at least one participant, and sometimes both. Thus, there is inherent uncertainty in the meaning of the words. Cultural differences in the use of all nonverbal channels add to the uncertainty. Decoders can never be as sure as they are in intracultural situations that they are interpreting signals and messages as originally intended by encoders.

Thus when interacting interculturally, one strategy many people attempt, especially initially, is to reduce the uncertainty (Berger, 1979; Berger & Calabrese, 1975). Research from three decades ago has provided support for this idea. Gudykunst and Nishida (1984) tested 100 American and 100 Japanese participants, assigning them to one of four experimental conditions: cultural and attitude similarity (intracultural communication), cultural dissimilarity (intercultural communication) and attitude similarity, cultural similarity and attitude dissimilarity, and cultural dissimilarity and attitude dissimilarity. Cultural similarity or dissimilarity was manipulated by having participants interact with a stranger from either their own culture or the other culture. Attitude similarity or dissimilarity was manipulated through a description of similar or dissimilar attitudes when introducing the stranger. For each participant, the researchers assessed intent to self-disclose, intent to interrogate, nonverbal affiliative expressions, attributional confidence, and interpersonal attraction. The intent to interrogate, intent to self-disclose, and nonverbal affiliative expressiveness were all higher in the cultural dissimilarity condition than in the cultural similarity condition. Uncertainty reduction theory predicted that these strategies would be used more extensively in communication contexts with higher levels of uncertainty.

8. *Conflict.* Intercultural communication is also marked by a greater potential for conflict. During intercultural encounters, chances are great that people's behaviors will not conform to our expectations. We often interpret those behaviors as transgressions against our value system and morality. They produce negative emotions, which are upsetting to our self-concepts. These conflicts arise in intercultural episodes not only with people but also with other agents of a cultural system (such as public transportation, the post office, shops, businesses). These interactions are bound to accentuate differences in process, which inevitably lead to conflict or misunderstanding.

Figure 10.6 illustrates why this conflict is highly likely. Because interactants cannot send or receive signals unambiguously, as they are accustomed to in intracultural situations, the intercultural communication episode can be frustrating and patience-testing. Tempers are quick to flare, and people can easily become distraught or turned off by the extra effort such interactions require. Even if interactants are somewhat successful in unpacking signals, the messages interpreted may be partial, ambiguous, or misunderstood. Messages may not be deciphered according to the sender's original intent, leading to miscommunication gaffes and problems later on.

Uncertainty contributes to this conflict. People may become impatient with or intolerant of the ambiguity, leading to anger, frustration, or resentment. Even after uncertainty is reduced, conflict can occur because of the differences in meaning of verbal language and nonverbal behaviors across cultures and the associated emotions and values inherent in the cultural system. The result is often differences in the interpretation of underlying intent among interactants. Of course this occurs in intracultural communication as well.

Research highlights how intercultural interactions may be difficult. In one study (Pekerti & Thomas, 2003), East Asian and Anglo-European students in New Zealand participated in a task with either another East Asian or Anglo-European student in which they had to rate the severity of crimes. Their communication behaviors during the 15-minute task were categorized according to an individualistic or collectivistic style. The Anglo-Europeans actually communicated in *more* individualistic ways than in the intracultural situation, and the East Asian students communicated in more collectivistic ways than in the intracultural situation. These findings suggested that in intercultural situations, cultural differences in communication may become *more* pronounced compared to intracultural situations.

Together, uncertainty and conflict make intercultural communication a complex yet fascinating process that challenges even the most practiced and interculturally sensitive people. Given these challenges, how can we develop our skills at intercultural communication and improve intercultural relationships?

Improving Intercultural Communication

Mindfulness and Uncertainty Reduction

mindfulness A Buddhist principle emphasizing close attention to the present moment, being aware of one's senses, breathing, and thoughts without judgment or evaluation. A strategy to improve intercultural communication that allows people to be conscious of their own habits, mental scripts, and cultural expectations concerning communication. Mindfulness is effective in reducing tension, anxiety, and stress and has been incorporated successfully in cognitive behavioral therapies.

Effective communication requires knowledge of and respect for cultural differences in worldviews and behaviors, as well as sensitivity to differences between high- and low-context communication patterns. **Mindfulness** may be especially important in dealing with conflict in intercultural communication (Ting-Toomey, 1996). Mindfulness allows people to be conscious of their own habits, mental scripts, and cultural expectations concerning communication. It allows one to continually create new mental categories, remain open to new information, and be aware of multiple perspectives. In short, mindfulness allows one to be conscious and conscientious about the various characteristics that are associated with ethnorelativism.

FIGURE 10.6 A Micromomentary Analysis of Intercultural Communication

Three components of mindfulness affect intercultural effectiveness: motivational, knowledge, and skill factors (Gudykunst, 1993; see Table 10.2). Motivational factors include the specific needs of the interactants, attraction between the interactants, social bonds, self-conceptions, and openness to new information. Knowledge factors include expectations, shared networks, knowledge of more than one perspective, knowledge of alternative interpretations, and knowledge of similarities and

TABLE 10.2 Three Components of Mindfulness

Motivational Factors	Knowledge Factors	Skill Factors
■ Needs	■ Multiple perspectives	■ Empathize
■ Attraction	■ Alternative interpretations	■ Tolerance of ambiguity
■ Social bonds	■ Similarities and differences	■ Adapt communication
■ Self-conceptions		■ Create new categories
■ Openness		■ Accommodate behavior
		■ Gather appropriate information

differences. Skill factors include the ability to empathize, tolerate ambiguity, adapt communication, create new categories, accommodate behavior, and gather appropriate information. These three factors influence the amount of uncertainty in a situation and the degree of anxiety or stress interactants actually feel. They influence the degree to which interactants are "mindful" of the communication episode—that is, the degree to which they take conscious and deliberate steps to think through their own and others' behaviors, and to plan and interpret the interaction appropriately as it unfolds. A high degree of mindfulness reduces uncertainty and anxiety, resulting in effective communication.

uncertainty reduction One of the major goals of initial intercultural encounters—to reduce the level of uncertainty and anxiety that one feels when attempting to decode intercultural messages.

   Uncertainty reduction is one of the major goals of initial intercultural encounters. Without uncertainty reduction, it is impossible for interactants to begin processing the content of signals and interpreting messages properly because uncertainty renders messages inherently ambiguous. If uncertainty is reduced, interactants can then focus on the content of the signals and messages that are being exchanged. Intercultural communication is like deciphering coded language: the first step is to decipher the code (reduce uncertainty); the second is to interpret and respond to the content, once deciphered.

Face

face The public appearance or image of a person.

When managing intercultural interactions, we should be mindful of the importance of "**face**" and its maintenance (Ting-Toomey, 1996). Although the concept of "face" appears to be uniquely Asian, people of all cultures experience the same phenomenon, as it refers to concerns with one's appearance in public or reputation, and the potential embarrassment or shame associated with a threat to that appearance. People working in *any* culture should be aware of face. Members of individualistic cultures who communicate with people from collectivistic cultures may consider being proactive in dealing with low-grade conflict situations; not be pushy; be sensitive to the importance of quiet, mindful observation; practice attentive listening skills, especially in relation to the feelings of others; discard the model of dealing with problems directly; and let go of conflict situations if the other party does not want to deal with them directly. Conversely, people from collectivistic cultures who must deal with conflicts in an individualistic context should be mindful of individualistic problem-solving assumptions; focus on resolving major issues and expressing their feelings and opinions openly; engage in assertive conflict behavior; take individual responsibility for dealing with conflict; provide verbal feedback; use direct verbal messages; and commit to working out the problem directly with the other person.

Emotion Regulation

Effective intercultural communication is riddled with challenges, and recent research has demonstrated a key role for a psychological process known as emotion regulation

(Matsumoto & LeRoux, 2003; Matsumoto, LeRoux, Bernhard, & Gray, 2004; Matsumoto et al., 2003; Matsumoto et al., 2001; Matsumoto, LeRoux, Robles, & Campos, 2007). As mentioned earlier, conflict and misunderstandings are inevitable, and our normal ethnocentric and stereotypic ways of thinking often lead us to make negative value judgments about those differences, conflicts, and misunderstandings. Negative emotions are often associated with these judgments. These negative reactions make it difficult for us to engage in more constructive methods of interacting; they keep us from appreciating differences and integrating with people who are different. As conflict is inevitable in intercultural communication, being able to control our negative emotional reactions becomes extremely important Those who can control their emotions will be able to engage in a more constructive intercultural process, opening the door to more successful intercultural interactions. Those who cannot will have that door closed to them. Emotions, therefore, hold the key to successful intercultural experiences.

When faced with cultural differences and conflict in intercultural communication, individuals who can somehow control their negative feelings—putting them on hold and not acting directly upon them or allowing them to overcome their thinking, acting, and feeling—will be able to engage in other processes that will help them broaden their appraisal and attribution of the causes of those differences. Once emotions are held in check, individuals can then engage in critical thinking about the origins of those differences, hopefully going beyond their own cultural framework to consider causes they may not have even been aware of. If this type of critical thinking can occur, individuals can be open to alternative hypotheses concerning the causes of those differences and have the flexibility to accept or reject them.

Regulating or controlling negative emotions, therefore, is a gatekeeper ability that allows us to become more mindful of our communication style and to engage in more constructive and open thought processes. Having the most complex mental model of effective intercultural communication will not help us one bit unless we are able to deal with the negative emotions that are bound to occur in intercultural communication episodes—to put them aside for the time being so that we can engage in more constructive thought processes that involve the creation of new mental categories via critical thinking. Regulating emotions is the key that allows us to open the door to these more advanced complex processes.

By creating expectations about some of the difficulties inherent in intercultural communication and having some ideas of how to overcome them, we can begin to ensure that intercultural interactions are not insurmountable obstacles. Instead, by clarifying expectations, we can create a platform for staging the development and exchange of ideas and the sharing of goals in new and exciting ways not actualized by intracultural communication.

▶ Bilingualism and Culture

Psychological Differences as a Function of Language

Although English is one of the most widely spoken languages in the world, the majority of individuals who speak English also speak at least one other language fluently. In fact, individuals who speak English and only English are a minority in the world of English speakers.

The fact that there are so many bilingual and multilingual individuals in the world raises interesting questions concerning the relationship between language and culture in these individuals. If, as we have discussed throughout this chapter, language is a symbol system of a culture, and if people can speak two or more languages fluently, that would suggest that bilinguals have two mental representations of culture—two different meaning systems—encoded in their minds. When speaking one language, speakers may access one cultural meaning system, but when the same person speaks another language, he or she may access a different meaning system.

Research has examined this issue for years. Ervin (1964), for example, compared responses from a sample of English–French bilinguals to pictures from the Thematic Apperception Test (a common test used in many cross-cultural studies). The subjects told their stories in response to the pictures once in English and then another time in French. Ervin found that subjects demonstrated more aggression, autonomy, and withdrawal in French than they did in English, and that females demonstrated a greater need for achievement in English than in French. Ervin attributed these differences to the higher value French culture placed on verbal prowess and to greater sex role differences.

How might the issue of bilingualism and culture be important for immigrants to the United States? Consider, for example, a Chinese–English bilingual raised in a monolingual Chinese-speaking home who learned English naturalistically only after migrating to the United States from China at age eight. She is now a 20-year-old college student, living with her parents. She uses Chinese as the only language in the home but English at school and with most of her peers. We might predict that when using Chinese, she would be likely to behave in ways appropriate to Chinese cultural norms in the home. In English, however, she might be more likely to behave in ways that are closer to European American norms.

Such differences have been reported with immigrant bilinguals (Hull, 1987; Dinges & Hull, 1992). In these studies, Chinese–English and Korean–English immigrant bilinguals were given the California Psychological Inventory (CPI), a widely used personality test. The immigrant bilinguals completed the CPI twice—once in their native language and once in English. These bilinguals presented different personalities depending on whether they were responding in their first language (Chinese or Korean) or in English (their second language). Immigrants are believed to have two clearly distinct cultural affiliations, accessible through the language in which much of this cultural knowledge was learned or is associated.

These findings are not limited to paper-and-pencil personality questionnaires; they have been replicated and extended not only to self-reports on personality tests but also to behavioral observations by others (Chen & Bond, 2010). Bilinguals also view facial expressions of emotion differently depending on which language they use when they are observing faces (Matsumoto, Anguas-Wong, & Martinez, 2008; Matsumoto & Assar, 1992).

A series of interesting studies by Benet-Martinez and her colleagues have shed more light on this important issue. They proposed that bilinguals are bicultural and must navigate between their multiple cultural identities based on the contextual cues afforded them in their environment (e.g., where they are, whom they are interacting with, etc.). Benet-Martinez and colleagues suggested that bilinguals engage in **code frame switching** when navigating different cultural identities, switching back and forth from one cultural meaning system to the other when accessing one language or another. In one of their studies (Hong, Morris, Chiu, & Benet-Martinez, 2000), Chinese American bicultural individuals were exposed to either stereotypically American images (e.g., Superman, the U.S. flag) or Chinese images (Chinese dragon, the Great Wall), shown some innocuous pictures, and then asked to make attributions about causality about events in the pictures. For example, the students saw the

code frame switching
The process by which bilinguals switch between one cultural meaning system and another when switching languages.

FIGURE 10.7 Stimulus Material Used as the Attributional Stimulus

Source: Reprinted from Hong, Y. Y., Morris, M., Chiu, C.-Y., & Benet-Martinez, V. (2000). Multicultural minds: A dynamic constructivist approach to culture and cognition. *American Psychologist*, 55, 709–720.

scene depicted in Figure 10.7. Students rated statements that reflected either internal or external motives of the fish. For example, if a student judged the one fish to be leading the other, this reflected more of an internal orientation. If a student judged the one fish to be chased by the others, this reflected more of an external orientation.

When they were primed with American images, the students tended to make more internal attributions, a typically American attributional style. When primed with the Chinese images, however, the students tended to make more external attributions (Figure 10.8), a more typically East Asian attributional style. In later studies, Benet-Martinez and colleagues (Benet-Martinez, Leu, Lee, & Morris, 2002) have shown that code frame switching actually occurs more with bicultural individuals who perceive themselves to be better integrated in both cultures.

A Bilingual Advantage for Cognitive Performance?

Recent research has raised interesting questions, and some debate, about whether or not bi- or multilingual individuals enjoy an advantage in some kinds of cognitive performance tasks. There is mounting evidence to support this belief. For example, studies have demonstrated that bilinguals can selectively attend to stimuli better than monolinguals, and can suppress interference from competing stimuli in attention (Engel de Abreu, Cruz-Santos, Tourinho, Martin, & Bialystok, 2012; Gollan, Schotter, Gomez, Murillo, & Keith, 2014); that thinking in a second language reduces biases when making decisions (Keysar, Hayakawa, & An, 2012); and that early exposure to a multilingual environment promotes effective communication (Fan, Liberman, Keysar, & Kinzler, 2015). Bilingual advantage effects have been documented as early as infancy, as bilingual infants can visually track silent video records of adult bilinguals switching languages but monolingual infants cannot (Sebastian-Galles, Albareda-Castellot, Weikum, & Werker, 2012). There is also some evidence to suggest

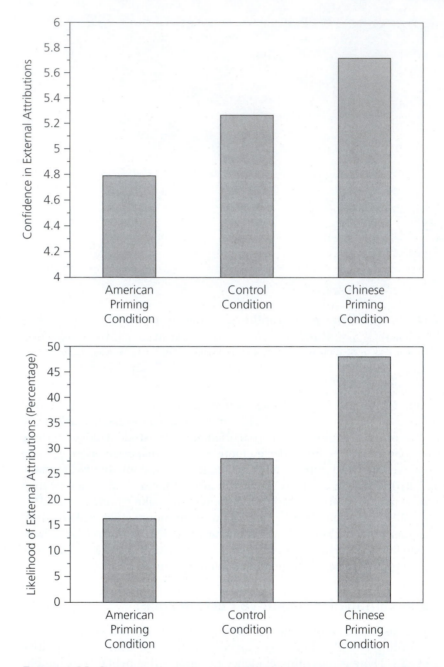

FIGURE 10.8 Results from Two Studies That Demonstrated Consistent Cultural Priming Effects in External Attributions about Fish Behavior among Hong Kong Chinese Bicultural Individuals

Source: Reprinted from Hong, Y. Y., Morris, M., Chiu, C.-Y., & Benet-Martinez, V. (2000). Multicultural minds: A dynamic constructivist approach to culture and cognition. *American Psychologist*, 55, 709–720.

that bilingualism produces these cognitive advantages because it affects the structure of white matter in the brain (Pliatsikas, Moschopoulou, & Saddy, 2015).

But beliefs about a cognitive advantage in bilingualism have recently been questioned. Paap and colleagues (Paap, Johnson, & Sawi, 2014, 2015), for example, have published reviews and data reporting no consistent evidence supporting the hypothesis that bilingualism enhances inhibitory control mechanisms, monitoring, or switching abilities. Instead, they have concluded that the bilingual advantages in cognitive functioning either do not exist or are restricted to very specific circumstances. Others have also suggested that the cognitive advantage in bilingualism may be the result of a bias to publish positive results to that effect (de Bruin, Treccani, & Della Sala, 2014). Future research may disentangle these difficult issues.

Perceptions of Bilinguals

The research described above demonstrates how closely language and culture are intertwined, presents the importance of language in everyday experience, and dispels the misconception that the existence of two personalities within an individual means that the individual is suffering from a mental disorder. Such a situation is a natural and healthy part of the bilingual and bicultural experience.

Other misconceptions persist, however. For example, negative impressions and stereotypes, particularly about intelligence, can occur when communicating with people in their second language because they may take more time in responding and appear to have cognitive difficulties while processing information. These difficulties, known as **foreign language processing difficulties**, arise because of nonfamiliarity or lack of fluency in speaking a language, and because of uncertainty or ambiguity about the intended meaning of messages when received in a foreign language. These difficulties are a normal part of learning a language and should not be used as a basis for negative inferences about intelligence or other dispositional characteristics of individuals who may be communicating in a second (or third) language.

Bilinguals may also experience difficulties in nonlinguistic thinking tasks; such difficulties are known as the **foreign language effect** (Takano & Noda, 1993). This term refers to a temporary decline in the thinking ability of people who are using a foreign language in which they are less proficient than their native language. The foreign language effect, seen in nonlinguistic thinking tasks, is a by-product of the foreign language processing difficulty seen in linguistic tasks. Takano and Noda (1993) demonstrated the existence of this effect in two studies involving Japanese–English bilinguals. In the first study, Japanese and American bilinguals performed a calculation task and responded to a question-and-answer task in either their first (native) or second (foreign) language. Performance for both groups of participants was lower when the question-and-answer task was in the foreign language. In the second study, the same basic methods were used with a different thinking task (nonverbal spatial reasoning) and a different linguistic task (sentence verification), producing the same results.

Takano and Noda (1995) reported two additional studies that showed the foreign language effect was larger when the discrepancy between the native and foreign languages was greater, and smaller when the difference between the native and foreign languages was smaller. Their first study used the same methods as the first study in Takano and Noda (1993), using native speakers of German and Japanese with English as a common foreign language. They found that the foreign language effect was larger for the Japanese. They explained this finding in terms of the greater difference between Japanese and English than between German and English. Their second study replicated the findings from the first, this time using native Korean and English speakers, with Japanese as the common foreign language.

Together, these studies indicated that interference in both linguistic (foreign language processing difficulty) and nonlinguistic (foreign language effect) tasks is a normal and expected occurrence in bilinguals. These interferences occur in the

foreign language processing difficulties Problems associated with learning a foreign language, such as taking more time to respond and experiencing cognitive difficulties while processing information.

foreign language effect A temporary decline in the thinking ability of people who are using a foreign language in which they are less proficient than their native tongue.

same way as interferences between any two cognitive tasks asked of the same person. Seen as normal cognitive interferences, these difficulties should not be used as a basis to form negative impressions or stereotypes of bilinguals. It is easy to fall into this trap, allowing our perceptions to be driven by ethnocentrism and, in some cases, an unconscious wish to validate preexisting stereotypes. The research clearly shows, however, that such perceptions have little basis in fact.

Monolingualism and Ethnocentrism

Recognition of the special relationship between language, culture, and behavior is especially important for students in the United States. Americans are notoriously ignorant of languages other than English, and this ignorance is often accompanied by an ethnocentric view rejecting the need to learn, understand, and appreciate other languages, customs, and cultures. Given that Americans are the most monolingual of all peoples of the world, that language is intimately tied to culture, and that multilingualism is associated with an appreciation of different cultures, it may be that Americans are actually the most ethnocentric of all people (which is a perception of Americans by many non-Americans). The fact that the United States is relatively geographically isolated from Europe and Asia, and is so economically and militarily powerful, produces a situation where many Americans don't feel the need to understand other points of view or interact with others. Our ignorance of languages other than English, and the potential ethnocentrism that often accompanies this ignorance, may be the root of a future downfall. For many who have little exposure to these issues in their everyday lives, now is the time to consider studying language and culture for a better understanding of the partners in our global village.

CONCLUSION

Language is the primary way we communicate with one another. It plays a critical role in the transmission, maintenance, and expression of our culture. In turn, culture has a pervasive influence on language, and language symbolizes what a culture deems important in our world. Both culture and language affect the structure of our thought processes. Understanding the culture—language relationship is an important step in becoming skillful intercultural communicators.

Communication in its broadest sense occurs both verbally (via language) and nonverbally. Despite the importance of nonverbal behaviors, however, we often take them for granted. Although we receive no formal training in how to send or receive nonverbal messages and signals, by adulthood we have become so skilled at it that we do so unconsciously and automatically. Nonverbal behaviors are just as much a language as any other. Just as verbal languages differ from culture to culture, so do nonverbal languages. Because we are aware of the differences between verbal languages, we do not hesitate to use dictionaries and other resources to help us understand different languages. But when it comes to nonverbal language, we often mistakenly assume that our systems of communicating nonverbally are all the same. Understanding cultural differences in nonverbal behavior is a step in the process of truly appreciating cultural differences in communication.

Communication is a rich and complex process that involves multiple messages sent via multiple signal systems. Culture has a pervasive influence on the encoding of both verbal and nonverbal signals, and the decoding of those signals. Because of this influence, conflict and misunderstanding are inevitable in intercultural communication. To overcome these obstacles, scholars have proposed a personal-growth model focusing on emotion regulation and mindfulness. Individuals who can engage in these processes can enhance their intercultural sensitivity, creating new mental categories, being respectful and open to cultural differences, and empathizing with others. Research on intercultural communication has made considerable progress in specifying the unique components of the intercultural communication process. The most recent studies have also shown that cultural differences in communication processes extend to computer-mediated communication such as e-mail and Facebook (DeAndrea et al., 2010; Rosette, Brett, Barsness, & Lytle, 2012). Future studies will undoubtedly examine the same processes in chatting, tweeting, and videoteleconferencing.

EXPLORATION AND DISCOVERY

Why Does This Matter to Me?

1. Have you ever had communication difficulties with someone who is not a native English speaker? What was difficult about it? How did it compare to communication difficulties you may have had with native English speakers?

2. When interacting with people who are not native English speakers, it may be a good idea to pay extra attention to the nonverbal behaviors. Facial expressions, gestures, tone of voice, and body posture may give additional clues about the messages that are being communicated.

3. When you are in another culture and do not speak the language, how do you communicate?

4. What kinds of stereotypes do you have of people whose mannerisms are different than yours? How would you feel if you spoke with someone who didn't look you in the eye when talking with you?

Suggestions for Further Exploration

1. Do bilinguals really act differently in all kinds of contexts? In which contexts may they act the same, and in which may their actions differ depending on the language they speak? Design a study that may tease out these different effects.

2. Say you wanted to find out about the gestures of a particular culture and their meaning. How would you go about doing that research? How would you know for sure that's what people actually did when they communicate in that culture?

3. Cultures develop norms for appropriate nonverbal behaviors, such as gesturing, interpersonal space, and touch. What happens when those norms are violated? Design a study to examine people's reactions to norm violations of any nonverbal behavior.

InfoTrac College Edition

Use InfoTrac College Edition to search for additional readings on topics of interest to you. For more information on topics in this chapter, use the following as search terms: communication and culture, culture and bilingualism, intercultural communication language and culture, monolingualism, nonverbal communication and language, Sapir–Whorf.

11 Culture and Health

CHAPTER CONTENTS

One major role of psychology is to improve the lives of the people we touch. Whether through research, service, or provision of primary or secondary health care, we look forward to the day when we can adequately prevent, diagnose, and treat diseases, and foster positive states of being in balance with others and the environment. This is not an easy task; a multitude of forces influences our health and the development of diseases.

As we strive to meet this challenge, the important role of culture in contributing to the maintenance of health and the etiology and treatment of disease has become increasingly clear. Although our goals of maintaining health and preventing and treating diseases may be the same across cultures, cultures vary in their perceptions of illness and their definitions of what is considered healthy and what is considered a disease. From anthropological and sociological perspectives, **disease** refers to a "malfunctioning or maladaptation of biologic and psychophysiologic processes in the individual" and **illness** refers to the "personal, interpersonal, and cultural reactions to disease or discomfort" (Kleinman, Eisenberg, & Good, 2006; p. 141). Thus, how we view health, disease, and illness, is strongly shaped by culture.

This chapter explores how cultural factors sway physical health and disease processes, and investigates our attempts to understand genetic, psychosocial, and sociocultural influences. We begin with an examination of cultural differences in the definition of health and present three indicators of health worldwide: life expectancy, infant mortality, and subjective well-being. We then review the considerable amount of research concerning the relationship between culture and heart disease, other physical disease processes, eating disorders, obesity, and suicide. Next, we explore differences in health care systems across countries. Finally, we summarize the research in the form of a model of cultural influences on health.

> ## Cultural Differences in the Definition of Health

Comparison across Cultures

Before we look at how culture influences health and disease processes, we need to examine exactly what we mean by health. More than 60 years ago, the World Health Organization (WHO) developed a definition at the International Health Conference, in which 61 countries were represented. They defined health as "a state of complete physical, mental, and social well-being, and not merely the absence of disease or infirmity." The WHO definition went on further to say that "The enjoyment of the highest attainable standard of health is one of the fundamental rights of every human being, without distinction of race, religion, political beliefs or economic and social conditions" (World Health Organization, 1948). This definition of health is still used by the WHO today.

In many Western countries, views of health have been heavily influenced by what many call the **biomedical model** of health and disease (Kleinman et al., 2006). Traditionally, this model views disease as resulting from a specific, identifiable cause such as a **pathogen** (an infectious agent such as a virus or bacteria), a genetic or developmental abnormality (such as being born with a mutated gene), or physical insult (such as being exposed to a carcinogen—a cancer-producing agent). From the perspective of the traditional biomedical model, the biological root of disease is primary and, subsequently, treatment focuses on addressing biological aspects of the disease.

Several decades ago, however, the biomedical model was strongly criticized by Engel, who proposed a **biopsychosocial model** to understand health and disease.

disease A malfunctioning or maladaptation of biologic and psychophysiologic processes in the individual.

illness Personal, interpersonal, and cultural reactions to disease or discomfort.

biomedical model A model of health that views disease as resulting from a specific, identifiable cause such as a pathogen (an infectious agent such as a virus or bacteria), a genetic or developmental abnormality (such as being born with a mutated gene), or physical insult (such as being exposed to a carcinogen—a cancer-producing agent).

pathogen An infectious agent such as a virus or bacteria.

biopsychosocial model A model of health that views disease as resulting from biological, psychological, and social factors.

Engel emphasized that health and disease need to be considered from several dimensions—not just the biological but also the psychological and social (Engel, 1977). This biopsychosocial model is now widely accepted. Adopting a biopsychosocial approach to health means that all three dimensions are highlighted—the biological (e.g., genetic, biological, and physiological functioning of the body), social (e.g., lifestyles and activities, quality of relationships, living conditions such as poverty), and psychological (e.g., beliefs and attitudes toward health, emotions, feelings of despair, positive thinking). All are important for a more accurate and complete understanding of health.

Views from other cultures suggest definitions of health that also include more than a person's biology. In China, the concept of health, based on Chinese religion and philosophy, focuses on the principles of *yin* and *yang*, which represent negative and positive energies, respectively. The Chinese believe that our bodies are made up of elements of *yin* and *yang*. Balance between these two forces results in good health; an imbalance—too much *yin* or too much *yang*—leads to poor health. Many things can disturb this balance, such as eating too many foods from one of the elements, a change in social relationships, the weather, the seasons, or even supernatural forces. Maintaining a balance involves not only the mind and body, but also the spirit and the natural environment. From the Chinese perspective, the concept of health is not confined to the individual but encompasses the surrounding relationships and environment— a view of health that is **holistic** (Yip, 2005). Balance between self and nature and across the individual's various roles in life is viewed as an integral part of health in many cultures around the world. This balance can produce a positive state in mind and body— a synergy of the forces of self, nature, and others—that many call health.

This notion of balance and imbalance, at least within the body, is a common concept across cultures (MacLachlan, 1997). The various systems of the body produce harmony and health when in balance, and illness and disease when in imbalance. A theory first developed by Hippocrates, which heavily influences views of the human body and disease in most industrialized countries and cultures today, suggests that the body is comprised of four humors: blood, phlegm, yellow bile, and black bile. Too much or too little of any of these throws the body out of balance, resulting in disease. Derivatives of these terms—such as *sanguine*, *phlegmatic*, and *choleric*—are widely used in health and medical circles today.

Another type of balance, common in theories of disease in many Latin American cultures, concentrates on hot and cold (MacLachlan, 1997). These terms do not refer to temperature, but to the intrinsic power of different substances in the body. Some illnesses or states are hot, others cold. A person who is in a hot condition is given cold foods to counteract the situation, and vice versa. The Chinese concept of *yin* and *yang* shows similarities to this concept.

In many cultures, then, we often hear about the importance of having a "balanced diet" and a "balanced lifestyle" (finding the optimal balance between work and play). The concept of **homeostasis** is all about balance—maintaining steady, stable functioning in our bodies when there are changes in the environment. When our bodies cannot maintain homeostasis over time, illness and disease may result. Thus, although there are differences across cultures in how health is conceived, there are also commonalities such as the notion of balance and imbalance that permeate discussions of health.

From this brief review of how different cultures define health, we can see how different beliefs of what leads to good health will affect how diseases are diagnosed and treated. If we believe that health is determined primarily by biological disturbances and individual choices, treatment may primarily focus on individual-level

holistic A view of health that focuses on the interconnections between the individual, his or her relationships, environment, and spiritual world.

homeostasis Maintaining steady, stable functioning in our bodies when there are changes in the environment.

factors. If we believe that health is determined by an individual's relationship with others, nature, and supernatural forces, treatment may primarily focus on correcting those relationships. Importantly, our choices of coping and treatment are closely tied to our attributions of the causes determining health, illness, and disease.

Comparison within Cultures

Concepts of health may differ not only between cultures but also within a pluralistic culture such as the United States or Canada. Health perspectives may differ between individuals from the dominant or mainstream culture and those of the nondominant social and ethnocultural group (Mulatu & Berry, 2001). Native Americans, for example, have a holistic view of health and consider good health to be living in harmony with oneself and one's environment. Poor health results when one does not live in harmony and engages in negative behaviors such as "displeasing the holy people of the past or the present, disturbing animal and plant life, misuse of sacred religious ceremonies, strong and uncontrolled emotions, and breaking social rules and taboos" (p. 52). Yurkovich and Lattergrass (2008) pointed out that while the WHO definition of health includes physical, mental, and social well-being, spiritual well-being is not mentioned. In Native American cultures, however, spiritual well-being—feeling connected to and in balance with the spiritual world—is a cornerstone of good health, both mental and physical. Figure 11.1 shows the Circle of Wellness, a model of health as conceptualized by Native Americans (Yurkovich & Lattergrass, 2008). The figure shows that, in contrast to the biopsychosocial model, spiritual well-being is central, or the focal point, for the other domains that contribute to health.

Although the concepts of health held by various ethnic and immigrant groups within a pluralistic country may differ from and even contradict the health concepts of the mainstream society, mainstream culture is also adapting and incorporating ideas of health that immigrants have brought with them, as seen in the rising popularity and interest in alternative health practices such as acupuncture, homeopathy, yoga, herbal medicines, and spiritual healing (Brodsky & Hui, 2006). Indeed, there is a growing field called complementary and alternative medicine (CAM) that incorporates medical and health care systems and practices that are not considered conventional medicine to treat illness and promote health. According to the U.S. National Health Interview Survey the percentage of U.S. adults doing yoga, one of the most popular CAM practices, has steadily increased in the last decade (Clark, Black, &

FIGURE 11.1

Circle of Wellness Model of Native American Health

Source: Yurkovich & Lattergrass (2008). Defining health and unhealthiness: Perceptions of Native Americans with persistent mental illness. *Mental Health, Religion, & Culture, 11,* 437–459.

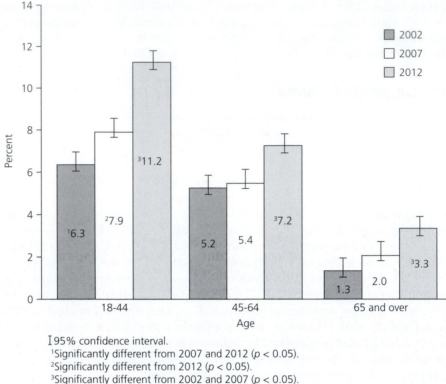

I 95% confidence interval.
[1]Significantly different from 2007 and 2012 (*p* < 0.05).
[2]Significantly different from 2012 (*p* < 0.05).
[3]Significantly different from 2002 and 2007 (*p* < 0.05).
NOTE: Estimates are based on household interviews of a sample of
the civilian noninstitutionalized population.
SOURCE: CDC/NCHS, National Health Interview Survey, 2002, 2007, and 2012.

FIGURE 11.2 Percentage of U.S. Adults Reporting Doing Yoga in the Last Year.
In Each Age Group There Is an Increase between 2002 and 2012, with the Largest
Increase in the 18–44 Age Group, Almost Doubling in the Last Decade

Stussman, 2015). See Figure 11.2. One thing is clear: with continued migration, immigration, and globalization, our views on health and how best to promote good health, are changing.

▶ Three Indicators of Health Worldwide

Life Expectancy

life expectancy
Average number of years a person is expected to live from birth.

Three indicators of health are used worldwide: life expectancy, infant mortality, and subjective well-being. **Life expectancy** refers to the average number of years a person is expected to live from birth (as opposed to calculating life expectancy from, e.g., age 65). Figure 11.3 shows the average life expectancy for selected countries, estimated for 2014. A comparison of 223 countries showed that the countries with the longest average life expectancies were Monaco (90 years), Macau and Japan (85), Singapore (84), San Marino, Andorra, Hong Kong (83), Switzerland, Guernsey, and Australia (82). The United States was ranked 42nd, at 80 years of age. Countries with the shortest life expectancies were Swaziland and Afghanistan (51), Guinea-Bissau, South Africa (50), and Chad (49) (CIA, The World Factbook, 2014).

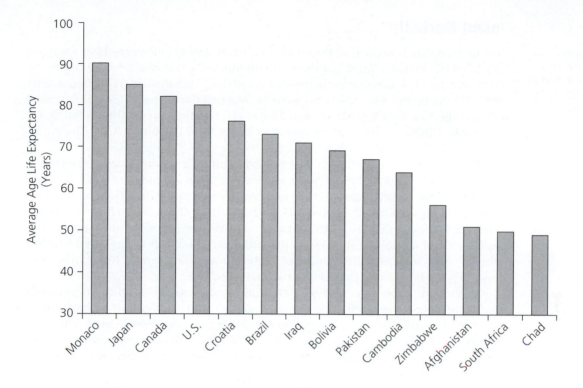

FIGURE 11.3 Average Life Expectancy in Selected Countries

Source: CIA Factbook.

A large part of explaining such drastic life expectancy differences is the general resources of a country (Barkan, 2010). Wealthier countries with greater resources have better access to better diet, nutrition, health care, and advanced technology to maintain health and prevent and treat diseases. Thus, life expectancy is lengthened. In contrast, poorer nations with the fewest resources are more likely to suffer from hunger, malnutrition, AIDS and other diseases, and lack of access to basics for survival such as clean water, sanitary waste removal, vaccinations, and other medications. Nations experiencing war and other disasters experience disruptions that challenge survival. Thus, life expectancy is shortened.

Importantly, disparities in life expectancies can vary widely within a country. In the United States, for instance, life expectancy differs by ethnicity (which is usually confounded with socioeconomic status). In 2011, for European Americans, life expectancy was 79 years. In contrast, for African Americans, life expectancy was 75 years. When gender was taken into account, the disparities were even greater: African American male life expectancy was 72 years, compared to European American females at 81 years (National Center for Health Statistics, 2011). These statistics show clear health disparities between ethnic groups in the United States. We will address possible reasons for these health disparities later in the chapter.

Across the globe, we are living longer. Worldwide, the average life expectancy in the 1950s was 46 years. In 2009 it was 69 years, and this is expected to increase to 75 years by 2050 (Barkan, 2010; United Nations Population Division, 2009). Nonetheless, great disparities across countries in average life expectancies mean that possibilities for good health and a long life are enjoyed by people in some countries, but not others.

Infant Mortality

infant mortality The number of infant deaths (one year of age or younger) per 1,000 live births.

Infant mortality is defined as the number of infant deaths (one-year-old or younger) per 1,000 live births. Figure 11.4 shows infant mortality rates for selected countries, estimated for 2014. Comparing across 224 countries, Afghanistan (117 infant deaths per 1,000 live births), Mali (104), and Somalia (100) had the highest rates of infant mortality while Norway (3), Japan (2), and Monaco (1) had the lowest. The United States was ranked 169th, with six infant deaths for every 1,000 live births (CIA, The World Factbook, 2014).

Compared to other industrialized countries, infant mortality rates in the United States are among the highest. There has, however, been a steady decrease in infant mortality in the United States over the past century—from 100 infant deaths per 1,000 births in 1900, to six infant deaths per 1,000 births in 2010. Similar to life expectancy, however, there are disparities by ethnic group. African American infants have the highest infant mortality rates (14 infant deaths per 1,000 births) compared to other ethnic groups such as Native American (8), European American (6), Mexican (6), and Asian/Pacific Islander (5) (MacDorman & Mathews, 2008).

In sum, life expectancy and infant mortality rates are broad indicators of health that show diversity in health outcomes around the world. A large part of these differences can be attributed to resources that ensure access to good nutrition, health care, and treatment (Barkan, 2010). To add to these objective indicators of health, researchers have focused more recently on an important *subjective* indicator of health—happiness, or subjective well-being.

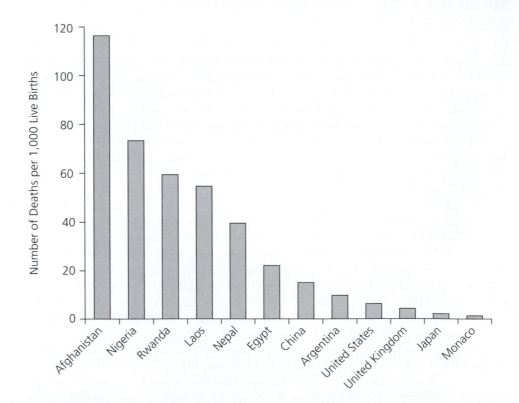

FIGURE 11.4 Infant Mortality Rates in Selected Countries
Source: CIA Factbook.

Subjective Well-Being

In contrast to life expectancy and infant mortality, **subjective well-being** (SWB) focuses on one's *perceptions* and *self-judgments* of health and well-being. Subjective well-being encompasses a person's feelings of happiness and life satisfaction (Diener & Ryan, 2009). Diener and Ryan (2009) state the importance of this subjective aspect of health.

The main applied goal of researchers who study subjective well-being is the improvement of people's lives beyond the elimination of misery. Because subjective well-being is a key component of quality of life, its measurement is crucial to understanding how to improve people's lives. In addition, a growing body of research shows that high levels of subjective well-being are beneficial to the effective functioning of societies beyond the advantages they bestow on individuals (p. 392).

Importantly, subjective well-being is positively related to physical health. In one study, researchers infected healthy people with a virus for the common cold. The findings showed that those who reported higher levels of SWB were less susceptible to the virus than those with lower levels of SWB (Cohen, Doyle, Turner, Alper, & Skoner, 2003). Others have found that people reporting higher SWB have stronger immune systems, fewer heart attacks, and less artery blockage (Diener & Biswas-Diener, 2008). These findings supported studies showing that higher SWB may lead to a longer life expectancy (Diener & Chan, 2011). It is worth noting that one reason why SWB may be related to better physical health is that people with higher SWB also tend to engage in healthier lifestyles (Diener & Biswas-Diener, 2008; Diener & Ryan, 2009).

The big question is, then: What predicts subjective well-being? In other words, what makes people happy? One major variable studied is affluence, or material wealth. Material wealth (as measured in greater household income) predicts an increase in satisfaction with one's financial situation, greater purchasing power, and greater optimism about the future (Diener Tay, & Oishi, 2013) These three factors predict greater SWB, for both richer and poorer countries.

Figure 11.5 shows levels of SWB in relation to per capita gross domestic product (GDP) across 88 countries. An interesting pattern emerges. The Latin American countries report higher SWB than would be expected based on their GDP; the former communist countries, lower SWB than would be expected. Thus, economic factors account for some, but not all, of the variation in levels of happiness across countries. Recent work on SWB shows that other nonmaterial factors such as feeling respected, having social support from friends and family, and feeling satisfied with the amount of freedom one has in life, are all related to greater SWB across many cultures (Ng & Diener, 2014). Thus, in addition to having enough material resources, our sense of autonomy and connection to others are essential to our happiness.

Research on SWB broadens our assessment of health beyond objective indicators such as life expectancy and infant mortality. It will be important in future research to examine how these three health indicators relate to one another, painting a more complete picture of variations in health and well-being around the world. We now turn to studies that have focused on specific factors that influence health and disease.

subjective well-being
A person's perceptions and self-judgments of his or her health and well-being that includes feelings of happiness and life satisfaction.

▶ Genetic Influences on Physical Health and Disease

While some diseases can be linked to mutations of a single gene (e.g., cystic fibrosis, sickle cell anemia), most diseases are linked to complex, multiple factors that include mutations in multiple genes that interact with environmental factors (e.g., stress, diet,

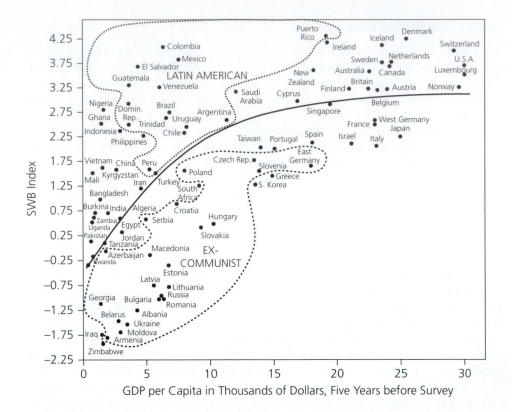

FIGURE 11.5 Subjective Well-Being (SWB) and per Capita Gross Domestic Product (GNP) in 88 Countries. SWB Is Based on Reported Life Satisfaction and Happiness, Using Mean Results from All Available Surveys Conducted 1995–2007

Source: Inglehart, Foa, Petersen, & Weltzel (2008). Development, freedom, and rising happiness: A global perspective (1987–2007). *Perspectives in Psychological Science*, 3(4), pp. 264–285. Copyright © 2008 by Sage Publications. Reprinted by permission of SAGE Publications.

health-related behaviors). Some of the most common complex-gene diseases are cancer, high blood pressure, heart disease, diabetes, and obesity (NIH, Genetics Home Reference).

The Human Genome Project, an international collaboration, completed one major aim of their project in 2003: to identify all 20,000–25,000 genes in human DNA (U.S. Department of Energy Genome Programs, http://genomics. energy.gov). This groundbreaking work has opened new avenues for exploring the role of genetics to understand disease. It has also spawned a renewed interest into whether racial, ethnic, or cultural groups may differ in their genetic makeup and whether some groups are more genetically vulnerable to certain diseases compared to others (Frank, 2007). For instance, sickle cell anemia is more common among African American and Mediterranean populations than Northern European, while the opposite is true for cystic fibrosis. Because humans living in the same geographical area tend to be more genetically similar to one another, this may partially explain the cultural variations we see in certain disease prevalence rates. Nonetheless, individuals of a particular racial or cultural background are not consistently genetically similar to other individuals of the same racial or cultural background. Indeed, there appears to be more genetic variation *within* racial and cultural groups than *between* (Jorde & Wooding, 2004; also recall our discussion of race in Chapter 1).

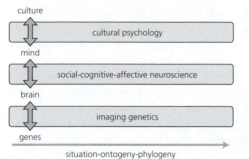

FIGURE 11.6

The Cultural Neuroscience Framework, Integrating Theory and Methods from Cultural Psychology, Neuroscience, and Genetics. The Aim Is to Understand How Culture, Mind, Brain, and Genes Interact to Produce Human Cultural Variations on Different Times Scales: Situation (in the Moment), Ontogeny (Individual Development) and Phylogeny (Species Development)

Source: Chiao, J. (2009). Cultural neuroscience: The once and future discipline. In J. Chiao (Ed.) *Progress in brain research,* 178, 247–304.

Research that examines how genes and environment interact over time is our best chance at illuminating why some diseases appear more often for some cultural groups compared to others. Francis (2009) argued for multilevel, interdisciplinary research programs to address questions such as how community, social, and societal forces contribute to how genes are regulated and expressed. Multilevel investigations study how genes interact with environments on various levels—cellular, individual, group, and societal. Interdisciplinary investigations include a collaboration of researchers from various fields—genetics, biology, psychology, sociology, and public policy.

In the last decade a new field of inquiry adopts this type of complex, multilevel and interdisciplinary approach, namely, **cultural neuroscience**. Researchers in this field combine recent advances in neuroscience with principles of cultural psychology and population genetics to understand the dynamic relations among culture, behavior, mind, brain, and genes (see Figure 11.6). Chiao, a leading theorist and researcher in cultural neuroscience, has studied why some cultures emphasize individualism versus collectivism as a result of both environmental factors (e.g., pathogen prevalence) and genetic selection (Chiao, Cheon, Pronpattananangkul, Mrazek, & Blizinsky, 2013). Her studies suggest that people living in areas around the world with a higher prevalence of infectious diseases (such as in hotter climates) are more likely to be more collectivistically oriented. Being more collectivistically oriented emphasizes connections with in-group members, which may serve as a way to reduce the spread of infectious diseases coming from outgroups. Studies in cultural neuroscience, then, aim to uncover how culture, genetic selection, and environmental pressures interact, leading to cultural traits (such as holding more individualistic or collectivistic orientations) that are adaptive for a particular environment. Ideally, future research should adopt multilevel, interdisciplinary research efforts to clarify the complex relation of how genes, environment, and culture interact and contribute to health and disease.

cultural neuroscience
An emerging research field that combines recent advances in neuroscience with principles of cultural psychology and population genetics to understand the dynamic relations among culture, behavior, mind, brain, and genes.

▶ Psychosocial Influences on Physical Health and Disease

Psychology as a whole has become increasingly aware of the important role that culture plays in the maintenance of health and the production of disease processes. This awareness can be seen on many levels, from more journal articles published on these topics to the establishment of new journals devoted to this area of research to the emergence of new fields such as cultural neuroscience. This increased awareness is related to a growing concern with psychosocial determinants of health and disease in general.

Some of the earliest research on psychosocial factors in health and disease processes examined the relationship between social isolation or social support and death. One of the best-known studies in this area is the Alameda County study (Berkman & Syme, 1979), named after the county in California where the data were collected. Researchers interviewed almost 7,000 individuals to discover their degree of social contact. Following the initial assessment interview, deaths were monitored over a nine-year period. The results were clear for both men and women: Individuals with the fewest social ties suffered the highest mortality rate. Those with the most social ties had the lowest. These findings held even when other factors were statistically or methodologically controlled for, including the level of physical health reported at the time of the initial questionnaire, the year of death, socioeconomic status (SES), and a number of health-related behaviors (such as smoking and alcohol consumption).

The Alameda County study was one of the first to demonstrate clearly the enormous impact that psychosocial factors have in the maintenance of physical health. Since then, many studies have found the same pattern: Individuals with few social supports tend to have poorer health. Further, it is the *perception* of having few social supports, or feeling lonely, that is important. Some people who have few social supports are not lonely, and some people with many social supports do feel lonely. Current reviews show that feeling lonely is linked to a host of health problems (Hawkley & Cacioppo, 2010; Steptoe & Kivimäki, 2013). People who report being lonely at more periods of time in their lives (such as during childhood, adolescence, and young adulthood), age faster on a number of indicators including body mass index, systolic blood pressure, cholesterol levels, and maximum oxygen consumption. All of these indicators are linked to cardiovascular health risks such as coronary heart disease, hypertension, and stroke. It truly is the case that loneliness weakens the heart.

A number of other important and interesting studies have documented the linkage between psychosocial factors and health or disease states. Steptoe and his colleagues in the United Kingdom have highlighted the links between unemployment and mortality, cardiovascular disease, and cancer; between negative life events and gastrointestinal disorders; between stress and the common cold; between bereavement and lymphocyte functions; between pessimistic explanatory styles and physical illnesses; between positive mood and heart rate and blood pressure; and between psychological well-being and mortality (e.g., Chida & Steptoe, 2008; Dockray & Steptoe, 2010; Steptoe, Dockray, & Wardle, 2009; Steptoe, Hamer, & Chida, 2007; Steptoe, Sutcliffe, Allen, & Coombes, 1991; Steptoe & Wardle, 1994). Indeed, the field has come a long way in demonstrating the close relationship between psychosocial factors and health or disease outcomes.

In multicultural countries such as the United States and the United Kingdom, researchers have focused on **health disparities**. Health disparities are differences in health outcomes by groups, for instance, between males and females, people of different ethnicities, and people of lower and higher SES. Disparity refers to the fact that one group shows worse (or better) health outcomes compared to another. Health disparities can result from social factors, such as a person's level of education, income, or occupational status (e.g., being employed versus unemployed or underemployed).

health disparities
Differences in health outcomes by groups such as between males and females, African Americans and European Americans, and people of lower and higher socioeconomic status (SES).

Adler and her colleagues (e.g., Adler, Boyce, Chesney, Cohen, Folkman, Kahn, & Syme, 1994; Adler & Rehkopf, 2008) have provided strong evidence that SES is consistently associated with health outcomes. People of higher SES enjoy better health than do people of lower SES (see Figure 11.7). This relationship has been found not only for mortality rates, but for almost every disease and condition studied. Adler and colleagues have suggested that health-related behaviors such as smoking, physical activity, and alcohol use may explain the relation between SES and health, as these

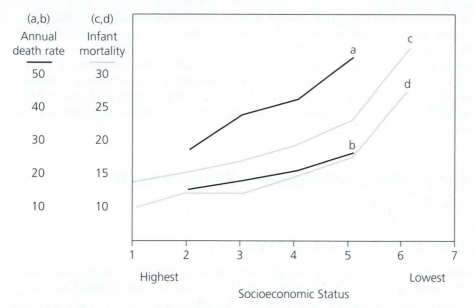

Note: (a) Annual death rate per 1,000 male (Feldman, Makuc, Kleinman, & Cornoni-Huntley, 1989),
(b) Annual death rate per 1,000 female (Feldman et al., 1989), (c) Infant mortality per 1,000 live
births male (Susser, Watson, & Hopper, 1985), (d) Infant mortality per 1,000 live births female
(Susser et al., 1985).

FIGURE 11.7 Mortality Rate by Socioeconomic Status Level

Source: Adler, N. E., T. Boyce, M. A. Chesney, S. Cohen, S. Folkman, R. L. Kahn, and S. L. Syme.
Socioeconomic Status and Health: The Challenge of the Gradient, American Psychologist, 49(1),
pp. 15–24, 1994. Copyright © American Psychological Association. Adapted with author permission.

behaviors have all been linked to SES. In addition, psychological characteristics such
as depression, stress, and social ordering (one's relative position in the SES hierarchy)
may also explain the relationship between SES and health. Interestingly, one's subjective *perception* of SES appears to better predict health and change in health rather than
an objective assessment of SES (Singh-Manoux, Marmot, & Adler, 2005).

An important psychosocial factor that may contribute to health disparities by
ethnic group is perceived racism and discrimination. One striking health disparity is the shorter life expectancy for African Americans versus other ethnic groups.
This disparity may be linked to stress-related health outcomes such as high blood
pressure (hypertension) due to racism and discrimination (Brondolo, Rieppi, Kelly,
& Gerin, 2003; Krieger, 1999; Mays, Cochran, & Barnes, 2007). Perceived racism has
been consistently linked to poorer physical health (such as a greater incidence of
cardiovascular disease) and premature biological aging among African Americans
(Chae, Nuru-Jeter, Adler, Brody, Lin, Blackburn, & Epel, 2014; Mays et al., 2007). For
African American women, racism-related stress and poorer physical health may subsequently contribute to negative pregnancy outcomes and explain some of the disparity between African American and European American infant mortality (Collins,
David, Handler, Walls, & Andes, 2004). Notably, the negative effects of racism can
carry on even to the next generation. In a racially stratified society such as the United
States, racism is a pervasive psychosocial stressor that has been consistently linked to
poorer physical health across various ethnic minority groups, contributing to significant health disparities (Pascoe & Richman, 2009).

In sum, research of the past several decades has demonstrated convincingly that psychosocial factors play an important role in maintaining and promoting health, and in the etiology and treatment of disease. Still, many avenues remain open for future research, including establishing direct links between particular psychosocial factors and specific disease outcomes, and identifying the specific mechanisms that mediate those relationships. Hopefully, research of the upcoming decades will be as fruitful as that of the past several decades in providing much-needed knowledge about these processes.

▶ Sociocultural Influences on Physical Health and Disease

Cultural Dimensions and Diseases

In addition to psychosocial factors, parallels can be drawn linking cultural factors and the development of diseases such as cardiovascular disease. Marmot and Syme (1976) studied Japanese Americans, classifying 3,809 participants into groups according to how "traditionally Japanese" they were (spoke Japanese at home, retained traditional Japanese values and behaviors, and the like). They found that those who were the "most" Japanese had the lowest incidence of coronary heart disease—comparable to the incidence in Japan. The group that was the "least" Japanese had a three to five times higher incidence. Moreover, the differences between the groups could not be accounted for by other coronary risk factors. These findings point to the contribution of cultural lifestyles to the development of heart disease.

Triandis, Bontempo, Villareal, Asai, and Lucca (1988) took this finding one step further, using the individualism–collectivism cultural dimension and examining its relationship to heart disease across eight different cultural groups. European Americans, the most individualistic of the eight groups, had the highest rate of heart attacks; Trappist monks, who were the least individualistic, had the lowest rate. Triandis and his colleagues (1988) suggested that social support or isolation was the most important factor that explained this relationship, a position congruent with the earlier research on social isolation. That is, people who live in more collectivistic cultures may have access to stronger and deeper social ties with others than do people in individualistic cultures. These social relationships, in turn, are considered a "buffer" against the stress and strain of living, reducing the risk of cardiovascular disease. People who live in individualistic cultures may not have access to the same types or degrees of social relationships; therefore, they may have less of a buffer against stress and are more susceptible to heart disease. Of course, this study was not conclusive, as many other variables confounded comparisons between Americans and Trappist monks (such as industrialization, class, and lifestyle). Nevertheless, the study was important because it was the first to examine the relationship between cultural dimensions and the incidence of a particular disease state.

Since this initial study, other researchers have expanded the focus of cultural dimensions beyond individualism and collectivism and have included many other diseases. Other dimensions of culture may be associated with the incidence of other disease processes. If members of individualistic cultures are indeed at higher risk for heart disease, for example, perhaps they are at lower risk for other disease processes. Conversely, if collectivistic cultures are at lower risk for heart disease, they may be at higher risk for other diseases. Matsumoto and Fletcher (1996) investigated this possibility by examining the relationship among multiple dimensions of culture and multiple disease processes, opening the door to this line of study. These researchers obtained the mortality rates for six different medical diseases: infections and parasitic diseases, malignant neoplasms (tumors), diseases of the circulatory system, heart diseases, cerebrovascular diseases, and respiratory system diseases. These epidemiological data, taken from the *World Health Statistics Quarterly* (WHO, 1991), were compiled across 28 countries widely distributed around the globe, spanning five continents, and representing many different ethnic, cultural, and socioeconomic backgrounds. In addition, incidence rates for each of the diseases were available at five age points for each country: at birth and at ages 1, 15, 45, and 65 years. To gather cultural data for each country, Matsumoto and Fletcher (1996) used Hofstede's (1980, 1983) four cultural dimensions: individualism versus collectivism (IC), power distance (PD), uncertainty avoidance (UA), and masculinity (MA). Matsumoto and Fletcher then correlated these cultural index scores with the epidemiological data.

The results were quite fascinating and pointed to the importance of culture in the development of these disease processes. See Table 11.1 for a summary of findings. The countries in this study differed economically as well as culturally, and it may have been that these economic differences—particularly with regard to the availability of treatment, diet, and sanitation—also contributed to disease. To deal with this possibility, Matsumoto and Fletcher (1996) recomputed their correlations controlling for per capita gross domestic product (GDP) of each country. Even when the effects of per capita GDP were accounted for, the predictions for infections and parasitic diseases, circulatory diseases, and heart diseases all survived. The predictions for UA and cerebrovascular and respiratory diseases, and MA and cerebrovascular diseases, also survived. Thus, these cultural dimensions predicted disease above and beyond what was accounted for by economic differences among the countries. Only the prediction for malignant neoplasms was not supported, indicating that economic differences among the countries cannot be disentangled from cultural differences in predicting the incidence of neoplasms.

How and why does culture affect medical disease processes? Triandis and colleagues (1988) suggested that culture—specifically, social support—is a major ingredient in mediating stress, which affects health. The findings of Matsumoto and Fletcher (1996), however, suggested a much more complex picture. Although collectivistic cultures were associated with lower rates of cardiovascular diseases, they were also associated with death from infectious and parasitic diseases and cerebrovascular diseases. Thus, although social support may be a buffer against life stress in the prevention of heart attacks, these data suggested that there is something else to collectivism

TABLE 11.1 Summary of Findings on the Relationship between Four Cultural Dimensions and Incidence of Diseases

Cultural Dimension	Rates of Disease
Higher Power Distance	■ Higher rates of infections and parasitic diseases ■ Lower rates of malignant neoplasm, circulatory disease, and heart disease
Higher Individualism	■ Higher rates of malignant neoplasms and heart disease ■ Lower rates of infections and parasitic diseases, cerebrovascular disease
Higher Uncertainty Avoidance	■ Higher rates of heart disease ■ Lower rates of cerebrovascular disease and respiratory disease
Higher Masculinity	■ Higher rates of cerebrovascular disease

that increases susceptibility to other disease processes. To be sure, these other factors may not be cultural per se. Collectivism, for example, is generally correlated with geographic location; countries nearer the equator tend to be more collectivistic. Countries nearer the equator also have hotter climates, which foster the spread of organisms responsible for infectious and parasitic diseases. The relationship between collectivism and death from these types of disease processes, therefore, may be related to geography in addition to culture.

Based on what we know from these studies, we see that different societies and countries develop different cultural ways of dealing with the problem of living. Each way is associated with its own specific and different set of stressors, each of which may take its toll on the human body. Because different cultural ways of living both punish and replenish the body, they are associated with different risk factors and rates for different disease processes. This view may be a more holistic account of how culture may influence health and disease processes.

Future research will need to investigate further the specific mechanisms that mediate the relationships between cultural dimensions and health. Some studies, for example, will need to examine more closely the relationship among culture, geography, and other noncultural factors in connection with disease incidence rates. Other studies will need to examine directly the relationship between culture and specific behavioral and psychological processes, to elucidate the possible mechanisms of health and disease. Matsumoto and Fletcher (1996), for example, suggested that culture influences human emotion and human physiology, particularly with respect to autonomic nervous system activity and the immune system. For example, the link between PD and circulatory and heart diseases may be explained by noting that cultures low on PD tend to minimize status differences among their members. As status and power differences diminish, people are freer to feel and express negative emotions, such as anger or hostility, to ingroup others. Containing negative emotions, as must be done in high-PD cultures, may have dramatic consequences for the cardiovascular system, resulting in a relatively higher incidence of circulatory and heart diseases in those cultures. A study showing that suppressing anger is related to greater cardiovascular risk (Harburg, Julius, Kaciroti, Gleiberman, & Schork, 2003) lent further credence to this hypothesis. Hopefully, future research will be able to address these and other possibilities.

Cultural Discrepancies and Physical Health

Although the studies described so far suggest that culture influences physical health, other research suggests that culture per se is not the only nonbiologically relevant variable. The discrepancy between one's personal cultural values and those of society may produce stress, which in turn leads to negative health outcomes. Researchers have tested this idea by asking university undergraduates to report what their personal cultural values were, as well as their perceptions of society's cultural values and ideal cultural values (Matsumoto, Kouznetsova, Ray, Ratzlaff, Biehl, & Raroque, 1999). Participants in this study also completed a scale assessing strategies for coping with stress; anxiety, depression, and other mood measures; and scales assessing physical health and psychological well-being. Discrepancy scores were computed by taking the differences between self and society, and self and ideal, ratings. These discrepancy scores were then correlated with the scores on the eight coping strategies assessed. The results indicated that discrepancies between self and ideal ratings were not related to coping. In contrast, discrepancies between self and society's cultural values were significantly correlated with all eight coping strategies, indicating that greater cultural discrepancies were associated with greater needs for coping. These coping strategies were significantly correlated with depression and anxiety, which in turn were significantly correlated with physical health symptoms. In particular, higher scores on anxiety were strongly correlated with greater health problems. The results of this study, therefore, suggested that greater discrepancy between self and societal cultural values may, at least indirectly, relate to more physical health problems.

A more recent study focused on another type of discrepancy—between an individual's emotional fit to the broader culture's emotional patterns (De Leersnyder, Mesquita, Kim, Eom, & Choi, 2014). To study this, the researchers first asked participants to describe an emotional experience for a particular situation (e.g., something that made them feel good) and within a particular context (e.g., family or work/school). They then calculated the degree to which this individual experience matched the country-level emotional profile for a similar situation and context. Using data gathered from Belgium, the United States, and Korea, the researchers found that those who fit better with their culture's emotional profile also reported greater well-being. Studies such as this one that focus on cultural discrepancies are important, as they specifically consider person–environment fit to understanding health. Future research will need to replicate these findings and elaborate on them. The current studies do suggest, however, the potential role of cultural discrepancies in mediating health outcomes, and open the door for new and exciting research in this area of psychology.

Culture, Body Shape, and Eating Disorders

Social and cultural factors are central in the perception of one's own and others' body shapes, and these perceptions influence the relationship between culture and health. Body shape ideals and body dissatisfaction (e.g., the discrepancy between one's perception of body shape with one's ideal body shape) has been widely studied because of links to eating disorders. For instance, greater body dissatisfaction is considered to be one of the most robust predictors of eating disorders (Stice, 2002). Evidence shows this link in several cultures such as the United States (Jacobi et al., 2004; Stice, 2002; Wertheim, Paxton, & Blaney, 2009), Greece (Bilali, Galanis, Velonakis, Katostaras, & Theofanis, 2010), and China (Jackson & Chen, 2011).

The International Body Project is a large-scale, cross-cultural study involving 26 countries from 10 world regions (North America, South America, Western Europe, Eastern Europe, Scandinavia, Oceania, Southeast Asia, East Asia, South and West Asia, and Africa) to assess body weight ideals and body dissatisfaction (Swami et al., 2010). In this project, almost 7,500 individuals were surveyed. The method to assess body weight ideals and dissatisfaction was Thompson and Gray's (1995) line-drawing figures of women. Nine figures, ranging from very thin to very overweight, were presented. Female participants were asked to select the figure that most closely resembled their actual body shape, and the figure that they would like to be (their ideal body shape). To measure body dissatisfaction, a difference score between actual and ideal preferences was calculated.

The results showed that body dissatisfaction varied across the world regions: North and South American women reported the highest levels of body dissatisfaction and West and South Asian the lowest. Further, in areas that were less economically developed (lower SES), such as in rural areas, heavier bodies were preferred. Conversely, in higher SES areas, thinner bodies were preferred. The authors suggested that in lower SES areas where resources (food, wealth) are scarce, being heavier is an indicator of greater resource security. The authors concluded that there may be fewer between-culture differences in body weight ideals and body dissatisfaction (at least between broad groupings such as "Western" and "non-Western" cultures) but rather, body weight ideals and body dissatisfaction appear to be more consistently linked to SES. Thus, targeting areas for eating disorders should rely also on the consideration of SES characteristics of a region. One limitation of this study was that it focused only on women's body dissatisfaction and did not include men's. Future research should also include men as body dissatisfaction is widespread and increasing among men, yet it is still under recognized (Jones & Morgan, 2010). Future research will also need to establish the links between perceptions of body shape and actual health-related behaviors in order to document the degree to which these perceptions influence health and disease processes.

Studies have also examined exposure to Western culture in relation to body dissatisfaction, eating attitudes, and behaviors. For instance, findings from the International Body Project showed that women who reported more exposure to Western media reported greater body dissatisfaction (Swami et al., 2010). A review of 36 countries found that body dissatisfaction is greater among those living in affluent countries with a Western lifestyle (defined as high-consuming with an individualistic orientation) (Holmqvist & Frisen, 2010). In line with these findings, a study of Pakistani females determined that exposure to Western culture significantly predicted more disturbed eating attitudes (Suhail & Nisa, 2002). A study of Mexican American females also found that those who reported greater orientation to Anglo American culture reported higher levels of eating disorders (Cachelin, Phinney, Schug, & Striegel-Moore, 2006).

Collectively, these studies demonstrate that attitudes toward body size and shape, and eating, are influenced by culture. Cultural values, attitudes, beliefs, and opinions about wealth, abundance, beauty and attractiveness, power, and other such psychological characteristics are likely significant factors in determining attitudes toward eating, thinness, and obesity. These latter attitudes, in turn, most likely have a direct effect on health-related behaviors such as eating, diet, and exercise. The research also suggests that these tendencies may be especially prevalent in the United States (Holmqvist & Frisen, 2009). Nonetheless, such tendencies are not solely an American or Western phenomenon. Cross-cultural research has pointed to similarities between Americans and members of other cultures—for example, the Japanese (Mukai & McCloskey, 1996)—in their attitudes toward eating and preoccupation with thinness. Indeed, although the prevalence of eating disorders in Japan is still lower than in the United States, it has risen significantly in the last 20 years (Chisuwa & O'Dea, 2009).

Culture and Obesity

In addition to eating disorders, increasing attention has been paid to the rapidly growing rates of being overweight and obesity around the world, especially among children and adolescents. This is a concern, as overweight and obese children and adolescents are more likely to become overweight and obese adults and are subsequently at much greater risk for developing serious health problems such as cardiovascular disease, diabetes, and cancer. Obesity has been an increasingly important public health concern across many countries in recent years.

The WHO's definition of overweight is body-mass index (BMI; calculated as the weight in kilograms divided by the square of the height in meters) at or above 25; for obesity, it is a BMI at or above 30. Data show that the United States has the highest rate of obesity (adults and children) compared to other economically similar countries (see Figure 11.8). In the United States, from 1974 to 2000, the obesity rate quadrupled for children (ages 6 to 11) and doubled for adolescents (ages 12 to 19) (Ogden, Flegal, Carroll, & Johnson, 2002). The trend has stabilized (Ogden & Caroll, 2010). Currently,

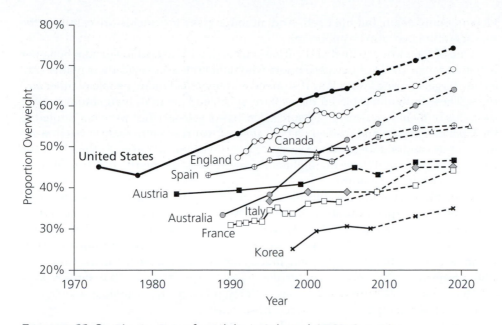

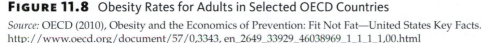

FIGURE 11.8 Obesity Rates for Adults in Selected OECD Countries

Source: OECD (2010), Obesity and the Economics of Prevention: Fit Not Fat—United States Key Facts. http://www.oecd.org/document/57/0,3343, en_2649_33929_46038969_1_1_1_1,00.html

it is estimated that almost one in six children and adolescents (2–19 years) and more than one in three adults are obese. Two main factors that may explain this disparity are diet (consumption of fast food and soft drinks) and lack of exercise. For instance, the rising epidemic of obese American children and adolescents is partly due to significant increases in soft-drink consumption in the past several decades (Malik, Schulze, & Hu, 2006). In addition to unhealthy drinks, many American children and adolescents eat unhealthy foods—both in school and out. Studies have also found that about one-third of American adolescents eat at least one fast-food meal a day and that as they get older (from early to late adolescence) their consumption of fast food increases (Bauer, Larson, Nelson, Story, & Neumark-Sztainer, 2009; Bowman, Gortmaker, Ebbeling, Pereira, & Ludwig, 2003). In sum, differences across cultures in food choice, behaviors, and lifestyles play a role in contributing to these striking differences in rates of overweight and obesity.

Future research will need to tackle the difficult question of exactly what it is about culture that influences attitudes about eating and stereotypes about thinness and obesity. Further study is also needed to determine where cultures draw the line between healthy patterns and disordered eating behaviors that have direct, negative impacts on health. Certainly, our body of knowledge will also benefit from a greater focus on tying specific eating behaviors to specific health and disease outcomes, and attempt to link culture with these relationships.

Culture and Suicide

No other behavior has health consequences as final as suicide—the taking of one's own life. Psychologists, sociologists, and anthropologists have long paid careful attention to suicide, and have studied this behavior across many cultures. The research to date suggests many interesting cross-cultural differences in the nature of suicidal behavior, all of which point to the different ways in which people of different cultures view not only death, but life itself. And although risks for suicide are complex, the role of culture may also be important.

One of the most glorified and curious cultures with regard to suicidal behavior is that of Japan. Tales of Japanese pilots who deliberately crashed their planes into enemy targets during World War II stunned and mystified many people of other cultures. These individuals placed the welfare, spirit, and honor of their country above the value of their own lives. To be sure, such acts of self-sacrifice were not limited to the Japanese, as men and women on both sides of war reach into themselves in ways many of us cannot understand to sacrifice their lives for the sake of others. But the Japanese case seems to have highlighted the mysterious and glorified nature of some acts of suicide in that culture.

Contemporary studies of culture and suicide have focused on factors, such as religious beliefs, to explain variations in prevalence of suicide across cultures. Data from suicide rates reported to the WHO showed that countries with religions that strongly condemned the act of suicide had lower reported rates of suicide than countries without religions that strongly condemned suicide (Kelleher, Chambers, Corcoran, Williamson, & Keeley, 1998). However, the researchers also suggested that the reports may have been biased. Those countries with religious sanctions against suicide may have been less willing to report and record suicides.

A more recent analysis of the WHO data showed that the relation between suicide and religion depends on the particular aspect of religion (Sisask et al., 2010). In general, Sisask and colleagues found that those who reported being part of a religious denomination and who perceived themselves to be religious (subjective religiosity) were less likely to engage in suicide ideation and attempts. It may be the case that being part of a religious denomination protects against suicide by providing social integration (having connections with other people) and regulation (moral guidelines to live by) (Durkheim, 1897/2002). Organizational religiosity (a person's involvement in his or her religious denomination as measured by attendance in worship services), however, showed differential effects across cultures—in some countries it showed a protective effect, in others no effect, and still others inconsistent or even a risk effect. The researchers concluded that culture and religion play important roles in understanding suicide but the relations are not straightforward.

Many studies have pointed to profound and traumatic large-scale sociocultural changes as another key determinant of suicidal behavior, such as forced migration of an entire cultural group and eradication of cultural heritage, practices, and language. This type of historic trauma and severance from cultural heritage has long been identified as a predictor of suicide among Native Americans (Isaak, Campeau, Katz, Enns, Elias, Sareen, & Swampy Cree Suicide Prevention Team, 2010) and Canadian Inuits (Leenaars, Anawak, & Taparti, 1998). The physical and psychological trauma associated with forced social and cultural changes have been implicated in the suicide rates of many indigenous cultural groups around the world (Lester, 2006).

In addition to sociocultural change, specific cultural dimensions predict suicide incidence rates (Rudmin, Ferrada-Noli, & Skolbekken, 2003). Rudmin and colleagues examined data for 33 countries gathered every 5 years over a 20-year period (between 1965 and 1985). They found that the cultural dimensions of power distance, uncertainty avoidance, and masculinity were negatively correlated with rates of suicide. In contrast, the cultural dimension of individualism was positively correlated with rates of suicide. The findings were further complicated, however, by showing that gender and age moderated these correlations. The researchers argued that the cultural dimensions are linked to suicide through many pathways—by affecting a person's thinking and emotions surrounding suicide, by influencing social institutions and organizations that may contribute to suicide, or by associations with other variables such as economic or political contexts, genetics, toxins, or climate. Although the link between culture and suicide is complex, this study attempted to pinpoint how certain cultural dimensions may foster specific beliefs or contexts that can either buffer or exacerbate rates of suicide across cultures.

Cross-cultural research on suicide over the past few decades has given us important glimpses into this difficult yet fascinating topic. Still, many questions remain unanswered. What is it about culture that produces differences in suicidal behaviors, and why? Why are there still considerable individual differences in attitudes toward suicide even in cultures where it is relatively more acceptable? Despite the glorified stories concerning suicide in Japan, for instance, there is still a relatively strong stigma against it and intense prejudice toward the mental disorders related to it, resulting in reluctance to seek help (Ando, Yamaguchi, Aoki, & Thornicroft, 2013). When may suicide be an acceptable behavior in any culture? Given recent and ongoing advances in medical technology and the aging population around the world, such questions that involve medicine, culture, and ethics are bound to increase in prominence. Future research within and between cultures may help to elucidate some of the important decision points as we approach these questions.

Up until now, we have discussed the importance of sociocultural factors, describing how cultural values and beliefs provide a context for understanding health and the development of disease. For pluralistic countries, another important issue is how these cultural values and beliefs may change with the acculturation process that immigrants and their families undergo. These changes may have profound consequences for health.

Acculturation and the Immigrant Paradox

On an individual level, **acculturation** refers to the process of individual change and adaptation as a result of continuous contact with a new, distinct culture (Berry, 2003; see also our discussion on immigration and acculturation in Chapter 12). In Berry's model of acculturation, two dimensions are important to consider: to what extent are individuals involved with the heritage culture and to what extent are individuals involved with the dominant, or mainstream culture. Thus, to understand how individuals with an immigrant background view health, it is important to first assess how connected and involved they are both with their heritage culture and dominant culture.

acculturation The process by which people adopt a different cultural system.

To illustrate, one study asked a group of Chinese Americans about their perceptions of health and also measured their level of acculturation by gathering information on generational status, language spoken, religious affiliation, and endorsement of traditional Chinese values (Quah & Bishop, 1996). The researchers found that those who rated themselves as being more Chinese believed that diseases were a result of imbalances in the body, such as excessive cold or excessive heat, in line with traditional Chinese views of illness. Those who rated themselves lower on being Chinese, in contrast, believed that diseases were a result of viruses, in line with the Western biomedical view of illness. The researchers also found that those who believed in the traditional Chinese views of health and disease were more likely to turn to a practitioner of traditional Chinese medicine when seeking medical help. Those "less" Chinese were more likely to turn to a mainstream medical practitioner. Thus, an immigrant's level of acculturation will determine, to some extent, his or her views on health and disease, and, importantly, the help they seek to treat poor health.

Acculturation also adds complexity to many health-related behaviors and outcomes. For instance, greater assimilation in the United States (being U.S. born or adopting more mainstream American values and behaviors) relates to positive behaviors (e.g., increased utilization of health services), negative behaviors (e.g., increased alcohol and drug use, poorer diet), or has mixed effects (e.g., related to both greater and fewer depressive symptoms) (Lara, Gamboa, Kahramanian, Morales, & Bautista, 2005; Salant & Lauderdale, 2003). Some of the mixed findings can be partially attributed to the multiple ways that acculturation is conceptualized and measured. Some studies examine proxies for acculturation (such as country of birth) while other studies use more in-depth measures, assessing acculturation values and behaviors for the heritage culture as well as mainstream culture. Nonetheless, despite inconsistencies in the measurement and conceptualization of acculturation, studies do show that acculturation is clearly linked to health—and sometimes in surprising ways—as discussed below.

immigrant paradox
Despite the many challenges of adapting and adjusting to a new country, immigrants tend to show better physical health compared to non-immigrants, and, with further assimilation, further negative health outcomes.

One intriguing phenomena that has received considerable attention in the United States, Canada, and Europe is the **immigrant paradox**. Immigrants face a multitude of challenges. Compared to nonimmigrants, they are more likely to have lower education, lower resources, live in poverty, experience adaptation challenges in terms of learning the language, customs, and lifestyles, experience discrimination, and are of lower status because of being a minority (Berry, 2003). But despite these challenges, researchers have found that as a population, immigrants, compared to nonimmigrants, appear to do better on a number of measures of health. This is the paradox—that despite the stress and challenges associated with immigration, immigrants do unexpectedly better than nonimmigrants in regards to health and that further assimilation leads to worse health outcomes (Garcìa Coll & Marks, 2012). For instance, large-scale studies of Latinos in the United States showed that foreign-born (immigrant) Latinos are healthier than U.S.-born Latinos in terms of lower infant mortality rates, less obesity, longer life expectancy, and fewer psychiatric and substance use disorders (Alegria et al., 2008; Hayes-Bautista, 2004; Mendoza, Javier, & Burgos, 2007). Figure 11.9 shows the prevalence rates of psychiatric disorders for different Latino

FIGURE 11.9
Rates of Any Lifetime Psychiatric Disorder by Immigrant Status and Ethnicity/Race Subgroups. The Immigrant Paradox Is Stronger for Some Groups (Non-Latino White and Mexican) Compared to Others

Source: Alegria, M., Canino, G., Shrout, P., Woo, M., Duan, N., Vila, D., Torres, M., Chen, C., Meng, X.-L. Prevalence of mental illness in immigrant and non-immigrant U.S. Latino groups. *American Journal of Psychiatry*, 165, 359–369.

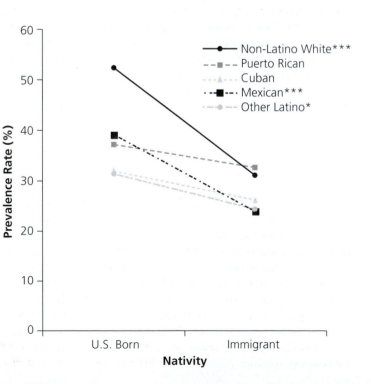

immigrant groups to the United States. The pattern is clear: Immigrants show a lower prevalence rate compared to those born in the United States.

What can explain the immigrant paradox? Scholars have suggested several factors where immigrants have an advantage: healthy behaviors (e.g., better diet, less drug use), social support (close family, kin, and community bonds), and immigrant selectivity (those who immigrate are the ones who are healthier and more robust) (Padilla, Hamilton, & Hummer, 2009; Suárez-Orozco, Rhodes, & Milburn, 2009). It will be important for future research to examine why immigrants seem to lose this protection and experience deteriorating health with each succeeding generation. This knowledge will be necessary for understanding how to reverse this negative trend.

Summary

Taken collectively, a growing literature is showing an increased awareness of sociocultural influences on a host of variables that ultimately have implications for health and disease. These include variables such as cultural definitions of health, attributions and beliefs about the cause of disease, and preferences with regard to lifestyles. For pluralistic countries with significant immigrant populations, understanding the role of acculturation to health is essential. Contemporary health practitioners and the institutions in which they work—clinics, hospitals, laboratories—have become increasingly sensitized to these issues, and are now struggling with the best ways to understand and incorporate them for maximum effectiveness.

▶ Differences in Health Care and Medical Delivery Systems

In this final section, we review how countries differ in how they deliver health care services to their populations. Different countries and cultures have developed their own unique ways of dealing with health care. A country's health care delivery system is a product of many factors, including social and economic development, technological advances and availability, and the influence of neighboring and collaborating countries. Also affecting health care delivery services are a number of social trends, including urbanization, industrialization, governmental structure, international trade laws and practices, demographic changes, demands for privatization, and public expenditures.

National health systems can be divided into four major types: entrepreneurial, welfare-oriented, comprehensive, and socialist (Roemer, 1991). Within each of these general categories, individual countries vary tremendously in terms of their economic level. The United States is an example of a country with a relatively high economic level that, until recently, endorsed an entrepreneurial system of health care, characterized by a substantial private industry covering individuals as well as groups. The Philippines and Ghana also use an entrepreneurial system of health care, but have moderate and low economic levels, respectively. France, Brazil, and Burma are examples of high-, moderate-, and low-income countries with welfare-oriented health systems. Likewise, Sweden, Costa Rica, and Sri Lanka have comprehensive health care systems, and the former Soviet Union, Cuba, and China have socialist health systems.

A quick review of the countries listed here suggests that cultural differences are related to the type of national health system a country is likely to adopt. It makes sense that an entrepreneurial system was used in the United States, for example, because of the highly individualistic nature of American culture. Likewise, it makes sense that socialist systems of health care are used in China and Cuba, given their collectivistic, communal nature. However, cultural influences cannot be separated from the other factors that contribute to the existence of national health care systems. In the complex interactions among culture, economy, technology, and government, social aspects of culture are inseparable from social institutions.

▶ A Model of Cultural Influences on Health: Putting It All Together

In this chapter, we have reviewed a considerable amount of literature concerning the influence of culture on health and disease processes. This research will affect the ways in which we deliver treatment and other services to people of varying cultural backgrounds, and the type of health care systems we create. It has also made scholars in the field more sensitive to the need to incorporate culture as a major variable in their studies and theories. Understanding the role that culture plays in the development and treatment of disease will take us a long way toward developing ways of preventing disease in the future.

So, just how does culture influence health and disease processes? Figure 11.10 summarizes what we know so far. We know that different cultures have different

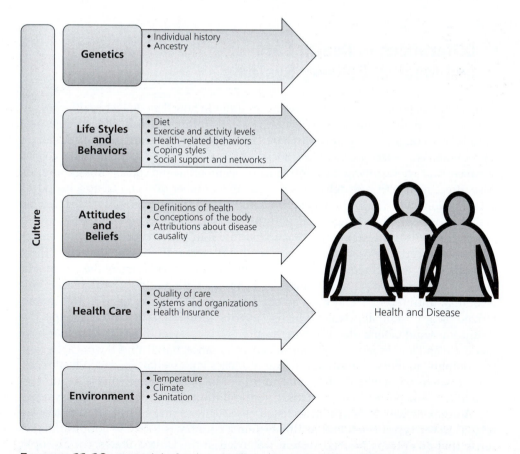

FIGURE 11.10 A Model of Cultural Influences on Health and Disease

definitions of health and disease and different conceptualizations of the body. We have reviewed a considerable amount of research that shows how culture relates to a number of diseases around the world. This literature complements the already large body of literature that highlights the importance of genetics and other psychosocial determinants of health and disease. We have also seen how individual cultural discrepancies may be related to health, and how culture influences specific behaviors such as eating, obesity, and suicide. Finally, although this chapter has focused primarily on the role of psychological and sociocultural factors in health and disease, we cannot ignore the contributions by the environment (temperature, climate) and available health care systems in promoting health and well-being.

Figure 11.10 provides a general overview of the factors that influence health. All these aspects will need to be fleshed out in greater detail, then tied together into a comprehensive and systematic whole to further our understanding of health and disease processes. Future research will also need to operationalize health according to dimensions other than mortality rates or incidence rates of various diseases. Incorporating cultural, genetic, environmental, social, and psychological factors in determining what leads to good health is an enormous job for the future, but it is one that we must work toward if we are to arrive at a clearer and more complete picture of the relative contribution of all these factors. A deep understanding of how culture influences our views of health, illness, and disease is vital to improving our ability to meet the health needs of culturally diverse populations.

EXPLORATION AND DISCOVERY

Why Does This Matter to Me?

1. How do you define good health for yourself? Does your definition resemble the WHO definition of health? Does it incorporate other aspects of health that are not mentioned in the WHO definition?

2. Many cultures have the notion of "balance" in their definitions of good health. In your definition of health from the previous question, did you mention the notion of balance? If yes, in what areas of your life is it important to have balance in order to maintain or promote good health?

3. What makes you happy? Do you think that at different times of your life, different things made you happy? Do you think that your happiness relates to better physical health? Or do you think better physical health leads to your happiness?

Suggestions for Further Exploration

1. We discussed three indicators of health that have been studied worldwide—infant mortality, life expectancy, and subjective well-being. What other indicators do you think are important for assessing a country's health and well-being? How would you measure it?

2. The immigrant paradox has been extensively studied in the United States, Canada, and Europe. The paradox refers to the finding that immigrants tend to do better than native-born individuals on a number of health indicators despite the many challenges associated with immigration. Do you think you would find the immigrant paradox in other countries with large numbers of immigrants? Think about how health beliefs, behaviors, norms, and social structures and institutions of different countries may affect whether health outcomes of immigrants versus native-born individuals may differ.

3. Choose a health outcome (such as obesity or other disease). Adopting a biopsychosocial perspective, identify and describe biological, psychological and social factors that may contribute to the development of the health outcome.

12 Culture and Psychological Disorders

CHAPTER CONTENTS

One important goal of psychology is to use the knowledge gained through research to help people suffering from **psychopathology** (psychological disorders that encompass behavioral, cognitive, and emotional aspects of functioning) to rid themselves of symptoms and lead more effective, productive, and happy lives. Several themes have guided research and practice in this area of psychology. First and foremost is the question concerning the definition of abnormality. What is considered abnormal? When are a person's behaviors, thinking, and emotions abnormal? A second question concerns the expression of a psychological disorder and our ability to detect it and classify it when it is expressed. These are questions concerning assessment and diagnosis. A third question concerns how we should treat a psychological disorder when it is detected. This chapter will address the first two questions; the next chapter will address the third.

psychopathology
Psychological disorders that encompass behavioral, cognitive, and emotional aspects of functioning.

Culture adds an important dimension to these basic questions. Incorporating culture into our psychological theories and concepts raises a number of significant issues with regard to psychological disorders (Marsella, 2000):

■ Do definitions of normality and abnormality vary across cultures, or are there universal standards of abnormality?

■ Do cultures vary in rates of psychological disorders?

■ Are psychological disorders expressed in the same way across cultures, or can we identify culturally distinct patterns?

■ Can the field develop cross-culturally reliable and valid ways of measuring, classifying, and diagnosing psychological disorders?

The answers to these questions have important implications for how we identify psychological disorders and intervene to affect change. Ignoring the ways in which psychological disorders are bound within the context of culture may lead to overdiagnosis, underdiagnosis, and/or misdiagnosis, with potentially harmful consequences to the individual (Marsella, 2009; Paniagua, 2000).

This chapter is devoted to the considerable amount of research and writing that seeks to address these questions and concerns. First, we will discuss the role of culture in defining abnormality. Second, we will discuss the role of culture in the assessment of psychological disorders, examine the classification schemes currently in use, and explore issues surrounding the measurement of abnormality. Third, we will look at how the measurement of personality has been used in assessing psychological disorders across cultures. Fourth, we will review studies of the prevalence (proportion of existing cases) and course of several of the most common psychological disorders (such as schizophrenia and depression) across cultures, and describe cultural concepts of distress. Finally, we will briefly review psychological disorders for traditionally understudied populations such as ethnic minorities, migrants, and refugees.

▶ Defining Abnormality: Some Core Issues

Psychologists and other social scientists have long been interested in the influence of culture on psychopathology. The literature has been somewhat divided between two points of view. One view suggests that culture and psychopathology are intertwined, and that disorders can be understood only in the cultural framework within which they occur. This perspective is known as **cultural relativism**. The contrasting view suggests that although culture plays a role in determining the exact behavioral and

cultural relativism
A viewpoint that suggests that psychological disorders can only be understood in the cultural framework within which they occur.

contextual manifestations of a psychological disorder, there are cross-cultural similarities, even universalities, in the underlying psychological mechanisms and subjective experiences of many psychological disorders. These two frameworks are evident when reviewing how the study of psychopathology across cultures has changed over time.

Historically, researchers have defined and described a particular psychopathology (the symptoms, diagnoses) within a particular culture and then have exported this definition to other cultures for comparative study (Kirmayer, 2007). More recently, researchers have demonstrated a greater commitment to questioning the cross-cultural validity of psychopathologies defined in one particular culture and are striving to understand disorders within the context of the local culture. To do so, researchers are paying close attention to how different cultures may have different attributions and beliefs about health, illness, and disease (see Chapter 11). Understanding local, culturally specific aspects of psychopathology as well as universals are important for identifying a common language and knowledge base to advance our understanding of psychopathologies globally (Gone & Kirmayer, 2010). One starting point to understanding what is culturally specific versus universal is to examine how we define what is abnormal.

Defining "Abnormal"

Consider, for example, the following scenario:

> A woman is in the midst of a group of people but seems totally unaware of her surroundings. She is talking loudly to no one in particular, often using words and sounds the people around her find unintelligible. When questioned later about her behavior, she reports that she had been possessed by the spirit of an animal and was talking with a man who had recently died.

Is this woman's behavior abnormal?

In defining what is abnormal, psychologists often use a statistical approach or apply criteria of impairment or inefficiency, deviance, or subjective distress. Using such a statistical approach, for example, we could define the woman's behavior as abnormal because its occurrence is rare or infrequent. Being out of touch with your surroundings, having delusions (mistaken beliefs) that you are an animal, and talking with the dead are not common experiences.

One problem with this approach to abnormality, however, is that not all rare behavior is disordered. Nor is all disordered behavior rare. Composing a concerto and running a four-minute mile are uncommon behaviors, yet we generally view them as highly desirable. Conversely, drinking to the point of drunkenness occurs quite frequently in the United States (and in many other countries of the world). Nevertheless, drunkenness is widely recognized as a sign of a possible substance-abuse disorder.

Another approach to defining abnormality focuses on whether an individual's behavior is associated with impairment, inefficiency, deviance, or subjective distress when carrying out customary roles. It is hard to imagine the woman described above carrying out normal day-to-day functions, such as caring for herself and working, while she believes herself to be an animal. In many instances, psychological disorders do involve serious impairments or a reduction in an individual's overall functioning. However, this is not always the case. Some people suffering from bipolar disorder (manic depression), for example, report enhanced productivity during manic episodes.

If we examine the woman's behavior in terms of deviance, we might also conclude that it is abnormal because it seems to go against social norms. But not all behavior that is socially deviant can be considered abnormal or psychologically disordered. For example, the American Psychological Association (APA) classified homosexuality as a psychological disorder until 1973. In China, the Chinese Psychiatric Association (CPA) classified homosexuality as a psychological disorder until 2010. Over time, our notions of what is socially deviant, changes. Thus, using societal norms as a criterion for abnormality is difficult not only because they are subjective (what one member of a society or culture considers deviant, another may accept as normal) but also because they change over time.

Reliance on reports of subjective distress to define abnormal behavior is also problematic. Whether a person experiences distress as a consequence of abnormal behavior may depend on how others treat him or her. For example, if the woman just described is ridiculed, shunned, and viewed as "sick" because of her behavior, she may well experience distress. Conversely, if she is seen as having special powers and is part of an accepting circle, she may not be distressed at all. Each of these ways of defining abnormality has advantages as well as disadvantages. These issues become even more complex when culture is considered.

As an alternative to these approaches, many cross-cultural scholars argue that we can understand and identify abnormality only if we take the cultural context into account. This viewpoint suggests that we must apply the principle of cultural relativism to abnormality. For example, the woman's behavior might appear disordered if it occurred on a street corner in a large city in the United States. It could, however, appear appropriate and understandable if it occurred in a shamanistic ceremony in which she was serving as healer. Cultures that believe in supernatural interventions are able to clearly distinguish when trance states and talking with spirits are an acceptable part of a healer's behavioral repertoire and when the same behaviors would be considered a sign of disorder (Murphy, 1976). Examples of such cultures include the Yoruba in Africa and some Inuits in Alaska. Along the same lines, behaviors associated with some religions (e.g., revivalist Christian groups in the United States), that involve speaking in tongues (glossolalia) and seeing visions, are widely practiced and accepted and may not indicate a psychological disorder (Loewenthal, 2007).

Abnormality and normality, then, are culturally determined concepts (Marsella & Yamada, 2007). Nonetheless, whether to accept universal or culturally relative definitions of abnormality is a source of continuing controversy in psychology. Examination of the cross-cultural literature provides clues on how to understand the role of culture in contributing to abnormality and psychological disorders.

▶ Culture and the Categorization and Assessment of Psychological Disorders

Assessment of psychological disorders involves identifying and describing an individual's symptoms in the broader context of his or her overall functioning, life history, and environment (Mezzich, Berganza, & Ruiperez, 2001). The tools and methods of assessment should be sensitive to cultural and other environmental influences on behavior and functioning. Although considerable progress has been made in the field over the years, the literature on standard assessment techniques indicates that there may be problems of bias or insensitivity when psychological tests and methods developed in one cultural context are used to assess behavior in a different context.

Culture and Categorization of Psychological Disorders

In assessing psychological disorders, psychologists seek to classify abnormal cognitions, behaviors, and emotions into categories—diagnoses—that are both reliable and valid. *Reliability*, as you will recall from Chapter 2, has to do with the degree to which the same diagnoses would be made consistently over time and by different clinicians; *validity* refers to the degree to which the diagnosis accurately portrays the clinical disorder it is supposed to describe.

Because culture exerts some degree of influence on the creation, maintenance, and definition of abnormality, cross-cultural issues arise concerning the reliability and validity of diagnoses, and even of the diagnostic categories used. If all psychological disorders were entirely etic in their expression and presentation—that is, entirely the same across cultures—then creating reliable and valid diagnostic categories would not be a problem. But just as individuals differ in their presentation of abnormality, cultures also vary; indeed, some psychological syndromes appear to be limited to only one or a few cultures. Thus, developing diagnostic systems and classifications that can be reliably and validly used across cultures around the world, or even across different cultural groups within a single country, becomes a significant challenge.

In the United States, the primary diagnostic classification system is the American Psychiatric Association's *Diagnostic and Statistical Manual of Mental Disorders* (DSM). The DSM, originally published in 1952, has undergone several major revisions and is now in its fifth edition (DSM-V, 2013). Notably, the revisions from the DSM-III to DSM-IV and now to the latest DSM-V represent the field's increasing recognition that culture is a critical aspect of diagnosis. In response to heavy criticism by cross-cultural psychiatrists that the DSM-III ignored the importance of a patient's cultural background, a section with a list of 25 "culture-bound syndromes" was added to the DSM-IV, albeit in the appendix. This addition was regarded as a rather weak attempt to acknowledge the role of culture in defining psychological disorders as it perpetuated the idea that only some, mostly non-Western, disorders are culture-bound, and not all (Hughes, 1998).

In the most recent version, the DSM-V, the section on culture-bound syndromes has been revised and replaced by three key concepts: (1) *cultural syndromes of distress*, patterns of symptoms that tend to cluster together for individuals in specific cultural groups, communities, or contexts; (2) *cultural idioms of distress*, ways that cultural groups and communities communicate and express their distressing thoughts, behaviors, and emotions; and (3) *cultural explanations of distress,* what cultural groups and communities believe is the cause of the distress, symptoms, or illness. In other words, how cultural groups and communities explain why symptoms are occurring. Together, the concepts of cultural syndromes, cultural idioms of distress, and cultural explanations represent **cultural concepts of distress (CCD)**. Cultural concepts of distress is a broader and more comprehensive construct than the DSM-IV's previous label of culture-bound syndromes. Importantly, the tenets of cultural concepts of distress are relevant for understanding *all* psychological disorders, not just those limited to the non-Western world (see Figure 12.1).

Another modification to the DSM-V to more comprehensively address culture is the inclusion of a reconceptualized and more detailed Cultural Formulation Interview (CFI). The CFI is a tool that clinicians can use to assess an individual's experience within his or her specific social and cultural context. Figure 12.2 shows the first page of the CFI. On the left hand side are notes for the interviewer outlining the rationale behind each question. On the right hand side are questions for the client.

cultural concepts of distress The shared ways in which cultural groups or communities experience, express, and interpret distress.

FIGURE 12.1

A Revised Formulation of Culture in Relation to Diagnosis: The Construct of Cultural Concepts of Distress in the DSM-V. Cultural Concepts of Distress Are Based on These Three Aspects of Cultural Understanding

Cultural Concepts of Distress

Cultural Syndromes of Distress	• Patterns of symptoms that tend to cluster together for individuals in specific cultural groups, communities, or contexts.
Cultural Idioms of Distress	• Ways that cultural groups and communities communicate and express their distressing thoughts, behaviors, and emotions.
Cultural Explanations of Distress	• What cultural groups and communities believe is the cause of the distress, symptoms, or illness.

Through these questions, the clinician elicits an individual's perspective on how he or she views and experiences his or her distress, paying special attention to the social and cultural context. This valuable information provides a stronger foundation for the clinician to diagnose and treat the person's distress.

One study reviewed over 300 medical records of clients with ethnic minority or immigrant backgrounds (Adeponle et al., 2012). When these cases were reevaluated using the cultural formulation interview (from the DSM-IV-TR), about half of the cases with a referral diagnosis of a psychotic disorder (e.g., schizophrenia) were rediagnosed as a nonpsychotic disorder (e.g., major depression, posttraumatic distress disorder). In other words, reevaluating the cases while taking a deeper account of culture led, in some instances, to a different conclusion concerning a diagnosis of psychosis. These findings suggested that use of the cultural formulation interview can be a useful tool for evaluating a person's symptoms and perspectives on distress. Studies with the newly revised DSM-V version of the cultural formulation interview are just beginning.

In sum, after over a decade of revisions, the DSM-V aims to offer a more inclusive account of psychological disorders that go beyond North American and Western European descriptions and experiences. Over the years, with each revision, the DSM has taken steps to incorporate the role of culture in understanding the expression and reliable classification of psychological disorders. Clearly, a better understanding is required for more effective treatment.

The other main classification system in use today is the *International Classification of Diseases*, 10th edition (ICD-10), endorsed and published by the World Health Organization (WHO, 1992). It is currently the most widely used classification system around the world and is used for global health reporting. Unlike the DSM-V, the majority of the ICD-10 focuses on physical diseases (e.g., infectious and parasitic diseases, diseases of the circulatory system), with one chapter focusing on "mental and behavioral disorders." The first time the ICD included psychological disorders was in 1949, in the ICD-6 manual. The ICD is intended to be descriptive and atheoretical. Although the ICD-10 is used around the world, reviews have suggested that it falls short of incorporating the importance of culture in influencing the expression and presentation of psychological disorders (e.g., Mezzich et al., 2001). Nonetheless, the 194 member states of the WHO are required by international treaty to gather health statistics using the ICD.

Cultural Formulation Interview (CFI)

Supplementary modules used to expand each CFI subtopic are noted in parentheses.

GUIDE TO INTERVIEWER	INSTRUCTIONS TO THE INTERVIEWER ARE *ITALICIZED.*
The following questions aim to clarify key aspects of the presenting clinical problem from the point of view of the individual and other members of the individual's social network (i.e., family, friends, or others involved in current problem). This includes the problem's meaning, potential sources of help, and expectations for services.	*INTRODUCTION FOR THE INDIVIDUAL:* I would like to understand the problems that bring you here so that I can help you more effectively. I want to know about **your** experience and ideas. I will ask some questions about what is going on and how you are dealing with it. Please remember there are no right or wrong answers.

CULTURAL DEFINITION OF THE PROBLEM

CULTURAL DEFINITION OF THE PROBLEM

(Explanatory Model, Level of Functioning)

Elicit the individual's view of core problems and key concerns. *Focus on the individual's own way of understanding the problem.* *Use the term, expression, or brief description elicited in question 1 to identify the problem in subsequent questions (e.g., "your conflict with your son").*	1. What brings you here today? *IF INDIVIDUAL GIVES FEW DETAILS OR ONLY MENTIONS SYMPTOMS OR A MEDICAL DIAGNOSIS, PROBE:* People often understand their problems in their own way, which may be similar to or different from how doctors describe the problem. How would *you* describe your problem?
Ask how individual frames the problem for members of the social network.	2. Sometimes people have different ways of describing their problem to their family, friends, or others in their community. How would you describe your problem to them?
Focus on the aspects of the problem that matter most to the individual.	3. What troubles you most about your problem?

CULTURAL PERCEPTIONS OF CAUSE, CONTEXT, AND SUPPORT

CAUSES

(Explanatory Model, Social Network, Older Adults)

This question indicates the meaning of the condition for the individual, which may be relevant for clinical care.	4. Why do you think this is happening to you? What do you think are the causes of your [PROBLEM]?
Note that individuals may identify multiple causes, depending on the facet of the problem they are considering.	*PROMPT FURTHER IF REQUIRED:* Some people may explain their problem as the result of bad things that happen in their life, problems with others, a physical illness, a spiritual reason, or many other causes.
Focus on the views of members of the individual's social network. These may be diverse and vary from the individual's.	5. What do others in your family, your friends, or others in your community think is causing your [PROBLEM]?

FIGURE 12.2 First page of the Cultural Formulation Interview (CFI) in the DSM-V (APA, 2013). On the left hand side is information for the interviewer that provides a rationale for each question. On the right hand side are questions to ask the individual being interviewed. The purpose of the CFI is to help the clinician understand a person's own perceptions of his or her distress, which is rooted in social and cultural contexts. To see the full cultural formulation interview, go to this website: http://www.psychiatry.org/practice/dsm/dsm5/online-assessment-measures#Disorder. If you want even more detail on additional questions to follow up the CFI (such as specific areas of cultural identity, or a cultural assessment of groups such as children, immigrants, and caregivers), go to the 12 supplementary modules on that website.

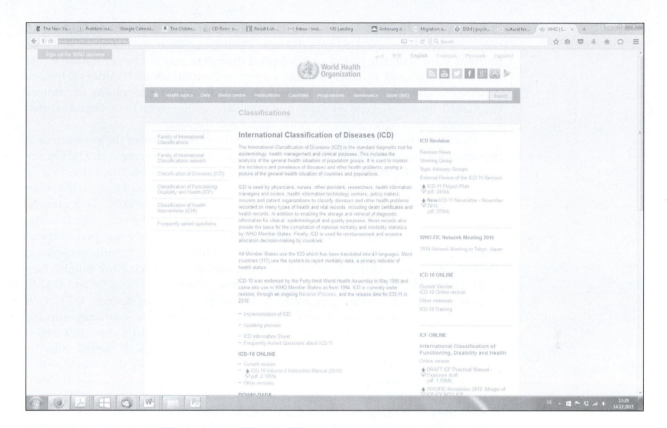

FIGURE 12.3 Website of the International Classification of Diseases (ICD). On this website you can access the ICD-10 online. According to their website, the ICD has been translated into 43 languages and is used by the world health organization members states to "monitor the incidence and prevalence of diseases and other health problems, providing a picture of the general health situation of countries and populations." http://www.who.int/classifications/icd/en/

The ICD-10 is undergoing revisions for a new edition, ICD-11, to be published in 2018. One of the main goals of the current revision is to develop a diagnostic system that has improved clinical utility. In other words, the revised ICD-11 should be able to be used effectively by all World Health Organization (WHO) countries to more reliably assess and diagnose health and mental health disorders. As we have learned throughout the chapter, the interpretation and experiences of health and illness are deeply rooted in culture. Creating a diagnostic manual that is reliable and valid for the almost 200 WHO member countries is quite a challenge. Nonetheless, it is a necessary step to better meet international public health goals.

The DSM and ICD diagnostic systems are similar in disorder categorizations, yet there are differences in what disorders are included, how disorders are named and defined, and how the categories are organized (Reed, 2010). A study with Sri Lankan Tamil immigrants in Canada, for instance, found that the lifetime prevalence rate of posttraumatic stress disorder was 5.8% based on DSM-IV criteria and doubled (12%) based on ICD-10 criteria (Beiser, Simich, Pandalangat, Nowakowski, & Tian, 2011). Rates of agreement in diagnosis using the DSM-IV and ICD-10 can range widely, from

83% agreement for depressive episodes, 64% for obsessive-compulsive disorder, and only 35% for posttraumatic stress disorder (Andrews, Slade, & Peters, 1999). These findings show that diagnosing psychological disorders may not be consistent across the two widely used systems of classification, at least for some disorders (Hyman, 2010; Reed, 2010). With the recent revision of the DSM-V and undergoing revision of the ICD-10, there have been efforts to align the two systems, with the recognition that each country may have country-specific versions of the ICD.

To address the problem of the lack of cultural considerations in the assessment of psychological disorders, local diagnostic systems have also been created. The *Chinese Classification of Mental Disorders* (CCMD), for example, has been heavily influenced by the DSM-IV and ICD-10 but has culture-specific features that do not exist in the other systems. The most recent edition, the CCMD-3, was revised in 2001. This manual includes disorders distinctive to Chinese culture, such as *lutu jingshen bing* (traveling disorder). Traveling disorder is a psychotic condition that occurs when people travel over long distances in overly crowded, poorly ventilated trains. Symptoms include illusions, delusions, hallucinations, panic, suicidal acts, and harming others (Lee, 2001). The CCMD also excludes disorders found in the previous DSM-IV and ICD-10 such as pathological gambling and some personality and sexual disorders (Mezzich et al., 2001). One study found that in 10% of the cases, there was a difference in the diagnosis of depression with Chinese patients using the DSM-IV versus CCMD-3 (Wang, Yang, & Zhang, 2008). Because there is no one-size-fits-all approach to the assessment and diagnosis of psychological disorders across cultures (Reed, 2010), international classification systems such as the ICD-10 should not replace local classification systems such as the CCMD-3 (Lee, 2001). Indeed, a recent survey of clinicians around the world found that those living and working outside the United States and Europe report the greatest need for country-specific diagnostic systems, beyond what the DSM and ICD can offer (Reed et al., 2013).

For all health professionals and the people they seek to help, having a reliable and valid classification system of diagnoses is essential. The DSM-V and ICD-10 have made major strides toward creating such a system. Still, work in this area is continually evolving, and we will see changes in this and other classification systems in the future. Hopefully, those changes will be informed by meaningful and relevant cross-cultural research. One such attempt to develop more culturally sensitive, valid, and reliable diagnoses can be found in *Culture, Medicine and Psychiatry,* an international research journal that devotes a special "Clinical Cases Section" to case studies of individuals within their specific cultural context. The case narratives include a clinical case history, cultural formulation, cultural identity, cultural explanation of the illness, cultural factors related to the psychosocial environment and levels of functioning, cultural elements of the clinician–patient relationship, and overall cultural assessment. Attempts such as this to document in detail how psychological disorders are embedded in and defined by culture should benefit the development of more culturally valid classification and diagnostic systems.

Cross-Cultural Assessment of Psychological Disorders

Not only is it important to have a reliable and valid system of classification of psychological disorders, it is also crucial to have a set of tools that can reliably and validly measure (assess) behaviors, feelings, and other psychological parameters related to mental illness. Those tools may include questionnaires, interview protocols, or standardized tasks that require some sort of behavioral and emotional response on the part of the test taker.

Needless to say, many of the issues that concern the valid and reliable measurement of any psychological variable cross-culturally for research purposes (see Chapter 2) are also relevant to discussions of measurement tools for abnormality. For instance, it may be difficult to adequately transfer and use a psychological assessment that has been developed in one culture to another because of culture-specific expressions of distress. Kleinman (1995) points out that many items of an assessment instrument may use wording that is so culture-specific (e.g., "feeling blue") that directly translating them to another culture would be nonsensical. Green (2009) reviewed a number of issues in developing culturally appropriate psychological assessments, including test construction, measurement error, construct validity, translations, social desirability, test administration, and interpretation. These issues, and others, make valid and reliable measurement of pathology across cultures difficult and complex.

A critical examination of how the tools in use fare across cultures provides a stark glimpse of reality. Tools of clinical assessment developed in one culture are based on that culture's definition of abnormality and use a set of classification criteria relevant to that culture for evaluating problematic behavior. Therefore, the tools may have little meaning in other cultures with varying definitions of abnormality, however well translated into the native language, and they may mask or fail to capture culturally specific expressions of disorder (Marsella, 2009).

The World Health Organization's (WHO) large-scale global studies of schizophrenia that started in the 1970s (described in detail later in this chapter) used the Present State Examination (PSE) to diagnose schizophrenia. At the time, the use of the PSE cross-culturally was criticized for the ethnocentric bias of procedures (Leff, 1986). In a psychiatric survey of the Yoruba in Nigeria, for instance, investigators had to supplement the PSE to include culture-specific symptoms such as feeling "an expanded head and goose flesh." The assessment problems encountered in studying schizophrenia globally illustrated the limitations of transporting assessment methods across cultures.

Transporting assessment methods within a multicultural country may also be problematic. In an extensive study of depression among Native Americans (Manson & Shore, 1981; Manson, Shore, & Bloom, 1985), the American Indian Depression Schedule was developed to assess and diagnose depressive illness. The investigators found that depression among the Hopi includes symptoms not measured by standardized measures of depression such as the Diagnostic Interview Schedule and the Schedule for Affective Disorders and Schizophrenia. These measures, based on diagnostic criteria found in the DSM-III (American Psychiatric Association, 1987), failed to capture the short but acute dysphoric moods sometimes reported by the Hopi (Manson et al., 1985).

Concerning children, the Child Behavior Checklist (CBCL) (Achenbach & Rescorla, 2001) is one of the most widely used measures to assess behavioral, emotional, and social problems of children around the world. The CBCL assesses both internalizing behaviors (e.g., withdrawn behavior, depressive symptoms, somatic complaints) and externalizing behaviors (e.g., attention problems, delinquent behavior, aggressive behavior). Informants, who are usually the parents or teachers, are asked to think about the child they are assessing and report whether behaviors described in the CBCL are not true (coded as 0), somewhat/sometimes true (coded as 1), or very/often true of the child (coded as 2). Some sample items are "Can't sit still, restless, or hyperactive," "Impulsive or acts without thinking," and "Gets into many fights." Higher scores, then, indicate greater behavior problems.

In the last two decades, researchers have conducted several major reviews of the use of this scale cross-culturally. The first set of reviews examined the CBCL (for children 6–17 years) across 12 countries—Australia, Belgium, China, Germany, Greece, Israel, Jamaica, the Netherlands, Puerto Rico, Sweden, Thailand, and the United States (Crijnen, Achenbach, & Verhulst, 1997, 1999). While these reviews showed the scale to be reliable and valid across these different cultures, they also show that clinical cutoff points (e.g., the threshold for what is considered a clinical disorder versus normal behavior) may vary by culture. A second set of reviews of the CBCL confirmed that the factor structure (e.g., the existence of specific dimensions such as being withdrawn, depressive symptoms, and somatic complaints, and two broader dimensions of internalizing and externalizing behaviors) was similar for studies of children and adolescents (6–18 years) from 20 to 30 countries representing Asia, Australia, the Caribbean, East, Western, Southern, and Northern Europe, the Middle East, and North America (Ivanova et al., 2007a, 2007b). Finally, the most recent review examined over 19,000 parent-ratings of their young children (1.5–5 years) using the CBCL across 23 countries (Ivanova et al., 2010). As with the previous reviews, this study confirmed a similar factor structure across the 23 countries for a younger sample. Thus, it appears that the CBCL can be appropriately used in many diverse cultures to capture behavioral, emotional, and social problems of children and adolescents.

Nonetheless, studies have also shown that the CBCL may not capture culture-specific dimensions of problematic behaviors. For instance, studies conducted in Thailand by Weisz and colleagues (2006) found other behavioral dimensions, such as delayed maturation and indirect aggression, not seen in the U.S. comparison group (Weisz, Weiss, Suwanlert, & Chaiyasit, 2006). Acknowledging that the CBCL may be missing culture-specific behaviors, additional culture-specific items have been developed that are not meant for cross-cultural comparison purposes (Achenbach, Becker, Dopfner, Heiervang, Roessner, Steinhausen, & Rothenberger, 2008). In sum, even when assessment tools appear to be reliable and valid for use in many different cultures, adopting an emic approach (review Chapter 1 for definitions of *etic* and *emic*) to identify culture-specific elements is still needed.

In addition to issues concerning the cross-culturally validity of assessment tools, other research has found that the cultural backgrounds of both therapist and client may contribute to the perception and assessment of psychological disorders. Li-Repac (1980) conducted a study to evaluate the role of culture in the diagnostic approach of therapists. In this study, Chinese American and European American male clients were interviewed and videotaped, then rated by Chinese American and European American male therapists on their level of psychological functioning. The results showed an interaction effect between the cultural backgrounds of therapist and client on the therapists' judgment of the clients. The Chinese American clients were rated as awkward, confused, and nervous by the European American therapists, but the same clients were rated as adaptable, honest, and friendly by the Chinese American therapists. In contrast, European American clients were rated as sincere and easygoing by European American therapists, but aggressive and rebellious by the Chinese American therapists. Furthermore, Chinese American clients were judged to be more depressed and less socially capable by the European American therapists, and European American clients were judged to be more severely disturbed by the Chinese American therapists.

Another study of mostly European American teachers showed that their assessments of normal behavior depended on the ethnicity of the child (Chang & Sue, 2003). In this study, teachers were presented with vignettes of overcontrolled (e.g., being anxious to please, feeling the need to be perfect, clinging to adults, and being shy and timid), undercontrolled (e.g., being disobedient, disrupting the class, talking out of turn, fidgeting), and normal (e.g., generally following rules, demonstrating normal play, having some friends) school behaviors that were paired with a picture of an European American, African American, or Asian American male child. Findings showed that teachers rated overcontrolled behaviors for Asian American children as more normative than for European American or African American children. The authors argued that if Asian American children are seen as typically overcontrolled, teachers may be more likely to miss problems associated with overcontrolled behaviors in this population compared to the other two. Thus, assessments of appropriate, healthy psychological functioning may differ depending on the cultural background, notions of normality, and cultural images and stereotypes of the person making the assessment, particularly if the person's sociocultural background differs from his or her client's. Culturally responsive assessment, then, requires more than an acknowledgement of the client's cultural background, but rather it needs an in-depth understanding of that client's culture, and, importantly, an understanding of one's own possible cultural biases (Okazaki, Okazaki, & Sue, 2009).

Finally, one interesting topic concerns language issues in psychological assessment. In more and more cases around the world today, patients or clients have a first language and culture that differ from the diagnostician's or clinician's. For instance, evaluation of English language learners as well as bilingual patients should be done in both languages, preferably by a bilingual clinician or with the help of an interpreter trained in mental health issues (Okazaki et al., 2009). The reason, as was discussed in Chapter 10, is that cultural nuances may be encoded in language in ways that are not readily conveyed in translation. That is, translations of key psychological phrases and constructs from one language to another may give the closest semantic equivalent, but may not have exactly the same nuances, contextualized meanings, and associations. Administration of assessments bilingually or with an interpreter may help to bridge this gap. Researchers have also suggested that assessing which language(s) the client is most comfortable with should be determined first before any assessment or therapy is started (Lim, Liow, Lincoln, Chan, & Onslow, 2008).

All of these issues of assessment (using culturally appropriate assessment tools, understanding a client's cultural background, being aware of one's own cultural biases, assessing client's level of comfort in language) are central for making appropriate diagnoses. Failure to address these issues may result in overpathologizing or underpathologizing (Lopez, 1989). **Overpathologizing** may occur when the clinician, unfamiliar with the client's cultural background, incorrectly judges the client's behavior as pathological when in fact the behaviors are normal variations for that individual's culture. **Underpathologizing** may occur when a clinician indiscriminately explains the client's behaviors as cultural—for example, attributing a withdrawn and flat emotional expression to a normal cultural communication style when in fact this behavior may be a symptom of depression. An important requirement to avoid over- or underpathologizing is a deep understanding of the client's cultural background that is woven throughout the assessment process.

overpathologizing
Misinterpreting culturally sanctioned behavior as expressions of pathological symptoms.

underpathologizing
Attributing pathological symptoms to normative cultural differences.

Measurement of Personality to Assess Psychopathology

One of the interesting ways in which personality tests are used cross-culturally involves the assessment not only of personality but also of clinical states and psychopathology. The most widely used scale in such cross-cultural assessments is the Minnesota Multiphasic Personality Inventory (MMPI). Two versions, the second edition of the MMPI (MMPI-2; Butcher, Dahlstrom, Graham, Tellegen, & Kaemmer, 1989) and a revised formulation of the second edition (MMPI-2-RF; Ben-Porath & Tellegen, 2008) are currently in use. The MMPI tests for the presence of abnormal behaviors in areas such as paranoia (level of trust), hypochondriasis (concern for own health), and social introversion (orientation toward people). If you were to take the MMPI, your score could be compared to scores based on a clinical population (those with a diagnosed psychological disorder) and a nonclinical population. In other words, a clinician could evaluate whether your score fits the profile of someone who may have a diagnosable psychological disorder versus someone who does not.

Although originally developed with a predominantly European American sample in Minnesota, the MMPI has been used extensively around the world. Butcher and colleagues (Butcher, Cheung, & Kim, 2003; Butcher, Derksen, Sloore, & Sirigatti, 2003; Butcher, Lim, & Nezami, 1998) have examined the use of the MMPI-2 in various cultures including countries in Asia, Europe, Australia, and the Middle East. They reported on the procedures most researchers used in adapting the MMPI-2 for use in their particular cultural milieu, including translation and back-translation, bilingual test–retest evaluation, and equivalency tests. They concluded:

> Clinical case studies involving the assessment of patients from different cultures have shown that MMPI-2 interpretations drawn from an American perspective generally produce congruent conclusions about clinical patients tested in other countries. . . . Computer-based MMPI-2 interpretations appear to have a high degree of accuracy when applied to patients from other countries. Computer-based reports derived on interpretive strategies developed for the United States were rated as highly accurate by clinicians when they were applied in Norway, Australia, and France. (Butcher et al., 1998, p. 207)

Thus, clinical studies involving personality scales such as the MMPI have been shown to be quite reliable and valid in assessing psychopathology and abnormal behavior across various cultures. This finding is once again consistent with the premise of a universal underlying personality structure that can be reliably and validly assessed by methods typically developed and refined in the United States or Europe. If such a universal personality structure exists and can be measured by some means, then deviations from that personality structure in the form of psychopathology should also be measurable using those same means.

Nonetheless, other research has strongly cautioned against the use of the MMPI-2 for specific populations. Pace and colleagues (Hill, Pace, & Robbins, 2010; Pace et al., 2006) have argued that the MMPI-2 may not accurately assess psychopathology for Native Americans. These researchers found that Native Americans score higher on several of the MMPI-2 scales compared to MMPI-2 norms. The researchers suggest that rather than implying higher levels of pathology in the Native American population, higher scores may reveal particular worldviews, knowledge, beliefs, and behaviors that are rooted in a history of trauma and oppression.

To examine the cultural validity of the MMPI-2 for Native Americans, the researchers adopted a mixed method approach (using surveys and interviews) to closely examine the items of the MMPI-2. In the interviews, they asked Native Americans to explain their responses to some of the MMPI-2 items. Through this analysis, the researchers argued that the set of items in the MMPI-2 assessing psychopathology if the person is preoccupied with contradictory beliefs, expectations, and self-descriptions could be interpreted by participants as the difficulty of living within and between two worlds—the white world and the Native American world—which are contradictory in their values, behaviors, and social norms. Another set of items in the MMPI-2 assesses psychopathology by feelings of isolation, alienation, and persecutory ideas. In the study, Native Americans reported racism and discrimination on a consistent basis that left them feeling isolated, wary, and distrustful. The researchers argue that the responses of Native Americans to these particular sets of items may appear to indicate pathological thinking while in fact, because of the unique and difficult history of Native Americans, the responses could be interpreted as normative. The authors conclude that using this personality assessment with Native Americans may result in pathologizing a Native American person's indigenous worldviews, experiences, and beliefs rather than accurately assess psychopathology. They suggest that the MMPI-2 with Native Americans should only be used by counselors and clinicians who are "well-versed about acculturation issues, who are capable of holistic and contextual interpretations, who understand the tribal person's unique medical history, and who are knowledgeable about the person's tribal affiliation(s) and traditional beliefs" (Pace et al., 2006, p. 331).

Because the standard MMPI-2 may not be culturally sensitive for some populations, there are efforts to modify the MMPI to account for cultural variations. One such effort is the development of the Korean MMPI-2 (Roberts, Han, & Weed, 2006). The Korean MMPI has been found to be valid and reliable in predicting *hwa-byung*, a pattern of symptoms unique to Koreans (Ketterer, Han, & Weed, 2010). Symptoms of *hwa-byung* include heart palpitations, digestive problems, anxiety, panic, insomnia, and fear of impending death. The development of the Korean MMPI-2 is an attempt to modify the MMPI-2 based on culturally specific conceptualizations of self, health, and abnormality (Butcher, Cabiya, Lucio, & Garrido, 2007).

Still others have taken a different approach and instead of revising the MMPI, they have developed culture-specific measures of personality, such as the Chinese Personality Assessment Inventory (CPAI) (Cheung, Kwong, & Zhang, 2003; Cheung, Fan, & To, 2009). The CPAI was created for use specifically with Chinese individuals and includes indigenous concepts from Chinese culture. The CPAI includes meaningful personality dimensions (e.g. "interpersonal relatedness") that are not included in the MMPI-2. The CPAI measure may be more valid and useful in assessing mental health with this population than purely imported assessments.

We have thus far reviewed issues of assessing and diagnosing psychological disorders. Although there are many critiques of the classifications and assessment tools used, many studies have attempted to compare the prevalence, prognosis, and outcome for people with psychological disorders across various cultures. We now turn to research that has examined psychological disorders cross-culturally.

▶ Cross-Cultural Research on Psychological Disorders

Cross-cultural research over the years has provided a wealth of evidence suggesting that psychological disorders have both universal and culture-specific aspects. In this section, we will look at a number of disorders that have been heavily researched cross-culturally: schizophrenia, depression, attention-deficit/hyperactivity disorder (ADHD), and a number of disorders that are specific to certain cultural groups.

Schizophrenia

Schizophrenia is characterized by delusions and hallucinations, lack of motivation, social withdrawal, impaired memory, and dysregulated emotions (van Os & Kapur, 2009). There is a common misperception that schizophrenia refers to having multiple or split personalities, due partly to the literal translation of the term *schizophrenia*, which means "split mind." Some have advocated for changing the term. Indeed, in Japan the term for schizophrenia has been changed from *Seishin Bunretsu Byo* (mind-split disease) to *Togo Shitcho Sho* (integration-dysregulation syndrome) (Sato, 2006). Sato reports that the name change has been well-received by clinicians and patients, removing some of the stigma attached to schizophrenia.

Some theories concerning the causes of schizophrenia give primacy to biological factors (e.g., excess dopamine or other biochemical imbalances). Other theories emphasize family dynamics such as parental separation and child trauma (e.g., neglect and abuse) and the broader environment such as living in a dense, urban city, socially fragmented neighborhood, or living in poverty (Morgan & Fisher, 2007; Morgan, Kirkbride, Hutchinson et al., 2008; Morgan et al., 2007; van Os, Rutten, & Poulton, 2008). The diathesis-stress model of schizophrenia suggests that it may develop in individuals with a genetic and biological predisposition to the disorder (diathesis) following exposure to environmental stressors (Walder, Faraone, Glatt, Tsuang, & Seidman, 2014). In one of the first global efforts to systemically study schizophrenia, the World Health Organization (1973, 1979, 1981) sponsored the International Pilot Study of Schizophrenia (IPSS) to compare the prevalence and course of the disorder of 1,202 patients in nine countries: Colombia, Czechoslovakia, Denmark, England, India, Nigeria, the Soviet Union, Taiwan, and the United States. Following rigorous training in using the research assessment tool, psychiatrists in each of the countries achieved good reliability in diagnosing schizophrenia in patients included in the study. As a result, WHO investigators were able to identify a set of symptoms present across all cultures in the adults with schizophrenia. These symptoms include lack of insight, auditory and verbal hallucinations, and ideas of reference (assuming one is the center of attention). The WHO studies are widely cited to bolster arguments for the universality of schizophrenia.

But some important cross-cultural differences emerged as well. In a finding that took the investigators by surprise, the course of the illness was shown to be more positive for patients in developing countries compared with those in highly industrialized countries. Patients in Colombia, India, and Nigeria recovered at faster rates than did those in England, the Soviet Union, and the United States. A study that followed the WHO participants 12–26 years later confirmed the surprising finding that outcomes were better for people in developing rather than developed countries (Hopper, Harrison, Janca, & Sartorius, 2007). This difference was attributed to factors in developing countries such as the presence of extended kin networks, community support, the tendency for patients to return to work fulltime, and being married (for instance, a majority [75%] of participants with schizophrenia in India were married during follow-up compared to a minority [33%] of patients in other developed countries). Importantly, however, the prognosis for those in developed countries is varied, suggesting that there is improvement for some.

The researchers also noted differences in symptom expression across cultures. Patients in the United States were less likely to demonstrate lack of insight and auditory hallucinations than were Danish or Nigerian patients. These findings may be related to cultural differences in values associated with insight and self-awareness, which are highly regarded in the United States but less well regarded in the other countries. Also, cultures may differ in their tolerance for particular symptoms; the Nigerian culture as a whole is more accepting of the presence of voices. Nigerian and Danish patients, however, were more likely to demonstrate catatonia (extreme withdrawal or agitation).

Lin and Kleinman (1988) have discussed some of the methodological problems that plagued the WHO studies—among them, an assessment tool that failed to tap culturally unique experiences and expressions of disorder. Lin and Kleinman also noted that the samples were made artificially homogeneous because of the selection criteria. They argued that the findings of cross-cultural differences might have been greater still had not the heterogeneity of the sample been reduced. Because the conclusions of the study emphasized the similarities and not the differences of schizophrenia across the various cultures, Kleinman (1995) states that we may have focused on and exaggerated the universal aspects of psychological disorders at the expense of revealing what is culturally specific. In other words, the biases of the investigators may have led them to search for cultural commonalities while overlooking important cultural differences.

More recent cross-cultural studies of patients with schizophrenia have tested the theory that expressed emotion—family communication characterized by hostility, criticism, and emotional overinvolvement—increases the risk of relapse. The expressed-emotion construct is important because it suggests that family and social interactions influence the course of schizophrenia. These interactions are influenced, in turn, by cultural values. In a review of research on expressed emotion and schizophrenia in various cultures, Bhugra and McKenzie (2010) report that expressed emotion consistently predicts relapse in Western samples (such as in the United States, United Kingdom, and Australia), but less so for other countries (such as India, Egypt, China, and Israel). One reason for this difference is the difficulties in using this construct in different cultures, particularly those that emphasize nonverbal communication (Bhugra & McKenzie, 2010; Kleinman, 1988). Core aspects of expressed emotion may have different meanings in different cultures. For instance, what is considered "overinvolvement" in one culture may be interpreted as normative care in another, and what is considered "high criticism" in one culture may be normative concern in another. These scholars question whether measures of expressed emotion developed in one cultural context have validity in another. Nonetheless, Bhurga and McKenzie's (2010) and other reviews (e.g., Weisman, 2005) show evidence that expressed emotion does predict relapse in a wide variety of cultures and ethnic groups.

In summary, the WHO studies provide evidence of a universal set of core symptoms that may be related to schizophrenia. Other studies, however, help to temper this interpretation by documenting specific cultural differences in the exact manifestations and experience of schizophrenia in different cultural contexts. We now turn to cross-cultural studies of depression, another one of the most common psychological disorders seen around the world.

Depression

Depression is one of the most widely studied disorders as it is one of the most prevalent disorders worldwide. By 2020, major depression is projected to be the second leading cause of illness-related disability affecting the world's population (WHO, 2015). Depressive disorder is characterized by physical changes (such as sleep and appetite disturbances), motivational changes (such as apathy and boredom), as well as emotional and behavioral changes (such as feelings of sadness, hopelessness, and loss of energy). The presence of a depressive disorder is experiencing these symptoms for at least two weeks, according to the DSM-V and ICD-10.

Women are more likely to experience depression than men, and this gender difference has held up across race, ethnicity, socioeconomics, and culture (Seedat et al., 2009). Developmentally, the incidence of depression increases dramatically around the time of puberty, and more so for females than for males (Cyranowski, Frank, Young, & Shear, 2000). This gender difference remains throughout adulthood. There is also evidence that the incidence of depression has risen over the past few decades, especially among adolescents (WHO, 2014).

A landmark study by the WHO (1983) investigated the symptoms of depression in four countries—Canada, Switzerland, Iran, and Japan—and found that the great majority of patients (76% of the 573 cases) reported cross-culturally constant symptoms, including "sadness, joylessness, anxiety, tension, lack of energy, loss of interest, loss of ability to concentrate, and ideas of insufficiency" (p. 61). More than half of this group (56 percent) also reported suicidal ideation. Based on these findings, Marsella (1980; Marsella, Sartorius, Jablensky, & Fenton, 1985) suggested that vegetative symptoms such as loss of enjoyment, appetite, or sleep are universal ways in which people experience depression. Nonetheless, Marsella (1979, 1980; Marsella, Kaplan, & Suarez, 2002; Marsella & Yamada, 2007) also argues for a culturally relative view of depression, suggesting that depressive symptom patterns differ across cultures because of cultural variations in sources of stress as well as in resources for coping with the stress.

As with schizophrenia, rates of depression also vary from culture to culture. Figure 12.4 shows 12-month prevalence rates for depressive episodes across 13 countries. Different manifestations of the disorder, however, render it somewhat difficult to interpret these differences in prevalence rates. While the DSM-V and ICD-10 may capture common symptoms across cultures, it may be missing other culturally specific symptoms. Lee, Kleinman, and Kleinman (2007) conducted in-depth interviews with Chinese psychiatric outpatients diagnosed with depression in southern China. Their findings support both universal and culturally specific aspects of depression. Patients reported symptoms that were similar to what is described in standard diagnostic systems such as loss of appetite, feelings of hopelessness, and suicidal ideation. Patients also reported, however, symptoms that are not included in these diagnostic systems. We highlight three of them here.

FIGURE 12.4 Twelve-Month Prevalence Rates (percent) of Depressive Episodes Based on the DSM-IV for Ages 18 and Above

Source: Kessler et al. (2010). Age differences in the prevalence and comorbidity of DSM-IV major depressive episodes: Results from the WHO World Mental Health Survey Initiative. *Depression and Anxiety, 27,* 351–364. Based on data from page 356.

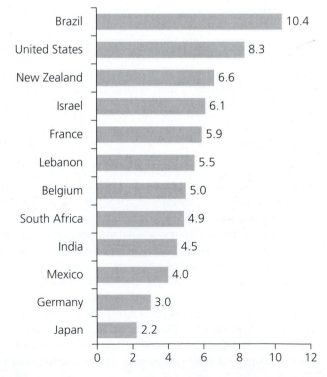

One symptom was "embodied emotional experiences" where emotional distress was combined with bodily experiences, especially centered around the heart:

> I felt my head swelling, very distressed and painful in the heart [*xin hen xinku*], my heart felt pressed … So … [sighing] … I felt my heart very irritated [*xin hen fan*], very upset … I felt my heart clutched and dysphoric [*xinyi*] … My brain swollen, so swollen inside. It is heart pressed and brain swollen [*xinyi naozhang*]. [case 29] (p. 4)

The patients described heart panic, heart dread, and heart pain. Importantly, Lee et al. (2007) argue that these symptoms are not simply **somatization** (bodily symptoms as expressions of psychological distress), because the Chinese view does not separate bodily and psychological symptoms but rather experience them as closely connected (Lee et al., 2007).

somatization Psychological distress expressed as bodily symptoms.

Another symptom was "distress of social harmony," referring to disrupted social relations within the family or work contexts:

> It seems everything is not smooth, and I want to vent my anger toward them. I want to wreak terrible vengeance toward others although they haven't done anything wrong to me. If they don't realize that I am suffering from depression, it will lead to quarrels. I will be misunderstood. They will think I am mischief making. [case 4] (p. 4)

In the DSM-V and ICO-10 criteria, impaired social relations is not a key marker of depression. For the Chinese patients, however, the distress associated with social disharmony was central to their experience of depression.

Finally, again unlike the DSM-V and ICD-10, insomnia was seen as a *cause*, not symptom, of depression:

> I suffered so hard [*xinku*] [to help the team at work], yet when I was not in fit condition, they kicked me out … So I was very unhappy and kept thinking about this, feeling very troubled, lost my sleep and couldn't sleep well … My friend advised me to come here for treatment. My condition improved after a period of consultation. I could sleep well and became better. So I stopped treatment, thinking that I had recovered. [case 29] (pp. 4–5)

The patients believed that if they could cure their insomnia, they could get rid of their depression. Clearly, these differences suggest that symptoms associated with depression are rooted in the particular cultural context. Future studies should continue to gather in-depth culturally based knowledge in order to uncover and describe experiences of psychological distress that may be unique to that particular culture.

One interesting study highlights the necessity of understanding psychological disorders within a particular cultural context by showing that expressions of depression may be based on deviations from cultural norms. In this study, the researchers compared European Americans and Asian Americans who were depressed with nondepressed people from the same cultural backgrounds in their emotional reactions to films to illicit sadness or happiness (Chentsova-Dutton, Chu, Tsai, Rottenberg, Gross, & Gotlib, 2007). In European American cultural contexts, people are encouraged to openly demonstrate their emotions. In Asian American cultural contexts, people are encouraged to maintain emotional balance and moderation. Because depression is characterized by emotional disturbances, the researchers hypothesized that those with depression would show inappropriate emotional reactivity, but relative to the specific cultural norm. Subsequently, European Americans who were depressed should show *less* emotional expression, whereas Asian Americans who were depressed should show *more* emotional expression. The results showed that there were no differences between depressed and nondepressed individuals when watching the happy film. However, for the sad film, depressed European Americans, as hypothesized, showed less emotional expression (less crying and less reported sadness) compared to nondepressed European Americans. Further, depressed Asian Americans, as hypothesized, showed more emotional expression (more crying and more reported sadness) compared to nondepressed Asian Americans. The researchers concluded that depression may impair emotional expression by suppressing or exacerbating the expression of a particular emotion depending on the cultural norms of that particular group. In sum, as with the cross-cultural work on schizophrenia, the literature on depression points to both universal and culture-specific ways in which the disorder may be expressed and experienced across cultures. Because depression is one of the most common mental health disorders worldwide, it will be important for future research to continue to uncover the etiology, expression, and prognosis of depression in different parts of the world.

Attention-Deficit/Hyperactivity Disorder

Up until now, we have discussed disorders affecting primarily adults. We now focus on one of the disorders most commonly diagnosed in childhood—attention-deficit/hyperactivity disorder (ADHD). Despite recognition of this disorder over a century ago, ADHD became more widely studied only within the last three decades (Lange, Reichl, Lange, Tucha, & Tucha, 2010). There are three main features of ADHD: inattentiveness (difficulty paying attention, easily distracted), impulsivity (having trouble waiting turns, interrupting others), and hyperactivity (fidgeting, cannot sit still). Importantly, these symptoms must interfere with social and academic functioning to be considered a disorder. Three subtypes have been identified: ADHD with symptoms of inattention, symptoms of hyperactivity and impulsivity, and symptoms of all three—inattention, hyperactivity, and impulsivity (DSM-V). In contrast, according to the ICD-10 criteria, all three types of symptoms must be present to diagnose ADHD. Thus, prevalence rates are difficult to compare across cultures if they use two different diagnostic systems.

There are two contrasting views of ADHD. One view focuses on the neurobiological component of the disorder, citing evidence of chemical imbalances in the brain as a primary cause of ADHD symptoms (Tripp & Wickens, 2009). The other view argues that ADHD is solely a social/cultural construct. Timimi (2004), for instance, contends that the stresses of modern Western culture (loss of extended family support, a busy and hyperactive family life, greater emphasis on schooling and achievement) have set the stage for the emergence of the disorder and higher rates of ADHD in recent years. These contrasting views have led to the current debate on the role of culture in the diagnosis, prevalence, and treatment of ADHD (Roessner et al., 2007).

In the last three decades, studies on ADHD from many different cultures have proliferated. A review of studies published on ADHD between 1987 and 2008 found that the core symptoms defining ADHD (inattention, hyperactivity, and impulsivity), were found in samples of school-age children from 15 countries in Africa, Arabian Peninsula, Asia, Europe, North America, Oceania, and South America—supporting the notion that ADHD is not merely a Western-based disorder (Bauermeister, Canino, Polanczyk, & Rohde, 2010). Further, there is one finding that is consistent across cultures: boys are more likely to be diagnosed with ADHD than girls (Polanczyk, de Lima, Horta, Biederman, & Rohde, 2007).

A review of 102 studies from seven world regions (Africa, the Middle East, Oceania, South America, North America, Europe, Asia) concluded that the prevalence of ADHD worldwide is about 5.29% (Polancyzk et al., 2007). The researchers found wide variations both within and between regions in ADHD rates. The wide variations were mainly due to methodological differences (e.g., different criteria used for diagnosing ADHD based on different versions of the DSM and ICD, sampling from community versus school contexts, gathering data from different sources such as parents versus teachers, and differences in sample size). When these methodological differences were taken into account and North America used as a comparison point, there were significant differences in prevalence rates between North America versus Africa and the Middle East (Africa and the Middle East report lower prevalence rates than North America) and no differences in rates between North America and Europe, South America, Asia, or Oceania. Based on these results, the authors concluded that there is more variation in prevalence rates due to methodological differences rather than geographical location. Evidence such as this bolsters the argument that ADHD may indeed be a universal psychological disorder among children—at least among those cultures where formal schooling is a normative feature of children's development.

Others acknowledge that ADHD may be universal, but that there are culture-specific variations. Norvilitis and Fang (2005) found both similarities and differences in the perception of ADHD among teachers in China and the United States. Both samples rated the importance of symptoms similarly to include both hyperactivity/impulsivity and inattentiveness. Where they differed was in their beliefs in the causes and treatment of ADHD. For instance, 60% of Chinese and 45% of U.S. teachers agreed with the statement that "ADHD is biologically based" and 71% of Chinese and only 13% of U.S. teachers agreed with the statement that "Children with ADHD are just bored and need more to do." The authors concluded that symptoms characterizing the disorder may be similar, yet the causes and treatment of the disorder may differ between the two countries.

International efforts such as the ADHD Working Group, consisting of clinicians and researchers from nine different nations (Australia, Brazil, France, Germany, South Korea, Mexico, the Philippines, the United Kingdom, and the United States), have gathered to discuss the etiology, diagnosis, and treatment of ADHD. The working group published a consensus statement arguing that ADHD is a valid disorder found in both developed and developing cultures, that it has a neurobiological basis, and that it is unrecognized, underdiagnosed, and subsequently, left untreated in many countries (Remschmidt, 2005). Research on ADHD around the world is growing, but there is still much more to be done. Future studies should include more representative samples of children from different parts of the world and conduct assessments longitudinally to confirm whether the etiology, course, and treatment outcome of ADHD is indeed similarly experienced by children from many different cultures.

▶ Cultural Syndromes of Distress

The approach used in cross-cultural studies of depression, schizophrenia, and ADHD can be characterized as etic; that is, it assumes universally accepted definitions of abnormality and methodology. In contrast to this etic approach are various reports of cultural syndromes of distress. As described earlier in the chapter, cultural syndromes of distress refers to patterns of symptoms that tend to cluster together for individuals in specific cultural groups, communities, or contexts. The term used previously to describe this phenomena was "culture-bound syndromes." The move away from using the term "culture-bound" acknowledges that all psychological disorders are culture-bound. The new term, then, is used to indicate that there are patterns of symptoms that tend to be localized to a particular group or community.

Findings concerning differential rates and courses of a disorder across cultures, and of culturally distinct forms of the disorder, suggest the importance of culture in shaping the expression of psychological disorders. In fact, reports of cultural syndromes of distress provide the strongest support for cultural relativism in understanding and dealing with abnormality.

Using primarily emic (culture-specific) approaches involving examinations of behavior within a specific cultural context, anthropologists and psychiatrists have identified several apparently unique forms of psychological disorders. Although some similarities between cultural symptoms of distress and those recognized across cultures have been observed, the particular pattern of symptoms listed below appear localized to a particular group.

Amok, the most widely observed cultural syndrome of distress, has been identified in several countries in Asia (Malaysia, Philippines, and Thailand). The disorder is characterized by sudden rage and homicidal aggression. It is thought to be brought on by stress, sleep deprivation, personal loss, or alcohol consumption (Carson, Butcher, & Coleman, 1988; Haque, 2008) and has been observed primarily in males. Several stages of the disorder have been identified, ranging from extreme withdrawal prior to the assaultive behavior to exhaustion and amnesia for the rage. The phrase *running amok* derives from observations of this disorder.

Zar is an altered state of consciousness observed among Ethiopian immigrants to Israel (Grisaru, Budowski, & Witztum, 1997). The belief in possession by Zar spirits, common in Africa, is expressed by involuntary movements, mutism, and incomprehensible language.

Baksbat is seen in Cambodia, recognized as symptoms based on cultural trauma that is distinct from PTSD (Chhim, 2013). The term *baksbat* means "broken courage." Symptoms include extreme fear, being overly submissive, being mute, and mistrusting other people as well as those in the spirit domain.

Susto is caused by a frightening event that may result in "soul loss" (Rubel, O'Nell, & Collado-Ardon, 1984; Weller, Baer, de alba Garcia, Rocha, 2008). It is characterized by sadness, sleep and eating disturbances, fear of unfamiliar places, impaired social relations with important others, and has been observed in Mexico, Central and South America, and Latinos in the United States.

Other cultural syndromes of distress are *latah* and *koro* (Haque, 2008). *Latah* is characterized by an extreme startle response, echolalia (involuntarily and immediately repeating words another person says), trancelike behavior, or other inappropriate, uncontrollable behavior. It is observed primarily in women in Malaysia. *Koro* is the extreme fear that one's genitals are shrinking or retracting into the body, causing death. *Koro* has been observed among males in Malaysia, Indonesia, and China. Many other cultural syndromes of distress have been documented around the world. See Figure 12.5.

Pfeiffer (1982) has identified three dimensions for understanding how cultural syndromes of distress emerge. First, he cites culture-specific areas of stress, including family and societal structure and ecological conditions. For example, *koro* might be best understood as resulting from the unique emphasis on potency in certain cultures that emphasize paternal authority. Second, culture-specific shaping of conduct and interpretations of conduct may mean that certain cultures implicitly approve patterns of exceptional behavior. An example is *amok*, in which aggression against others "broadly follows the patterns of societal expectations" (p. 206). Third, Pfeiffer argues

Examples of Disorders That Demonstrate Similarities in Symptoms across Cultures		Examples of Disorders That Appear to Be Localized to a Particular Culture, Community, or Context	
	Symptoms		**Symptoms**
Schizophrenia	Delusions and hallucinations, lack of motivation, social withdrawal, impaired memory, dysregulated emotions	Amok	Sudden rage and homicidal aggression
Depression	Sleep and appetite disturbances, apathy, feelings of sadness, hopelessness, loss of energy, for at least two weeks	Zar	An altered state of consciousness, involuntary movements, mutism, and incomprehensible language
ADHD	Difficulty paying attention, impulsivity, and hyperactivity that interferes with social and academic functioning	Baksbat	Extreme fear, being mute, and mistrusting other people as well as those in the spirit domain

FIGURE 12.5 Some Psychological Disorders Show Similarities across Cultures, and Others Appear to Be More Specific to a Culture. All Psychological Disorders Are Culturally Bound

that how a culture interprets exceptional behavior will be linked to culture-specific interventions.

Some disorders that were once considered to be culture-specific have become less so over time. One example is anorexia nervosa. Before 1980, anorexia nervosa was limited to Western countries and primarily to white, middle to upper class females (Mezzich, Kleinman, Fabrega, & Parron, 2002; Miller & Pumariega, 2001). The disorder is characterized by a distorted body image, fear of becoming fat, and a serious loss of weight associated with restraining from eating food or purging after eating. Anorexia nervosa is no longer limited to Europe and North America, but is now found in many parts of the world such as Hong Kong, Japan, and China (Gordon, 2001; Lau, Lee, Lee, & Wong, 2006; Tetsuro, Murakami, Washizuka, Ikuta, Nishizono, & Miyake, 2005; Tong et al., 2011). In countries where attention is not drawn to the female figure and the female body is usually entirely covered, such as in Saudi Arabia, eating disorders such as anorexia nervosa have not been mentioned in psychiatric literature until recently (Al-Subaie & Alhamad, 2000).

The particular criteria for being anorexic may differ among different cultural groups. For instance, distinctive reasons for self-imposed starvation in China are not a fear of getting fat (fat phobia), but having an "extreme distaste for food" or being "intolerably full" (Lee-Sing, Leung, Wing, & Chiu, 1991). Other studies of immigrants have also found differences. A comparison of white British and Southeast Asian British adolescent females diagnosed with anorexia found that fear of fat was not part of the anorexia profile for Southeast Asian British adolescents (Tareen, Hodes, & Rangel, 2005). Interestingly, however, a study examining patients with anorexia nervosa in Hong Kong between the years 1987 and 2008 found that fat phobia became more and more prevalent over the years, to the extent that the clinical profile of this disorder now mirrors the profile of those in the West (Lee, Ng, Kwok, & Fung, 2010). This raises the question of whether the symptoms (such as fat phobia) have been "imported" or better recognized as more diagnoses are being made. Either way, this once cultural syndrome of distress no longer appears to be geographically restricted.

Cultural syndromes of distress share some overlap with, but are distinct from, other disorders that are considered universal. Anxiety and panic disorders are universal, but there is great cultural variation in the presentation, meaning, and alleviation of the symptoms (Lewis-Fernández, Gorritz, Raggio, Peláez, Chen, & Guarnaccia, 2010). *Ataque de nervios*, for instance, is observed among Puerto Ricans and other Caribbean Latinos (Febo San Miguel, Guarnaccia, Shrout, Lewis-Fernandez, Canino, & Ramirez, 2006; Lewis-Fernández et al., 2010; Guarnaccia & Pincay, 2008; Guarnaccia et al., 2010). A core symptom is feeling out of control. Other symptoms include trembling, uncontrollable shouting, intense crying, heat in the chest rising to the head, and dizziness. This disorder is more common among women and tends to surface during stressful family events, such as funerals, divorce or separation, or witnessing an accident involving a family member. Lewis-Fernández et al. (2010) describe how *ataque de nervios* shares symptoms with the DSM criteria of panic attacks, but also shows other symptoms not included in the DSM criteria. Because of this, they argue that relying on standard diagnostic systems such as the DSM may be inadequate for diagnosing certain disorders in some populations. In a national sample of Latinos in the United States, Guarnaccia et al. (2010) found that people reporting symptoms of *ataque de nervios* were more likely to report experiencing other illnesses such as mood, anxiety, and substance use disorders. As such, these researchers argue that this particular cultural syndrome of distress is an appropriate and useful indicator in assessing the mental health and vulnerabilities of individuals with Latino backgrounds.

Guarnaccia and Pincay (2008) propose that considerable research still needs to be done to better understand cultural syndromes of distress. In addition to elaborating and systematically studying cultural syndromes of distress on their own, researchers should also study how cultural syndromes of distress relate to current "mainstream" diagnoses. Cultural syndromes of distress may or may not be subsumed under DSM or ICD diagnoses, may be comorbid (occurring together) with other diagnoses, or may share some overlap with other diagnoses. They suggest that instead of trying to fit cultural syndromes of distress into mainstream diagnoses, researchers engage in intensive research focusing more deeply on specific aspects that make these diagnoses unique.

What conclusions can be made concerning cultural syndromes of distress? The new terminology is one step forward, replacing the term "culture-bound syndromes" originated by Yap in 1967. Designating some disorders as "culture-bound" while others are not fostered the assumption (or perception) that one set of disorders (usually those defined by Western researchers and clinicians) was more valid, true, based on knowledge, and universal, while the other (usually those disorders originating in non-Western cultures) was more exotic, folk, based on beliefs, and culturally specific (Gone & Kirmayer, 2010). In reality, no psychological disorder can escape cultural encoding, shaping, and presentation; thus, the term "culture-bound" was inaccurate (Marsella, 2000). An important lesson is to be learned from the concept of cultural syndromes of distress—that it is necessary to consider cultural values, beliefs, practices, and social situations in determining how to help someone who is suffering.

Summary

The material reviewed in this section suggests that there may be universal aspects of symptoms and disease expression for at least some of the major psychological disorders such as depression, schizophrenia, and ADHD. At the same time, however, the existence of cultural syndromes of distress also suggests that psychopathologies are heavily influenced by culture, especially in terms of the specific behavioral and contextual manifestations of the disorder, and the meaning of the disorder to the life-styles and lives of individuals.

We began this section by positing two viewpoints about the relation between culture and psychological disorders: the universalist position and the cultural-relativist position. The research reviewed here provides evidence for both positions, indicating that psychopathology across cultures contains both universal and culturally specific components. Although the debate continues, one bright spot is that there is much greater recognition of culture's important role in psychopathology compared to even a decade ago.

▶ Mental Health of Ethnic Minorities, Migrants, and Refugees

In this final section of the chapter, we will first discuss rates of psychopathology among four ethnic minority groups in the United States that have been a focus of recent research: African Americans, Asian Americans, Latino Americans, and Native Americans. Second, we will discuss the mental health of migrants and refugees both within and outside the United States. We devote a separate section to these groups as historically, studies of psychological disorders, health, and well-being have overlooked these populations. With globalization and an increasingly diverse social world, it will be important to continue focusing on potential within and between country variations concerning the assessment, diagnosis, prevalence, and prognosis of psychological disorders.

African Americans

African Americans constitute 13.2% of the U.S. population (U.S. Census Bureau, 2014). To understand the mental health of African Americans, it is necessary to recognize that the unique historical context of slavery and exclusion from social, economic, and educational opportunities continues to contribute to their psychological health and well-being today (U.S. Department of Health and Human Services, 2001). Despite a history of major challenges, African Americans have shown resilience. National epidemiological surveys have found that African Americans report lower lifetime and 12-month prevalence rates of major depression and panic disorder compared to European Americans (Breslau, Kendler, Su, Aguilar-Gaxiola, & Kessler, 2005; Levine, Himle, Taylor, Abelson, Matsusko, Moroff, & Jackson, 2013; Smith, Stinson, & Dawson, 2006). Strong family, community, and religious networks have been identified as protective factors against mental illness in this population (U.S. Department of Health and Human Services, 2001). And yet, African Americans report higher lifetime prevalence rates of bipolar disorder (Breslau et al., 2005; Smith et al., 2006) and schizophrenia (Blow, Zeber, McCarthy, Valenstein, Gillon, & Bingham, 2004). Some of these disparities may be explained by disparities in SES, as studies by Nancy Krieger (discussed in Chapter 7) clearly showed that lower SES is related to poorer health outcomes.

Some studies have focused on the heterogeneity within the African American population. The National Survey of American Life (NSAL) is a comprehensive study of the mental health of African Americans in the United States that distinguishes between those who were born in the United States with U.S.-born parents versus those who were born in a Caribbean country or had parents who were born in a

Caribbean country (Jackson et al., 2004). These two groups differ on a number of variables including geographical residence, family income, college attendance, and experiences of racial discrimination (Broman, Neighbors, Delva, Torres, & Jackson, 2008). Thus, aggregating these two groups masks important differences that may contribute to the development of psychological disorders. Analyses of the NSAL have found both differences and similarities in prevalence of psychological disorders between the two groups. The findings are complex. The prevalence of substance abuse disorders was higher among African American women compared to Caribbean Black women (Broman, Neighbors, Delva, Torres, & Jackson, 2008). Caribbean blacks who were foreign-born were less likely (but U.S.-born more likely) than African Americans to report substance abuse disorders. These findings suggest much within group variation based on immigration status. Using data from the same national survey, however, other studies have found similarities between African Americans and Caribbean blacks, for instance, in lifetime and 12-month obsessive-compulsive disorders (Himle et al., 2008). Future research should continue to examine what contributes to similarities and differences in psychological disorders between these two groups to better understand the heterogeneity within the African American population.

Latino Americans

Latino Americans are among the fastest-growing population in the United States and constitute 17.1% of the population (U.S. Census Bureau, 2014). The first comprehensive national study in the United States examining the prevalence of psychiatric disorders and service use among various Latino and Asian American groups is the National Latino and Asian American Study (NLAAS), headed by Maria Alegria and David Takeuchi. The NLAAS was launched in 2002 (Alegria et al., 2004). One significant advancement in this study is the inclusion of cultural syndromes of distress that are relevant for Latinos, such as *ataque de nervios* (Guarnaccio et al., 2010).

Analyses of the NLAAS dataset show variations in rates of mental illness among different Latino groups (e.g., higher among Puerto Ricans compared with Cuban, Mexican, and other Latinos). A review of Latino mental health in the United States indicates that factors such as reception of immigration (being hostile or supportive), history of immigration (experiencing colonization or not), varying SES, experiences with discrimination, and strength of ethnic community may explain differing rates among Latino groups (Guarnaccia, Martinez, & Acosta, 2005). For instance, to explain why Cubans are less likely to report psychological distress, these authors suggest that their unique immigration experiences, such as receiving strong support from the United States (e.g., loans to start businesses, easy transfer of professional credentials for doctors and lawyers), having access to a vibrant ethnic enclave in Miami with political and cultural status and power, and enjoying relatively high SES, have reduced potential life stressors and, subsequently, reduced their risk for psychological disorders compared with other, less well-supported Latino groups. The review highlights how variations in contexts and policies have implications for adaptation, and, subsequently, one's mental health.

Analysis combining the NLAAS dataset with another nationally representative dataset, the National Comorbidity Survey Replication, found that psychological disorders for Latinos differed by immigration status; foreign-born Latinos reported lower rates of psychological disorders compared to U.S.-born Latinos (Alegria et al., 2008). These results seem to support the immigrant paradox (see Chapter 7). However, when the researchers analyzed the different ethnic groups separately, they found that the immigrant paradox held for some groups but not others. The paradox was evident for Mexican individuals concerning anxiety, mood, and substance abuse disorders. For Cuban and other Latinos the immigrant paradox was evident only for substance abuse disorders. And for Puerto Rican individuals, there was no evidence for the immigrant paradox (e.g., there was no difference in prevalence rates by immigration status). These results, along with the previous analysis, point to important variation in prevalence rates of psychological disorders within the broad category of "Latino," highlighting the need to disaggregate the different groups by ethnicity and immigration status (Alegria et al., 2008).

Asian Americans

Asian Americans are among the fastest growing population in the United States and constitute 5.3% of the population (U.S. Census Bureau, 2014). It is difficult to paint an accurate picture of the prevalence of psychological disorders in Asian Americans because, until recently, they have not been included in epidemiological studies (Takeuchi et al., 2007). Furthermore, being stereotyped as a "model minority" masks the fact that Asian Americans may also be at risk for poor mental health (Wong & Halgin, 2006). And, as with the other ethnic groups, the Asian American population is extremely heterogeneous in terms of culture, language, and history of immigration (Okazaki et al., 2009). Thus, describing the mental health of the Asian American population is a challenge.

One study based on the National Epidemiologic Survey on Alcohol and Related Conditions in the United States found that overall, compared to other ethnic groups, Asian Americans reported the lowest 12-month prevalence of disorders including major depression, mania, panic disorder, and anxiety disorders (Smith et al., 2006). One drawback of this large study, however, was that it did not distinguish between the different Asian ethnic groups. This is a critical oversight, as there is substantial variation within the Asian American population depending on the specific ethnic background, generational status, and immigrant or refugee status. The NLAAS (described earlier) addressed this limitation by sampling several Asian ethnic groups (Chinese, Filipino, Vietnamese, other Asian) of varying generation and immigration statuses. One analysis of the NLAAS dataset found that Chinese women were more likely to report a depression disorder compared to Vietnamese women and that Filipino men were more likely to report a substance abuse disorder than Chinese men (Takeuchi et al., 2007). The analyses showed that beyond Asian subgroup differences, prevalence rates varied depending on gender and immigration-related factors. For women, those who were foreign-born were less likely to have an anxiety, depression, or substance abuse disorder compared to those who were U.S.-born. For men, those who were foreign-born were less likely to report a substance abuse disorder than those who were born in the United States. Further, males who spoke English well were less likely to report any anxiety or depression disorder than those who did not speak English well. Proficiency in English was not related to lifetime prevalence rates of disorders for women. The results showed that to understand mental health disorders among Asian Americans, gender and immigration-related factors must be taken into account (Hong, Walton, Tamaki, & Sabin, 2014). The results also showed that studies need to include different types of immigration-related factors such as place of birth and English proficiency. These two aspects of immigration most likely tap into different aspects of the acculturation process. English proficiency may be a proxy for how well the individual is able to integrate into a wider range of communities that may offer expanded opportunities for access to social and economic resources, possibly supporting better mental health. One limitation of this study is the inclusion of only major DSM disorders, and not disorders that may be more specific to those with Asian backgrounds.

Although not nationally representative, smaller studies of regional areas with high numbers of Asian Americans have found ethnic group variation. In California, Vietnamese adults self-reported higher rates of poor health compared to other Asian groups (Tseng, McDonnell, Takahashi, Ho, Lee, & Wong, 2010), and Vietnamese and Filipino youth reported feeling more depressed compared to other Asian groups (API Youth Violence Prevention Center, 2007). Southeast Asians (such as the Vietnamese) were more likely to have refugee status and lower socioeconomic status and resources, which may account for their poorer health and mental health. As with all of the major categories of ethnic groups, each subgroup has their specific histories, reasons for immigration, culture, language, and context and community in which they settle, that may play a role in the development and prevalence of psychological disorders. Clearly, the wide variation we see within this and other ethnic groups demonstrates that sweeping generalizations about each group cannot be made.

Native Americans

Native Americans constitute 1.2% of the U.S. population (U.S. Census Bureau, 2014). Because of their small numbers, very few epidemiological surveys of mental health and mental disorders have included this ethnic group. To address this limitation, the National Epidemiological Survey of Alcohol and Related Conditions included and targeted this population specifically. The findings from this nationally representative dataset suggest that the prevalence of depression and other mood and anxiety disorders is higher for Native Americans relative to other ethnic groups (Hasin, Goodwin, Stinson, & Grant, 2005; Smith, Smith et al., 2006). Moreover, rates of alcohol abuse and suicide among Native Americans are also significantly higher (Centers for Disease Control and Prevention 2009; Huang et al., 2006). The higher rates of psychological disorders in this population could be due to historical trauma (e.g., forced removal and relocation of tribal communities, loss of sacred places, prohibition of language and cultural practices, family separation), community-wide poverty, segregation, and marginalization, which may translate into greater risk for mental health problems (Organista, Organista, & Kurasaki, 2003).

Nonetheless, as with other ethnic groups, variations within the Native American community should not be overlooked. One large epidemiological study—the American Indian Service Utilization, Psychiatric Risk, and Protective Factors Project (Beals, Novins, Whitesell, Spicer, Mitchell, & Manson, 2005)—involved two Native American tribes. This study reported that the Southwest Tribe and Northern Planes Tribe differed significantly in 12-month prevalence of mood and anxiety disorders. Tribal communities vary in the extent to which they preserve and promote traditional culture. One study found that preserving and promoting traditional culture acted as a strong protective factor in reducing severe psychological distress (Chandler, Lalonde, Sokol, & Hallett, 2003). Thus, depending on the particular community and resources available, the prevalence of psychiatric disorders starkly differed across tribes.

In sum, there are several issues relevant for all four ethnic minority groups in understanding the prevalence of psychological disorders. One is paying attention to the heterogeneity within each of the broad ethnic categories. Most studies have found some within ethnic group variation for mental health when the different subgroups are disaggregated. Also, for African American, Latino, and Asian American groups, immigration status, or place of birth, is another important variable to consider. Studies have shown, in general, that immigration status is a protective factor against psychological disorders. Historically, too, ethnic minorities in general have not had the same access to social, economic, and educational opportunities and resources as ethnic majority individuals. These challenges provide a context for understanding why psychological disorders may develop, and must not be ignored. Future studies will need to be more precise by taking a more fine-grained approach to examine the heterogeneity as well as commonalities within the different ethnic groups. Doing so will provide a more complete and accurate knowledge base to inform public policy and treatment services for these traditionally underserved populations.

Immigrants

Immigration has become increasingly common across the globe, generating an increased interest in the mental health of immigrants. Immigrants adapting to a new cultural environment are confronted with many challenges, such as learning the customs and language of the host culture, while at the same time maintaining aspects of their traditional culture (Berry, 2003). This process of acculturation is key to understanding the mental health of immigrants (see Chapter 11 for a discussion on acculturation). Berry and Sam (Berry & Sam, 1997; Sam, 2000) report that depression, anxiety, and psychosomatic problems are common among individuals undergoing acculturation. Based on these findings, Berry and others have proposed an acculturation stress hypothesis—that experiencing stresses associated with acculturation (e.g., learning a new language, dealing with unfamiliar customs, values, beliefs, experiencing discrimination, leaving social networks behind, and attempting to establish new networks) may set the stage for poorer mental health.

Nonetheless, as discussed in Chapter 11 (Health), evidence for the immigrant paradox challenges the notion that immigration is inherently stressful and leads to poor adaptation. The immigrant paradox is a population-level phenomenon that refers to the counterintuitive finding that immigrants report better physical and mental health outcomes compared to their U.S.-born peers despite the fact that immigrants are, in general, more likely to experience poorer socioeconomic conditions, have less education, and are unfamiliar with the new environment. Figure 12.6 illustrates the immigrant paradox by showing how native (U.S.)-born adults report higher levels of antisocial behaviors compared to immigrant adults. Another study using a nationally representative sample also found that native born adults report greater mood, anxiety, and personality disorders compared to immigrant adults (Salas-Wright, Kagotho, & Vaughn, 2014). Factors such as strong ties to the family and access to a supportive ethnic community may partly account for positive mental health among immigrants (Padilla et al., 2009; Suárez-Orozco et al., 2009).

Other studies have found that the acculturation process is related to mental health, but in complex ways. Some studies have reported that poor mental health is predicted by low involvement in the majority culture (Shim & Schwartz, 2007; Wang & Mallinckrodt, 2006), whereas others have showed that poor mental health is predicted by high involvement in the majority culture (Oh, Koeske, & Sales, 2002). Furthermore, a study of Vietnamese American immigrant adolescents found that those who were more involved in their Vietnamese culture reported more depressive symptoms (Nguyen, Messe, & Stollack, 1999). In contrast, a study of Chinese American adolescents found that those who were more involved in their Chinese culture reported fewer depressive symptoms (Juang & Cookston, 2009).

To reconcile these divergent findings regarding acculturation's link to mental health, the contexts of acculturation must be considered. In other words, taking into account important aspects of the community such as the tolerance for and acceptance

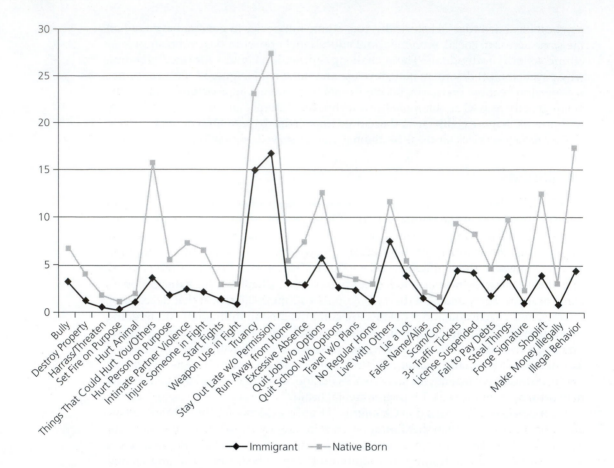

FIGURE 12.6 An Illustration of the Immigrant Paradox: Lifetime Prevalence of Violent and Nonviolent Antisocial Behavior among Native-Born Americans and Immigrants from Asia, Africa, Europe, and Latin America, Aged 18 and Older in the United States

Source: Vaughn, M. G., Salas-Wright, C. P., DeLisi, M., & Maynard, B. R. (2014). The immigrant paradox: Immigrants are less antisocial than native-born Americans. *Social Psychiatry and Psychiatric Epidemiology, 49,* 1129–1137.

of cultural diversity, policies that may prevent the acculturating group from participating fully in the larger society, and the existence of a network of supports, may clarify how acculturation relates to the mental health of immigrants and their children (Berry, 2003; Oppedal, Roysamb, & Sam, 2004). For example, Asian-heritage adolescents living in a small town in the Midwest in the United States where there are few cultural supports and resources for Asian-heritage families, are at greater risk for emotional and behavioral distress if they are highly involved in their heritage culture. However, in a culturally diverse environment such as San Francisco where Asian-heritage traditions are supported, encouraged, and celebrated, Asian-heritage adolescents who strongly maintain the attitudes, values, and behaviors of their heritage culture are less at risk for emotional and behavioral distress (Juang & Cookston, 2009; Nguyen et al., 1999). These findings speak to the importance of the particular communities in which people live in order to understand how acculturation relates to well-being.

In addition to relating to levels of distress, an individual's level of acculturation may also contribute to the content and expression of his or her distress, with implications for the assessment, diagnosis, and treatment of acculturating individuals at risk for mental disorders. If it is assumed that highly assimilated individuals are culturally similar to members of the dominant society, then they may also be similar in the way they express psychological distress. However, psychological symptoms among less-assimilated individuals may not follow this pattern. By definition, less-assimilated individuals are culturally different from the groups for whom conventional symptom scales have been developed. Thus, the question of whether standard measures of psychological symptoms fit the realities of ethnic minority groups remains to be tested (Cortes, 2003).

Refugees

The acculturation, adaptation, and mental health of refugees—migrants who are forced to flee from their countries because of political violence, social unrest, war, or civil conflicts—have also received increasing attention. About 59.5 million people worldwide were forcibly displaced as of 2014 (UNHCR, 2015). Because of traumatic experiences marked by profound losses and upheavals, refugees tend to show higher rates of posttraumatic stress disorder (PTSD), depression, and anxiety than those who migrated voluntarily (American Psychological Association, 2010; Bhui, Craig, & Mohamud, 2006; Kinzie & Sack, 2002; van Ommeren, Sharma, Sharma, Komproe, Cardena, & de Jong, 2002). Using in-depth interviews and surveys, a study of Cambodian refugees demonstrated long-lasting effects on their mental health (Marshall, Schell, Elliott, Berthold, & Chun, 2005). Even after two decades of being in the United States, many refugees were still suffering; 51 percent had major depression, compared with the general rate of 9.5 percent of U.S. adults with major depression. Furthermore, 62 percent had had PTSD in the past year, compared with 3.6 percent in the general U.S. population. The researchers also found that the greater the trauma experienced before arriving in the United States, the greater the toll on their mental health. This has been called a "dose effect," whereby greater severity of trauma is associated with a higher likelihood of experiencing a psychological disorder (Ellis, MacDonald, Lincoln, & Cabral, 2008).

Work with Bosnian refugees living in the United States suggests that postmigration factors are just as important in predicting a refugee's emotional distress and psychopathology as premigration traumatic experiences (Miller, Worthington, Muzurovic, Tipping, & Goldman, 2002). Based on intensive, in-depth narrative interviews with Bosnian refugees, Miller et al. found that postmigration factors such as social isolation and loss of community, the loss of life projects such as building a home or running a business, and the loss of social roles and meaningful activity all contributed to refugees' posttraumatic stress reactions and emotional and physical distress.

Beiser and colleagues (Beiser, 2006; Beiser, 2009; Beiser & Hou, 2001; Simich, Beiser, Stewart, & Mwakarimba, 2005) have followed the adjustment of Chinese, Vietnamese, and Laotian refugees in Canada. Their project is one of the few longitudinal studies of refugee adaptation and mental health. Using a longitudinal perspective has proved invaluable, as predictors of mental health may change across time. For instance, they found that learning the language of the new country did not have immediate mental health benefits but did yield benefits in the long term, predicting less depression. Refugees who learned the new culture's language well were less likely to be diagnosed with depression several years later. The researchers also found that having the strong social support of members of the same ethnic group helped in the early years of resettlement (acting as a springboard for adaptation). However, social support was also associated with a complex set of outcomes in the long term, such as becoming isolated from the larger society. As the number of refugees increases around the world, research that can inform treatment and policies to prevent psychiatric disorders and promote positive adaptation among this population is sorely needed.

Summary

Increasingly, studies have included traditionally understudied populations such as ethnic minority, immigrant, and refugee groups in examining the prevalence of mental illness. To understand ethnic and immigrant status variations in rates of mental disorders, broader contextual factors such as poverty, discrimination, and stresses associated with being an ethnic minority or immigrant to a new country need to be taken into account (Berry, Phinney, Sam, & Vedder, 2006; Chae et al., 2008). Importantly, protective factors such as strong ties to family and ethnic networks within communities are an asset that can counteract these stresses and contribute to the development of positive mental health. Future research should not only continue to examine the prevalence of mental illnesses in more diverse populations, but also move beyond adopting a merely comparative approach to explore which protective factors may help prevent these illnesses (Mossakowski, 2003; Newberg & Lee, 2006).

CONCLUSION

Psychiatric diagnoses, classification schemes, and measurement of abnormality are complex and difficult issues. To the extent that there are both etic and emic aspects of psychopathology, classification systems and assessment methods need to contain both etic and emic elements. Where to draw the lines, and how to measure psychological traits and characteristics within this fluid, dynamic, and ever-changing system, is the challenge that faces this area of psychology today. Although the field has made vast improvements in this area in the past few years, future research will need to elaborate even further on these issues so that classification and measurement can be more precise, meaningful, and relevant. Inclusion of more diverse populations in pluralistic countries is also needed in this area of research. The significance of this is not trivial, as the proper understanding, assessment, and diagnosis of mental disorders is a necessary step to develop effective preventions and treatments that improve and enhance people's lives.

EXPLORATION AND DISCOVERY

Why Does This Matter to Me?

1. How have the studies reviewed in this chapter challenged you in thinking about whether psychological disorders are universal versus culture-specific? Do you believe that disorders like depression are universal? Why or why not? Think about the stresses that people around the world have to deal with. Are there universal stressors that may lead to universal psychological disorders?

2. Think about a time when you were feeling sad. If you are bilingual, describe how you felt in one language, and then describe how you felt in your other language. Were the ways that you described your sadness similar or different when using

those two languages? Do you think language and vocabulary have consequences for how we understand and experience pain and distress?

3. In the beginning of the chapter, a scenario was presented where a woman was talking loudly to no one in particular. Later she reported that she had been possessed by the spirit of an animal and was talking with a man who had recently died. In your culture, is this considered abnormal behavior? Why or why not? How does your explanation clarify what you believe is abnormal versus normal?

Suggestions for Further Exploration

1. There are many ways to describe feeling sad and depressed. In your culture, what are different idioms for expressing feelings of sadness and depression (such as "feeling blue" or "down in the dumps")? Now ask someone from a different culture for idioms expressing sadness and depression. What do different idioms say about how feelings of sadness and depression are understood and experienced in different cultures?

2. Can you think of any psychological disorders that only appear in your particular culture? How would you go about studying whether a particular disorder is specific only to your culture?

3. Timimi (2004) proposes that ADHD is solely a social/cultural construct, arguing that the stresses of modern Western culture have set the stage for the emergence of the disorder. Think about stresses that are prevalent in today's society that might not have existed 50 years ago (such as the stresses associated with the possibility of being plugged into technology 24 hours a day). What kinds of disorders might we see now that we would not have seen 50 years ago? Be creative and come up with one or more new disorders, labeling the disorder and describing the etiology, symptoms, and prognosis.

13 Culture and Treatment for Psychological Disorders

CHAPTER CONTENTS

One of the primary goals of psychology is to use the knowledge generated by research to help people improve their lives. In Chapter 12, we discussed the important role that culture plays in defining abnormality. Culture influences how disorders are expressed and our ability to reliably and validly assess and diagnose when abnormalities have developed into psychopathology. The proper assessment and diagnosis of psychopathology is a necessary step toward helping people with mental disorders improve their lives. In this chapter, we discuss a common approach to addressing psychopathology—namely, psychotherapy. In doing so, we will address the question of whether psychotherapy, which emerged from Western European culture, is applicable and useful in other cultures. Next, we discuss psychotherapy within a pluralistic culture such as the United States, and cover various issues such as why some ethnic minorities are less likely to seek treatment and more likely to end treatment prematurely. Then we describe the field of community-clinical psychology as another avenue for treating psychological disorders. Finally, we end with a discussion of culture and clinical training that prepares the next generation of clinicians and researchers.

▶ Culture and Psychotherapy

Among the many ways in which practicing or applied psychologists pursue the goal of improving people's lives is through psychological interventions with people who have psychological disorders, and whose lives are dysfunctional because of those disorders. One primary vehicle for delivering such intervention is **psychotherapy**. Psychotherapy broadly refers to a method of healing that emphasizes an explicit focus on the self, encouraging deeper self-awareness and self-reflection. The key method of psychotherapy is healing through talking—about one's emotions, thoughts, feelings, and relationships (Kirmayer, 2007).

psychotherapy A method of healing that emphasizes an explicit focus on the self.

Traditional Psychotherapy

Traditional psychotherapy has its origins in Western Europe and can be traced to Sigmund Freud, the father of psychoanalysis. In Vienna, Freud discovered that patients under the influence of hypnosis would talk more freely and emotionally about their problems, conflicts, and fears. Recalling and reliving earlier traumatic experiences appeared to alleviate some of the patients' symptoms. Through individual therapy sessions, he encouraged his patients to explore their memories and unconscious thoughts, much as an archaeologist explores a buried city (Hothersall, 1990). His observations led him to develop the psychoanalytic model, a comprehensive theory on the structure of personality that contributes to our knowledge about the origins of psychopathology.

Freud's theory caught the attention of American psychologists, and psychotherapy was introduced to the United States in the early 1900s. Carl Rogers (1942), an American psychologist, later modified Freud's psychoanalysis techniques and developed what became known as a "client-centered" approach to psychotherapy. Rogers moved away from the role of the therapist as the interpreter of the patient's troubles to emphasize the client's self-propelled growth while the therapist remained empathically sensitive to the feelings and emotions of the client. Despite these modifications, traditional psychotherapy clearly stems from and is bound by a uniquely Western cultural perspective on the understanding and treatment of individuals.

Contemporary Psychotherapy

Over the course of the past century, traditional psychoanalytic psychotherapy has evolved into many different forms and types of psychotherapeutic approaches. These approaches may differ in their theoretical perspective, activity or passivity of the therapist, guidance, focus of treatment on actual behaviors or underlying psychology, and a host of other factors. They are all similar, however, in their goal of improving the patient's or client's life, their one-on-one approach, and the use of psychological principles to affect cognitive, emotional, and behavioral change within an individual.

Modified psychotherapeutic approaches that have developed since Freud's time include **cognitive behavioral therapy** (Beck, 1967, 1976; Ellis, 1962), one of the most commonly used therapies today. Cognitive behavioral interventions emphasize the development of strategies for teaching cognitive skills (Hollon & Beck, 1994). Underlying these types of therapy is an assumption that by changing our thinking we can change our behaviors, and vice versa. These therapeutic approaches originated in the treatment of depression, in which depressed individuals presumably maintain negative thoughts and evaluations of themselves, the world, and the future. Helping such individuals to understand and control their thought patterns and emotions, and changing their maladaptive views to become more adaptive, can help them to recover.

It is important to note that contemporary psychotherapeutic techniques are infused with cultural assumptions, such as the inherent separation of thoughts and behaviors and the emphasis on deep self-awareness. The recognition that psychotherapy is a distinctively Western approach has led some psychologists to challenge the use of psychotherapy with individuals of non-Western backgrounds.

cognitive behavioral therapy Interventions that emphasize the development of strategies for teaching cognitive skills. Underlying these types of therapy is an assumption that by changing our thinking we can change our behaviors, and vice versa.

Cultural Limitations of Psychotherapy

In a diverse world, many psychologists have come to see psychotherapeutic approaches as effective for some people, but less so for others, particularly those of non-European descent. Kirmayer (2007) argues that psychotherapy itself is inescapably bound to a particular cultural framework. This notion makes sense for several reasons. First, as we have seen, expressions of abnormality, and their underlying psychological causes, are at least partly bound to culture. Second, psychotherapy requires probing into the self, and cultures differ on notions of the self—some cultures focus on the independent sense of self, while others concentrate more on the interdependent sense of self (see Chapter 5). Third, the ability of the therapist or clinician to assess and deal with such behaviors is intimately related to his or her knowledge, understanding, and appreciation of the cultural context within which the behaviors occur. Fourth, if the goal of psychotherapy is to help people to become more functional within their society, then functionality itself is culturally determined; that is, different cultures and societies would necessitate different outcomes.

In examining the roots and history of the development of psychotherapy, some writers have suggested that psychoanalysis—the basis for contemporary psychotherapy—was developed specifically within a Jewish cultural framework, and that it shares features with Jewish mysticism (Langman, 1997). In fact, the development of other psychotherapeutic approaches, such as behavioral (e.g., cognitive-behavioral therapy) or humanistic approaches (e.g., client-centered therapy), could be considered a "culturalization" of traditional psychoanalysis to American culture and society. Viewed in this fashion, psychotherapy can be considered a cultural product, reflecting and reproducing a cultural context. Because cultural context is in part composed of moral traditions embedded in political structures, psychotherapy is itself unavoidably a moral practice with political consequences embedded within a cultural framework. In this sense, there can be no value-free psychotherapy because all psychotherapy is bound to a particular cultural framework, and cultures are inextricably tied to moral values and systems. It is useful to take a step back and examine how our approaches to psychotherapy are bound to our cultural norms, values, and beliefs (Kirmayer, 2007).

Recognizing that cultures vary in the understanding of the self will affect the psychotherapy used. In traditional and contemporary psychotherapy, individuals are encouraged and expected to express verbally their private emotions, thoughts, and feelings, and to engage in self-reflection and self-disclosure in order to arrive at insights into their own behavioral and thought patterns underlying the mental illness (Kirmayer, 2007). Thus, for Western psychologists, focusing on oneself, talking about feelings, openly expressing emotions, and being in touch with one's inner self are important to understanding and treating distressed individuals. In other cultures, however, this approach may run counter to what is considered constructive for treating a psychological disorder. Persons from collectivistic cultures might find this focus on the self unusual and uncomfortable. Consequently, using this type of therapy may be less effective. More effective may be treatment that includes the family or community to acknowledge that the fundamental unit of analysis and intervention is the individual *in relation* to others (Kirmayer, 2007). In Dwairy's (2009) work with Arab-Muslim clients she focuses on a person's relation to his or her family (what are the norms, expectations, and values surrounding this person–family relationship) rather than focusing primarily on the person's personality to uncover intrapsychic feelings, thoughts, attitudes, and expectations (Dwairy, 2009).

In sum, depending on a culture's view of the self—as primarily unique and individual, or inextricably connected to others, or bound to the broader ecological or cosmic system—the most effective mode of healing may differ. Table 13.1 outlines several possibilities of different healing systems. Kirmayer (2007) also points out that views of self and cultures are complex, so that these different views and values described

TABLE 13.1 Cultural Configurations of the Self and Healing Systems

	Self Defined By	**Dominant Values**	**Locus of Agency**	**Healing System**
Egocentric	Personal history Accomplishments	Individualism Autonomy Achievement Materialism Monotheism	Individual	Psychotherapy
Sociocentric	Family Clan Lineage Community	Collectivism Interdependence Cooperation Honor Filial piety Familism	Group	Collective ritual family therapy
Ecocentric	Environment Ecology	Balance Harmony Exchange Animism	Animals Natural elements	Shamanism
Cosmocentric	Ancestors	Cosmic order Holism Polytheism	Gods Spirits	Possession Divination

Source: Reproduced with permission from Kirmayer, L. J., Psychotherapy and the cultural concept of the person. *Transcultural Psychiatry, 44*(2), 232–257. Copyright © Kirmayer, L. J. 2007. By permission of Sage Publications Ltd. www.sagepub.co.uk

in the table are not mutually exclusive, and probably all can be found in each culture, though one view of the self is probably more prominent than another.

Despite critiques of the historically Eurocentric bias in the development of psychotherapy, it continues to be implemented with culturally diverse populations around the world. Perhaps because self-reflection and self-awareness are human universals (Spiro, 1993), psychotherapy may be relevant for people of many different cultures. But because the ways in which our views of the self are structured and expressed are culturally bound (Kirmayer, 2007), recent work with diverse populations has modified psychotherapies to be more culturally relevant.

Psychotherapy in Diverse Cultures

Psychotherapy has been exported to diverse cultures such as Singapore (Devan, 2001), Pakistan (Naeem, Waheed, Gobbi, Ayub, & Kingdon, 2011), India (Arulmani, 2009), Malaysia (Azhar & Varma, 2000), Africa (Mwiti, 2014), and China (Zhang, Young, & Lee, 2002). Psychologists in these cultures have attempted to incorporate essential elements of their culture to make psychotherapy useful. Because religion plays an essential role in people's lives from all corners of the world, some have argued that incorporating religion into psychotherapy can provide valuable tools for dealing with psychological distress (Abu Raiya & Pargament, 2010; Ahammed, 2010). In Malaysia, for example, integrating religious beliefs and behaviors, such as prayer and focusing on verses of the Koran that address "worry" are some techniques to make psychotherapy more culturally relevant (Azhar & Varma, 2000). Studies comparing Muslim patients with a variety of disorders, including anxiety disorder and depression, suggest that religious psychotherapy is more effective and encourages more rapid improvement compared to supportive psychotherapy (Razali, Aminah, & Khan, 2002; Razali, Hasanah, Aminah, & Subramaniam, 1998). In China, Taoist and Confucian principles are embedded in psychotherapy techniques. Verses from Taoist writings that highlight main principles, such as restricting selfish desires, learning how to be content, and learning to let go, are read and reflected on by the patient. One study found that this approach, called Chinese Taoist cognitive psychotherapy, was more effective in the long term in reducing anxiety disorders than treating the patient with medications (Zhang et al., 2002).

Zhang (2014) argued that effective counseling in China depends on "localizing" therapies that originated in Western cultures. For instance, there is a preference for engaging in family versus individual psychotherapy. Family therapy aligns with the traditional cultural view of the primacy of the family, family obligations, and family interdependence in relation to the self. Further, because of increasing globalization and the continuous exchange of ideas from multiple cultures, adapting psychotherapies and seeking out psychotherapy is increasing in rapidly changing countries such as China. In China, the first ever mental health law was enacted in 2012 and became effective in 2013. The goal of this law is to promote greater awareness of mental health, further develop the field of mental health, create consistent mental health services, and ensure that people with psychological disorders are guaranteed rights and protection (Zhao & Dawson, 2014). This is a historic formal recognition and support of the importance of mental health issues to address and treat. This recognition may prompt an increase in interest in treatments for psychological disorders, including psychotherapy.

Although psychotherapy has been transported to many different cultures for some time, only recently have there been enough studies conducted on the effectiveness of culturally modified psychotherapies to conduct a formal meta-analysis. A recent meta-analysis of studies that have used the traditional gold standard of evaluation research—randomly assigning people to different treatment groups to assess outcomes over time—reported that culturally modified psychotherapies were more effective than non-modified psychotherapy to treat depressive disorders (Chowdhary et al., 2014). Modifications included using colloquial language, integrating local remedies and health practices into the therapy, and using culturally meaningful materials such as local stories, idioms, and symbols (such as beads for counting thoughts) that were familiar to the clients. Thus, although there is still much work to be done to carefully examine whether psychotherapy is the most appropriate and effective way to treat psychological disorders in a variety of cultures around the world, there is some evidence that modifying existing therapies may, indeed, be successful.

Psychotherapy in Diverse Cultures in the United States: An Example of Within Culture Variation

With increasing recognition that our current approaches must include a cultural understanding of how clients respond to psychotherapy, researchers and practitioners have advocated for the expansion and adoption of appropriate cultural elements to promote successful treatment. For example, because psychotherapy has been developed primarily from a Western, middle-class cultural perspective, the American Psychological Association has created guidelines for providing mental health services to diverse linguistic and ethnic groups in the United States. Other researchers and clinicians are developing culturally driven theoretical approaches to treatment, such as the theory of multicultural counseling and therapy (Sue & Sue, 2003, 2007).

Although cognitive behavioral therapy (CBT) developed specifically within a Western cultural context, this particular type of therapy has been modified and implemented with diverse populations such as African American (Kohn, Oden, Muñoz, Robinson, & Leavitt, 2002), Native American (De Coteau, Anderson, & Hope, 2006), Latino (Miranda, Nakamura, & Bernal, 2003), and Vietnamese and Cambodian refugee (Hinton, Pham, Tran, Safren, Otto, & Pollack, 2004; Hinton, Chhean, Pich, Safren, Hofmann, & Pollack, 2005) populations. Adaptations can include modifying language (such as incorporating vocabulary specific to a cultural group, or having bilingual therapists and materials), a focus on culturally specific content (such as focusing on issues related to living life on a reservation), and an emphasis on culturally appropriate patterns of communication (such as on *respeto* and forms of address).

As a more detailed example, Hinton and colleagues' work (Hinton et al., 2004; 2005) with Vietnamese and Cambodian refugees to the United States demonstrated the utility of culturally adapted CBT that included culturally appropriate visualization techniques. For instance, clients are asked to visualize a lotus bloom spinning in the wind at the end of a stem to relax the neck muscles (the neck being a focal point for symptoms of panic among Cambodian refugees). Clients also work on relaxation techniques through the framework of **mindfulness**, a Buddhist principle emphasizing close attention to the present moment, being aware of one's senses, breathing, and thoughts without judgment or evaluation (Roemer & Orsillo, 2002). Hinton et al. (2004; 2005) proposed that particularly for Asian-heritage populations, using mindfulness as a framework for treatment strategies is a culturally salient way to modify and enhance cognitive behavioral therapies.

Is psychotherapy, and especially culturally adapted psychotherapy, useful for diverse populations within a pluralistic country such as the United States? Earlier studies with African Americans found treatment outcomes to be poorer compared to those from other groups (Sue, Fujino, Hu, Takeuchi, & Zane, 1991; Sue, Zane, & Young, 1994). However, a more recent study of a clinical trial of low-income African American

mindfulness A Buddhist principle emphasizing close attention to the present moment, being aware of one's senses, breathing, and thoughts without judgment or evaluation. Mindfulness is effective in reducing tension, anxiety, and stress and has been incorporated successfully in cognitive behavioral therapies.

and Latino women found psychotherapy to be an effective treatment for depression, even one year later (Miranda, Green, & Krupnick, 2006). Indeed, a review of empirically rigorous studies with randomized trials found that CBT can be very effective for depression for African American and Latinos with improvement as good as for European Americans (Miranda, Bernal, Lau, Kohn, Hwang, & LaFromboise, 2005). Miranda et al.'s review also showed that psychotherapy can be used successfully, for instance, with Southeast Asian Americans dealing with posttraumatic distress disorder or depression. Many changes in the fields of clinical and counseling psychology, such as promoting a greater awareness of the need for culturally sensitive psychotherapy, proposing theories that highlight the role of culture in counseling and treatment, and providing guidelines for culturally competent services (Sue, Zane, Hall, & Berger, 2009; Sue & Sue, 2013), have no doubt provided a stronger foundation to develop effective psychotherapy treatments for people of many different backgrounds.

Still, more work needs to be done. One immediate area of need is figuring out exactly what aspects of culture are critical to ensuring that psychotherapeutic treatment is efficacious (Miranda et al., 2005). As noted throughout this textbook, culture is a fuzzy concept, not static, and continually evolving (recall our discussion in Chapter 1). To tackle culture and treatment, Lau (2006) has proposed a strategy to develop culturally adapted evidence-based treatments. She suggested that researchers need to thoroughly review the literature, research studies, and data (such as epidemiological data) to first understand what mental health problems are experienced in a particular cultural community. In other words, it is important to figure out what particular risk factors (e.g., poverty, specific stresses) and resilience factors (e.g., strong family ties) that characterize a particular cultural community may lead to certain psychological disorders as being more prominent. Next, researchers need to identify culturally salient aspects of the population that may be targeted for use in treatment and intervention programs.

As an example, Zayas and colleagues (2005; 2015; 2011) have identified a serious mental health issue in the Latino community in the United States: one in five Latina teens attempts to commit suicide, higher than any other ethnic group (Substance Abuse and Mental Health Administration, 2003). Based on a thorough review of literature, research studies, and in-depth interviews with Latinas who attempted suicide, they theorized that acculturation-based conflicts may explain, at least partly, these higher rates. More specifically, they contended that Latinas are pulled in two different directions culturally—the dominant, mainstream culture emphasizes individual autonomy while traditional Latino culture emphasizes the importance of fulfilling family obligations. These contrasting pulls are more severe for females than males as there is a strong emphasis for females to uphold more responsibilities to the family. The researchers proposed a model whereby Latinas who experience these pulls experience greater emotional vulnerability, especially if combined with low parental support, high conflict with parents, and poorer communication with parents. This emotional vulnerability, coupled with a sense of a deep family crisis, may set the stage for some Latinas to consider suicide as a way out of this difficult struggle. Based on their knowledge of culture-specific risks for suicide, Zayas and colleagues are developing family-based treatments to address this serious mental health issue and are rigorously evaluating the treatments to test for efficacy.

Summary

Psychotherapy is widely used within North America and Europe, and, to a lesser extent, in other parts of the world. Because of its roots in Western notions of the self, distress, and healing, the usefulness of psychotherapy with individuals who do not originate from these cultural groups has been challenged. This brings us back to the issue we raised in Chapter 12: there are two contrasting viewpoints—cultural relativism and universalism—that help us understand whether psychotherapy is exportable. All of the issues raised for assessing and diagnosing psychological disorders are relevant for the treatment of psychological disorders. More specifically, the cultural relativist position would argue that psychotherapy was developed in a specific culture with specific stresses and assumptions about the self and, subsequently, evolved into specific ideas on what is normative functioning. Subsequently, it cannot be exported to other cultures that differ in types of stresses and assumptions about the self. A universalist position, however, would argue that there are aspects of psychotherapy that are probably relevant for all people, and that psychotherapies that are culturally sensitive and adapted can be useful. In the literature we reviewed, we see some evidence for the latter position. Recent research has modified psychotherapy to be more salient to specific populations. There is some evidence that these culturally adapted psychotherapies are, indeed, effective for disorders such as depression and anxiety disorders for diverse populations (Chowdhary et al., 2014; Miranda et al., 2005). Our review of indigenous approaches (later in this chapter) provides support for the cultural relative position and for developing therapies from an emic approach. As with many issues discussed in this textbook, the truth probably lies somewhere in between.

There is a continued need for studies of evidence-based treatments—treatments that have been shown, through empirical studies, to be effective (Lau, 2006). More rigorous and systematic studies are also needed to identify which elements of psychotherapy may be universally effective, and which elements may be culture-specific. And more studies are needed that focus on a broader array of psychological disorders. Only by evaluating the efficacy of our treatments can we determine whether we are truly helping individuals in alleviating psychological distress.

▶ Receiving Treatment and Barriers to Treatment

Disparities in Receiving Treatment

Even if appropriate and effective therapies are available for many different populations, not all people are equally likely to receive treatment. In 1998 the World Health Organization established the World Mental Health Survey to assess the prevalence, severity, and service use (treatment) from a range of low- to high-income countries. This cross-national comparison showed that those in the lower income countries are, in general, less likely to receive treatment compared to those in higher-income countries (Wang et al., 2007). When the data were broken down into mild, moderate, and serious disorders, the disparities for receiving treatment for those falling into the "serious" category are shown in Figure 13.1.

The pattern is clear: individuals from countries with fewer economic resources are less likely to receive mental health treatment and services than those with greater economic resources. This is a cause for concern as a significant number of even those with serious diagnosed disorders, especially in lower income countries, are not receiving treatment.

We also see disparities in utilizing services within countries. For instance, disparities can be seen throughout the life span—in adolescence, adulthood, and old age, in the United States. A study using a nationally representative dataset (the National Comorbidity Survey-Adolescent Supplement) examined lifetime mental health

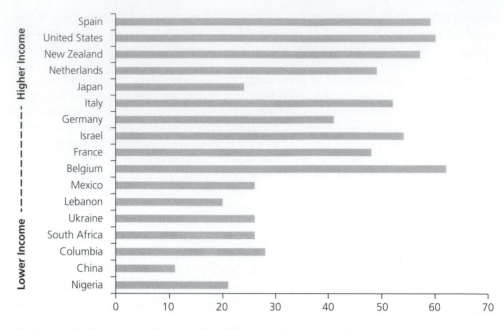

FIGURE 13.1 Percent of Those Classified with a "Serious" Diagnosis Reporting Using Mental Health Services in the Last 12 Months

Source: Wang et al. (2007). Worldwide use of mental health services for anxiety, mood, and substance disorders: Results from 17 countries in the WHO World Mental Health (WMH) surveys. *Lancet, 370,* 841–850.

service use for almost 6,500 adolescents aged 13–18 years (Merikangas et al., 2011). The results are sobering. Overall, only about one third of adolescents with a diagnosable psychological disorder (ranging from attention deficit hyperactivity disorder [ADHD], mood and anxiety disorders, and behavioral disorders) received treatment. Even for those with the most severe case of the disorder, only half had ever received treatment. Foreshadowing a trend that continues through adulthood and old age, African American and Latino adolescents were less likely than European American adolescents to receive treatment, even after controlling for variables such as socioeconomic status and severity of the disorder.

Another study of "high-risk" youth (6- to 18-year-olds who received services in a publicly funded institution such as child welfare and juvenile justice) also showed that mental health utilization differed by racial or ethnic group (Garland, Lau, Yeh, McCabe, Hough, & Landsverk, 2005). In this rigorous study, the researchers controlled for numerous confounding factors that might explain the disparity in racial or ethnic groups. Even after controlling for age, sex, family factors (such as caregiver depression, caregiver stress), family resources (income, college education), insurance status, and DSM-IV diagnosis, the researchers found that African American and Asian American youth were only half as likely as European American youth to utilize mental health services. This pattern of findings supported an earlier study of adolescents over a five-year period in Los Angeles (Bui & Takeuchi, 1992). This earlier study also found that Asian American adolescents were more likely to remain in treatment longer than European American adolescents (the authors suggested this may be due to the specific context of Los Angeles, which has a high density of Asians and thus perhaps more culturally accessible treatment), and that African American adolescents remained in treatment for the shortest time. Thus, there are disparities not only in

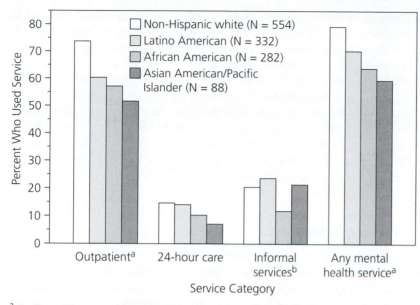

FIGURE 13.2
Mental Health Service Use among Youths Aged 6–18 Years in a Large, Publicly Funded System of Care by Racial/Ethnic Group (N = 1,256)
Source: Garland, et al., 2005. Page 1338.

[a] Significant difference among racial/ethnic groups (p<0.001, chi-square test).
[b] Significant difference among racial/ethnic groups (p<0.02, chi-square test).

mental service utilization, but also in length of treatment. Length of treatment is a critical variable to look at because studies have shown that the more time spent in treatment, the more likely it is that change will occur (Hansen, Lambert, & Forman, 2002).

In adults, a pioneering study of ethnic differences in response to standard mental health services was conducted by Stanley Sue (1977). He found lower rates of utilization of services by Asian Americans and Native Americans than by European Americans and African Americans. He also found that all other groups had higher dropout rates and poorer treatment outcomes relative to those of European Americans. Several decades later, do we find the same pattern? A review by Snowden and Yamada (2005) suggested, yes. Reviewing several studies using national datasets, there was a consistent finding that ethnic minorities in the United States are less likely than European Americans to utilize mental health services. Their review also highlighted that when ethnic minorities do seek treatment, they are more likely to end treatment prematurely (Armistead, Clark, Barber, Dorsey, Hughley, & Favors, 2004; Gallagher-Thompson, Solano, Coon, & Arean, 2003). These findings are part of a general disparity between ethnic groups in many different areas of health that has been a focus of increasing research.

Much attention has been focused on the Asian American population as studies have found they tend to be the least likely to seek treatment (Leong & Lau, 2001). One study of Chinese Americans found, for instance, that only 15% of those with a diagnosable psychological disorder received mental health services (Kung, 2003). However, there are important variations by immigration status. In a study using the National Latino and Asian American Study dataset (see Chapter 12), Asian Americans who were born in the United States (and especially those who also had parents born in the United States—the third generation) reported being more likely to seek services than those born outside of the United States (Abe-Kim et al., 2007). Importantly, they were also more likely to rate the services they received as being helpful compared to those born outside the United States. Similarly, Mexican Americans who were born in the United States reported being more likely to utilize health services compared to those born in Mexico (Dubard & Gizlice, 2008). These findings suggested there is still a lot of work to be done, particularly in targeting immigrant populations to encourage them to seek mental-health services when needed.

Although data are more limited for the elderly, racial or ethnic group disparities in mental health appear to continue into old age. Studies show that older African Americans reported greater psychotic symptoms than older European Americans, but were less likely to perceive needing and receive needed services (Cohen, Magai, Yaffee, & Walcott-Brown, 2004). In sum, there are disparities concerning mental health utilization starting in adolescence that persist throughout old age. It will be important to address these disparities, targeting people at younger ages to prevent disparities from continuing throughout the life span.

Barriers to Seeking Treatment

To understand why there are significant disparities between ethnic groups in seeking treatment and services, researchers have identified barriers in many different areas—ranging from individual level factors (e.g., language barriers) to cultural factors (e.g., cultural beliefs regarding health, illness, and treatment) to structural factors (e.g., availability of services within the neighborhood, state and national policies on health care that determine insurance and coverage) (Snowden & Yamada, 2005). Here we review some of the most common barriers that have been identified.

Language Barriers

One important barrier to seeking treatment is language differences. A study reviewing mental health services in 16 European countries reported that having difficulty with the mainstream language was one of the most important barriers to seeking mental health services (Watters, 2002). In the United States, there is strong evidence that those with limited English proficiency are less likely to use mental health services (Alegría et al., 2008; Kim, Loi, Chiriboga, Jang, Parmelee, & Allen, 2011; Snowden & Yamada, 2005; Ta, Juon, Gielen, Steinwachs, & Duggan, 2008). In one community, when language assistance measures were taken (providing translation for written materials, having linguistically capable staff or interpreters, providing information to the community on what language assistance was available), there was an increase in the number of people with limited English proficiency seeking out mental health services (Snowden, Masland, Peng, Lou, & Wallace, 2011). Nonetheless, this increase did not last in the long term, suggesting that language barriers, while a very important factor in understanding access to mental health services, is not the only factor that is relevant for encouraging individuals to seek mental health services.

Stigma and Mistrust

For some groups, there is a greater stigma attached to seeking mental health services. For Asian Americans, feelings of shame and loss of face associated with having a mental illness may partially explain low mental health service utilization rates (Chow, Jaffe, & Snowden, 2003; Jimenez, Bartels, Cardenas, & Alegrìa, 2013; Leong & Lau, 2001; Snowden & Yamada, 2005). Both U.S.-born African American and immigrant black Caribbean women, more so than European American women, noted that stigma associated with mental illness was a reason why they did not seek services (Nadeem, Lange, Edge, Fongwa, Belin, & Miranda, 2007). For Arab Americans, using mental health services may also be stigmatizing, especially for women. For women, being involved with conventional mental health services could damage their marriageability or increase the likelihood of separation or divorce (Al-Krenawi & Graham, 2000). Some research also indicated that Mexican Americans associate seeking help outside the family for treatment of mental disturbances with shame, weakness of character, and disgrace (Leong, Wagner, & Tata, 1995). As with Asian Americans, the primary source of support and help during times of difficulty are the extended family and folk healers (Koss-Chioino, 2000). Hence, formal mental health professionals such as clinicians or psychiatrists may be a last resort, at least for very traditional Mexican Americans.

In addition to stigma, some communities may be mistrustful of mental health professionals. African Americans were more likely than European Americans to voice mistrust toward formal mental health services, fearing hospitalization and treatment (Sussman, Robins, & Earls, 1987). Mistrust among African Americans may stem from their history and experiences of segregation, racism, and discrimination (Nadeem et al., 2007). African Americans have historically been subject to severely unethical medical treatment. The notorious Tuskegee experiment was a study sponsored by the U.S. government that started in the 1930s and lasted until the 1970s. In this experiment, African American men living in Alabama who were infected with syphilis were recruited and enrolled in the study. They were told that they would be receiving free health care and treatment. Remarkably, however, they were never told they had syphilis and were not treated even though there was a treatment readily available in the form of penicillin. The purpose of the experiment was to document the "natural" course of the disease. Not surprisingly, events such as this have fostered a deep mistrust in the professional medical system. Similarly, the history and experiences of Native Americans have also left many of them mistrustful of formal mental health services (Gone, 2010).

Beliefs on Health and Illness

Various cultural groups may hold beliefs on health and illness that may lead to less reliance on seeking formal treatment for psychological disorders. Some African Americans may be encouraged to depend on their own willpower to confront problems, to be self-reliant, and to "tough out" difficult situations (Broman, 1996; Snowden, 2001). A study of Puerto Rican individuals found that those who reported high levels of self-reliance were much less likely to seek treatment compared to those who reported lower levels of self-reliance (Ortega & Alegria, 2002). And a study of Chinese Americans found that those who rated themselves higher on having a "hardy" personality were also less likely to seek treatment compared to those who rated themselves as less hardy (Kung, 2003). The reduced utilization of services by Native Americans may be the result of cultural beliefs that sickness comes from disharmony with one's community, nature, and spiritual world. Thus, seeking help from formal mental health services, which traditionally do not focus on such a holistic view of mental health, may not be desirable (Gone, 2010).

Prayers are an important aspect of psychological and physical healing for some Latino communities, and it may be the case that only when religious and folk healers cannot help are mental health professionals acknowledged. Likewise, in Arab American families, individuals may first seek help from informal systems of support, such as the extended family or traditional healers, before turning to more conventional mental health services (Al-Krenawi & Graham, 2000). It may be fruitful for mental health professionals to collaborate with churches and religious organizations to provide information about mental health services and to consider incorporating religious and spiritual values and practices into the provision of treatment (Abu Raiya & Pargament, 2010).

Social Structures and Policies

Finally, structural factors such as lack of availability of mental health services in the community, health insurance coverage, and culturally competent services have been identified as important barriers to seeking mental health services. Availability of mental health services depends on where you live. More mental health professionals and services are found in urban areas, and much fewer in rural areas in the United States (Ziller, Anderson, & Coburn, 2010). Even for those living in urban areas where there may be greater availability, financial barriers may prevent people from seeking treatment. Some of the racial or ethnic disparities we see in seeking mental health services are linked to insurance coverage. Ethnic minorities are more likely to be uninsured compared to European Americans (Kaiser Family Foundation, 2013). There is evidence that universal coverage does, not surprisingly, increase access and use of health care services (Siddiqi, Zuberi, & Nguyen, 2009).

Removing Barriers to Treatment

A major concern in the treatment of psychological disorders is the consistent finding that certain populations tend to seek and utilize needed mental health services much less compared to others. These disparities are evident throughout adolescence, adulthood, and old age. A major focus has been to illuminate barriers that may lead to these disparities and examine how these barriers may interact with a person's racial or ethnic background, immigration status, and socioeconomic status.

Researchers and mental health professionals have taken the next step to identify strategies to overcome these barriers to treatment. Hiring bilingual and bicultural staff, increasing outreach (activities in the community to promote awareness and give referrals), having flexible hours, and increasing the number of practitioners in the community, facilitates seeking treatment (Snowden, Masland, Ma, & Clemens, 2006). Other strategies aim at reducing stigma associated with mental illness. A recent review of studies (notably, published in English and non-English journals with samples drawn from 14 countries) examined which strategies attempting to reduce public stigma regarding mental illness was most effective for adults and adolescents (Corrigan et al., 2012). The review found that for adults, programs that promoted and required interpersonal contact with persons with mental illness were more effective than providing education (e.g., listening to public service announcements, reading factual information about mental health illness). For adolescents, however, education was more effective than interpersonal contact, possibly because adolescents are more likely than adults to be still forming their ideas and beliefs on mental illness and thus more likely to be responsive to educational efforts (Corrigan et al., 2012). The researchers concluded that both types of strategies are effective for reducing stigma but that it is necessary to carefully consider characteristics of the target population in developing the most successful strategies.

In countries such as China where there is a history of very strong stigma against mental illness, there is some evidence of change. Zhang (2014) reports that "World Mental Health Day" was formally recognized by the Chinese government in 2000. Starting in 2005 the China Central Television station (CCTV) aired a popular television show called "Psychology Sessions" (*xinli fangtan*) where a client, therapist, and host sit together to talk about problems in relationships, family, marriage, and school. Although this show has prompted critiques (Yang, 2013), some argue that this show has also popularized counseling and has helped to reduce stigma associated with psychological disorders (Zhang, 2014). At the very least, shows such as this has raised visibility in the general public about mental health awareness and treatment. Only by tackling stigma on multiple levels from various sources, will stigma be reduced.

▶ Treatment Issues

Contemporary mental health services must deal effectively with the emotional concerns of a wide variety of people. This section highlights some of the challenges that may arise during treatment when the clinician and patient differ with respect to their cultural backgrounds.

One issue, especially relevant when treating recent immigrants, is understanding culturally different ways of thinking about illness and expressing thoughts about illness. Moreover, when language difficulties and culturally different ways of communicating are thrown into the picture, it can be a challenge for the clinician and patient to communicate effectively. Consequently, treatment may be compromised.

Counselors also need to be sensitive to variations in communication patterns of different ethnic groups. In line with the notion of *respeto* and deference to authority in many Latino communities, it may be appropriate for counselors to address clients more formally (instead of by their first name) and to have clients also address them formally, at least for Latinos who may be more oriented toward their traditional cultures (Sue et al., 2009). Of course, showing respect is important for dealing with clients of all cultural backgrounds, but how that respect is specifically conveyed will be culturally determined. In addition to being sensitive to aspects of verbal communication, interpreting nonverbal aspects of communication correctly is also important (recall our discussions in Chapters 9 and 10). In some cultures, making direct eye contact is disrespectful, such as in traditional Native American and Mexican cultures (Andrews & Boyle, 2003). If the therapist of a different cultural background is not familiar with this cultural norm, he or she might falsely assume that the client is showing a lack of interest, resisting treatment, or even being rude.

Taking into account cultural variations in the importance of hierarchy in interpersonal relationships is also important. For traditional Asian American and Latino families, therapists should pay attention to hierarchical family roles, for instance by initially reinforcing the father's role as head of the family (Szapocznik et al., 2003). Likewise, it may be inappropriate for the therapist to treat the child and his or her parents as equals for families adhering to cultural family values of hierarchy, respect, and obedience. If the therapist tries to alter power hierarchies or role patterns, parents may feel that the therapist is undermining their authority and this may well alienate the family.

Treatment expectations may also differ across cultural groups. For instance, for some groups, the therapist is the authority and is expected to be directive, make suggestions, and give reassurance. For Native American clients, more directive and strategic interventions are preferred over client-centered or reflective therapy (LaFromboise, Trimble, & Mohatt, 1990). The introspective approach may lead to impatience and prematurely terminating therapy. Other studies have also found that Latino and Asian Americans prefer active or direct approaches to therapy instead of inactive or indirect approaches that emphasize self-disclosure, insight, and "talk" therapy (Leong, Lee, & Kalibatseva, 2015).

Finally, in many cultures, the extended family is a primary source of support in times of distress. Recognizing and involving members of the extended family instead of focusing on the individual and nuclear family may be useful and may present a more familiar approach to problem solving. It is also important to note that with many ethnic minority families, nonblood kin may also be considered family, such as neighbors and ministers in African American families, godparents in Latino families, and elders in Asian communities (Sue, 2003).

We have highlighted just some of the many issues that come into play when counseling clients from diverse cultural origins. What may work best in treating one population may not necessarily work for another. Developing responses to psychological distress that are sensitive to each individual's cultural outlook, beliefs, and practices is the goal for many psychologists working with diverse populations (Sue et al., 2009). In the next section, we discuss some ways in which researchers and mental health professionals are promoting more culturally appropriate treatment and services.

▶ Culturally Competent Services

An extensive body of literature by researchers and practitioners has prompted mental health professionals to stress the need for culturally competent services in order to improve utilization and effectiveness of treatment for individuals from diverse cultural backgrounds. This literature has evolved to address the traditional exclusion of cultural and minority groups in the fields of counseling and clinical psychology (Sue et al., 2009). Understanding and respecting the histories, traditions, beliefs, and value systems of various cultural groups underlies culturally competent services.

To fashion more culturally sensitive services, Sue and colleagues (Sue & Sue, 2003, 2007; Sue et al., 2009) suggested that treatment methods should be modified to improve their fit with the worldviews and experiences of culturally diverse clients. For example, traditional psychoanalytic approaches are derived from a worldview that assumes that unconscious conflicts (often sexual) give rise to abnormal behavior. This worldview may reflect the experience of the well-to-do Austrian women Freud treated and on which he based many of his theoretical assumptions. However, a therapeutic approach based on such a worldview may be inappropriate for cultures that attribute abnormality either to natural factors (e.g., physical problems or being out of harmony with the environment) or supernatural causes (e.g., spirit possession). Cultural systems of cure and healing may be effective precisely because they operate within a particular culture's worldview (Moodley & Sutherland, 2010). For example, a spiritual ceremony performed by a native shaman (priest or healer) may be a more effective treatment for the cultural syndrome of distress *susto* than a mainstream cognitive-behavioral approach.

There is also some indication that culturally diverse clients prefer to see therapists who are similar to them in cultural background and gender. But research indicates that similarity of worldviews and attitudes to treatment between client and therapist may be more important than simply ethnic similarity (Sue & Sue, 2003). For instance, matching a Korean American client who does not consider herself to be very Korean (she does not speak Korean and does not identify herself with Korean values and attitudes) with a Korean-heritage therapist may not make much difference compared with pairing her with a therapist of another ethnicity. Thus, acculturation status and ethnic identity may be more important determinants of client responses to treatment (Sue et al., 2009).

Indeed, there is robust literature demonstrating individual variation in ethnic identity (e.g., one's sense of belonging to one's ethnic group and salience to overall identity) (Phinney, 2003). A study with African Americans found that those who identified strongly with African American culture preferred an ethnically similar therapist, compared to those who did not identify strongly with African American culture (Ponterotto, Alexander, & Hinkston, 1988). Likewise, in a study with Mexican American college students, only those who expressed a strong commitment to Mexican American culture desired an ethnically matched counselor

(Sanchez & Atkinson, 1983). Mexican American students who primarily identified themselves with the majority culture were not concerned that their counselor be of the same ethnicity.

Not only do client views of the therapist differ depending on the match between therapist and client; therapist views of clients also differ. In one study, the records of thousands of African American, Asian American, Mexican American, and European American outpatient clients in the Los Angeles County mental health system were examined for ethnic match with their therapist (Russell, Fujino, Sue, Cheung, & Snowden, 1996). In this study, a black therapist–black client dyad or Chinese therapist–Chinese client dyad was considered an ethnic match. However, for Asian Americans, a Chinese therapist–Japanese client was not a match. Results indicated that ethnically matched therapists tended to judge clients to have higher mental functioning than did mismatched therapists. This finding held even after controlling for variables such as age, gender, marital status, and referral source. Thus, how the therapist perceived the client differed according to whether the therapist was of the client's ethnic group or not.

Although matching may be beneficial in the therapy process, it may not be *essential* for effective counseling (Chang & Berk, 2009). A meta-analysis of seven studies conducted in the 1990s on ethnic matching found that the effect sizes were very small (ranging from $r = .01$ to $r = .04$) for outcomes such as dropping out, number of treatment sessions, and assessment of client functioning at the end of treatment (Maramba & Nagayama Hall, 2002). Another meta-analysis of studies focused on ethnic matching for African American and European American clients and clinicians (Shin, Chow, Camacho-Gonsalves, Levy, Allen, & Leff, 2005). Similar to the previous meta-analysis, the researchers found that ethnic matching did not predict better overall functioning, dropout rate, and number of treatment sessions. Thus, other factors, such as cognitive matching (in attitudes toward therapy and problems discussed in therapy) (Zane et al., 2005), cultural matching (in worldviews, cognitive styles, and language), level of cultural sensitivity and responsiveness of the therapist, and client characteristics and preferences, may be more crucial to whether therapy leads to improvement in outcomes (Chang & Berk, 2009; Sue et al., 2009).

In sum, ethnic matching may be more important for those whose ethnicity is very salient to their overall identity (e.g., having a strong ethnic identity). And clinicians who are sensitive to the client's cultural background and who take the time and effort to understand the client within his or her cultural context can still be very effective in providing useful treatment.

So what are the specific competencies and knowledge base necessary for conducting sensitive and effective treatment across cultures? Based on the research literature of the past two decades, Sue et al. (2009, p. 529) proposed that every counselor must possess the following three characteristics (see Table 13.2).

- *Cultural awareness and beliefs:* The counselor is sensitive to her or his personal values and biases and how these may influence perceptions of the client, the client's problem, and the counseling relationship.
- *Cultural knowledge:* The counselor has knowledge of the client's culture, worldview, and expectations for the counseling relationship.
- *Cultural skills:* The counselor has the ability to intervene in a manner that is culturally sensitive and relevant.

Sue et al. (2009) also emphasize that it is important to attend to individual histories and circumstances to avoid stereotyping and assuming that cultural background is the only salient characteristic of the individual to the exclusion of other important

TABLE 13.2 Characteristics of Culturally Competent Counselors

Cultural Awareness and Beliefs	Cultural Knowledge	Cultural Skills
• The counselor is sensitive to her or his personal values and biases and how these may influence perceptions of the client, the client's problem, and the counseling relationship.	• The counselor has knowledge of the client's culture, worldview, and expectations for the counseling relationship.	• The counselor has the ability to intervene in a manner that is culturally sensitive and relevant.

Source: (Sue et al., 2009, Page 529).

characteristics, such as gender or sexual orientation. A very assimilated Latino individual, for instance, may share more similarities in beliefs and expectations for treatment with a European American counselor compared to a more traditional Latino individual. In the end, a sensitive assessment of the role of culture in shaping the person is needed. Consequently, training counselors to offer culturally competent services is one important way to reduce health disparities (Sue et al., 2009).

Despite significant advances made in providing culturally competent therapy and services to diverse populations, there remains much work to be done. Future research should continue to examine what specific aspects (e.g., skills) of cultural competency are the most effective in treatment, and develop theoretical models to explain why cultural competency may lead to better outcomes. Importantly, future research must also explore what culturally competent treatment strategies may be effective universally, across many diverse populations, and what treatment strategies may be effective locally, only for specific cultural or ethnic populations (Sue et al., 2009). Hopefully, the next two decades of research will make significant advances in these areas to offer effective ways to alleviate the suffering of people with mental health disorders.

▶ Indigenous and Traditional Healing

indigenous healing Helping beliefs and practices that originate within a given culture or society for treating the inhabitants of the given group.

traditional medicine Treatments that have a long history within a culture and that are indigenous to that culture.

complementary medicine Treatments offered in a culture that do not originate within that culture.

Recent discussions of culture and the treatment of psychological disorders has focused on culture-specific interventions, or indigenous healing. **Indigenous healing** encompasses therapeutic beliefs and practices that are rooted within a given culture. In other words, these beliefs and practices are not imported from outside cultures but are indigenously developed to treat the native population (Sue & Sue, 2007). The World Health Organization (2013) uses the term **traditional medicine** to refer to treatments that have a long history within a culture and that are indigenous to that culture while **complementary medicine** (or alternative medicine) refers to treatments that do not originate within that culture (see Table 13.3). Acupuncture, for instance, is traditional medicine originating in China. However, it is one of the most popular complementary treatments around the world: over 80% of WHO member states report using acupuncture (Figure 13.3). The WHO emphasizes that for a majority of the world, indigenous, traditional healers and doctors are the primary systems of care used to treat people. In Africa, for example, there is one traditional healer for every 500 people and one medical doctor for every 40,000. Thus, in order to address health issues on a global level, a greater understanding, integration, and collaboration between traditional and complementary medicine is needed.

Many indigenous methods of healing around the world differ widely from traditional Western notions of healing. Many indigenous treatments are rooted in religion and spirituality, not biomedical science (Sue & Sue, 2007; Yeh, Hunter, Madan-Bahel, Chiang,

TABLE 13.3 The World Health Organization Definitions of Traditional (Indigenous) and Complementary (Alternative) Medicine

Traditional Medicine (TM)	Complementary Medicine (CM)	Traditonal and Complementary Medicine (T&CM)
Traditional medicine has a long history. It is the sum total of the knowledge, skill, and practices based on the theories, beliefs, and experiences indigenous to different cultures, whether explicable or not, used in the maintenance of health as well as in the prevention, diagnosis, improvement or treatment of physical and mental illness. (http://www.who.int/medicines/areas/traditional/definitions/en/).	The terms "complementary medicine" or "alternative medicine" refer to a broad set of health care practices that are not part of that country's own tradition or conventional medicine and are not fully integrated into the dominant health-care system. They are used interchangeably with traditional medicine in some countries. (http://www.who.int/medicines/areas/traditonal/definitions/en/).	T&CM merges the terms TM and CM, encompassing products, practices and practitioners.

Source: WHO Traditional Medicine Strategy 2014–2023, page 15.

& Arora, 2004). Indigenous healing shares several commonalities (Lee, Oh, & Mountcastle, 1992; Mpofu, 2006). One is the heavy reliance on family and community networks as both the context and instrument for treatment. For instance, family and community are used in Saudi Arabia to protect the disturbed individual, in Korea to reconnect and reintegrate the individual with members of the family, and in Nigeria to solve problems in the context of a group. Another commonality is the incorporation of traditional, spiritual, and religious beliefs as part of the treatment—such as, reading verses from the Koran, opening treatment with a prayer, or conducting treatment in religious houses or churches. Finally, another commonality is the use of shamans in treatment.

A review by a group of counseling psychologists has identified several indigenous treatments originating in Japan, China, Egypt, and India that are gaining acceptance in various parts of the world (Yeh et al., 2004). *Reiki* refers to a "universal life energy" and is a Japanese practice used for relaxation, reducing stress, and promoting healing. In Reiki therapy, this life energy is used for healing by balancing the physical, emotional, mental, and spiritual elements of our bodies through the laying

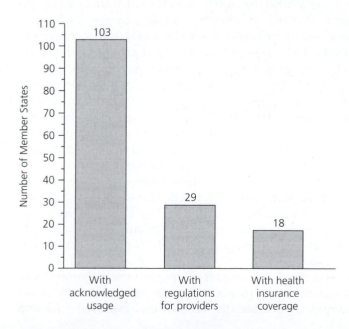

FIGURE 13.3

Over 80% of 129 WHO Member States Report Using Acupuncture as Part of Their Complementary Health Care Practices

Source: Interim data from 2nd WHO TRM global survey as of June 11, 2012.

on of hands very lightly or just above the person in need of healing. *Qigong* refers to "flow of air" or "vital energy" and is a Chinese method that emphasizes breathing, movement, and physical postures for maintaining and improving one's health. *Prana* refers to "life force" and pranic healing is based on the principle that healing is possible by increasing the life force on the unhealthy part of the physical body. All three of these therapies endorse the holistic notion that our physical health is intertwined with our emotional, mental, and spiritual health, and healing begins by connecting these various energies. Currently, there is a movement in many countries and cultures to integrate indigenous therapies with contemporary cognitive and behavioral therapies (Jilek & Draguns, 2008; World Health Organization, 2013). In this next section, we describe an attempt to do so.

An Example of Blending Indigenous Healing Practices with Traditional Western-Based Treatment Approaches

In 1990, a seminal article was published in *The Counseling Psychologist* that argued for a blending or integration of traditional healing and psychotherapy for Native American populations (LaFromboise et al., 1990). Since then, those in the counseling and clinical field have further explored ways to rely on traditional healing to ensure greater access and effectiveness to mental health services. The work of James Gone with Native American populations (2007, 2010, 2011) is an excellent example of how this can be done. Gone argued that in order to integrate the two very disparate traditions of healing, in-depth comparisons between indigenous healing practices with regard to psychotherapy must first be documented and explained. His review of the literature revealed that there are still very few published case studies of traditional healing (Gone, 2010). Next, there must be careful consideration and understanding of traditional healing within the broader historical and sociocultural contexts. For Native American populations in particular, there are major challenges to understanding traditional healing. Many traditional healing practices were suppressed and eradicated for many years; thus, for those communities who managed to preserve and pass on traditional healing, there is much distrust and reluctance to discuss these practices with outsiders and researchers. Only through years of working closely with the community has Gone been able to document, in detail, traditional healing beliefs and practices.

In his work, Gone uncovered that traditional healing in the Native American community "emphasizes rank, status, role, relationship, and protocol much more than personal dispositions, private sentiments, or inner states or processes" (p. 186). In other words, the relationship and ceremony occurring between the healer, patient, community members, and nonhuman persons (spiritual, other world) comprised the healing therapy rather than the patient expressing and reflecting on her or his thoughts, beliefs, and psychological state. Gone described how a deep understanding of these traditional ways of healing can then be integrated into contemporary psychotherapy. For instance, by utilizing psychotherapeutic methods such as having one-on-one discussions and reframing problems to be understood from a Native American worldview. Gone described the work of Eduardo Duran (2006) to illustrate this reframing and building from indigenous ways of healing to fit into aspects of contemporary psychotherapy. Duran's therapeutic work with Native Americans starts with the assumption that the colonization and genocide of the Native American population has affected individuals on a very deep "soul level"; subsequently, treatment should focus on healing the "soul wound." From this perspective, the language Duran uses with his patients moves away from "psychologizing to spiritualizing" (Gone, 2010, p. 190). Here is an excerpt from a session between Duran (Therapist, T) with a patient (P) with an alcohol problem to illustrate this reframing (Duran, 2006 as cited in Gone, 2010, pp. 194–195). In this account, Gone also interprets Duran's guidance.

T: "You know, when you drink or use drugs, it is a ceremony? Let me explain this to you …. You step up to the bar, leave your token just like when you go to a medicine person …, and request the kind of medicine you want…. Then you proceed to drink…. You have completed your ceremony. Now, the contract is in place. The medicine will give you what you want. It will keep its part of the bargain. Now it will be up to you to fulfill your part."

P: Not surprisingly, the gravity of the situation for the patient begins to settle in: P: "It sounds really serious when you talk about it like that. It sounds hopeless. I mean I already did these ceremonies to the spirit of alcohol. I can't undo that. What do I do?"

T: There are ways. In the spirit world, it's all about etiquette and manners. So far, you have forgotten these. All traditions have manners when it comes to dealing with these forces. Spiritual transactions, of course, require ritual accommodations."

Duran readily incorporates prayer, offerings, and "power objects" or "fetishes" in explicit recognition that "therapy is a ceremony" (Duran, 2006, p. 42):

T: "Since you want to let go of the spirit of alcohol, you need to talk to it and ask what it wants in exchange for your spirit. I'm sure you can work out a deal. [Duran reaches for a "fetish" resembling a bottle of cheap "Dark Eyes" vodka.] Here is my friend. We can talk to it now… . Dark Eyes is already wondering if you're going to have manners. You know as part of your Step 4 through Step 8 [in Alcoholics Anonymous] that you also need to make amends to the medicine here."

P: "How do I do that? What do I say?"

T: "When you make an offering, you know what to do. You can offer tobacco, cornmeal, food, water, and such. It's the intent that is important, and the spirit of alcohol will recognize the honesty of your spirit as you go into this new way of relating with awareness."

Now that the patient has reconceptualized his problem with alcohol by virtue of the "decolonization" process facilitated in the preceding therapeutic interactions, a renewed relationship to himself, his community, and his cultural heritage will together support a renewed relationship to alcohol. In the end, beyond merely recovering from addiction, it is Duran's hope that such patients will experience a "deeper healing of the spirit" (Duran, 2006, p. 18) involving "an existential reconnection with who they are as a Native person" (Duran, 2006, p. 66). Perhaps even more significantly, according to Duran, such patients "restore their humanity in a way that is harmonious with natural laws" (Duran, 2006, p. 14).

In this account, one can see how elements from indigenous healing, psychotherapy, and other treatment programs (Alcoholics Anonymous) were fused and integrated in treating the individual. In this approach, indigenous healing served as the foundation for incorporating other treatments rather than the other way around. More detailed, in-depth research as rigorous and thoughtful as Gone's work is needed to arrive at a more complete understanding of culture, therapy, and effectiveness of treatment beyond a superficial or stereotypical understanding of culture to help a person in distress.

▶ A Community Approach to Treatment

Much of our discussion in this chapter has focused on a particular treatment based on a medical model—namely, psychotherapy. Even with modifications to psychotherapy, this type of treatment may still not be wholly appropriate with people of many cultures. In the medical model, treatment is designed and directed at the individual. Some assumptions of this model are that the problem resides in the individual and that highly trained professionals such as clinicians should provide the treatment. Recognizing the limitations of the medical model, the field of community psychology, led by researchers such as Kelly (2007) and Trickett (2009), combine traditional principles of clinical psychology with an emphasis on the multiple and diverse ecologies of individuals to create alternative conceptual frameworks for understanding abnormal behavior. Community psychologists go beyond the traditional focus of responding to a person's distress on an individual level to include an analysis of mental health at the community level. In other words, understanding how to treat individuals successfully requires a recognition of the relationship between the individual and her or his daily interactions within diverse social settings and contexts in the community.

Based on these considerations, some community-oriented psychologists describe a different approach to the treatment of emotional distress. Miller and colleagues (1999; Miller & Rasco, 2004) proposed a community-based treatment to complement traditional psychotherapy:

> In contrast to the medical model, which focuses on the individual as the unit of analysis and intervention, and which emphasizes the treatment of pathology by highly trained experts, the ecological model emphasizes the relationships between people and the settings they live in; the identification of naturally occurring resources within communities that can promote healing and healthy adaptation; the enhancement of coping and adaptational strategies that enable individuals and communities to respond effectively to stressful events and circumstances; and the development of collaborative, culturally grounded community interventions that actively involve community members in the process of solving their own problems. (1999, p. 288)

Community-based treatments may be especially relevant for helping populations such as immigrants and refugees, who are unfamiliar with the host culture, who tend not to seek out professional help, and who tend to underuse mental health services. Such approaches can also be a useful alternative in developing countries, where access to professional mental health services and resources are scarce.

In sum, researchers and clinicians are exploring how various communities can use cultural informants and community structure to provide mental health services in ways that differ from traditional one-on-one psychotherapy. From a community psychology perspective, healing is based on the strengths and resources of the community and is aimed not only at individuals but toward the health of the community as a whole. The community-level approach offers a promising and powerful addition to the medical model of clinical psychology for understanding and responding to psychological distress in culturally diverse populations.

▶ Culture and Clinical Training

Because of all the issues discussed in this chapter, and throughout the book, all accredited programs of clinical training in some countries (such as the United States) have, for some time now, been mandated to incorporate culture and diversity in their training programs. Clinical psychologists who will be in the field actually applying psychological knowledge and principles to people who seek help need to have a base for understanding the role of culture in the expression and presentation of mental illness, the difficulties and complexities involved in psychological assessment, and the issues regarding culturally sensitive yet effective treatment. Beyond these factors, however, contemporary clinicians and therapists receive training in the broad base of culture's influence on all aspects of psychology, from perception and sensation through development to social behavior and personality. It is only with this broad base of training that contemporary psychologists can gain the perspective necessary to work effectively with their clients and patients to help them improve their lives. Of course, this need for a broad understanding of the influence of culture on psychology applies to the training and practice of psychologists globally. Moreover, the implications of psychologists' training in other cultures, learning culturally bound methods of treatment, and then returning home to practice has not been studied.

The increasing number of bilingual or bicultural individuals seeking help raises its own set of special issues, including the language and cultural framework within which psychotherapy and healing will occur. A number of writers have suggested that language proficiency, level of acculturation, and the degree to which cultural expressions represent symptoms should be considered in the development of an effective treatment plan. The need for fluency in multiple languages and cultures adds to the growing list of requirements for culturally competent therapists.

In Canada, a clinical training program at McGill University that is well known for its attention to culture has three main emphases (Kirmayer, Rousseau, Guzder, & Jarvis, 2008). One, rather than learning about the cultures of "others" (which may inadvertently foster cultural or ethnic group stereotypes), students focus on becoming aware of and understanding the culture of their own professional field. In other words, students examine cultural assumptions that drive the theories and practices of contemporary clinicians in their professional field. In so doing, the emphasis is on understanding how their own individual and professional worldviews affect the way they interpret, assess, diagnose, and treat people of different cultural backgrounds. Two, there is an emphasis on how most individuals, due to globalization, migration, and mass media, probably do not have a monocultural background but rather a much more complex, multicultural background. This adds another layer of complexity to assessment, diagnosis, and treatment. Three, there is an emphasis on respect, empathy, and humility in recognizing that individuals have unique histories, experiences, and situations that may not be fully understood by the clinician. Kirmayer et al. (2008) propose that students training to be clinicians "must learn to use their own identity, both in terms of self-understanding and, with an awareness of how they appear to others … as a tool to explore patient identity, illness meanings, the social context of illness and adaptation, and the clinical relationship itself" (p. 315).

CONCLUSION

In this chapter, we have discussed the important role culture plays in attempting to help people with mental disorders improve their lives. The material in this chapter is not only relevant on its own, but is informed by material in the entire book, showing the pervasive influence of culture on all aspects of our psychological composition. It is only within this larger perspective of the influence of culture that we can begin to truly grasp and appreciate the difficulties and complexities of diagnosing and treating psychological disorders in a diverse world.

The difficulties presented, however, should be viewed as challenges, not obstacles. Through the study of culture, psychopathology, assessment, and psychotherapy, we are afforded the chance to expand our theoretical and conceptual horizons regarding abnormality and treatment, and to help our treatment systems evolve into bigger and better systems effectively serving larger and larger groups of people. We are currently engaged in the search for principles and knowledge that will help us achieve those goals.

Continued cross-cultural research on clinical issues—such as defining and assessing abnormality and designing treatment approaches that effectively mobilize healing forces within clients—is a must. But research on these major issues of definition, assessment, and treatment should proceed cautiously and systematically. Future research will need to explore the efficacy of different treatment approaches that address both etic and emic concerns, blending traditional and culture-specific methods in an overall, comprehensive fashion.

EXPLORATION AND DISCOVERY

Why Does This Matter to Me?

1. Look back at Table 13.1. "Cultural Configurations of the Self and Healing Systems. *Source*: Kirmayer (2007)." Consider your own worldviews. Where would you fit in this table? Which healing system would you feel most comfortable with? Think about your parents. Where would they fit in this table? Which healing system would they feel most comfortable with?

2. To be successful in college, some would argue it is important to have a mentor, someone who cares about your personal and academic development and who can guide you throughout your academic career to help you make important decisions about life and school. If you were to choose a mentor, what characteristics would she or he have? Would it be important that she or he is of

the same ethnicity as you are? Would it be important that she or he is the same gender as you are? Would it be important that she or he share similar worldviews as you do? How would her or his characteristics influence the way you heed (or not heed) her/his advice?

3. In the Canadian clinical training program described toward the end of the chapter, one of the emphases was to move away from learning about people of other cultures, and instead focus on learning and understanding one's own cultural background and assumptions. One reason for this emphasis was to discourage cultural and ethnic group stereotyping. In your opinion, do you think that learning about people of other cultures would tend to foster cultural stereotypes? Why or why not?

Suggestions for Further Exploration

1. We have reviewed several barriers to seeking mental health services that may explain racial or ethnic disparities. Think about the category of gender. Do you think there would also be gender disparities in seeking out and utilizing mental health services? If so, explain what specific barriers may account for these disparities.

2. With globalization, increasing numbers of people will be of multiple racial or ethnic backgrounds. In this chapter, we have primarily discussed people of a single racial or ethnic group. How might issues discussed in this chapter (e.g., ethnic

matching in the counselor–patient relationship, barriers to seeking treatment) be similar or different for those who are of multiple racial or ethnic backgrounds?

3. After reading this chapter, what is your view—are you more of a cultural relativist or universalist on the issue of whether psychotherapy, developed in a Western European context, can be exported successfully to other diverse cultures? Ask at least one other student what her or his view is and discuss.

Culture and Social Behavior

14

CHAPTER CONTENTS

All mankind is of one author, and is one volume; when one man dies, one chapter is not torn out of the book, but translated into a better language; and every chapter must be so translated.... As therefore the bell that rings to a sermon, calls not upon the preacher only, but upon the congregation to come: so this bell calls us all: but how much more me, who am brought so near the door by this sickness.... No man is an island, entire of itself; every man is a piece of the continent, a part of the main. If a clod be washed away by the sea, Europe is the less, as well as if a promontory were, as well as if a manor of thy friend's or of thine own were. Any man's death diminishes me, because I am involved in mankind; and therefore never send to know for whom the bell tolls; it tolls for thee.

(John Donne, 1624)

People of all cultures have a universal need to form meaningful bonds with others, have intimate relationships, and to belong to social groups (Baumeister & Leary, 1995). Creating these bonds and relationships is associated with many things that aid in our survival. Humans are social animals, and all of us are fundamentally interconnected with each other in our lives. All individuals need others to live, work, play, and function in our societies and cultures. Without others, we can neither function effectively nor achieve our goals. Relationships help ensure reproduction by finding mates, aid in our caring for offspring and the elderly, and in buffering many of life's trials and tribulations. People with meaningful social relationships live longer and are healthier (as discussed in Chapter 11).

Yet while the need for affiliation is universal, how people address that need and interact with others can be different depending on their culture. This is one of the richest areas of research in cultural psychology. In this chapter, we will discuss how cultures affect social behaviors. We begin our discussion by examining how we perceive others, and then about how culture influences how we interpret the world around us in our attributions. We will discuss finding mates, love, and marriage, and how cultures influence conformity, obedience, compliance, and cooperation. We then turn our attention to intergroup relations, discussing ingroups versus outgroups, ethnocentrism, prejudice, stereotypes, and discrimination. We will discuss the relationship between culture and aggression, and end with a discussion of acculturation—how we adapt and adjust to new cultures.

▶ Cultural Influences on How We Perceive People

Person Perception and Impression Formation

We form many reliable impressions of people based on our perceptions, including judgments of appearance, attractiveness, personality traits, and even recognizing others. **Person perception** refers to the process of forming them. For example, greater height, which is generally considered attractive, has been associated with leadership ability, competence, and high salary (Deck, 1968; Patzer, 1985). Size is generally associated with strength and dominance, even when perceived by infants (Thomsen, Frankenhuis, Ingold-Smith, & Carey, 2011). Adults with baby-face features tend to be judged as warm, kind, naive, and submissive; adults with more mature facial features tend to be judged

person perception
The process of forming impressions of others.

as strong, worldly, and dominant (Berry & McArthur, 1985, 1986). People who are neat dressers are thought to be conscientious (Albright, Kenny, & Malloy, 1988). People with poor eye contact are often judged to be dishonest (DePaulo, Stone, & Lassiter, 1985).

Individuals can generally identify the ethnicity of individuals based on their looks and accents (Rakic, Steffens, & Memmendey, 2011). Individuals across cultures also tend to agree on the personality traits they infer from faces, and these inferences can be predictive of important outcomes. For example, there is high agreement between American and Chinese individuals in judgments of personality traits associated with photographs of faces (Zebrowitz, 1997). In one well-known study, naïve ratings of competence of the faces of U.S. congressional candidates predicted the winners of elections (Todorov, Mandisodza, Goren, & Hall, 2005).

But there are also cultural differences. In a recent study, American and Japanese participants made naïve inferences of traits from the faces of U.S. and Japanese political candidates (Rule et al., 2010). There was high agreement in the ratings of the faces across cultures, replicating previous findings. Both sets of judgments were predictive of the percentage of votes that each candidate received in the actual election, also replicating previous findings. But the traits predicting electoral success differed depending on culture. American judgments were predictive of American election outcomes but not of Japanese elections, whereas Japanese judgments were predictive of Japanese election outcomes but not American elections.

There are also cultural differences in judgments of truthworthiness. Some research suggests that people who smile tend to cooperate more, and that smiling partners are trusted more than nonsmiling partners (Scharlemann, Eckel, Kacelnik, & Wilson, 2001). A study testing American and Japanese observers who were shown smiling faces of Americans and Japanese individuals reported that Americans trusted the faces with greater intensity in the smiling mouths, while Japanese trusted the faces with greater intensity in the smiling eyes (Ozono et al., 2010). This finding might have occurred because Americans believe smiling faces are more intelligent than neutral faces, whereas Japanese believe neutral faces are more intelligent than smiling faces (Matsumoto & Kudoh, 1993). Thus, not all smiles may be interpreted in the same way across cultures.

Weisbuch, Pauker, and Ambady (2009) conducted two studies that have suggested that subtle, unconscious nonverbal cues imbedded in culture—in media, Internet, magazines, movies, and so on—exert powerful influences on the way we perceive others. In the first study, the nonverbal behaviors toward white and black characters on 11 popular TV shows were analyzed. There were more negative nonverbal behaviors toward black characters than toward white. Subsequent studies showed that exposure to the pro-white nonverbal bias increased viewers' biases unconsciously, even though the viewers could not report the patterns of nonverbal behaviors that produced the bias.

Culture and Face Recognition

In order to create meaningful bonds with others we need to be able to recognize them when we see them. Early research in this area showed the existence of a same-race bias in this ability. Malpass and Kravitz (1969) showed photographs of either African American or European American individuals to observers in either a predominantly African American or European American university. Observers recognized individuals of their own race better than they did people of the other race. These results were replicated a number of times (e.g., Malpass, 1974) using different methods (Wright, Boyd, & Tredoux, 2001) and have been supported in meta-analyses (e.g., Bothwell, Brigham, & Malpass, 1989; Meissner & Brigham, 2001). Research has documented this effect for Asian faces as well (O'Toole, Deffenbacher, Valentin, & Abdi, 1994). There also appears to be a same-race bias in discriminating between male and female faces (O'Toole, Peterson, & Deffenbacher, 1996). This bias exists in children as young as three months old (Bar-Haim, Ziv, Lamy, & Hodes, 2006; Kelly, Quinn, Slater, Lee, Gibson, Smith et al., 2005).

Why might this bias exist? Meissner and Brigham (2001) suggested that attitudes toward people of same and other races, social orientation, task difficulty, and experience all contribute to this differential recognition ability. Their meta-analysis also suggested that the explanation provided by intergroup contact theories—that differential recognition stems from limited experience with members of other groups—has received only weak support in the research literature. Orienting strategies may provide an explanation. Devine and Malpass (1985) found no difference in recognition rates when observers in their study were told that they were participating in a reaction-time experiment and would later be asked to make differential judgments about the people they observed. Different schemas about faces of different races may account for the same-race bias (Levy, Lysne, & Underwood, 1995). Or, same-race and other-race faces may be perceived and classified differently, with race features being coded differently in same-race and other-race perceptions (Levin, 1996).

Culture and Attractiveness

Do people of different cultures differ in their judgments of attractiveness? On one hand, beauty may be in the eye of the beholder. On the other hand, evolutionary theories predict that there may be a universal standard of attractiveness because attractiveness increases the chances of reproduction, a standard that may be reinforced by today's mass media. Early studies on this topic provided evidence for both sides of the argument. Daibo, Murasawa, and Chou (1994), for example, demonstrated that attractiveness ratings were associated with different facial features in Japan and Korea. But, Cunningham, Roberts, Barbee, Druen, and Wu (1995) conducted three studies involving European Americans and African Americans, Asian and Hispanic immigrants, and Taiwanese observers who judged faces of individuals from various ethnicities. There were high correlations among the judge groups in their attractiveness ratings, and the ratings by all groups correlated with the same facial characteristics, which included the nature of the eyes, nose, cheeks, chin, and smile.

More recent studies have provided stronger evidence for a possible universal standard of attractiveness. For example, leg-to-body ratio is associated with attractiveness across cultures, with short and excessively long legs judged as less attractive (Sorokowski et al., 2011). A meta-analysis reviewing 1,800 articles and 919 findings indicated that raters agree both within and across cultures about who is and is not attractive (Langlois, Kalakanis, Rubenstein, Larson, Hallam, & Smoot, 2000). Men prefer low female waist-to-hip ratios, and this is true even of blind men (Karremans, Frankenhuis, & Arons, 2010), suggesting that this preference may not be learned through visual input. Research across nine cultures also has demonstrated that small foot size is generally judged as more attractive and preferred, while average foot size is preferred for males (Fessler et al., 2005).

But even if people across cultures agree on what is attractive, there are cultural differences in the meaning of attractiveness. Research with North Americans has consistently shown that people tend to ascribe desirable personality characteristics to those who are good-looking, seeing them as more sensitive, kind, sociable, pleasant, likable, and interesting than those who are unattractive (Dion, 1986; Patzer, 1985). Attractive people are also judged to be more competent and intelligent (Ross & Ferris, 1981).

Attractiveness ratings are strongly correlated with social competence, adjustment, potency, and intellectual competence, and negatively with modesty (Eagly, Ashmore, Makhijani, & Longo, 1991); and are strongly correlated with social skills, sociability, mental health, dominance, intelligence, and sexual warmth, and again negatively with modesty (Feingold, 1992). These studies have demonstrated quite consistent agreement in findings involving North American participants with regard to the psychological meanings attributed to attractive people.

Many, but not all, of these effects have been replicated in other cultures. For example, Wheeler and Kim (1997) showed photos of Korean males and females to Korean university students, who made judgments of social competence, intellectual competence, concern for others, integrity, adjustment, potency, sexual interest or warmth, and modesty. Consistent with research involving North American judges, they found that Korean students rated attractive faces as more socially and intellectually competent, better adjusted, more sexually interesting, and less modest. Contrary to previous research with North Americans, however, the Koreans did not rate attractive faces as more potent, and they rated them as having more integrity and concern for others, which was not found in studies with Americans.

Thus, there may be a universal standard for attractiveness, but there are cultural differences in the specific features of a person that are more or less relevant in judgments of attractiveness, and the meaning of attractiveness is different across cultures. As with person perception, subtle, unconscious nonverbal cues imbedded in culture influence the way we perceive others' attractiveness (Weisbuch & Ambady, 2009). And there are large individual differences in judgments of attractiveness; on the individual level beauty really is in the eye of the beholder.

▶ Culture and Attributions

What Are Attributions, and Where Do They Come From?

Attributions are the inferences people make about the causes of events or behaviors, their own as well as others. For instance, you might attribute a friend's failure to show up for a date to irresponsibility, too much traffic, or just forgetting. You might attribute your success on an exam to your effort or to luck. Attributions represent the ways we understand the world around us and the behaviors of others.

attributions Beliefs about the underlying causes of behavior.

In Chapter 1 we discussed some of the unique cognitive abilities that humans have that allow us to create human cultures. One of these was the ability to infer agency in oneself and others, that is, to know that other people are *intentional agents*. People have needs, motives, desires, and goals, and their behaviors are often the direct result of these. Knowing that this is true for oneself, others, and especially that others make those inferences about oneself, is one of the most important cognitive building blocks of human culture.

This same cognitive ability enables humans to create attributions. Attributions allow us to explain things, to put things in order, and to make sense of the world. Because the cognitive abilities to understand that oneself and others are intentional agents are universal to humans, the process of making attributions is a universal psychological process. All people of all cultures make attributions. This probably reflects a universal need to know—a universal motive for humans to derive meaning from events and behaviors. This would explain why humans personalize inanimate objects or random acts of nature (e.g., hurricanes) and make causal inferences—attributions—about them. By creating attributions, we exert psychological control over the world.

Immediately after the terror attacks of September 11, 2001, for instance, searching for meaning in the attacks led to a high stress response (greater posttraumatic stress response symptoms); finding meaning in the attacks also led to better adjustment, less stress symptoms, and less fear of future attacks (Updegraff, Silver, & Holman, 2008).

The study of attributions has a rich history in social psychology. An important concept in attribution research is the distinction between internal and external attributions. **Internal attributions** specify the cause of behavior within a person; these are also known as **dispositional attributions**. **External attributions** locate the cause of behavior outside a person, such as other people, nature, or acts of God; these are also known as **situational dispositions**.

Early Research on Cultural Differences in Attributional Styles

Because attributions are creations of the mind, they may or may not be rooted in an objective reality and are subjected to many possible biases in ways of thinking. One of these biases is known as the **fundamental attribution error** (Ross, 1977), which refers to bias toward inferences about an actor's disposition even if the presence of very obvious situational constraints. Fundamental attribution error is also known as **correspondence bias**. One of the earliest studies to show this bias was Jones and Harris's (1967) study of attributions about an essay supporting Fidel Castro in Cuba. Participants inferred that the author must have a favorable attitude toward Castro. Furthermore, such dispositional inferences occurred even when the participants were explicitly told that the writer was assigned to write a pro-Castro essay and no choice was given. The participants ignored these situational constraints and erroneously drew inferences about the author's disposition. Fundamental attribution error has been replicated many times in American psychological experiments.

Early cross-cultural research, however, suggested that it may not be as robust or pervasive among people of other cultures. For example, J. G. Miller (1984) examined patterns of social explanation in Americans and Hindu Indians. Both Hindu and American respondents were asked to describe someone they knew well who either did something good for another person or did something bad to another person. After describing such a person, the respondents were asked to explain why the person committed that good or bad act. American respondents typically explained the person's behavior in terms of general dispositions (e.g., "She is very irresponsible"). The Hindus, contrastingly, were much less likely to offer dispositional explanations. Instead, they tended to provide explanations in terms of the actor's duties, social roles, and other situation-specific factors (see also Shweder & Bourne, 1984).

Another type of attributional bias is known as **self-serving bias**, which refers to the tendency to attribute one's successes to personal factors and one's failures to situational factors (Heider, 1976). Research for many decades has shown that Americans often exhibit a self-serving bias. If a student fails an exam, for instance, that student may attribute his or her failure to situational causes such as a poorly constructed test, lousy teaching, distractions, or a bad week at home. If that same student aced an exam, however, he or she would be more likely to attribute that success to dispositional causes such as effort, intelligence, or ability.

Many early studies demonstrated cultural differences in this bias. Hau and Salili (1991), for example, asked junior and senior high-school students in Hong Kong to rate the importance and meaning of 13 specific causes of academic performance. Effort, interest, and ability—all internal attributions—were rated the most important causes, regardless of success or failure. Crittenden (1991) also found that Taiwanese women used more external and self-effacing attributions about themselves than

internal attributions Attributions that specify the cause of behavior within a person; also known as **dispositional attributions**, because they are attributions about people's dispositions.

dispositional attributions Attributions about people's internal characteristics, traits, or personality.

external attributions Attributions that locate the cause of behavior outside a person, such as other people, nature, or acts of God; these are also known as **situational dispositions**.

fundamental attribution error A tendency to explain the behaviors of others using internal attributions but to explain one's own behaviors using external attributions; also known as **correspondence bias**.

correspondence bias See Fundamental Attribution Error.

self-serving bias A bias in which people tend to attribute good deeds and successes to their own internal attributes but attribute bad deeds or failures to external factors.

did American women. Crittenden suggested that the Taiwanese women did this to enhance their public and private self-esteem by using an attributional approach that conformed to a feminine gender role. Earlier, Bond, Leung, and Wan (1982) found that self-effacing Chinese students were better liked by their peers than those who adopted this attributional style less often.

Other cross-cultural studies on attributions concerning academic performance peppered the literature with findings that challenged American notions of attribution. Kashima and Triandis (1986) showed that Japanese use a more group-oriented, collective approach to attribution with regard to attention and memory achievement tasks. Compared to their American counterparts, Japanese subjects attributed failure to themselves more and attributed success to themselves less. Kashima and Triandis interpreted this finding as suggestive of American and Japanese cultural differences in degree of responsibility taking.

Many cross-cultural studies of attributions in nonacademic areas as well also showed cultural differences. For example, Moghaddam, Ditto, and Taylor (1990) examined the attributional processes of high- and low-distressed Indian female immigrants to Canada in relation to the degree to which they have adjusted to life in Canada. They found that the Indian women were more likely to attribute both successes and failures to internal causes. Forgas, Furnham, and Frey (1989) documented broad cross-national differences in the importance of different types of specific attributions for wealth. Their study included 558 subjects from the United Kingdom, Australia, and the Federal Republic of Germany. The British considered family background and luck as the most important determinants of wealth. Germans also considered family background the most important determinant. Australians, however, rated individual qualities the most important determinant of wealth. Romero and Garza (1986) examined differences between Hispanic and Anglo women in their attributions concerning occupational success and failure, and found that Chicanas tended to make more attributions on the basis of luck, ethnicity, or gender; in making attributions about failure, Anglo females tended to attribute less competence to the actor than did the Chicana females.

Cultural differences in attributions exist in mass media as well. Morris and Peng (1994) found that U.S. newspaper articles were more likely to attribute the cause of a murder to an individual's personality traits, attitudes, and beliefs (such as "bad temper," "psychologically disturbed"), but Chinese newspapers were more likely to attribute the cause to situational factors (such as "didn't get along with his advisor," "isolated from his community"). Lee, Hallahan, and Herzog (1996) coded Hong Kong and U.S. newspaper articles concerning sporting events for attributional style and judged the extent to which events were attributed to personal or situational factors. As hypothesized, they found that attributions by Hong Kong reporters were more situational and less dispositional than those of U.S. reporters.

Contemporary Research: Universality and Culture-Specificity of Attributional Styles

Cultural differences in attributional styles clearly exist. But are there contexts in which attributional styles may be universal as well? Two comprehensive reviews of the literature shed some light on this topic.

Many of the cultural differences in attributional styles demonstrated that North Americans committed the fundamental attribution error while East Asians did not. Choi, Nisbett, and Norenzayan (1999) concluded that East Asians did not commit the error because they have a greater sensitivity to context and situationalism. To demonstrate this, they conducted a study in which Korean and American participants predicted the behaviors of a group of individuals based on situational information, and the behavior of a single individual based on both personality and situational information. When dispositional (personality) information was not available or applicable, the Koreans used situational information more than did the American participants, suggesting a stronger belief in situational influence in the Koreans than the Americans. When both dispositional and situational information was present, however, there were no cultural differences in the attributions of the Koreans or the Americans.

In the second review, Mezulis, Abramson, Hyde, and Hankin (2004) conducted a meta-analysis of 266 studies that produced 503 effects. Across all studies, there was a very large effect for the self-serving bias. This bias was present in nearly all samples, indicating universality. When data were analyzed separately for different cultures, there were *no* differences in the size of the bias among European, African, Asian, Hispanic, Native, and multiethnic Americans; they all showed the self-serving bias to a large degree. The sizes of the effects for Asian cultures were lower but still showed evidence for the self-serving bias. Moreover, there were differences among the Asian countries. There was almost no degree of bias in Japan, while Mainland China and South Korea were associated with large self-serving biases at levels comparable to the United States.

These findings suggested that simple explanations based on individualism versus collectivism *cannot* account for cultural differences in self-serving bias because many of the Asian cultures share some similarities in collectivism. Instead, religious affiliation or backgrounds and dialectic thinking (the tendency to think that apparently mutually dichotomous events are not necessarily dichotomous; see Chapter 8) may be more important variables in explaining cultural differences in attributional styles (Norenzayan & Lee, 2010).

Thus, attributional biases such as the self-serving bias or fundamental attribution error may be universal. This makes sense, given the view of the origin of attributions we discussed earlier, and the role that self-esteem and cultural worldviews play in maintaining our self-image (recall our discussion of tactical self-enhancement in Chapter 5). All people of all cultures appear to have a universal need to maintain their self-image and protect their self-integrity; attributions are one of the ways in which this is achieved. There are cultural differences, however, in the specific ways in which attributional processes are used, and how much. This cultural influence probably starts early; Bornstein and associates (1998), for example, examined attributions of mothers of 20-month-olds in Argentina, Belgium, France, Israel, Italy, Japan, and the United States with regard to success and failure in seven parenting tasks. They found only a few cross-cultural similarities, but many differences, especially with regard to degree of competence and satisfaction in parenting. Child age could not be a factor, as it was controlled in the study, and child gender did not influence the data either. These types of findings provide us with ideas about how and why parents transmit valuable cultural information to their children, resulting in specific styles of attribution (among many other psychological effects).

▶ Mate Selection, Love, and Marriage across Cultures

Culture and Mate Selection

What do people look for in a mate, and is it different across cultures? In one of the best-known studies on this topic (Buss, 1989, 1994), more than 10,000 respondents in 37 cultures from 33 countries completed two questionnaires, one dealing with factors in choosing a mate and the second dealing with preferences concerning potential mates.

TABLE 14.1 Sex Differences in Preferred Traits in a Mate across Cultures

Male Preferences in Females	Female Preferences in Males
▪ Younger	▪ Financial prospects
▪ Good looking	▪ Ambition
▪ Less/no sexual experiences	▪ Industriousness
	▪ Older

Source: Adapted from Buss (1989)

In 36 of the 37 cultures, females rated financial prospects as more important than did males; in 29 of those 36 cultures, females also rated ambition and industriousness as more important than did males. In all 37 cultures, males preferred younger mates and females preferred older mates; in 34 of the cultures, males rated good looks as more important than did females; and in 23 of the cultures, males rated chastity as more important than did females (see Table 14.1). Buss (1989) concluded that females value cues related to resource acquisition in potential mates more highly than males do, whereas males value reproductive capacity more highly than do females. These findings were predicted by an evolutionary-based framework that generated hypotheses related to evolutionary concepts of parental involvement, sexual selection, reproductive capacity, and certainty of paternity or maternity. The degree of agreement in sex differences across cultures has led Buss (1989) and his colleagues to view these mate-selection preferences as universal, arising from different evolutionary selection pressures on males and females.

But culture also plays a role in influencing mate preferences. Hatfield and Sprecher (1995) studied American, Russian, and Japanese students and reported that Americans preferred expressivity, openness, and sense of humor more than did the Russians, who in turn preferred these traits more than did the Japanese. Russians desired skill as a lover most while Japanese preferred it least. The Japanese gave lower ratings than the other two cultures on kind and understanding, good conversationalist, physical attractiveness, and status. Similarly, the most important traits reported by both men and women in the United States when looking for a partner were kindness, consideration, honesty, and a sense of humor (Goodwin, 1990).

Thus mate selection is influenced by both evolutionary forces and culture. But what about trying to romantically attract someone who is *already* in a romantic relationship—that is, stealing someone else's mate? This is known as **mate poaching**. A study involving 16,954 participants in 53 countries showed that it was most common in Southern Europe, South America, Western Europe, and Eastern Europe, and relatively less frequent in Africa, South and Southeast Asia, and East Asia (Schmitt, 2004). In all regions studied, men were more likely to have attempted mate poaching and to be the victims of mate-poaching attempts by others. Across all regions of the world, mate poachers tended to be more extroverted, disagreeable, unconscientious, unfaithful, and erotophilic—being comfortable in talking about sex. In all regions, successful mate poachers were more open to new experiences, were sexually attractive, were not exclusive in their relationships, exhibited less sexual restraint, and were more erotophilic. Men and women in all regions who were the targets of mate-poaching attempts were more extroverted, open to experience, sexually attractive, erotophilic, and low on relationship exclusivity.

There were also some cultural differences in mate poaching. Cultures with more economic resources had higher rates of mate-poaching attempts. Women were more likely to engage in mate poaching in countries with more women than men; this was not the case for men, however. Sex differences in mate poaching tended to be smaller in cultures that were more gender egalitarian.

mate poaching Attracting someone who is already in a romantic relationship with someone else.

Culture and Love

Love is one of the uniquely human sentiments, and it is important because it aids in our finding potential mates and creating a social support system to buffer the stresses of life. Love, it is said, "is a many-splendored thing," and "love conquers all." In the United States, love seems to be a prerequisite to forming a long-term romantic relationship. But is that so in other cultures as well?

Maybe not; many studies have demonstrated cultural differences in attitudes about love. Ting-Toomey (1991), for instance, compared ratings of love commitment, disclosure maintenance, ambivalence, and conflict expression by 781 participants from France, Japan, and the United States. The French and Americans had significantly higher ratings than the Japanese on love commitment and disclosure maintenance. Americans also had significantly higher ratings than the Japanese on relational ambivalence. The Japanese and the Americans, however, had significantly higher ratings than the French on conflict expression.

Simmons, vom Kolke, and Shimizu (1986) examined attitudes toward love and romance among American, German, and Japanese students. Romantic love was valued more in the United States and Germany than in Japan. These researchers explained this cultural difference by suggesting that romantic love is more highly valued in cultures with few strong, extended family ties, and less valued in cultures in which kinship networks influence and reinforce the relationship between marriage partners.

Thus although love may be a universal and uniquely human sentiment, it is valued differently in different cultures. Additionally, there are many forms of love (Hatfield, 1988; Hatfield & Rapson, 1996; Sternberg, 1988) and we do not know exactly what kinds of cultural similarities and differences exist for what specific types of love. Future research will need to explore this interesting question.

Culture and Marriage

Marriage is an institutionalized relationship that publicly recognizes the long-term commitment that two people make to each other. About 90% of people in most societies get married, or whatever is the equivalent of marriage in their societies (Carroll & Wolpe, 1996). A study involving 17,804 participants in 62 cultures around the world found that 79% of the romantic attachments people had could be considered "secure"—that is, one in which both the self and the other are considered valuable and worthy of trust; they are characterized as being responsive, supportive, and comfortable in their mutual interdependence (Schmitt et al., 2004). This suggested a large degree of normality around the world in the way people form romantic attachments with others, and that there is something universal in the fact that people need and want to make such commitments with someone else.

But there are cultural differences in the ways in which people around the world form romantic attachments and view the role of love in marriage. For example, individuals in South, Southeast, and East Asia tend to score higher on preoccupied romantic attachment, in which attachments to others are relatively more dependent on the value that they provide to others and that others provide to themselves (Schmitt et al., 2004). That is, they tend to strive more for the approval of highly valued others in romantic relationships.

In the United States today, there is decreasing pressure, especially on women, to get married before a certain age or to have children. Yet there are many people in many other cultures of the world that harbor many traditional values concerning marriage, including the belief that women should get married before a certain age, such as 25, and have children before 30. These values are at conflict within cultures and societies that are, at the same time, becoming more affluent and individualistic. As children in these cultures leave to visit and/or study in cultures such as the United States, those types of conflicts come to a head, especially for women, who on the one hand, want to get an education, job, and career, and yet on the other, feel the pressure to get married, settle down, have children, and raise a family. Families who provide the financial support for their children to get an international education may not perceive the value of an education for their children, especially if they insist on an early marriage and child-rearing.

There are cultural differences in the perceived role of love in marriage. Levine, Sato, Hashimoto, and Verma (1995), for instance, asked students in India, Pakistan, Thailand, Mexico, Brazil, Japan, Hong Kong, the Philippines, Australia, England, and the United States to rate the importance of love for both the establishment and the maintenance of a marriage. Individualistic cultures were more likely to rate love as essential to the establishment of a marriage, and to agree that the disappearance of love is a sufficient reason to end a marriage. Countries with a large gross domestic product also showed this tendency—not surprising, given the high correlation between affluence and individualism. Countries with high marriage and divorce rates, and low fertility rates, assigned greater importance to romantic love. Divorce rates were highly correlated with the belief that the disappearance of love warranted the dissolution of a marriage.

Jankowiak and Fischer (1992) compared 186 traditional cultures on love and showed that in every culture but one, young people reported falling passionately in love; experienced the euphoria and despair of passionate love; knew of poems, stories, and legends about famous lovers; and sang love songs. Nonetheless, this did not mean that the young people from these cultures could pursue these feelings of love and marry the person they fell in love with. Instead, in many of these cultures, arranged marriages were the norm.

Arranged marriages are quite common in many cultures of the world. In India, arranged marriages date back 6,000 years (Saraswathi, 1999), although the practice is rarer today. Sometimes parents arrange marriages far before the age at which the couple can even consider marriage. In other cases, marriage meetings are held between prospective couples, who may then date for a while to decide whether to get married or not. In these cultures, marriage is seen as more than just the union of two individuals, but rather as a union and alliance between two families (Dion & Dion, 1993b; Stone, 1990). Love between the two individuals is often not part of this equation but is something that should grow in the marriage relationship. People from these cultures often report that they "love the person they marry," not "marry the person they love."

Hatfield and Rapson (1996) reported that getting married based on romantic love is a relatively new concept—about 300 years old in the West and much newer in non-Western cultures. With globalization, however, young people from these countries are opting for selecting their own mates. For instance, over 20 years ago, 40% of young people in India intended to find a marriage partner on their own (Sprecher & Chandak, 1992). This trend is currently reflected in other countries as well, such as Japan, China, Egypt, and Turkey (Arnett, 2001).

arranged marriages
A marriage in which someone other than the couple being married makes the decision about who will be wed. Oftentimes, this can be the parents of the individuals being wed.

Intercultural Marriages

Marriage in any culture is not easy because two people from two different backgrounds, and often two different cultures within a culture, come together to live, work, and play. Being together with anyone 24/7 is tough and is bound to bring about its own share of conflicts and struggles. Any marriage requires work from both partners to be successful, regardless of how "successful" is defined.

Intercultural marriages bring with them their own special problems and issues. Conflicts in intercultural marriages arise in several major areas, including the expression of love and intimacy, the nature of commitment and attitudes toward the marriage itself, and approaches to child-rearing (see Cottrell, 1990, for a review). Other potential sources of conflict include differences in perceptions of male–female roles, especially with regard to division of labor (McGoldrick & Preto, 1984; Romano, 1988), differences in domestic money management (Ho, 1984; Hsu, 1977; Kiev, 1973; McGoldrick & Preto, 1984), differences in perceptions of relationships with extended family (Cohen, 1982; Markoff, 1977), and differences in the definitions of marriage itself (Markoff, 1977).

Sometimes couples in intercultural marriages experience conflicts with regard to intimacy and love expression. As described in Chapter 9, people of different cultures can vary in their expression of basic emotions such as anger, frustration, and happiness (because of cultural display rules). And cultures differ on the degree to which emotions such as love and intimacy are seen as important ingredients of a successful marriage. These differences arise from a fundamental difference in attitudes toward marriage. Americans tend to view marriage as a companionship between two individuals in love. People of many other cultures view marriage more as a partnership formed for succession (that is, for producing offspring) and for economic and social bonding. Love does not necessarily have to enter the equation for people in these cultures, at least in the beginning. With such fundamental differences, it is no wonder that intercultural marriages can be difficult.

Another conflict area is around issues of child-rearing, and sometimes the differences between two people involved in an intercultural marriage do not arise until they have children. This is no surprise because of the enormous differences in socialization practices and the role of parenting in the development of culture, as discussed in Chapter 3. Although it has been a common belief that children of intracultural marriages have stronger ethnic identities than children of intercultural marriages, research does not tend to support this claim (e.g., Parsonson, 1987). Children tend to develop strong or weak ethnic identities based not on their parents' similarities or differences, but on their upbringing, especially with regard to attitudes, values, and behaviors regarding their single or dual cultures. Children with stronger ethnic identities, however, are more likely to want to marry within their own ethnic group (Parsonson, 1987).

In many ways, intercultural marriages are the prime example of intercultural relationships. For them to be successful, both partners need to be flexible, compromising, and committed to the relationship. If these ingredients are in play, couples will find ways to make their relationships work. Perhaps it all comes down to how much both spouses are willing to work to negotiate differences, compromise, and stay together—a good recipe for all marriages.

conformity Yielding to real or imagined social pressure.

compliance Yielding to social pressure in one's public behavior, even though one's private beliefs may not have changed.

obedience A form of compliance that occurs when people follow direct commands, usually from someone in a position of authority.

▶ Culture and Conformity, Compliance, and Obedience

Conformity means yielding to real or imagined social pressure. **Compliance** is generally defined as yielding to social pressure in one's public behavior even though one's private beliefs may not have changed. **Obedience** is a form of compliance that occurs when people follow direct commands, usually from someone in a position of authority.

Two of the best-known studies on these topics are the Asch and Milgram studies. In his earliest experiments, Asch (1951, 1955, 1956) examined a participant's response to a simple judgment task after other "subjects" (actually experimental confederates) had all given the same incorrect response. For example, a subject would be placed in a room with others, shown objects (lines, balls, and so forth), and asked to make a judgment about the objects (such as relative sizes). The answer was often obvious, but participants were asked to give their answers only after a number of confederates had given theirs. Asch (1956) reported that 36.8% of the participants conformed by giving the wrong answer even though it was obviously wrong. Across studies and trials, group size and group unanimity were the influencing factors; conformity peaked when the group contained seven people and was unanimous in its judgments (even though the judgments were clearly wrong).

In Milgram's (1974) famous study, participants were brought into a laboratory ostensibly to study the effects of punishment on learning. They were instructed to administer shocks to another person (actually a confederate) when the latter gave the wrong response or no response. The shock meter was labeled from "Slight Shock" to "DANGER: Severe Shock" and the confederate's behaviors ranged from simple utterances of pain through pounding on the walls, pleas to stop, and then deathly silence. No shock was actually administered. Milgram reported that 65 percent of the subjects obeyed the commands of the experimenter and administered the most severe levels of shock.

The Asch experiments were rather innocuous in the actual content of the compliance (e.g., judgments of the length of lines), and compliance resulted from subtle, implied pressure. But in the real world, compliance can occur in response to explicit rules, requests, and commands. We can imagine how forceful and pervasive group pressure to conform and comply is in the real world if it can operate in a simple laboratory environment among people unknown to the subject on a task that has relatively little meaning. The Milgram studies highlighted the potential negative and harmful effects of compliance and obedience. To this day, it stands as one of the best-known studies in American social psychology. Its findings spoke for themselves on the power of group influence.

A number of cross-cultural studies have attempted to replicate the Asch experiment. For example, a replication of the Asch experiment in Japan using only ingroup members (teammates in sport clubs) also reported a conformity rate of 25.2%, which was comparable to four other behavioral studies in Japan using the same paradigm (Takano & Sogon, 2008). Bond and Smith (1996) conducted a meta-analysis analyzing 133 studies conducted in 17 countries, and reported that the mean conformity rate was 25%. There were considerable cultural differences, however. Conformity was higher when the majority that tried to influence the conforming participant was larger and with a greater proportion of female participants. Conformity was also greater when the majority did not consist of outgroup members and when the stimuli were more ambiguous. Conformity was higher in collectivistic countries than in individualistic ones.

Smith and Bond (1999) also reviewed nine studies that used the Milgram paradigm across nine countries. These studies indicated a broad range in the percentage of participants obeying the experimenter, spanning from a low of 16% among females in Australia to a high of 92% in the Netherlands. These differences may have reflected real cultural differences in obedience, but they may have also reflected other types of differences, including differences in the meaning of the particular tasks used in the studies, the specific instructions given to the participants, and the nature of the confederate who supposedly received the shocks.

Recent research has suggested that the source of these cultural differences may be in the historical prevalence of disease-causing pathogens: cultures in which pathogens were more prevalent in history may have facilitated cultural norms promoting greater conformity in order to deal with increased risk of disease. In an ecological-level study (recall our discussion of these in Chapter 2), pathogen prevalence was positively associated with the amount of conformity in behavioral experiments and in the percentage of population who prioritize obedience. Prevalence was also negatively correlated with within-country dispositional variability and the percentage of the population that were left-handed (Murray, Trudeau, & Schaller, 2011).

That conformity differs across cultures makes sense. Traditional American culture fosters individualistic values, endorsing behaviors and beliefs contrary to conformity. To conform in American culture is to be "weak" or somehow deficient. But many other cultures foster more conforming values; in those cultures, conformity, obedience, and compliance enjoy much higher status and are viewed positively. In these cultures, conformity is viewed not only as "good" but as necessary for the successful functioning of the culture, its groups, and the interpersonal relationships of its members. This probably explains why the best-known studies of conformity and obedience conducted in the United States are negative in their connotation. Although the Asch studies are rather innocuous, the Milgram studies are clearly a powerful indictment of the potential negative consequences of obedience. Have any studies been conducted by American social psychologists that might show positive outcomes of conformity, compliance, or obedience? If not, perhaps we need to examine the possible biases of American social scientists in approaching these topics. Conformity and obedience are important constructs in any social system as a way of reinforcing behaviors (Lachlan, Janik, & Slater, 2004).

▶ Culture and Cooperation

cooperation People's ability to work together toward common goals.

Cooperation refers to people's ability to work together toward common goals. Trust and cooperation are necessary for the efficient functioning and survival of any social group, human or animal. Yet humans differ from animals in important ways. Whereas cooperative behavior in nonhuman primates exists, it is generally limited to kin and reciprocating partners and is virtually never extended to strangers; humans, on the other hand, give blood, volunteer, recycle, and are willing to incur costs to help even strangers in one-shot interactions (Silk, Brosnan, Vonk, Henrich, Povinelli, Richardson, et al., 2005). Cooperation, trust, and giving allow people to care for others' children, even those of strangers, and to help out victims of tragedies, even if we do not know them. This does not happen in the nonhuman animal world. Human trust and cooperation appears to be based on unique human cognitive abilities (see Chapter 1), including empathy and concern for the welfare of others (Silk et al., 2005), memory (Pennisi, 2005), and shared intentions; reciprocity and cooperation can be practiced only by those who can remember who was helpful and who was not.

One of the most well-known lines of research on cooperation and culture is that of Yamagishi and colleagues. In one study, Yamagishi (1986) categorized Japanese participants as high and low trusters; they then participated in an experiment in which they could cooperate with three other players by giving money to them, either with or without a sanctioning system that provided for punishments. The conditions, therefore, were the presence or absence of the sanctioning system. The sanctioning system involved the participants donating any or all of their earnings at the end of the experiment into a "punishment fund," which was then subtracted from the earnings of the participant who contributed the least to the totals for all players. High trusters did indeed cooperate more than low trusters without the sanctioning system; when the sanctioning system was in effect, however, low trusters cooperated more than did the high trusters. Yamagishi (1988) replicated this study in the United States and compared the American and Japanese responses. He found the same results for Americans as he did for the Japanese; when there was no sanctioning system, high-trusting Americans cooperated more than low-trusting Americans. When there was a sanctioning system, the findings reversed. Moreover, there were no differences between the Americans and the Japanese when the sanctioning system was in effect. These findings have been replicated numerous times (Mashima, Yamagishi, & Macy, 2004; Yamagishi, Makimura, Foddy, Matsuda, Kiyonari, & Platow, 2005) and suggest that cultural differences in cooperation exists because of the sanctioning system within which individuals exist; when people are placed in the same type of system, they behave in similar ways.

These conclusions are consistent with other studies that have examined punishment as the source of cooperation. All populations of the world studied to date demonstrate some willingness to administer costly punishment in response to unequal behavior and that costly punishment positively correlates with altruistic behavior across countries (Henrich et al., 2006). The size of the communities within which people live is positively associated with punishment—the larger the communities, the greater the punishments. The degree of market integration based on exchanges of goods and services is positively associated with fairness across cultures (Henrich et al., 2010). The most recent review in this area, covering 83 studies with 7,361 participants in 18 societies, revealed the punishment more strongly promotes cooperation in societies with high rather than low trust (Balliet & Van Lange, 2013).

Many studies have reported that intercultural interactions produce increased competitiveness and less cooperation. In one recent study, students played a game of cooperation and competition (Prisoner's Dilemma) either with a same-sex student of the same ethnicity or a different ethnicity. The participant pairs were strangers to each other prior to the experiment. Different ethnicity pairs produced less positive outcomes and cooperative behaviors, and more competition than same ethnicity pairs, and the increased competitive play occurred with both players from the start of the game (Matsumoto & Hwang, 2011).

But these findings may be limited to specific types of behaviors and targets. Allik and Realo (2004), for instance, examined the relationship between individualism and social capital across the states in the United States and across 42 cultures around the world. **Social capital** was broadly defined as interpersonal trust, civic engagement, and time spent with friends. The results were clear: both states in the United States and countries around the world that were more individualistic were associated with greater social capital; people are more trusting of others and engaged with them (see Figure 14.1). Kemmelmeier, Jambor, and Letner (2006) also showed that in the United States, states that were more individualistic also had higher rates of charitable giving and volunteerism.

Thus cultural differences in cooperative behavior may exist but these are most likely related to the specific situational constraints that individuals are in at the time when a behavior occurs. Some contexts foster some types of cooperative behavior with some people; others do not. Culture provides the environment that defines the situational constraints and contexts. The effects of culture, therefore, are specific to type of behavior and context.

social capital This refers to the social resources available to a person that can be used to obtain one's goals. These include social factors such as interpersonal trust, civic engagement, and time spent with friends.

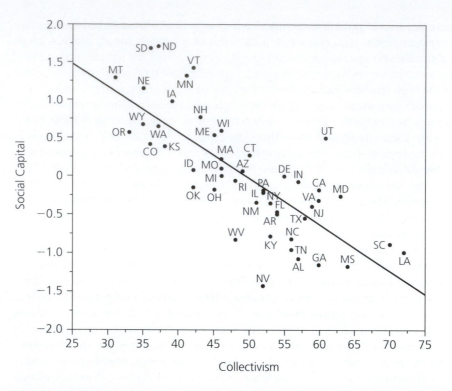

FIGURE 14.1 Social Capital and Individualism–Collectivism in the United States

Source: van de Vijver, F. J. R., *Journal of Cross-Cultural Psychology*, vol. 35, no. 1, pp. 29–49, Jan 2004. Copyright © 2004 by Jueri Allik and Anu Realo. Reprinted by Permission of Sage Publications Inc.

▶ # Culture and Intergroup Relations

Ingroups and Outgroups

ingroups A category of individuals people of all cultures create. Ingroup members generally have a history of shared experiences and an anticipated future that produces a sense of intimacy, familiarity, and trust.

Individuals in all societies need to make distinctions among the individuals with whom they interact because they are necessary for both individual and group functioning and ultimately for survival. One type of meaningful social distinction that people of all societies make is known as ingroups and outgroups (Brewer & Kramer, 1985; Messick & Mackie, 1989; Tajfel, 1982). **Ingroups** include individuals with a history of shared experiences and an anticipated future that produces a sense of intimacy, familiarity, and trust. **Outgroups** are individuals who lack these qualities. In all societies, enculturation involves learning who constitute ingroups and who do not.

outgroups A category of individuals people of all cultures create. Outgroup members generally include all individuals who are not in one's ingroup. Outgroup members generally lack a history of shared experiences and do not have an anticipated future.

People perceive groups as real entities, not just collections of individuals (Campbell, 1958); this is known as group entitativity. That means that groups may be perceived as having real intentions and the capacity for planned actions (Sacchi, Castano, & Brauer, 2008). Differentiating between ingroups and outgroups, therefore, is associated with interesting psychological consequences. People tend to expect greater similarities between themselves and their ingroups relative to their outgroups (Robbins & Krueger, 2005). Perceptions of outgroups are often association with **infrahumanization**—the belief that others are less human. For example, people tend to attribute more uniquely human emotions such as contentment, delight, or resignation, to their ingroups, but more primary, basic emotions such as happiness or anger

infrahumanization The belief that others lack human qualities.

to outgroups (Cortes, Demoulin, Rodriguez, Rodriguez, & Lyens, 2005), as well as values and adjectives thought to be uniquely human and to describe human essence (Haslam, Bain, Douge, Lee, & Bastian, 2005).

Cultural Differences in Ingroup/Outgroup Relationships

One of the important functions of culture is to ascribe different meanings to ingroup and outgroup relationships (Triandis, Bontempo, Villareal, Asai, & Lucca, 1988). These differences produce many cultural differences in the specific nature and function of self-ingroup and self-outgroup relationships. For instance, work colleagues may be ingroups in one culture but outgroups in another, and we cannot assume that people from another culture will interpret and act on those relationships in exactly the same way.

Self-ingroup and self-outgroup relationships differ in individualistic and collec-tivistic cultures (Triandis et al., 1988). In individualistic cultures, people often belong to multiple ingroups. For example, in the United States, many people belong to sev-eral ingroups—music groups, sports groups, church groups, social groups, and so forth. Children may belong to football teams during football season, basketball teams during basketball season, and baseball teams during baseball season. They may take swimming lessons, piano and/or violin lessons, belong to Boy or Girl Scouts, and gen-erally just be the busiest people around.

In contrast, members of collectivistic cultures typically belong to fewer ingroups. But in exchange for belonging to fewer groups, people in collectivistic cultures have greater commitments to the groups to which they belong, and deeper quality of com-mitments and relationships. They also identify more strongly with those groups. Members of individualistic cultures do not necessarily identify with their ingroups as much as people from collectivistic cultures. They have fewer commitments to their ingroups and move much more easily from ingroup to ingroup. Groups take on spe-cial importance in collectivistic cultures. Thus collectivistic cultures require a greater degree of harmony, cohesion, and cooperation within their ingroups and place greater burdens on individuals to identify with the group and conform to group norms. Sanc-tions usually exist for nonconformity. Individualistic cultures depend less on groups and more on the uniqueness of their individuals. The pursuit of personal goals rather than collective ones is of primary importance. As a result, individualistic cultures require less harmony and cohesion within groups and place less importance on con-formity of individuals to group norms.

These differences in the meaning of self-ingroup relationships between indi-vidualistic and collectivistic cultures have consequences for behavior. In collectivistic cultures, people are more willing to make sacrifices for their ingroups in pursuit of group goals, and people try harder to cooperate with one another, even if it means that they must suppress their feelings, thoughts, behaviors, or goals to maintain har-mony and cohesion. Similarly, people in collectivistic cultures try to find ways of agreeing with each other, downplaying and minimizing interpersonal differences for the sake of harmony. In individualistic cultures, people are less willing to sacrifice their individual goals, needs, and desires for the sake of a common good. People are more expressive of their own feelings, attitudes, and opinions, without as much fear or worry about the consequences for group harmony or cohesion. These concepts are summarized in Table 14.2.

Self-outgroup relationships also differ. In collectivistic cultures, relationships with outgroups are marked by a relatively greater lack of concern, distancing, aloof-ness, and even discrimination to outgroups compared to members of individualistic cultures. In individualistic cultures, people are more likely to treat outgroup per-sons more equally, with relatively less distinction between ingroups and outgroups.

TABLE 14.2 Self-Ingroup and Self-Outgroup Relationship Differences as a Function of Individualism and Collectivism

Type of Culture	Characteristics
In individualistic cultures ...	1. People have more ingroups.
	2. People are not as attached to any single ingroup because there are numerous ingroups to which they can be attached.
	3. Survival of the individuals and the society is more dependent on the successful and effective functioning of individuals rather than groups.
	4. People make relatively fewer distinctions between ingroups and outgroups.
In collectivistic cultures ...	1. People have fewer ingroups.
	2. People are very attached to the ingroups to which they belong.
	3. Survival of the individuals and the society is more dependent on the successful and effective functioning of the groups rather than individuals.
	4. People make greater distinctions between ingroup and outgroup others.

Source: Adapted from Triandis et al. (1988).

ingroup derogation
Negative attitudes or beliefs about one's own ingroup.

Members of individualistic cultures engage in positive, relationship-building behaviors with outgroup others that members of collectivistic cultures would reserve only for ingroup others. These consequences of the cultural differences in self-ingroup and -outgroup relationships are summarized in Table 14.3.

There are interesting cultural differences in **ingroup derogation**—the degree to which individuals have negative attitudes or beliefs about their own ingroup. For example, East Asian individuals, relative to Americans, tend to rate their relationships, lovers, friends, universities, cities, countries, and sports teams less favorably (Endo, Heine, & Lehman, 2000; Heine & Lehman, 1997; Snibbe, Kitayama, Markus, & Suzuki, 2003). These attitudes may be related to cultural differences in dialecticism—the degree to which individuals can tolerate contradictory thoughts (see Chapter 5) (Ma-Kellams, Spencer-Rodgers, & Peng, 2011).

The Cultural Origins of Ingroup Favoritism

A number of studies have provided evidence that ingroup favoritism co-evolved along with the emergence of cultures. For instance, a 73-nation study of three types of ingroup favoritism—patriotism, nepotism, and familism—showed that these

TABLE 14.3 Some Consequences of Cultural Differences in Ingroup-Outgroup Relationships

	Individualistic Cultures	Collectivistic Cultures
Ingroup Relationships	People are less willing to sacrifice personal needs, wants, and desires for the sake of the ingroup	People are more willing to sacrifice personal needs, wants, and desires for the sake of the ingroup
	People try less to cooperate with each other, and express their contradictory thoughts and feelings more freely	People try harder to cooperate with each other, even if that means they need to suppress their thoughts and feelings
		People find ways of being agreeable, maintaining harmony
Outgroup Relationships	People are more willing to treat outsiders as equals	People exhibit greater distancing, aloofness, or hostility and discrimination

variables were related to both climate and resources (Van de Vliert, 2011). Favoritism was highest in countries with demanding climates and low income, and lowest in countries with demanding climates but high income.

Arbitrary symbolic markers, although initially meaningless, also can evolve to play a key role in cultural group formation and ingroup favoritism (Efferson, Lalive, & Fehr, 2008). In this study, pairs of participants played a coordination game that required each player to produce a behavior that had consequences for payoffs for self and others. Players also selected a shape—a triangle or circle—to denote themselves and their plays. Over a number of plays, players came to see the linkage between the shapes and the behaviors, and exhibited an increased inclination to request partners with the same shape (because their behaviors were predictable and had positive consequences). Thus, cultural groups were formed on the basis of the linkage between an observable trait, which may start out as rather innocuous, and behaviors that are important for social coordination. If cultural groups can form to innocuous shapes, imagine how they form according to more permanent and meaningful traits of individuals such as ethnicity or sex.

Stereotypes

Stereotypes are generalized images that we have about groups of people, particularly about their underlying psychological characteristics or personality traits (Lee, Jussin, & McCauley, 1995). Stereotypes can be either positive or negative. For example, a common positive stereotype is that Asians are hardworking, the "model minority" (Wong, Lai, Nagasawa, & Lin, 1998), or that Germans are industrious and scientifically minded.

Stereotypes based on some degree of "factual" observation are called *sociotypes* (Triandis, 1994). But stereotypes can also be totally baseless. Because stereotypes can be perpetuated without direct observation of the behaviors of others, some stereotypes have no factual connection to the target group. Even when we convince ourselves that a stereotype is based on direct observations, we have to question the validity of those observations and the interpretations based on them because of the cultural and psychological biases inherent in those processes.

People have stereotypes about their own groups as well as about other groups. Stereotypes about one's own group are called **autostereotypes**; stereotypes about other groups are called **heterostereotypes**. There is often a considerable degree of overlap between a group's autostereotypes and the heterostereotypes that others hold about that group. Iwao and Triandis (1993), for example, asked Japanese and American undergraduate students to respond to three scenarios describing conflicts among individuals and to rate stereotypes of Americans and Japanese. When respondents from the two cultures were similar in their interpretations of an episode, the relationship between autostereotypes and heterostereotypes was high; when they were dissimilar in their interpretations, the relationship was low. The Japanese viewed themselves as passively accepting inconsistencies between their public and private selves, acting according to group norms, whereas Americans tried to reduce the discrepancy between their private and public selves. Similar findings have been reported elsewhere also (Nichols & McAndrew, 1984; Walkey & Chung, 1996).

The Origins of Stereotypes

Stereotypes are products of normal psychological processes, including selective attention, attribution, concept formation, and memory. They occur because people categorize concepts. A **concept** is a mental category we use to classify events, objects,

stereotypes Generalized images we have about groups of people, particularly about their underlying psychological characteristics or personality traits.

autostereotypes Stereotypes about your own group.

heterostereotypes Stereotypes about other groups.

concept A mental category we use to classify events, objects, situations, behaviors, or even people with respect to what we perceive as common properties.

categorization The process by which objects are grouped or classified together based on their perceived similarities

situations, behaviors, and people with respect to what we perceive as common properties. We use these common properties to aid us in classification or **categorization**, which refers to the process by which psychological concepts are grouped together. We form concepts so that we can evaluate information, make decisions, and act accordingly. It is easier and more efficient to create categories of information and to evaluate and act on those categories than it is to process each individual item. As general categories of mental concepts, stereotypes are aids that help us keep information about the world organized in our mental representations. We have such categorical representations about many objects in the world, and there is no way we could keep track of the world without them.

Stereotypes also occur because people make attributions about causes of their own and other people's behavior (see earlier this chapter), and because they have emotions that reinforce important cultural concepts and very complex emotional reactions to people of different groups (Cottrell & Neuberg, 2005). Forgas and colleagues have reported an interesting line of research on the role of emotion in person perception, intergroup discrimination, and stereotype judgments and have suggested the existence of mood-congruent bias in such judgments of others. In one study, Forgas and Moylan (1991) induced happy, sad, or neutral moods in participants, who then formed impressions about Asians or Caucasians interacting with same-race or other-race partners. Participants who were happy had more positive judgments of the target persons; participants who were sad had more negative judgments. The influence of mood on judgment was larger when the participants were judging mixed-race dyads. On the basis of these and similar findings (e.g., Forgas & Bower, 1987; Forgas & Fiedler, 1996), Forgas has suggested that the role of emotion or mood in these types of judgments may be greatest when participants engage in substantive processing, which requires them to select, learn, and interpret novel stimuli and to relate this information to preexisting knowledge (for a review of this affect infusion model, see Forgas, 1992, 1994). Forgas (1994) also suggested that stereotypic judgments of others are probably the least affected by emotion or mood when they involve the retrieval of preexisting stereotypes.

A recent study demonstrated how cultural stereotypes of social groups can be created spontaneously from random bits of information. In this study (Martin et al., 2014), information about novel social groups was passed down a chain of individuals. What was initially a random set of associations evolved into information about the group that was simplified and categorically structured. Over time, new stereotypes eventually emerged that were easy to learn and allowed for generalizations to be made with any prior exposure or knowledge to the social targets.

Although stereotypes are an inevitable aspect of our psychological life, problems occur because negative stereotypes are relatively easy to develop because our cultural upbringing, cultural filters, and inherent ethnocentrism and prejudice, all of which create a set of expectations in us about the behaviors and traits of others. That is, when we observe people from a different cultural background, we are often exposed to behaviors, activities, or situations that do not match our initial expectations based on our own cultural backgrounds. These observations can lead to negative attributions about the causes of those events or the underlying intentions or psychological characteristics of the actors being observed. Because such events are unexpected, they often require what Forgas (1994) would call "substantive processing," which is the type of processing most affected by emotion. If the emotion at the time is negative, which is a natural and the usual reaction to our witnessing something outside of our expectations, then that negative emotion will be more likely to contribute to negatively valenced attributions about the other person or group. Such negatively valenced attributions can form the core of a mental concept that may then be placed in a category of people. This negative attribution will also have a reinforcing effect on the value and expectation system that began the process. The result is a negative stereotype.

Once developed, stereotypes are easily reinforced. Our expectations change according to our stereotypes. We may selectively attend to events that appear to support our stereotypes, ignoring, albeit unconsciously, events and situations that challenge those stereotypes (Johnston, Hewstone, Pendry, & Frankish, 1994); that is, it is easy to vindicate our stereotypic ways of thinking. The *cocktail party phenomenon* illustrates how selective attention may contribute to stereotypes. People can often hear their own names across the room at a party even though many other sounds are occurring at the same time. People who believe an individual's characteristics are relatively fixed tend to pay more attention to stereotypic-consistent information than do people who believe an individual's characteristics are malleable, which may work to reinforce stereotypic thinking in the former group and hinder revising their stereotypes (Plaks, Stroessner, Dweck, & Sherman, 2001). Lyons and Kashima (2001) found that when people were presented with stereotypical and nonstereotypical information about a certain group (football players), they tended to remember and communicate to other people the stereotypical information rather than the nonstereotypical.

Even when events occur that are contrary to our stereotypic beliefs, we selectively do not attend to them, or come up with unique attributional processes to convince ourselves that our stereotype is correct. We may suggest that the observed event was a fluke or that the person observed was not a good representative of the group to which the stereotype applies. Such dismissals can occur quickly, with little conscious thought or effort, and are resistant to emotion at the time. In this case the question of why an individual would maintain a stereotype in the face of opposing data is interesting.

Stereotypes can also be created and perpetuated in individuals merely by communication of verbal labels from generation to generation, with no actual interaction with the people who are the target of the stereotype (Brislin, 1993). Stereotypes that are most easily talked about are most likely to persist over time. An understanding of the communicability of stereotypes is helpful in predicting the maintenance and modification in the contents of stereotypes of real groups in the real world (Schaller, Conway, & Tanchuk, 2002).

Stereotypes can be created and reinforced by television, movies, magazines, the Internet, and other media. Gender and class stereotypes are reinforced in popular television shows (Croteau & Hoynes, 2000). Men are more likely than women to be portrayed as having high status, traditionally male jobs (such as doctors or lawyers), and are less likely to be shown in the home. Fathers in working-class families are usually portrayed as incompetent yet lovable buffoons (e.g., Al Bundy, Homer Simpson), while middle-class fathers are depicted as competent at their jobs and as parents (Butsch, 1992).

It is important to distinguish between stereotype activation and application (Bargh, 1996; Devine, 1989; Gilbert & Hixon, 1991). Well-learned stereotypes are activated automatically (Blair, 2001), but whether people apply the stereotype or not depends on factors such as whether they are motivated to be nonprejudiced (Monteith, Sherman, & Devine, 1998) or are encouraged to be aware of egalitarian norms and standards (Macrae, Bodenhausen, & Milne, 1998).

Stereotypes can also change depending on major events. Bal-Tal and Labin (2001) conducted a longitudinal study of Israeli adolescents and their stereotypes of Palestinians, Jordanians, and Arabs. They administered surveys at a relatively peaceful time, directly after an attack by an extreme Palestinian group, and then again a few months later. Stereotypic judgments concerning Palestinians became more negative directly after the attack, but after a few months they returned to the initial baseline level. Their results supported the view that stereotypes are "fluid, variable, and context-dependent" (Oakes, Haslam, & Turner, 1994, p. 211). Thus, situational factors are also important.

Stereotypes may be formed through limited exposure to members of the target group or to exposure based on a "biased" sample. Stereotypes can be formed and reinforced in a person on the basis of very limited exposure, or no exposure at all, to the target group. The complex interplay of these external factors with our own cultural and psychological processes make stereotypes a difficult problem to deal with.

Stereotypes of ourselves (autostereotypes) and others are difficult to change because they become part of our self-system. They are intimately tied to our emotions, values, and core self and, as such, are difficult to change once we acquire them. Stereotypes are also tied to our emotion and value systems.

The Content of Stereotypes

Studies spanning many years have examined the content of stereotypes. In one of the oldest and most often cited studies, Katz and Braly (1933) gave undergraduate students a list of adjectives and asked them to select the traits they considered representative of ten different racial/ethnic groups. The 12 traits most frequently assigned to each group by the students are shown in the first column of Table 14.4. This study was followed up on the same university campus in 1951 (Gilbert, 1951) and again in 1969 (Karlins, Coffman, & Walters, 1969). There were a number of surprising changes over the years, both in stereotypes and in students' willingness to ascribe stereotypic traits to the various groups. The 12 traits most frequently selected for each group in 1951 and 1969 are listed in the second and third columns of Table 14.4.

To aid in interpreting the data, Karlins et al. (1969) asked a separate group of students to rate the favorableness of each of the adjectives used in the stereotype study, and then computed average favorableness scores for each of the ethnic groups rated across the adjectives selected for them. The results are given in Table 14.5. There were interesting changes in overall favorableness for the various groups across the years surveyed. Americans and Italians dropped in perceived favorableness, while Chinese, Japanese, and Jews increased in favorableness.

Madon and colleagues (2001) replicated and extended the original 1933, 1951, and 1969 studies in two studies. They obtained stereotype ratings of the various groups by European American and non-European American participants. In the first study, they used the same set of adjectives that Katz and Braly (1933) had used. In the second study, they used a more comprehensive list of trait adjectives. Stereotypes of all groups except the Irish had changed significantly across time; the biggest changes occurred in stereotypes of African Americans. Moreover, there was overall agreement in stereotypes between European Americans and non-European American raters. The results for ratings of European- and African Americans are in Tables 14.6 and 14.7.

People in all cultures have stereotypes of others, and in many cases, there are many commonalities in these stereotypes, even across cultures (Nichols & McAndrew, 1984; Smith, Griffith, Griffith, & Steger, 1980; Forgas & O'Driscoll, 1984; Walkey & Chung, 1996; Williams & Best, 1994). There is often ingroup bias in one's stereotypes, with the exception of white Americans, who have been demonstrated to have ingroup derogation (Burton, Greenberger, & Hayward, 2005). Having stereotypes, therefore, is a universal phenomenon, and the content of many stereotypes may also share some universal features.

But there are also cultural differences in stereotypes. For example, citizens of smaller nations tend to have more negative stereotypes about larger nations, especially if they border each other, whereas citizens of larger nations tend to have more positive stereotypes about smaller nations (Van Oudenhoven, Selenko, & Otten, 2009).

TABLE 14.4 The 12 Traits Most Frequently Assigned to Various Racial and National Groups by Princeton Students from 1933 to 1969

Trait	Percentage Checking Trait		
	Katz and Braly (1933)	Gilbert (1951)	Karlins, Coffman, and Walters (1969)
Germans			
Scientifically minded	78	62	47
Industrious	65	50	59
Stolid	44	10	9
Intelligent	32	32	19
Methodical	31	20	21
Extremely nationalistic	24	50	43
Progressive	16	3	13
Efficient	16	—	46
Jovial	15	—	5
Musical	13	—	4
Persistent	11	—	4
Practical	11	—	9
Aggressive[a]	—	27	30
Arrogant[a]	—	23	18
Ambitious[b]	—	—	15
Italians			
Artistic	53	28	30
Impulsive	44	19	28
Passionate	37	25	44
Quick-tempered	35	15	28
Musical	32	22	9
Imaginative	30	20	7
Very religious	21	33	25
Talkative	21	23	23
Revengeful	17	—	0
Physically dirty	13	—	4
Lazy	12	—	0
Unreliable	11	—	3
Pleasure loving[a]	—	28	33
Loyal to family ties[b]	—	—	26
Sensual[b]	—	—	19
Argumentative[b]	—	—	19

Trait	Percentage Checking Trait		
	Katz and Braly (1933)	Gilbert (1951)	Karlins, Coffman, and Walters (1969)
Negroes			
Superstitious	84	41	13
Lazy	75	31	26
Happy-go-lucky	38	17	27
Ignorant	38	24	11
Musical	26	33	47
Ostentatious	26	11	25
Very religious	24	17	8
Stupid	22	10	4
Physically dirty	17	—	3
Naïve	14	—	4
Slovenly	13	—	5
Unreliable	12	—	6
Pleasure loving[a]	—	19	26
Sensitive[b]	—	—	17
Gregarious[b]	—	—	17
Talkative[b]	—	—	14
Imitative[b]	—	—	13
Irish			
Pugnacious	45	24	13
Quick-tempered	39	35	43
Witty	38	16	7
Honest	32	11	17
Very religious	29	30	27
Industrious	21	8	8
Extremely nationalistic	21	20	41
Superstitious	18	—	11
Quarrelsome	14	—	5
Imaginative	13	—	3
Aggressive	13	—	5
Stubborn	13	—	23

(continues)

TABLE 14.4 (*Continued*)

Trait	Percentage Checking Trait			Trait	Percentage Checking Trait		
	Katz and Braly (1933)	Gilbert (1951)	Karlins, Coffman, and Walters (1969)		Katz and Braly (1933)	Gilbert (1951)	Karlins, Coffman, and Walters (1969)
Tradition loving[b]	—	—	25	**Americans**			
Loyal to family ties[b]	—	—	23	Industrious	48	30	23
Argumentative[b]	—	—	20	Intelligent	47	32	20
Boastful[b]	—	—	17	Materialistic	33	37	67
English				Ambitious	33	21	42
Sportsmanlike	53	21	22	Progressive	27	5	17
Intelligent	46	29	23	Pleasure-loving	26	27	28
Conventional	34	25	19	Alert	23	7	7
Tradition-loving	31	42	21	Efficient	21	9	15
Conservative	30	22	53	Aggressive	20	8	15
Reserved	29	39	40	Straightforward	19	—	9
Sophisticated	27	36	47	Practical	19	—	12
Courteous	21	17	17	Sportsmanlike	19	—	9
Honest	20	11	17	Individualistic[a]	—	26	15
Industrious	18	—	17	Conventional[b]	—	—	17
Extremely nationalistic	18	—	7	Scientifically minded[b]	—	—	15
Humorless	17	—	11	Ostentatious[b]	—	—	15
Practical[b]	—	—	25	**Chinese**			
Jews				Superstitious	34	18	8
Shrewd	79	47	30	Sly	29	4	6
Mercenary	49	28	15	Conservative	29	14	15
Industrious	48	29	33	Tradition-loving	26	26	32
Grasping	34	17	17	Loyal to family ties	22	35	50
Intelligent	29	37	37	Industrious	18	18	23
Ambitious	21	28	48	Meditative	19	—	21
Sly	20	14	7	Reserved	17	18	15
Loyal to family ties	15	19	19	Very religious	15	—	6
Persistent	13	—	9	Ignorant	15	—	7
Talkative	13	—	3	Deceitful	14	—	5
Aggressive	12	—	23	Quiet	13	19	23
Very religious	12	—	7	Courteous[b]	—	—	20
Materialistic[b]	—	—	46	Extremely Nationalistic[b]	—	—	19
Practical[b]	—	—	19	Humorless[b]	—	—	17
				Artistic[b]	—	—	15

TABLE 14.4 (Continued)

Trait	Percentage Checking Trait			Trait	Percentage Checking Trait		
	Katz and Braly (1933)	Gilbert (1951)	Karlins, Coffman, and Walters (1969)		Katz and Braly (1933)	Gilbert (1951)	Karlins, Coffman, and Walters (1969)
Japanese				**Turks**			
Intelligent	45	11	20	Cruel	47	12	9
Industrious	43	12	57	Very religious	26	6	7
Progressive	24	2	17	Treacherous	21	3	13
Shrewd	22	13	7	Sensual	20	4	9
Sly	20	21	3	Ignorant	15	7	13
Quiet	19	—	14	Physically dirty	15	7	14
Imitative	17	24	22	Deceitful	13	—	7
Alert	16	—	11	Sly	12	7	7
Suave	16	—	0	Quarrelsome	12	—	9
Neat	16	—	7	Revengeful	12	—	6
Treacherous	13	17	1	Conservative	12	—	11
Aggressive	13	—	19	Superstitious	11		5
Extremely nationalistic[a]	—	18	21	Aggressive[b]	—	—	17
Ambitious[b]	—	—	33	Quick Tempered[b]	—	—	13
Efficient[b]	—	—	27	Impulsive[b]	—	—	12
Loyal to family ties[b]	—	—	23	Conventional[b]	—	—	10
Courteous[b]	—	—	22	Pleasure loving[b]	—	—	11
				Slovenly[b]	—	—	10

Source: Karlins et al. (1969).

a - Additional traits added by Gilbert (1951)
b - New traits added in 1967 to account for 10 most frequently selected traits then

TABLE 14.5 Favorableness Ratings of Traits from Karlins et al. (1969)

Ethnic Group	1933	1951	1969
Americans	.99	.86	.49
Chinese	−.12	.25	.46
English	.63	.59	.51
Germans	.89	.57	.77
Irish	.14	.00	−.13
Italians	.48	.44	.27
Japanese	.66	−.14	.84
Jews	.24	.45	.66
Negroes	−.70	−.37	−.07
Turks	−.98	−.103	−.62

TABLE 14.6 American Stereotypes

Attribute	Katz and Braly (1933)	Gilbert (1951)	Karlins, Coffman, and Walters (1969)	Study 1		Study 2	
				EA	NEA	EA	NEA
Industrious	48.5	30.0	23.0	23.2	15.8	12.9	11.8
Intelligent	47.5	32.0	20.0	17.9	26.3	6.5	11.8
Materialistic	33.3	37.0	67.0	53.6	36.8	25.8	29.4
Ambitious	33.3	21.0	42.0	10.7	10.5	16.1	5.9
Progressive	27.3	5.0	17.0	10.7	7.9	6.5	5.9
Pleasure loving	26.3	27.0	28.0	26.8	26.3	16.1	12.5
Alert	23.2	7.0	7.0	1.8	2.6	12.9	5.9
Efficient	21.2	9.0	15.0	3.6	2.6	6.5	5.9
Aggressive	20.2	8.0	15.0	12.5	15.8	19.4	11.8
Straightforward	19.2	—	9.0	8.9	7.9	12.9	0.0
Practical	19.2	—	12.0	1.8	5.3	9.7	0.0
Sportsmanlike	19.2	—	9.0	7.1	15.8	9.7	11.8
Individualistic	—	26.0	15.0	28.6	31.6	22.6	5.9
Conventional	—	—	17.0	5.4	5.3	9.7	0.0
Scientifically minded	—	—	15.0	7.1	7.9	9.7	12.5
Ostentatious	—	—	15.0	8.9	7.9	6.9	0.0
Lazy	—	—	—	30.4	15.8	22.6	23.5
Extremely nationalistic	—	—	—	19.6	15.8	9.7	17.7
Ignorant	—	—	—	16.1	13.2	9.7	0.0
Impulsive	—	—	—	16.1	7.9	22.6	11.8
Arrogant	—	—	—	14.3	15.8	19.4	5.9
Rude	—	—	—	14.3	7.9	16.1	11.8
Diverse[a]	—	—	—	—	—	64.5	41.2
Democratic[a]	—	—	—	—	—	32.3	23.5
Listen to a lot of music[a]	—	—	—	—	—	32.3	17.7
Flirtatious[a]	—	—	—	—	—	30.0	6.3
Competitive[a]	—	—	—	—	—	29.0	17.7
Loud	—	—	—	—	—	29.0	5.9
Outspoken[a]	—	—	—	—	—	29.0	5.9
Stubborn	—	—	—	—	—	29.0	5.9
Interests wide[a]	—	—	—	—	—	26.7	6.3
Adventurous[a]	—	—	—	—	—	25.8	12.5
Boastful	—	—	—	—	—	25.8	5.9
Cool[a]	—	—	—	—	—	25.8	0.0
Hard-headed[a]	—	—	—	—	—	25.8	5.9
Independent[a]	—	—	—	—	—	25.8	5.9
Leaders[a]	—	—	—	—	—	25.8	11.8

TABLE 14.6 *(Continued)*

Attribute	Katz and Braly (1933)	Gilbert (1951)	Karlins, Coffman, and Walters (1969)	Study 1 EA	Study 1 NEA	Study 2 EA	Study 2 NEA
Liberal[a]	—	—	—	—	—	25.8	11.8
Opinionated[a]	—	—	—	—	—	25.8	18.8
Rebellious[a]	—	—	—	—	—	25.8	23.5
Prejudiced[a]	—	—	—	—	—	19.4	35.3
Superficial[a]	—	—	—	—	—	12.9	29.4
Emotional[a]	—	—	—	—	—	9.7	25.0
Complaining[a]	—	—	—	—	—	16.1	23.5
Cruel	—	—	—	—	—	12.9	23.5
Greedy[a]	—	—	—	—	—	19.4	23.5
Patriotic[a]	—	—	—	—	—	16.1	23.5
Politically active[a]	—	—	—	—	—	6.5	23.5
Proud[a]	—	—	—	—	—	19.4	23.5
Racists[a]	—	—	—	—	—	16.1	23.5
Show-offs[a]	—	—	—	—	—	*22.6*	*23.5*
Spoiled[a]	—	—	—	—	—	22.6	23.5

NOTE: EA refers to the European American samples; NEA refers to the non–European American samples. For the Princeton trilogy and Study 1, values reflect the percentage of participants who endorsed an attribute as one of the five most characteristic of Americans. For Study 2, values reflect the percentage of participants who endorsed an attribute as "much more characteristic of Americans than other people." Attributes without superscripts are from Katz and Braly's attribute list. Values in italics correspond to the 10 most frequently endorsed attributes for Studies 1 and 2. In the case of ties, attributes with the same percentages are listed.

Source: Reprint of Madon et al. (2001) Reference Crediting: Madon, S., Guyll, M., Aboufadel, K., Montiel, E., Smith, A., Palumbo, P., & Jussim, L. (2001). Ethnic and national stereotypes: The Princeton trilogy revisited and revised. Personality and Social Psychology Bulletin, 27(8), 996–1010.

a. Identifies attributes added in Study 2.

TABLE 14.7 African American Stereotypes

Attribute	Katz and Braly (1933)	Gilbert (1951)	Karlins, Coffman, and Walters (1969)	Study 1 EA	Study 1 NEA	Study 2 EA	Study 2 NEA
Superstitious	84.0	41.0	13.0	1.7	5.3	0.0	4.2
Lazy	75.0	31.0	26.0	12.1	10.5	0.0	4.2
Happy-go-lucky	38.0	17.0	27.0	0.0	7.9	0.0	4.2
Ignorant	38.0	24.0	11.0	10.3	13.2	3.5	0.0
Musical	26.0	33.0	47.0	27.6	39.5	3.5	33.3
Ostentatious	26.0	11.0	25.0	8.6	5.3	0.0	4.6
Very religious	24.0	17.0	8.0	19.0	13.2	6.9	16.7
Stupid	22.0	10.0	4.0	1.7	0.0	0.0	0.0
Physically dirty	17.0	—	3.0	0.0	0.0	3.5	0.0
Naive	14.0	—	4.0	1.7	0.0	0.0	0.0
Slovenly	13.0	—	5.0	3.5	7.9	0.0	0.0

(continues)

TABLE 14.7 (*Continued*)

Attribute	Katz and Braly (1933)	Gilbert (1951)	Karlins, Coffman, and Walters (1969)	Study 1		Study 2	
				EA	NEA	EA	NEA
Unreliable	12.0	—	6.0	5.2	5.3	0.0	0.0
Pleasure loving	—	19.0	26.0	5.2	0.0	0.0	25.0
Sensitive	—	—	17.0	5.2	0.0	0.0	4.2
Gregarious	—	—	17.0	6.9	5.3	0.0	8.7
Talkative	—	—	14.0	10.3	13.2	6.9	20.8
Imitative	—	—	13.0	1.7	0.0	3.5	8.3
Loyal to family ties	—	—	—	22.4	13.2	3.5	12.5
Loud	—	—	—	20.7	52.6	6.9	20.8
Tradition loving	—	—	—	20.7	7.9	3.5	8.3
Aggressive	—	—	—	15.5	18.4	0.0	16.7
Artistic	—	—	—	13.8	5.3	3.5	8.3
Quick tempered	—	—	—	13.8	15.8	6.9	16.7
Revengeful	—	—	—	13.8	5.3	0.0	8.3
Rude	—	—	—	13.8	26.3	0.0	20.8
Quarrelsome	—	—	—	8.6	18.4	0.0	20.8
Sportsmanlike	—	—	—	12.1	15.8	6.9	25.0
Intelligent	—	—	—	3.5	13.2	0.0	4.2
Materialistic	—	—	—	8.6	13.2	0.0	8.3
Passionate	—	—	—	8.6	13.2	0.0	16.7
Straightforward	—	—	—	12.1	13.2	6.9	21.7
Listen to a lot of music[a]	—	—	—	—	—	17.2	25.0
Noisy[a]	—	—	—	—	—	17.2	25.0
Athletic[a]	—	—	—	—	—	13.8	26.1
Have an attitude[a]	—	—	—	—	—	13.8	25.0
Prejudiced[a]	—	—	—	—	—	13.8	20.8
Sing and dance well[a]	—	—	—	—	—	13.8	20.8
Cultural[a]	—	—	—	—	—	10.7	8.3
Democratic[a]	—	—	—	—	—	10.3	4.2
Angry[a]	—	—	—	—	—	10.3	20.8
Masculine[a]	—	—	—	—	—	10.3	8.3
Opinionated[a]	—	—	—	—	—	10.3	29.2
Outspoken[a]	—	—	—	—	—	10.3	12.5
Tough[a]	—	—	—	—	—	6.9	33.3
Humorous[a]	—	—	—	—	—	3.5	30.4
Rebellious[a]	—	—	—	—	—	0.0	29.2
Active[a]	—	—	—	—	—	0.0	25.0
Bossy[a]	—	—	—	—	—	0.0	25.0

TABLE 14.7 (*Continued*)

Attribute	Katz and Braly (1933)	Gilbert (1951)	Karlins, Coffman, and Walters (1969)	Study 1		Study 2	
				EA	NEA	EA	NEA
Energetic[a]	—	—	—	—	—	0.0	25.0
Outgoing[a]	—	—	—	—	—	0.0	25.0
Proud[a]	—	—	—	—	—	3.5	25.0
Show-offs[a]	—	—	—	—	—	0.0	25.0
Strong[a]	—	—	—	—	—	3.5	25.0

NOTE: EA refers to the European American samples; NEA refers to the non–European American samples. For the Princeton trilogy and Study 1, values reflect the percentage of participants who endorsed an attribute as one of the five most characteristic of African Americans. For Study 2, values reflect the percentage of participants who endorsed an attribute as "much more characteristic of African Americans than other people." Attributes without superscripts are from Katz and Braly's attribute list. Values in italics correspond to the 10 most frequently endorsed attributes for Studies 1 and 2. In the case of ties, attributes with the same percentages are listed.

Source: Reprint of Madon et al. (2001) Reference Crediting: Madon, S., Guyll, M., Aboufadel, K., Montiel, E., Smith, A., Palumbo, P., & Jussim, L. (2001). Ethnic and national stereotypes: The Princeton trilogy revisited and revised. Personality and Social Psychology Bulletin, 27(8), 996–1010.

a - Refers to traits added in Study 2.

Although stereotypes are useful as categories in terms of helping us organize information, they are dangerous if applied to people uniformly without recognizing the vast individual differences that occur within any cultural or ethnic group. Recall, for instance, the construct of stereotype threat that we discussed in Chapter 8. Cohen and Garcia (2005) also demonstrated the existence of **collective threat**: the fear that an ingroup member's behavior can reinforce negative stereotypes about one's group. Collective threat resulted in lower self-esteem, lower academic performance, self-stereotyping, and physical distancing from the ingroup member whose behavior reinforced the negative stereotype. Even the **model minority stereotype** of Asian Americans in the United States has its drawbacks, because it has been demonstrated that this stereotype has two components: excessive competence coupled with deficient sociality (Lin, Kwan, Cheung, & Fiske, 2005).

collective threat The fear that an ingroup member's behavior can reinforce negative stereotypes about one's group.

model minority stereotype The stereotype of Asian Americans as overachievers.

Ethnocentrism and Prejudice

Ethnocentrism is the tendency to view the world through one's own cultural filters. With this definition, and understanding about how we acquire those filters, it follows that just about everyone in the world is ethnocentric. That is, everyone learns a certain way of behaving, and in doing so learns a certain way of perceiving and interpreting the behaviors of others. This way of perceiving and making interpretations about others is a normal consequence of growing up in society. A large goal of enculturation (Chapter 3) is learning what is normal, right, appropriate, and good. By doing so, however, we also learn what is abnormal, incorrect, inappropriate, and bad. Just as we learn how to attach these labels to our own behavior, we use those standards to judge others' behaviors. Herein lies the beginnings of ethnocentrism in all of us. In this sense, ethnocentrism per se is neither bad nor good; it merely reflects the state of affairs—that we all have our cultural filters when we perceive others.

ethnocentrism The tendency to view the world through one's own cultural filters.

Prejudice refers to the tendency to prejudge others on the basis of their group membership. Prejudice has a cognitive (thinking) component and an affective (feeling) component. Stereotypes form the basis of the cognitive component of prejudice. The affective component comprises one's feelings toward other groups of people, which

prejudice The tendency to prejudge others on the basis of their group membership.

may include anger, contempt, resentment, or disdain, or even compassion, sympathy, and closeness (Fiske, Cuddy, Glick, & Xu, 2002). Although the cognitive and affective components are often related, they need not be, and may exist independently of each other within the same person. That is, a person may have feelings about a particular group of people without being able to specify a stereotype about them; and a person may have stereotypic beliefs about others that are detached from their feelings.

explicit prejudice
Prejudice that is verbalized and thus made public.

Ethnocentrism and prejudice can be explicit or implicit. **Explicit prejudice** refers to prejudice that is verbalized and thus made public. Conducting studies on prejudice using explicit measures, however, is difficult, because respondents may be biased to respond in socially desirable or politically correct ways (see Chapter 2). Unsurprisingly, researchers who have examined studies on explicit prejudice over the past half-century have concluded that explicit prejudice is actually on the decline (Wittenbrink, Judd, & Park, 1997).

implicit prejudice
Prejudicial attitudes, values, or beliefs that are unspoken and perhaps even outside conscious awareness.

In recent years, an interesting test has been developed that supposedly measures **implicit prejudice**, which refers to prejudicial attitudes, values, or beliefs that are unspoken and perhaps even outside conscious awareness. This test is called the Implicit Association Test (IAT) (Greenwald, McGhee, & Schwartz, 1998). Participants are shown pairs of stimuli, such as faces of European American or African American individuals, and adjectives such as good and bad, and are asked to make an evaluation of the pair (such as whether the pairing is accurate or not). Implicit attitudes are measured by the amount of time respondents take to make their judgments; faster times supposedly reflect stronger implicit beliefs. Studies that have used both explicit (e.g., questionnaires) and implicit measures (like the IAT) have reported that they are correlated, but to a very small degree (Hoffman, Gawronski, Gschwendner, Le, & Schmitt, 2005).

Pena, Sidanius, and Sawyer (2004) used both implicit and explicit measures to determine prejudice toward whites and blacks in four countries—the United States, Cuba, Dominican Republic, and Puerto Rico. There were no differences in attitudes on the explicit measure; on the implicit measure, however, whites were judged more favorably than blacks by all groups, which included both white and black participants (see Figure 14.2). This finding is interesting because the implicit racial prejudice against blacks was found among Latin American participants with African heritage as well.

Prejudicial attitudes and judgments are quick, automatic, and often based on physical features such as in the face (Blair, Judd, & Fallman, 2004; Maddox, 2005). Individuals from racial and ethnic groups other than one's own are often associated unconsciously with fear, among both white and black Americans (Olsson, Ebert, Banaji, & Phelps, 2005). Ethnocentric, prejudicial attitudes are more strongly related to the strength of one's own ingroup attitudes (Duckitt, Callaghan, & Wagner, 2005).

Social identity theory (Tajfel & Turner, 1986) is helpful in understanding stereotypes and prejudice. According to this theory, we categorize people into social groups and place ourselves within a category. We are motivated to positively evaluate our own social group (ingroup) in comparison to other groups (outgroups) in order to maintain a positive social identity.

The Origins of Prejudice

There are many factors that contribute to the apparent universality of ethnocentrism and prejudice. One may be that they are the outcomes of social biology and evolution (see, for example, Van den Berghe, 1981). This argument suggests that sentiments about ethnicity and race are logical extensions of kinship sentiment—that is, the favoring of kin over nonkin. Kinship sentiments are biologically and evolutionarily functional, increasing the likelihood of one's own genes being transmitted to future generations. Because racial and ethnic groups may be viewed as extensions of kin, these sentiments may predispose people to behave more favorably to such kin.

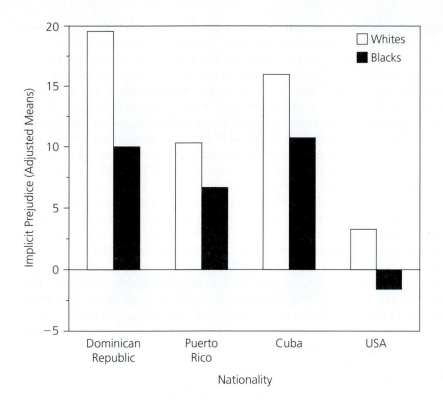

FIGURE 14.2 Symbols Used to Evaluate Good and Bad

Source: van de Vijver, F. J. R., *Journal of Cross-Cultural Psychology*, vol. 35, no. 6, Nov. 2004, p. 754.
Copyright © 2004 by Fons J. R. van de Vijver. Reprinted by Permission of Sage Publications, Inc.

If kinship sentiments apply to ethnicity and race, this argument continues, prejudice and discrimination may indeed be fundamental and inevitable.

Theories concerning intergroup conflict and power also explain ethnocentrism and prejudice (Duckitt, 1992; Healey, 1998). These suggest that the competition that naturally occurs among groups in any society—whether for power, prestige, status, or wealth—produces prejudicial and discriminatory thoughts, feelings, and actions among both those in power (the "haves") and those without (the "have-nots"). Such prejudice and discrimination on both sides, but especially on the part of the haves, can serve as a justification to exploit the have-nots. As such, prejudice and discrimination require an identifying variable or characteristic to which they can become attached. Race, ethnicity, or social class is often used as that marker (see also Mirande, 1985; Moore, 1988).

Social and cultural factors also play a role, in that society may promote ideological prejudice and institutional discrimination in order to impose inferior status on some groups. This inferior status reinforces ideological prejudice and institutional discrimination, which themselves further reinforce the inferior status. Children growing up in such societies, whether as members of the "inferior" or the "superior" group, become enculturated in these ways of thinking, feeling, and acting, which become a part of their own operating culture, thus ensuring the reenactment of this cycle of exploitation. Jane Elliot, a schoolteacher in the 1960s, is well known for her Blue-Eyed/Brown-Eyed classroom exercises, in which she demonstrated how quickly children can learn to become discriminatory simply based on the messages they are told about a particular group. In this exercise, she divided the children into brown-eyed and blue-eyed groups and told one group they were superior, more talented, and better than the other. She found that in a short time the children actually took on the stereotypes of these groups and began to act in discriminatory ways toward one another.

Some aspects of personality may also contribute to prejudice. Of particular note is the work on the relationship between authoritarian personality and prejudice (Adorno, Frenkel-Brunswick, Levinson, & Sanford, 1950, cited in Healey, 1998). Early work suggested that prejudicial thoughts and feelings and discriminatory behaviors are an integral part of authoritarian personalities, and that people with such personalities in fact require prejudicial thoughts and feelings to function effectively in their lives and in society. More recent research, however, has suggested a more precise relationship between authoritarianism and prejudice. Verkuyten and Hagendoorn (1998), for example, conducted two studies that examined the interaction of self-categorization, authoritarian personality, ingroup stereotypes, and prejudicial attitudes. Participants were instructed to focus on themselves either as unique individuals (personal identity condition) or as members of a larger group (national identity condition). They also completed an authoritarian personality questionnaire, provided data about their stereotypes regarding their own group, and rated three different outgroups in terms of prejudicial attitudes. Authoritarian personality predicted prejudicial attitudes only when the participants focused on their personal identities. When participants focused on their national identities, their ingroup stereotypes predicted their prejudicial attitudes, but authoritarianism did not. Personality variables may be salient only when the reference for prejudicial thought is oneself as an individual, and not as a member of a larger group.

The Contact Hypothesis

contact hypothesis
The proposition that contact between groups is especially effective in reducing prejudice.

Many years ago, Allport (1954) made a famous proposition, claiming that contact between groups is especially effective in reducing prejudice. This became known as the **contact hypothesis** in intergroup relations. Allport also claimed that the effects of contact would be optimal if four conditions were met: there was equal status between the groups in the situation, they had common goals, the situation required cooperation, and they received support from authorities, law, or custom. Research over the years has tended to support the hypothesis; Pettigrew and Tropp (2006) conducted a meta-analysis involving 713 samples from 515 studies, and reported that not only did intergroup contact tend to reduce intergroup prejudice, but contact under the four optimal conditions proposed by Allport led to greater reductions in prejudice. These authors suggested therefore that future work should identify the negative factors that prevent intergroup contact from occurring in the first place.

Research involving longitudinal designs has extended this finding. Individuals who were ethnic minorities or majorities in Germany, Belgium, and England were assessed on intergroup friendship, anxiety, and prejudice at two times, six months apart (Binder et al., 2009). Contact indeed reduced prejudice, as predicted by the contact hypothesis, but prejudice also reduced contact. Contact effects were negligible for minority members, replicating previous findings (Tropp & Pettigrew, 2005), and which suggested interesting limitations to the contact hypothesis.

Discrimination

discrimination The unfair treatment of others based on their group membership.

Discrimination refers to the unfair treatment of others based on their group membership. The difference between prejudice and discrimination is the difference between thinking/feeling (prejudice) and doing (discrimination). Like stereotypes and prejudice, discrimination can include preferential or positive treatment as well as deferred or negative treatment. The important issue in defining discrimination revolves around the concept of fairness and treatment based on group membership.

When prejudice and discrimination occur on the group or organizational level, they are known as various "-isms" and institutional discrimination. Racism, classism, and sexism are a few of the many examples of the prejudicial thoughts and feelings that can be harbored by people about groups. Although prejudice can be either positive or negative in content, -isms are usually negative and derogatory, used to justify inferior status on the part of the people being characterized. *Prejudice* describes preferential thoughts and feelings held by an individual; *-isms* are prejudices that are held by one group of people about another. As such, they generally constitute systems of ideas, beliefs, and opinions held by a large group of people and are often woven into the social and cultural fabric of that group. They constitute an ideology that can be communicated from one generation to the next, much as other elements of culture are communicated (see Healey, 1998).

Institutional discrimination is discrimination that occurs on the level of a large group, society, organization, or institution. It is unequal or unfair patterns of behavior or preferential treatment of people by a large group or organization solely on the basis of group membership. Institutional discrimination can exist in the explicit or explicit rules or norms of an organization, such as in the recruitment, hiring, reward and punishment systems. These patterns of treatment may or may not be conscious and deliberate. Allegations concerning such institutional discrimination are all around us in the daily news, involving the educational system, places of business and work, the legal and criminal justice systems, and professional sports.

Experiencing discrimination across the lifespan is linked with negative mental health outcomes such as major depression and generalized anxiety disorder (Sellers & Shelton, 2003). These effects are comparable to the effects of traumatic life events, such as sexual assault or combat exposure (Kessler, Mickelson, & Williams, 1999). Chronic exposure to racial discrimination has been linked with greater daily discrimination and greater psychological distress (Ong, Fuller-Rowell, & Burrow, 2009). These findings highlight the need for us, as psychologists and concerned citizens of the world, to gather as much data as possible about the social and psychological consequences of programs and policies related to allegations of -isms or institutional discrimination and to become fully educated and informed about the issues.

institutional discrimination Discrimination that occurs on the level of a large group, society, organization, or institution.

▶ Culture and Aggression

Aggression is any act or behavior that intentionally hurts another person, either physically or psychologically. Culture plays an important role in contributing to aggression because culture facilitates or prohibits the channeling of the expression of aggressive behaviors as a means of social control (Bond, 2004a); that is, aggression can be considered a form of coercive control occurs in all cultures. As we discussed in Chapter 1, all cultures represent some form of solutions to a universal set of problems that humans face around the world in order to survive. These problems concern how to distribute desired materials, goods, and resources among group members, while at the same time maintaining social order and harmony. In order to do this, all cultures develop norms. Norms often favor some people while not favoring others. Violations of norms by individuals or groups who are perceived as competitors for those same resources are conceptualized as aggressive; these perceptions, in turn, stimulate a process of counterattack, which further escalates violence.

Understanding aggression and violence requires an understanding of the cultural context within which it occurs. This is apparent in examining cultures of honor. *Honor* refers to respect, esteem, or admiration, and some cultures can be characterized as **cultures of honor**, in which norms place a strong emphasis on status and

aggression Any act or behavior that intentionally hurts another person, either physically or psychologically.

cultures of honor Cultures in which norms place a strong emphasis on status and reputation.

reputation. In these cultures, insults, threats, and sexual infidelity especially threaten one's honor, which can lead to violence and aggression. Higher rates of violent crimes and other aggressive acts in the U.S. South, for instance, have been linked to a "Southern culture of honor" (Nisbett, 1993). In one study (Cohen, Nisbett, Bowdle, & Schwarz, 1996), participants were purposefully bumped by a research confederate and called an "asshole." Individuals born and raised in the northern United States were relatively unaffected by the insult; those from the South, however, were more likely to believe that their masculinity was threatened, were more upset, more physiologically and cognitively primed for aggression, and were more likely to actually engage in aggressive behavior. These acts were interpreted as attempts to restore lost honor. Cortisol and testosterone levels were elevated in the Southern sample.

The culture of honor is also at work in many cases of domestic violence, especially by males toward females because of actual or perceived infidelity or promiscuity. In cultures of honor, female infidelity or promiscuity is considered to bring dishonor and disgrace to a man and his family. The damage to the reputation can be restored through violence, and women in such relationships are expected to remain loyal to the man and family despite such violence (Vandello & Cohen, 2003). Cultural values emphasizing female loyalty, sacrifice, and male honor may be used to sanction violence toward women who even remain in abusive relationships (Vandello, Cohen, Grandon, & Franiuk, 2009). Norms regarding male-honor-related aggression may have been created years ago and persist in the U.S. South even though they are no longer functional (Vandello, Cohen, & Ransom, 2008).

Honor culture may also play a role in depression and suicide. Osterman and Brown (2011) conducted three studies and reported that honor states in the United States had significantly higher rates of both male and female suicide than did non-honor states, especially in rural areas, and that levels of major depression was higher in honor states. The authors suggested that the honor culture allows people in those cultures to consider death as an option when failure occurs or threats to honor or reputation happens.

Honor is an important cultural construct in many countries of the world, especially around the Mediterranean and the Middle East (Rodriguez Mosquera, Manstead, & Fischer, 2002). Life in the Pashtun region of Afghanistan, for instance, is organized around *Pashtunwali*—or way of the Pashtun (Rubin, 2010). The foundation of this code is a man's honor, which is evaluated by three possessions—gold, land, and women. If injury is caused to a man's gold, land, or women, it is a matter of honor to exact revenge. If a woman is disloyal, disrespectful, or caught in infidelity, it is a matter of honor to be violent toward the woman and others involved.

The culture-of-honor construct is not the only one at work in influencing aggression across cultures. Archer (2006) analyzed data across 52 nations and showed that the rates and types of physical aggression between partners differed across cultures. Cultures that were more individualistic and egalitarian had less female victimization and more male victimization. Across countries, rates of murder and other crimes have been correlated with levels of stress and social support systems (Landau, 1984). Countries with hotter and more humid climates have been associated with higher murder rates (Robbins, DeWalt, & Pelto, 1972), and this tendency has also been documented for U.S. states (Anderson & Anderson, 1996). Exposure to violent video games appears to cause increased aggressive behavior, and this effect occurs across cultures (Anderson et al., 2010). Some cultures have norms of aggression, such as the Yanomami of Venezuela and Brazil, a cultural group well known for its aggressive tendencies both within the group and toward outsiders, and often referred to as the "fierce people" (Sponsel, 1998).

Both ecological and individual-level factors predict homicide rates. In one study involving 56 countries, homicide was predicted by economic inequality, lower per capita gross national product (GNP), and the ratio of males to females in the society (negatively) on the ecological level. On the individual level, lower trust in fellow citizens, belief in less social complexity, and preference for mates of higher status as opposed to love also predicted national homicide rates (Lim, Bond, & Bond, 2005). Recent research even among mobile forager band societies has shown that most lethal aggression events are perpetrated by lone individuals and stem from accidents, interfamilial disputes, within-group executions, or interpersonal motives (such as competition over a woman) rather than coalitionary-type group-based action against other groups (i.e., war; see Fry & Soderberg, 2013).

Climate also has a strong influence on aggression and conflict. A recent review involving 60 quantitative studies from archeology, criminology, economics, geography, history, political science, and psychology indicated convincingly that changes in climate to either warmer temperatures or more extreme rainfalls were associated with increases in both interpersonal and intergroup violence. More specifically, for each 1 standard deviation change in climate, there was a 4% increase in interpersonal violence, and a 14% increase in intergroup violence (Hsiang, Burke, & Miguel, 2013).

Cultures also facilitate racial microaggressions, which are "brief and commonplace daily verbal, behavioral and environmental indignities, whether intentional or unintentional, that communicate hostile, derogatory, or negative racial slights and insults to the target person or group" (Sue et al., 2007, p. 271). They often appear in everyday situations, such as when talking to a sales clerk, or with your employer or even friends and acquaintances. They have consequences for the mental and physical health of the targets, create a hostile environment, and lower productivity and problem solving abilities. They trigger difficult dialogues in the classroom (Sue, Lin, Torino, Capodilupo, & Rivera, 2009), and more negative emotions in ethnic minorities compared to the same microaggressions against ethnic majority individuals (Wang, Leu, & Shoda, 2011).

Examining the influence of culture on aggression and violence can provide us with different ways of understanding why violence and wars occur around the world. Across time in history, for example, many wars can be considered clashes of culture, and the potential for such clashes to occur may increase as our world becomes a functionally smaller place with improvements in communication and transportation technologies. Culture is a vital construct to incorporate in understanding terrorism, suicide bombers, and genocide (Atran & Axelrod, 2007; Ginges, Hansen, & Norenzayan, 2009; Rudmin, 2004), all of which are central topics in the lives of all citizens of the world today. Hopefully, recognizing the contributions of culture to this process can lead to more peaceful ways of being.

▶ Acculturation

The final topic we explore in this chapter concerns **acculturation**, which is the process by which people adapt to and adopt a different cultural system. Understanding the process of acculturation is important for many individuals in the world today, including not only immigrants and sojourners (such as international students), but also refugees, asylum seekers, and those whose countries are overcome by war. Examining acculturation involves the understanding of two related but different components: **intercultural adaptation**, which refers to how people *adapt* or *change their behaviors*

acculturation The process by which people adopt a different cultural system. The process of individual change and adaptation as a result of continuous contact with a new, distinct, or different culture.

intercultural adaptation How people change their behaviors or ways of thinking in a new cultural environment.

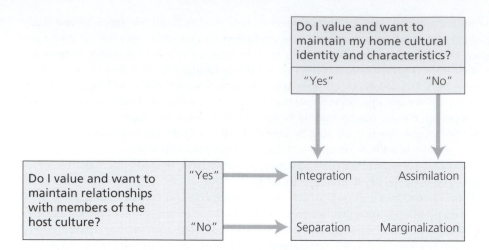

FIGURE 14.3 Berry's Four Basic Acculturation Strategies

Source: Berry, J. W., U. Kim, and P. Boski (1988). Psychological Acculturation of Immigrants. *International and Intercultural Communication Annual* (vol. 11, pp. 62–89). Newbury Park, CA: Sage.

intercultural adjustment The subjective experiences people have as they adapt their behaviors and thinking.

or ways of thinking in a new cultural environment; and **intercultural adjustment**, which refers to how people *feel* as they are making those changes (or not). We believe that distinguishing between these two constructs is important because some people can adapt (that is, change their behaviors and ways of thinking to some degree) and feel great about it, while others may adapt their behaviors but be very stressed out.

One influential model of acculturation is Berry's (Berry, Kim, & Boski, 1988; Berry & Sam, 1997), in which immigrants and sojourners basically ask themselves two questions:

1. Do I value and want to maintain *my home* cultural identity and characteristics?

2. Do I value and want to maintain relationships with people from the *host* culture as well?

An individual's acculturation style can be described depending on one's answers to these questions (see Figure 14.3). People who answer *yes* to the first but no to the second are known as *separators* because they essentially live in their own immigrant communities, speaking their native language and interacting with their home-culture friends, with minimal contact with host-culture individuals. Individuals who answer no to the first and yes to the second are called *assimilators;* these individuals typically reject their home culture and totally assimilate to the host culture. They minimize interactions with people from their home culture, and typically speak the language of the host culture, even when interacting with people from their home culture. People who answer *no* to both questions are known as *marginalizers*. They reject both home and host cultures, and do not do well in either. They live on the fringes of both cultures, not really being able to immerse themselves in either. Finally, people who answer *yes* to both questions are known as *integrators*. These individuals are able to move from one cultural context to another, switching their cultural styles as they go along in accordance with the cultural system they are in. They are likely to be bilingual or multilingual as well as bicultural or multicultural.

While Berry's model may describe how people behave (adaptation), is one strategy better than another when it comes to how well people adjust in a new culture? Although it may seem that integration is the "best" pattern of adaptation, research has been equivocal in terms of whether it actually produces the best outcomes in terms of adjustment. On one hand, reviews of research with bicultural individuals (who are supposedly integrators in the Berry model) spanning 83 studies and 23,197 individuals have shown significant, strong, and positive associations between biculturalism and adjustment (Nguyen & Benet-Martinez, 2013). Bicultural individuals also show enhanced creativity and greater professional success than monocultural individuals (Tadmor, Galinsky, & Maddux, 2012), and less negative intergroup bias (Tadmor, Hong, Chao, Wiruchnipawan, & Wang, 2012). Other reviews, however, examining differences in adjustment outcomes for the various adaptation strategies have shown that integration is not necessarily associated with the best adjustment outcomes (Rudmin, 2003). In fact, people can be relatively happy and well adjusted, at least in terms of their own self-report, regardless of what kind of adaptational strategies they use as part of their acculturation process. Many members of immigrant groups in the United States live happy, productive lives, not speaking very much English and not interacting very much with host Americans. Recent research on economically based immigration has also suggested different factors that are at work for acculturation for individuals who immigrate to other countries to find work to survive and make a living (Boski, 2013).

So what psychological factors may predict intercultural adaptation and adjustment? With regard to the former, certainly changing one's behaviors and ways of thinking would be helped if one knew what they would have to be changed to. Thus, knowledge of the target culture's norms, beliefs, attitudes, and values, would seem to be a prerequisite for adaptation. This is exactly what Kurman and Ronen-Eilon (2004) found in their study of immigrants and individuals from the former Soviet Union in Israel. Another study found that knowledge of a host culture's gestures (see Chapter 10) was positively correlated with length of stay in a foreign country and negatively correlated with communication problems (Molinsky, Krabbenhoft, Ambady, & Choi, 2005).

With regard to intercultural adjustment, several factors seem to be important. One is "cultural fit," or the degree to which a person's characteristics match those of the new cultural environment in which he or she will acculturate (Ward & Chang, 1997). Ward and colleagues have provided evidence for the **cultural fit hypothesis**, showing that individuals with better fits have better adjustment; those with worse fits have worse adjustment, that is, they are less happy while at the same time more depressed, stressed, or anxious. Research involving a similar construct known as "person-culture match" has produced similar effects (Fulmer et al., 2010). Relatedly, acculturation also brings about short- and long-term changes in personality (Zimmermann & Neyer, 2013).

cultural fit hypothesis The proposition that immigrants and sojourners with characteristics that match their host cultures will adjust better than those with less match.

Another factor that is important for intercultural adjustment is emotion regulation, which is the ability to monitor and manage one's emotional reactions in order to achieve constructive outcomes. A series of studies has demonstrated that emotion regulation is one of the keys to successful intercultural adjustment (Matsumoto, LeRoux, Bernhard, & Gray, 2004; Matsumoto, LeRoux, Iwamoto, Choi, Rogers, et al., 2003; Matsumoto, LeRoux, Ratzlaff, Tatam, Uchida et al., 2001). This makes sense, because intercultural adaptation is fraught with inevitable conflicts that bring about many stresses for both home and host culture members (West, Shelton, & Trail, 2009). Such interactions deplete the psychological resources we have to make good decisions and adapt effectively (Richeson & Trawalter, 2005). The ability to adjust successfully requires one to be able to handle the many inevitable stresses that occur when living in a new culture. Part of this ability requires us to not be overcome with emotions when they occur; instead, we need to be able to keep emotions in check but channel their energies toward useful goals.

CONCLUSION

We began this chapter by noting that "no man is an island," and we have discussed how true that really is. No matter how we look at it, we cannot ignore the fact that we are fundamentally connected with other people in our world. Our behaviors, thoughts, and feelings are all influenced by others, and we in turn influence those around us.

As we close this chapter, we cannot help but feel that, despite the great differences across cultures in people's social behaviors, there are considerable underlying similarities as well. There are many universal psychological processes; culture produces differences in how we define goals to address universal needs and motives, and in their behavioral manifestations. Yet at the core of it all, perhaps there is some culture-constant belief or value that we all operate on as human beings. The seminal review by Amir and Sharon (1988) on the cross-cultural validity of social psychological laws speaks to this point. They indicated that original findings are often replicated across studies in statistical main effects—that is, in broad ways transcending culture. Somehow, cross-cultural psychology and research should attempt to engage this core, seeking similarities as well as differences at various levels of our psychological lives.

EXPLORATION AND DISCOVERY

Why Does This Matter to Me?

1. What kinds of stereotypes and prejudices do you have about people of other cultures? Do you find ways of vindicating those stereotypes or challenging them? What kinds of stereotypes do people of other cultures have about your culture? How do these stereotypes interfere, or not, with actual interactions?

2. Do you feel that you are a fairly obedient and compliant person, or not? Where do these behaviors originate?

3. Do you know of people from different cultures than your own who are different in how they interact with others? Treat their friends and families differently? How are those behaviors adaptive for them but not for you?

4. If you were to live in a foreign country for a short while, what would you do to prepare? If you were to learn some simple phrases to help you get along, what would those be, and why?

Suggestions for Further Exploration

1. Take the list of adjectives in Table 14.2 and conduct a survey of people's stereotypes of others from different cultural groups. Is there a pattern to the findings? Are there differences for different cultural groups?

2. Is there a universal standard for attractiveness? How would you design a study that would test

that idea? How would you test that differently for men and women?

3. How frequent are racial microaggressions? How would you conduct a survey to examine how frequently they occur in real life?

Culture and Organizations

15

CHAPTER CONTENTS

An organization is a structure created by people to achieve certain objectives. Organizations are composed of people who work collectively to address the goals of the organization. Different people or groups may be specialized according to role, objective or task, and rank or status within a hierarchy may differentiate them from one another; but theoretically they should all collectively address a common goal (e.g., building a car, selling groceries).

We all spend a major portion of our lives in organizations. In fact, most of you reading this book are probably doing so within the educational system—an organization that plays an important part in many people's lives and is an important agent of socialization in the development and maintenance of culture (recall our discussion of this topic in Chapters 3 and 4). The companies that we work for are also organizations. Churches, sport teams, government, community centers, the military, and small businesses are all different types of organizations to which we all belong. We are witness to culture and organizational issues in everyday news, from events involving the United Nations to clashes between groups, religions, and countries.

In this chapter, we describe how culture influences people's behaviors in organizations and the organizations themselves. We will focus on work organizations because they have been the topic of many cross-cultural studies and provide the context for our knowledge of the effects of culture on organizations. The work context is an interesting place to study the influence of culture on psychological processes because it may enhance or diminish differences. Sanchez-Burks, Lee, Choi, Nisbett, Zhao, and Koo (2003), for instance, demonstrated that American versus East Asian cultural differences in attention to indirect meaning were actually larger at work compared to nonwork settings. Still, it's important to remember that the information gained in understanding the relationship between culture and work organizations can be useful in understanding the many other organizations that are part of our lives as well.

We begin by examining cross-cultural research analyzing organizational culture first through work-related values, focusing on Hofstede's five major dimensions of culture, because of the major contributions this work has made to this area of cultural psychology. Using the Hofstede dimensions as a base, we then describe how culture influences organizations, and individuals within organizations, including attitudes about work, motivation and productivity, leadership and management, and decision making. We examine intercultural issues related to business and work, and discuss the important issue of sexual harassment across cultures.

► Cultural Differences in Work-Related Values: Hofstede's Cultural Dimensions

The most well-known work on culture and organizations has been the study of employees' work-related values by Geert Hofstede (1980, 1984). Although this work has its roots in the study of organizational culture, it has aided scientists in understanding national cultures as well, which we discussed in Chapter 1 and throughout this book. His study began in the 1960s and involved employees at International Business Machines (IBM), a multinational corporation with branch offices and subsidiaries in many different countries. In his original report in 1980, Hofstede reported data collected from workers in 40 different countries. In his 1984 study, he reported data from an additional 10 countries. In 2001, he reported data from 72 countries involving the responses of more than 117,000 employees, spanning over 20 different languages and seven occupational levels to his 63 work-related values items (Hofstede, 2001). Hofstede identified five major dimensions of work-related values and computed overall scores for each country on each of these four dimensions. As we discussed in Chapter 1, the five dimensions were power distance, uncertainty avoidance, individualism–collectivism, masculinity–femininity, and long- versus short-term orientation. Each of the dimensions is related to concrete differences in attitudes, opinions, beliefs, and behaviors within organizations, and each forms the basis for understanding certain societal norms in each of the countries in Hofstede's studies. These dimensions also have consequences for organizational structure and interorganizational behavior. We focus here on what they mean in terms of organizational culture.

Power Distance

Organizations need vertical or hierarchical relationships based on status and power. Differentiating people according to their roles, functions, and positions is vital to the successful operation of any organization. The various statuses afforded to different individuals within a hierarchy come with certain benefits, rights, privileges, and power not afforded to others. The "chain of command" within an organization identifies the players and their roles.

The basic hierarchical relationship is that between a boss and his or her immediate subordinate. In most cases, an employee is involved in a hierarchical relationship both with someone of higher status and with others of lower status. People within each organization develop ways of interacting with others according to the status differential that exists between the individual and the person with whom he or she is interacting. Power distance *refers to the degree to which different cultures encourage or maintain power and status differences between interactants*. Organizations (and cultures) high on power distance are hierarchical; they develop rules, mechanisms, and rituals that serve to maintain and strengthen the status relationships among their members. Cultures low on power distance are more egalitarian; they minimize those rules and customs.

Uncertainty Avoidance

Uncertainty is a fact of life. This is true for individuals as well as for organizations. Today's profits can easily turn into tomorrow's losses and vice versa. How a market will react to a new product, revisions in old products, corporate restructuring, mergers and acquisitions, and all the other changes that occur within organizations and in the business world are all major sources of uncertainty. The future of churches, schools, community centers, and sports teams depends heavily on membership and performance, both of which are not guarantees, and thus bring about uncertainty. With this uncertainty can come confusion, stress, and anxiety.

Every society and organization develops its own ways of dealing with the anxiety and stress associated with uncertainty. These ways involve the development of rituals, informal or written, concerning a code of conduct among employees, as in intracompany policies regarding communication or interpersonal relationships. These rules may also govern behavior between companies within a society, or across cultures, as in domestic and international laws governing business and interbusiness relationships.

Uncertainty avoidance refers to *the degree to which different organizations develop ways to deal with the anxiety and stress of uncertainty*. Organizations (and cultures) high on uncertainty avoidance develop highly refined rules and rituals that are mandated and become part of the company rubric and normal way of operating. Companies in these cultures may be considered rule-oriented. In Hofstede's survey, Greece, Portugal, Belgium, and Japan were the four countries with the highest scores on this dimension. Cultures low on uncertainty avoidance are less concerned with rules and rituals to deal with the stress and anxiety of uncertainty. Companies in these cultures have a more relaxed attitude concerning uncertainty and ambiguity and mandate fewer rules and rituals for their employees. In Hofstede's study, Sweden, Denmark, and Singapore had the lowest scores on uncertainty avoidance.

Individualism–Collectivism

As described throughout this book, individualism–collectivism has been used to explain, understand, and predict cultural differences in a variety of contexts. It is also a very important dimension in relation to work organizations. This dimension refers to *the degree to which individuals will sacrifice personal goals for the sake of their ingroup*. Individualistic cultures foster less sacrifice for the group and prioritize individual goals, wishes, and desires. Collectivistic cultural values foster more compliance with company policies and more conformity in group, section, or unit behavior. Collectivism also fosters a greater degree of reliance on group work and group orientation to company and organizational tasks. Harmony within groups, sections, or business units is valued more in collectivistic cultures; members are more likely to engage in behaviors that ensure harmony and to refrain from behaviors that threaten harmony.

In Hofstede's study, the United States, Australia, Great Britain, and Canada had the highest scores on individualism–collectivism. Workers in these countries were characterized as being the most individualistic of all workers in the study. It is interesting to note that each of these countries has a strong historical link to Great Britain. Peru, Pakistan, Colombia, and Venezuela had the lowest scores on individualism–collectivism and were the most collectivistic.

Masculinity–Femininity

Biological differences between men and women are a given. The question that every society, culture, and individual has to deal with is the degree to which the biological differences translate to practical differences in social roles, functions, or positions. Traditionally, American culture has expected men to be more assertive, dominant, and the primary wage earner and women to be more nurturing, caring, and primarily concerned with family and childcare issues (see also Chapter 7). This picture has been changing rapidly in the United States and many other cultures. Values concerning equity and equality have infused the workplace, and many American companies are still in transition toward providing gender equity in the workplace.

Each culture and society must deal with the issue of sex roles and gender differences. According to Hofstede, masculinity–femininity refers to *the degree to which cultures foster or maintain differences between the sexes in work-related values*. Cultures high on masculinity–femininity—such as Japan, Austria, Venezuela, and Italy—were associated with the greatest degree of sex differences in work-related values. Cultures low on masculinity–femininity—such as Denmark, the Netherlands, Norway, and Sweden—had the fewest differences between the sexes.

Interestingly, Hofstede's original definition of this dimension was not so related to sex differences as it was related to competitiveness and achievement orientation and was labeled simply as Masculinity (Hofstede, 1980). Over the years, the label for this dimension and its description was transformed to a bipolar comparison with femininity.

Long- versus Short-Term Orientation

The long- versus short-term orientation dimension originated from Hofstede's research in Asia, where he and his collaborators found that there was an additional dimension that characterized organizational cultures there (Chinese Culture Connection, 1987; Hofstede & Bond, 1988). This dimension refers *to the degree to which cultures encourage delayed gratification of material, social, and emotional needs among its members*. The most long-term-oriented cultures in Hofstede's study were China, Hong Kong, and Taiwan; the most short-term-oriented were Poland, West Africa, and Spain.

Cultures with long-term orientations are based on two principles:

- Unequal status relationships lead to a stable society.
- The family is typical of all social organizations.

These principles translate to abstract values that play an important role not only in interpersonal relationships in business but also as organizational goals and principles. For example, cultures and organizations high in long-term orientation differentiate more between elders and youngers, and between brothers and sisters; believe that humility is a great human virtue, focus on building relationships and market position rather than bottomline profits, integrate business and family lives, and coordinate more hierarchically and horizontally (Hofstede, 2001).

Hofstede's is not the only research on work-related values across cultures. There have been several other large-scale attempts to measure organizational culture around the world, and these have aided our understanding of national culture as well. For example, Smith, Dugan, and Trompenaars (1996) reported two universal value orientations in their work in organizations; House, Hanges, Javidan, Dorfman, and Gupta (2004) reported nine value orientations related to leadership; and Inglehart (1997) reported two attitudinal-belief-value orientations (Table 15.1). Thus, in reality,

TABLE 15.1 Four Major Sets of Dimensions of Cultural Variability Found in Studies of Work-Related Values

Framework	Dimensions
Hofstede's (2001) dimensions of work-related values	Individualism–collectivism
	Power distance
	Uncertainty avoidance
	Masculinity–femininity
	Long- vs. short-term orientation
Smith, Dugan, and Trompenaars's (1996) dimensions of values	Egalitarian commitment vs. conservatism
	Utilitarian involvement vs. loyal involvement
	Performance orientation
	Assertiveness orientation
House, Hanges, Javidan, Dorfman, and Gupta's (2004) dimensions of leadership values	Future orientation
	Human orientation
	Institutional collectivism
	Family collectivism
	Gender egalitarianism
	Power distance
	Uncertainty avoidance
Inglehart's (1997) dimensions of attitudes, values, and beliefs	Traditional vs. secular-rational orientation
	Survival vs. self-expression values

there is a wide range of cultural dimensions to use in developing cultural theories and accounting for between-country differences.

Many of these dimensions, however, are theoretically and empirically related to each other. Hofstede (1996), for instance, reanalyzed Trompenaars's (1993) data, and reported that Trompenaars's dimensions were statistically correlated with his own. And, Hofstede's work has arguably had the largest impact on the field. In the next section, we will use Hofstede's work as a base to describe cultural differences in organizational cultures and behavior.

▶ Organizational Culture and Organizational Climate

Cultural Differences in Organizational Culture

Each organization is unique, and because each contains a group of people with a way of existence, they have culture. This is known as "organizational culture" or "corporate culture" (O'Reilly, 1989; O'Reilly, Chatman, & Caldwell, 1991). Recall that in Chapter 1 we defined *culture* as a meaning and information system, shared by a group and transmitted across generations, that allows the group to meet basic needs of survival, pursue happiness and well-being, and derive meaning from life. Likewise, **organizational culture** can be defined as a meaning and information system shared within an organization and transmitted across successive generations of members, which allows the organization to survive and potentially thrive.

The concept of organizational culture needs to be compared with another closely related construct, **organizational climate**. This refers to a shared awareness of "the way things are around here" (Reichers & Schneider, 1990)—a shared perception of organizational policies, practices, and procedures. The term contains nuances of an emotional climate—that is, how people generally feel in their normal, everyday business practices. Climate can probably be best understood as a manifestation of organizational culture (Reichers & Schneider, 1990; Schein, 1985), or a perception of how things are. Organizational culture generally refers to a deeper, less consciously held set of values, attitudes, and meanings.

The concept of organizational climate is a long-standing one in the field of industrial and organizational psychology. Reichers and Schneider (1990), in their review of these two constructs, pointed out that writing appeared as early as 1939 on organizational climate and its relationship to work behaviors. Organizational culture, on the other hand, first appeared in the literature in 1979 and has currently become an important catchphrase. Most of the cross-cultural research on organizations has focused on culture, not climate.

Organizations differ according to Hofstede's dimensions (Table 15.2). For example, in low power distance cultures, employees are less afraid of disagreeing with their boss, and generally show more cooperativeness. In high power distance cultures, however, employees have greater fear of disagreeing with their boss and are more reluctant to trust each other. This makes sense because high power distance cultures encourage greater status and power differences between bosses and subordinates and likely produce institutional procedures and rules to maintain those status differences. Low power distance cultures minimize such differences and thus encourage greater conflict and disagreement across status hierarchies.

Other aspects of organizational culture are also different across other Hofstede dimensions. For example, there are more women in jobs with mixed-sex composition

organizational culture A dynamic system of rules involving attitudes, values, beliefs, norms, and behaviors that are shared among members of an organization.

organizational climate A shared perception of organizational policies, practices, and procedures, and how people feel about them.

TABLE 15.2 Differences in Organizational Processes According to Hofstede's Cultural Dimensions

Power Distance		Uncertainty Avoidance		Individualism vs. Collectivism		Masculinity vs. Femininity	
Low	High	Low	High	Collectivistic	Individualistic	Feminine	Masculine
Employees less afraid of disagreeing with their boss.	Employees fear to disagree with their boss.	Competition between employees can be fair and right.	Competition between employees is emotionally disapproved of.			More traditional time-use pattern.	More modern time-use pattern.
Employees show more cooperativeness	Employees reluctant to trust each other.	Rules may be broken for pragmatic reasons.	Company rules should not be broken.			More women in jobs with mixed-sex composition.	Fewer women in jobs with mixed-sex composition.
		Conflict in organizations is natural.	Conflict in organizations is undesirable.			Smaller or no value differences between men and women in the same jobs.	Greater value differences between men and women in the same jobs.

and smaller or no value differences between the sexes in the same jobs in feminine cultures, whereas the opposite is true in masculine cultures. Conflict in organizations is seen as natural in low uncertainty avoidance cultures, whereas it is undesirable in high uncertainty avoidance cultures.

Culture and Person-Organization Fit

One topic that has gained prominence not only in the scientific literature but also in applied work is the issue of cultural fit between person and company. (This topic is also related to the person-culture match discussed in the section on acculturation in Chapter 14.) Given the work conducted in the past two decades on organizational culture, and the work that has been done for years on individual culture, a logical question concerns the match between employees and the cultures they come from and a company and its organizational culture. Do "mismatches" create conflicts? Do successful "matches" lead to more productive companies?

Abrams, Ando, and Hinkle (1998) examined cross-cultural differences in organizational identification and subjective norms as predictors of workers' turnover intentions. In their study, employees of companies in Great Britain and Japan completed questionnaires related to turnover intentions, attitudes toward leaving the organization, subjective norms regarding perceived approval for leaving, and organizational identification. In the British sample, turnover intentions were predicted by organizational identification; workers with stronger identifications with the company had lower turnover intentions. In the Japanese sample, however, turnover intentions were associated with both organizational identification and subjective norms. These findings suggested that although social identity is strongly associated with employee turnover in both cultures, subjective normative aspects of group membership play a larger role in predicting turnover in Japan than they do in Great Britain.

Research has documented positive aspects of employee–company cultural congruence. Meglino, Ravlin, and Adkins (1989), for example, questioned 191 production workers, 17 supervisors, and 13 managers on job satisfaction and organization commitment; they also collected objective data concerning attendance, performance, and efficiency. Two measures of employees' values congruence were computed and correlated with all psychological and behavioral data. Workers who were more satisfied and committed had values that were congruent with those of their supervisor.

These findings raise important questions concerning the nature of personnel selection in companies today, especially in cultures with a diverse workforce population. Adding to the complexity of these issues are the cultural and ethnic differences in career choices of today's young adults (Kim, 1993) and perceived past and future barriers to career development (Luzzo, 1993). Finding an appropriate match between employer and employee is a daunting task for both individuals and organizations, as neither side profits from an unsuitable relationship or unhappy employees.

But there is also some evidence that person–organization fit may not be that important in some contexts, especially in developing countries (Nyambegera, Daniels, & Sparrow, 2001). Thus, more research is certainly necessary on organizational culture and the fit between employee and company in different cultures and contexts. These are real-life issues that have important implications in our everyday lives. Organizations today struggle with the issue of cultural match between employee and company, and innovative ways of assimilating newcomers into organizations are constantly being developed from a cultural perspective (see, for example, Hess, 1993). Although most research approaches this issue from the organization's point of view, some researchers have also addressed efforts by employees to assess the fit between themselves and the culture of the organization to which they are applying (e.g., Pratt, 1993). We still have much to learn. What constitutes a "successful" or "unsuccessful" match? How do we make these assessments? In some cultures, making such assessments may be counter to the prevailing cultural norms. And how valid is the suggestion that all personnel election decisions should be informed by matches? Are there optimal levels of mismatches that may spur on maximal performance? For example, although individualism is usually associated with creativity and initiative, at least one study has shown that innovation and entrepreneurship is highest under conditions of balanced individualism and collectivism, and lowest in either highly individualistic or highly collectivistic corporations (Morris, Avila, & Allen, 1993). Could such an effect exist within organizations as well?

▶ Culture and Attitudes about Work and Organizations

People construe themselves and their existence in relation to work differently across cultures and those differences are related to meaningful dimensions of cultural variability. Again Hofstede's dimensions are useful in understanding cultural differences in attitudes about work. For instance, people in low power distance cultures have a stronger perceived work ethic and a strong disbelief that people dislike work, whereas the opposite is true for people in high power distance cultures. Duty in life appeals to people in collectivistic cultures while enjoyment in life appeals to people in individualistic cultures. People in higher performance capabilities in masculine cultures feel empowered to make decisions and seek opportunities to voice their opinions, whereas people with less capabilities in feminine cultures value the importance of nurturing people with lower capability (van den Bos et al., 2010). See Table 15.3.

People of different cultures differ in their levels of **organizational commitment**, and what factors are important to it. A meta-analysis by Meyer and colleagues (2002) showed that **normative commitment**—the degree to which one's ties to the

organizational commitment The degree to which a person is committed, identifies with, and makes efforts for, his or her organization.

normative commitment The degree to which one's ties to the organization are bound by duty and obligation.

TABLE 15.3 Differences in the Meaning of Work According to Hofstede's Cultural Dimensions

| Power Distance | | Uncertainty Avoidance | | Individualism vs. Collectivism | | Masculinity vs. Femininity | |
Low	High	Low	High	Collectivistic	Individualistic	Feminine	Masculine
Stronger perceived work ethic, strong disbelief that people dislike work.	Weaker perceived work ethic, more frequent belief that people dislike work.	Prefers manager career over specialist career.	Prefers specialist career over manager career.	Duty in life appeals to employees.	Enjoyment in life appeals to employees.	People prefer shorter working hours to more salary.	People prefer more salary to shorter working hours.
		Higher tolerance for ambiguity in looking at own job (lower satisfaction scores).	Lower tolerance for ambiguity in looking at own job (higher satisfaction).	Managers choose duty, expertness, and prestige as life goals.	Managers choose pleasure, affections, and security as life goals.	Employees like small companies.	Employees like large corporations.
				More years of schooling needed to do a given job.	Fewer years of schooling needed to do a given job.	Lower job stress.	Higher job stress.
						Less skepticism as to factors leading to getting ahead.	Skepticism as to factors leading to getting ahead.
Optimism about people's amount of initiative, ambition, and leadership skills.	Pessimism about people's amount of initiative, ambition, and leadership skills.			Importance of provisions by company (training, physical conditions).	Importance of employees' personal life (time).	"Theory X" (employees dislike work) strongly rejected.	"Theory X" gets some support.

(continues)

TABLE 15.3 (*Continued*)

Power Distance		Uncertainty Avoidance		Individualism vs. Collectivism		Masculinity vs. Femininity	
High	Low	Low	High	Collectivistic	Individualistic	Feminine	Masculine
		Preference for broad guidelines.	Preference for clear requirements and instructions.	Emotional dependence on company.	Emotional independence from company.	Relationship with manager, cooperation, friendly atmosphere, living in a desirable area, and employment security relatively more important to employees.	Earnings, recognition, advancement, and challenge relatively more important to employees.
		Less hesitation to change employers.	Tendency to stay with the same employer.	Large company attractive.	Small company attractive.	Work less central in people's lives.	Greater work centrality.
		Loyalty to employer is not seen as a virtue.	Loyalty to employer is seen as a virtue.	Moral involvement with company.	Calculative involvement with company.	Company's interference in private life rejected.	Company's interference in private life accepted.
		Preference for smaller organizations as employers.	Preference for larger organizations as employers.				
		Employee optimism about the motives behind company activities.	Employee pessimism about the motives behind company activities.				

organization are bound by duty and obligation—and **affective commitment**—the level of personal feelings associated with one's relationship to an organization—both were predictive of organizational commitment, but to different degrees across cultures. Some people view their work groups and the organizations to which they belong as a fundamental part of themselves. In collectivistic cultures, work, colleagues, and the organization become synonymous with the self. The bonds between the people and their colleagues, and between themselves and the organization, are stronger and qualitatively different from those of people in individualistic cultures. In individualistic cultures, people have an easier time separating themselves from their organizations. They make greater distinctions between "work time" and "personal time," and between company-based expense accounts and personal expenses. They also make greater distinctions between social and work activities, with regard to both their work colleagues and their business associates (potential clients, customers, and so forth).

Cultural differences in the meaning of work can manifest themselves in other ways. For example, in American culture, it is easy to think of work simply as a means to make money and a living. In other cultures, especially collectivistic ones, work may be seen more as fulfilling an obligation to a larger group. In such cultures there is less movement of individuals from one job to another because of the individual's social obligations toward the work organization to which he or she belongs and to the people comprising that organization. In individualistic cultures, it is easier to consider leaving one job and going to another because it is easier to separate jobs from the self. A different job will just as easily accomplish the same goals.

The work in this area points to differences in the nature of the **psychological contracts** that exist between organizations and their members (Rosseau & Schalk, 2000). These are the perceptions of mutual obligations that exist between organizations and their members, and they differ across cultures.

Also one cannot ignore the large influence of socioeconomics. In many cultures, people young and old alike are without work and have many difficulties making a living for themselves and their families. The inability to work, related to the unavailability of work, has major consequences for individuals and societies, causing unrest and hardship at both levels. To many around the world, having a job—any job—is a luxury. A glance at the differences in per capita gross domestic product at purchasing power parity, which is an index of the purchasing power of the average individual in each country controlled for the cost of living, gives one an idea of these differences (Table 15.4).

Regardless of the type of work one does, in many cultures of the world, people who have work come to perceive their work as their lifework. That is, people tend to ascribe important meaning to what they are doing. The ability to ascribe meaning to things is unique to humans because of the unique cognitive skills humans have, as we discussed in Chapter 1. People's views of their lifework are an important aspect of human culture.

affective commitment
The level of personal feelings associated with one's relationship to an organization.

psychological contracts The perceptions of mutual obligations that exist between organizations and their members, which differ across cultures.

▶ Culture, Motivation, and Productivity

One important issue all organizations must address is the degree to which their members will be productive in various types of settings. All organizations want to maximize productivity while minimizing costs, whether a company, church, or sport team. This concern has led to an important area of research on productivity as a function of group size.

Early research on group productivity in the United States showed that individual productivity tends to decline in larger groups (Latané, Williams, & Harkins, 1979).

TABLE 15.4 Selected Countries' GDP per Capita (PPP) in 2014 from the International Monetary Fund (in International Dollars)

Country	PPP	Country	PPP
Qatar (1)	143,426.98	United States (11)	54,596.65
Luxembourg (2)	92,048.55	Taiwan (21)	45,853.74
Singapore (3)	82,762.15	Canada (22)	44,843.44
Brunei Darussalam (4)	73,233.03	Korea (32)	35,277.35
Kuwait (5)	71,020.25	Russia (50)	24,805.49
Norway (6)	66,937.46	Mexico (67)	17,880.51
United Arab Emirates (7)	64,478.67	People's Republic of China (91)	12,879.85
San Marino (8)	60,664.33	Egypt (99)	10,877.19
Switzerland (9)	58,087.21	India (125)	5,855.31
Hong Kong (10)	54,722.12	Afghanistan (165)	1,936.72

social loafing The common finding in research on group productivity in the United States that individual productivity tends to decline in larger groups.

These findings contributed to the coining of the term **social loafing**. Two factors appeared to have contributed to this phenomenon. One is reduced efficiency resulting from a lack of coordination among workers' efforts, resulting in lack of activity or duplicate activity. The second is a reduction in effort by individuals when they work in groups as compared to when they work by themselves. Latané (1981) and his colleagues (Latané et al., 1979) conducted a number of studies investigating group size, coordination, and effort and found that in larger groups, both lack of coordination and reduced effort resulted in decreased productivity. Latané (1981) attributed these findings to a diffusion of responsibility in groups. As group size increases, the responsibility for getting a job done is divided among more people, and group members ease up because their individual contribution is less recognizable.

Early cross-cultural research on groups and their productivity, however, found the opposite in other cultures. Earley (1989) examined social loafing in an organizational setting among managerial trainees in the United States and in the People's Republic of China. Participants in both cultures worked on a task under conditions of low or high accountability and low or high shared responsibility. Social loafing occurred with the Americans, whose individual performances in a group were less than when working alone, but not for the Chinese.

Shirakashi (1985) and Yamaguchi, Okamoto, and Oka (1985) also reported that social loafing did not occur in studies involving Japanese participants; instead, working in a group enhanced individual performance rather than diminished it. Gabrenya, Wang, and Latané (1985) demonstrated this **social striving** in a sample of Chinese schoolchildren. These authors speculated that cultures such as China and Japan fostered interpersonal interdependence and group collective functioning more than did the American culture, thus fostering group productivity because of increasing coordination among ingroup members. These cultures also placed higher values on individual contributions in group settings.

social striving The opposite of social loafing; the finding in many cultures that working in a group enhances individual performance rather than diminishes it.

This trend may also be occurring in the United States in recent decades (see Ebrahimpour & Johnson, 1992; Hodgetts, Luthans, & Lee, 1994), and several studies involving American participants have begun to challenge the traditional notion of social loafing (e.g., Harkins, 1987; Harkins & Petty, 1982; Shepperd & Wright, 1989; Wagner, 1995; Weldon & Gargano, 1988; Zaccaro, 1984). Jackson and Williams (1985), for instance, reported that Americans working collectively improved performance and productivity.

Westaby (1995) asked participants in the United States and Japan to complete a paper-and-pen tracing task, either individually or in the presence of a group. Although the author expected that the Japanese would perform better in the group situation, the effect of group presence was the same for Americans and Japanese. Participants of both cultures had higher productivity and job quality in the presence of a group than when working alone. Further analyses indicated that although Japanese participants had higher productivity than American participants in general (regardless of social context), there was no difference in the quality of the work. Thus, notions of social loafing and group productivity have been challenged not only cross-culturally but also within American culture. Indeed, workaholism seems be a growing concern for many, and some research suggests that the relationship between workaholism and work–life imbalance is not influenced by culture (Aziz, Adkins, Walker, & Wuensch, 2009).

How does social striving work in the United States? Clearly, the same processes that work in one culture may or may not work in another. Bagozzi, Werbeke, and Gavino (2003), for instance, showed that while shame produced positive effects in Filipino employees (enhanced customer relationship building and civic virtue), it had negative effects in Dutch employees (diminished sales volume, and problems in communication and relationships). Some scholars have suggested that one way in which work groups and teams can become more productive in cultures like the United States is through the use of constructive thought patterns that help to transform self-managing teams into self-leading teams (for example, Manz, 1992; Neck & Manz, 1994). The idea is that employees become empowered to influence strategic issues concerning what they do and why, in addition to how they do their work. These suggestions highlight the notion that different bases may underlie productivity or nonproductivity in different cultural groups.

Hofstede's dimensions also provide some understanding of cultural differences in motivation and productivity. There is generally greater achievement motivation in low uncertainty avoidance cultures compared to high, and in masculine cultures compared to feminine. Individual initiative is encouraged in individualistic cultures, whereas it is looked down upon in collectivistic cultures, which encourage group achievement. In high masculine cultures, achievement is defined in terms of recognition and wealth, whereas achievement is defined in terms of personal relationships in feminine cultures. And the relationship between job satisfaction and job performance is stronger in Individualistic, low power distance, low uncertainty avoidance, and masculine cultures (Ng, Sorenson, & Yim, 2009). See Table 15.5.

Not only are the factors that influence motivation and productivity different across cultures, but leaders' perceptions of the motivations of subordinates also differ. In one study (DeVoe & Iyengar, 2004), for example, North American and Latin American managers' perceptions of their subordinates' intrinsic motivation was a better predictor of performance appraisal, whereas perceptions of both subordinate intrinsic and extrinsic motivations were better predictors of performance appraisals for Asian managers.

▶ Culture, Leadership, and Management Styles

Culture and the Meaning of Leadership

In many industrialized cultures, leadership can be defined as the "process of influence between a leader and followers to attain group, organizational, or societal goals" (Hollander, 1985, p. 486). Leaders may be autocratic, dictatorial, democratic, and so

TABLE 15.5 Differences in Motivation and Productivity According to Hofstede's Cultural Dimensions

Power Distance		Uncertainty Avoidance		Individualism vs. Collectivism		Masculinity vs. Femininity	
Low	High	Low	High	Collectivistic	Individualistic	Feminine	Masculine
		Stronger achievement motivation.	Less achievement motivation.	Moral importance attached to training and use of skills in jobs.	More importance attached to freedom and challenge in jobs.	Employees less interested in recognition.	Employees aspire to recognition (admiration for the strong).
		Stronger ambition for individual advancement.	Lower ambition for individual advancement.	Individual initiative is socially frowned upon; fatalism.	Individual initiative is socially encouraged.	Weaker achievement motivation.	Stronger achievement motivation.
						Achievement defined in terms of human contacts and living environment.	Achievement defined in terms of recognition and wealth.

on. In common language, we speak of "strong" and "effective" leaders as opposed to "weak" and "ineffective" ones. In many organizations, especially in the United States, we expect leaders to have vision, authority, and power and to give subordinates tasks that have meaning in a larger picture. In American culture, leaders are expected to be decision makers—"movers and shakers" of organizations and of people.

In other cultures, leaders may share many of these same traits, but their leadership and managerial styles are not necessarily seen as dynamic or action-oriented. For example, some of the most effective leaders and managers in organizations in India have been seen as much more nurturing, taking on a parental role within the company and in relation to their subordinates (Sinha, 1979). These leaders are more participative, guiding and directing their subordinates' tasks and behaviors as opposed to merely giving directives. Still leaders and managers in India need to be flexible, at times becoming very authoritative in their work roles. Thus, the optimal leadership style in India, according to Sinha, is somewhere between participative and authoritative styles.

Another way leadership and managerial styles differ across cultures is in the boundaries of that leadership. In American culture, for example, workers make a clear distinction between work and personal life. When 5:00 P.M. arrives, many American workers consider themselves "off" from work and on their personal time. The boundary between work and their personal lives is very clear. Leaders, bosses, and others in the company should have nothing to say about how members of the company live their personal lives (e.g., where they should live or whom they should marry or what they do in their personal time). In other cultures, however, the boundaries between work and personal life are less clear. In many countries, the individual's existence at work becomes an integral part of the self. Thus, the distinction between work and company, on the one hand, and one's personal life, on the other, is fuzzy and blurred. Needless to say, leaders in such cultures can request overtime work from their subordinates and expect to receive it with much less complaining than in American culture.

As the distinction between work and self becomes blurred, so do the boundaries of jurisdiction for leaders. For example, leaders and managers in India and Japan are expected to look after their subordinates in terms of their work and existence within the company; but it is not uncommon for leaders to be concerned with their subordinates' private lives as well. Subordinates in these cultures often will not hesitate to consult with their bosses about problems at home and to seek advice and help from them about those problems. Leaders, more often than not, will see helping their subordinates with this part of their lives as an integral and important part of their jobs. In such cultures, it is not uncommon for bosses to find marriage partners for their subordinates and to look after them inside as well as outside the company. The bond between them extends well beyond the company.

Culture and Leadership Behaviors

Given these cross-cultural differences in the definition of leadership, it is not surprising that many cross-cultural studies report differences in specific leadership behaviors (see, for example, Black & Porter, 1991, on managerial differences in the United States and Hong Kong; Okechuku, 1994, on managers' ratings of subordinates in Canada, Hong Kong, and China; Smith, Peterson, & Schwartz, 2002, on sources of guidance of managers in 47 nations). Smith, Peterson, and Misumi (1994), for instance, obtained effectiveness ratings of work teams in electronics assembly plants in Japan, Great Britain, and the United States, as well as ratings of ten event-management processes used by superiors. For the Japanese, work performance depended on the relatively frequent use of manuals and procedures and on relatively frequent guidance from supervisors (related to high uncertainty avoidance). American and British supervisors, however, favored more contingent responses, suggesting that the preferred managerial response depends on the specific event or task they face.

Many other studies have documented cross-cultural differences in leadership and managerial style, and many of their findings can be summarized using Hofstede's dimensions. For example, leaders in high power distance cultures tend to be autocratic or paternalistic in their decision making and interactional style, while leaders and managers in low power distance cultures tend to be more participative and consensual. Managers in high uncertainty avoidance cultures tend to be selected on the basis of seniority, whereas in low uncertainty avoidance cultures they tend to be selected on other criteria, such as merit. In individualistic cultures, autonomy is important to managers, whereas in collectivistic cultures security is more important (Table 15.6).

Not all cross-cultural research on this topic, however, has shown cultural differences; a substantial amount of literature documents cultural similarities in leadership behaviors as well. For example, Smith, Peterson, Misumi, and Bond (1992) examined work teams in Japan, Hong Kong, the United States, and Great Britain and found that leaders who were rated high in behaviors related to task performance and group maintenance all achieved higher work quality. Smith (1998) also found consistent themes in a survey of managers' handling of day-to-day work events in Brazil, Mexico, Colombia, and Argentina. Many other studies (see review by Bond & Smith, 1996) showed similar cross-cultural consistencies in some aspects of managerial behavior.

How are we to make sense of the literature that shows both similarities and differences across cultures in leadership and managerial behaviors? Misumi (1985) suggested that management involves general and universal functions that all effective leaders must carry out, but that the specific ways in which they are carried out may differ. Misumi contrasted functions related to task performance and group maintenance, and suggested that both domains involve universal leadership goals that are consistent across cultures and companies. Different specific behaviors may be used to accomplish these managerial goals, however; depending on situations, companies,

TABLE 15.6 Differences in Leadership and Management Styles According to Hofstede's Cultural Dimensions

Power Distance		Uncertainty Avoidance		Individualism vs. Collectivism		Masculinity vs. Femininity	
Low	High	Low	High	Collectivistic	Individualistic	Feminine	Masculine
Close supervision negatively evaluated by subordinates.	Close supervision positively evaluated by subordinates.	Managers selected on criteria other than seniority.	Managers selected on basis of seniority.	Managers aspire to conformity and orderliness.	Managers aspire to leadership and variety.	Managers relatively less interested in leadership, independence, and self-realization.	Managers have leadership, independence, and self-realization ideal.
Managers more satisfied with participative superior.	Managers more satisfied with directive or persuasive superior.	A manager need not be an expert in the field he/she manages.	A manager must be an expert in the field he or she manages.	Managers rate having security in their position more important.	Managers rate having autonomy more important.	Managers have more of a service ideal.	Managers relatively less attracted by service role.
Subordinates' preference for manager's decision-making style clearly centered on consultative, give-and-take style.	Subordinates' preference for manager's decision-making style polarized between autocratic-paternalistic and majority rule.	Delegation to subordinates can be complete.	Initiative of subordinates should be kept under control.			Managers endorse "traditional" points of view, not supporting employee initiative and group activity.	Managers endorse "modern" points of view on stimulating employee initiative and group activity.
Managers like seeing themselves as practical and systematic; they admit a need for support.	Managers like seeing themselves as benevolent decision makers.	Acceptance of foreigners as managers.	Suspicion toward foreigners as managers.				
Managers seen as showing more consideration.	Managers seen as showing less consideration.						
Mixed feeling about employees' participation in management.	Ideological support for employees' participation in management.						
Mixed feelings among managers about the distribution of capacity for leadership and initiative.	Ideological support among managers for a wide distribution of capacity for leadership and initiative.						

and cultures, these behaviors will vary. This approach invites us to examine and understand human behavior on multiple levels—one level involving cross-cultural universals or similarities in functions and goals, and the other involving differences in culture- and context-specific instrumental behaviors.

In addition to cultural explanations of differences in leadership behaviors, an emerging line of research has demonstrated the potential effects of climate and national wealth on leadership. In an interesting series of studies, Van de Vliert and colleagues have shown that the climate of a country—whether hot, cold, or mild—is related to levels of poverty and workers' wages (Van de Vliert, 2003), motives for volunteer work (Van de Vliert, Huang, & Levine, 2004), happiness and altruism (Van de Vliert, Huang, & Parker, 2004), domestic violence (Van de Vliert, Schwartz, Huismans, Hofstede, & Daan, 1999), and leader reliance on subordinates (Van de Vliert & Smith, 2004). Van de Vliert (2006) examined the relationship between climate and autocratic leadership, in which superiors act in more self-centered ways, make decisions unilaterally, and supervise subordinates' activities more closely. The sample included 17,370 middle managers from companies in 61 cultures. He reported that autocratic leadership styles were less effective in rich countries with a demanding (very harsh hot or cold) climate, but more effective in poor countries with a demanding climate (Figure 15.1).

One of the largest and most influential studies on the characteristics of leaders has been the Global Leadership and Organizational Behavior Effectiveness Project (the GLOBE Project; House, Hanges, Javidan, Dorfman, & Gupta, 2003). In this project, perceptions of leadership were assessed in 62 cultures involving about 17,000 middle managers. There were two characteristics of leadership that were universally endorsed: charisma and team orientation. Cultures differed, however, on the relative degree of importance they placed on both of these attributes. Charisma was relatively less important in high power distance and collectivistic cultures, whereas it was relatively more important in low power distance, individualistic cultures.

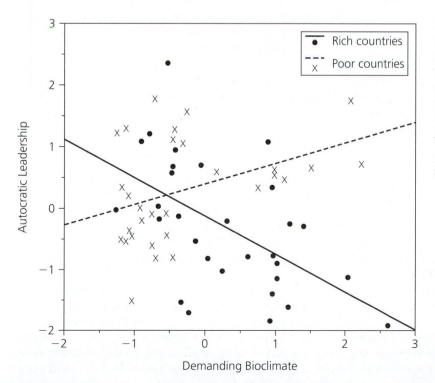

FIGURE 15.1 Autocratic Leadership as a Joint Function of Demanding Bioclimate and National Wealth

Source: Evert Van de Vliert. "Autocratic Leadership Around the Globe: Do Climate and Wealth Drive Leadership Culture?," *Journal of Cross-Cultural Psychology,* 18(1), p. 53, Copyright © 2006 by Sage Publications. Reprinted by permission of SAGE Publications.

▶ Culture and Decision-Making Processes

How are decisions made in the organizations of which you are a part? How is pay determined? How are members recognized for their efforts? How is change implemented? These and other decisions are some of the most important things any organization does. Culture influences organizational decision-making processes.

Organizational Decisions

One way of making decisions many Americans are familiar with is a democratic decision-making procedure (although there are many different definitions and types of "democracies"). In this procedure, every person involved has a say in the decision, usually by way of a vote; once votes are tallied, the decision of the majority prevails. This procedure has advantages and disadvantages. A major advantage to this procedure is that everyone has an equal say in the process. Democratic decision making is associated with an individualistic cultural viewpoint, which tends to see each person as a separate, autonomous being.

The democratic process can also lead to considerable red tape and bureaucracy. Many organizations, in fact, are not so much democracies as oligarchies (Ferrante, 1992). An **oligarchy** is an organizational structure characterized by rule- or decision-making power of a few. Decisions are typically made by people "at the top," who then impose their decisions on subordinates. Sometimes the size of organizations necessitates that they be oligarchies if decisions are to be made at all. If everyone were to be involved in all types of decisions, the bureaucratic process would simply be too unwieldy and time-consuming. This top-down approach to business decision-making is characteristic of many American companies.

Decision making is different in different cultures. The Japanese process, for instance, is known as the **ringi** system. In a Japanese organization, there is no formal system by which every person is ensured a vote. Instead, a proposal is circulated among all people who will be affected by it regardless of status, rank, or position. Initiatives for proposals can come from top, middle, or lower management, or from subordinates. Even before a proposal is formally circulated among all interested parties, there is often considerable discussion and debate about the proposal. All views are taken into account so that the proposal, when written and formally circulated, addresses concerns and negative consequences raised by as many parties as possible. There is considerable consultation about the proposal on as broad a basis as possible, and consensus is achieved before the proposal is formally implemented. This broad-based, consensus-building procedure is called **nemawashi**. If proposals do not achieve consensus by this procedure, they do not appear formally. Proposals that have gone through this procedure and have received the blessing of all those affected are then put in the form of a formal proposal on paper. A routing of the proposal involves all section chiefs and managers before it gets to the person or persons on top, who then put their formal stamp of approval on it. Needless to say, by the time something gets to that stage, it has met with the approval of many people throughout the organization.

Like all decision-making procedures, the Japanese system has advantages and disadvantages. One of the disadvantages is the time-consuming nature of the process. The inability of Japanese managers to make a decision on the spot in international negotiations has been a source of frustration for American negotiators, who are used to dealing with single decision makers. The Japanese negotiator, however, must contact all the people within the company affected by the impending decision prior to making that decision. An advantage of the Japanese system, however, is the speed

oligarchy An organizational structure characterized by rule- or decision-making power of a few. Decisions are typically made by people "at the top," who impose their decisions on subordinates.

ringi The Japanese process of decision making, which involves circulating a proposal among all people who will be affected by it, addressing concerns and negative consequences raised by as many parties as possible, consulting on as broad a basis as possible about the proposal, and achieving consensus before the proposal is formally implemented.

nemawashi The broad-based consensus-building procedure that occurs within the Japanese ringi system of decision making.

with which decisions can be implemented. Although the Japanese typically take much more time making a decision, they can usually implement it relatively quickly. No doubt, having everyone briefed in advance about the proposal aids in speedy implementation. Also, people in a collectivistic culture are more likely to get behind a decision that is for the good of the company, whatever their personal feelings about it.

One problem that has plagued decision making in groups is **groupthink**—a collective pattern of thinking that hinders effective group decisions. Groupthink is generally characterized by direct pressure; self-censorship; illusions of invulnerability, unanimity, or morality; mind guarding; collective rationalization; and shared stereotypes (Janis, 1983). These types of processes may underlie social loafing, which we discussed earlier, and general apathy toward work and productivity. Such destructive thought patterns, however, can be transformed into constructive ones, or **teamthink** (Neck & Manz, 1994). Teamthink involves the encouragement of divergent views, open expression of concerns and ideas, awareness of limitations and threats, recognition of members' uniqueness, and discussion of collective doubts. These constructive patterns lead to more effective decision making. Such a process may be critical for many organizations in many cultures, and especially for increasingly diversified companies in the United States, because it may be one way of maintaining individuality while serving the collective common good of the organization.

Hofstede's dimensions also provide a way of understanding cultural differences in decision making. In low power distance cultures, managers are seen as making decisions after consulting with subordinates, and informal employee consultation is very possible. In high power distance cultures, however, managers are seen as making decisions autocratically and paternalistically. Organizations in low uncertainty avoidance cultures engage in more risk taking, whereas organizations in high uncertainty avoidance cultures exercise more restraint in taking risks (see Table 15.7).

groupthink A collective pattern of thinking that hinders effective group decisions.

teamthink Teamthink involves the encouragement of divergent views, open expression of concerns and ideas, awareness of limitations and threats, recognition of members' uniqueness, and discussion of collective doubts.

Organizational Fairness

Leaders and organizations often rely on being perceived as fair in order to have any sense of effectiveness. But cultures differ on definitions of fairness and procedures

TABLE 15.7 Differences in Decision Making According to Hofstede's Cultural Dimensions

Power Distance		Uncertainty Avoidance		Individualism vs. Collectivism		Masculinity vs. Femininity	
Low	**High**	**Low**	**High**	**Collectivistic**	**Individualistic**	**Feminine**	**Masculine**
Managers seen as making decisions after consulting with subordinates.	Managers seen as making decisions autocratically and paternalistically.	More risk-taking.	Less risk-taking.	Group decisions are considered better than individual decisions.	Individual decisions are considered better than group decisions.	Belief in group decisions.	Belief in the independent decision maker.
Informal employee consultation possible without formal participation.	Formal employee participation possible without informal consultation.	More sympathy for individual and authoritative decisions.	Ideological appeal of consensus and of consultative leadership.				

equity Refers to whether one's contributions and efforts are considered in making organizational decisions.

equality Refers to whether the demographic characteristics of individuals such as age or seniority in the organization are considered primarily in making organizational decisions.

distributive justice Fairness regarding the distribution of resources, such as pay, the corner office, or perks.

procedural justice Fairness associated with the procedures and processes that organizations use to make decisions.

by which to achieve it. One way to understand fairness is by delineating whether decisions are made on the basis of equity or equality. **Equity** refers to whether one's contributions and efforts are considered in making organizational decisions. **Equality** refers to whether the demographic characteristics of individuals such as age or seniority in the organization are considered primarily in making organizational decisions. Cross-cultural research on these topics has provided mixed results. One meta-analysis of the literature showed that equity was preferred in individualistic cultures, while equality was preferred in collectivistic cultures (Sama & Papamarcos, 2000). Another, however, showed that individualism versus collectivism was not related to reward allocation preferences (Fischer & Smith, 2003). It may be that who is making the decision and who is the recipient of the decision contribute to these conflicting findings. If the individual making the decision is also the person receiving the benefits of the decision, then it appears that individuals in collectivistic cultures prefer equality; if individuals making the decisions are not recipients of the benefits of the decision, however, individuals in both individualistic and collectivistic cultures tend to prefer equity (Leung, 1997).

Another important line of research in this area examines outcomes of decisions regarding the distribution of resources such as pay (**distributive justice**) and on the process of making decisions (**procedural justice**). Morris and Leung (2000) reviewed the research in this area, and classified cross-cultural studies or distributive justice into two types: studies examining cross-cultural differences in the criteria by which decisions are made, and studies examining cross-cultural differences in the behaviors judged to match the criteria. With regard to the former, Morris and Leung noted many inconsistencies in the literature across studies in the findings, and concluded that people of different cultures apply different criteria in making allocation decisions, and that these criteria are based on situational cues. Different situations in different cultures produce different cues which, in turn, are associated with different criteria to be used in making allocating decisions.

With regard to the behaviors judged to match criteria, Americans' judgments of fairness are more likely to be tied to judgments of performance and merit, whereas many East Asians' judgments are more tied to seniority, education, and family size (Hundley & Kim, 1997). Morris and Leung's analysis of these studies suggested that these types of judgments are not static; as cultural beliefs, values, and opinions change across time, their judgments of this aspect of fairness also shift across time. In Japan today, for example, there is a much larger concern for performance and merit-based rewards than seniority and education, as compared with 20 or 30 years ago (Matsumoto, 2002a), and such changes are occurring in many cultures around the world that are undergoing cultural evolution.

As with distributive justice, Morris and Leung (2000) separated studies related to procedural justice into studies examining criteria and then the behaviors associated with the criteria. They suggested that in hierarchical, high-power-distance cultures, people in legitimate positions of authority can treat subordinates more harshly before this behavior is seen as unfair. A meta-analysis examining 25 studies in 14 cultures (Fischer & Smith, 2003) indicated that the hierarchical nature of cultures was important in influencing reward allocation. Specifically, they found that rewards such as pay and promotions were distributed in hierarchical cultures differentially on the basis of equity and performance, whereas more egalitarian, horizontal cultures preferred equality over equity. Also individualism–collectivism was not as important in determining reward allocations as the hierarchical, power dimensions of culture were.

Consumer Decisions

One interesting area of research that has blossomed in recent years has been cross-cultural research on consumer decision making. While consumer and economic decision making in general has been a major area of research for many years, it has only been in the recent decade or two that cross-cultural research has taken hold. Recent studies, for example, have shown that compared to European Americans, Asian Americans typically choose more brand-name products, and this difference appears to be related to greater social status concerns among Asian Americans than European Americans (Kim & Drolet, 2009). Certainly this kind of knowledge is important to marketing products, goods, and services.

In the study of consumer behavior, the role of emotion in consumer decision making has also gained importance in recent years. While emotion is a universal phenomenon, people of different cultures differ in how much they express and experience emotions, and control them (see Chapter 9). These psychological processes are at work in consumer behavior as well. In one study, when given an unexpected gift, East Asians reported less surprise and pleasure than Americans. This difference appeared to have been associated with East Asian's motivations to maintain balance and emotional control. But when the unexpected gift was attributed to good luck, East Asians experienced greater pleasure than Westerners (Valenzuela, Mellers, & Strebel, 2009).

Another interesting line of research on consumer behaviors concerns the **endowment effect**. This refers to the tendency for owners and potential sellers of goods and products to value those products more than potential buyers do. Although this effect has been widely studied in the United States, a recent study showed that the size of the effect differs across cultures. East Asians demonstrated a smaller endowment effect compared to Americans and Canadians, and this difference was attributed to the idea that ownership of the product enhanced the self more in individualistic contexts like the United States and Canada than in Asia (Maddux et al., 2010).

endowment effect
This refers to the tendency for owners and potential sellers of goods and products to value those products more than potential buyers do.

▶ Culture and Negotiation

In the United States, Americans generally approach negotiation with a certain set of assumptions that are rooted in our culture and values. For example, we view time as a commodity ("time is money"), and we believe we are in control of our lives (recall our discussion of control in Chapter 6). Americans value specialization, pragmatism, equal opportunity, independence, and competition (Kimmel, 1994). Thus, in the United States, negotiation is a business, not a social activity. The objective of the negotiation is to get a job done, which usually requires a mixture of problem solving and bargaining. Communication is direct and verbal, with little deliberate or intentional use of nonverbal behaviors in the communication process. Sometimes it is confrontational and competitive.

Negotiation processes in other cultures challenge many of these American assumptions. In the arena of international negotiation, negotiators come as representatives not only of their companies but of their cultures as well. They bring all the issues of culture—customs, rituals, rules, and heritage—to the negotiating table. Factors that we are not even aware of play a role in these negotiating sessions, such as who sits where, the amount of space between people, how to greet each other, what to call each other, and what kinds of expectations we have of each other. The "diplomatic dance" that has been observed between American and Arab negotiators is but one example. People from

Arab cultures tend to interact with others at a much closer distance than Americans are accustomed to. As the Arabs move closer, Americans unconsciously edge backward, whereupon the Arabs unconsciously edge forward, until they are almost chasing each other around the room (recall our discussion of interpersonal spacing in Chapter 10).

Cross-cultural studies on negotiation challenge many American assumptions about it (see, for example, Allerheiligen, Graham, & Lin, 1985; Goldman, 1994; Graham, 1983, 1984, 1993; Graham & Andrews, 1987). One interesting cultural difference between American approaches to negotiation from those in many other cultures concerns the role of socializing. Americans are used to "sitting down at the table and hammering out a deal." East Asian negotiators may want to have dinner, go for drinks, or play golf. Negotiation in the Middle East and many other parts of the world will start with tea, and many times negotiators have to get through many intermediaries before they can talk to decision makers. People of cultures that take their time in negotiations are more willing to engage in these activities because they are generally more interested in developing a relationship with their business partners as people. It also gives them a good opportunity to make judgments about the character or integrity of potential partners, which is an important aspect of their business decisions. Contrastingly, Americans are primarily concerned with "the deal" and what is right for the organization's bottom line. Many American business negotiators not used to a more relationship-based style of negotiating often become impatient with these activities, feeling as though they never get to talk business. By the same token, negotiators in many other cultures feel put on the spot by Americans, as though they have been thrust into a situation and forced to make a decision they cannot possibly make. Needless to say, these cultural differences in negotiation styles have led to many a breakdown in international negotiations.

Cultural differences exist in many other aspects of negotiation as well. Expressing anger elicits more concessions from European Americans, probably because of the often competitive and contentious nature of negotiation; but expressing anger elicits smaller concessions from Asian and Asian American negotiators, probably because it violates cultural norms of appropriateness (Adam, Shirako, & Maddux, 2010), and thus says something about the people.

Gelfand and colleagues (2006) have argued that relational self-construals—that is, viewing oneself as fundamentally connected with others—is an important aspect to understanding negotiation. Negotiation starts with individuals coming with their own sense of relational self, which is influenced by the culture from which they come. One of the goals of negotiation is to align the relational self-construal of the negotiators so that they are congruent. Congruence between the relational self-construals of the negotiators aids in the production of relational behaviors, creates value, and eventually economic or relational capital. One implication of this model is that even if behaviors are adapted to the situation, negotiation may not be as fruitful as it can be unless the relational self-construals of the negotiators are aligned through the negotiation process.

Although research has documented many major cultural differences in negotiation (summarized in Table 15.8), the available research tells us little about the degree to which negotiators adjust their cultural practices depending on whom they are negotiating with, and on what parameters such adjustment occurs. Nor has cross-cultural research done much to elucidate the ingredients of a "successful" negotiation. A review of cross-cultural studies on negotiation (Gelfand & Dyer, 2000) suggested that factors such as proximal social conditions (deadlines, negotiator relationships), the negotiators' psychological states (implicit theories and metaphors, judgment biases), and behaviors (tactics) are also important in understanding international or intercultural discussions and negotiations. Indeed, Gelfand and Dyer's model of the

TABLE 15.8 Typical U.S. Assumptions about Negotiation

Topic	Typical U.S. Beliefs	Alternative Beliefs about Negotiation in Many Other Cultures
Conception of the negotiation process	Negotiation is a business, not a social activity. The object is to get a job done, which usually requires a mixture of problem-solving and bargaining activities. Most negotiations are adversarial, and negotiators are trying to get as much as possible for their side. The flow of a negotiation is from prenegotiation strategy sessions to opening sessions to give-and-take (bargaining) to final compromises to signing and implementation of agreements. All parties are expected to give up some of their original demands. Success can be measured in terms of how much each party achieves its bottom-line objectives.	Negotiation is based on human relationships, and thus must be built on social activity. The object is to develop a long-term relationship with someone or another organization that can be mutually beneficial for a long time. Thus negotiation should be collegial and collaborative. Success can be measured in terms of how both parties mutually benefit.
Type of issues	Substantive issues are more important than social and emotional issues. Differences in positions are seen as problems to be solved.	Relationships are of prime importance. Differences in positions are of personal importance.
Protocol	Negotiations are scheduled occasions that require face-to-face interactions among the parties involved. Efficiency of time centering on substantive tasks is valued over ceremony and social amenities. During negotiation, standardized procedures of interaction should be followed; social interactions are informal and should occur elsewhere.	Negotiation can occur anytime, anywhere, and especially in social settings such as dinners, tea, golf outings, and the like.
Reliance on verbal behaviors	Communication is direct and verbal. What is said is more important than how it is said, or what is not said. Communications tend to be spontaneous and reactive after presentation of initial positions.	Actions speak louder than words.
Nature of persuasive arguments	Tactics such as bluffing are acceptable in the bargaining process. Current information and ideas are more valid than history or tradition.	History and tradition are extremely important. Lying may be acceptable.
Individual negotiator's latitude	The representatives who negotiate have a great deal of latitude in reaching agreements for their companies.	Individuals who represent a group may not have much latitude.
Bases of trust	Negotiators trust the other parties until they prove untrustworthy. Trust is judged by the behavior of others.	Other parties are untrustworthy until proven trustworthy.
Risk-taking propensities	Negotiators are open to different or novel approaches to problem issues. Brainstorming is good. Avoiding uncertainty is not important in the negotiation process. Fixed ideological positions and approaches are not acceptable.	Time tested solutions are often the best. Ideology is sometimes non-negotiable and sacred.
Value of time	Time is very important. Punctuality is expected. A fixed time is allotted for concluding a negotiation.	Time is open ended and fluid.
Decision-making system	Majority voting and/or authoritative decisions are the rule. Certain team members are expected to be authorized to make binding decisions.	The decision of a single leader is final and absolute. What the leader says goes.
Forms of satisfactory agreement	Oral commitments are not binding. Written contracts that are exact and impersonally worded are binding. There is the expectation of contractual finality. Lawyers and courts are the final arbitrators in any arguments after contracts have been signed.	People are taken on their word. A person's word is everything.

Source: The U.S. beliefs are adapted from Kimmel (1994).

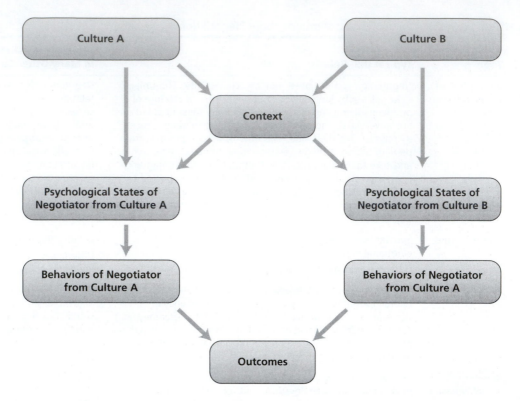

FIGURE 15.2 A Dynamic and Psychological Model of Culture and Negotiation

Source: Gelfand, Michele J. A Cultural Perspective on Negotiation: Progress, Pitfalls and Prospects, *Applied Psychology: An International Review, 49*(1), 77, 2000, Blackwell Publishing. Reprinted with permission.

influence of culture on the negotiation process identifies many important variables that indicate that the process is very complex (Figure 15.2).

Because of cultural differences in negotiation practices, communication becomes especially important in intercultural negotiations. Findings from studies examining communication in these situations, however, typically have shown that the quality of communication is lower in intercultural negotiations than in same-culture negotiations (recall our discussion in Chapter 14 on studies comparing inter- and intracultural dyads on cooperation as well). Better quality of communication experiences lead to better negotiation outcomes, and these beneficial effects tend to be better in intercultural compared to intracultural contexts (Liu, Chua, & Stahl, 2010).

▶ Intercultural Issues Regarding Business and Work

In the past, the American workforce was less racially, ethnically, and culturally diverse than it is today. With less cultural diversity, the expectations of the members of any work organization were generally similar. Communication, lines of authority, and hierarchical structure were established with less conscious awareness of differences among people. Members of organizations had implicit, tacit knowledge about how to behave around one another and how to work together, because cultures and organizations were relatively more homogeneous.

Organizations were more isolated from issues of culture in yet another way, as many companies in the past were much less international or intercultural. Most of the work-related issues companies dealt with were confined to the United States and its culture. And most of the companies that competed or cooperated with one another were based in the same country and culture.

This national work environment is now a thing of the past. Not only is the American workforce culturally diverse, but many companies today operate in an international arena. The workplace of the world now includes unprecedented numbers of **multinational and international corporations**—work organizations that have subsidiaries, satellite offices, and work units in more than one country. Increasingly, these companies need to deal with people of diverse and varied backgrounds. Today, transfers from one business unit to another within the same company can mean a transfer from one country to another. This internationalization of business brings with it more intercultural issues and challenges.

multinational and international corporations Work organizations that have subsidiaries, satellite offices, and work units in more than one country.

Even domestic companies that are not multinational in their structure must face the challenge of internationalization, with its associated intercultural issues. Trade laws and treaties, along with the Internet, have brought more business and competitors from distant cultures, as well as increased opportunities for opening markets in other countries and cultures. Advances in communication and transportation allow companies and individuals to work more easily today than ever before over vast physical and cultural distances. Technological changes in communication—telephones, fax machines, videoteleconferencing, and e-mail—have forced the issue of culture to the forefront of our work lives. More companies today than ever before are concerned with currency exchange rates, and the value of goods, services, and labor in other countries. The business world has become a global village, in which there are few boundaries.

As companies become increasingly dependent on other companies in other countries and cultures for survival and success, people today are facing an ever-larger number of intercultural issues in the workplace. Add to these organizational developments the increasingly porous and flexible nature of national borders, and the result is a large number of people of different cultural backgrounds, lifestyles, values, and behaviors living and working together. These social trends and changes bring their own particular set of issues, challenges, and opportunities regarding intercultural interactions in the workplace and other work-related situations.

For multinational corporations, international business is not just international; it is intercultural. As we have seen throughout this chapter, business organizations are affected in many ways by the cultures in which they reside. Organizational structures and decision-making procedures differ, and people differ—in their definitions of work, work-related values, identification between self and company, and rules of interacting with other workers. Today's international business world requires that business organizations, and the people within them, gain intercultural competence as well as business competence.

In this section, we will discuss two broad areas in which intercultural issues have come to the fore in recent decades: overseas assignments and working with an increasingly diverse workforce population.

Overseas Assignments and Culture Shock

Many corporations with subsidiaries and business partners in other countries are finding it increasingly necessary to send workers abroad for extended periods. Worker exchanges and overseas assignments are used to train employees and business units in another country in skills that are found only there. Such overseas assignments can give rise to myriad problems, not only because of all the cultural differences discussed in this chapter, but also because of limited language skills and differing expectations of the person on assignment and his or her hosts.

American companies today would not hesitate to send "the most qualified person" on assignment, either for negotiation or for the long term, regardless of sex, race, or ethnicity. Many other cultures, however, are not accustomed to women in important positions in business, or a young person, and may not be receptive to people of different perceived races or ethnicities. In many contexts, a woman would not be taken as seriously as a man, and racial or ethnic stereotypes may dominate interactions. The resulting frustrations might include not being looked at during a conversation and having questions directed to a man when a woman is the recognized leader or expert on an assignment team.

Many of the most pressing problems for people on overseas assignments occur not at work but in other aspects of living in a foreign country. Major differences in lifestyle, customs, and behaviors often overshadow cultural differences at work. If an individual goes on an overseas assignment with his or her family, there is the added problem of their adjustment to the new culture, especially if school-age children are involved. The entire spectrum of intercultural adjustment and acculturation becomes important for all involved (as we discussed in Chapter 14). Even when workers do well in their work environment, they may do poorly in their home and community adjustment. While employees may find a safe haven during the workday in a milieu with which they are somewhat familiar, their families are often left bearing the brunt of intercultural adaptation.

culture shock The disorientation, anxiety, confusion, doubt, distress, or nervousness that occurs when a person is confronted with and needs to deal with a new and different culture.

Many individuals who travel to other cultures for a sustained period of time experience **culture shock**, which can be defined as the disorientation, anxiety, confusion, doubt, distress, or nervousness that occurs when a person is confronted with and needs to deal with a new and different culture. Oberg (1960) was the first to identify this construct over half a century ago, and since that time it has been well studied and documented by many scholars (e.g., Furnham & Bochner, 1982; Pederson, 1995; Ward, Bochner, & Furnham, 2001). While there are minor differences across writers, most scholars agree that individuals often pass through four stages of culture shock. The first is the *honeymoon phase*, in which engaging with a different culture is new, wonderful, exciting, and refreshing. The second stage is the *negotiation stage*, where differences between the familiar and unfamiliar cultures become more prominent and conscious; the greater awareness of differences can create frustration, confusion, anxiety, distress, or depression. The third stage is the *adjustment phase*, in which individuals adopt new behavioral routines and adjust their mind-sets to their new situation and context. Things start to become more normal again. The fourth stage is the *mastery phase*, in which individuals are more able to participate and immerse themselves in the new culture more fully (see Figure 15.3).

reverse culture shock The culture shock that individuals experience upon returning to their home cultures and realizing that things are not the same as when they left.

Individuals are not only at risk for culture shock when they go abroad. Culture shock can occur within the same culture, such as when people from one part of a country go to school in another, such as has been documented when African Americans go to elite, predominantly European American universities (Torres, 2009). After returning home from a sojourn elsewhere, individuals can experience **reverse culture shock**, especially after one has adapted and adjusted fully to another culture (e.g., see Gaw, 2000; Yoshida et al., 2002). This refers to the culture shock that individuals experience upon returning to their home cultures and realizing that things are not the same as when they left. Having adapted and adjusted to a new and different culture, people often find themselves in the situation of having to re-adjust again to their original, home culture.

STAGES *of* CULTURE SHOCK

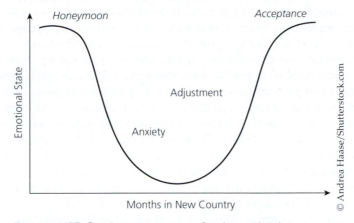

FIGURE 15.3 The Four Stages of Culture Shock

Of course, adaptation and adjustment to a new culture is not all negative. On the positive side, people who go on overseas assignments have a tremendous opportunity to learn new skills and new ways of doing their work that can help them when they return. They may learn a new language and customs, broadening their perspectives. They may make new friends and business acquaintances, and this type of networking may have business as well as personal payoffs in the future. Foreign assignment is an important aspect of today's international business world that promises to play an even larger role in the global village of the future. Completing these assignments to the best of our abilities requires us to understand all the influences of culture, both inside and outside the workplace. In the future, these types of skills will be even more valuable than they are today. Little systematic, formal research exists on this topic in the published literature, but the situation is slowly changing (e.g., Kaye & Taylor, 1997; Selmer, 1999). Future research on this important topic will help in the design of intercultural adjustment programs for company employees, allowing them to be more effective in their overseas assignments.

Working with an Increasingly Diverse Workforce Population

Organizations all around the world are dealing with an increasingly diverse workforce population. For example, American companies are increasingly hosting workers from other countries. Joint ventures between American and Asian and European companies have increased over the past 20 years—most visibly beginning with automobile manufacturing, but also in computers and semiconductors, communication technology, and many other fields. One result is an influx of workers from these countries and cultures to the United States.

Many of the problems that arise when American workers go overseas also arise when foreign workers come to the United States. Often, managers from another culture come to oversee and supervise production or assembly, bringing with them all the expectations, customs, and rituals of their home country. Not surprisingly, they find that those ways of doing business do not work in the United States, because the people are different and the system is different. Similarly, many of the problems experienced by American families abroad are also experienced by the families of workers who come to the United States.

One early study highlighted some of the problems and issues that may arise in these situations. Graham (1993) spent six months as a hidden participant observer at a Japanese automobile plant near Lafayette, Indiana (Subaru/Isuzu Automotive). During this time, the author was able to document worker resistance to Japanese management practices in the form of sabotage, protest, agitation, and confrontation. The results of this study brought into question the validity and worth of simply "transferring" the Japanese management model to the American milieu. The data also failed to support the contention that participation schemes (such as teamwork) automatically increase worker control or that decentralized authority structures increase worker autonomy.

Another study focused on cultural differences in ways of handling disagreement. In this study (Smith, Dugan, Peterson, & Leung, 1998), managers and supervisors from a variety of organizations in 23 countries completed a questionnaire about how they handled disagreements in their work unit. The responses were aggregated for each country, and the country mean values on the questionnaire were correlated with the country's scores on Hofstede's dimensions described earlier. The results indicated that power distance (PD) significantly predicted the frequency of disagreements between work groups. In handling disagreements, people in low-PD cultures tended to rely on subordinates and coworkers. People of individualistic countries relied more on their own personal experience and training, whereas people of collectivistic cultures relied more on formal rules and procedures. Although this study involved participants in different countries, these types of psychological differences based on power distance and individualism–collectivism may be important in understanding cultural differences within a single multicultural organization.

Despite the potential problems associated with receiving foreign workers, many of the advantages of overseas assignments also apply to receiving people from abroad. The ability to reap these benefits depends on the openness of the host organization to learn and on the goodwill and intent of the employee and the company to engage in a mutually beneficial partnership.

Even without international joint ventures and worker exchanges, many American companies are dealing with increasing diversity solely on the basis of the increasing diversity of the American population. The United States is home to people of many different races, ethnicities, and cultures. Within this "mixed salad" of cultures are generational differences, from recent immigrants to second-, third-, and multiple-generation Americans of wide-ranging ethnic and cultural backgrounds. The problems that can occur when two cultures clash can be magnified many times over when people from multiple cultures are thrust together to interact and work toward a common goal.

Many of the issues raised in dealing with people across countries and cultures are relevant for domestic work organizations dealing with an increasingly diverse American workforce as well. People come to work with different expectations, and different expectations can lead to intercultural clashes. Cultural differences in the management of time and people, in identification with work, and in making decisions all provide areas for conflict. People in the United States come to work with differences in work-related values and the degree to which they respect or minimize power and status differences between them. People come to work with different views regarding sex differences and how to manage uncertainty.

Many successful companies have met these challenges by making explicit what kinds of communication styles, decision making, productivity, and worker behaviors are important for the success of the company. Many companies today actively train their employees in intercultural issues ranging from communication to expectations (Goldman, 1992); the most successful of these programs undoubtedly have important positive, practical implications in many areas of people's lives. Many companies have created temporary organizational cultures in which their employees can move and adapt without fear of losing themselves or their own personal cultures. They have designed ways not only of avoiding problems but also of handling problems effectively and constructively when they do arise. Negotiating all these issues requires additional work and effort by companies and people alike, but organizations that can do so successfully are likely to realize long-term benefits to the bottom line.

▶ Culture and Sexual Harassment

You are the boss of a company that is trying to close a major deal with another company in another country. Your best negotiator is a woman, whom you trust and has been with the company for years. You have been told, however, that the other company will not deal with a woman. When previous negotiating teams have been sent, their negotiators clearly ignore the woman and talk only to the male, even though the male is the woman's assistant. What would you do?

Complex issues concerning gender and sex are commonplace in organizations that work cross-culturally. One of these is sexual harassment. **Sexual harassment** is defined by the Equal Employment Opportunity Commission as unwelcome sexual advances, requests for sexual favors, or other verbal or physical conduct of a sexual nature in which submission to such behavior is a condition to employment and employment decisions affecting the individual (such as promotion), and where the behavior interferes with the individual's work environment or creates an intimidating, offensive, or hostile work environment. The past few decades have seen a dramatic increase in awareness to issues concerning sexual harassment in the U.S. workplace. The increase in the number of intercultural contacts in work organizations brought about by the creation of multinational companies and transfer of employees across borders has brought about an increase in the awareness of these issues cross-culturally as well.

To our knowledge, there is not yet formal research across a wide range of cultures documenting the incidence of sexual harassment, but we believe it is also widespread across cultures. This may be true for a variety of cultural reasons (Luthar & Luthar, 2002). For one, sex- and gender-based discriminatory actions—both in terms of behaviors and words—may be tolerated more across different cultures. Recall, for example, our discussion of cultural differences in masculinity versus femininity (Chapter 7). Cultures differ greatly in the degree to which they differentiate behaviors between men and women. One may even say that these differences are not only tolerated but also expected and natural; thus, what may be construed as sexual harassment in the United States may not be seen as such in other cultures. Moreover, there are large cultural differences in sex roles, which contribute to this situation. Differences across cultures in power and hierarchy also contribute to this state of affairs, because power differences contribute to the maintenance of sex and gender differences within a culture, and in many cultures males have more powerful roles in organizations.

When it occurs, sexual harassment may have the same effects across cultures. Studies examining the experiences of individuals have shown that there are three major types of sexual harassment-related experiences: sexist hostility, sexual hostility, and unwanted sexual advances (Fitzgerald, Gelfand, & Drasgow, 1995); these same clusters of experiences were reported by Latina women as well (Cortina, 2001). Fitzgerald and colleagues (Fitzgerald, Drasgow, Hulin, Gelfand, & Magley, 1997) demonstrated that sexual harassment in the U.S. workplace affects job satisfaction, health conditions, and psychological conditions. Subsequently, these same types of effects

sexual harassment
Unwelcome sexual advances, requests for sexual favors, or other verbal or physical conduct of a sexual nature in which submission to such behavior is a condition to employment and employment decisions affecting the individual (such as promotion), and where the behavior interferes with the individual's work environment or creates an intimidating, offensive, or hostile work environment.

have been shown to occur in Turkey (Wasti, Bergman, Glomb, & Drasgow, 2000) and among Latinas (Cortina, Fitzgerald, & Drasgow, 2002).

Being the victim of sexual harassment can be stressful for anyone, and research shows that women across a wide range of cultures attempt to cope with these experiences in a variety of ways, including avoidance, denial, negotiation, advocacy seeking, and social coping (Cortina & Wasti, 2005; Wasti & Cortina, 2002). Research has demonstrated acculturation effects as well; in one study, Hispanic women with greater affiliation to mainstream American cultures experienced more sexual harassment than Hispanic women with less affiliation (Shupe, Cortina, Ramos, Fitzgerald, & Salisbury, 2002). Clearly, more cross-cultural research on this very important topic is needed, as well as education across many strata of society in many cultures.

CONCLUSION

The cultural differences that people bring with them to an organization present us with challenges unprecedented in the modern industrialized period of history. To meet these challenges, business, government, and private organizations look to research and education about cultural diversity as it relates to work. Intercultural communication and competence training and organizational consulting with regard to managing diversity have become major growth industries.

Too often, the idea of managing diversity rests on the underlying assumption that diversity is an unwanted by-product of our work environment—a nuisance variable that must be dealt with in order to maximize efficiency. As we move toward a greater appreciation of cultural similarities and differences, however, we may gain a better appreciation for the different approaches to work, management, and leadership that have worked for different cultures. As we confront the challenges of diversity in the future, we need to move away from the notion of managing a nuisance variable to viewing it as a potential resource for tapping into products, services, and activities that will make companies more efficient, productive, and profitable than ever before. By leveraging diversity rather than managing it, perhaps we can increase international and intercultural cooperation not only in business but among people in general.

EXPLORATION AND DISCOVERY

Why Does This Matter to Me?

1. Have you ever encountered difficulties working in groups, either at school or your job? What kind of problems occurred? Do you think some of these problems may have been the result of cultural differences? How did you resolve them? Do you think you would try to resolve such problems differently in the future?

2. How do the organizations to which you belong make decisions? Is it top-down, bottom-up, or something else? How does it compare to the Japanese system described in the text? What system would work best, and why?

3. Have you ever experienced culture shock, or reverse culture shock? In what situations do you think you can expect yourself to have those types of experiences?

4. Have you ever experienced sexual harassment? What would you do if you were sexually harassed in a job interview? Most people say they would not tolerate such treatment and be angry and confrontative, but in a study that examined what people actually did, the very same people who said they would be angry and confrontative actually tolerated it and were polite and respectful (Woodzicka & LaFrance, 2001). How about you?

Suggestions for Further Exploration

1. How would you study the culture of your organization? Design a study that would examine what an organization's culture is like. Why did you select the variables you did?

2. What kind of training would you provide to a person who was going to be moved to another country for work? Would your training program be limited to the employee, or include the employee's family as well?

3. What kinds of reward systems work best in different organizational and national cultures? How would you design a study that examined cultural differences in reward systems?

4. Interview an international student and see what their experiences have been like adapting to and adjusting to a new culture. Did they experience culture shock?

GLOSSARY

Accommodation the process of changing one's understanding of the world to accommodate ideas that conflict with existing concepts.

Acculturation the process by which people adopt a different cultural system.

The process of individual change and adaptation as a result of continuous contact with a new, distinct, or different culture.

Acquiescence bias the tendency to agree rather than disagree with items on questionnaires.

Affect feelings, or subjective experience.

Affective commitment the level of personal feelings associated with one's relationship to an organization.

Aggression any act or behavior that intentionally hurts another person, either physically or psychologically.

Allocentrism refers to collectivism on the individual-level. On the cultural level, collectivism refers to how a culture functions. Allocentrism refers to how individuals may act in accordance with collectivistic cultural frameworks.

Ambivalent attachment a style of attachment in which children are uncertain in their response to their caregiver, going back and forth between seeking and shunning the caregiver.

Analytic perception context-independent perceptual processes that focuses on a salient object independently from the context in which it is embedded.

Androgyny a gender identity that involves endorsement of both male and female characteristics.

Animism the belief that all things, including inanimate objects, are alive.

Appraisal the process by which people evaluate the events, situations, or occurrences that lead to their having emotions.

Arable land the type of land that can sustain life by food production of some sort.

Arranged marriages a marriage in which someone other than the couple being married makes the decision about who will be wed. Oftentimes, this can be the parents of the individuals being wed.

Assimilation the process of fitting new ideas into a preexisting understanding of the world.

Attachment the special bond that develops between the infant and his or her primary caregiver and provides the infant with emotional security. The quality of attachment has lifelong effects on our relationships with loved ones.

Attention the focusing of our limited capacities of consciousness on a particular set of stimuli, more of whose features are noted and processed in more depth than is true of nonfocal stimuli.

Attitudes evaluations of objects occurring in ongoing thoughts about the objects, or stored in memory.

Attributions Beliefs and inferences about the causes of events and self and other behaviors.

Authoritarian parent a style of parenting in which the parent expects unquestioned obedience and views the child as needing to be controlled.

Authoritative parent a style of parenting that is viewed as firm, fair, and reasonable. This style is seen as promoting psychologically healthy, competent, independent children who are cooperative and at ease in social situations.

Autostereotypes stereotypes about your own group.

Avoidant attachment a style of attachment in which children shun their caregiver.

Back translation a technique of translating research protocols that involves taking the protocol as it was developed in one language, translating it into the target language, and having someone else translate it back to the original. If the back-translated version is the same as the original, they are generally considered equivalent. If it is not, the procedure is repeated until the back-translated version is the same as the original.

Basic emotions a small set of emotion categories, or families of emotions, that are considered to be universal to all humans, biologically based and genetically coded, and evolutionarily based. Humans come into the world with programs for these basic emotions; social and cultural learning then influences how they are used in life.

Behavioral inhibition an aspect of temperament where a child shows signs of wariness, discomfort, or distress when confronted with novel, challenging, or unfamiliar situations. Also known as fearfulness or shyness.

Beliefs a proposition that is regarded as true. People of different cultures have different beliefs.

Better than average effect (also known as the false uniqueness effect) the tendency for individuals to underestimate the commonality of desirable traits and to overestimate their uniqueness.

Bias differences that do not have exactly the same meaning within and across cultures; a lack of equivalence.

Biomedical model a model of health that views disease as resulting from a specific, identifiable cause such as a pathogen (an infectious agent such as a virus or bacteria), a genetic or developmental abnormality (such as being born with a mutated gene), or physical insult (such as being exposed to a carcinogen—a cancer-producing agent).

Biopsychosocial model a model of health that views disease as resulting from biological, psychological, and social factors.

Biosocial model a model that suggests that biological differences between the sexes interact with the environment to produce culture-specific sex roles that are adaptations to the environment.

Blind spot a spot in our visual field where the optic nerve goes through the layer of receptor cells on its way back toward the brain, creating a lack of sensory receptors in the eye at that location.

Carpentered world theory a theory of perception that suggests that people (at least most Americans) are used to seeing things that are rectangular in shape, and thus unconsciously expect things to have square corners.

Categorization the process by which objects are grouped or classified together based on their perceived similarities.

Centration the tendency to focus on a single aspect of a problem.

Channels the specific sensory modalities by which signals are sent and messages are retrieved.

Code frame switching the process by which bilinguals switch between one cultural meaning system and another when switching languages.

Cofigurative culture a culture in which change occurs rapidly. Both adults and peers socialize young people. Young people may have to turn to one another for advice and information in this type of culture.

Cognition a term denoting all mental processes we use to transform sensory input into knowledge.

Cognitive behavioral therapy interventions that emphasize the development of strategies for teaching cognitive skills. Underlying these types of therapy is an assumption that by changing our thinking we can change our behaviors, and vice versa.

Cognitive development a specialty in psychology that studies how thinking skills develop over time. One major theory of cognitive development is that of Piaget.

Collective control a type of control in which one attempts to control the environment as a member of a group, and the group serves as the agent of control.

Collective identity a form of identity that refers to our recognition that we belong to social categories, such as occupation, religion, or culture.

Collective intelligence the general ability of a group to perform a wide variety of tasks.

Collective threat the fear that an ingroup member's behavior can reinforce negative stereotypes about one's group.

Compliance yielding to social pressure in one's public behavior, even though one's private beliefs may not have changed.

Concept a mental category we use to classify events, objects, situations, behaviors, or even people with respect to what we perceive as common properties.

Conceptual bias the degree to which a theory or set of hypotheses being compared across cultures are equivalent—that is, whether they have the same meaning and relevance in all the cultures being compared.

Conformity yielding to real or imagined social pressure.

Conservation an awareness that physical quantities remain the same even when they change shape or appearance.

Contact hypothesis the proposition that contact between groups is especially effective in reducing prejudice.

Context variables variables that operationalize aspects of culture that researchers believe produce differences in psychological variables. These variables are actually measured in unpackaging studies.

Contextual factors any variable that can explain, partly or fully, observed cross-cultural differences. These may involve characteristics of the participants (such as socioeconomic status, education, and age) or their cultures (such as economic development and religious institutions).

Conventional morality the second stage of Kohlberg's theory of moral development, emphasizing conformity to rules that are defined by others' approval or society's rules.

Cooperation people's ability to work together toward common goals.

Correspondence bias see Fundamental Attribution Error.

Counterfactual thinking hypothetical beliefs about the past that could have occurred in order to avoid or change a negative outcome.

Cross-cultural comparisons a study that compares two or more cultures on some psychological variable of interest, often with the hypothesis that one culture will have significantly higher scores on the variable than the other(s).

Cross-cultural research a research methodology that tests the cultural parameters of psychological knowledge. Traditionally, it involves research on human behavior that compares psychological processes between two or more cultures. In this book, we also incorporate knowledge contrasting human cultures versus nonhuman animal cultures. This approach is primarily concerned with testing the possible limitations of knowledge gleaned from one culture by studying people of different cultures.

Cross-cultural validation study a study that examines whether a measure of a psychological construct that was originally generated in a single culture is applicable, meaningful, and thus equivalent in another culture.

Cultural attribution fallacies a mistaken interpretation in cross-cultural comparison studies. Cultural attribution fallacies occur when researchers infer that something cultural produced the differences they observed in their study, despite the fact that they may not be empirically justified in doing so because they did not actually measure those cultural factors.

Cultural concepts of distress the shared ways in which cultural groups or communities experience, express, and interpret distress.

Cultural decoding rules these are rules that people of all cultures learn from early childhood about how to decode or decipher speech and behavior. They form the basis for the cultural filters we have in interpreting the world, and are associated with implicit (and sometimes explicit) judgments of appropriateness, goodness, socialization, or right-wrong.

Cultural display rules culturally prescribed rules that govern how universal emotions can be expressed. These rules center on the appropriateness of displaying emotion, depending on social circumstances. Learned by people early in their lives, they dictate how the universal emotional expressions should be modified according to the social situation. By adulthood, these rules are quite automatic, having been very well practiced.

Cultural explanations of distress what communities and cultural groups believe is the cause of the distress, symptoms, or illness.

Cultural fit hypothesis the proposition that immigrants and sojourners with characteristics that match their host cultures will adjust better than those with less match.

Cultural identity this refers to individuals' psychological membership in a distinct culture.

Cultural idioms of distress ways that communities and cultural groups communicate and express their distressing thoughts, behaviors, and emotions.

Cultural neuroscience an emerging research field that combines recent advances in neuroscience with principles of cultural psychology and population genetics to understand the dynamic relations between culture, behavior, mind, brain, and genes.

Cultural psychology a subdiscipline within psychology that examines the cultural foundations of psychological processes and human behavior. It includes theoretical and methodological frameworks that posit an important role for culture and its influence on mental processes behavior, and vice versa.

Cultural reaffirmation effect the amplified endorsement of home cultural values by bicultural individuals.

Cultural relativism a viewpoint that suggests that psychological disorders can only be understood in the cultural framework within which they occur.

Cultural syndromes patterns of symptoms that tend to cluster together for individuals in specific cultural groups, communities, or contexts.

Cultural worldviews culturally specific belief systems about the world. They contain attitudes, beliefs, opinions, and values about the world. People have worldviews because of evolved, complex cognition; thus, having a worldview is a universal psychological process. The specific content of worldviews, however, is specific to and different for each culture.

Culture a unique meaning and information system, shared by a group and transmitted across generations, that allows the group to meet basic needs of survival, pursue happiness and well-being, and derive meaning from life.

Culture shock the disorientation, anxiety, confusion, doubt, distress, or nervousness that occurs when a person is confronted with and needs to deal with a new and different culture.

Cultures of honor cultures in which norms place a strong emphasis on status and reputation.

Culture-specific a psychological process that is considered to be true for some people of some cultures but not for others.

Cyberbullying bullying through electronic means, for example, using the Internet, social media, or sending text messages.

Decenter the concept underlying the procedure of back translation that involves eliminating any culture-specific concepts of the original language or translating them equivalently into the target language.

Decoding the process by which a person receives signals from an encoder and translates these signals into meaningful messages.

Decoding rules rules that govern the interpretation and perception of emotion. These are culturally dependent rules learned early in life that govern how emotional expressions are perceived, recognized, interpreted, evaluated, and acted on.

Developmental contextualism a contemporary theoretical perspective proposing that the multiple levels of a developing child—ranging from the inner biological, psychological, social relational, and sociocultural—are inextricably intertwined and function as an integrated system. Developmental contextualism stresses that it is the *relation* between these changing multiple levels that constitutes human development.

Deviation from temperate climate the degree to which the average temperature of a given region will differ from what is considered to be the relatively "easiest" temperature to live in, which is 22°C (about 72°F).

Dialectical thinking the tendency to accept what seem to be contradictions in thought or beliefs.

Difficult temperament a type of temperament that is characterized by an intense, irregular, withdrawing style that is generally marked by negative moods.

Direct control a type of control in which the self acts as an agent, and individuals feel themselves to be more self-efficacious when their agency is made explicit, leading to greater feelings of autonomy and efficacy. Direct control may be the preferred mode of behavior in cultural contexts that promote independence or autonomy, such as in the United States.

Discrimination the unfair treatment of others based on their group membership.

Disease a malfunctioning or maladaptation of biologic and psychophysiologic processes in the individual.

Dispositional attributions attributions about people's internal characteristics, traits, or personality.

Distributive justice fairness regarding the distribution of resources, such as pay, the corner office, or perks.

Easy temperament a type of temperament that is defined by a very regular, adaptable, mildly intense style of behavior that is positive and responsive.

Ecological (cultural) level studies a study in which countries or cultures, not individuals, are the unit of analysis.

Egocentrism the inability to step into another's shoes and understand the other person's point of view.

Emblems nonverbal gestures that carry meaning, like a phrase or sentence.

Emics aspects of life that appear to differ across cultures; truths or principles that are culture-specific.

Emotion antecedents the events or situations that elicit or trigger an emotion.

Emotion response system coherence the idea that the various response components of an emotion—facial expressions, voice, physiological reactions, movements, etc.—are related to each other in a coordinated fashion that prepares individuals to do something vis-à-vis the emotion aroused.

Emotional complexity the idea that positive and negative emotions can co-occur and be experienced simultaneously.

Emotions transient, neurophysiological reactions to events that have consequences for our welfare, and require an immediate behavioral response. They include feelings, but also physiological reactions, expressive behaviors, behavioral intentions, and cognitive changes.

Encoding the process by which people select, consciously or unconsciously, a particular modality and method by which to create and send a message to someone else.

Enculturation the process by which individuals learn and adopt the ways and manners of their specific culture.

Endowment effect this refers to the tendency for owners and potential sellers of goods and products to value those products more than potential buyers do.

Episodic memory the recollection of specific events that took place at a particular time and place in the past.

Equality refers to whether the demographic characteristics of individuals such as age or seniority in the organization are considered primarily in making organizational decisions.

Equity refers to whether one's contributions and efforts are considered in making organizational decisions.

Equivalence a state or condition of similarity in conceptual meaning and empirical method between cultures that allows comparisons to be meaningful; a lack of bias.

Ethic of autonomy moral reasoning that emphasizes individual rights and justice. Individual choices and freedoms are important to the extent that they do not harm others and others' choices and freedoms.

Ethic of community moral reasoning that emphasizes interpersonal relationships and community. One's duties, obligations, and roles within the group are highlighted.

Ethic of divinity moral reasoning that emphasizes the centrality of religious beliefs and spirituality.

Ethnic identity individuals' psychological membership in a distinct ethnic group.

Ethnocentrism the tendency to view the world through one's own cultural filters.

Etics aspects of life that appear to be consistent across different cultures; universal or pancultural truths or principles.

Everyday cognition an area of study that examines cognitive skills and abilities that are used in everyday functioning that appear to develop without formal education, but from performing daily tasks of living and working.

Experiments studies in which researchers create conditions to establish cause–effect relationships. Participants are generally assigned randomly to participate in the conditions, and researchers then compare results across conditions.

Explicit prejudice prejudice that is verbalized and thus made public.

Exploratory studies studies designed to examine the existence of cross-cultural similarities or differences. These are generally simple, quasi-experimental designs comparing two or more cultures on a psychological variable.

External attributions attributions that locate the cause of behavior outside a person, such as other people, nature, or acts of God; these are also known as **situational dispositions**.

Extreme response bias the tendency to use the ends of a scale regardless of item content.

Face the public appearance or image of a person.

Factor analysis a statistical technique that allows researchers to group items on a questionnaire. The theoretical model underlying factor analysis is that groups of items on a questionnaire are answered in similar ways because they are assessing the same, single underlying psychological construct (or trait). By interpreting the groupings underlying the items, therefore, researchers make inferences about the underlying traits that are being measured.

Foreign language effect a temporary decline in the thinking ability of people who are using a foreign language in which they are less proficient than their native tongue.

Foreign language processing difficulties problems associated with learning a foreign language, such as taking more time to respond and experiencing cognitive difficulties while processing information.

Front-horizontal foreshortening theory a theory of perception that suggests that we interpret vertical lines as horizontal lines extending into the distance. Because we interpret the vertical line in the horizontal–vertical illusion as extending away from us, we see it as longer.

Fundamental attribution error a tendency to explain the behaviors of others using internal attributions but to explain one's own behaviors using external attributions; also known as **correspondence bias**.

Gender the behaviors or patterns of activities a society or culture deems appropriate for men and women. These behavioral patterns may or may not be related to sex and sex roles, although they often are.

Gender identity the degree to which a person has awareness of or recognition that he or she has adopted a particular gender role.

Gender role the degree to which a person adopts the gender-specific behaviors ascribed by his or her culture.

Gender role ideology judgments about what gender roles in a particular culture ought to be.

Gender stereotype the psychological or behavioral characteristics typically associated with men and women.

Gender stratification hypothesis the idea that gender differences are related to cultural variations in opportunity structures for girls and women.

Gestures movements of the body, usually the hands, that are generally reflective of thought or feeling.

Goodness of fit how well a child's temperament fits into the expectations and values of the parents, environment, and culture.

Group entitativity the belief that groups are like people in that they have intentions and the ability to plan actions.

Groupthink a collective pattern of thinking that hinders effective group decisions.

Haptics the use of touch in interpersonal interactions.

Health disparities differences in health outcomes by groups such as between males and females, African Americans and European Americans, and people of lower and higher socioeconomic status (SES).

Heterostereotypes stereotypes about other groups.

High-context cultures cultures that promote communication in which many messages are conveyed indirectly in context rather than directly in verbal language.

Hindsight bias the process in which individuals adjust their memory for something after they find out the true outcome.

Holistic health a perspective on health that considers the physical, social, environmental and sometimes spiritual needs of the individual.

Holistic perception context-dependent perceptual processes that focus on the relationships between objects and their contexts.

Homeostasis maintaining steady, stable functioning in our bodies when there are changes in the environment.

Honorific speech speech styles in certain languages that denote status differences among interactants.

Hypercognition relatively greater amounts and forms of knowledge, awareness, and thought about something that go beyond the usual. This term was coined by Levy to refer to cultures that create (hypercognize) many words to differentiate many different emotional states.

Hypocognition relatively fewer amounts and forms of knowledge, awareness, and thought about something compared to the usual. This term was coined by Levy to refer to cultures that lack (hypocognize) words to differentiate emotional states.

Hypothesis-testing studies studies designed to test why cultural differences exist. They go beyond simple quasi-experimental designs by either including context variables or by using experiments.

Identity the way individuals understand themselves and are recognized by others. Our perceived roles in life, aggregate role and life experiences, narratives, values, and motives.

Identity denial when an individual is not recognized as a member of a group to which he or she identifies.

Idiocentrism refers to individualism on the individual level. On the cultural level, individualism refers to a how a culture functions. Idiocentrism refers to how individuals may act in accordance with individualistic cultural frameworks.

Illness personal, interpersonal, and cultural reactions to disease or discomfort.

Immigrant paradox despite the many challenges of adapting and adjusting to a new country, immigrants tend to show better physical health compared to non-immigrants, and, with further assimilation, further negative health outcomes.

Implicit prejudice prejudicial attitudes, values, or beliefs that are unspoken and perhaps even outside conscious awareness.

Independent construal of self a sense of self that views the self as a bounded entity, clearly separated from relevant others.

Indigenous cultural studies studies that use rich, complex, and in-depth descriptions of cultures and cultural differences to predict and test for differences in a psychological variable.

Indigenous healing helping beliefs and practices that originate within a given culture or society for treating the inhabitants of the given group.

Indigenous personalities conceptualizations of personality developed in a particular culture that are specific and relevant only to that culture.

Indirect control a type of control in which one's agency is hidden or downplayed; people pretend as if they are not acting as an agent even though they are doing so in reality.

Individual-level measures of culture measures that assess psychological dimensions related to meaningful dimensions of cultural variability and that are completed by individuals. They are often used as context variables to ensure that samples in different cultures actually harbor the cultural characteristics thought to differentiate them.

Infant mortality the number of infant deaths (one year of age or younger) per 1,000 live births.

Infrahumanization the belief that others lack human qualities.

Ingroups a category of individuals people of all cultures create. Ingroup members generally have a history of shared experiences and an anticipated future that produces a sense of intimacy, familiarity, and trust.

Ingroup advantage the hypothesis that individuals can recognize emotions expressed by members of their own culture relatively better than of those from a different culture.

Ingroup derogation negative attitudes or beliefs about one's own ingroup.

Ingroup relationships relationships characterized by some degree of familiarity, intimacy, and trust. We feel close to people around us we consider to be in our ingroup. Self-ingroup relationships develop through bonds that tie the ingroup together through common friendship or relationships or goals.

Institutional discrimination discrimination that occurs on the level of a large group, society, organization, or institution.

Intercultural adaptation how people change their behaviors or ways of thinking in a new cultural environment.

Intercultural adjustment the subjective experiences people have as they adapt their behaviors and thinking.

Intercultural communication the exchange of knowledge, ideas, thoughts, concepts, and emotions among people of different cultural backgrounds.

Interdependent construal of self a sense of self that views the self as unbounded, flexible, and contingent on context. This sense of self is based on a principle of the fundamental connectedness among people.

Internal attributions attributions that specify the cause of behavior within a person; also known as **dispositional attributions**, because they are attributions about people's dispositions.

Internal reliability the degree to which different items in a questionnaire are related to each other, and give consistent responses.

Intracultural communication communication that occurs among people of the same cultural background.

Irreversibility the inability to imagine "undoing" a process.

Leadership the "process of influence between a leader and followers to attain group, organizational, or societal goals" (Hollander, 1985).

Level-oriented studies studies that examine cultural differences in mean levels of variables.

Lexicon the words contained in a language, the vocabulary.

Life expectancy average number of years a person is expected to live from birth.

Linguistic bias refers to the degree of semantic equivalence between protocols (instruments, instructions, questionnaires, etc.) used in a cross-cultural comparison study.

Linkage studies studies that attempt to measure an aspect of culture theoretically hypothesized to produce cultural differences and then empirically link that measured aspect of culture with the dependent variable of interest.

Locus of control people's attributions of control over their behaviors and relationships as internal or external to themselves. People with an internal locus of control see their behavior and relationships with others as dependent on their own behavior. People with an external locus of control see their behavior and relationships as contingent on forces outside themselves and beyond their control.

Low-context cultures cultures that promote direct communication in which messages are conveyed primarily and directly in verbal languages and the effects of context are minimized.

Machismo a concept related to Mexican American gender role differentiation that is characterized by many traditional expectations of the male gender role, such as being unemotional, strong, authoritative, and aggressive.

Mate poaching attracting someone who is already in a romantic relationship with someone else.

Measurement bias the degree to which measures used to collect data in different cultures are equally valid and reliable.

Messages the meanings that encoders intend to convey and decoders interpret.

Microsaccades micro eye movements that help our brains fill in scenes so it looks as if we see everything.

Mindfulness a Buddhist principle emphasizing close attention to the present moment, being aware of one's senses, breathing, and thoughts without judgment or evaluation. A strategy to improve intercultural communication that allows people to be conscious of their own habits, mental scripts, and cultural expectations concerning communication. Mindfulness is effective in reducing tension, anxiety, and stress and has been incorporated successfully in cognitive behavioral therapies.

Model minority stereotype the stereotype of Asian Americans that they are overachievers.

Morphemes the smallest and most basic units of meaning in a language.

Multi-level studies studies that involve data collection at multiple levels of analysis, such as the individual level, context, community, and national culture.

Multinational and international corporations work organizations that have subsidiaries, satellite offices, and work units in more than one country.

Mutual self-enhancement self-enhancement that is achieved through the giving and receiving of compliments between partners in close relationships.

Naïve dialectivism a constellation of lay beliefs about the nature of the world (rather than a cognitive style as suggested by dialectical thinking). Naïve dialecticism is characterized by the doctrine of the mean, or the belief that the truth is always somewhere in the middle.

National character the perception that each culture has a modal personality type, and that most persons in that culture share aspects of it.

Nemawashi the broad-based consensus-building procedure that occurs within the Japanese ringi system of decision making.

Nonverbal behaviors all the dynamic behaviors, other than words, that convey messages, including facial expressions; movements and gestures of hands, arms, and legs; posture; vocal characteristics such as pitch, rate, intonation, and silence; interpersonal space; touching behaviors; and gaze and visual attention.

Normative commitment the degree to which one's ties to the organization are bound by duty and obligation.

Norms a generally accepted standard of behavior within a cultural or sub-cultural group.

Obedience a form of compliance that occurs when people follow direct commands, usually from someone in a position of authority.

Oligarchy an organizational structure characterized by rule- or decision-making power of a few. Decisions are typically made by people "at the top," who impose their decisions on subordinates.

Operationalization the ways researchers conceptually define a variable and measure it.

Optical illusions perceptions that involve an apparent discrepancy between how an object looks and what it actually is.

Organizational climate a shared perception of organizational policies, practices, and procedures, and how people feel about them.

Organizational commitment the degree to which a person is committed, identifies with, and makes efforts for, his or her organization.

Organizational culture a dynamic system of rules involving attitudes, values, beliefs, norms, and behaviors that are shared among members of an organization.

Outgroups a category of individuals people of all cultures create. Outgroup members generally include all individuals who are not in one's ingroup. Outgroup members generally lack a history of shared experiences and do not have an anticipated future.

Outgroup relationships relationships that lack the familiarity, intimacy, and trust characteristic of relationships with ingroup others.

Overpathologizing misinterpreting culturally sanctioned behavior as expressions of pathological symptoms.

Paralinguistic cues aspects of the voice that convey information, such as tone, intonation, pitch, speech rate, use of silence.

Parental ethnotheories parental cultural belief systems.

Pathogen an infectious agent such as a virus or bacteria.

Perception the process of gathering information about the world through our senses; our initial interpretations of sensations.

Permissive parents a style of parenting in which parents allow children to regulate their own lives and provide few firm guidelines.

Person perception the process of forming impressions of others.

Personal identity a form of identity characterized by the qualities and attributes that distinguish oneself from others.

Personality a set of relatively enduring behavioral and cognitive characteristics, traits, or predispositions that people take with them to different situations, contexts, and interactions with others, and that contribute to differences among individuals.

Phonemes the smallest and most basic units of sound in a language.

Phonology the system of rules governing how words should sound (pronunciation, "accent") in a given language.

Population density the number of people living within a given unit of space. In a place like a city in which a large number of people live in a relatively small space, the population density is higher than in a rural area where fewer people live in each similar amount of space.

Positive logical determinism a tendency to see contradictions as mutually exclusive categories, as either-or, yes-no, one-or-the-other types of categories.

Postconventional morality the third stage of Kohlberg's theory of moral development, emphasizing moral reasoning on the basis of individual principles and conscience.

Postfigurative culture a culture in which change is slow and socialization occurs primarily by elders transferring their knowledge to their children. Elders hold the knowledge necessary for becoming a successful and competent adult.

Pragmatics the system of rules governing how language is used and understood in given social contexts.

Preconventional morality the first stage of Kohlberg's theory of moral development, emphasizing compliance with rules to avoid punishment and gain rewards.

Prefigurative culture a culture that is changing so rapidly that young people may be the ones to teach adults cultural knowledge.

Prejudice the tendency to prejudge others on the basis of their group membership.

Priming a method used to determine if one stimulus affects another.

Priming studies studies that involve experimentally manipulating the mindsets of participants and measuring the resulting changes in behavior.

Problem solving the process by which we attempt to discover ways of achieving goals that do not seem readily attainable.

Procedural bias the degree to which the procedures used to collect data in different cultures are equivalent to each other.

Procedural justice fairness associated with the procedures and processes that organizations use to make decisions.

Proxemics the use of space in interpersonal relationships.

Proxy control refers to control by someone else for the benefit of oneself. This is a form of control that can be used when personal control—either direct or indirect—is not available or inappropriate. These are third-party interventions.

Psychological contracts the perceptions of mutual obligations that exist between organizations and their members, which differ across cultures.

Psychometric equivalence the degree to which different measures used in a cross-cultural comparison study are statistically equivalent in the cultures being compared—that is, whether the measures are equally valid and reliable in all cultures studied.

Psychopathology psychological disorders that encompass behavioral, cognitive, and emotional aspects of functioning.

Psychotherapy a method of healing that emphasizes an explicit focus on the self.

Racial identity individuals' psychological membership in a distinct racial group.

Racial microaggressions brief and commonplace indignities that communicate negative slights and insults.

Ratchet effect the concept that humans continually improve on improvements, that they do not go backward or revert to a previous state. Progress occurs because improvements move themselves upward, much like a ratchet.

Reference group effect the idea that people make implicit social comparisons with others when making ratings on scales. That is, people's ratings will be influenced by the implicit comparisons they make between themselves and others, and these influences may make comparing responses across cultures difficult.

Relational identity a form of identity that refers to our qualities of ourselves in relation to others.

Reliability the degree to which a finding, measurement, or statistic is consistent.

Religion organized systems of beliefs that tie together many attitudes, values, beliefs, worldviews, and norms. They provide guidelines for living.

Response bias a systematic tendency to respond in certain ways to items or scales.

Reverse culture shock the culture shock that individuals experience upon returning to their home cultures and realizing that things are not the same as when they left.

Ringi the Japanese process of decision making, which involves circulating a proposal among all people who will be affected by it, addressing concerns and negative consequences raised by as many parties as possible, consulting on as broad a basis as possible about the proposal, and achieving consensus before the proposal is formally implemented.

Sacred values values considered to be nonnegotiable. They differ from normal values because they incorporate moral beliefs that drive action in ways dissociated from prospects for success. Across the world, people believe that devotion to core values (such as the welfare of their family and country or their commitment to religion, honor, and justice) is, or ought to be, absolute and inviolable. Such values outweigh other values, particularly economic ones.

Sampling bias the degree to which different samples in different cultures are equivalent to each other.

Sapir–Whorf hypothesis the proposition that speakers of different languages think differently, and that they do so because of the differences in their languages. Also referred to as linguistic relativity.

Secure attachment a style of attachment in which infants are described as warm and responsive to their caregiver.

Self-concept the cognitive representations of who one is, that is, the ideas or images that one has about oneself, especially in relation to others, and how and why one behaves. The sum of one's idea about one's self, including physical, mental, historical, and relational aspects, as well as capacities to learn and perform. Self-concept is usually considered central to personal identity and change over time. It is usually considered partially conscious and partially unconscious or inferred in a given situation.

Self-conscious emotions emotions that focus on the self, such as shame, guilt, pride, or embarrassment. They are important in studies of culture because humans universally have a unique knowledge of self that is different from that of other animals, thus giving rise to self-conscious emotions.

Self-effacement the tendency to downplay one's virtues.

Self-enhancement a collection of psychological processes by which individuals maintain or enhance their self-esteem.

Self-esteem the cognitive and affective evaluations we make about ourselves.

Self-other referents the words used in a language to refer to oneself and others.

Self-serving bias a bias in which people tend to attribute good deeds and successes to their own internal attributes but attribute bad deeds or failures to external factors.

Semantics what words mean.

Sensation the feelings that result from excitation of the sensory receptors such as touch, taste, smell, sight, or hearing.

Serial position effect the finding that people tend to remember something better if it is either the first or the last item in a list.

Sex roles the behaviors and patterns of activities men and women may engage in that are directly related to their biological differences and the process of reproduction.

Sex the biological and physiological differences between men and women, the most obvious being the anatomical differences in their reproductive systems.

Sexual harassment unwelcome sexual advances, requests for sexual favors, or other verbal or physical conduct of a sexual nature in which submission to such behavior is a condition to employment and employment decisions affecting the individual (such as promotion), and where the behavior interferes with the individual's work environment or creates an intimidating, offensive, or hostile work environment.

Sexual identity the degree of awareness and recognition by an individual of his or her sex and sex roles.

Shared intentionality knowledge about motivations concerning behaviors that are common among people in a group.

Signals the specific words and behaviors that are sent during communication that convey messages.

Slow-to-warm-up a type of temperament in which infants need time to make transitions in activity and experiences. Though they may withdraw initially or respond negatively, given time and support they will adapt and react positively.

Social axioms general beliefs and premises about oneself, the social and physical environment, and the spiritual world. They are assertions about the relationship between two or more entities or concepts; people endorse and use them to guide their behavior in daily living, such as "belief in a religion helps one understand the meaning of life."

Social capital this refers to the social resources available to a person that can be used to obtain one's goals. These include social factors such as interpersonal trust, civic engagement, and time spent with friends.

Social loafing the common finding in research on group productivity in the United States that individual productivity tends to decline in larger groups.

Social orientation hypothesis the hypothesis that cultural differences in individualism versus collectivism are associated with differences in social orientation patterns that affect the ways individuals attend to and think about their worlds.

Social striving the opposite of social loafing; the finding in many cultures that working in a group enhances individual performance rather than diminishes it.

Socialization and enculturation agents the people, institutions, and organizations that exist to help ensure that socialization and enculturation occurs.

Socialization the process by which we learn and internalize the rules and patterns of behavior that are affected by culture. This process, which occurs over a long time, involves learning and mastering societal and cultural norms, attitudes, values, and belief systems.

Socially desirable responding tendencies to give answers on questionnaires that make oneself look good.

Socially disengaging emotions emotions that occur as a result of themes grounded in independence and autonomy of the self, and its separateness from others.

Socially engaging emotions emotions that occur as a result of themes derived from social interdependence and relationships with others.

Speech illustrators nonverbal behaviors, often gestures, that accompany speech and are used to illustrate or highlight speech.

Stereotype threat the threat that others' judgments or one's own actions will negatively stereotype one in a domain (such as academic achievement).

Stereotypes generalized images we have about groups of people, particularly about their underlying psychological characteristics or personality traits.

Structural equivalence the degree to which a measure used in a cross-cultural study produces the same factor analysis results in the different countries being compared.

Structure-oriented studies studies that examine whether constructs are conceptualized the same way across cultures, the relationship of a construct to other constructs, or the measurement of a construct.

Subjective experience of emotion an individual's inner feelings or experiences of an emotion.

Subjective well-being a person's perceptions and self-judgments of his or her health and well-being that includes feelings of happiness and life satisfaction.

Symbolizing three dimensions in two a theory of perception that suggests that

people in Western cultures focus more on representations on paper than do people in other cultures, and in particular spend more time learning to interpret pictures.

Syntax and grammar the system of rules governing word forms and how words should be strung together to form meaningful utterances.

Tactical self-enhancement the idea that people of different cultures all self-enhance, but they choose to do it in different ways (i.e., tactically).

Teamthink teamthink involves the encouragement of divergent views, open expression of concerns and ideas, awareness of limitations and threats, recognition of members' uniqueness, and discussion of collective doubts.

Temperament qualities of responsiveness to the environment that exist from birth and evoke different reactions from people in the baby's world. Temperament is generally considered to be a biologically based style of interacting with the world.

Terror management theory the theory that suggests that, because humans have unique cognitive abilities, they are the only animals that are aware of the fact that we will die eventually, and we are afraid, terrified in fact, of that inevitable death. Because inevitable death is terrifying to us, we create psychological phenomena as a buffer against the terror of dying.

Tightness versus looseness a dimension of cultural variability that refers to the variability within a culture of its members to norms. Tight cultures have less variability and are more homogeneous with respect to norms; loose cultures have more variability and are more heterogeneous.

Trait a characteristic or quality distinguishing a person. It refers to a consistent pattern of behavior that a person would usually display in relevant circumstances.

Uncertainty reduction one of the major goals of initial intercultural encounters—to reduce the level of uncertainty and anxiety that one feels when attempting to decode intercultural messages.

Underpathologizing attributing pathological symptoms to normative cultural differences.

Uninvolved parents a style of parenting in which parents are often too absorbed in their own lives to respond appropriately to their children and may seem indifferent to them.

Universal a psychological process that is found to be true or applicable for all people of all cultures.

Universal psychological toolkit a set of basic psychological skills and abilities that people can use to meet their needs. These include complex cognitive skills, language, emotions, and personality traits.

Universality studies a series of studies that demonstrated the pancultural universality of facial expressions of emotion.

Unpackaging studies studies that unpackage the contents of the global, unspecific concept of culture into specific, measurable psychological constructs and examine their contribution to cultural differences.

Validity the degree to which a finding, measurement, or statistic is accurate, or represents what it is supposed to.

Values trans-situational goals that serves as a guiding principle in the life of a person or group (e.g., kindness, creativity). Values motivate and justify behavior and serve as standards for judging people, actions, and events.

Zone of proximal development the gap between the actual developmental level of a child versus the potential developmental level that the child is capable of, with some assistance by more knowledgeable others (such as parent, teacher, or more experienced peers).

Abbott, S. (1992). Holding on and pushing away: Comparative perspectives on an Eastern Kentucky child-rearing practice. *Ethos, 20,* 33–65.

Abe-Kim, J., Takeuchi, D. T., Hong, S., Zane, N., Sue, S., Spencer, M. S., … Alegría, M. (2007). Use of mental health-related services among immigrant and U.S.-born Asian Americans: Results from the National Latino and Asian American study. *American Journal of Public Health, 97*(1), 91–98.

Abrams, D., Ando, K., & Hinkle, S. (1998). Psychological attachment to the group: Cross-cultural differences in organizational identification and subjective norms as predictors of workers' turnover intentions. *Personality and Social Psychology Bulletin, 24*(10), 1027–1039.

Abu Raiya, H., & Pargament, K. I. (2010). Religiously integrated psychotherapy with Muslim clients: From research to practice. *Professional Psychology: Research and Practice, 41*(2), 181–188.

Achenbach, T., Becker, A., Dopfner, M., Heiervang, E., Roessner, V., Steinhausen, H. C., & Rothenberger, A. (2008). Multicultural assessment of child and adolescent psychopathology with ASEBA and SDQ instruments: Research findings, applications, and future directions. *Journal of Child Psychology and Psychiatry, 49,* 251–275.

Achenbach, T. M., & Rescorla, L. A. (2001). *Manual for the ASEBA school-age forms & profiles.* Burlington, VT: University of Vermont, Research Center for Children, Youth, & Families.

Acioly, N. M., & Schliemann, A. D. (1986). *Intuitive mathematics and schooling in understanding a lottery game.* Paper presented at the Tenth PME Conference, London.

Adam, H., Shirako, A., & Maddux, W. W. (2010). Cultural variance in the interpersonal effects of anger in negotiations. *Psychological Science, 21,* 882–889.

Adeponle, A. B., Thombs, B. D., Groleau, D., Jarvis, E., & Kirmayer, L. J. (2012). Using the cultural formulation to resolve uncertainty in diagnoses of psychosis among ethnoculturally diverse patients. *Psychiatric Services, 63*(2), 147–153. doi: 10.1176/appi.ps.201100280

Adler, N. E., Boyce, T., Chesney, M. A., Cohen, S., Folkman, S., Kahn, R. L., & Syme, S. L. (1994). Socioeconomic status and health: The challenge of the gradient. *American Psychologist, 49*(1), 15–24.

Adler, N. E., & Rehkopf, D. H. (2008). U.S. disparities in health: Descriptions, causes, and mechanisms. *Annual Review of Public Health, 29,* 235–252.

Adorno, T. W., Frenkel-Brunswick, E., Levinson, D. J., & Sanford, R. N. (1950). *The authoritarian personality.* New York: Harper & Row.

Ahammed, S. (2010). Applying Qur'anic metaphors in counseling. *International Journal for the Advancement of Counselling, 32*(4), 248–255.

Ainsworth, M. D. S. (1967). *Infancy in Uganda: Infant care and the growth of love.* Baltimore: Johns Hopkins University Press.

Ainsworth, M. D. S. (1977). Attachment theory and its utility in cross-cultural research. In P. H. Leiderman, S. R. Tulkin, & A. Rosenfeld (Eds.), *Culture and infancy: Variations in the human experience* (pp. 49–67). San Diego, CA: Academic Press.

Akin-Ogundeji, O. (1988). An African perspective on personality: A case study of the Ibo. *Journal of Human Behavior and Learning, 5*(1), 22–26.

Akpinar, E., & Berger, J. (2015). Drivers of cultural success: The case of sensory metaphors. *Journal of Personality and Social Psychology, 109,* 20–34. doi: http://dx.doi.org/10.1037/pspa0000025

Albright, L., Kenny, D. A., & Malloy, T. E. (1988). Consensus in personality judgments at zero acquaintance. *Journal of Personality and Social Psychology, 55,* 387–395.

Alegria, M., Canino, G., Shrout, P., Woo, M., Duan, N., Vila, D., Torres, M., Chen, C., & Meng, X.-L. (2008). Prevalence of mental illness in immigrant and non-immigrant U.S. Latino groups. *American Journal of Psychiatry, 165*(3), 359–369.

Alegría, M., Chatterji, P., Wells, K., Cao, Z., Chen, C.-N., Takeuchi, D. T., … Meng, X.-L. (2008). Disparity in depression treatment among racial and ethnic minority populations in the United States. *Psychiatric Services, 59*(11), 1264–1272.

Alegría, M., Takeuchi, D. T., Canino, G., Duan, N., Shrout, P. E., Meng, X., … Gong, F. (2004). Considering context, place and culture: The National Latino and Asian American Study. *International Journal of Methods and Psychiatric Research, 13*(4), 208–220.

Al-Krenawi, A., & Graham, J. R. (2000). Culturally sensitive social work practice with Arab clients in mental health settings. *Health & Social Work, 25*(1), 9–22.

Allamani, A., Voller, F., Kubicka, L., & Bloomfield, K. (2000). Drinking cultures and the position of women in nine European countries. *Substance Abuse, 21*(4), 231–247.

Allen, M. W., Ng, S. H., Ikeda, K. I., Jawan, J. A., Sufi, A. H., Wilson, M., & Yang, K.-S. (2007). Two decades of change in cultural values and economic development in eight East Asian and Pacific Island nations. *Journal of Cross-Cultural Psychology, 38*(3), 247–269.

Allerheiligen, R., Graham, J. L., & Lin, C.-Y. (1985). Honesty in interorganizational negotiations in the United States, Japan, Brazil, and the Republic of China. *Journal of Macromarketing, 5*(2), 4–16.

Allik, J., & McCrae, R. R. (2002). A Five-Factor Theory perspective. In R. R. McCrae & J. Allik (Eds.), *The Five-Factor Model of personality across cultures* (pp. 303–322). New York: Kluwer Academic/Plenum Publishers.

Allik, J., & McCrae, R. R. (2004). Towards a geography of personality traits: Patterns of profiles across 36 cultures. *Journal of Cross-Cultural Psychology, 35,* 13–28.

Allik, J., Mottus, R., Borkenau, P., Kupens, P., & Hrebickova, M. (2010). How people see others is different from how people see themselves: A replicable pattern across cultures. *Journal of Personality and Social Psychology, 99,* 870–882. doi: 10.1037/a0020963

Allik, J., Mottus, R., & Realo, A. (2010). Does national character reflect mean personality traits when they are both measured by the same instrument? *Journal of Research in Personality, 44,* 62–69.

Allik, J., Mottus, R., Realo, A., Pullman, H., Trifonova, A., McCrae, R. R., ... Korneeva, Ekaterina E. (2009). Personality profiles and the "Russian soul": Literary and scholarly views evaluated. *Journal of Cross-Cultural Psychology, 40,* 372–389.

Allik, J., & Realo, A. (2004). Individualism-collectivism and social capital. *Journal of Cross-Cultural Psychology, 35,* 29–49.

Allport, G. W. (1936). *Personality: A psychological interpretation.* New York: Holt.

Allport, G. W. (1954). *The nature of prejudice.* Cambridge, MA: Addison-Wesley.

Al-Subaie, A., & Alhamad, A. (2000). Psychiatry in Saudi Arabia. In I. Al-Junun (Ed.), *Mental illness in the Islamic world* (pp. 205–233). Madison, CT: International Universities Press.

American Psychiatric Association. (1987). *Diagnostic and statistical manual of mental disorders* (3rd ed.) [DSM-IIIR]. Washington, DC: Author.

American Psychological Association. (2010). *Resilience and recovery after war: Refugee children and families in the United States.* Washington, DC: Author.

American Psychiatric Association. (2013). *Diagnostic and statistical manual of mental disorders, fifth edition (DSM-5).* Arlington, VA: American Psychiatric Association.

Amir, Y., & Sharon, I. (1988). Are social psychological laws cross-culturally valid? *Journal of Cross-Cultural Psychology, 18*(4), 383–470.

Anderson, C. A., & Anderson, K. B. (1996). Violent crime rate studies in philosophical context: A destructive testing approach to heat and southern culture of violence effects. *Journal of Personality, 70*(4), 740–756.

Anderson, N. B., & Nickerson, K. J. (2005). Genes, race, and psychology in the genome era. *American Psychologist, 60,* 5–8.

Anderson, C. A., Shibuya, A., Ihori, N., Swing, E. L., Bushman, B. J., Sakamoto, A., ... Saleem, M. (2010). Violent video game effects on aggression, empathy, and prosocial behavior in Eastern and Western

countries: *A meta-analytic review. Psychological Bulletin, 136*(2), 151–173.

Ando, S., Yamaguchi, S., Aoki, Y., & Thornicroft, G. (2013). Review of mental-health-related stigma in Japan. *Psychiatry and Clinical Neurosciences, 67,* 471–482.

Andrews, M. M., & Boyle, J. (2003). *Transcultural concepts in nursing care (3rd ed.).* Pennsylvania, PA: Lippincott Williams and Wilkins.

Andrews, G., Slade, T., Peters, L. (1999). Classification in psychiatry: ICD-10 versus DSM-IV. *British Journal of Psychiatry, 174,* 3–5.

API Youth Violence Prevention Center. (2007). *Under the microscope: Asian and Pacific Islander youth in Oakland: Needs, issues, and solutions.* Oakland, CA: National Council on Crime and Delinquency.

Archer, J. (2006). Cross-cultural differences in physical aggression between partners: A social-role analysis. *Personality and Social Psychology Review, 10*(2), 133–153.

Argyle, M., & Cook, M. (1976). *Gaze and mutual gaze.* New York: Cambridge University Press.

Armistead, L. P., Clark, H., Barber, C. N., Dorsey, S., Hughley, J., & Favors, M. (2004). Participant retention in the Parents Matter! program: Strategies and outcome. *Journal of Child and Family Studies, 13*(1), 67–80.

Arnett, J. J. (2001). *Adolescence and emerging adulthood: A cultural approach.* Upper Saddle River, NJ: Prentice Hall.

Arnett, J. J. (2008). The neglected 95%: Why American psychology needs to become less American. *American Psychologist, 63*(7), 602–614.

Arulmani, G. (2009). Tradition and modernity: The cultural-preparedness framework for counselling in India. In L. H. Gerstein, P. P. Heppner, S. Ægisdóttir, S.-M. A. Leung, & K. L. Norsworthy (Eds.), *International handbook of cross-cultural counseling: Cultural assumptions and practices worldwide* (pp. 251–262). Thousand Oaks, CA U.S.: Sage Publications, Inc.

Asch, S. E. (1951). Effects of group pressure upon the modification and distortion of judgments. In H. Guetzkow (Ed.), Groups, leadership and men: *Research in human relations* (pp. 177–190). Pittsburgh: Carnegie Press.

Asch, S. E. (1955). Opinions and social pressures. *Scientific American, 193,* 31–35.

Asch, S. E. (1956). Studies of independence and conformity: A minority of one against a unanimous majority. *Psychological Monographs, 70*(9), 1–70.

Atran, S., & Axelrod, R. (2007). Sacred barriers to conflict resolution. *Science, 317,* 1039–1040.

Au, T. K. (1983). Chinese and English counterfactuals: The Sapir-Whorf hypothesis revisited. *Cognition, 15,* 155–187.

Azhar, M. Z., & Varma, S. L. (2000). Mental illness and its treatment in Malaysia. In I. Al-Junun (Ed.), *Mental illness in the Islamic world* (pp. 163–186). Madison, CT: International Universities Press.

Aziz, S., Adkins, C. T., Walker, A. G., & Wuensch, K. L. (2009). Workaholism and work-life imbalance: Does cultural origin influence the relationship? *International Journal of Psychology, 45*(1), 72–79.

Bagozzi, R. P., Werbeke, W., & Gavino Jr., J. C. (2003). Culture moderates the self-regulation of shame and its effects on performance: The case of salespersons in the Netherlands and the Philippines. *Journal of Applied Psychology, 88,* 219–233.

Bagozzi, R. P., Wong, N., & Yi, Y. (1999). The role of culture and gender and the relationship between positive and negative affect. *Cognition and Emotion, 3,* 641–672.

Balliet, D., & Van Lange, P. A. M. (2013). Trust, punishment, and cooperation across 18 societies: A meta analysis. *Perspectives on Psychological Science, 8,* 363–379. doi: 10.1177/1745691613488533

Bal-Tal, D., & Labin, D. (2001). The effect of a major event on stereotyping: Terrorist attacks in Israel and Israeli adolescents' perceptions of Palestinians, *Jordanians and Arabs. European Journal of Social Psychology, 31,* 265–280.

Balter, M. (2010). Did working memory spark creative culture? *Science, 328,* 160–163.

Bargh, J. (1996). Automaticity in social psychology. In E. Higgins & A. Kruglanski (Eds.), *Social psychology: Handbook of basic principles* (pp. 169–183). New York: Guilford.

Bar-Haim, Y., Ziv, T., Lamy, D., & Hodes, R. M. (2006). Nature and nurture in own-face face processing. *Psychological Science, 17,* 159–163.

Barkan, S. (2010). *Sociology: Exploring and changing the social world.* Nyack, NY: Flat World Knowledge.

Barlett, C. P., Gentile, D. A., Anderson, C. Suzuki, K., Sakamoto, A., Yamaoka, A., & Katsura, R. (2014). Cross-Cultural Differences in Cyberbullying Behavior: A Short-Term Longitudinal Study. *Journal of Cross-Cultural Psychology, 45,* 300–313.

Barna, L. M. (1996). Stumbling blocks in intercultural communication. In L. A. Samovar & R. E. Porter (Eds.), *Intercultural communication: A reader* (8th ed., pp. 370–379). Belmont, CA: Wadsworth.

Barnlund, D. C., & Araki, S. (1985). Intercultural encounters: The management of compliments by Japanese and Americans. *Journal of Cross-Cultural Psychology, 16*(1), 9–26.

Barnlund, D. C., & Yoshioka, M. (1990). Apologies: Japanese and American styles. *International Journal of Intercultural Relations, 14,* 193–206.

Barry, H. (1980). Description and uses of the Human Relations Area Files. In H. C. Triandis & J. W. Berry (Eds.), *Handbook of cross-cultural psychology: Vol. 2. Methodology* (pp. 445–478). Boston: Allyn & Bacon.

Barry, H., Josephson, L., Lauer, E., & Marshall, C. (1976). Agents and techniques for child training. *Ethnology, 16,* 191–230.

Barstow, D. G. (1999). Female genital mutilation: The penultimate gender abuse. *Child Abuse and Neglect, 23,* 501–510.

Bartlett, F. C. (1932). *Remembering.* Cambridge: Cambridge University Press.

Bauer, K., Larson, N., Nelson, M., Story, M., & Neumark-Sztainer, D. (2009). Preventive medicine: Fast food intake among adolescents: Secular and longitudinal trends from 1999 to 2004. *An International Journal Devoted to Practice and Theory, 48*(3), 284–287.

Bauermeister, J. J., Canino, G., Polanczyk, G., & Rohde, L. A. (2010). ADHD across cultures: Is there evidence for a bidimensional organization of symptoms? *Journal of Clinical Child and Adolescent Psychology, 39*(3), 362–372.

Baumeister, R. F. (2005). *The cultural animal: Human nature, meaning, and social life.* New York: Oxford University Press.

Baumeister, R. F., Campbell, J. D., Krueger, J. I., & Vohs, K. D. (2003). Does high self-esteem cause better performance, interpersonal success, happiness, or healthier lifestyles? *Psychological Science in the Public Interest, 4*(1), 1–44.

Baumeister, R. F., Ciarocco, N. J., & Twenge, J. M. (2005). Social exclusion impairs self-regulation. *Journal of Personality and Social Psychology, 88*(4), 589–604.

Baumeister, R. F., & Leary, M. R. (1995). The need to belong: Desire for interpersonal attachments as a fundamental human motivation. *Psychological Bulletin, 117,* 497–529.

Baumrind, D. (1967). Child care practices anteceding three patterns of preschool behavior. *Genetic Psychology Monographs, 75,* 43–88.

Baumrind, D. (1971). Current patterns of parental authority. *Developmental Psychology Monograph, 4*(No. 1, Pt. 2), 1–103.

Baumrind, D. (1991). The influence of parenting style on adolescent competence and substance use. *Journal of Early Adolescence,* Special Issue: The work of John P. Hill: *Theoretical, Instructional, and Policy Contributions 11*(1), 56–95.

Baydar, N., & Brooks-Gunn, J. (1998). Profiles of grandmothers who help care for their grandchildren in the United States. *Family Relations: Interdisciplinary Journal of Applied Family Studies,* Special Issue: The family as a context for health and well-being, *47*(4), 385–393.

Beals, J., Novins, D. K., Whitesell, N. R., Spicer, P., Mitchell, C., & Manson, S. M. (2005). Prevalence of mental disorders and utilization of mental health services in two American Indian reservation populations: Mental health disparities in a national context. *American Journal of Psychiatry, 162*(9), 1723–1732.

Beck, A. T. (1967). *Depression: Clinical, experimental and theoretical aspects.* New York: Harper and Row.

Beck, A. T. (1976). *Cognitive therapy and the emotional disorders.* New York: International Universities Press.

Becker, E. (1971). *The birth and death of meaning* (2nd ed.). New York: Free Press.

Becker, E. (1973). *The denial of death.* New York: Academic Press.

Becker, M., Vignoles, V. L., Owe, E., Brown, R., Smith, P. B., .Easterbrook, M., . . . Yamakoğlu, N. (2012). Culture and the distinctiveness motive: Constructing identity in individualistic and collectivistic contexts. *Journal of Personality and Social Psychology, 102,* 833–855.

Becker, M., Vignoles, V. L., Owe, E., Easterbrook, M. J., Brown, R., Smith, P. B., . . . Koller, S. H. (2014). Cultural bases for self-evaluation: Seeing oneself positively in different cultural contexts. *Personality and Social Psychology Bulletin, 40,* 657–675.

Behrensmeyer, A. K. (2006). Climate change and human evolution. *Science, 311,* 476–478.

Beier, E. G., & Zautra, A. J. (1972). Identification of vocal communication of emotions across cultures. *Journal of Consulting & Clinical Psychology, 39*(1), 166.

Beiser, M. (2006). Longitudinal research to promote effective refugee resettlement. *Transcultural Psychiatry, 43*(1), 56–71.

Beiser, M. (2009). Resettling refugees and safeguarding their mental health: Lessons learned from the Canadian Refugee Resettlement Project. *Transcultural Psychiatry, 46*(4), 539–583. doi: 10.1177/1363461509351373

Beiser, M., & Hou, F. (2001). Language acquisition, unemployment and depressive disorder among Southeast Asian refugees: A 10-year study. *Social Science & Medicine, 53*(10), 1321–1334.

Beiser, M., Simich, L., Pandalangat, N., Nowakowski, M., & Tian, F. (2011). Stresses of passage, balms of resettlement, and posttraumatic stress disorder among Sri Lankan Tamils in Canada. *The Canadian Journal of Psychiatry / La Revue canadienne de psychiatrie, 56*(6), 333–334.

Beit-Hallahmi, B. (1972). National character and national behavior in the Middle East conflict: The case of the "Arab personality." *International Journal of Group Tensions, 2*(3), 19–28.

Bem, S. L. (1981). The BSRI and gender schema theory: A reply to Spence and Helmreich. *Psychological Review, 88*(4), 369–371.

Ben-Porath, Y. S., & Tellegen, A. (2008). Empirical correlates of the MMPI-2 Restructured Clinical (RC) scales in mental health, forensic, and nonclinical settings: An introduction. *Journal of Personality Assessment, 90*(2), 119–121. doi: 10.1080/00223890701845120

Benet-Martinez, V., Leu, J., Lee, F., & Morris, M. (2002). Negotiating biculturalism: Cultural frame-switching in biculturals with "Oppositional" vs. "Compatible" cultural identities. *Journal of Cross-Cultural Psychology, 33*, 492–516.

Benet-Martinez, V., & Waller, N. G. (1995). The big-seven factor model of personality description: Evidence for its cross-cultural generality in a Spanish sample. *Journal of Personality and Social Psychology, 69*, 701–718.

Benet-Martinez, V., & Waller, N. G. (1997). Further evidence for the cross-cultural generality of the big-seven factor model: Indigenous and imported Spanish personality constructs. *Journal of Personality, 65*, 567–598.

Berger, C. R. (1979). Beyond initial interaction. In H. Giles & R. St. Claire (Eds.), *Language and social psychology* (pp. 122–144). Oxford: Basil Blackwell.

Berger, C. R., & Calabrese, R. J. (1975). Some explorations in initial interaction and beyond: Toward a developmental theory of interpersonal communication. *Human Communication Research, 10*, 179–196.

Berkman, L. F., & Syme, S. L. (1979). Social networks, host resistance, and mortality: A nine-year follow-up study of Alameda County residents. *American Journal of Epidemiology, 109*, 186–204.

Berlin, B., & Kay, P. (1969). *Basic color terms: Their universality and evolution.* Berkeley: University of California Press.

Berry, D. S., & McArthur, L. Z. (1985). Some components and consequences of a babyface. *Journal of Personality and Social Psychology, 48*, 312–323.

Berry, D. S., & McArthur, L. Z. (1986). Perceiving character in faces: The impact of age-related craniofacial changes in social perception. *Psychological Bulletin, 100*, 3–18.

Berry, J. W. (1966). Temne and Eskimo perceptual skills. *International Journal of Psychology, 1*, 207–229.

Berry, J. W. (1969). On cross-cultural comparability. *International Journal of Psychology, 4*, 119–128.

Berry, J. W. (1976). Sex differences in behavior and cultural complexity. *Indian Journal of Psychology, 51*, 89–97.

Berry, J. W. (2003). Conceptual approaches to acculturation. In K. M. Chun, P. Balls Organista, & G. Marín (Eds.), *Acculturation: Advances in theory, measurement, and applied research* (pp. 17–37). Washington, DC: U.S. American Psychological Association.

Berry, J. W., Kim, U., & Boski, P. (1988). Psychological acculturation of immigrants. In Y. Y. Kim & W. B. Gudykunst (Eds.), *Cross-cultural adaptation: Current approaches. International and intercultural communication annual* (Vol. 11, pp. 62–89). Newbury Park, CA: Sage.

Berry, J. W., Phinney, J. S., Sam, D. L., & Vedder, P. (2006*). Immigrant youth in cultural transition: Acculturation, identity, and adaptation across national contexts.* New Jersey: Lawrence Erlbaum.

Berry, J. W., Poortinga, Y. H., Segall, M. H., & Dasen, P. R. (1992). *Cross-cultural psychology: Research and applications.* New York: Cambridge University Press.

Berry, J. W., & Sam, D. L. (1997). Acculturation and adaptation. In J. W. Berry, M. H. Segall, & C. Kagitcibasi (Eds.), *Handbook of cross-cultural psychology: Vol 3. Social behavior and applications* (2nd ed., pp. 291–326). Boston: Allyn & Bacon.

Betancourt, H., & Lopez, R. S. (1993). The study of culture, ethnicity, and race in American psychology. *American Psychologist, 48*(6), 629–637.

Bhawuk, D., & Brislin, R. (1992). The measurement of intercultural sensitivity using the concepts of individualism and collectivism. *International Journal of Intercultural Relations, 16*(4), 413–436.

Bhui, K., Craig, T., & Mohamud, S. (2006). Mental disorders among Somali refugees: Developing culturally appropriate measures and assessing socio-cultural risk factors. *Social Psychiatry and Psychiatric Epidemiology, 41*(5), 400–408.

Bhurga, D., & McKenzie, K. (2010). Expressed emotion across cultures. In R. Bhattacharya, S. Cross, &

D. Bhugra (Eds.), *Clinical topics in cultural psychiatry* (pp. 52–67). London, England: Royal College of Psychiatrists.

Biederman, I., Yue, X., & Davidoff, J. (2009). Representation of shape in individuals from a culture with minimal exposure to regular, simple artifacts: Sensitivity to nonaccidental versus metric properties. *Psychological Science, 20*(12), 1437–1442.

Biehl, M., Matsumoto, D., Ekman, P., Hearn, V., Heider, K., Kudoh, T., ... Ton, V. (1997). Matsumoto and Ekman's Japanese and Caucasian Facial Expressions of Emotion (JACFEE): Reliability Data and Cross-National Differences. *Journal of Nonverbal Behavior, 21*, 3–21.

Bilali, A., Galanis, P., Velonakis, E., & Katostaras, T. (2010). Factors associated with abnormal eating attitudes among Greek adolescents. *Journal of Nutrition Education and Behavior, 42*(5), 292–298.

Binder, J., Zagefka, H., Brown, R., Funke, F., Kessler, T., Mummendey, A., ... Leyens, J.-P. (2009). A longitudinal test of the contact hypothesis among majority and minority groups in three European countries. *Journal of Personality and Social Psychology, 96*(4), 843–856.

Bissilat, J., Laya, D., Pierre, E., & Pidoux, C. (1967). La notion de lakkal dans la culture Djerma-Songhai [The concept of lakkal in Djerma-Songhai culture]. *Psychopathologie Africaine, 3*, 207–264.

Black, J. S., & Porter, L. W. (1991). Managerial behavior and job performance: A successful manager in Los Angeles may not succeed in Hong Kong. *Journal of International Business Studies, 22*, 99–113.

Blair, I. V. (2001). Implicit stereotypes and prejudice. In G. B. Moskowitz (Ed.), *Cognitive social psychology: The Princeton symposium on the legacy and future of social cognition* (pp. 359–374). Mahwah, NJ: Erlbaum.

Blair, I. V., Judd, C. M., & Fallman, J. L. (2004). The automaticity of race and afrocentric facial features in social judgments. *Journal of Personality and Social Psychology, 87*, 763–778.

Blau, Z. S. (1981). *Black children-white children: Competence, socialization, and social structure.* New York: Free Press.

Block, J. (1983). Differential premises arising from differential socialization of the sexes: Some conjectures. *Child Development, 54,* 1335–1354.

Bloom, A. H. (1981). *The linguistic shaping of thought: A study in the impact of language on thinking in China and the West.* Hillsdale, NJ: Erlbaum.

Blow, F. C., Zeber, J. E., McCarthy, J. F., Valenstein, M., Gillon, L., & Bingham, C. R. (2004). Ethnicity and diagnostic patterns in veterans with psychoses. *Social Psychiatry Psychiatric Epidemiology, 39*(10), 841–851.

Boas, F., Efron, D., & Foley, J. P. A. (1936). A comparative investigation of gestural behavior patterns in "racial" groups living under different as well as similar environmental conditions. *Psychological Bulletin, 33,* 760.

Boesch, C. (2003). Is culture a golden barrier between human and chimpanzee? *Evolutionary Anthropology, 12,* 82–91.

Bond, M. H. (2004a). Culture and aggression: From context to coercion. *Personality and Social Psychology Review, 8,* 62–78.

Bond, M. H. (2004b, August). *The third stage of cross-cultural psychology: Some personal prescriptions for our future.* Paper presented at the 17th International Congress of the International Association for Cross-Cultural Psychology, Xian, China.

Bond, M. H., Leung, K., & Wan, K. C. (1982). The social impact of self-effacing attributions: The Chinese case. *Journal of Social Psychology, 118*(2), 157–166.

Bond, M. H., Leung, K., Au, A., Tong, K. K., Reimel de Carrasquel, S., Murakami, F., … Lewis, J. R. (2004). Culture-level dimensions of social axioms and their correlates across 41 cultures. *Journal of Cross-Cultural Psychology, 35,* 548–570.

Bond, M. H., & Smith, P. B. (1996). Cross-cultural social and organizational psychology. *Annual Review of Psychology, 47,* 205–235.

Bond, M. H., & Tak-Sing, C. (1983). College students' spontaneous self concept: The effect of culture among respondents in Hong Kong, Japan, and the United States. *Journal of Cross-Cultural Psychology, 14,* 153–171.

Bond, M. H., & Wang, S. (1983). China: Aggressive behavior and the problems of mainstreaming order and harmony. In A. P. Goldstein &

M. H. Segall (Eds.), *Aggression in global perspective* (pp. 58–74). New York: Pergamon.

Borkenau, P., & Ostendorf, F. (1998). The Big Five as states: How useful is the five-factor model to describe intraindividual variations over time? *Journal of Research in Personality, 32*(2), 202–221.

Bornstein, M. (2012). Cultural approaches to parenting. *Parenting: Science and Practice, 12,* 212–221.

Bornstein, M. H., Haynes, O. M., Azuma, H., Galperin, C, Maital, S., & Ogino, M., … Wright, B. (1998). A cross-national study of self-evaluations and attributions in parenting: Argentina, Belgium, France, Israel, Italy, Japan and the United States. *Developmental Psychology, 34*(4), 662–676.

Boroditsky, L., Fuhrman, O., & McCormick, K. (2011). Do English and Mandarin speakers think about time differently? *Cognition, 118*(1), 126–132.

Boroditsky, L., & Gaby, A. (2010). Remembrances of times east: Absolute spatial representations of time in an Australian aboriginal community. *Psychological Science, 21*(11), 1635–1639.

Boski, P. (2013). A psychology of economic migration. *Journal of Cross-Cultural Psychology, 44,* 1067–1093. doi: 10.1177/0022022112471895

Bothwell, R. K., Brigham, J. C., & Malpass, R. S. (1989). Cross-racial identification. *Personality and Social Psychology Bulletin, 25*(1), 19–25.

Bouchard, T. J., & Loehlin, J. C. (2001). Genes, evolution, and personality. *Behavior Genetics, 31,* 243–273.

Bouchard, T. J., Lykken, D. T., & McGue, M. (1994). Sources of human psychological differences: The Minnesota study of twins reared apart. *Science, 250,* 223–228.

Bouchard, T. J., Jr., & McGue, M. (1981). Familial studies of intelligence: A review. *Science, 212,* 1055–1059.

Boucher, J. D., & Brandt, M. E. (1981). Judgment of emotion: American and Malay antecedents. *Journal of Cross-Cultural Psychology, 22*(3), 272–283.

Boucher, H. C., Peng, K., Shi, J., & Wang, L. (2009). Culture and implicit self-esteem: Chinese are "good" and "bad" at the same time. *Journal of Cross-Cultural Psychology, 40,* 24–45.

Bouhmama, D. (1984). Assessment of Kohlberg's stages of moral

development in two cultures. *Journal of Moral Education, 13*(2), 124–132.

Bowlby, J. (1969). *Attachment and loss: Vol. 1. Attachment.* New York: Basic Books.

Bowman, S. A., Gortmaker, S. L., Ebbeling, C. B., Pereira, M. A., & Ludwig, D. S. (2003). Effects of fast-food consumption on energy intake and diet quality among children in a national household survey. *Pediatrics, 113,* 112–118.

Boyer, P. (2000). Evolutionary psychology and cultural transmission. *American Behavioral Scientist, 43,* 987–1000.

Bradley, R. H., Caldwell, B. M., & Corwyn, R. F. (2003). The Child Care HOME Inventories: Assessing the quality of family child care homes. *Early Childhood Research Quarterly, 18*(3), 294–309.

Bradley, R. H., & Corwyn, R. (2005). Caring for children around the world: A view from HOME. *International Journal of Behavioral Development, 29*(6), 468–478.

Brandt, M. E., & Boucher, J. D. (1985). Judgment of emotions from antecedent situations in three cultures. In I. Lagunes & Y. Poortinga (Eds.), *From a different perspective: Studies of behavior across cultures* (pp. 348–362). Lisse, Netherlands: Swets & Zeitlinger.

Brandt, M. E., & Boucher, J. D. (1986). Concepts of depression in emotion lexicons of eight cultures. *International Journal of Intercultural Relations, 10,* 321–346.

Brandt, M. J. (2011). Sexism and gender inequality across 57 societies. *Psychological Science, 22,* 1413–1418. doi: 10.1177/0956797611420445

Breslau, J., Kendler, K. S., Su, M., Aguilar-Gaxiola, S., & Kessler, R. C. (2005). Lifetime risk and persistence of psychiatric disorders across ethnic groups in the United States. *Psychological Medicine, 35*(3), 317–327.

Breugelmans, S. M., Zeelenberg, M., Gilovich, T., Huang, W.-H., & Shani, Y. (2014). Generality and cultural variation in the experience of regret. *Emotion, 14*(6), 1037. doi: 10.1037/a0038221

Brewer, M. B. (2004). Taking the origins of human nature seriously: Toward a more imperialist social psychology. *Personality and Social Psychology Review, 8*(2), 107–113.

Brewer, M. B., & Kramer, R. M. (1985). The psychology of intergroup attitudes and behavior. *Annual Review of Psychology, 36,* 219–243.

Brislin, R. (1970). Back translation for cross-cultural research. *Journal of Cross-Cultural Psychology, 1,* 185–216.

Brislin, R. (1993). *Understanding culture's influence on behavior.* Fort Worth, TX: Harcourt Brace Jovanovich.

Brodsky, M., & Hui, K.-K. (2006). Complementary and alternative medicine. In D. Wedding & M. Stuber (Eds.), *Behavior and medicine* (4th ed., pp. 281–285). Ashland, OH: Hogrefe & Huber.

Broman, C. L. (1996). Coping with personal problems. In H. W. Neighbors & J. S. Jackson (Eds.), *Mental health in black America* (pp. 117–129). Thousand Oaks, CA: Sage.

Broman, C. L., Neighbors, H. W., Delva, J., Torres, M., & Jackson, J. S. (2008). Prevalence of substance use disorders among African Americans and Caribbean Blacks in the national survey of American life. *American Journal of Public Health, 98*(6), 1107–1114.

Brondolo, E., Rieppi, R., Kelly, K. P., & Gerin, W. (2003). Perceived racism and blood pressure: A review of the literature and conceptual and methodological critique. *Annals of Behavioral Medicine, 25*(1), 55–65.

Bronfenbrenner, U. (1979). *The ecology of human development.* Cambridge, MA: Harvard University Press.

Bronfenbrenner, U., & Morris, P. A. (1998). The ecology of environmental processes. In W. Damon (Series Ed.) & R. M. Lerner (Vol. Ed.), *Handbook of child psychology* (5th ed., Vol. 1, pp. 993–1028). New York: Wiley.

Broota, K. D., & Ganguli, H. C. (1975). Cultural differences in perceptual selectivity. *Journal of Social Psychology, 95,* 157–163.

Brown, D. E. (1991). *Human universal.* Philadelphia, PA: Temple University.

Brown, J. D., Cai, H., Oakes, M. A., & Deng, C. (2009). Cultural similarities in self-esteem functioning: East is East and West is West, but sometimes the twain do meet. *Journal of Cross-Cultural Psychology, 40,* 140–157.

Brown, R. P., Carvallo, M., & Imura, M. (2014). Naming patterns reveal cultural values patronyms, matronyms, and the US culture of honor. *Personality and Social Psychology Bulletin, 40,* 250–262. doi: 10.1177/0146167213509840

Brown, J. D., & Kobayashi, C. (2002). Self-enhancement in Japan and America. *Asian Journal of Social Psychology, 5,* 145–168.

Bruner, J. S., Oliver, R. R., & Greenfield, P. M. (1966). *Studies in cognitive growth.* New York: Wiley.

Bui, K.-V. T., & Takeuchi, D. T. (1992). Ethnic minority adolescents and the use of community mental health care services. *American Journal of Community Psychology, 20,* 403–417.

Buist, K. L. (2010). Sibling relationship quality and adolescent delinquency: A latent growth curve approach. *Journal of Family Psychology, 24*(4), 400–410.

Burton, M. L., Greenberger, E., & Hayward, C. (2005). Mapping the ethnic landscape: Personal beliefs about own group's and other group's traits. *Cross-Cultural Research, 39,* 351–379.

Buss, D. M. (1988). The evolution of human intrasexual competition: Tactics of mate attraction. *Journal of Personality & Social Psychology, 54,* 616–628.

Buss, D. M. (1989). Sex differences in human mate preferences: Evolutionary hypotheses tested in 37 cultures. *Behavioral & Brain Sciences, 12,* 1–49.

Buss, D. M. (1991). Evolutionary personality psychology. *Annual Review of Psychology, 42,* 459–491.

Buss, D. M. (1994). *The evolution of desire: Strategies of human mating.* New York: Basic Books.

Buss, D. M. (2001). Human nature and culture: An evolutionary psychological perspective. *Journal of Personality, 69,* 955–978.

Buss, D. M., & Schmitt, D. P. (1993). Sexual strategies theory: An evolutionary perspective on human mating. *Psychological Review, 100,* 204–232.

Buss, D. M., Shackelford, T. K., Kirkpatrick, L. A., Choe, J. C., Lim, H. K., & Hasegawa, M. (1999). Jealousy and the nature of beliefs about infidelity: Test of competing hypotheses about sex differences in the United States, Korea, and Japan. *Personal Relationships, 6,* 125–150.

Butcher, J. N., Cabiya, J., Lucio, E. M., & Garrido, M. (2007). *Assessing Hispanic clients using the MMPI-2 and MMPI-A.* Washington, DC: American Psychological Association.

Butcher, J. N., Cheung, F. M., & Kim, J. (2003). Use of the MMPI-2 With Asian Populations. *Psychological Assessment, 15*(3), 248–256.

Butcher, J. N., Dahlstrom, W. G., Graham, J. R., Tellegen, A., & Kaemmer, B. (1989). MMPI-2: *Manual for administration and scoring.* Minneapolis: University of Minnesota Press.

Butcher, J. N., Derksen, J., Sloore, H., & Sirigatti, S. (2003). Objective personality assessment of people in diverse cultures: European adaptations of the MMPI–2. *Behaviour Research and Therapy, 41,* 819–840.

Butcher, J. N., Kim, J., & Nezami, E. (1998). Objective study of abnormal personality in cross-cultural settings: The Minnesota Multiphasic Personality Inventory (MMPI-2). *Journal of Cross-Cultural Psychology, 29*(1), 189–211.

Butsch, R. (1992). Class and gender in four decades of television situation comedy. *Critical Studies in Mass Communication, 9,* 387–399.

Cachelin, F. M., Phinney, J. S., Schug, R. A., & Striegel-Moore, R. M. (2006). Acculturation and eating disorders in a Mexican American community sample. *Psychology of Women Quarterly, 30*(4), 340–347.

Callister, L., Vehvilainen-Julkunen, K., & Lauri, S. (2001). Giving birth: Perceptions of Finnish childbearing women. *American Journal of Maternal/Child Nursing, 26*(1), 28–32.

Campbell, D. T. (1958). Common fate, similarity, and other indices of the status of aggregates of person as social entities. *Behavioural Science, 3,* 14–25.

Camras, L., Oster, H., Campos, J. J., & Bakeman, R. (2003). Emotional facial expressions in European-American, Japanese, and Chinese infants. In P. Ekman, J. J. Campos, R. J. Davidson, & F. B. M. de Waal (Eds.), *Emotions inside out: 130 years after Darwin's "the expression of the emotions in man and animals"* (Vol. 1000, pp. 135–151). New York: New York Academy of Sciences.

Carroll, J. B., & Casagrande, J. B. (1958). The function of language classifications in behavior. In E. E. Maccoby, T. M. Newcomb, & E. L. Hartley (Eds.), *Readings in social psychology* (pp. 18–31). New York: Holt.

Carroll, J. L., & Wolpe, P. R. (1996). *Sexuality and gender in society.* New York: Harper Collins.

Carson, R. C., Butcher, J. N., & Coleman, J. C. (1988). *Abnormal psychology and modern life* (8th ed.). Glenview, IL: Longman.

Casey, R. J. (1993). Children's emotional experience: Relations among expression, self-report, and understanding. *Developmental Psychology, 29,* 119–129.

Cassidy, W., Faucher, C., & Jackson, M. (2013). Cyberbullying among youth: A comprehensive review of current international research and its implications and application to policy and practice. *School Psychology International, 34,* 575–612.

Caudill, W., & Frost, L. (1974). A comparison of maternal care and infant behavior in Japanese-American, American, and Japanese families. In W. P. Lebra (Ed.), *Youth, socialization, and mental health: Vol. 3. Mental health research in Asia and the Pacific* (pp. 3–15). Honolulu: University Press of Hawaii.

Caudill, W., & Weinstein, H. (1969). Maternal care and infant behavior in Japan and America. Psychiatry: *Journal for the Study of Interpersonal Processes, 32*(1), 12–43.

Cederblad, M. (1988). Behavioral disorders in children from different cultures. *Acta Psychiatrica Scandinavia Supplementum, 344,* 85–92.

Centers for Disease Control and Prevention. (2009). Youth suicide, 2009. National Center for Injury Prevention and Control, Division of Violence Prevention. Retrieved: http://www.cdc.gov/violenceprevention/pub/youth_suicide.html

Centola, D., & Baronchelli, A. (2015). The spontaneous emergence of conventions: An experimental study of cultural evolution. *Proceedings of the National Academy of Sciences, 112*(7), 1989–1994.

Central Intelligence Agency. (2014). *The world factbook.* Retrieved from https://www.cia.gov/library/publications/resources/the-world-factbook/rankorder/2091rank.html

Chae, D. H., Nuru-Jeter, A. M., Adler, N. E., Brody, G. H., Lin, J., Blackburn, E. H., & Epel, E. S. (2014). Discrimination racial bias, and telomere length in African-American men. *American Journal of Preventive Medicine, 46,* 103–111.

Chae, D. H., Takeuchi, D. T., Barbeau, E. M., Bennett, G. G., Lindsey, J., &

Krieger, N. (2008). Unfair treatment, racial/ethnic discrimination, ethnic identification, and smoking among Asian Americans in the National Latino and Asian American Study. *American Journal of Public Health, 98*(3), 485–492.

Chandler, M. J., Lalonde, C. E., Sokol, B. W., & Hallett, D. (2003). Personal persistence, identity development, and suicide: A study of Native and non-Native North American adolescents. *Monographs of the Society for Research in Child Development, 68*(2), vii–130.

Chang, D. F., & Berk, A. (2009). Making cross-racial therapy work: A phenomenological study of clients' experiences of cross-racial therapy. *Journal of Counseling Psychology, 56*(4), 521–536.

Chang, D. F., & Sue, S. (2003). The effects of race and problem type on teachers' assessment of school behavior. *Journal of Consulting and Clinical Psychology, 71,* 235–242.

Chao, R. K. (1994). Beyond parental control and authoritarian parenting style: Understanding Chinese parenting through the cultural notion of training. *Child Development, 65,* 1111–1119.

Chao, R. K. (1996). Chinese and European American mothers' beliefs about the role of parenting in children's school success. *Journal of Cross-Cultural Psychology, 27*(4), 403–423.

Chao, R. (2000). Cultural explanations for the role of parenting in the school success of Asian-American children. In R. Taylor & M. Wang (Eds.), *Resilience across contexts: Family, work, culture, and community* (pp. 333–363). Mahwah, NJ: Erlbaum.

Chao, R. (2001). Extending research on the consequences of parenting style for Chinese Americans and European Americans. *Child Development, 72*(6), 1832–1843.

Chao, R., & Tseng, V. (2002). Parenting of Asians. In M. H. Bornstein & M. H. Bornstein (Eds.), *Handbook of parenting: Vol. 4: Social conditions and applied parenting* (2nd ed., pp. 59–93). Mahwah, NJ: Lawrence Erlbaum Associates Publishers.

Charlesworth, W. R., & Kreutzer, M. A. (1973). Facial expressions of infants

and children. In P. Ekman (Ed.), *Darwin and facial expression* (pp. 91–168). New York: Academic Press.

Chaudhary, N. (2004). *Listening to culture: Constructing culture from everyday talk.* New Delhi: Sage.

Chen, G. M. (1995). Differences in self-disclosure patterns among Americans versus Chinese: A comparative study. *Journal of Cross-Cultural Psychology, 26,* 84–91.

Chen, W-W. (2014). The relationship between perceived parenting style, filial piety, and life satisfaction in Hong Kong. *Journal of Family Psychology, 28,* 308–314.

Chen, S. X., & Bond, M. H. (2010). Two languages, two personalities? Examining language effects on the expression of personality in a bilingual context. *Personality and Social Psychology Bulletin, 36*(11), 1514–1528.

Chen, J., Chiu, C.-Y., Roese, N. J., Tam, K.-P., & Lau, I. Y.-M. (2006). Culture and counterfactuals: On the importance of life domains. *Journal of Cross-Cultural Psychology, 37*(1), 75–84.

Chen, X., Dong, Q., & Zhou, H. (1997). Authoritative and authoritarian parenting practices and social and school performances in Chinese children. *International Journal of Behavioral Development, 21*(4), 855–873.

Chen, X., Rubin, K. H., Li, B., & Li, D. (1999). Adolescent outcomes of social functioning in Chinese children. *International Journal of Behavioral Development, 23*(1), 199–223.

Chen, X., Rubin, K. H., & Sun, Y. (1992). Social reputation and peer relationships in Chinese and Canadian children: A cross-cultural study. *Child Development, 63*(6), 1336–1343.

Chen, X., Wang, L., & DeSouza, A. (2006). Temperament, socioemotional functioning, and peer relationships in Chinese and North American children. In X. Chen, D. French, & B. Schneider (Eds.), *Peer relationships in cultural context,* (pp. 123–147). Cambridge: Cambridge University Press.

Chen, X., Wang, L., & Wang, Z. (2009). Shyness-sensitivity and social, school, and psychological adjustment in rural migrant and urban children in China. *Child Development, 80*(5), 1499–1513. doi: 10.1111/j.1467-8624.2009.01347.x

Cheng, C., Cheung, S.-F., Chio, J. H.-M., & Chan, M.-P. S. (2013). Cultural meaning of perceived control: A meta-analysis of locus of control and psychological symptoms across 18 cultural regions. *Psychological Bulletin, 139*, 152–188. doi: 10.1037/a0028596

Chentsova-Dutton, Y. E., Chu, J. P., Tsai, J. L., Rottenberg, J., Gross, J. J., & Gotlib, I. H. (2007). Depression and emotional reactivity: Variation among Asian Americans of East Asian descent and European Americans. *Journal of Abnormal Psychology, 116*(4), 776–785.

Cheryan, S., & Monin, B. (2005). "Where are you really from?": Asian Americans and identity denial. *Journal of Personality and Social Psychology, 89*(5), 717–730.

Cheung, F. M., Cheung, S. F., Leung, K., Ward, C., & Leong, F. T. (2003). The English version of the Chinese personality assessment inventory. *Journal of Cross-Cultural Psychology, 34*, 433–452.

Cheung, F. M., Cheung, S. F., Wada, S., & Zhang, J. (2003). Indigenous measures of personality assessment in Asian countries: A review. *Psychological Assessment, 15*, 280–289.

Cheung, F. M., Fan, W., & To, C. (2009). Teaching and learning guide for: The Chinese Personality Assessment Inventory as a culturally relevant personality measure in applied settings. *Social and Personality Psychology Compass, 3*(6), 1113–1119.

Cheung, F. M., Kwong, J. Y. Y., & Zhang, J. (2003). Clinical validation of the Chinese Personality Assessment Inventory. *Psychological Assessment, 15*(1), 89–100.

Cheung, F. M., Leung, K., Fan, R. M., Song, W. Z., Zhang, J. X., & Zhang, J. P. (1996). Development of the Chinese Personality Assessment Inventory. *Journal of Cross-Cultural Psychology, 27*, 181–199.

Cheung, F. M., Leung, K., Zhang, J.-X., Sun, H.-F., Gan, Y.-Q., Song, W.-Z., ... Xie, D. (2001). Indigenous Chinese personality constructs: Is the five-factor model complete? *Journal of Cross-Cultural Psychology, 32*, 407–433.

Cheung, F. M., van de Vijver, F. J. R., & Leong, F. T. L. (2011). Toward a new approach to the study of personality in culture. *American Psychologist, 66*, 593–603.

Chevalier-Skolnikoff, S. (1973). Facial expression of emotion in nonhuman primates. In P. Ekman (Ed.), *Darwin and facial expression* (pp. 11–89). New York: Academic Press.

Chhim, S. (2013). Baksbat (broken courage): A trauma-based cultural syndrome in Cambodia. *Medical Anthropology, 32*(2), 160–173. doi: 10.1080/01459740.2012.674078

Chiao, J. Y., Cheon, B., Pronpattananangkul, N., Mrazek, A. J., & Blizinsky, K. D. (2013). Cultural neuroscience: Progress and promise. *Psychological Inquiry, 24*, 1–19.

Chida, Y., & Steptoe, A. (2008). Positive psychological well-being and mortality: A quantitative review of prospective observational studies. *Psychosomatic Medicine, 70*(7), 741–756.

Chinese Culture Connection. (1987). Chinese values and the search for culture-free dimensions of culture. *Journal of Cross-Cultural Psychology, 18*, 143–164.

Chirkov, V., Ryan, R. M., Kim, Y., & Kaplan, U. (2003). Differentiating autonomy from individualism and independence: A self-determination theory perspective on internalization of cultural orientations and well-being. *Journal of Personality and Social Psychology, 84*, 97–110.

Chirkov, V. I., Ryan, R. M., & Willness, C. (2005). Cultural context and psychological needs in Canada and Brazil: Testing a self-determination approach to the internalization of cultural practices, identity and well-being. *Journal of Cross-Cultural Psychology, 36*, 423–443.

Chisholm, J. S. (1981). Prenatal influences on Aboriginal - white Australian differences in neonatal behavior. *Ethology and Sociobiology, 2*, 67–73.

Chisholm, J. S. (1983). *Navajo infancy.* New York: Aldine.

Chisholm, J. S., Woodson, R. H., & da Costa Woodson, E. (1978). Maternal blood pressure in pregnancy and newborn irritability. *Early Human Development, 2*(3), 171–178.

Chisuwa, N., & O'Dea, J. A. (2009). Body image and eating disorders amongst japanese adolescents: A review of the literature. *Appetite, 51*(1), 5–15.

Chiu, L. H. (1972). A cross-cultural comparison of cognitive styles in Chinese and American children. *International Journal of Psychology, 7*, 235–242.

Choi, S.-C., Kim, U., & Choi, S.-H. (1993). Indigenous analysis of collective representations: A Korean perspective. In U. Kim & J. W. Berry (Eds.), *Indigenous psychologies: Research and experience in cultural context* (pp. 193–210). Newbury Park, CA: Sage.

Choi, I., & Nisbett, R. (2000). Cultural psychology of surprise: Holistic theories and recognition of contradiction. *Journal of Personality and Social Psychology, 79*, 890–905.

Choi, I., Nisbett, R., & Norenzayan, A. (1999). Causal attribution across cultures: Variation and universality. *Psychological Bulletin, 125*(1), 47–63.

Chow, J. C.-C., Jaffee, K., & Snowden, L. R. (2003). Racial/ethnic disparities in the use of mental health services in poverty areas. *American Journal of Public Health, 93*(5), 792–797.

Chowdhary, N., Jotheeswaran, A. T., Nadkarni, A., Hollon, S. D., King, M., Jordans, M. J. D., ... Patel, V. (2014). The methods and outcomes of cultural adapations of psychological treatments for depressive disorders: A systematic review. *Psychological Medicine, 44*, 1131–1146.

Christopher, J. C., Wendt, D. C., Marecek, J., & Goodman, D. M. (2014). Critical cultural awareness. *American Psychologist, 69*(7), 645–655.

Chua, A. (2011). *Battle hymn of the Tiger Mother.* New York: Penguin Press.

Church, A. T. (2000). Culture and personality: Toward an integrated cultural trait psychology. *Journal of Personality, 68*, 651–703.

Church, A. T., Alvarez, J. M., Mai, N. T. W., French, B. F., & Katigbak, M. S. (2011). Are cross-cultural comparisons of personality profiles meaningful? Differential item and facet functioning in the Revised NEO Personality Inventory. *Journal of Personality and Social Psychology, 101*, 1068–1089. doi: 10.1037/a0025290

Church, A. T., Anderson-Harumi, C. A., del Prado, A. M., Curtis, G. J., Tanaka-Matsumi, J., Valdez-Medina, J. L., ... Katigbak, M. S. (2008). Culture, cross-role consistency, and adjustment: Testing trait and cultural psychology perspectives. *Journal of Personality and Social Psychology, 95*(3), 739–755.

Church, A. T., Katigbak, M. S., & Reyes, J. A. (1998). Further exploration of Filipino personality structure using the lexical approach: Do the big-five or big-seven dimensions emerge? *European Journal of Personality, 12,* 249–269.

Church, A. T., Katigbak, M. S., del Prado, A. M., Ortiz, F. A., Mastor, K. A., Harumi, Y., ... Cabrera, H. F. (2006). Implicit theories and self-perceptions of traitedness across cultures: Toward integration of cultural and trait psychology perspectives. *Journal of Cross-Cultural Psychology, 37*(6), 694–716.

Church, A. T., & Lonner, W. J. (Eds.). (1998). The cross-cultural perspective in the study of personality: Rationale and current research. *Journal of Cross-Cultural Psychology, 29*(1), 32–62.

Church, A. T., Reyes, J. A., Katigbak, M. S., & Grimm, S. D. (1997). Filipino personality structure and the big-five model: A lexical approach. *Journal of Personality, 65,* 477–528.

CIA, The World Factbook. (2010). Retrieved https://www.cia.gov/library/publications/the-world-factbook/rankorder/2102rank.html.

Clarke, T. C., Black. L., & Stussman, B. J. (2015). Trends in the use of complementary health approaches among adults: United States, 2002–2012. National health statistics reports; no. 79. Hyattsville, MD: National Center of Health Statistics.

Cohen, N. (1982). Same or different? A problem of identity in cross-cultural marriages. *Journal of Family Therapy, 4*(2), 177–199.

Cohen, S., Doyle, W. J., Turner, R. B., Alper, C. M., & Skoner, D. P. (2003). Emotional style and susceptibility to the common cold. *Psychosomatic Medicine, 65,* 652–657.

Cohen, G. L., & Garcia, J. (2005). "I" am "us": Negative stereotypes as collective threats. *Journal of Personality and Social Psychology, 89,* 566–582.

Cohen, C. I., Magai, C., Yaffee, R., & Walcott-Brown, L. (2004). Racial differences in paranoid ideation and psychoses in an older urban population. *The American Journal of Psychiatry, 161*(5), 864–871.

Cohen, D., Nisbett, R., Bowdle, B. F., & Schwarz, N. (1996). Insult, aggression, and the southern culture of honor: An "experimental ethnography". *Journal of Personality and Social Psychology, 70*(5), 945–960.

Cole, M. (2006). Culture and cognitive development in phylogenetic, historical, and ontogenetic perspective. In W. Damon, R. M. Lerner, D. Kuhn, & R. S. Siegler (Eds.), *Handbook of child psychology: Vol. 2. Cognition, perception, and language* (6th ed., pp. 636–683). New York: Wiley.

Cole, M., Gay, J., Glick, J. A., & Sharp, D. W. (1971). *The cultural context of learning and thinking: An exploration in experimental anthropology.* New York: Basic Books.

Cole, M., & Scribner, S. (1974). *Culture and thought: A psychological introduction.* New York: Wiley.

Coll, C. G. (1990). Developmental outcome of minority infants: A process-oriented look into our beginnings. *Child Development, 61*(2), 270–289.

Collins, J. W., Jr., David, R. J., Handler, A., Wall, S., & Andes, S. (2004). Very low birthweight in African American infants: The role of maternal exposure to interpersonal racial discrimination. *American Journal of Public Health, 94*(12), 2132–2138.

Collins, W., Maccoby, E., Steinberg, L., Hetherington, M., & Bornstein, M. H. (2000). Contemporary research on parenting: The case for nature and nurture. *American Psychologist, 55*(2), 218–232.

Comas-Diaz, L. (1992). The future of psychotherapy with ethnic minorities. *Psychotherapy, 29,* 88–94.

Connection, C. C. (1987). Chinese values and the search for culture-free dimensions of culture. *Journal of Cross-Cultural Psychology, 18,* 143–174.

Conyers, L. M. (2003). Disability culture: A cultural model of disability. *Rehabilitation Education, 17*(3), 139–154.

Corrigan, P. W., Morris, S. B., Michaels, P. J., Rafacz, J. D., & Rüsch, N. (2012). Challenging the public stigma of mental illness: A meta-analysis of outcome studies. *Psychiatric Services, 63*(10), 963–973. doi: 10.1176/appi.ps.201100529

Cortes, B. P., Demoulin, S., Rodriguez, R. T., Rodriquez, A. P., & Lyens, J.-P. (2005). Infrahumanization or familiarity? Attribution of uniquely human emotions to the self, the ingroup, and the out-group. *Personality and Social Psychology Bulletin, 31,* 243–253.

Cortes, D. E. (2003). Idioms of distress, acculturation and depression: The Puerto Rican experience. In K. M. Chun, P. B. Organista, & G. Marin (Eds.), *Acculturation: Advances in theory, measurement, and applied research* (pp. 207–222). Washington, DC: American Psychological Association.

Cortina, L. M. (2001). Assessing sexual harassment among Latinas: Development of an instrument. *Cultural Diversity & Ethnic Minority Psychology, 7,* 164–181.

Cortina, L. M., Fitzgerald, L. F., & Drasgow, F. (2002). Contextualizing Latina experiences of sexual harassment: Preliminary tests of a structural model. *Basic and Applied Social Psychology, 24,* 295–311.

Cortina, L. M., & Wasti, S. A. (2005). Profiles in coping: Responses to sexual harassment across persons, organizations, and cultures. *Journal of Applied Psychology, 90,* 182–192.

Costa, P. T., & McCrae, R. R. (1992). *Revised Neo-Personality Inventory (NEO-PI-R) and Neo Five Factor Inventory (NEO-FFI).* Odessa, FL: Psychological Assessment Resources.

Costa, P. T., Terracciano, A., & McCrae, R. R. (2001). Gender differences in personality traits across cultures: Robust and surprising findings. *Journal of Personality & Social Psychology, 81*(2), 322–331.

Cottrell, A. B. (1990). Cross-national marriages: A review of literature. *Journal of Comparative Family Studies, 21*(2), 151–169.

Cottrell, C. A., & Neuberg, S. L. (2005). Different emotional reactions to different groups: A sociofunctional threat-based approach to "prejudice." *Journal of Personality and Social Psychology, 88,* 770–789.

Cousins, S. D. (1989). Culture and self-perception in Japan and the United States. *Journal of Personality and Social Psychology, 56,* 124–131.

Creanza, N., Ruhlen, M., Pemberton, T. J., Rosenberg, N. A., Feldman, M. W., & Ramachandran, S. (2015). A comparison of worldwide phonemic and genetic variation in human populations. *Proceedings of the National Academy of Sciences, 112,* 1265–1272. doi: 10.1073/pnas.1424033112

Crijnen, A. A. M., Achenbach, T. M., & Verhulst, F. C. (1997). Comparisons of problems reported by parents of children in 12 cultures: Total problems, externalizing, and internalizing. *Journal of the American Academy of Child & Adolescent Psychiatry, 36*(9), 1269–1277.

Crijnen, A. A. M., Achenbach, T. M., & Verhulst, F. C. (1999). Problems reported by parents of children in multiple cultures: The child behavior checklist syndrome constructs. *American Journal of Psychiatry, 156*(4), 569–574.

Crittenden, K. S. (1991). Asian self-effacement or feminine modesty? Attributional patterns of women university students in Taiwan. *Gender and Society, 5,* 98–117.

Crittenden, P. M. (2000). A dynamic-maturational exploration of the meaning of security and adaptation: Empirical, cultural, and theoretical considerations. In P. M. Crittenden & A. H. Claussen (Eds.), *The organization of attachment relationships: Maturation, culture, and context* (pp. 358–383). New York: Cambridge University Press.

Crook, T. H., Youngjohn, J. R., Larrabee, G. J., & Salama, M. (1992). Aging and everyday memory: *A cross-cultural study. Neuropsychology, 6*(2), 123–136.

Cross, S., & Morris, M. L. (2003). Getting to know you: The relational self-construal, relational cognition, and well-being. *Personality and Social Psychology Bulletin, 29*(4), 512–523.

Cross, S., Morris, M. L., & Gore, J. S. (2002). Thinking about oneself and others: The relational-interdependent self-construal and social cognition. *Journal of Personality and Social Psychology, 82*(5), 399–418.

Croteau, D., & Hoynes, W. (2000). *Media/society: Industries, images and audiences* (2nd ed.). Thousand Oaks, CA: Sage.

Crozier, G., & Davies, J. (2006). Family matters: A discussion of the Bangladeshi and Pakistani extended family and community in supporting the children's education. *The Sociological Review, 54*(4), 678–695.

Csikszentmihalyi, M. (1999). Implications of a systems perspective for the study of creativity. In R. J. Sternberg (Ed.), *Handbook of creativity* (pp. 313–335). New York: Cambridge University Press.

Cunningham, M. R., Roberts, A. R., Barbee, A. P., Druen, P. B., & Wu, C. (1995). "Their ideas of beauty are, on the whole, the same as ours": Consistency and variability in the cross-cultural perception of female physical attractiveness. *Journal of Personality and Social Psychology, 68*(2), 261–279.

Cyranowski, J. M., Frank, E., Young, E., Shear, M. K. (2000). Adolescent onset of the gender difference in lifetime rates of major depression. *Archives of General Psychiatry, 57,* 21–27.

Daibo, I., Murasawa, H., & Chou, Y. (1994). Attractive faces and affection of beauty: A comparison in preference of feminine facial beauty in Japan and Korea. *Japanese Journal of Research on Emotions, 1*(2), 101–123.

Dalsky, D. J., Gohm, C. L., Noguchi, K., & Shiomura, K. (2008). Mutual self-enhancement in Japan and the United States. *Journal of Cross-Cultural Psychology, 39,* 215–223.

Dandash, K. F., Refaat, A. H., & Eyada, M. (2001). Female genital mutilation: A descriptive study. *Journal of Sex and Marital Therapy, 27,* 453–458.

Darwin, C. (1859). *The origin of species.* New York: Modern Library.

Darwin, C. (1872). *The expression of emotion in man and animals.* London: John Murray.

Dasen, P. R. (1975). Concrete operational development in three cultures. *Journal of Cross-Cultural Psychology, 6,* 156–172.

Dasen, P. R., Dembele, B., Ettien, K., Kabran, L., Kamagate, D., Koffi, D. A., & N'Guessean, A. (1985). N'glouele, l'intelligence chez les Baoule [N'glouele: Intelligence among the Ivory Coast Baoule]. *Archives de Psychologie, 53,* 293–324.

Dasen, P. R., Lavallee, M., & Retschitzki, J. (1979). Training conservation of quantity (liquids) in West African (Baoulé) children. *International Journal of Psychology, 14,* 57–68.

Dasen, P. R., Ngini, L., & Lavalle, M. (1979). Cross-cultural training studies of concrete operations. In L. Eckensberger, Y. Poortinga, & W. Lonner (Eds.), *Cross-cultural contributions to psychology.* Amsterdam: Swets & Zeitlinger.

Davidson, R. J. (2003). Parsing the subcomponents of emotion and disorders of emotion: Perspectives from affective neuroscience. In R. J. Davidson, K. R. Scherer, & H. H. Goldsmith (Eds.), *Handbook of affective sciences* (pp. 8–24). New York: Oxford University Press.

Davis, F. G. (1991). *Who is black? One nation's definition.* University Park: Pennsylvania State University Press.

de Bruin, A., Treccani, B., & Della Sala, S. (2014). Cognitive advantage in bilingualism: An example of publication bias? *Psychological Science, 26,* 99–107. doi: First published on 4 December 2014; doi: 10.1177/0956797614557866

De Clerck, G. A. M. (2010). Deaf epistemologies as a critique and alternative to the practice of science: An anthropological perspective. *American Annals of the Deaf, 154*(5), 435–446.

De Coteau, T., Anderson, J., & Hope, D. (2006). Adapting manualized treatments: Treating anxiety disorders among Native Americans. *Cognitive and Behavioral Practice, 13*(4), 304–309.

de la Fuente, J., Santiago, J., Roman, A., Dumitrache, C., & Casasanto, D. (2014). When you think about it, your past is in front of you: How culture shapes spatial conceptions of time. *Psychological Science, 25,* 1682–1690. doi: 10.1177/0956797614534695

De Leersnyder, J. Mesquita, B., Kim, H., Eom, K., & Choi, H. (2014). Emotional fit with culture: A predictor of individual differences in relational well-being. *Emotion, 14,* 241–245.

De Raad, B., Perugini, M., Hrebickova, M., & Szarota, P. (1998). Lingua franca of personality: Taxonomies and structures based on the psycholexical approach. *Journal of Cross-Cultural Psychology, 29*(1), 212–232.

de Silva, S., Stiles, D., & Gibbons, J. (1992). Girls' identity formation in the changing social structure of Sri Lanka. *Journal of Genetic Psychology, 153*(2), 211–220.

de Waal, F. B. M. (2002). Apes from Venus: Bonobos and human social evolution. In F. B. M. de Waal (Ed.), *Tree of origin: What primate behavior can tell us about human social evolution* (pp. 39–68). Cambridge, MA: Harvard University Press.

De Waal, F. B. M. (2013). Animal conformists. *Science, 340,* 437–438.

De Wolff, M. S. and van IJzendoorn, M. H. (1997). Sensitivity and attachment: A meta-analysis on parental antecedents of infant attachment. *Child Development, 68,* 571–591

Dean, L. G., Kendal, R. L., Schapiro, S. J., Thierry, B., & Laland, K. N. (2012). Identification of the social and cognitive processes underlying human cumulative culture. *Science, 335,* 1114–1118.

DeAndrea, D. C., Shaw, A. S., & Levine, T. R. (2010). Online language: The role of culture in self-expression and self-construal on Facebook. *Journal of Language and Social Psychology, 29*(4), 425–442. doi: 10.1177/0261927X10377989

Deci, E. L., & Ryan, R. M. (1985). *Intrinsic motivation and self-determination theory in human behavior.* New York: Plenum.

Deck, L. P. (1968). Buying brains by the inch. *Journal of College and University Personnel Associations, 19,* 33–37.

Degler, C. N. (1971). *Neither black nor white: Slavery and race relations in Brazil and the United States.* Madson, WI: University of Wisconsin Press.

Dehaene, S., Izard, V., Pica, P., & Spelke, E. (2006). Core knowledge of geometry in an Amazonian indigene group. *Science, 311,* 381–384.

Dehaene, S., Izard, V., Spelke, E., & Pica, P. (2008). Log or linear? Distinct intuitions of the number scale in Western and Amazonian indigene cultures. *Science, 320,* 1217–1220.

Denham, S. A., Renwick, S. M., & Holt, R. W. (1997). Working and playing together: Prediction of preschool social-emotional competence from mother-child interaction. *Child Development, 62*(2), 242–249.

DePaulo, B. M., Stone, J., & Lassiter, G. D. (1985). Deceiving and detecting deceit. In B. R. Schlenker (Ed.), *The self and social life* (pp. 323–370). New York: McGraw-Hill.

Desjarlais, R. R. (1991). Dreams, divination, and Yolmo ways of knowing. Dreaming: *Journal of the Association for the Study of Dreams, 1*(3), 211–224.

Devan, G. S. (2001). Culture and the practice of group psychotherapy in Singapore. *International Journal of Groups Psychotherapy, 51,* 571–577.

Devine, P. G. (1989). Stereotypes and prejudice: Their automatic and controlled components. *Journal of Personality and Social Psychology, 56,* 5–18.

Devine, P. G., & Malpass, R. S. (1985). Orienting strategies in differential face recognition. *Personality and Social Psychology Bulletin, 11*(1), 33–40.

DeVoe, S. E., & Iyengar, S. S. (2004). Manager's theories of subordinates: A cross-cultural examination of manager perceptions of motivation and appraisal of performance. *Organizational Behavior and Human Decision Processes, 93,* 47–61.

Devos, T., & Banaji, M. R. (2005). American = White? *Journal of Personality and Social Psychology, 88*(3), 447–466.

DeVries, M. W. (1984). Temperament and infant mortality among the Masai of East Africa. *The American Journal of Psychiatry, 141*(10), 1189–1194.

DeVries, M. W. (1989). Difficult temperament: A universal and culturally embedded concept. In W. B. Carey & S. C. McDevitt (Eds.), *Clinical and educational applications of temperament research* (pp. 81–85). Lisse Netherlands: Swets & Zeitlinger Publishers.

Diaz-Loving, R. (1998). Contributions of Mexican ethnopsychology to the resolution of the etic-emic dilemma in personality. *Journal of Cross Cultural Psychology, 29*(1), 104–118.

Diener, E., & Biswas-Diener, R. (2008). *Happiness: Unlocking the mysteries of psychological wealth.* Malden, MA: Blackwell Publishing.

Diener, E., & Chan, M. Y. (2011). Happy people live longer: Subjective well-being contributes to health and longevity. *Applied Psychology: Health and Well-Being, 3,* 1–43.

Diener, E., & Ryan, K. (2009). Subjective well-being: A general overview. *South African Journal of Psychology, 39*(4), 391–406.

Diener, E., Tay, L., & Oishi, S. (2013). Rising income and the subjective well-being of nations. *Journal of Personality and Social Psychology, 104,* 267–276.

Dinges, N. G., & Hull, P. (1992). Personality, culture, and international studies. In D. Lieberman (Ed.), *Revealing the world: An interdisciplinary reader for international studies* (pp. 133–162). Dubuque, IA: Kendall-Hunt.

Dion, K. K. (1986). Stereotyping based on physical attractiveness: Issues and conceptual perspectives. In C. P. Herman, M. P. Zanna, & E. T. Higgins (Eds.), *Ontario symposium on personality and social psychology* (Vol. 3, pp. 7-21). Hillsdale, NJ: Erlbaum.

Dion, K. K., & Dion, K. L. (1993b). Individualistic and collectivistic perspectives on gender and the cultural context of love and intimacy. *Journal of Social Issues, 49,* 53–69.

Dockray, S., & Steptoe, A. (2010). Positive affect and psychobiological processes. *Neuroscience and Biobehavioral Reviews, 35*(1), 69–75.

Dodds, P. S., Clark, E. M., Desu, S., Frank, M. R., Reagan, A. J., Williams, J. R., . . . Bagrow, J. P. (2015). Human language reveals a universal positivity bias. *Proceedings of the National Academy of Sciences.* doi: 10.1073/pnas.1505647112

Doi, T. (1973). *The anatomy of dependence.* Tokyo: Kodansha.

Donne, J. (1999). Meditation xvii. *Devotions upon emergent occasions, 1624,* 344–345.

DuBard, C. A., & Gizlice, Z. (2008). Language spoken and differences in health status, access to care, and receipt of preventive services among U.S. Hispanics. *American Journal of Public Health, 98,* 2021–2028.

Duckitt, J. (1992). Psychology and prejudice: A historical analysis and integrative framework. *American Psychologist, 47,* 1182–1194.

Duckitt, J., Callaghan, J., & Wagner, C. (2005). Group identification and outgroup attitudes in four south African ethnic groups: A multidimensional approach. *Personality and Social Psychology Bulletin, 31,* 633–646.

Dumas, F. (1932). La mimique des aveugles [facial expression of the blind]. *Bulletin de I'Academie de Medecine, 107.*

Dunn, J. (1988). *The beginnings of social understanding.* Cambridge, MA: Harvard University Press.

Duran, E. (2006). *Healing the soul wound: Counseling with American Indians and other Native peoples.* New York: Teacher's College.

Durkheim, E. (1897; 2002). *Suicide: A study in sociology.* London and New York: Routledge Classics.

Dwairy, M. (2009). Culture analysis and metaphor psychotherapy with Arab-Muslim clients. *Journal of Clinical Psychology, 65*(2), 199–209.

Dwairy, M., Achoui, M., Abouseire, R., & Farah, A. (2006). Parenting styles, individuation, and mental health of Arab adolescents: A third cross-regional research study. *Journal of Cross-Cultural Psychology, 37*(3), 262–272.

Dweck, C. (2008). The secret to raising smart kids. *Scientific American Mind, 18,* 36–43.

Dyal, J. A. (1984). Cross-cultural research with the locus of control construct. In H. M. Lefcourt (Ed.), *Research with the locus of control construct* (Vol. 3, pp. 209–306). New York: Academic Press.

Eagly, A. H. (1987). Sex differences in social behavior: *A social role interpretation.* Hillsdale, NJ: Lawrence Erlbaum Associates, Inc.

Eagly, A. H., Ashmore, R. D., Makhijani, M. G., & Longo, L. C. (1991). What is beautiful is good, but…: A meta analytic review of research on the physical attractiveness stereotype. *Psychological Bulletin, 110*(1), 109–128.

Earley, P. C. (1989). Social loafing and collectivism: A comparison of the United States and the People's Republic of China. *Administrative Science Quarterly, 34,* 565–581.

Eberhardt, J. L., & Randall, J. L. (1997). The essential notion of race. *Psychological Science, 8*(3), 198–203.

Ebrahimpour, M., & Johnson, J. L. (1992). Quality, vendor evaluation and organizational performance: A comparison of U.S. and Japanese firms. *Journal of Business Research, 25,* 129–142.

Eccles, J. S., & Roeser, R. W. (2011). Schools as developmental contexts during adolescence. *Journal of Research on Adolescence, 21*(1), 225–241. doi: 10.1111/j.1532-7795.2010.00725.x

Economic and Social Research Council. (2005). Who is a sister and a brother? Biological and social ties. Retrieved http://www.esrcsocietytoday.ac.uk/ESRCInfoCentre/PO/releases/2005/may/index2.aspx.

Eddey, G. E., & Robey, K. L. (2005). Considering the culture of disability in cultural competence education. *Academic Medicine, 80*(7), 706–712.

Efferson, C., Lalive, R., & Fehr, E. (2008). The coevolution of cultural groups and ingroup favoritism. *Science, 321,* 1844–1849.

Efron, D. (1941). *Gesture and environment.* Oxford, England: King's Crown Press.

Eibl-Eibesfeldt, I. (1973). The expressive behavior of the deaf-and-blind born. In M. von Cranach & I. Vine (Eds.), *Social communication and movement* (pp. 163–194). London: Academic Press.

Ekman, P. (1972). Universal and cultural differences in facial expression of emotion. In J. R. Cole (Ed.), *Nebraska symposium on motivation, 1971* (pp. 207–283). Lincoln: University of Nebraska Press.

Ekman, P. (1973). *Darwin and facial expression: A century of research in review.* New York: Academic Press.

Ekman, P. (1976). Movements with precise meanings. *Journal of Communication, 26*(3), 14–26.

Ekman, P. (1999). Basic emotions. In T. Dalgleish & T. Power (Eds.), *The handbook of cognition and emotion* (pp. 45–60). Sussex: John Wiley and Sons, Ltd.

Ekman, P., Davidson, R. J., & Friesen, W. V. (1990). The Duchenne smile: Emotional expression and brain physiology: II. *Journal of Personality & Social Psychology, 58,* 342–353.

Ekman, P., & Friesen, W. V. (1969). The repertoire of nonverbal behavior: Categories, origins, usage, and coding. *Semiotica, 1,* 49–98.

Ekman, P., & Friesen, W. V. (1971). Constants across culture in the face and emotion. *Journal of Personality and Social Psychology, 17,* 124–129.

Ekman, P., & Friesen, W. V. (1986). A new pan-cultural facial expression of emotion. *Motivation & Emotion, 10,* 159–168.

Ekman, P., Friesen, W. V., & Ellsworth, P. (1972). *Emotion in the human face.* New York: Garland.

Ekman, P., Friesen, W. V., O'Sullivan, M., Chan, A., Diacoyanni-Tarlatzis, I., Heider, K., … Tzavaras, A. (1987). Universals and cultural differences in the judgments of facial expressions of emotion. *Journal of Personality & Social Psychology, 53,* 712–717.

Ekman, P., Friesen, W. V., O'Sullivan, M., & Scherer, K. R. (1980). Relative importance of face, body, and speech in judgments of personality and affect. *Journal of Personality and Social Psychology, 38,* 270–277.

Ekman, P., & Heider, K. G. (1988). The universality of a contempt expression: A replication. *Motivation & Emotion, 12,* 303–308.

Ekman, P., & Oster, H. (1979). Facial expressions of emotion. *Annual Review of Psychology, 30,* 527–554.

Ekman, P., Levenson, R. W., & Friesen, W. V. (1983). Autonomic nervous system activity distinguishes among emotions. *Science, 221,* 1208–1210.

Ekman, P., Sorenson, E. R., & Friesen, W. V. (1969). Pancultural elements in facial displays of emotion. *Science, 164,* 86–94.

Elfenbein, H. A., & Ambady, N. (2002). On the universality and cultural specificity of emotion recognition: A meta-analysis. *Psychological Bulletin, 128,* 205–235.

Elfenbein, H. A., & Ambady, N. (2003a). Cultural similarity's consequences: A distance perspective on cross-cultural differences in emotion recognition. *Journal of Cross-Cultural Psychology, 34,* 92–110.

Elfenbein, H. A., & Ambady, N. (2003b). When familiarity breeds accuracy: Cultural exposure and facial emotion recognition. *Journal of Personality and Social Psychology, 85,* 276–290.

Elfenbein, H. A., Mandal, M. K., Ambady, N., & Harizuka, S. (2002). Cross-cultural patterns in emotion recognition: Highlighting design and analytic techniques. *Emotion, 2,* 75–84.

Elfenbein, H. A., Mandal, M. K., Ambady, N., Harizuka, S., & Kumar, S. (2004). Hemifacial differences in the in-group advantage in emotion recognition. *Cognition & Emotion, 18,* 613–629.

Ellis, A. (1962). *Reason and emotion in psychotherapy.* Secaucus, NJ: Prentice-Hall.

Ellis, B. H., MacDonald, H. Z., Lincoln, A. K., & Cabral, H. J. (2008). Mental health of Somali adolescent refugees: The role of trauma, stress, and perceived discrimination. *Journal of Consulting and Clinical Psychology, 76,* 184–193.

Else-Quest, N. M., Hyde, J. S., & Linn, M. C. (2010). Cross-national patterns of gender differences in mathematics: A meta analysis. *Psychological Bulletin, 136*(1), 103–127.

Endo, Y., Heine, S. J., & Lehman, D. R. (2000). Culture and positive illusions in close relationships: How my relationships are better than yours. *Personality and Social Psychology Bulletin, 26*(12), 1571–1586.

Engel, G. L. (1977). The need for a new medical model: A challenge for biomedicine. *Science, 196,* 129–136.

Engel de Abreu, P. M. J., Cruz-Santos, A., Tourinho, C. J., Martin, R., & Bialystok, E. (2012). Bilingualism enriches the poor: Enhanced cognitive control in low-income minorities. *Psychological Science, 23,* 1364–1671. doi: 10.1177/0956797612443836

Enriquez, V. G. (1992). *From colonial to liberation psychology: The Philippine experience.* Manila: De La Salle University Press.

Ervin, S. M. (1964). Language and TAT content in bilinguals. *Journal of Abnormal and Social Psychology, 68,* 500–507.

Espin, O. M. (1993). Feminist theory: Not for or by white women only. *Counseling Psychologist, 21,* 103–108.

Espin, O. M. (1997). *Latina realities: Essays on healing, migration, and sexuality.* Boulder, CO: Westview.

Everett, C., Blasi, D. E., & Roberts, S. G. (2015). Climate, vocal folds, and tonal languages: Connecting the physiological and geographic dots. *Proceedings of the National Academy of Sciences, 112*, 1322–1327. doi: 10.1073/pnas.1417413112

Exline, R. V., Jones, P., & Maciorowski, K. (1977). *Race, affiliative-conflict theory and mutual visual attention during conversation.* Paper presented at the American Psychological Association Annual Convention, San Francisco.

Eysenck, H. J. (1983). Is there a paradigm in personality research? *Journal of Research in Personality, 27*(4), 369–397.

Fabrega, H. (1989). Language, culture, and the neurobiology of pain: A theoretical exploration. *Behavioral Neurology, 2*(4), 235–260.

Fagot, B., Leinbach, M. D., & Hagen, R. (1986). Gender labeling and adoption of sex-typed behaviors. *Developmental Psychology, 22*, 440–443.

Falk, C. F., Heine, S. J., Yuki, M., & Takemura, K. (2009). Why do Westerners self-enhance more than East Asians? *European Journal of Personality, 23*, 183–203.

Fan, S. P., Liberman, Z., Keysar, B., & Kinzler, K. D. (2015). The exposure advantage: Early exposure to a multilingual environment promotes effective communication. *Psychological Science.* doi: first published online, May 8, 2015; doi: 10.1177/0956797615574699

Febo San Miguel, V. E., Guarnaccia, P. J., Shrout, P. E., Lewis-Fernandez, R., Canino, G. J., & Ramirez, R. R. (2006). A quantitative analysis of ataque de nervios in Puerto Rico: Further examination of a cultural syndrome. *Hispanic Journal of Behavioral Sciences, 28*(3), 313–330.

Fehr, B. J., & Exline, R. V. (1987). Social visual interactions: A conceptual and literature review. In A. W. Siegman & S. Feldstein (Eds.), *Nonverbal behavior and communication* (Vol. 2, pp. 225–326). Hillsdale, NJ: Lawrence Erlbaum.

Feingold, A. (1992). Good-looking people are not what we think. *Psychological Bulletin, 111*(2), 304–341.

Ferber, R. (1985). *Solve your child's sleep problems.* New York: Fireside.

Ferber, R. (2006). *Solve your child's sleep problems*: New, revised, and expanded edition. New York: Fireside.

Fernandez, A. M., Sierra, J. C., Zubeidat, I., & Vera-Villarroel, P. (2006). Sex differences in response to sexual and emotional infidelity among Spanish and Chilean students. *Journal of Cross-Cultural Psychology, 37*(4), 359–365.

Ferrante, J. (1992). *Sociology: A global perspective.* Belmont, CA: Wadsworth.

Fessler, D. M. T., Nettle, D., Afshar, Y., de Andrade Pinheiro, I., Bolyanatz, A., Borgerhoff Mulder, M., . . . Zbarauskaite, A. (2005). A cross-cultural investigation of the role of foot size in physical attractiveness. *Archives of Sexual Behavior, 34*, 267–276. doi: IO.lOO7/sU)5(lK-OO.V3115-4

Field, T., Diego, M., Hernandez-Reif, M., Schanberg, S., Kuhn, C., Yando, R., & Bendell, D. (2003). Pregnancy anxiety and comorbid depression and anger: Effects on the fetus and neonate. *Depression and Anxiety, 17*(3), Special Issue: Anxiety disorders in women, 140–151.

Fischer, R., & Smith, P. B. (2003). Reward allocation and culture: A metaanalysis. *Journal of Cross-Cultural Psychology, 34*(3), 251–268.

Fishman, J. A. (1960). A systematization of the Whorfian hypothesis. *Behavioral Science, 5*, 323–339.

Fiske, A. P. (2000). Complementarity theory: Why human social capacities evolved to require cultural complements. *Personality and Social Psychology Review, 4*(1), 76–94.

Fiske, S. T., Cuddy, A. J. C., Glick, P., & Xu, J. (2002). A model of (often mixed) stereotype content: Competence and warmth respectively follow from perceived status and competition. *Journal of Personality and Social Psychology, 82*, 878–902.

Fitch, W. T., & Hauser, M. D. (2004). Computational constraints on syntactic processing in a nonhuman primate. *Science, 303*(2004), 377–380.

Fitzgerald, L. F., Drasgow, F., Hulin, C. L., Gelfand, M. J., & Magley, V. J. (1997). Antecedents and consequences of sexual harassment in organizations: A test of an integrated model. *Journal of Applied Psychology, 82*, 578–589.

Fitzgerald, L. F., Gelfand, M. J., & Drasgow, F. (1995). Measuring sexual harassment: Theoretical and psychometric advances. *Basic and Applied Social Psychology, 17*, 425–445.

Flores, N. M., & Huo, Y. J. (2012). "We" are not all alike: Consequences of neglecting national origin identities among Asians and Latinoes. *Social Psychological and Personality Science, 4*, 143–150.

Forgas, J. P. (1992). On mood and peculiar people: Affect and person typicality in impression formation. *Journal of Personality & Social Psychology, 62*(5), 863–875.

Forgas, J. P. (1994). The role of emotion in social judgments: An introductory review and an affect infusion model (AIM). *European Journal of Social Psychology, 24*, 1–24.

Forgas, J. P., & Bower, H. G. (1987). Mood effects on person perception judgments. *Journal of Personality and Social Psychology, 53*(1), 53–60.

Forgas, J. P., & Fiedler, K. (1996). Us and them: Mood effects on intergroup discrimination. *Journal of Personality and Social Psychology, 70*, 28–40.

Forgas, J. P., Furnham, A., & Frey, D. (1989). Cross-national differences in attributions of wealth and economic success. *Journal of Social Psychology, 129*, 643–657.

Forgas, J. P., & Moylan, J. S. (1991). Affective influences on stereotype judgments. *Cognition and Emotion, 5*(5/6), 379–395.

Forgas, J. P., & O'Driscoll, M. (1984). Cross-cultural and demographic differences in the perception of nations. *Journal of Cross-Cultural Psychology, 15*(2), 199–222.

Forston, R. F., & Larson, C. U. (1968). The dynamics of space: An experimental study in proxemics behavior among Latin Americans and North Americans. *Journal of Communication, 18*(2), 109–116.

Fox, N. A., Henderson, H. H., Rubin, K., Calkins, S. D., & Schmidt, L. A. (2001). Continuity and discontinuity of behavioral inhibition and exuberance: Psychophysiological and behavioral influences across the first four years of life. *Child Development, 72*, 1–21.

Francis, D. D. (2009). Conceptualizing child health disparities: A role for developmental neurogenomics. *Pediatrics, 124*, S196–S202.

Frank, R. (2007). What to make of it? The (Re)emergence of a biological conceptualization of race in health disparities research. *Social Science & Medicine, 64*(10), 1977–1983.

Freedman, D. G. (1964). Smiling in blind infants and the issue of innate versus acquired. *Journal of Child Psychology and Psychiatry, 5,* 171–184.

Freedman, D. G. (1974). *Human infancy: An evolutionary perspective.* New York: Wiley/ Halstead.

Friedman, H. S. (1978). The relative strength of verbal versus nonverbal cues. *Personality and Social Psychology Bulletin, 4,* 147–150.

Friesen, W. V. (1972). *Cultural differences in facial expressions in a social situation: An experimental test of the concept of display rules.* Unpublished doctoral dissertation, University of California, San Francisco.

Friesen, W. V., Ekman, P., & Wallbott, H. (1979). Measuring hand movements. *Journal of Nonverbal Behavior, 4*(2), 97–112.

Frome, P., & Eccles, J. S. (1996, March). *Gender-role identity and self-esteem.* Paper presented at the biennial meeting of the Society for Research on Adolescence, Boston.

Fry, D. P., & Soderberg, P. (2013). Lethal aggression in mobile forager bands and implications for the origins of war. *Science, 341,* 270–273. doi: 10.1126/science.1235675

Fu, A., & Markus, H. (2014). My mother and me: Why tiger mothers motivate Asian Americans but not European Americans. *Personality and Social Psychology Bulletin, 40,* 739–749.

Fuhrman, O., & Boroditsky, L. (2010). Cross-cultural differences in mental representations of time: Evidence from an implicit nonlinguistic task. *Cognitive Science: A Multidisciplinary Journal, 34*(8), 1430–1451.

Fukumizu, M., Kaga, M., Kohyama, J., & Hayes, M. (2005). Sleep-related nighttime crying (Yonaki) in Japan: A community-based study. *Pediatrics, 115,* 217–224

Fulcher, J. S. (1942). "Voluntary" facial expression in blind and seeing children. *Archives of Psychology, 272,* 5–49.

Fuligni, A., & Stevenson, H. W. (1995). Time-use and mathematics achievement among American, Chinese, and Japanese high school students. *Child Development, 66,* 830–842.

Fulmer, C. A., Gelfand, M. J., Kruglanski, A., Kim-Prieto, C., Diener, E., Pierro, A., & Higgins, E. T. (2010). On "feeling right" in cultural contexts: How person-culture match affects self-esteem and subjective well-being. *Psychological Science, 21,* 1563–1569. doi: 10.1177/0956797610384742

Funder, D. (2001). Personality. *Annual Review of Psychology, 52,* 197–221.

Furnham, A., & Bochner, S. (1982). Social difficulty in a foreign culture: An empirical analysis of culture shock. In S. Bochner (Ed.), *Cultures in contact: Studies in cross-cultural interactions* (pp. 161–198). Oxford: Pergamon.

Gabrenya, W. K., Jr., Wang, Y., & Latane, B. (1985). Social loafing on an optimizing task: Cross-cultural differences among Chinese and Americans. *Journal of Cross-Cultural Psychology, 16,* 223–242.

Gaertner, L., Sedikides, C., & Chang, K. (2008). On pancultural self-enhancement: Well-adjusted Taiwanese self-enhance on personally valued traits. *Journal of Cross-Cultural Psychology, 39,* 463–477.

Galambos, N., Petersen, A., Richards, M., & Gitelson, I. (1985). The Attitudes Towards Women Scale for Adolescents (AWSA): A study of reliability and validity. *Sex Roles, 5/6,* 343–356.

Galati, D., Scherer, K. R., & Ricci-Bitti, P. E. (1997). Voluntary facial expression of emotion: Comparing congenitally blind with normally sighted encoders. *Journal of Personality and Social Psychology, 73,* 1363–1379.

Gallagher-Thompson, D., Solano, N., Coon, D., & Arean, P. (2003). Recruitment and retention of Latino dementia family caregivers in intervention research: Issues to face, lessons to learn. *Gerontologist, 43*(1), 45–51.

Garcia-Coll, C. T. (1990). Developmental outcomes of minority infants: A process oriented look at our beginnings. *Child Development, 61,* 270–289.

Garcia Coll, C., & Marks, A. (2012). *The immigrant paradox in children and adolescents: Is becoming American a developmental risk?* Washington, DC: American Psychological Association.

Garcia-Moreno, C., Heise, L., Jansen, H. A. F. M., Ellsberg, M., & Watts, C. (2005). Violence against women. *Science, 310,* 1282–1283.

Gardner, H. (1983). *Frames of mind.* New York: Basic Books.

Gardner, W. L., Gabriel, S., & Lee, A. Y. (1999). "I" value freedom, but "we" value relationships: Self-construal priming mirrors cultural differences in judgment. *Psychological Science, 10*(4), 321–326.

Garland, A. F., Lau, A. S., Yeh, M., McCabe, K. M., Hough, R. L., & Landsverk, J. A. (2005). Racial and ethnic differences in utilization of mental health services among high-risk youths. *The American Journal of Psychiatry, 162*(7), 1336–1343.

Garro, L. C. (1986). Language, memory, and focality: A reexamination. *American Anthropologist, 88*(1), 128–136.

Gartstein, M., Slobodskaya, H., Z– ylicz, P., Gosztyła, D., & Nakagawa, A. (2010). A cross-cultural evaluation of temperament: Japan, USA, Poland, and Russia. *International Journal of Psychology & Psychological Therapy, 10*(1), 55–75

Gaw, K. F. (2000). Reverse culture shock in students returning from overseas. *International Journal of Intercultural Relations, 24,* 83–104.

Geen, T. (1992). Facial expressions in socially isolated nonhuman primates: Open and closed programs for expressive behavior. *Journal of Research in Personality, 26,* 273–280.

Geertz, C. (1975). From the natives' point of view: On the nature of anthropological understanding. *American Scientist, 63,* 47–53.

Gelfand, M. J., & Dyer, N. (2000). A cultural perspective on negotiation: Progress, pitfalls, and prospects. Applied Psychology: *An International Review, 49*(1), 62–99.

Gelfand, M. J., Major, V. S., Raver, J. L., Nishii, L. H., & O'Brien, K. (2006). The dynamics of the relational self in negotiations. *Academy of Management Review, 31,* 427–451.

Gelfand, M. J., Raver, J. L., Nishii, L., Leslie, L. M., Lun, J., Lim, B. C., ... Yamaguchi, S. (2011). Differences between tight and loose cultures: A 33-nation study. *Science, 332*(6033), 1100–1104.

Georgas, J., Berry, J. W., van di Vijver, F. J. R., Kagitcibasi, C., & Poortinga, Y. H. (2006). *Families across cultures: A 30 nation psychological study.* New York: Cambridge University Press.

Gerber, E. (1975). *The cultural patterning of emotions in Samoa.* Unpublished doctoral dissertation, University of California, San Diego.

Gergen, K. J., Gulerce, A., Lock, A., & Misra, G. (1996). Psychological science in cultural context. *American Psychologist, 52*(5), 496–503.

Gibbons, J., Bradford, R., & Stiles, D. A. (1989). Madrid adolescents express interest in gender roles and work possibilities. *Journal of Early Adolescence, 9*(1–2), 125–141.

Gibbons, J., Stiles, D. A., Schnellman, J. D., & Morales-Hidalgo, I. (1990). Images of work, gender, and social commitment among Guatemalan adolescents. *Journal of Early Adolescence, 10*(1), 89–103.

Gibbons, J., Stiles, D. A., & Shkodriani, G. M. (1991). Adolescents' attitudes toward family and gender roles: An international comparison. *Sex Roles, 25*(11–12), 625–643.

Gibbs, J., Basinger, K., Grime, R., & Snarey, J. (2007). Moral judgment development across cultures: Revisiting Kohlberg's universality claims. *Developmental Review, 27*(4), 443–500.

Gilbert, D. T., & Hixon, J. G. (1991). The trouble of thinking: Activation and application of stereotypic beliefs. *Journal of Personality and Social Psychology, 60*(4), 509–517.

Gilbert, G. M. (1951). Stereotype persistence and change among college students. *Journal of Abnormal and Social Psychology, 46*, 245–254.

Gilligan, C. (1982). *In a different voice: Psychological theory and women's development.* Cambridge, MA: Harvard University Press.

Gilovich, T., & Medvec, V. H. (1995). The experience of regret: What, when, and why. *Psychological Review, 102*, 379–395.

Gilovich, T., Medvec, V. H., & Kahneman, D. (1998). Varieties of regret: A debate and partial resolution. *Psychological Review, 105*, 602–605.

Gilovich, T., Wang, R. F., Regan, D., & Nishina, S. (2003). Regrets of action and inaction across cultures. *Journal of Cross-Cultural Psychology, 34*, 61–71.

Ginges, J., Atran, S., Medin, D., & Shikaki, K. (2007). Sacred bounds on rational resolution of violent political conflict. *Proceedings from the National Academy of Sciences, 104*, 7357–7360.

Ginges, J., Hansen, I., & Norenzayan, A. (2009). Religion and support for suicide attacks. *Psychological Science, 20*(2), 224–230.

Gladwin, H., & Gladwin, C. (1971). Estimating market conditions and profit expectations of fish sellers at Cape Coast, Ghana. In G. Dalton (Ed.), *Studies in economic anthropology* (Anthropological Studies No. 7, pp. 122–143). Washington, DC: American Anthropological Association.

Gladwin, T. (1970). *East is a big bird: Navigation and logic on Puluwat Atoll.* Cambridge, MA: Harvard University Press.

Glick, P., Lameiras, M., Fiske, S. T., Eckes, T., Masser, B., Volpato, C., … Wells, R. (2004). Bad but bold: Ambivalent attitudes toward men predict gender inequality in 16 nations. *Journal of Personality and Social Psychology, 86*(5), 713–728.

The Global Deception Research Team. (2006). A world of lies. *Journal of Cross-Cultural Psychology, 37*, 60–74.

Glover, G. (2001). Parenting in Native American families. In N. B. Webb (Ed.), *Culturally diverse parent-child and family relationships: A guide for social workers and other practitioners* (pp. 205–231). New York: Columbia University Press.

Grisaru, N., Budowski, D., & Witztum, E. (1997). Possession by the "zar" among Ethiopian immigrants to Israel: Psychopathology or culture-bound syndrome? *Psychopathology, 30*(4), 223–233.

Goldman, A. (1992). Intercultural training of Japanese for U.S. Japanese interorganizational communication. *International Journal of Intercultural Relations, 16*, 195–215.

Goldman, A. (1994). The centrality of "ningensei" to Japanese negotiating and interpersonal relationships: Implications for U.S.-Japanese communication. *International Journal of Intercultural Relations, 18*(1), 29–54.

Gollan, T. H., Schotter, E. R., Gomez, J., Murillo, M., & Keith, R. (2014). Multiple levels of bilingual advantage control: Evidence from language intrusions in reading aloud. *Psychological Science, 25*, 585–595. doi: First published on 23 December 2013; doi: 10.1177/0956797613512661

Goncalo, J. A., & Staw, B. M. (2006). Individualism-collectivism and group creativity. *Organizational Behavior and Human Decision Processes, 100*, 96–109.

Gone, J. P. (2007). 'We never was happy living like a Whiteman': Mental health disparities and the postcolonial predicament in American Indian communities. *American Journal of Community Psychology, 40*(3–4), 290–300.

Gone, J. P. (2010). Psychotherapy and traditional healing for American Indians: Exploring the prospects for therapeutic integration. *The Counseling Psychologist, 38*(2), 166–235.

Gone, J. P. (2011). 'I came to tell you of my life': Narrative expositions of 'mental health' in an American Indian community. In M. S. Aber, K. I. Maton, & E. Seidman (Eds.), *Empowering settings and voices for social change* (pp. 134–154). New York: Oxford University Press.

Gone, J. P., & Kirmayer, L. J. (2010). On the wisdom of considering culture and context in psychopathology. In T. Millon, R. F. Krueger, & E. Simonsen (Eds.), *Contemporary directions in psychopathology: Scientific foundations of the DSM-V and ICD-11.* (pp. 72–96). New York: Guilford Press.

Goodenough, F. L. (1932). Expression of emotions in a blind-deaf child. *Journal of Abnormal and Social Psychology, 27*, 328–333.

Goodwin, R. (1990). Sex differences among partner preferences: Are the sexes really very similar? *Sex Roles, 23*, 501–503.

Goodnow, J. (1988). Parents' ideas, actions and feelings: Models and methods from developmental and social psychology. *Child Development, 59*, 289–320.

Gordon, P. (2004). Numerical cognition without words: Evidence from Amazonia. *Science Express, 306*, 496–499.

Gordon, R. A. (2001). Eating disorders East and West: A culture-bound syndrome unbound. In M. Nasser & M. A. Katzman (Eds.), *Eating disorders and cultures in transition* (pp. 1–16). New York: Brunner-Routledge.

Gottman, J. M. (1994). *What predicts divorce?* Hillsdale, NJ: Erlbaum.

Gottman, J. M., & Levenson, R. W. (2002). A two-factor model for predicting when a couple will divorce: Exploratory analyses using 14-year longitudinal data. *Family Process, 41*, 83–96.

Graham, J. L. (1983). Brazilian, Japanese, and American Business Negotiations. *Journal of International Business Studies, 14*, 47–61.

Graham, J. L. (1984). *Smart bargaining: Doing business with the Japanese.* Cambridge, MA: Ballinger.

Graham, J. L. (1993). The Japanese negotiation style: Characteristics of a distinct approach. *Negotiation Journal, 9*(2), 123–140.

Graham, J. L., & Andrews, J. D. (1987). A holistic analysis of Japanese and American business negotiations. *Analysis of Business Negotiations, 24*(4), 63–77.

Green, B. A. (2009). Culture and mental health assessment. In S. Eshun & R. A. R. Gurung (Eds.), *Culture and mental health: Sociocultural influences, theory, and practice* (pp. 19–33). Wiley-Blackwell.

Greenberg, J., Solomon, S., & Pyszczynski, T. (1997). Terror management theory of self-esteem and cultural worldviews: Empirical assessments and conceptual refinements. In M. P. Zanna (Ed.), *Advances in experimental social psychology* (pp. 61–139). San Diego, CA: Academic Press.

Greenfield, P. M. (1997). You can't take it with you: Why ability assessments don't cross cultures. *American Psychologist, 52*, 1115–1124.

Greenfield, P. M., Reich, L. C., & Oliver, R. R. (1966). On culture and equivalence II. In J. S. Bruner, R. R. Oliver, & P. M. Greenfield (Eds.), *Studies in cognitive growth* (pp. 270–318). New York: Wiley.

Greenwald, A. G., McGhee, D. E., & Schwartz, J. L. K. (1998). Measuring individual differences in implicit cognition: The implicit association test. *Journal of Personality and Social Psychology, 74*, 1464–1480.

Greenwald, A. G., & Pratkanis, A. R. (1984). The self. In R. S. Wyer & T. K. Srull (Eds.), *Handbook of social cognition* (Vol. 3, pp. 129–178). Hillsdale, NJ: Erlbaum.

Grossman, K. E., & Grossmann, K. (1990). The wider concept of attachment in cross-cultural research. *Human Development, 33*, 31–47.

Grusec, J. E., & Davidov, M. (2010). Integrating different perspectives on socialization theory and research: A domain-specific approach. *Child Development, 81*(3), 687–709.

Guarnaccia, P. J., Lewis-Fernández, R., Pincay, I. M., Shrout, P. E., Guo, J., Torres, M., … Alegria, M. (2010). Ataque de nervios as a marker of social and psychiatric vulnerability: Results from the NLAAS. *International Journal of Social Psychiatry, 56*(3), 298–309.

Guarnaccia, P. J., Martinez, I., & Acosta, H. (2005). Mental health in the Hispanic immigrant community: An overview. *Journal of Immigrant and Refugee Services, 3*, 21–46.

Guarnaccia, P., & Pincay, I. M. (2008). Culture-specific diagnoses and their relationship to mood disorders. In S. Loue & M. Sajatovic (Eds.), *Diversity issues in the diagnosis, treatment and research of mood disorders* (pp. 32–53). New York: Oxford University Press.

Gudykunst, W. B. (1993). Toward a theory of effective interpersonal and intergroup communication: An anxiety/uncertainty management (AUM) perspective. In R. L. Wiseman, J. Koester (Eds.), *International and inter-cultural communication annual: Vol. 17. Intercultural communication competence* (pp. 33–71). Newbury Park, CA: Sage.

Gudykunst, W. B., & Nishida, T. (1984). Individual and cultural influences on uncertainty reduction. *Communication Monographs, 51*, 23–36.

Gudykunst, W. B., & Nishida, T. (1986). Attributional confidence in low and high context cultures. *Human Communication Research, 12*(4), 525–549.

Gudykunst, W. B., Yoon, Y., & Nishida, T. (1987). The influence of individualism-collectivism on perceptions of communication in ingroup and outgroup relationships. *Communication Monographs, 54*, 295–306.

Guilford, J. P. (1985). The structure of intellect model. In B. B. Wolman (Ed.), *Handbook of intelligence: Theories, measurements, and applications* (pp. 225–265). New York: Wiley.

Guisinger, S., & Blatt, S. J. (1994). Individuality and relatedness: Evolution of a fundamental dialectic. *American Psychologist, 49*, 104–111.

Guo, T., Ji, L.-J., Spina, R., & Zhang, Z. (2012). Culture, temporal focus, and values of the past and future. *Personality and Social Psychology Bulletin, 38*, 1030–1040. doi: 10.1177/0146167212443895

Gurven, M., von Rueden, C., Massenkoff, M., & Kaplan, H. (2012). How universal is the Big Five? Testing the Five-Factor Model of personality variation among forager-farmers in the Bolivian Amazon. *Journal of Personality and Social Psychology, 104*, 354–370. doi: http://dx.doi.org/10.1037/a0030841

Haidt, J. (2001). The emotional dog and its rational tail: A social intuitionist approach to moral judgment. *Psychological Review, 108*, 814–834.

Hall, E. T. (1963). A system for the notation of proxemic behaviors. *American Anthropologist, 65*, 1003–1026.

Hall, E. T. (1966). *The hidden dimension*. New York: Doubleday.

Hall, E. T. (1973). *The silent language*. New York: Anchor.

Hamid, P. N. (1994). Self-monitoring, locus of control, and social encounters of Chinese and New Zealand students. *Journal of Cross-Cultural Psychology, 25*(3), 353–368.

Hammack, P. L. (2008). Narrative and the cultural psychology of identity. *Personality and Social Psychology Review, 12*, 222–247.

Hansen, N. B., Lambert, M. J., & Forman, E. M. (2002). The psychotherapy dose response effect and its implications for treatment delivery services. *Clinical Psychology: Science and Practice, 9*, 329–343.

Haque, A. (2008). Culture-bound syndromes and healing practices in Malaysia. *Mental Health, Religion & Culture, 11*(7), 685–696.

Harb, C., & Smith, P. B. (2008). Self-construals across cultures: Beyond independence-interdependence. *Journal of Cross-Cultural Psychology, 39*(2), 178–197.

Harburg, E., Julius, M., Kaciroti, N., Gleiberman, L., & Schork, M. A. (2003). Expressive/suppressive anger-coping responses, gender, and types of mortality: A 17-year follow-up (Tecumseh, Michigan, 1971–1988). *Psychosomatic Medicine, 65*(4), 588–597.

Hardin, E. E. (2006). Convergent evidence for the multidimensionality of self construal. *Journal of Cross-Cultural Psychology, 37*(5), 516–521.

Hardin, E. E., Leong, F. T. L., & Bhagwat, A. A. (2004). Factor structure of the self-construal scale revisited: Implications for the multidimensionality of self-construal. *Journal of Cross-Cultural Psychology, 35*(3), 327–345.

Harkins, S. G. (1987). Social loafing and social facilitation. *Journal of Experimental Social Psychology, 23*, 1–18.

Harkins, S. G., & Petty, R. E. (1982). Effects of task difficulty and task uniqueness on social loafing. *Journal of Personality and Social Psychology, 43*, 1214–1229.

Harkness, S., & Super, C. M. (2006). Themes and variations: Parental ethnotheories in Western culture. In K. Rubin

& O. Chung (Eds.), *Parenting beliefs, behaviors, and parent-child relations* (pp. 61–79). New York: Psychology Press.

Harris, A. C. (1996). African Americans and Anglo American gender identities: An empirical study. *Journal of Black Psychology, 22*(2), 182–194.

Hasin, D. S., Goodwin, R. D., Stinson, F. S., & Grant, B. F. (2005). Epidemiology of major depressive disorder: Results from the national epidemiologic survey on alcoholism and related conditions. *Archives of General Psychiatry, 62*, 1097–1106.

Haslam, N., Bain, P., Douge, L., Lee, M., & Bastian, B. (2005). More human than you: Attributing humanness to self and others. *Journal of Personality and Social Psychology, 89*, 937–950.

Hatfield, E. (1988). Passionate and companionate love. In R. J. Sternberg & M. L. Barnes (Eds.), *The psychology of love* (pp. 191–217). New Haven, CT: Yale University Press.

Hatfield, E., & Rapson, R. L. (1996). *Love and sex: Cross-cultural perspectives.* Boston: Allyn & Bacon.

Hatfield, E., & Sprecher, S. (1995). Men's and women's preferences in marital partners in the United States, Russia, and Japan. *Journal of Cross-Cultural Psychology, 26*(6), 728–750.

Hau, K., & Salili, F. (1991). Structure and semantic differential placement of specific causes: Academic causal attributions by Chinese students in Hong Kong. *International Journal of Psychology, 26*, 175–193.

Haun, D. B. M., Rekers, Y., & Tomasello, M. (2014). Children conform to the behavior of peers; other great apes stick with what they know. *Psychological Science, 25*(12), 2160–2167. doi: 10.1177/0956797614553235

Hauser, M. (1993). Right hemisphere dominance for the production of facial expression in monkeys. *Science, 261*, 475–477.

Hawkley, L. C., & Cacioppo, J. T. (2010). Loneliness matters: A theoretical and empirical review of consequences and mechanisms. *Annals of Behavioral Medicine, 40*(2), 218–227.

Hayes-Bautista, D. (2004). *La Nueva California: Latinos in the Golden State.* Los Angeles: University of California Press.

Healey, J. F. (1998). *Race, ethnicity, gender, and class: The sociology of group conflict and change.* Thousand Oaks, CA: Pine Forge.

Heaven, P. C. L., & Rajab, D. (1983). Correlates of self-esteem among a South African minority group. *Journal of Social Psychology, 121*(2), 269–270.

Heelas, P., & Lock, A. (1981). *Indigenous psychologies: An anthropology of the self.* London: Academic Press.

Heider, E. R., & Oliver, D. (1972). The structure of the color space in naming and memory for two languages. *Cognitive Psychology, 3*, 337–354.

Heider, F. (1976). A conversation with Fritz Heider. In J. H. Harvey, W. J. Ickes, & R. F. Kidd (Eds.), *New directions in attribution research* (Vol. 1, pp. 47–61). Hillsdale, NJ: Erlbaum.

Heine, S. J., & Buchtel, E. E. (2009). Personality: The universal and the culturally specific. *Annual Review of Psychology, 60*, 369–394.

Heine, S. J., & Hamamura, T. (2007). In search of East Asian self-enhancement. *Personality and Social Psychology Review, 11*(1), 1–24.

Heine, S. J., & Lehman, D. R. (1996). Hindsight bias: A cross-cultural analysis. *Japanese Journal of Experimental Social Psychology, 35*, 317–323.

Heine, S. J., & Lehman, D. R. (1997). Culture, dissonance, and self-affirmation. *Personality and Social Psychology Bulletin, 23*(4), 389–400.

Heine, S. J., Harihara, M., & Niiya, Y. (2002). Terror management in Japan. *Asian Journal of Social Psychology, 5*, 187–196.

Heine, S. J., Lehman, D. R., Markus, H. R., & Kitayama, S. (1999). Is there a universal need for positive self-regard? *Psychological Review, 106*, 766–794.

Heine, S. J., Lehman, D. R., Peng, K., & Greenholz, J. (2002). What's wrong with cross-cultural comparisons of subjective likert scales? The reference-group problem. *Journal of Personality and Social Psychology, 82*, 903–918.

Heine, S. J., & Renshaw, K. (2002). Interjudge agreement, self-enhancement, and liking: Cross-cultural divergences. *Personality and Social Psychology Bulletin, 28*, 578–587.

Helms, J. E., Jernigan, M., & Mascher, J. (2005). The meaning of race in psychology and how to change it. *American Psychologist, 60*, 27–36.

Henderson, N. D. (1982). Human behavior genetics. *Annual Review of Psychology, 33*, 403–440.

Henrich, J., Ensminger, J., McElreath, R., Barr, A., Barrett, C., Bolyanatz, A., … Ziker, J. (2010). Markets, religion, community size, and the evolution of fairness and punishment. *Science, 327*, 1480–1484.

Henrich, J., Heine, S. J., & Norenzayan, A. (2010). The weirdest people in the world? *Behavioral and Brain Sciences, 33*(2–3), 61–83.

Henrich, J., McElreath, R., Barr, A., Ensminger, J., Barrett, C., Bolyanatz, A., … Ziker, J. (2006). Costly punishment across human societies. *Science, 312*, 1767–1770.

Hepper, E. G., Sedikides, C., & Cai, H. (2013). Self-enhancement and self-protection strategies in China: Cultural expressions of a fundamental human motive. *Journal of Cross-Cultural Psychology, 44*, 5–23.

Hepper, E. G., Wildschut, T., Sedikides, C., Ritchie, T. D., Yung, Y.-F., Hansen, N., . . . Demassosso, D. B. (2014). Pancultural nostalgia: Prototypical conceptions across cultures. *Emotion, 14*(4), 733. doi: 10.1037/a0036790

Herdt, G., & Howe, C. (Eds.). (2007). *21st century sexualities: Contemporary issues in health, education, and rights.* London: Routledge Chapman & Hall.

Hermans, H. J. M., & Kempen, H. J. G. (1998). Moving cultures: The perilous problems of cultural dichotomies in a globalizing society. *American Psychologist, S3*, 1111–1120.

Hess, J. A. (1993). Assimilating newcomers into an organization: A cultural perspective. *Journal of Applied Communication Research, 21*(2), 189–210.

Hiatt, L. R. (1978). Classification of the emotions. In L. R. Hiatt (Ed.), *Australian aboriginal concepts* (pp. 182–187). Princeton, NJ: Humanities Press.

Higgins, E. T. (1987). Self-discrepancy: A theory relating self and affect. *Psychological Review, 94*, 319–340.

Hill, J. S., Pace, T. M., & Robbins, R. R. (2010). Decolonizing personality assessment and honoring indigenous voices: A critical examination of the MMPI-2. *Cultural Diversity and Ethnic Minority Psychology, 16*(1), 16–25.

Himle, J. A., Muroff, J. R., Taylor, R. J., Baser, R. E., Abelson, J. M., Hanna, G. L., Abelson, J. L., & Jackson, J. S. (2008). Obsessive-compulsive disorder among African Americans and blacks of Caribbean descent: Results from the National Survey of American Life. *Depression and Anxiety, 25*(12), 993–1005.

Hinton, D. E., Chhean, D., Pich, V., Safren, S. A., Hofmann, S. G., & Pollack, M. H. (2005). A randomized controlled trial of cognitive-behavior therapy for Cambodian refugees with treatment-resistant PTSD and panic attacks: A cross-over design. *Journal of Traumatic Stress, 18*(6), 617–629.

Hinton, D. E., Pham, T., Tran, M., Safren, S. A., Otto, M. W., & Pollack, M. H. (2004). CBT for Vietnamese refugees with treatment-resistant PTSD and panic attacks: A pilot study. *Journal of Traumatic Stress, 17*(5), 429–433.

Hippler, A. E. (1974). The North Alaska Eskimos: A culture and personality perspective. *American Ethnologist, 2*(3), 449–469.

Hirschfield, L. A. (1996). *Race in the making: Cognition, culture, and the child's construction of human kinds.* Cambridge, MA: MIT Press.

Ho, D. Y. (1998). Indigenous psychologies: Asian perspectives. *Journal of Cross Cultural Psychology, 29*(1), 88–103.

Ho, M. K. (1984). Social group work with Asian/Pacific-Americans. *Social Work with Groups, 7*(3), 49–61.

Hochschild, A., & Machung, A. (1989). *The second shift.* New York: Penguin Books.

Hodgetts, R. M., Luthans, F., & Lee, S. M. (1994). New paradigm organizations: From total quality to learning to world-class. *Organizational Dynamics, 22*(3), 5–19.

Hoffman, W., Gawronski, B., Gschwendner, T., Le, H., & Schmitt, M. (2005). A meta-analysis on the correlation between the implicit association test and explicit self-report measures. *Personality and Social Psychology Bulletin, 31*, 1369–1385.

Hofstede, G. H. (1980). *Culture's consequences: International differences in work-related values.* Beverly Hills, CA: Sage.

Hofstede, G. H. (1983). Dimensions of national cultures in fifty countries and three regions. In J. B. Deregowski, S. Dziurawiec, & R. C. Annis (Eds.), *Expectations in cross-cultural psychology* (pp. 335–355). Amsterdam: Swets & Zeithnger.

Hofstede, G. H. (1984). *Culture's consequences: International differences in work-related values* (abridged ed.). Beverly Hills, CA: Sage.

Hofstede, G. H. (1996). Riding the waves of commerce: A test of Trompenaars' "model" of national culture differences. *International Journal of Intercultural Relations, 20*(2), 189–198.

Hofstede, G. H. (2001). *Culture's consequences: Comparing values, behaviors, institutions, and organizations across nations* (2nd ed.). Thousand Oaks, CA: Sage.

Hofstede, G. H., & Bond, M. (1984). Hofstede's cultural dimensions: An independent validation using Rokeach's value survey. *Journal of Cross-Cultural Psychology, 15*, 417–433.

Hofstede, G. H., & Bond, M. (1988). Confucius and economic growth: New trends in culture's consequences. *Organizational Dynamics, 16*(4), 4–21.

Hofstede, G. H., Bond, M., & Luk, C.-L. (1993). Individual perceptions of organizational cultures: A methodological treatise on levels of analysis. *Organization Studies, 14*, 483–503.

Hogan, R. (1982). A socioanalytic theory of personality. In M. Page (Ed.), *Nebraska symposium on motivation* (Vol. 30, pp. 55–89). Lincoln, NE: University of Nebraska Press.

Hollander, E. (1985). Leadership and power. In G. Lindzey & E. Aaronson (Eds.), *The handbook of social psychology* (3rd ed., Vol. 2, pp. 485–537). New York: Random House.

Hollon, S. D., & Beck, A. T. (1994). Cognitive and cognitive behavioral therapies. In A. E. Bergin & S. L. Garfield (Eds.), *Handbook of psychotherapy and behavior change* (4th ed., pp. 428–466). New York: Wiley.

Holloway, R. A., Waldrip, A. M., & Ickes, W. (2009). Evidence that a simpatico self-schema accounts for differences in the self-concepts and social behavior of Latinoes versus Whites (and Blacks). *Journal of Personality and Social Psychology, 96*(5), 1012–1028.

Holmes, L. D., Tallman, G., & Jantz, V. (1978, Fall). Samoan personality. *Journal of Psychological Anthropology, 2*(4), 453–469.

Holmqvist, K., & Frisén, A. (2010). Body dissatisfaction across cultures: Findings and research problems. *European Eating Disorders Review, 18*(2), 133–146. doi: 10.1002/erv.965

Hong, Y.-Y., Morris, M., Chiu, C.-Y., & Benet-Martinez, V. (2000). Multicultural minds: A dynamic constructivist approach to culture and cognition. *American Psychologist, 55*, 709–720.

Hong, S., Walton, E., Tamaki, E., & Sabin, J. A. (2014). Lifetime prevalence of mental disorders among Asian Americans: Nativity, gender, and sociodemographic correlates. *Asian American Journal of Psychology, 5*(4), 353–363. doi: 10.1037/a0035680

Hoosain, R. (1986). Language, orthography and cognitive process: Chinese perspectives for the Sapir-Whorf hypothesis. *International Journal of Behavioral Development, 9*(4), 507–525.

Hoosain, R. (1991). *Psycholinguistic implications for linguistic relativity: A case study of Chinese.* Hillsdale, NJ: Erlbaum.

Hopper, K., Harrison, G., Janca, A., & Sartorius, N. (2007). *Recovery from schizophrenia: An international perspective: A report from the WHO Collaborative Project, the international study of schizophrenia.* New York: Oxford University Press.

Hornsey, M. J., & Jetten, J. (2004). The individual within the group: Balancing the need to belong with the need to be different. *Personality and Social Psychology Review, 8*(3), 248–264.

Hothersall, D. (1990). *History of psychology* (2nd ed.). New York: McGraw-Hill.

House, R. J., Hanges, P. J., Javidan, M., Dorfman, P., & Gupta, V. (2003). *GLOBE, cultures, leadership, and organizations: GLOBE study of 62 societies.* Newbury Park, CA: Sage.

House, R. J., Hanges, P. J., Javidan, M., Dorfman, P. W., & Gupta, V. (2004). *Culture, leadership, and organizations: The GLOBE study of 62 societies.* Thousand Oaks, CA: Sage.

Howell, S. (1981). Rules not words. In P. Heelas & A. Lock (Eds.), *Indigenous psychologies: The anthropology of the self* (pp. 133–143). San Diego: Academic Press.

Hsiang, S. M., Burke, M., & Miguel, E. (2013). Quantifying the influence of climate on human conflict. *Science, 341*, 1235367. doi: http://dx.doi.org/10.1126/science.1235367; http://www.ncbi.nlm.nih.gov/pmc/articles/PMC2847360/; https://kaiserfamilyfoundation.files.wordpress.com/2014/07/8423-health-coverage-by-race-and-ethnicity.pdf

Hsiao, J. H., & Cottrell, G. W. (2009). Not all visual expertise is holistic, but it may be leftist. *Psychological Science, 20*(4), 455–463.

Hsu, L. (1977). An examination of Cooper's test for monotonic trend. *Educational and Psychological Measurement, 37*(4), 843–845.

Huang, B., Grant, B. F., Dawson, D. A., Stinson, F. S., Chou, S. P., Saha, T. D., . . . Pickering, R. P. (2006). Race-ethnicity and the prevalence and co-occurrence of Diagnostic and Statistical Manual of Mental Disorders, Fourth Edition, alcohol and drug use disorders and Axis I and II disorders: United States, 2001 to 2002. *Comprehensive Psychiatry, 47*(4), 252–257.

Huang, L. N., & Ying, Y. (1989). Chinese American children and adolescents. In J. T. Gibbs & L. N. Huang (Eds.), *Children of color* (pp. 30–66). San Francisco: Jossey-Bass.

Huang, Y. Y., & Chou, C. (2010). An analysis of multiple factors of cyber-bullying among junior high school students in Taiwan. *Computers in Human Behavior, 26*(6), 1581–1590.

Hudson, W. (1960). Pictorial depth perception in subcultural groups in Africa. *Journal of Social Psychology, 52*, 183–208.

Hughes, C. C. (1998). The glossary of 'culture-bound syndromes' in DSM-IV: A critique. *Transcultural Psychiatry, 35*(3), 413–421. doi: 10.1177/136346159803500307

Hui, C. H. (1984). *Individualism-collectivism: Theory, measurement, and its relation to reward allocation.* Unpublished doctoral dissertation, University of Illinois.

Hui, C. H. (1988). Measurement of individualism-collectivism. *Journal of Research in Personality, 22*, 17–36.

Hull, P. V. (1987). *Bilingualism: Two languages, two personalities? Resources in education, educational resources clearinghouse on education.* Ann Arbor: University of Michigan Press.

Hundley, G., & Kim, J. (1997). National culture and the factors affecting perceptions of pay fairness in Korea and the United States. *International Journal of Organizational Analysis, 5*, 325–341.

Huntington, R. L., Fronk, C., & Chadwick, B. A. (2001). Family roles of contemporary Palestinian women. *Journal of Comparative Family Studies, 32*(1), 1–19.

Hwang, H. C., & Matsumoto, D. (2016). Facial expressions. In D. Matsumoto, H. C. Hwang, & M. G. Frank (Eds.), *APA handbook of nonverbal communication* (pp. 257–287). Washington, DC: American Psychological Association.

Hyman, S. E. (2010). The diagnosis of mental disorders: The problem of reification. *Annual Review of Clinical Psychology, 6*, 155–179.

Hyson, M. C., & Izard, C. E. (1985). Continuities and changes in emotion expressions during brief separation at 13 and 18 months. *Developmental Psychology, 21*, 1165–1170.

Inglehart, R. (1997). *Modernization and post-modernization: Cultural, economic and political change in 43 societies.* Princeton, NJ: Princeton University Press.

Inglehart, R. (1998). *Modemizacion y postmodemizacion. El cambio cultural, economico y polotico en 43 sociedades.* Madrid, Spain: CIS.

Inglehart, R., Foa, R., Petersen, C., & Weltzel, C. (2008). Development, freedom, and rising happiness: A global perspective (1987–2007). *Perspectives in Psychological Science, 3*, 264–285.

Isaak, C., Campeau, M., Katz, L. Y., Enns, M. W., Elias, B., Sareen, J., & Swampy Cree Suicide Prevention Team. (2010). Community-based suicide prevention research in remote on-reserve First Nations communities. *International Journal of Mental Health and Addiction, 8*, 258–270.

Ivanova, M. Y., Dobrean, A., Dopfner, M., Erol, N., Fombonne, E., Fonseca, A. C., . . . Chen, W. J. (2007a). Testing the 8-syndrome structure of the Child Behavior Checklist in 30 societies. *Journal of Clinical Child and Adolescent Psychology, 36*(3), 405–417.

Ivanova, M. Y., Achenbach, T. M., Rescorla, L., Dumenci, L., Almqvist, F., Bathiche, M., ... Verhulst, F.C. (2007b). Testing the teacher's report from syndromes in 20 societies. *School Psychology Review, 36*(3), 468–483.

Ivanova, M. Y., Achenbach, T. M., Rescorla, L. A., Harder, V. S., Ang, R. P., Bilenberg, N., ... Verhulst, F. C. (2010). Preschool psychopathology reported by parents in 23 societies: Testing the seven-syndrome model of the Child Behavior Checklist for ages 1.5–5. *Journal of the American Academy of Child & Adolescent Psychiatry, 49*(12), 1215–1224.

Iwao, S., & Triandis, H. C. (1993). Validity of auto-and heterostereotypes among Japanese and American students. *Journal of Cross-Cultural Psychology, 24*(4), 428–444.

Izard, C. E. (1971). *The face of emotion.* East Norwalk, CT: Appleton-Century-Crofts.

Izard, C. E. (2007). Basic emotions, natural kinds, emotion schemas, and a new paradigm. *Perspectives on Psychological Science, 2*(3), 260–280.

Jackson, J. M., & Williams, K. D. (1985). Social loafing on difficult tasks: Working collectively can improve performance. *Journal of Personality and Social Psychology, 49*, 937–942.

Jackson, J. S., Torres, M., Caldwell, C. H., Neighbors, H. W., Nesse, R. M., Taylor, R. J., … Williams, D. (2004). The National Survey of American Life: A study of racial, ethnic and cultural influences on mental disorders and mental health. *International Journal of Methods in Psychiatric Research, 13*, 196–207.

Jackson, T., & Chen, H. (2011). Risk factors for disordered eating during early and middle adolescence: Prospective evidence from mainland Chinese boys and girls. *Journal of Abnormal Psychology, 120*, 454–464.

Jacobi, C., Hayward, C., de Zwaan, M., Kraemer, H. C., & Agras, W. S. (2004). Coming to terms with risk factors for eating disorders: Application of risk terminology and suggestions for a general taxonomy. *Psychological Bulletin, 130*(1), 19–65.

Jahoda, G. (1984). Do we need a concept of culture? *Journal of Cross-Cultural Psychology, 15*, 139–151.

Janis, I. L. (1983). *Group think.* Boston: Houghton Mifflin.

Jankowiak, W. R., & Fischer, E. F. (1992). A cross-cultural perspective on romantic love. *Ethology, 32*, 149–155.

Jencks, C., Smith, M., Acland, H., Bane, M. J., Cohen, D., Gintis, H., Heyns, B., & Michaelson, S. (1972). *Inequality: A reassessment of the effect of family and schooling in America.* New York: Harper & Row.

Jensen, A. R. (1968). Social class, race and genetics: Implications for education. *American Educational Research Journal, 5*(1), 1–42.

Jensen, A. R. (1969). How much can we boost IQ and scholastic achievement? *Harvard Educational Review, 39*, 1–123.

Jensen, A. R. (1971). Twin differences and race differences in I.Q.: A reply to Burgess and Jahoda. *Bulletin of the British Psychological Society, 24*(84), 195–198.

Jensen, A. R. (1973). Personality and scholastic achievement in three ethnic groups. *British Journal of Educational Psychology, 43*(20), 115–125.

Jensen, A. R. (1977). Cumulative deficit in IQ of Blacks in the rural South. *Developmental Psychology, 13*(93), 184–191.

Jensen, A. R. (1980). *Bias in mental testing*. New York: Free Press.

Jensen, A. R. (1981). *Straight talk about mental tests*. London: Methuen.

Jensen, A. R. (1983). Effects of inbreeding on mental-ability factors. *Personality and Individual Differences, 4*(1), 71–87.

Jensen, A. R. (1984). The black-white difference on the K-ABC: Implications for future tests. *Journal of Special Education, 18*(3), 377–408.

Jensen, L. A. (1991). *Coding manual: Ethics of autonomy, community, and divinity*. Unpublished manuscript, University of Chicago.

Jensen, L. A. (1997). Different worldviews, different morals: America's culture war divide. *Human Development, 40*(6), 325–344.

Jensen, L. A. (2008). Through two lenses: A cultural–developmental approach to moral psychology. *Developmental Review, 28*(3), 289–315.

Jensen, L. A. (2011). The cultural-developmental theory of moral psychology: A new synthesis. In L. A. Jensen (Ed.), *Bridging cultural and developmental approaches to psychology: New syntheses in theory, research, and policy* (pp. 3–25). New York: Oxford University Press.

Ji, L. J., Zhang, Z., & Nisbett, R. (2004). Is it culture or is it language? Examination of language effects in cross-cultural research on categorization. *Journal of Personality and Social Psychology, 87*, 57–65.

Jilek, W. G., & Draguns, J. G. (2008). Interventions by traditional healers: Their impact and relevance within their cultures and beyond. In U. P. Gielen, J. G. Draguns, & J. M. Fish (Eds.), *Principles of multicultural counseling and therapy* (pp. 353–371). New York: Routledge/Taylor & Francis Group.

Jimenez, D. E., Bartels, S. J., Cardenas, V., & Alegría, M. (2013). Stigmatizing attitudes toward mental illness among racial/ethnic older adults in primary care. *International Journal of Geriatric Psychiatry, 10*, 1061–1068.

Johnson, T., Kulesa, P., Cho, Y. I., & Shavitt, S. (2004). The relation between culture and response styles: Evidence from 19 countries. *Journal of Cross-Cultural Psychology, 36*, 264–277.

Johnston, L., Hewstone, M., Pendry, L., & Frankish, C. (1994). Cognitive models of stereotype change: IV. Motivational and cognitive influences.
European Journal of Social Psychology, 24(2), 237–265.

Jones, E. F., Forrest, J. D., Goldman, N., Henshaw, S. K., Lincoln, R., Rosoff, J. I., ... Wulf, D. (1985). Teenage pregnancy in developed countries: Determinants and policy implications. *Family Planning Perspectives, 17*, 53–63.

Jones, E. E., & Harris, V. A. (1967). The attribution of attitudes. *Journal of Experimental Social Psychology, 3*, 1–24.

Jones, W. R., & Morgan, J. F. (2010). Eating disorders in men: A review of the literature. *Journal of Public Mental Health, 9*(2), 23–31.

Jorde, L. B., & Wooding, S. P. (2004). Genetic variation, classification and 'race', *Nature Genetics, 36*, S28–S33.

Joseph, R. A., Markus, H. R., & Tafarodi, R. W. (1992). Gender differences in the source of selfesteem. *Journal of Personality and Social Psychology, 63*, 1017–1028.

Juang, L. P., & Cookston, J. T. (2009). A longitudinal study of family obligation and depressive symptoms among Chinese American adolescents. *Journal of Family Psychology, 23*(3), 396–404.

Juang, L. P., Qin, D. B., & Park, I. J. K. (2013). (Special issue Eds). Deconstructing the myth of the "tiger mother": An introduction to the special issue on tiger parenting, Asian-heritage families, and child/adolescent well-being. *Asian American Journal of Psychology, 4*, 1–6.

Juni, S. (1996). Review of the revised NEO Personality Inventory. In J. C. Conoley & J. C. Impara (Eds.), *12th mental measurements yearbook* (pp. 863–868). Lincoln: University of Nebraska Press.

Kagan, J., Snidman, N., Arcus, D., & Reznick, J. (1994). *Galen's prophecy: Temperament in human nature*. New York: Basic Books.

Kagan, J., Snidman, N., Kahn, V., & Towsley, S. (2007). The preservation of two infant temperaments into adolescence. *Monographs of the Society for Research in Child Development, 72*, 1–75.

Kagitcibasi, C. (1996a). The autonomous-relational self: A new synthesis. *European Psychologist, 1*(3), 180–186.

Kagitcibasi, C. (1996b). *Family and human development across cultures: A view from the other side*. Mahwah, NJ: Erlbaum.
Kaiser Family Foundation. (2013). Health coverage by race and ethnicity. Retrieved https://kaiserfamilyfoundation.files.wordpress.com/2014/07/8423-health-coverage-by-race-and-ethnicity.pdf

Kan, K.-J., Wicherts, J. M., Dolan, C. V., & van der Maas, H. L. J. (2013). On the nature and nurture of intelligence and specific cognitive abilities: The more heritable, the more culture dependent. *Psychological Science, 24*, 2420–2428. doi: 10.1177/0956797613493292

Kane, C. M. (1994). Differences in the manifest dream content of Anglo-American, Mexican-American, and African-American college women. *Journal of Multicultural Counseling and Development, 22*, 203–209.

Karavasilis, L., Doyle, A., & Markiewicz, D. (2003). Associations between parenting style and attachment to mother in middle childhood and adolescence. *International Journal of Behavioral Development, 27*(2), 153–164.

Karlins, M., Coffman, T. L., & Walters, G. (1969). On the fading of social stereotypes: Studies in three generations of college students. *Journal of Personality and Social Psychology, 13*(1), 1–16.

Karremans, J. C., Frankenhuis, W. E., & Arons, S. (2010). Blind men prefer a low waist-to-hip ratio. *Evolution and Human Behavior, 31*, 182–186.

Kashima, E. S., & Hardie, E. A. (2000). The development and validation of the Relational, Individualism, and Collectivism self-aspects (RIC) Scale. *Asian Journal of Social Psychology, 3*, 19–48.

Kashima, E. S., & Kashima, Y. (1998). Culture and language: The case of cultural dimensions and personal pronoun use. *Journal of Cross-Cultural Psychology, 29*, 461–486.

Kashima, Y., Kokubo, T., Kashima, E. S., Boxall, D., Yamaguchi, S., & Macrae, K. (2004). Culture and self: Are there within-culture differences in self between metropolitan areas and regional cities? *Personality and Social Psychology Bulletin, 30*(7), 816–823.

Kashima, Y., & Triandis, H. C. (1986). The self-serving bias in attributions as a coping strategy: A cross-cultural study. *Journal of Cross-Cultural Psychology, 17*, 83–97.

Kashima, Y., Yamaguchi, S., Kim, U., & Choi, S. C. (1995). Culture, gender, and self: A perspective from individualism-collectivism research. *Journal of Personality & Social Psychology, 69,* 925–937.

Katigbak, M. S., Church, A. T., Guanzon-Lapena, M. A., Carlota, A. J., & del Pilar, G. H. (2002). Are indigenous personality dimensions culture specific? Philippine inventories and the five-factor model. *Journal of Personality and Social Psychology, 82*(1), 89–101.

Katz, D., & Braly, K. (1933). Racial stereotypes of one hundred college students. *Journal of Abnormal and Social Psychology, 28,* 280–290.

Kay, P., & Kempton, W. (1984). What is the Sapir-Whorf hypothesis? *American Anthropologist, 86,* 65–89.

Kaye, M., & Taylor, W. G. K. (1997). Expatriate culture shock in China: A study in the Beijing hotel industry. *Journal of Managerial Psychology, 12,* 496–510. doi: http://dx.doi.org/10.1108/02683949710189102

Keats, D. M. (1982). Cultural bases of concepts of intelligence: A Chinese versus Australian comparison. In P. Sukontasarp, N. Yongsiri, P. Intasuwan, N. Jotiban, & C. Suvannathat (Eds.), *Proceedings of the Second Asian Workshop on Child and Adolescent Development* (pp. 67–75). Bangkok: Burapasilpa Press.

Kelleher, M. J., Chambers, D., Corcoran, P., Williamson, E., & Keeley, H. S. (1998). Religious sanctions and rates of suicide worldwide. *Crisis, 19,* 78–86.

Keller, H. (2013). Attachment and culture. *Journal of Cross-Cultural Psychology, 44*(2), 175–194. doi: 10.1177/0022022112472253

Keller, H., Borke, J., Chaudhary, N., Lamm, B., & Kleis, A. (2010). Continuity in parenting strategies: A cross-cultural comparison. *Journal of Cross-Cultural Psychology, 41*(3), 391–409.

Keller, M., Edelstein, W., Schmid, C., Fang, F.-X., & Fang, G. (1998). Reasoning about responsibilities and obligations in close relationships: A comparison across two cultures. *Developmental Psychology, 34*(4), 731–741.

Kelley, M., & Tseng, H. (1992). Cultural differences in child rearing: A comparison of immigrant Chinese and Caucasian American mothers. *Journal of Cross-Cultural Psychology, 23*(4), 444–455.

Kelly, D. J., Quinn, P. C., Slater, A. M., Lee, K., Gibson, A., Smith, M., ... Pascalis, O. (2005). Three-month-olds, but not newborns, prefer own-race faces. *Developmental Science, 8,* F31–F36.

Kelly, J. G. (2007). The system concept and systemic change: Implications for community psychology. *American Journal of Community Psychology, 39,* 415–418. Special Issue: Systems change.

Keltner, D., & Haidt, J. (1999). Social functions of emotion at four levels of analysis. *Cognition and Emotion, 13*(5), 505–521.

Kemmelmeier, M., & Cheng, B. Y.-M. (2004). Language and self-construal priming: A replication and extension in a Hong Kong sample. *Journal of Cross-Cultural Psychology, 35*(6), 705–712.

Kemmelmeier, M., Jambor, E., & Letner, J. (2006). Individualism and good works: Cultural variation in giving and volunteering across the United States. *Journal of Cross-Cultural Psychology, 37,* 327–344.

Kerr, M., Stattin, H., & Özdemir, M. (2012). Perceived parenting style and adolescent adjustment. Revisiting direction of effects and the role of parental knowledge. *Developmental Psychology, 48,* 1540–1553.

Kessler, R. C., Mickelson, K. D., & Williams, D. R. (1999). The prevalence, distribution, and mental health correlates of perceived discrimination in the United States. *Journal of Health and Social Behavior, 40,* 208–230.

Kessler, R. C., Birnbaum, H. G., Shahly, V., Bromet, E., Hwang, I., McLaughlin, K. A., ... Stein, D. J. (2010). Age differences in the prevalence and co-morbidity of DSM-IV major depressive episodes: Results from the WHO World Mental Health Survey Initiative. *Depression and Anxiety, 27*(4), 351–364.

Ketterer, H., Han, K., & Weed, N. C. (2010). Validation of a Korean MMPI-2 Hwa-Byung scale using a Korean normative sample. *Cultural Diversity and Ethnic Minority Psychology, 16*(3), 379–385.

Keysar, B., Hayakawa, S. L., & An, S. G. (2012). The foreign-language effect: Thinking in a foreign tongue reduces decision biases. *Psychological Science, 23,* 661–668. doi: 10.1177/0956797611432178

Khaleefa, O. H., Erdos, G., & Ashria, I. H. (1996). Creativity in an indigenous Afro-Arab Islamic culture: The case of Sudan. *Journal of Creative Behavior, 30*(4), 268–282.

Kiev, A. (1973). The psychiatric implications of interracial marriage. In I. R. Stuart & L. E. Abt (Eds.), *Interracial marriage: Expectations and realities* (pp. 162–176). New York: Grossman.

Kim, E. Y. (1993). Career choice among second-generation Korean-Americans: Reflections of a cultural model of success. *Anthropology and Education Quarterly, 24*(3), 224–248.

Kim, G., Loi, C. X. A., Chiriboga, D. A., Jang, Y., Parmelee, P., & Allen, R. S. (2011). Limited English proficiency as a barrier to mental health service use: A study of Latino and Asian immigrants with psychiatric disorders. *Journal of Psychiatric Research, 45*(1), 104–110.

Kim, H. S. (2002). We talk, therefore we think? A cultural analysis of the effect of talking on thinking. *Journal of Personality and Social Psychology, 83,* 828–842.

Kim, H. S., & Drolet, A. (2009). Express your social self: Cultural differences in choice of brand-name versus generic products. *Personality and Social Psychology Bulletin, 35*(12), 1555–1566.

Kim, H. S., & Markus, H. R. (1999). Deviance or uniqueness, harmony or conformity? A cultural analysis. *Journal of Personality and Social Psychology, 77*(4), 785–800.

Kim, S. Y., Wang, Y., Orozco-Lapray, D., Shen, Y., & Murtuza, M. (2013). Does "tiger parenting" exist? Parenting profiles of Chinese Americans and adolescent developmental outcomes. *Asian American Journal of Psychology, 4,* 7–18.

Kim, U. (2001). Culture, science, and indigenous psychologies: An integrated analysis. In D. Matsumoto (Ed.), *Handbook of culture and psychology* (pp. 51–75). Oxford: Oxford University Press.

Kim, U., & Berry, J. W. (1993). Introduction. In K. Uichol & J. W. Berry (Eds.), *Indigenous psychologies: Research and experience in cultural context* (Cross-cultural research: Indigenous and methodology series, Vol. 17, pp. 1–29). Newbury Park, CA: Sage.

Kim, Y.-H., Cohen, D., & Au, W.-T. (2010). The jury and abjury of my peers: The self in face and dignity cultures. *Journal of Personality and Social Psychology, 98*(6), 904–916.

Kimmel, P. R. (1994). Cultural perspectives on international negotiations. *Journal of Social Issues, 50*(1), 179–196.

King, J. E., & Figueredo, A. J. (1997). The Five-Factor Model plus dominance in chimpanzee personality. *Journal of Research in Personality, 31*(2), 257–271.

Kinzie, J. D., & Sack, W. (2002). The psychiatric disorders among Cambodian adolescents: The effects of severe trauma. In F. J. C. Azima & N. Gnzenko (Eds.), *Immigrant and refugee children and their families: Clinical, research, and training issues* (pp. 95–112). Madison, CT: International Universities Press.

Kirmayer, L. J. (2007). Psychotherapy and the cultural concept of the person. *Transcultural Psychiatry, 44*(2), 232–257.

Kirmayer, L. J., Rousseau, C., Guzder, J., & Jarvis, G. E. (2008). Training clinicians in cultural psychiatry: A Canadian perspective. *Academic Psychiatry, 32*(4), 313–319.

Kitayama, S., & Markus, H. R. (Eds.). (1994). *Emotions and culture: Empirical studies of mutual influence.* Washington, DC: American Psychological Association.

Kitayama, S., Markus, H. R., & Matsumoto, H. (1995). Culture, self, and emotion: A cultural perspective on "self-conscious" emotions. In J. P. Tangney & K. W. Fischer (Eds.), *Self-conscious emotions: The psychology of shame, guilt, embarrassment, and pride* (pp. 439–464). New York: Guilford Press.

Kitayama, S., Matsumoto, H., Markus, H. R., & Norasakkunkit, V. (1997). Individual and collective processes in the construction of the self: Self-enhancement in the United States and self-criticism in Japan. *Journal of Personality and Social Psychology, 72,* 1245–1267.

Kitayama, S., Mesquita, B., & Karasawa, M. (2006). Cultural affordances and emotional experience: Socially engaging and disengaging emotions in Japan and the United States. *Journal of Personality and Social Psychology, 91*(5), 890–903.

Kleinknecht, R. A., Dinnel, D., Kleinknecht, E. E., Hiruma, N., & Harada, N. (1997). Cultural factors in social anxiety: A comparison of social phobia symptoms and taijin kyofusho. *Journal of Anxiety Disorders, 11,* 157–177.

Kleinman, A. (1988). *Rethinking psychiatry: From cultural category to personal experience.* New York: Free Press.

Kleinman, A. (1995). Do psychiatric disorders differ in different cultures? The methodological questions. In N. R. Goldberger & J. B. Veroff (Eds.), *The culture and psychology* (pp. 631–651). New York: New York University Press.

Kleinman, A., Eisenberg, L., & Good, B. (2006). Culture, illness, and care: Clinical lessons from anthropologic and cross-cultural research. *Focus, 4*(1), 140–149.

Kobayashi, C., & Brown, J. D. (2003). Self-esteem and self-enhancement in Japan and America. *Journal of Cross-Cultural Psychology, 34*(5), 567–580.

Kobayashi, C., & Greenwald, A. G. (2003). Implicit-explicit differences in self-enhancement for Americans and Japanese. *Journal of Cross-Cultural Psychology, 34*(5), 522–541.

Kohlberg, L. (1976). Moral stages and moralization: The cognitive-developmental approach. In J. Lickona (Ed.), *Moral development behavior: Theory, research and social issues* (pp. 31–53). New York: Holt, Rinehart & Winston.

Kohlberg, L. (1984). *The psychology of moral development: The nature and validity of moral stages* (Vol. 2). New York: Harper & Row.

Kohn, L. P., Oden, T., Muñoz, R. F., Robinson, A., & Leavitt, D. (2002). Adapted cognitive behavioral group therapy for depressed low-income African American women. *Community Mental Health Journal, 38*(6), 497–504.

Koltko-Rivera, M. E. (2004). The psychology of worldviews. *Review of General Psychology, 8,* 3–58.

Koo, H., Kwak, K., & Smith, P. K. (2008). Victimization in Korean schools: The nature, incidence, and distinctive features of Korean bullying or wang-ta. *Journal of School Violence, 7*(4), 119–139.

Koopmann-Holm, B., & Tsai, J. L. (2014). Focusing on the negative: Cultural differences in expression of sympathy. *Journal of Personality and Social Psychology, 107,* 1092–1115. doi: 10.1037/a0037684

Kosmitzki, C. (1996). The reaffirmation of cultural identity in cross-cultural encounters. *Personality and Social Psychology Bulletin, 22,* 238–248.

Koss-Chioino, J. D. (2000). Traditional and folk approaches among ethnic minorities. In J. F. Aponte & J. Wohl (Eds.), *Psychological intervention and cultural diversity* (2nd ed., pp. 149–166). Boston: Allyn & Bacon.

Krappmann, L. (1996). Amicitia, drujba, shin-yu, philia, freundschaft, friendship: On the cultural diversity of a human relationship. In W. M. Bukowski, A. F. Newcomb, & W. W. Hartup (Eds.), *The company they keep: Friendship in childhood and adolescence* (pp. 19–40). Cambridge: Cambridge University Press.

Krieger, N. (1999). Embodying inequality: A review of concepts, measures, and methods for studying health consequences of discrimination. *International Journal of Health Services, 29,* 295–352.

Kroeber, A. L., & Kluckholn, C. (1952/1963). *Culture: A critical review of concepts and definitions.* Cambridge, MA: Harvard University.

Kung, W. W. (2003). Chinese Americans' help seeking for emotional distress. *Social Services Review, 77,* 110–113.

Kurman, J. (2001). Self-enhancement: Is it restricted to individualistic cultures? *Personality and Social Psychology Bulletin, 27*(12), 1705–1716.

Kurman, J., & Ronen-Eilon, C. (2004). Lack of knowledge of a culture's social axioms and adaptation difficulties among immigrants. *Journal of Cross-Cultural Psychology, 35,* 192–208.

Lachlan, R. F., Janik, V. M., & Slater, P. J. B. (2004). The evolution of conformity-enforcing behaviour in cultural communication systems. *Animal Behaviour, 68,* 561–570.

LaFrance, M., & Mayo, C. (1976). Racial differences in gaze behavior during conversations: Two systematic observational studies. *Journal of Personality and Social Psychology, 33*(5), 547–552.

LaFromboise, T. D., Trimble, J. E., & Mohatt, G. V. (1990). Counseling intervention and American Indian tradition: An integrative approach. *The Counseling Psychologist, 18*(4), 159–182, 628–654.

Lalwani, A. K., Shavitt, S., & Johnson, T. (2006). What is the relation between cultural orientation and socially desirable responding? *Journal of Personality and Social Psychology, 90,* 165–178.

Lamoreaux, M., & Morling, B. (2012). Outside the head and outside individualism-collectivism: Further meta-analyses of cultural products. *Journal of Cross-Cultural Psychology, 43*(2), 299–327.

Landau, M. S. (1984). The effects of spatial ability and problem presentation format on mathematical problem solving performance of middle school students. *Dissertation Abstracts International, 45*(2-A), 442–443.

Lange, K. W., Reichl, S., Lange, K. M., Tucha, L., & Tucha, O. (2010). The history of attention deficit hyperactivity disorder. *Attention Deficit and Hyperactivity Disorders, 2*(4), 241–255. http://doi.org/10.1007/s12402-010-0045-8

Langlois, J. H., Kalakanis, L., Rubenstein, A. J., Larson, A., Hallam, M., & Smoot, M. (2000). Maxims or myths of beauty? A meta-analytic and theoretical review. *Psychological Bulletin, 126,* 390–423.

Langman, P. F. (1997). White culture, Jewish culture and the origins of psychotherapy. *Psychotherapy: Theory, Research, Practice, Training, 34,* 207–218.

Lara, M., Gamboa, C., Kahramanian, M. I., Morales, L. S., & Bautista, D. E. (2005). Acculturation and Latino health in the United States: A review of the literature and its sociopolitical context. *Annual Review of Public Health, 26,* 367–397.

Latane, B. (1981). The psychology of social impact. *American Psychologist, 36,* 343–356.

Latane, B., Williams, K., & Harkins, S. (1979). Many hands make light the work: The causes and consequences of social loafing. *Journal of Personality and Social Psychology, 37,* 322–332.

Lau, A. S. (2006). Making the case for selective and directed cultural adaptations of evidence-based treatments: Examples from parent training. *Clinical Psychology: Science and Practice, 13*(4), 295–310.

Lau, L., Lee, S., Lee, E., & Wong, W. (2006). Cross-cultural validity of the eating disorder examination: A study of Chinese outpatients with eating disorders in Hong Kong. *Hong Kong Journal of Psychiatry, 16,* 132–136.

Lau, S. (1989). Sex role orientation and domains of self-esteem. *Sex Roles, 21*(5–6), 415–422.

Leadbeater, B. J., & Way, N. (2001). *Growing up fast: Transitions to early adulthood of inner-city adolescent mothers.* Mahwah, NJ: Erlbaum.

Lee, C. C., Oh, M. Y., & Mountcastle, A. R. (1992). Indigenous models of helping in nonwestern countries: Implication for multicultural counseling. *Journal of Multicultural Counseling and Development, 20,* 3–10.

Lee, D. T. S., Kleinman, J., & Kleinman, A. (2007). Rethinking depression: An ethnographic study of the experiences of depression among Chinese. *Harvard Review of Psychiatry, 15*(1), 1–8.

Lee, F., Hallahan, M., & Herzog, T. (1996). Explaining real life events: How culture and domain shape attributions. *Personality and Social Psychology Bulletin, 22*(7), 732–741.

Lee, H. E., Park, H. S., Imai, T., & Dolan, D. (2012). Cultural differences between Japan and the United States in uses of "apology" and "thank you" in favor asking messages. *Journal of Language and Social Psychology, 31,* 263–289. doi: 10.1177/0261927X12446595

Lee, S. (2001). From diversity to unity: The classification of mental disorders in 21st century China. *Cultural Psychiatry: International Perspectives, 24*(3), 421–431.

Lee, S., Ng, K. L., Kwok, K., & Fung, C. (2010). The changing profile of eating disorders at a Tertiary Psychiatric Clinic in Hong Kong (1987–2007). *International Journal of Eating Disorders, 43*(4), 307–314.

Lee, V. K., & Dengerink, H. A. (1992). Locus of control in relation to sex and nationality: A cross-cultural study. *Journal of Cross-Cultural Psychology, 23*(4), 488–497.

Lee, Y.-T., Jussin, L. J., & McCauley, C. R. (Eds.). (1995). *Stereotype accuracy: Toward appreciating group differences.* Washington, DC: American Psychological Association.

Leenaars, A. A., Anawak, J., & Taparti, L. (1998). Suicide among the Canadian Inuit. In R. J. Kosky & H. S. Hadi (Eds.), *Suicide prevention: The global context* (pp. 111–120). New York: Plenum Press.

Lee-Sing, C. M., Leung, Y. K., Wing, H. F., & Chiu, C. N. (1991). Acne as a risk factor for anorexia nervosa in Chinese. *Australian and New Zealand Journal of Psychiatry, 25*(1), 134–137.

Leff, J. (1973). Culture and the differentiation of emotional states. *British Journal of Psychiatry, 123,* 299–306.

Leff, J. (1986). The epidemiology of mental illness. In J. L. Cox (Ed.), *Transcultural psychiatry* (pp. 23–36). London: Croom Helm.

Leong, F. T. L., & Lau, A. S. L. (2001). Barriers to providing effective mental health services to Asian Americans. *Mental Health Services Research, 3*(4), 201–214.

Leong, F. T., Lee, J. D., & Kalibatseva, Z. (2015). Counseling Asian Americans: Client and therapist variables. In P. B. Pedersen, W. J. Lonner, J. G. Draguns, J. E. Trimble, & M. Scharrón del Rìo (Eds.), *Counseling across cultures* (7th ed., pp. 121–142). Thousand Oaks, CA: Sage Publications.

Leong, F. T. L., Wagner, N. S., & Tata, S. P. (1995). Racial and ethnic variations in help-seeking attitudes. In J. G. Ponterotto & J. M. Casas (Eds.), *Handbook of multicultural counseling* (pp. 415–438). Thousand Oaks, CA: Sage.

Lerner, R. M. (2006). Developmental science, developmental systems, and contemporary theories of human development. In R. M. Lerner & W. Damon (Eds.), *Handbook of child psychology (6th ed.): Vol 1, Theoretical models of human development* (pp. 1–17). Hoboken, NJ: John Wiley & Sons Inc.

Lester, D. (2006). Suicide among indigenous peoples: A cross-cultural perspective. *Archives of Suicide Research, 10*(2), 117–124.

Leung, K. (1996). The role of beliefs in Chinese culture. In M. H. Bond (Ed.), *The handbook of Chinese psychology* (pp. 247–262). Hong Kong: Oxford University Press.

Leung, K. (1997). Negotiation and reward allocations across cultures. In P. C. Earley & M. Erez (Eds.), *New perspectives on international industrial/organizational psychology* (pp. 640–675). San Francisco: New Lexington/Jossey-Bass.

Leung, K., Bond, M. H., de Carrasquel, S. R., Muñoz, C., Hernández, M., Murakami, F., … Singelis, T. M. (2002). Social axioms: The search for universal dimensions of general beliefs about how the world functions. *Journal of Cross-Cultural Psychology, 33*(3), 286–302.

Levenson, R. W., Carstensen, L. L., Friesen, W. V., & Ekman, P. (1991). Emotion, physiology, and expression in old age. *Psychology & Aging, 6*, 28–35.

Levenson, R. W., & Ekman, P. (2002). Difficulty does not account for emotion-specific heart rate changes in the directed facial action task. *Psychophysiology, 39*, 397–405.

Levenson, R. W., Ekman, P., & Friesen, W. V. (1990). Voluntary facial action generates emotion-specific autonomic nervous system activity. *Psychophysiology, 27*, 363–384.

Levenson, R. W., Ekman, P., Heider, K., & Friesen, W. (1992). Emotion and autonomic nervous system activity in the Minangkabau of West Sumatra. *Journal of Personality and Social Psychology, 62*(6), 972–988.

Levin, H. M. (1996). Accelerated schools after eight years. In L. Schauble & R. Glaser (Eds.), *Innovations in learning: New environments for education* (pp. 329–352). Mahwah, NJ: Erlbaum.

Levine, D. S., Himle, J. A., Taylor, R. J., Abelson, J. M., Matusko, N., Muroff, J., & Jackson, J. (2013). Panic disorder among African Americans, Caribbean blacks and non-Hispanic whites. *Social Psychiatry and Psychiatric Epidemiology, 48*(5), 711–723. doi: 10.1007/s00127-012-0582-x

Levine, J. B. (1991). The role of culture in the representation of conflict in dreams: A comparison of Bedouin, Irish, and Israeli children. *Journal of Cross-Cultural Psychology, 22*, 472–490.

LeVine, R. A. (1977). Child rearing as cultural adaptation. In P. H. Leiderman, S. R. Tulkin, & A. Rosenfeld (Eds.), *Culture and infancy* (pp. 15–27). New York: Academic Press.

LeVine, R. A. (1997). Mother-infant interaction in cross-cultural perspective. In N. L. Segal & G. Weisfeld (Eds.), *Uniting psychology and biology: Integrative perspectives on human development* (pp. 339–354). Washington, DC: American Psychological Association.

Levine, R. V., & Bartlett, K. (1984). Pace of life, punctuality, and coronary heart disease in six countries. *Journal of Cross-Cultural Psychology, 15*, 233–255.

Levine, R. V., & Norenzayan, A. (1999). The pace of life in 31 countries. *Journal of Cross-Cultural Psychology, 30*, 178–205.

Levine, R. V., Lynch, K., Miyake, K., & Lucia, M. (1989). The Type A city: Coronary heart disease and the pace of life. *Journal of Behavioral Medicine, 12*, 509–524.

Levine, R., Sato, S., Hashimoto, T., & Verma, J. (1995). Love and marriage in eleven cultures. *Journal of Cross-Cultural Psychology, 26*(5), 554–571.

Levine, T. R., Bresnahan, M. J., Park, H. S., Lapinski, M. K., Wittenbaum, G. M., Shearman, S. M., … Ohashi, R. (2003). Self-construal scales lack validity. *Human Communication Research, 29*(2), 210–252.

Levy, G., Lysne, M., & Underwood, L. (1995). Children's and adults' memories for self-schema consistent and inconsistent content. *Journal of Social Psychology, 135*(1), 113–115.

Levy, R. I. (1973). *Tahitians*. Chicago: University of Chicago Press.

Levy, R. I. (1983). Introduction: Self and emotion. *Ethos, 11*, 128–134.

Lewis-Fernández, R., Gorritz, M., Raggio, G. A., Peláez, C., Chen, H., & Guarnaccia, P. J. (2010). Association of trauma-related disorders and dissociation with four idioms of distress among Latino psychiatric outpatients. *Culture, Medicine and Psychiatry, 34*(2), 219–243.

Lewontin, R. C., Rose, S., & Kamin, L. J. (1984). *Not in our genes: Biology, ideology and human nature*. New York: Pantheon.

Li, H.-Z. (2003). Inter- and intra-cultural variations in self-other boundary: A qualitative-quantitative approach. *International Journal of Psychology, 38*(3), 138–149.

Li, S., Jin, X., Yan, C., Wu, S., Jiang, F., & Shen, X. (2009). Factors associated with bed and room sharing in Chinese school-aged children. *Child: Care, Health and Development, 35*(2), 171–177.

Liebal, K., Pika, S., & Tomasello, M. (2004). Social communication in siamangs (Symphalangus syndactylus): Use of gestures and facial expressions. *Primates, 45*, 41–57.

Lightfoot-Klein, H. (1989). *Prisoners of ritual: An odyssey into female genital circumcision in Africa*. New York: Harrington Park Press.

Lijembe, J. (1967). The valley between: A Muluyia's story. In L. Fox (Ed.), *East African Childhood* (pp. 4–7). Nairobi: Oxford University Press.

Lim, F., Bond, M. H., & Bond, M. K. (2005). Linking societal and psychological factors to homicide rates across nations. *Journal of Cross-Cultural Psychology, 36*(5), 515–536.

Lim, V. P., Liow, S. J. R., Lincoln, M., Chan, Y. H., & Onslow, M. (2008). Determining language dominance in English-Mandarin bilinguals: Development of a self-report classification tool for clinical use. *Applied Psycholinguistics, 29*(3), 389–412.

Lin, E. J.-L., & Church, A. T. (2004). Are indigenous Chinese personality dimensions culture-specific? *Journal of Cross-Cultural Psychology, 35*, 586–605.

Lin, K.-M., & Kleinman, A. M. (1988). Psychopathology and clinical course of schizophrenia: A cross-cultural perspective. *Schizophrenia Bulletin, 14*(4), 555–567.

Lin, M. H., Kwan, V. S. Y., Cheung, A., & Fiske, S. T. (2005). Stereotype content model explains prejudice for an envied outgroup: Scale of anti-Asian American stereotypes. *Personality and Social Psychology Bulletin, 31*, 34–47.

Lin, P., & Schwanenflugel, P. (1995). Cultural familiarity and language factors in the structure of category knowledge. *Journal of Cross-Cultural Psychology, 26*(2), 153–168.

Lindsey, D. T., & Brown, A. M. (2009). World color survey: Color naming reveals universal motifs and their within-language diversity. *Proceedings from the National Academy of Sciences, 106*(47), 19785–19790.

Linton, R. (1936). *The study of man: An introduction*. New York: Appleton.

Linville, P. W., & Carlston, D. E. (1994). Social cognition perspective on self. In P. G. Devine, D. L. Hamilton, & T. M. Ostrom (Eds.), *Social cognition: Contributions to classic issues in social psychology* (pp. 143–193). New York: Springer-Verlag.

Li-Repac, D. (1980). Cultural influences on clinical perception: A comparison between Caucasian and Chinese-American therapists. *Journal of Cross-Cultural Psychology, 11*, 327–342.

Little, K. B. (1968). Cultural variations in social schemata. *Journal of Personality and Social Psychology, 10*(1), 1–7.

Little, T. D., Miyashita, T., Karasawa, M., Mashima, M., Oettingen, G., Azuma, H., & Baltes, P. B. (2003). The links among action-control beliefs, intellective skill, and school performance in Japanese, US, and German school children. *International Journal of Behavioral Development, 27*(1), 41–48.

Little, T. D., Oettingen, G., Stetsenko, A., & Baltes, B. P. (1995). Children's action-control beliefs about school performance: How do American children compare with German and Russian children? *Journal of Personality and Social Psychology, 69*(4), 686–700.

Liu, J. H., Goldstein-Hawes, R., Hilton, D., Huang, L.-L., Gastardo-Conaco, C., Dresler-Hawke, E., … Hidaka, Y. (2005). Social representations of events and people in world history across 12 cultures. *Journal of Cross-Cultural Psychology, 36*(2), 171–191.

Liu, J. H., Paez, D., Slawuta, P., Cabecinhas, R., Techio, E., Kokdemir, D., … Zlobina, A. (2009). Representing world history in the 21st century: The impact of 9/11, the Iraq war, and the nation-state on dynamics of collective remembering. *Journal of Cross-Cultural Psychology, 40*(4), 667–692.

Liu, L. A., Chua, C. H., & Stahl, G. K. (2010). Quality of communication experience: Definition, measurement, and implications for intercultural negotiations. *Journal of Applied Psychology, 95*, 469–487.

Liu, L. G. (1985). Reasoning counterfactually in Chinese: Are there any obstacles? *Cognition, 21*(3), 239–270.

Liu, O. L. (2009). An investigation of factors affecting gender differences in standardized math performance: Results from U.S. and Hong Kong 15 year olds. *International Journal of Testing, 9*(3), 215–237.

Lockenhoff, C. E., Chan, W., McCrae, R. R., De Fruyt, F., Jussim, L., De Bolle, M., . . . Terracciano, A. (2014). Gender stereotypes of personality: Universal and accurate? *Journal of Cross-Cultural Psychology, 45*, 675–694. doi: 10.1177/0022022113520075

Loewenthal, K. (2007). *Religion, culture, and mental health.* New York: Cambridge University Press.

Lonner, W. J. (1980). The search for psychological universals. In J. W. Berry, Y. H. Poortinga & J. Pandey (Eds.), *Handbook of cross-cultural psychology, vol. 1: Theory and method* (pp. 43–83). Boston: Allyn and Bacon.

Loo, K. K., Ohgi, S., Zhu, H., Akiyama, T., Howard, J., & Chen, L. (2005). Cross-cultural comparison of the neurobehavioral characteristics of Chinese and Japanese neonates. *Pediatrics International, 47*, 446–451.

Lopez, S. R. (1989). Patient variable biases in clinical judgment: Conceptual overview and methodological considerations. *Psychological Bulletin, 106*(2), 184–203.

Lott, D. F., & Hart, B. L. (1977). Aggressive domination of cattle by Fulani herdsmen and its relation to aggression in Fulani culture and personality. *Ethos, 5*(2), 174–186.

Lucy, J. A. (1992). *Language diversity and thought: A reformation of the linguistic relativity hypothesis.* Cambridge: Cambridge University Press.

Lueptow, L. B., Garovich, L., & Lueptow, M. B. (1995). The persistence of gender stereotypes in the face of changing sex roles: Evidence contrary to the socio-cultural model. *Ethology and Sociobiology, 16*(6), 509–530.

Luthar, V. K., & Luthar, H. K. (2002). Using Hofstede's cultural dimensions to explain sexually harassing behaviors in an international context. *International Journal of Human Resource Management, 13*, 268–284.

Lutz, C. (1980). *Emotion words and emotional development on Ifaluk Atoll.* Unpublished doctoral dissertation, Harvard University.

Lutz, C. (1982). "The domain of emotion words in Ifaluk." *American Ethnologist, 9*, 113–128.

Lutz, C. (1983). Parental goals, ethnopsychology, and the development of emotional meaning. *Ethos, 11*, 246–262.

Luzzo, D. A. (1993). Ethnic differences in college students' perceptions of barriers to careers development. *Journal of Multicultural Counseling and Development, 21*, 227–236.

Lykes, V. A., & Kemmelmeier, M. (2013). What predicts loneliness? Cultural difference between individualistic and collectivistic societies in Europe. *Journal of Cross-Cultural Psychology, 45*(3), 468–490. doi: 10.1177/0022022113509881

Lyons, A., & Kashima, Y. (2001). The reproduction of culture: Communication processes tend to maintain cultural stereotypes. *Social Cognition, 19*(3), 372–394.

Ma, H. K. (1997). The affective and cognitive aspects of moral development: A Chinese perspective. In H. S. R. Kao & D. Sinha (Eds.), *Asian perspectives on psychology* (pp. 93–109). Thousand Oaks, CA: Sage Publications, Inc.

Maccoby, E. E., & Jacklin, C. N. (1974). *The psychology of sex differences.* Stanford, CA: Stanford University Press.

Maccoby, E. E., & Martin, J. A. (1983). Socialization in the context of the family: Parent-child interaction. In E. M. Hetherington (Ed.), *Handbook of child psychology: Vol. 4. Socialization, personality, and social development* (4th ed., pp. 1–101). New York: Wiley.

MacDonald, K. (1991). A perspective on Darwinian psychology: The importance of domain-general mechanisms, plasticity, and individual differences. *Ethology and Sociobiology, 12*(6), 449–480.

MacDonald, K. (1998). Evolution, culture, and the Five Factor Model. *Journal of Cross-Cultural Psychology, 29*(1), 119–150.

MacDorman, M. F., & Mathews, T. J. (2008). Recent trends in infant mortality in the United States. NCHS data brief, no 9. Hyattsville, MD: National Center for Health Statistics.

MacLachlan, M. (1997). *Culture and health.* Chichester, UK: Wiley.

Macrae, C. N., Bodenhausen, G. V., & Milne, A. B. (1998). Saying no to unwanted thoughts: Self-focus and the regulation of mental life. *Journal of Personality and Social Psychology, 74*(3), 578–589.

Maddox, K. B. (2005). Perspectives on racial phenotypicality bias. *Personality and Social Psychology Review, 8*, 383–401.

Maddux, W. W., Adam, H., & Galinsky, A. D. (2010). When in Rome…Learn why the Romans do what they do: How multicultural learning experiences facility creativity. *Personality and Social Psychology Bulletin, 36*(6), 731–741.

Maddux, W. W., & Galinsky, A. D. (2009). Cultural borders and mental barriers: The relationship between living abroad and creativity. *Journal of Personality and Social Psychology, 96*(5), 1047–1061.

Maddux, W. W., Yang, H., Falk, C. F., Adam, H., Adair, W. L., Endo, Y., … Heine, S. J. (2010). For whom is parting with possessions more painful? Cultural differences in the endowment effect. *Psychological Science. 21*, 1910–1917.

Madon, S., Guyll, M., Aboufadel, K., Montiel, E., Smith, A., Palumbo, P., & Jussim, L. (2001). Ethnic and national stereotypes: The Princeton trilogy revisited and revised. *Personality and Social Psychology Bulletin, 27,* 996–1010.

Ma-Kellums, C., Blascovich, J., & McCall, C. (2012). Culture and the body: East-west differences in visceral perception. *Journal of Personality and Social Psychology, 102,* 718–728. doi: http://dx.doi.org/10.1037/a0027010

Ma-Kellams, C., Spencer-Rodgers, J., & Peng, K. (2011). I am against us? Unpacking cultural differences in ingroup favoritism via dialecticism. *Personality and Social Psychology Bulletin, 37*(1), 15–27.

Malik, V., Schulze, M., & Hu, F. (2006). Intake of sugar-sweetened beverages and weight gain: A systematic review. *American Journal of Clinical Nutrition, 84,* 274–288.

Malpass, R. S. (1974). Racial bias in eyewitness identification. *Personality and Social Psychology Bulletin, 1*(1), 42–44.

Malpass, R. S., & Kravitz, J. (1969). Recognition for faces of own and other race. *Journal of Personality and Social Psychology, 13*(4), 330–334.

Manson, S. M., & Shore, J. H. (1981). Psychiatric epidemiological research among American Indian and Alaska Natives: Some methodological issues. *White Cloud Journal, 2,* 48–56.

Manson, S. M., Shore, J. H., & Bloom, J. D. (1985). The depressive experience in American Indian communities: A challenge for psychiatric theory and diagnosis. In A. Kleinman & B. Good (Eds.), *Culture and depression: Studies in the anthropology and cross-cultural psychiatry of affect and disorder* (pp. 331–368). Berkeley: University of California Press.

Manz, C. C. (1992). Self-leading work teams: Moving beyond self-management myths. *Human Relations, 45*(11), 1119–1140.

Maramba, G. G., & Nagayama Hall, G. C. (2002). Meta-analysis of ethnic match as a predictor of dropout, utilization, and level of functioning. *Cultural Diversity and Ethnic Minority Psychology, 8,* 290–297.

Markoff, R. (1977). Intercultural marriage: Problem areas. In W. S. Tsent, J. F. McDermott, Jr., and T. W. Maretzk (Eds.), *Adjustment in intercultural marriage* (pp. 51–61). Honolulu: University of Hawaii Press.

Markus, H. R. (1977). Self-schemata and processing information about the self. *Journal of Personality and Social Psychology, 35,* 63–78.

Markus, H. R., & Kitayama, S. (1991). Culture and the self: Implications for cognition, emotion, and motivation. *Psychological Review, 98*(2), 224–253.

Markus, H. R., & Kitayama, S. (1991a). Cultural variation in self-concept. In G. R. Goethals & J. Strauss (Eds.), *Multidisciplinary perspectives on the self* (pp. 18–48). New York: Springer-Verlag.

Markus, H. R., & Kitayama, S. (1991b). Culture and the self: Implications for cognition, emotion, and motivation. *Psychological Review, 98,* 224–253.

Markus, H. R., & Kitayama, S. (1998). The cultural psychology of personality. *Journal of Cross Cultural Psychology, 29*(1), 63–87.

Markus, H. R., Mullally, P. R., & Kitayama, S. (1997). Selfways: Diversity in modes of cultural participation. In U. Neisser & D. Jopling (Eds.), *The conceptual self in context: Culture, experience, self-understanding* (pp. 13–61). Cambridge: Cambridge University Press.

Markus, H. R., & Wurf, E. (1987). The dynamic self-concept: A social psychological perspective. *Annual Review of Psychology, 38,* 299–337.

Marmot, M. G., & Syme, S. L. (1976). Acculturation and coronary heart disease in Japanese Americans. *American Journal of Epidemiology, 104,* 225–247.

Marsella, A. J. (1979). Cross-cultural studies of mental disorders. In A. J. Marsella, G. DeVos, & F. L. K. Hsu (Eds.), *Perspectives on cross-cultural psychology* (pp. 233–262). New York: Academic Press.

Marsella, A. J. (1980). Depressive experience and disorder across cultures. In H. C. Triandis & J. Draguns (Eds.), *Handbook of cross-cultural psychology: Vol. 6. Psychopathology* (pp. 237–289). Boston: Allyn & Bacon.

Marsella, A. J. (2000). Culture bound disorders. In A. Kazdin (Ed.), *The encyclopedia of psychology.* Washington, DC: American Psychological Association Press/ Oxford University Press.

Marsella, A. J. (2009). Some reflections on potential abuses of psychology's knowledge and practices. *Psychological Studies, 54*(1), 23–27.

Marsella, A. J., Kaplan, A., & Suarez, E. (2002). Cultural considerations for understanding, assessing, and treating depressive experience and disorder. In M. Reinecke & M. Davison (Eds.), *Comparative treatments of depression* (pp. 47–78). New York: Springer.

Marsella, A. J., Sartorius, N., Jablensky, A., & Fenton, F. R. (1985). Cross-cultural studies of depressive disorders. In A. Kleinman & B. Good (Eds.), *Culture and depression* (pp. 299–324). Berkeley: University of California Press.

Marsella, A. J., & Yamada, A. M. (2007). Culture and psychopathology: Foundations, issues, and directions. In S. Kitayama & D. Cohen (Eds.), *Handbook of cultural psychology* (pp. 797–818). New York: Guilford Press.

Marshall, G. N., Schell, T. L., Elliott, M. N., Berthold, S. M., & Chun, C.-A. (2005). Mental health of Cambodian refugees 2 decades after resettlement in the United States. *JAMA, 294,* 571–579.

Martin, D., Hutchison, J., Slessor, G., Urquhart, J., Cunningham, S. J., & Smith, K. (2014). The spontaneous formation of stereotypes via cumulative cultural evolution. *Psychological Science, 25,* 1777–1786. doi: 10.1177/0956797614541129

Marvin, R. S., VanDevender, T. L., Iwanaga, M. I., LeVine, S., & LeVine, R. A. (1977). Infant—caregiver attachment among the Hausa of Nigeria. In H. M. McGurk (Ed.), *Ecological factors in human development* (pp. 247–260). Amsterdam: North-Holland.

Mashima, R., Yamagishi, T., & Macy, M. (2004). Trust and cooperation: A comparison of ingroup preference and trust behavior between American and Japanese students (in Japanese). *Japanese Journal of Psychology, 75*(4), 308–315.

Masuda, T., Ellsworth, P. C., Mesquita, B., Leu, J., Tanida, S., & Van de Veerdonk, E. (2008). Placing the face in context: Cultural differences in the perception of facial emotion. *Journal of Personality and Social Psychology, 94*(3), 365–381.

Masuda, T., & Nisbett, R. (2001). Attending holistically versus analytically: Comparing the context sensitivity of Japanese and Americans. *Journal of Personality and Social Psychology, 81,* 922–934.

Matsumoto, D. (1989). Cultural influences on the perception of emotion. *Journal of Cross-Cultural Psychology, 20*, 92–105.

Matsumoto, D. (1992). More evidence for the universality of a contempt expression. *Motivation & Emotion, 16*, 363–368.

Matsumoto, D. (2001). Culture and emotion. In D. Matsumoto (Ed.), *The handbook of culture and psychology* (pp. 171–194). New York: Oxford University Press.

Matsumoto, D. (2002a). *The new Japan*. Yarmouth, ME: Intercultural Press.

Matsumoto, D. (2006a). Are cultural differences in emotion regulation mediated by personality traits? *Journal of Cross-Cultural Psychology, 37*(4), 421–437.

Matsumoto, D. (2006b). Culture and cultural worldviews: Do verbal descriptions about culture reflect anything other than verbal descriptions about culture? *Culture and Psychology, 22*(1), 33–62.

Matsumoto, D. (2007a). Individual and cultural differences in status differentiation: The status differentiation scale. *Journal of Cross-Cultural Psychology, 38*(4), 413–431.

Matsumoto, D. (2007b). Playing catch with emotions. *Journal of Intercultural Communication, 10*, 39–49.

Matsumoto, D., Anguas-Wong, A. M., & Martinez, E. (2008). Priming effects of language on emotion judgments in Spanish-English bilinguals. *Journal of Cross-Cultural Psychology, 39*(3), 335–342.

Matsumoto, D., & Assar, M. (1992). The effects of language on judgments of universal facial expressions of emotion. *Journal of Nonverbal Behavior, 16*(2), 85–99.

Matsumoto, D., Consolacion, T., Yamada, H., Suzuki, R., Franklin, B., Paul, S., et al. (2002). American-Japanese cultural differences in judgments of emotional expressions of different intensities. *Cognition & Emotion, 16*, 721–747.

Matsumoto, D., & Ekman, P. (1989). American-Japanese cultural differences in intensity ratings of facial expressions of emotion. *Motivation and Emotion, 13*, 143–157.

Matsumoto, D., & Ekman, P. (2004). The relationship between expressions, labels, and descriptions of contempt. *Journal of Personality and Social Psychology, 87*, 529–540.

Matsumoto, D., & Fletcher, D. (1996). Cultural influences on disease. *Journal of Gender, Culture, and Health, 1*, 71–82.

Matsumoto, D., Frank, M. G., & Hwang, H. C. (2015). The role of intergroup emotions on political violence. *Current Directions in Psychological Science, 24*(5), 369–373. doi: 10.1177/0963721415595023

Matsumoto, D., Grissom, R., & Dinnel, D. (2001). Do between-culture differences really mean that people are different? A look at some measures of cultural effect size. *Journal of Cross-Cultural Psychology, 32*, 478–490.

Matsumoto, D., & Hwang, H. C. (2016). The cultural bases of nonverbal communication. In Matsumoto, D., Hwang, H. C., & Frank, M. G. (Eds.), *APA handbook of nonverbal communication*. Washington, DC: American Psychological Association.

Matsumoto, D., Hwang, H. C., & Frank, M. G. (2013). Emotions expressed by leaders in videos predict political aggression. *Behavioral Sciences of Terrorism and Political Aggression*. doi: 10.1080/19434472.2013.769116

Matsumoto, D., Hwang, H. C., & Frank, M. G. (2014). Emotions expressed in speeches by leaders of ideologically motivated groups predict aggression. *Behavioral Sciences of Terrorism and Political Aggression, 6*(1), 1–18. doi: 10.1080/19434472.2012.716449

Matsumoto, D., & Hwang, H. S. (2011). Cooperation and competition in intercultural interactions. *International Journal of Intercultural Relations, 35*(5), 677–685.

Matsumoto, D., & Hwang, H. S. (2012). Culture and emotion: The integration of biological and cultural contributions. *Journal of Cross-Cultural Psychology, 43*(1), 91–118.

Matsumoto, D., Kasri, F., & Kooken, K. (1999). American-Japanese cultural differences in judgments of expression intensity and subjective experience. *Cognition and Emotion, 13*(2), 201–218.

Matsumoto, D., Keltner, D., Shiota, M. N., Frank, M. G., & O'Sullivan, M. (2008). What's in a face? Facial expressions as signals of discrete emotions. In M. Lewis, J. M. Haviland, & L. Feldman Barrett (Eds.), *Handbook of emotions* (pp. 211–234). New York: Guilford Press.

Matsumoto, D., & Kishimoto, H. (1983). Developmental characteristics in judgments of emotion from nonverbal vocal cues. *International Journal of Intercultural Relations, 7*(4), 415–424.

Matsumoto, D., Kouznetsova, N., Ray, R., Ratzlaff, C., Biehl, M., & Raroque, J. (1999). Psychological culture, physical health, and subjective well being. *Journal of Gender, Culture, and Health, 4*(1), 1–18.

Matsumoto, D., & Kudoh, T. (1993). American-Japanese cultural differences in attributions of personality based on smiles. *Journal of Nonverbal Behavior, 17*, 231–243.

Matsumoto, D., Kudoh, T., & Takeuchi, S. (1996). Changing patterns of individualism and collectivism in the United States and Japan. *Culture and Psychology, 2*, 77–107.

Matsumoto, D., & LeRoux, J. A. (2003). Measuring the psychological engine of intercultural adjustment: The Intercultural Adjustment Potential Scale (ICAPS). *Journal of Intercultural Communication, 6*, 27–52.

Matsumoto, D., LeRoux, J. A., Bernhard, R., & Gray, H. (2004). Personality and behavioral correlates of intercultural adjustment potential. *International Journal of Intercultural Relations, 28*(3–4), 281–309.

Matsumoto, D., LeRoux, J. A., Iwamoto, M., Choi, J. W., Rogers, D., Tatani, H., et al. (2003). The robustness of the Intercultural Adjustment Potential Scale (ICAPS). *International Journal of Intercultural Relations, 27*, 543–562.

Matsumoto, D., LeRoux, J. A., Ratzlaff, C., Tatani, H., Uchida, H., Kim, C., et al. (2001). Development and validation of a measure of intercultural adjustment potential in Japanese sojourners: The Intercultural Adjustment Potential Scale (ICAPS). *International Journal of Intercultural Relations, 25*, 483–510.

Matsumoto, D., LeRoux, J. A., Robles, Y., & Campos, G. (2007). The Intercultural Adjustment Potential Scale (ICAPS) predicts adjustment above and beyond personality and general intelligence. *International Journal of Intercultural Relations, 31*, 747–759.

Matsumoto, D., Nezlek, J. B., & Koopmann, B. (2007). Evidence for universality in phenomenological emotion response system coherence. *Emotion, 7*(1), 57–67. doi: 10.1037/1528-3542.7.1.57

Matsumoto, D., Olide, A., & Willingham, B. (2009). Is there an ingroup advantage in recognizing spontaneously expressed emotions? *Journal of Nonverbal Behavior, 33*, 181–191.

Matsumoto, D., Takeuchi, S., Andayani, S., Koutnetsouva, N., & Krupp, D. (1998). The contribution of individualism-collectivism to cross-national differences in display rules. *Asian Journal of Social Psychology, 1*, 147–165.

Matsumoto, D., & van de Vijver, F. J. R. (2011). *Cross-Cultural Research Methods in Psychology*. New York: Cambridge University Press.

Matsumoto, D., Weissman, M., Preston, K., Brown, B., & Kupperbusch, C. (1997). Context-specific measurement of individualism-collectivism on the individual level: The IC Interpersonal Assessment Inventory (ICIAI). *Journal of Cross-Cultural Psychology, 28*, 743–767.

Matsumoto, D., & Willingham, B. (2006). The thrill of victory and the agony of defeat: Spontaneous expressions of medal winners at the 2004 Athens Olympic games. *Journal of Personality and Social Psychology, 91*, 568–581.

Matsumoto, D., & Willingham, B. (2009). Spontaneous facial expressions of emotion of congenitally and non-congenitally blind individuals. *Journal of Personality and Social Psychology, 96*(1), 1–10.

Matsumoto, D., & Yoo, S. H. (2006). Toward a new generation of cross-cultural research. *Perspectives on Psychological Science, 2*(3), 234–250.

Matsumoto, D., Yoo, S. H., Fontaine, J. R. J., Alexandre, J., Altarriba, J., Anguas-Wong, A. M., … Zengaya, A. (2009). Hypocrisy or maturity: Culture and context differentiation. *European Journal of Personality, 23*, 251–264.

Matsumoto, D., Yoo, S. H., Fontaine, J., Anguas-Wong, A. M., Arriola, M., Ataca, B., … Zengeya, A. (2008). Mapping expressive differences around the world: The relationship between emotional display rules and individualism v. collectivism. *Journal of Cross-Cultural Psychology, 39*, 55–74.

Matsumoto, D., Yoo, S. H., Hirayama, S., & Petrova, G. (2005). Validation of an individual-level measure of display rules: The Display Rule Assessment Inventory (DRAI). *Emotion, 5*(1), 23–40.

Matsumoto, D., Yoo, S. H., Nakagawa, S., Alexandre, J., Altarriba, J.,

Anguas-Wong, A. M., et al. (2008). Culture, emotion regulation, and adjustment. *Journal of Personality and Social Psychology, 94*(6), 925–937.

Matsuzawa, T. (2001). *Primate origins of human cognition and behavior*. New York: Springer-Verlag.

Matsuyama, Y., Hama, H., Kawamura, Y., & Mine, H. (1978). Analysis of emotional words. *Japanese Journal of Psychology, 49*, 229–232.

Mauro, R., Sato, K., & Tucker, J. (1992). The role of appraisal in human emotions: A cross-cultural study. *Journal of Personality and Social Psychology, 62*(2), 301–317.

Mauss, I. B., Levenson, R. W., McCarter, L., Wilhelm, F. L., & Gross, J. J. (2005). The tie that binds? Coherence among emotion experience, behavior, and physiology. *Emotion, 5*, 175–190.

Maynard, A. E. (2008). What we thought we knew and how we came to know it: Four decades of cross-cultural research from a Piagetian point of view. *Human Development, 51*(1), Special Issue: Celebrating a Legacy of Theory with New Directions for Research on Human Development, 56–65.

Maynard, A. E., & Greenfield, P. M. (2003). Implicit cognitive development in cultural tools and children: Lessons from Maya Mexico. *Cognitive Development, 18*(4), 489–510.

Mays, V. M., Cochran, S. D., & Barnes, N. W. (2007). Race, race-based discrimination, and health outcomes among African Americans. *Annual Review of Psychology, 58*, 201–225.

McCarthy, A., Lee, K., Itakura, S., & Muir, D. W. (2006). Cultural display rules drive eye gaze during thinking. *Journal of Cross-Cultural Psychology, 37*(6), 717–722.

McCluskey, K. W., & Albas, D. C. (1981). Perception of the emotional content of speech by Canadian and Mexican children, adolescents and adults. *International Journal of Psychology, 16*, 119–132.

McCrae, R. R. (2000). Trait psychology and the revival of personality and culture studies. *American Behavioral Scientist, 44*(1), 10–31.

McCrae, R. R. (2001). Trait psychology and culture: Exploring intercultural comparisons. *Journal of Personality, 69*(6), 819–846.

McCrae, R. R. (2002). NEO-PI-R data from 36 cultures: Further intercultural comparisons. In R. R. McCrae &

J. Allik (Eds.), *The Five-Factor Model of personality across cultures* (pp. 105–125). New York: Kluwer Academic/Plenum Publishers.

McCrae, R. R., & Costa, P. T. (1997). Personality trait structure as a human universal. *American Psychologist, 52*(5), 509–516.

McCrae, R. R., & Costa, P. T. (1999). A Five-Factor Theory of personality. In L. A. Pervin & O. John (Eds.), *Handbook of personality: Theory and research* (2nd ed., pp. 139–153). New York: Guilford.

McCrae, R. R., & Costa, P. T. (2003). *Personality in adulthood: A five-factor theory perspective* (2nd ed.). New York: Guilford Press.

McCrae, R. R., Costa, P. T., & Martin, T. A. (2005). The NEO PI-3: A more readable Revised NEO Personality Inventory. *Journal of Personality Assessment, 84*(3), 261–270.

McCrae, R. R., Costa, P. T., Del-Pilar, G. H., & Rolland, J. P. (1998). Cross-cultural assessment of the five-factor model: The revised NEO personality inventory. *Journal of Cross Cultural Psychology, 29*(1), 171–188.

McCrae, R. R., Terracciano, A., Khoury, B., Nansubuga, F., Knezevic, G., Djuric Jocic, D., et al. (2005). Universal features of personality traits from the observer's perspective: Data from 50 cultures. *Journal of Personality and Social Psychology, 88*(3), 547–561.

McCrae, R. R., Terracciano, A., Leibovich, N. B., Schmidt, V., Shakespeare-Finch, J., Neubauer, A., et al. (2005). Personality profiles of cultures: Aggregate personality traits. *Journal of Personality and Social Psychology, 89*(3), 407–425.

McCrae, R. R., Terracciano, A., Realo, A., & Allik, J. (2007). Climactic warmth and national wealth: Some culture-level determinants of national character stereotypes. *European Journal of Personality, 21*, 953–976.

McGoldrick, M., & Preto, N. G. (1984). Ethnic intermarriage: Implications for therapy. *Family Process, 23*(3), 347–364.

McGrew, W. C. (2004). *The cultured chimpanzee: Reflections on cultural primatology*. New York: Cambridge University Press.

McGurk, H., & Jahoda, G. (1975). Pictorial depth perception by children in Scotland and Ghana. *Journal of Cross-Cultural Psychology, 6*(3), 279–296.

McHale, S. M., Crouter, A. C., & Whiteman, S. D. (2003). The family contexts of gender development in childhood and adolescence. *Social Development, 22*(1), 125–148.

McHale, S., Updegraff, K. A., Helms-Erikson, H., & Crouter, A. (2001). Sibling influences on gender development in middle childhood and early adolescence: A longitudinal study. *Developmental Psychology, 37*(1), 115–125.

McKenna J. J., & McDade T. (2005). Why babies should never sleep alone: A review of the co-sleeping controversy in relation to SIDS, bedsharing and breastfeeding. *Paediatric Respiratory Reviews, 6,* 134–152.

McNeely, C. A., & Barber, B. K. (2010). How do parents make adolescents feel loved? Perspectives on supportive parenting from adolescents in 12 cultures. *Journal of Adolescent Research, 25*(4), 601–631

Mead, M. (1975). *Growing up in New Guinea.* New York: William Morrow. (Originally published in 1930.)

Mead, M. (1978). *Culture and commitment.* Garden City, NY: Anchor. (Original work published 1928.)

Meglino, B. M., Ravlin, E. C, & Adkins, C. L. (1989). A work values approach to corporate culture: A field test of the value congruence process and its relationship to individual outcomes. *Journal of Applied Psychology, 74*(3), 424–432.

Meissner, C. A., & Brigham, J. C. (2001). Thirty years of investigating the own-race bias in memory for faces: A meta-analytic review. *Psychology, Public Policy, and Law, 7,* 3–35.

Mendoza, F. S., Javier, J. R., & Burgos, A. E. (2007). Health of children in immigrant families. In J. Lansford, K. Deater-Deckard, M. H. Bornstein, (Eds.), *Immigrant families in contemporary society* (pp. 30–50). New York: Guilford Press.

Merikangas, K. R., He, J.-P., Burstein, M., Swendsen, J., Avenevoli, S., Case, B., … Olfson, M. (2011). Service utilization for lifetime mental disorders in U.S. adolescents: Results of the national comorbidity survey-adolescent supplement (NCSA). *Journal of the American Academy of Child & Adolescent Psychiatry, 50*(1), 32–45.

Mesquita, B. (2001). Emotions in collectivist and individualist contexts. *Journal of Personality and Social Psychology, 80*(1), 68–74.

Mesquita, B., & Karasawa, M. (2002). Different emotional lives. *Cognition & Emotion, 16*(1), 127–141.

Messick, D. M., & Mackie, D. M. (1989). Intergroup relations. *Annual Review of Psychology, 40,* 45–81.

Meyer, J. P., Stanley, D. J., Herscovitch, L., & Topolnytsky, L. (2002). Affective, continuous, and normative commitment to the organization: A meta-analysis of antecedents, correlates, and consequences. *Journal of Vocational Behavior, 61,* 20–52.

Mezulis, A. H., Abramson, L. Y., Hyde, J. S., & Hankin, B. L. (2004). Is there a universal positivity bias in attributions? A meta-analytic review of individual, developmental, and cultural differences in the self-serving attributional bias. *Psychological Bulletin, 130*(5), 711–747.

Mezzich, J. E., Berganza, C. E., & Ruiperez, M. A. (2001). Culture in DSM-IV, ICD-10, and evolving diagnostic systems. *Psychiatric Clinics of North America, 24,* 407–419.

Mezzich, J. E., Kleinman, A., Fabrega, H. Jr., & Parron, D. (Eds.). (2002). *Culture and psychiatric diagnosis, a DSM-IV perspective,* Washington, DC: American Psychiatric Association.

Michel, J.-B., Shen, Y. K., Aiden, A. P., Veres, A., Gray, M. K., Team, T. G. B., … Aiden, E. L. (2011). Qunatitative analysis of culture using millions of digitized books. *Science, 331,* 176–182.

Milgram, S. (1974). *Obedience to authority.* New York: Harper & Row.

Millennium Cohort Study: Family Demographics. (2007). Taken from Chapter 3 of Millennium Cohort Study Second Survey: A User's Guide to Initial Findings, Lisa Calderwood.

Miller, J. G. (1984). Culture and the development of everyday social explanation. *Journal of Personality and Social Psychology, 46,* 961–978.

Miller, J. G., & Bersoff, D. M. (1992). Culture and moral judgment: How are conflicts between justice and interpersonal responsibilities resolved? *Journal of Personality and Social Psychology, 62,* 541–554.

Miller, J. G., & Das, R. (2011). Culture and the role of choice in agency. *Journal of Personality and Social Psychology, 101,* 46–61.

Miller, K. E. (1999). Rethinking a familiar model: Psychotherapy and the mental health of refugees. *Journal of Contemporary Psychotherapy, 29,* 283–306.

Miller, K. E., & Rasco, L. M. (2004). An ecological framework for addressing the mental health needs of refugee communities. In K. E. Miller & L. Rasco (Eds.), *The mental health of refugees: Ecological approaches to healing and adaptation* (pp. 1–64). Mahwah, NJ: Lawrence Erlbaum Associates.

Miller, K. E., Worthington, G. J., Muzurovic, J., Tipping, S., & Goldman, A. (2002). Bosnian refugees and the stressors of exile: A narrative study. *American Journal of Orthopsychiatry, 72*(3), 341–354.

Miller, K. M., Kelly, M., & Zhou, X. (2005). Learning mathematics in China and the United States: Cross-cultural insights into the nature and course of preschool mathematical development. In J. Campbell (Ed.), *Handbook of mathematical cognition* (pp. 163–177). New York: Psychology Press.

Miller, M. N., & Pumariega, A. J. (2001). Culture and eating disorders: A historical and cross-cultural review. *Psychiatry, 64,* 93–110.

Minami, M., & McCabe, A. (1995). Rice balls and bear hunts: Japanese and North American family narrative patterns. *Journal of Child Language, 22*(2), 423–445.

Minkov, M., Blagoev, V., & Bond, M. H. (2015). Improving research in the emerging field of cross-cultural sociogenetics: The case of serotonin. *Journal of Cross-Cultural Psychology, 46,* 336–354. doi: 10.1177/0022022114563612

Miranda, J., Bernal, G., Lau, A., Kohn, L., Hwang, W.-C., & LaFromboise, T. (2005). State of the science on psychosocial interventions for ethnic minorities. *Annual Review of Clinical Psychology, 1*(1), 113–142.

Miranda, J., Green, B. L., & Krupnick, J. L. (2006). One-year outcomes of a randomized clinical trial treating depression in low-income minority women. *Journal of Consulting and Clinical Psychology, 74*(1), 99–111.

Miranda, J., Nakamura, R., & Bernal, G. (2003). Including ethnic minorities in mental health intervention research: A practical approach to a long-standing problem. *Culture, Medicine and Psychiatry, 27*(4), 467–486.

Mirande, M. (1985). *The Chicano experience: An alternative perspective*. Notre Dame, IN: University of Notre Dame Press.

Mishra, R. C. (2014). Piagetian studies of cognitive development in India. *Psychological Studies, 59*(3), 207–222. doi: 10.1007/s12646-014-0237-y

Misumi, J. (1985). *The behavioral science of leadership: An interdisciplinary Japanese research program*. Ann Arbor: University of Michigan Press.

Miura, I. T., Okamoto, Y., Vladovic-Stetic, V., Kim, C., & Han, J. (1999). Language supports for children's understanding of numerical fractions: Cross-national comparisons. *Journal of Experimental Child Psychology, 74*(4), Special Issue: The development of mathematical cognition: Numerical processes and concepts, pp. 356–365.

Miyamoto, Y., Nisbett, R., & Masuda, T. (2006). Culture and the physical environment: Holistic versus analytic perceptual affordances. *Psychological Science, 17*, 113–119.

Moghaddam, F. M., Ditto, B., & Taylor, D. M. (1990). Attitudes and attributions related to psychological symptomatology in Indian immigrant women. *Journal of Cross-Cultural Psychology, 21*, 335–350.

Molinsky, A. L., Krabbenhoft, M. A., Ambady, N., & Choi, Y. S. (2005). Cracking the nonverbal code: Intercultural competence and gesture recognition across cultures. *Journal of Cross-Cultural Psychology, 36*, 380–395.

Monteith, M., Sherman, J., & Devine, P. (1998). Suppression as a stereotype control strategy. *Personality and Social Psychology Review, 1*, 63–82.

Moodley, R., & Sutherland, P. (2010). Psychic retreats in other places: Clients who seek healing with traditional healers and psychotherapists. *Counselling Psychology Quarterly, 23*(3), 267–282.

Moore, J. T. (1988). *Pride against prejudice: The biography of Larry Doby*. New York: Greenwood Press.

Morelli, G. A., Oppenheim, D., Rogoff, B., & Goldsmith, D. (1992). Cultural variations in infant sleeping arrangements: Questions of independence. *Developmental Psychology, 28*, 604–613.

Morgan, C., & Fisher, H. (2007). Environmental factors in schizophrenia: Childhood trauma—a critical review. *Schizophrenia Bulletin, 33*, 3–10.

Morgan, C., Kirkbride, J., Hutchinson, G., Craig, T., Morgan, K., Dazzan, P., . . . Fearon, P. (2008). Cumulative social disadvantage, ethnicity and first-episode psychosis: A case-control study. *Psychological Medicine, 38*, 1701–1715.

Morgan, C., Kirkbride, J., Leff, J., Craig, T., Hutchinson, G., McKenzie, K., ... Fearon, P. (2007). Parental separation, loss and psychosis in different ethnic groups: A case-control study. *Psychological Medicine: A Journal of Research in Psychiatry and the Allied Sciences, 37*(4), 495–503.

Morling, B., & Lamoreaux, M. (2008). Measuring culture outside the head: A meta-analysis of individualism-collectivism in cultural products. *Personality and Social Psychology Review, 12*, 199–221.

Morris, D., Collett, P., Marsh, P., & O'Shaughnessy, M. (1980). *Gestures: Their origins and distribution*. New York: Scarborough.

Morris, M. H., Avila, R. A., & Allen, J. (1993). Individualism and the modern corporation: Implications for innovation and entrepreneurship. *Journal of Management, 19*(3), 595–612.

Morris, M. W., Chiu, C-Y., & Liu, Z. (2015). Polycultural psychology. *Annual Review of Psychology, 66*, 631–659.

Morris, M. W., & Leung, K. (2000). Justice for all? Progress in research on cultural variation in the psychology of distributive and procedural justice. *Applied Psychology: An International Research Journal, 49*, 100–132.

Morris, M. W., & Peng, K. (1994). Culture and cause: American and Chinese attributions for social and physical events. *Journal of Personality and Social Psychology, 67*(6), 949–971.

Mossakowski, K. N. (2003). Coping with perceived discrimination: Does ethnic identity protect mental health? *Journal of Health and Social Behavior, Special Issue: Race, Ethnicity and Mental Health 44*(3), 318–331.

Mpofu, E. (2006). Editorial: Majority world health care traditions intersect indigenous and complementary and alternative medicine. *International Journal of Disability, Development and Education, 53*(4), 375–379.

Mukai, T., & McCloskey, L. (1996). Eating attitudes among Japanese and American elementary schoolgirls. *Journal of Cross-Cultural Psychology, 27*(4), 424–435.

Mulatu, M. S., & Berry, J. W. (2001). Health care practice in a multicultural context: Western and non-Western assumptions. In S. S. Kazanan & D. R. Evans (Eds.), *Handbook of Cultural Health psychology* (pp. 45–61). San Diego: Academic Press.

Mule, P., & Barthel, D. (1992). The return to the veil: Individual autonomy and social esteem. *Sociological Forum, 7*(2), 323–333.

Munro, D. (1979). Locus-of-control attribution: Factors among Blacks and Whites in Africa. *Journal of Cross-Cultural Psychology, 10*(2), 157–172.

Murdock, G. P., Ford, C. S., & Hudson, A. E. (1971). *Outline of cultural materials* (4th ed.). New Haven, CT: Human Relations Area Files.

Murdock, G. P., & White, D. R. (1969). Standard cross-cultural sample. *Ethnology, 9*, 329–369.

Muret-Wagstaff, S. and S. G. Moore. (1989). The Hmong in America: Infant behavior and child rearing practices. In J. K. Nugent, B. M. Lester, and T. B. Brazelton (Eds.), *The cultural context of literacy: Biology, culture, and infant development* (pp. 319–339). Norwood, NJ: Ablex.

Murphy, J. M. (1976). Psychiatric labeling in cross-cultural perspective. *Science, 191*, 1019–1028.

Murray, D. R. (2014). Direct and indirect implications of pathogen prevalence for scientific and technological innocation. *Journal of Cross-Cultural Psychology, 45*, 971–985. doi: 10.1177/0022022114532356

Murray, D. R., & Schaller, M. (2010). Historical prevalence of infectious diseases within 230 geopolitical regions: A tool for investigating origins of culture. *Journal of Cross-Cultural Psychology, 41*(1), 99–108.

Murray, D. R., Trudeau, R., & Schaller, M. (2011). On the origins of cultural differences in conformity: Four tests of the pathogen prevalence hypothesis. *Personality and Social Psychology Bulletin, 37*(3), 318–329.

Mwiti, G. (2014). African indigenous psychotherapy. *Journal of Psychology and Christianity, 33*, 171–178.

Myers, D. (1987). *Social psychology* (2nd ed.). New York: McGraw-Hill.

Myers, F. R. (1979). Emotions and the self: A theory of personhood and political order among Pintupi aborigines. *Ethos, 7*, 343–370.

Nadeem, E., Lange, J. M., Edge, D., Fongwa, M., Belin, T., & Miranda, J. (2007). Does stigma keep poor young immigrant and U.S.-born black and Latina women from seeking mental health care? *Psychiatric Services, 58*(12), 1547–1554.

Naeem, F., Waheed, W., Gobbi, M., Ayub, M., & Kingdon, D. (2011). Preliminary evaluation of culturally sensitive CBT for depression in Pakistan: Findings from developing culturally-sensitive CBT project (DCCP). *Behavioural and Cognitive Psychotherapy, 39*(2), 165–173.

Narayanan, S., & Ganesan, V. (1978). The concept of self among the Irulas of Palamalai. *Journal of Psychological Researches, 22*(2), 127–134.

National Center for Education Statistics. (2009). Trends in international math and science study, 2007. Retrieved http://nces.ed.gov/timss/results07. asp

National Center for Health Statistics. (2011). Deaths: Final data for 2011. Retrieved http://www.cdc.gov/nchs/data/nvsr/nvsr63/nvsr63_03.pdf

Nayak, S., Shiflett, S., Eshun, S., & Levine, F. (2000). Culture and gender effects in pain beliefs and the prediction of pain tolerance. *Cross-Cultural Research: The Journal of Comparative Social Science, 34*(2), 135–151.

Neck, C. P., & Manz, C. C. (1994). From groupthink to teamthink: Toward the creation of constructive thought patterns in self-managing work teams. *Human Relations, 47*(8), 929–951.

Nenty, H. J. (1986). Cross-culture bias analysis of Cattell Culture-Fair Intelligence Test. *Perspectives in Psychological Researches, 9*(1), 1–16.

Newberg, A. B., & Lee, B. Y. (2006). The relationship between religion and health. In P. McNamara (Ed.), *Where god and science meet: How brain and evolutionary studies alter our understanding of religion (Vol. 3): The psychology of religious experience* (pp. 51–81). Westport, CT: Praeger/Greenwood.

Ng, S. H., Han, S., Mao, L., & Lai, J. C. L. (2010). Dynamic bicultural brains: fMRI study of their flexible neural representation of self and significant others in response to culture primes. *Asian Journal of Social Psychology, 13*, 83–91.

Ng, T. W. H., Sorenson, K. L., & Yim, F. H. K. (2009). Does the job satisfaction-job performance relationship vary across cultures? *Journal of Cross-Cultural Psychology, 40*(5), 761–796.

Ng, W., & Diener, E. (2014). What matters to the rich and the poor? Subjective well-being, financial satisfaction, and postmaterialist needs across the world. *Journal of Personality and Social Psychology, 107*, 326–338.

Nguyen, A.-M. T. D., & Benet-Martinez, V. (2013). Biculturalism and adjustment: A meta-analysis. *Journal of Cross-Cultural Psychology, 44*, 122–159. doi: 10.1177/0022022111435097

Nguyen, H. H., Messe, L., & Stollak, G. (1999). Toward a more complex understanding of acculturation and adjustment: Cultural involvements and psychosocial functioning in Vietnamese youth. *Journal of Cross-Cultural Psychology, 30*(1), 5–31.

Nichols, R. K., & McAndrew, T. F. (1984). Stereotyping and autostereotyping in Spanish, Malaysian, and American college students. *Journal of Social Psychology, 124*, 179–189.

Niedenthal, P., & Beike, D. (1997). Interrelated and isolated self-concepts. *Personality and Social Psychology Review, 1*(2), 106–128.

Nisbett, R. (1993). Violence and U.S. regional culture. *American Psychologist, 48*, 441–449.

Nisbett, R. E. (2003). *The geography of thought: How Asians and westerners think differently. And why.* New York: The Free Press.

Nisbett, R. E., & Miyamoto, Y. (2005). The influence of culture: Holistic versus analytic perception. *Trends in Cognitive Sciences, 9*(10), 467–473.

Nisbett, R. E., Peng, K., Choi, I., & Norenzayan, A. (2001). Culture and systems of thought: Holistic versus analytic cognition. *Psychological Review, 108*, 291–310.

Noesjirwan, J. (1977). Contrasting cultural patterns on interpersonal closeness in doctors: Waiting rooms in Sydney and Jakarta. *Journal of Cross-Cultural Psychology, 8*(3), 357–368.

Noesjirwan, J. (1978). A rule-based analysis of cultural differences in social behavior: Indonesia and Australia. *International Journal of Psychology, 13*, 305–316.

Nomura, N., & Barnlund, D. (1983). Patterns of interpersonal criticism in Japan and United States. *International Journal of Intercultural Relations, 7*(1), 1–18.

Norenzayan, A., & Heine, S. J. (2005). Psychological universals: What are they and how can we know? *Psychological Bulletin, 131*, 763–784.

Norenzayan, A., & Lee, A. (2010). It was meant to happen: Explaining cultural variations in fate attributions. *Journal of Personality and Social Psychology, 98*(5), 702–720.

Norvilitis, J. M., & Fang, P. (2005). Perceptions of ADHD in China and the United States: A preliminary study. *Journal of Attention Disorders, 9*(2), 413–424.

Nucci, L. P., & Turiel, E. (1978). Social interactions and the development of social concepts in preschool children. *Child Development, 49*(2), 400–407.

Nyambegera, S. M., Daniels, K., & Sparrow, P. (2001). Why fit doesn't always matter: The impact of HRM and cultural fit on job involvement of Kenyan employees. *Applied Psychology: An International Research Journal, 50*, 109–140.

Oakes, P. J., Haslam, S. A., & Turner, J. C. (1994). *Stereotyping and social reality.* Oxford: Basil Blackwell.

Oberg, K. (1960). Culture shock: Adjustment to new cultural environments. *Practical Anthropologist, 7*, 177–182.

Odden, H., & Rochat, P. (2004). Observational learning and enculturation. *Educational and Child Psychology, 21*(2), 39–50.

Ogbu, J. U. (1981). Origins of human competence: A cultural-ecological perspective. *Child Development, 52*, 413–429.

Ogden, C., & Caroll, M. (2010). Prevalence of obesity among children and adolescents: United States, trends 1963–1965 through 2007–2008. National Center for Health Statistics. Retrieved: http://www.cdc.gov/nchs/data/hestat/obesity_child_07_08/obesity_child_07_08.htm

Ogden, C. L., Flegal, K. M., Carroll, M. D., & Johnson, C. L. (2002). Prevalence and trends in overweight among US children and adolescents, 1999–2000. *JAMA, 288*, 1728–1732.

Oh, Y., Koeske, G. F., Sales, E. (2002). Acculturation, stress and depressive symptoms among Korean immigrants in the United States. *Journal of Social Psychology, 142*(4), 511–526.

Okazaki, S., Okazaki, M., & Sue, S. (2009). Clinical personality assessment with Asian Americans. In J. N. Butcher (Ed.), *Oxford handbook of personality assessment* (pp. 377–395). New York: Oxford University Press

Okechuku, C. (1994). The relationship of six managerial characteristics to the assessment of managerial effectiveness in Canada, Hong Kong and People's Republic of China. *Journal of Occupational and Organizational Psychology, 67*(1), 79–86.

Olsson, A., Ebert, J. P., Banaji, M. R., & Phelps, E. A. (2005). The role of social groups in the persistence of learned fear. *Science, 309*, 785–787.

Olweus, D. (1993). *Bullying at school: What we know and what we can do.* Cambridge, MA: Blackwell Publishers.

Omi, M., & Winant, H. (1994). *Racial formation in the United States: From the 1960s to the 1990s* (2nd ed.). New York: Routledge.

Ong, A. D., Fuller-Rowell, T., & Burrow, A. L. (2009). Racial discrimination and the stress process. *Journal of Personality and Social Psychology, 96*(6), 1259–1271.

Oppedal, B., Roysamb, E., & Sam, D. L. (2004). The effect of acculturation and social support on change in mental health among young immigrants. *International Journal of Behavioral Development, 28*(6), 481–494.

O'Reilly, C. A. (1989). Corporations, culture, and commitment: Motivation and social control in organizations. *California Management Review, 31*, 9–25.

O'Reilly, C. A., Chatman, J., & Caldwell, D. F. (1991). People and organizational culture: A profile-comparison approach to assessing person-organization fit. *Academy of Management Journal, 34*, 487–516.

Organista, P. B., Organista, K. C., & Kurasaki, K. (2003). The relationship between acculturation and ethnic minority health. In K. M. Chun & P. B. Organista (Eds.), *Acculturation: Advances in theory, measurement, and applied research* (pp. 139–161). Washington, DC: American Psychological Association.

Orr, E., & Ben-Eliahu, E. (1993). Gender differences in idiosyncratic sex-typed self-images and self-esteem. *Sex Roles, 29*(3/4), 271–296.

Ortega, A. N., & Alegría, M. (2002). Self-reliance, mental health need, and the use of mental healthcare among island Puerto Ricans. *Mental Health Services Research, 4*(3), 131–140.

Ortega, J. E., Iglesias, J., Fernandez, J. M., & Corraliza, J. A. (1983). La expresion facial en los ciegos congenitos [facial expression in the congenitally blind]. *Infancia y Aprendizaje, 21*, 83–96.

Oster, H. (2005). The repertoire of infant facial expressions: An ontogenetic perspective. In J. Nadel & D. Muir (Eds.), *Emotional development* (pp. 261–292). New York: Oxford University Press.

Osterman, L. L., & Brown, R. P. (2011). Culture of honor and violence against the self. *Personality and Social Psychology Bulletin, 37*, 1611–1623. doi: 10.1177/0146167211418529

Ostrov, J. M., Crick, N. R., & Staffacher, K. (2006). Relational aggression in sibling and peer relationships during early childhood. *Journal of Applied Developmental Psychology, 27*(3), 241–253.

O'Sullivan, M., Ekman, P., Friesen, W. V., & Scherer, K. R. (1985). What you say and how you say it: The contribution of speech content and voice quality to judgments of others. *Journal of Personality & Social Psychology, 48*(1), 54–62.

O'Toole, A. J., Deffenbacher, K. A., Valentin, D., & Abdi, H. (1994). Structural aspects of face recognition and the other-race effect. *Memory and Cognition, 22*(2), 208–224.

O'Toole, A. J., Peterson, J., & Deffenbacher, K. A. (1996). An "other-race effect" for categorizing faces by sex. *Perception, 25*(6), 669–676.

Otto, H., Potinius, I., & Keller, H. (2014). Cultural differences in stranger–child interactions: A comparison between German middle-class and Cameroonian Nso stranger–infant dyads. *Journal of Cross-Cultural Psychology, 45*(2), 322–334. doi: 10.1177/0022022113509133

Oyserman, D. (1993). The lens of personhood: Viewing the self and others in a multicultural society. *Journal of Personality and Social Psychology, 65*(5), 993–1009.

Oyserman, D., Coon, H. M., & Kemmelmeier, M. (2002). Rethinking individualism and collectivism: Evaluation of theoretical assumptions and metaanalyses. *Psychological Bulletin, 128*(1), 3–72.

Oyserman, D., Gant, L., & Ager, J. (1995). A socially contextualized model of African American identity: Possible selves and school persistence. *Journal of Personality and Social Psychology, 69*(6), 1216–1232.

Oyserman, D., & Lee, S. W.-S. (2008). Does culture influence what and how we think? Effects of priming individualism and collectivism. *Psychological Bulletin, 134*(2), 311–342.

Oyserman, D., Sorenson, N., Reber, R., & Chen, S. X. (2009). Connecting and separating mind-sets: Culture as situated cognition. *Journal of Personality and Social Psychology, 97*, 217–235.

Ozono, H., Watabe, M., Yoshikawa, S., Nakashima, S., Rule, N. O., Ambady, N., & Adams, R. B. (2010). What's in a smile? Cultural differences in the effects of smiling on judgments of trustworthiness. *Letters on Evolutionary Behavioral Science, 1*(1), 15–18.

Paap, K. R., Johnson, H. A., & Sawi, O. (2014). Are bilingual advantages dependent upon specific tasks or specific bilingual experiences? *Journal of Cognitive Psychology, 26*, 615–639. doi: http://dx.doi.org/10.1080/20445911.2014.944914

Paap, K. R., Johnson, H. A., & Sawi, O. (2015). Bilingual advantages in executive functioning either do not exist or are restricted to very specific and undetermined circumstances. Cortex, 69, 265-278

Pace, T. M., Robbins, R. R., Choney, S. K., Hill, J. S., Lacey, K., & Blair, G. (2006). A cultural-contextual perspective on the validity of the MMPI-2 with American Indians. *Cultural Diversity and Ethnic Minority Psychology, 12*(2), 320–333.

Padilla, Y. C., Hamilton, E. R., & Hummer, R. A. (2009). Beyond the epidemiological paradox: The health of Mexican-American children at age five. *Social Science Quarterly, 90*(5), Special Issue: Health policy and healthy populations, 1072–1088.

Paez, D., Liu, J. H., Techio, E., Slawuta, P., Zlobina, A., & Cabecinhas, R. (2008). "Remembering" World War II and willingness to fight: Sociocultural factors in the social representation of historical warfare across 22 societies. *Journal of Cross-Cultural Psychology, 39*(4), 373–380.

Paguio, L. P., Robinson, B. E., Skeen, P., & Deal, J. E. (1987). Relationship between fathers' and mothers' socialization practices and children's locus of control in Brazil, the Philippines, and the United States. *Journal of Genetic Psychology, 148*(3), 202–313.

Paik, J. H., & Mix, K. S. (2003). U.S. and Korean children's comprehension of fraction names: A reexamination of cross-national differences. *Child Development, 74*(1), 144–154.

Pang, O. V. (1991). The relationship of test anxiety and math achievement to parental values in Asian American and European American middle school students. *Journal of Research and Development in Education, 24*(4), 1–10.

Paniagua, F. A. (2000). Culture-bound syndromes, cultural variations and psychopathology. In I. Cuellar & F. A. Paniagua (Eds.), *Handbook of multicultural mental health: Assessment and treatment of diverse populations* (pp. 139–169). San Diego: Academic Press.

Park, H. S., & Lee, H. E. (2012). Cultural differences in "Thank You". *Journal of Language and Social Psychology, 31,* 138–156. doi: 10.1177/0261927X12438536

Parke, R. (2004). Development in the family. *Annual Review of Psychology, 55,* 365–399.

Parsonson, K. (1987). Intermarriages: Effects on the ethnic identity of the offspring. *Journal of Cross-Cultural Psychology, 18*(3), 363–371.

Pascoe, E. A., & Richman, L. (2009). Perceived discrimination and health: A meta-analytic review. *Psychological Bulletin, 135*(4), 531–554.

Patzer, G. L. (1985). *The physical attractiveness phenomena.* New York: Plenum Press.

Paulhus, D. L. (1984). Two-component models of socially desirable responding. *Journal of Personality and Social Psychology, 46,* 598–609.

Paunonen, S. V., & Ashton, M. C. (1998). The structured assessment of personality across cultures. *Journal of Cross-Cultural Psychology, 29*(1), 150–170.

Pederson, A. K., King, J. E., & Landau, V. I. (2005). Chimpanzee (Pan troglodytes) personality predicts behavior. *Journal of Research in Personality, 39,* 534–549.

Pederson, P. (1995). *The five stages of culture shock: Critical incidents around the world.* Westwood, CT: Greenwood Press.

Pekerti, A. A., & Thomas, D. C. (2003). Communication in intercultural interaction: An empirical investigation of idiocentric and sociocentric communication styles. *Journal of Cross-Cultural Psychology, 34*(2), 139–154.

Pelto, P. J. (1968). The differences between "tight" and "loose" societies. *Transaction, 37–40.*

Pelto, P. J., & Pelto, G. H. (1975). Intracultural diversity: Some theoretical issues. *American Ethnologist, 2,* 1–18.

Pena, Y., Sidanius, J., & Sawyer, M. (2004). Racial democracy in the Americas: A Latin and U.S. comparison. *Journal of Cross-Cultural Psychology, 35,* 749–762.

Peng, K., & Nisbett, R. (1999). Culture, dialectics, and reasoning about contradiction. *American Psychologist, 54*(9), 741–754.

Peng, K., Nisbett, R. E., & Wong, Y. C. (1997). Validity problems comparing values across cultures and possible solutions. *Psychological Methods, 2*(4), 329–344.

Peng, K., Spencer-Rodgers, J., & Zhong, N. (2006). Naive dialecticism and the Tao of Chinese thought. In U. Kim, K.-S. Yang, & K. K. Hwang (Eds.), *Indigenous and cultural psychology: Understanding people in context* (pp. 247–262). New York: Springer.

Penke, L., Denissen, J. J. A., & Miller, G. F. (2007). The evolutionary genetics of personality. *European Journal of Personality, 21*(5), 549–587.

Pennisi, E. (2005). How did cooperative behavior evolve? *Science, 309,* 93.

Pe-Pua, R. (1989). Pagtatanong-Tanong: A cross-cultural research method. *International Journal of Intercultural Relations, 13,* 147–163.

Pettigrew, T. F., & Tropp, L. R. (2006). A meta-analytic test of intergroup contact theory. *Journal of Personality and Social Psychology, 90,* 751–783.

Pew Research Center. (2010). The return of the multigenerational household. A social and demographic trends report. Retrieved http://pewsocialtrends.org/2010/03/18/the-return-of-the-multi-generational-family-household/

Pfeiffer, W. M. (1982). Culture-bound syndromes. In I. Al-Issa (Ed.), *Culture and psychopathology* (pp. 201–218). Baltimore: University Park Press.

Phinney, J. S. (1996). When we talk about American ethnic groups, what do we mean? *American Psychologist, 51*(9), 918–927.

Phinney, J. S. (2003). Ethic identity and acculturation. In K. M. Chun, P. Balls Organista, & G. Marín (Eds.), *Acculturation: Advances in theory, measurement, and applied research* (pp. 63–81).

Washington, DC: American Psychological Association.

Piaget, J.-P. (1952). *The origins of intelligence in children.* New York: International Universities Press.

Piaget, J. (1972). Intellectual evolution from adolescence to adulthood. *Human Development, 15,* 1–12.

Piers, G., & Singer, M. B. (1971). *Shame and guilt: A psychoanalytic and a cultural study.* Oxford, England: W. W. Norton.

Pika, S., Nicoladis, E., & Marentette, P. (2009). How to order a beer: Cultural differences in the use of conventional gestures for numbers. *Journal of Cross-Cultural Psychology, 40*(1), 70–80.

Pike, K. L. (1954). *Language in relation to a unified theory of the structure of human behavior, Pt. 1* (Preliminary ed.). Glendale, CA: Summer Institute of Linguistics.

Piker, S. (1998). Contributions of psychological anthropology. *Journal of Cross-Cultural Psychology, 29*(1), 9–31.

Pinker, S. (1995). *The language instinct: How the mind creates language.* New York: Harper Collins.

Plaks, J. E., Stroessner, S. J., Dweck, C. S., & Sherman, J. W. (2001). Person theories and attention allocation: Preferences for stereotypic versus counterstereotypic information. *Journal of Personality and Social Psychology, 80*(6), 876–893.

Pliatsikas, C., Moschopoulou, E., & Saddy, J. D. (2015). The effects of bilingualism on the white matter structure of the brain. *Proceedings of the National Academy of Sciences, 112,* 1334–1337. doi: 10.1073/pnas.1414183112

Plomin, R. (1990). *Nature and nurture: An introduction to human behavioral genetics.* Pacific Grove, CA: Brooks/Cole.

Pohl, R. F., Bender, M., & Lachmann, G. (2002). Hindsight bias around the world. *Experimental Psychology, 49,* 270–282.

Polanczyk, G., de Lima, M. S., Horta, B. L., Biederman, J., & Rohde, L. A. (2007). The worldwide prevalence of ADHD: A systematic review and metaregression analysis. *American Journal of Psychiatry, 164,* 942–948.

Pollack, R. H., & Silvar, S. D. (1967). Magnitude of the Mueller-Lyer illusion in children as a function of the pigmentation of the fundus oculi. *Psychonomic Science, 8,* 83–84.

Pong, S. L., Johnston, J., & Chen, V. (2010). Authoritarian parenting and Asian adolescent school performance: Insights from the U.S. and Taiwan. *International Journal of Behavioral Development, 34*(1), 62–72.

Ponterotto, J. G., Alexander, C. M., & Hinkston, J. A. (1988). Afro-American preferences for counselor characteristics: A replication and extension. *Journal of Counseling Psychology, 35*(2), 175–182.

Poortinga, H. Y. (1989). Equivalence of cross-cultural data: An overview of basic issues. *International Journal of Psychology, 24,* 737–756.

Poortinga, H. Y. (1990). *Presidential address IACCP: Towards a conceptualization of culture for psychology.* Unpublished paper, Tilburg University, The Netherlands.

Poortinga, Y. H., van de Vijver, F. J. R., Joe, R. C., & van de Koppel, J. M. H. (1987). Peeling the onion called culture: A synopsis. In C. Kagitcibasi (Eds.), *Growth and progress in cross-cultural psychology* (pp. 22–34). Lisse: Swets and Zeitlingcr.

Pratt, G. (1993). Should I take this job? The organizational culture dimension to career decisions. *Educational Psychology in Practice, 8*(4), 222–224.

Pratto, F., Liu, J. H., Levin, S., Sidanius, J., Shih, M., Bachrach, H., & Hegarty, P. (2000). Social dominance orientation and the legitimization of inequality across cultures. *Journal of Cross-Cultural Psychology, 31,* 369–409.

Pratto, F., Sidanius, J., Stallworth, L. M., & Malle, B. F. (1994). Social dominance orientation: A personality variable predicting social and political attitudes. *Journal of Personality and Social Psychology, 67,* 741–763.

Premack, D. (2004). Is language the key to human intelligence? *Science, 303,* 318–320.

Pugh, J. F. (1991). The semantics of pain in Indian culture and medicine. *Culture, Medicine and Psychiatry, 15*(1), 19–43.

Punamaeki, R. L., & Joustie, M. (1998). The role of culture, violence, and personal factors affecting dream content. *Journal of Cross-Cultural Psychology, 29*(2), 320–342.

Pyszczynski, T., Greenberg, J., Solomon, S., Arndt, J., & Schimel, J. (2004). Why do people need self-esteem? A theoretical and empirical review. *Psychological Bulletin, 130*(3), 435–468.

Quah, S., & Bishop, G. D. (1996). Seeking help for illness: The roles of cultural orientation and illness cognition. *Journal of Health Psychology, 1,* 209–222.

Rakic, T., Steffens, M. C., & Memmendey, A. (2011). Blinded by the accent! The minor role of looks in ethnic categorization. *Journal of Personality and Social Psychology, 100,* 16–29. doi: http://dx.doi.org/10.1037/a0021522

Razali, S. M., Aminah, K., & Khan, U. A. (2002). Religious-cultural psychotherapy in the management of anxiety patients. *Transcultural Psychiatry, 39,* 130–136.

Razali, S. M., Hasanah, C. I., Aminah, K., & Subramaniam, M. (1998). Religious sociocultural psychotherapy in patients with anxiety and depression. *Australian and New Zealand Journal of Psychiatry, 32,* 867–872.

Realo, A., Allik, J., Verkasalo, M., Lonnquist, J. E., Kwiatowska, A., Koots, L., ... Renge, V. (2009). Mechanisms of the national character stereotype: How people in six neighboring countries of Russia describe themselves and the typical Russian. *European Journal of Personality, 23,* 229–249.

Redican, W. K. (1982). An evolutionary perspective on human facial displays. In P. Ekman (Ed.), *Emotion in the human face* (pp. 212–280). New York: Cambridge University Press.

Reed, G. M. (2010). Toward ICD-11: Improving the clinical utility of WHO's International Classification of mental disorders. *Professional Psychology: Research and Practice, 41*(6), 457–464

Reed, G. M., Roberts, M. C., Keeley, J., Hooppell, C., Matsumoto, C., Sharan, P., ... Medina-Mora, M. E. (2013). Mental health professionals' natural taxonomies of mental disorders: Implications for the clinical utility of the ICD-11 and the DSM-5. *Journal of Clinical Psychology, 69*(12), 1191–1212. doi: 10.1002/jclp.22031

Reichers, A. E., & Schneider, B. (1990). Climate and culture: An evolution of constructs. In B. Schneider (Ed.), *Organizational climate and culture* (pp. 5–39). San Francisco: Jossey-Bass.

Remschmidt, H. (2005). Global consensus on ADHD/HKD. *European Child & Adolescent Psychiatry, 14*(3), 127–137.

Rhee, E., Uleman, J. S., & Lee, H. K. (1996). Variations in collectivism and individualism by ingroup and culture: Confirmatory factor analyses. *Journal of Personality and Social Psychology, 71*(5), 1037–1054.

Richeson, J. A., & Trawalter, S. (2005). Why do interracial interactions impair executive function? A resource depletion account. *Journal of Personality and Social Psychology, 88*(6), 934–947.

Riesman, P. (1977). *Freedom in Fulani social life: An introspective ethnography* (M. Fuller, Trans.). Chicago: University of Chicago Press. (Original work published 1974).

Rivers, W. H. R. (1905). Observations on the senses of the Todas. *British Journal of Psychology, 1,* 321–396.

Robbins, J. M., & Krueger, J. I. (2005). Social projection to ingroups and outgroups: A review and meta-analysis. *Personality and Social Psychology Review, 9,* 32–47.

Robbins, M. C., DeWalt, B. R., & Pelto, P. J. (1972). Climate and behavior: A biocultural study. *Journal of Cross-Cultural Psychology, 3*(4), 331–344.

Roberts, B. W. (2006). Personality development and organizational behavior. In B. M. Shaw (Ed.), *Research on organizational behavior* (pp. 1–41). New York: Elsevier Science/JAI Press.

Roberts, B. W., Caspi, A., & Moffitt, T. E. (2003). Work experiences and personality development in young adulthood. *Journal of Personality and Social Psychology, 84,* 582–593.

Roberts, B. W., & DelVecchio, W. F. (2000). The rank-order consistency of personality traits from childhood to old age: A quantitative review of longitudinal studies. *Psychological Bulletin, 126*(1), 3–25.

Roberts, B. W., & Helson, R. (1997). Changes in culture, changes in personality: The influence of individualism in a longitudinal study of women. *Journal of Personality and Social Psychology, 72,* 644–651.

Roberts, B. W., Helson, R., & Klohnen, E. C. (2002). Personality development and growth in women across 30 years: Three perspectives. *Journal of Personality, 70,* 79–102.

Roberts, B. W., Walton, K. E., & Viechtbauer, W. (2006). Patterns of mean-level change in personality traits across the life course: A meta-analysis of longitudinal studies. *Psychological Bulletin, 132,* 1–25.

Roberts, M. E., Han, K., & Weed, N. C. (2006). Development of a scale to assess hwa-byung, a Korean culture-bound syndrome, using the Korean MMPI-2. *Transcultural Psychiatry, 43*(3), 383–400.

Rodriguez Mosquera, P. M., Manstead, A. S. R., & Fischer, A. H. (2002). Honor in the Mediterranean and Northern Europe. *Journal of Cross-Cultural Psychology, 33*(1), 16–36.

Rodriguez, D., Wigfield, A., & Eccles, J. S. (2003). Changing competence perceptions, changing values: Implications for youth sports. *Journal of Applied Sport Psychology, 15*, 67–81.

Roemer, L., & Orsillo, S. M. (2002). Expanding our conceptualization of and treatment for generalized anxiety disorder: Integrating mindfulness/acceptance-based approaches with existing cognitive-behavioral models. *Clinical Psychology: Science and Practice, 9*(1), 54–68.

Roemer, M. I. (1991). *National health systems of the world*. New York: Oxford University Press.

Roessner, V., Becker, A., Rothenberger, A., Rohde, L. A., & Banaschewski, T. (2007). A cross-cultural comparison between samples of Brazilian and German children with ADHD/HD using the Child Behavior Checklist. *European Archives of Psychiatry and Clinical Neuroscience, 257*(6), 352–359.

Rogers, C. R. (1942). *Counseling and psychotherapy*. Boston: Houghton Mifflin.

Rogoff, B. (2003). *The cultural nature of human development*. New York: Oxford University Press.

Rogoff, B., Baker-Sennett, J., Lacasa, P., & Goldsmith, D. (1995). Development through participation in sociocultural activity. In J. Goodnow, P. Miller, & F. Kessel (Eds.), *Cultural practices as contexts for development* (pp. 45–65). San Francisco: Jossey-Bass.

Rogoff, B., & Chavajay, P. (1995). What's become of research on the cultural basis of cognitive development? *American Psychologist, 50*(10), 859–877.

Rogoff, B., Moore, L., Najafi, B., Dexter, A., Correa-Chávez, M., & Solís, J. (2007). Children's development of cultural repertoires through participation in everyday routines and ractices. In J. E. Grusec, P. D. Hastings, J. E. Grusec, & P. D. Hastings (Eds.), *Handbook of socialization: Theory and research* (pp. 490–515). New York: Guilford Press.

Rohner, R. P. (1984). Toward a conception of culture for cross-cultural psychology. *Journal of Cross-Cultural Psychology, 15*, 111–138.

Romano, J. L. (1988). Stress management counseling: From crisis to intervention. *Counseling Psychology Quarterly, 2*(2–3), 211–219.

Romero, G. J., & Garza, R. T. (1986). Attributes for the occupational success/failure of ethnic minority and non-minority women. *Sex Roles, 14*, 445–452.

Rosch, E. (1973). On the internal structure of perceptual categories. In T. E. Moore (Ed.), *Cognitive development and the acquisition of language* (pp. 111–144). San Diego: Academic Press.

Rosch, E. (1978). Principles of categorization. In E. Rosch & B. B. Lloyd (Eds.), *Cognition and categorization* (pp. 28–48). Hillsdale, NJ: Erlbaum.

Roseman, I. J., Dhawan, N., Rettek, S. I., Nadidu, R. K., & Thapa, K. (1995). Cultural differences and cross-cultural similarities in appraisals and emotional responses. *Journal of Cross-Cultural Psychology, 26*, 23–48.

Rosenberg, M. (1965). *Society and the adolescent self-image*. Princeton, NJ: Princeton University Press.

Rosette, A. S., Brett, J. M., Barsness, Z., & Lytle, A. L. (2012). When cultures clash electronically: The impact of email and social norms on negotiation behavior and outcomes. *Journal of Cross-Cultural Psychology, 43*, 628–643. doi: 10.1177/0022022111407190

Rosmus, C, Halifax, N. S., Johnston, C., Chan-Yip, A., & Yang, F. (2000). Pain response in Chinese and non-Chinese Canadian infants: Is there a difference? *Social Science and Medicine, 51*(2), 175–184.

Ross, B. M., & Millson, C. (1970). Repeated memory of oral prose in Ghana and New York. *International Journal of Psychology, 5*, 173–181.

Ross, J., & Ferris, K. R. (1981). Interpersonal attraction and organizational outcome: A field experiment. *Administrative Science Quarterly, 26*, 617–632.

Ross, L. (1977). The intuitive psychologist and his shortcomings: Distortions in the attribution process. In L. Berkowitz (Ed.), *Advances in experimental social psychology* (Vol. 10, pp. 174–221). New York: Academic Press.

Rosseau, D. M., & Schalk, R. (2000). *Psychological contracts in employment: Cross-national perspectives*. Thousand Oaks, CA: Sage.

Rothbart M. K. (1981). Measurement of temperament in infancy. *Child Development, 52*, 569–578.

Rothbart, M. K., & Bates, J. E. (2006). Temperament. In N. Eisenberg, W. Damon, & R. M. Lerner (Eds.), *Handbook of child psychology: Vol. 3, Social, emotional, and personality development* (6th ed.). (pp. 99–166). Hoboken, NJ: John Wiley & Sons Inc.

Rothbart, M., Sheese, B., & Conradt, E. (2009). Childhood temperament. In P. Corr, & G. Matthews (Eds.), *The Cambridge handbook of personality psychology* (pp. 177–190). New York: Cambridge University Press.

Rothbaum, F., Weisz, J. R., Pott, M. Miyake, K., & Morelli, G. (2000). Attachment and culture: Security in the United States and Japan. *American Psychologist, 55*, 1093–1104.

Rotter, J. B. (1954). *Social learning and clinical psychology*. Englewood Cliffs, NJ: Prentice-Hall.

Rotter, J. B. (1966). Generalized expectancies for internal versus external control of reinforcement. *Psychological Monographs, 80*, 1–28.

Rowe, D. C. (1994). *The limits of family influence: Genes, experience, and behavior*. New York: Guilford Press.

Rozin, P., Lowery, L., Imada, S., & Haidt, J. (1999). The cad triad hypothesis: A mapping between three moral emotions (contempt, anger, disgust) and three moral codes (community, autonomy, divinity). *Journal of Personality and Social Psychology, 75*, 574–585.

Rubel, A., O'Nell, C. W., & Collado-Ardon, R. (1984). *Susto: A folk illness*. Berkeley: University of California Press.

Rubin, E. (2010). Veiled rebellion. *National Geographic, 218*(6), 28–53.

Rubin, K. H., Chen, X., McDougall, P., Bower, A., & McKinnon, J. (1995). The Waterloo longitudinal project: Predicting internalizing and externalizing problems in adolescence. *Development and Psychopathology, 7*, 751–764.

Rubin, K. H., Hemphill, S. A., Chen, X., Hastings, P., Sanson, A., Coco, A. L., … Cui, L. (2006). A cross-cultural study of behavioral inhibition in toddlers: East-West-North-South. *International Journal of Behavioral Development, 30*(3), 219–226.

Rudmin, F. (2003). Critical history of the acculturation psychology of assimilation, separation, integration, and marginalization. *Review of General Psychology, 7*, 3–37.

Rudmin, F. W. (2004). Historical notes on the dark side of cross-cultural psychology: Genocide in Tasmania. *Peace Research, 36*(1), 57–64.

Rudmin, F. W., Ferrada-Noli, M., & Skolbekken, J.-A. (2003). Questions of culture, age and gender in the epidemiology of suicide. *Scandinavian Journal of Psychology, 44*(4), 373–381.

Rugani, R., Vallortigara, G., Priftis, K., & Regolin, L. (2015). Number-space mapping in the newborn chick resembles humans' mental number line. *Science, 347*, 534–536.

Rule, N. O., Ishii, K., Ambady, N., Rosen, K. S., & Hallett, K. C. (2011). Found in translation: Cross-cultural consensus in the accurate categorization of male sexual orientation. *Personality and Social Psychology Bulletin, 37*, 1499–1507. doi: 10.1177/0146167211415630

Rule, N. R., Ambady, N., Adams, R. B., Ozono, H., Nakashima, S., Yoshikawa, S., & Watabe, M. (2010). Polling the face: Prediction and consensus across cultures. *Journal of Personality and Social Psychology, 98*(1), 1–15.

Russell, G. L., Fujino, D. C., Sue, S., Cheung, M., & Snowden, L. R. (1996). The effects of the therapist-client ethnic match in the assessment of mental health functioning. *Journal of Cross-Cultural Psychology, 27*(5), 598–615.

Russell, J. A. (1991). Culture and the categorization of emotions. *Psychological Bulletin, 110*, 426–450.

Russell, S. T., Crockett, L. J., & Chao, R. K. (2010). *Asian American parenting and parent–adolescent relationships.* New York: Springer Science + Business Media.

Ryan, R. M., & Deci, E. L. (2000). Self-determination theory and the facilitation of intrinsic motivation, social development and well-being. *American Psychologist, 55*, 68–78.

Sacchi, S., Castano, E., & Brauer, M. (2008). Perceiving one's nation: Entitativity, agency, security in the international arena. *International Journal of Psychology, 44*(5), 321–332.

Saco-Pollitt, C. (1989). Ecocultural context and developmental risk: Birth in the high altitudes (Peru). In J. K. Nugent, B. M. Lester, & T. Brazelton (Eds.), *The cultural context of infancy, Vol. 1: Biology, culture, and infant development* (pp. 3–25). Westport, CT: Ablex Publishing.

Sakamoto, Y., & Miura, T. (1976). An attempt to understand Japanese personality from a family psychiatry point of view. *Australian and New Zealand Journal of Psychiatry, 10*(1-A), 115–117.

Salant, T., & La uderdale, D. S. (2003). Measuring culture: A critical review of acculturation and health in Asian immigrant populations. *Social Science & Medicine, 57*(1), 71–90.

Salas-Wright, C. P., Kagotho, N., & Vaughn, M. G. (2014). Mood, anxiety, and personality disorders among first and second-generation immigrants to the United States. *Psychiatry Research, 220*(3), 1028–1036. doi: 10.1016/j.psychres.2014.08.045

Salzman, M. (2001). Cultural trauma and recovery: Perspectives from terror management theory. *Trauma, Violence, and Abuse: A Review Journal, 2*(2), 172–191.

Sam, D. L. (2000). Psychological adaptation of adolescents with immigrant backgrounds. *Journal of Social Psychology, 140*(1), 5–25.

Sama, L. M., & Papamarcos, S. D. (2000). Hofstede's IC dimension as predictive of allocative behaviors: A meta analysis. *Journal of Value-Based Management, 13*, 173–188.

Sampson, E. E. (1988). The debate on individualism: Indigenous psychologies and their role in personal and societal functioning. *American Psychologist, 43*, 15–22.

Sanchez, A. R., & Atkinson, D. R. (1983). Mexican-American cultural commitment, preference for counselor ethnicity, and willingness to use counseling. *Journal of Counseling Psychology, 30*(2), 215–220.

Sanchez-Burks, J., Lee, F., Choi, I., Nisbett, R., Zhao, S., & Koo, J. (2003). Conversing across cultures: East-West communication styles in work and nonwork contexts. *Journal of Personality and Social Psychology, 85*, 363–372.

Santa, J. L., & Baker, L. (1975). Linguistic influences on visual memory. *Memory and Cognition, 3*(4), 445–450.

Santrock, J. W. (2007). *Child development* (11th ed.). New York: McGraw-Hill Companies, Inc.

Saraswathi, T. (1999). Adult-child continuity in India: Is adolescence a myth or an emerging reality? In T. Saraswathi (Ed.), *Culture, socialization, and human development: Theory, research,* and applications in India (pp. 213–232). Thousand Oaks, CA: Sage.

Sargent, C. (1984). Between death and shame: Dimensions of pain in Bariba culture. *Social Science and Medicine, 19*(12), 1299–1304.

Saroglou, V., & Cohen, A. B. (2011). Psychology of culture and religion: Introduction to the JCCP Special Issue. *Journal of Cross-Cultural Psychology, 42*(8), 1309–1319.

Sato, M. (2006). Renaming schizophrenia: A Japanese perspective. *World Psychiatry, 5*(1), 53–55.

Satoh, K. (1996). Expression in the Japanese kindergarten curriculum. *Early Child Development and Care, 123*, 193–202.

Saucier, G., Georgiades, S., Tsaousis, I., & Goldberg, L. R. (2005). The factor structure of Greek personality adjectives. *Journal of Personality and Social Psychology, 88*, 856–875.

Sauter, D. A., & Eimer, M. (2010). Rapid detection of emotion from human vocalizations. *Journal of Cognitive Neuroscience, 22*(3), 474–481.

Sauter, D. A., Eisner, F., Ekman, P., & Scott, S. K. (2010). Cross-cultural recognition of basic emotions through nonverbal emotional vocalizations. *Proceedings from the National Academy of Sciences, 107*(6), 2408–2412.

Scarr, S., & Weinberg, R. A. (1976). I.Q. test performance of black children adopted by white families. *American Psychologist, 31*, 726–739.

Schaller, M., Conway, L. G., & Tanchuk, T. L. (2002). Selective pressures on the once and future contents of ethnic stereotypes: Effects of the communicability of traits. *Journal of Personality and Social Psychology, 82*(6), 861–877.

Scharlemann, J. P. W., Eckel, C. C., Kacelnik, A., & Wilson, R. K. (2001). The value of a smile: Game theory with a human face. *Journal of Economic Psychology, 22*, 617–640.

Schein, E. H. (1985). *Organizational culture and leadership: A dynamic view.* San Francisco: Jossey-Bass.

Scheper-Huges, N. (1992). *Death without weeping: The violence of everyday life in Brazil.* Berkeley: University of California Press.

Scherer, K. R. (1986). Vocal affect expression: Review and a model for future research. *Psychological Bulletin, 99*, 143–165.

Scherer, K. R. (1997a). Profiles of emotion-antecedent appraisal:

Testing theoretical predictions across cultures. *Cognition & Emotion, 11,* 113–150.

Scherer, K. R. (1997b). The role of culture in emotion-antecedent appraisal. *Journal of Personality & Social Psychology, 73,* 902–922.

Scherer, K. R., & Wallbott, H. (1994). Evidence for universality and cultural variation of differential emotion response patterning. *Journal of Personality & Social Psychology, 66,* 310–328.

Schimmack, U. (1996). Cultural influences on the recognition of emotion by facial expressions. *Journal of Cross-Cultural Psychology, 27,* 37–50.

Schimmack, U., Oishi, S., & Diener, E. (2002). Cultural influences on the relation between pleasant and unpleasant emotions: Asian dialectic philosophies or individualism-collectivism. *Cognition and Emotion, 16,* 705–719.

Schimmack, U., Oishi, S., & Diener, E. (2005). Individualism: A valid and important dimension of cultural differences between nations. *Personality and Social Psychology Review, 9*(1), 17–31.

Schliemann, A. D., & Carraher, D. W. (2001). Everyday cognition: Where culture, psychology, and education come together. In D. Matsumoto (Ed.), *Handbook of culture and psychology* (pp. 137–150). New York: Oxford University Press.

Schmitt, D. P. (2004). Patterns and universals of mate poaching across 53 nations: The effects of sex, culture, and personality on romantically attracting another person's partner. *Journal of Personality and Social Psychology, 86*(4), 560–584.

Schmitt, D. P., Alcalay, L., Allensworth, M., Allik, J., Ault, L., Austers, I., ... Zupanèiè, A. (2004). Patterns and universals of adult romantic attachment across 62 cultural regions. *Journal of Cross-Cultural Psychology, 35,* 367–402.

Scholz, U., Dona, B., Sud, S., & Schwarzer, R. (2002). Is general self-efficacy a universal construct? *European Journal of Psychological Assessment, 18,* 242–251.

Schwartz, S. H. (1994). Are there universal aspects in the structure and contents of human values? *Journal of Social Issues, 50*(4), 19–45.

Schwartz, S. H. (2004). Mapping and interpreting cultural differences around the world. In H. Vinken, J. Soeters, & P. Ester (Eds.), *Comparing cultures, dimensions of culture in a comparative perspective* (pp. 43–73). Leiden, The Netherlands: Brill.

Schwartz, S. H., & Bardi, A. (2001). Value hierarchies across cultures: Taking a similarities perspective. *Journal of Cross-Cultural Psychology, 32*(3), 268–290.

Schwartz, S. H., & Ros, M. (1995). Values in the west: A theoretical and empirical challenge to the individualism-collectivism cultural dimension. *World Psychology, 1,* 91–122.

Scribner, S. (1974). Developmental aspects of categorized recall in a West African society. *Cognitive Psychology, 6*(4), 475–494.

Scribner, S. (1979). Modes of thinking and ways of speaking: Culture and logic reconsidered. In I. O. Freedle (Ed.), *New directions in discourse processing* (pp. 223–243). Norwood, NJ: Ablex.

Sebastian-Galles, N., Albareda-Castellot, B., Weikum, W. M., & Werker, J. F. (2012). A bilingual advantage in visual language discrimination in infancy. *Psychological Science, 23,* 994–999. doi: First published on 18 July 2012, doi: 10.1177/0956797612436817

Sedikides, C., Gaertner, L., & Toguchi, Y. (2003). Pancultural self-enhancement. *Journal of Personality and Social Psychology, 84*(1), 60–79.

Sedikides, C., Gaertner, L., & Vevea, J. L. (2005). Pancultural self-enhancement reloaded: A meta-analytic reply. *Journal of Personality and Social Psychology, 89*(4), 539–551.

Seedat, S., Scott, K. M., Angermeyer, M. C., Berglund, P., Bromet, E. J., Brugha, T. S., ... Kessler, R. C. (2009). Cross-national associations between gender and mental disorders in the World Health Organization World Mental Health Surveys. *Archives of General Psychiatry, 66*(7), 785–795.

Segall, M. H. (1979). *Cross-cultural psychology: Human behavior in global perspective.* Pacific Grove, CA: Brooks/Cole.

Segall, M. H. (1984). More than we need to know about culture, but are afraid to ask. *Journal of Cross-Cultural Psychology, 15*(2), 153–162.

Segall, M. H., Campbell, D. T., & Hersokovits, J. (1963). Cultural differences in the perception of geometric illusions. *Science, 193,* 769–771.

Segall, M. H., Campbell, D. T., & Hersokovits, J. (1966). *The influence of culture on visual perception.* Indianapolis: Bobbs-Merrill.

Segall, M. H., Dasen, P. R., Berry, J. W., & Poortinga, Y. H. (1990). *Human behavior in global perspective: An introduction to cross-cultural psychology.* New York: Pergamon Press.

Sellers, R. M., & Shelton, J. N. (2003). The role of racial identity in perceived racial discrimination. *Journal of Personality and Social Psychology, 84,* 1079–1092.

Selmer, J. (1999). Culture shock in China? Adjustment pattern of western expatriate business managers. *International Business Review, 8,* 515–534.

Shakin, M., Shakin, D., & Sternglanz, S. H. (1985). Infant clothing: Sex labeling for strangers. *Sex Roles, 12*(9–10), 955–964.

Shand, N., & Kosawa, Y. (1985). Culture transmission: Caudill's model and alternative hypotheses. *American Anthropologist, 87*(4), 862–871.

Shane, S., Venkataraman, S., & MacMillan, I. (1995). Cultural differences in innovation championing strategies. *Journal of Management, 21*(5), 931–952.

Sheldon, K. M. (2004). *The psychology of optimal being: An integrated, multi-level perspective.* Mahwah, NJ: Erlbaum.

Shepperd, J., & Wright, R. (1989). Individual contributions to a collective effort: An incentive analysis. *Personality and Social Psychology Bulletin, 15,* 141–149.

Shiller, V. M., Izard, C. E., & Hembree, E. A. (1986). Patterns of emotion expression during separation in the strange-situation procedure. *Developmental Psychology, 22,* 378–382.

Shim, Y., & Schwartz, R. (2007). The relationship between degree of acculturation and adjustment difficulties among Korean immigrants living in a western society. *British Journal of Guidance & Counseling, 35,* 409–426.

Shin, S.-M., Chow, C., Camacho-Gonsalves, T., Levy, R., Allen, I., & Leff, H. (2005). A meta-analytic review of racial-ethnic matching for African American and Caucasian American clients and clinicians. *Journal of Counseling Psychology, 52*(1), 45–56.

Shirakashi, S. (1985). Social loafing of Japanese students. *Hiroshima Forum for Psychology, 10,* 35–40.

Shteynberg, G., Gelfand, M. J., & Kim, K. (2009). Peering into the "magnum mysterium" of culture: The explanatory power of descriptive norms. *Journal of Cross-Cultural Psychology, 40*(1), 46–69.

Shupe, E. I., Cortina, L. M., Ramos, A., Fitzgerald, L. F., & Salisbury, J. (2002). The incidence and outcomes of sexual harassment among Hispanic and non-Hispanic white women: A comparison across levels of cultural affiliation. *Psychology of Women Quarterly, 26*, 295–308.

Shuter, R. (1976). Proxemics and tactility in Latin America. *Journal of Communication, 26*(3), 46–52.

Shuter, R. (1977). A field study of nonverbal communication in Germany, Italy, and the United States. *Communication Monographs, 44*(4), 298–305.

Shweder, R. A. (1979a). Rethinking culture and personality theory: I. A critical examination of two classical postulates. *Ethos, 7*(3), 255–278.

Shweder, R. A. (1979b). Rethinking culture and personality theory: II. A critical examination of two more classical postulates. *Ethos, 7*(4), 279–311.

Shweder, R. A. (1980). Rethinking culture and personality theory: III. From genesis and typology to hermeneutics and dynamics. *Ethos, 8*(1), 60–94.

Shweder, R. A. (1990). In defense of moral realism: Reply to Gabennesch. *Child Development, 61*, 2060–2067.

Shweder, R. A. (1991). *Thinking through cultures: Expeditions in cultural psychology.* Cambridge, MA: Harvard University Press.

Shweder, R. A. (1993). Liberalism as destiny. In B. Puka (Ed.), *Moral development: A compendium* (Vol. 4: The great justice debate: Kohlberg criticism, pp. 71–74). New York: Garland Publishing.

Shweder, R. A., & Bourne, E. J. (1984). Does the concept of the person vary cross-culturally? In R. A. Shweder & R. A. LeVine (Eds.), *Culture theory: Essays on mind, self, and emotion* (pp. 158–199). Cambridge, UK: Cambridge University Press.

Shweder, R. A., Goodnow, J. J., Hatano, G., LeVine, R. A., Markus, H. R., & Miller, P. J. (2006). The cultural psychology of development: One mind, many mentalities. In R. M. Lerner, W. Damon, R. M. Lerner, & W. Damon (Eds.), *Handbook of child psychology (6th ed.): Vol 1, Theoretical models of human development* (pp. 716–792). Hoboken, NJ: John Wiley & Sons Inc.

Shweder, R. A., Mahapatra, M., & Miller, J. G. (1987). Culture and moral development. In J. Kagan & S. Lamb (Eds.), *The emergence of morality in young children* (pp. 1–83). Chicago, IL: University of Chicago Press.

Shweder, R. A., Minow, M., & Markus, H. R. (Eds.). (2002). *Engaging cultural differences: The multicultural challenge in liberal democracies.* New York: Russell Sage Foundation.

Shweder, R. A., Much, N. C., Mahapatra, M., & Park, L. (1997). The "big three" of morality (autonomy, community, divinity), and the "big three" explanations of suffering. In A. Brandt & P. Rozin (Eds.), *Morality and health.* New York: Routledge.

Sidanius, J., Henry, P. J., Pratto, F., & Levin, S. (2004). Arab attributions for the attack on America: The case of Lebanese Subelites. *Journal of Cross-Cultural Psychology, 35*, 403–416.

Siddiqi, A., Zuberi, D., & Nguyen, Q. C. (2009). The role of health insurance in explaining immigrant versus non-immigrant disparities in access to health care: Comparing the United States to Canada. *Social Science & Medicine, 69*(10), 1452–1459.

Silk, J. B., Brosnan, S. F., Vonk, J., Henrich, J., Povinelli, D. J., Richardson, A. S., ... Schapiro, Steven J. (2005). Chimpanzees are indifferent to the welfare of unrelated group members. *Nature, 437*, 1357–1359.

Simich, L., Beiser, M., Stewart, M., & Mwakarimba, E. (2005). Providing social support for immigrants and refugees in Canada: Challenges and directions. *Journal of Immigrant Health, 7*(4), 259–268.

Simmons, C. H., vom Kolike, A., & Shimizu, H. (1986). Attitudes toward romantic love among American, German and Japanese students. *Journal of Social Psychology, 126*, 327–336.

Simon-Thomas, E. R., Keltner, D., Sauter, D. A., Sinicropi-Yao, L., & Abramson, A. (2009). The voice conveys specific emotions: Evidence from vocal burst displays. *Emotion, 9*(6), 838–846.

Simonton, D. K. (1996). Presidents' wives and First Ladies: On achieving eminence within a traditional gender role. *Sex Roles, 35*(5–6), 309–336.

Singelis, T. M. (1994). The measurement of independent and interdependent self-construals. *Personality and Social Psychology Bulletin, 20*(5), 580–591.

Singelis, T. M. (2000). Some thoughts on the future of cross-cultural social psychology. *Journal of Cross-Cultural Psychology, 31*(1), 76–91.

Singelis, T. M., Bond, M., Sharkey, W. F., & Lai, C. S. Y. (1999). Unpackaging culture's influence on self-esteem and embarassability. *Journal of Cross-Cultural Psychology, 30*, 315–341.

Singelis, T. M., Triandis, H. C., Bhawuk, D., & Gelfand, M. J. (1995). Horizontal and vertical dimensions of individualism and collectivism: A theoretical and measurement refinement. *Cross-Cultural Research, 29*(3), 241–275.

Singh-Manoux, A., Marmot, M. G., & Adler, N. E. (2005). Does subjective social status predict health and change in health status better than objective status? *Psychosomatic Medicine, 67*(6), 855–861.

Sinha, D. (1993). Indigenization of psychology in India and its relevance. In U. Kim & J. W. Berry (Eds.), *Indigenous psychologies: Research and experience in cultural context* (pp. 30–43). Newbury Park, CA: Sage.

Sinha, J. B. P. (1979). The authoritative leadership: A style of effective management. *Indian Journal of Industrial Relations, 2*(3), 381–389.

Sisask, M., Värnik, A., Kõlves, K., Bertolote, J. M., Bolhari, J., Botega, N. J., ... Wasserman, D. (2010). Is religiosity a protective factor against attempted suicide: A cross-cultural case-control study. *Archives of Suicide Research, 14*(1), 44–55.

Smedley, A., & Smedley, B. D. (2005). Race as biology is fiction, racism as a social problem is real: Anthropological and historical perspectives on the social construction of race. *American Psychologist, 60*, 16–26.

Smith, J. R., Griffith, E. J., Griffith, K. H., & Steger, J. M. (1980). When is a stereotype a stereotype? *Psychological Reports, 46*, 643–651.

Smith, P. B. (1998, October). *Leadership in high power distance cultures: An event management perspective.* Paper presented at the Third Latin-American Reunion of Cross-Cultural Psychology, Toluca, Mexico.

Smith, P. B., & Bond, M. H. (1999). *Social psychology: Across cultures* (2nd ed.) Boston: Allyn & Bacon.

Smith, P. B., Dugan, S., Peterson, M. F., & Leung, K. (1998). Individualism-collectivism and the handling of disagreement: A 23-country study. *International Journal of Intercultural Relations, 22*(3), 351–367.

Smith, P. B., Dugan, S., & Trompenaars, F. (1996). National culture and the values of organizational employees. *Journal of Cross-Cultural Psychology, 27*(2), 231–264.

Smith, P. B., Dugan, S., & Trompenaars, F. (1997). Locus of control and affectivity by gender and occupational status: A 14-nation study. *Sex Roles, 36*(1–2), 51–77.

Smith, P. B., Peterson, M. F., & Misumi, J. (1994). Event management and work team effectiveness in Japan, Britain and USA. *Journal of Occupational and Organizational Psychology, 67*, 33–43.

Smith, P. B., Peterson, M., Misumi, J., & Bond, M. (1992). A cross-cultural test of the Japanese PM leadership theory. Applied Psychology: *An International Review, 41*, 5–19.

Smith, P. B., Peterson, M. F., & Schwartz, S. H. (2002). Cultural values, sources of guidance, and their relevance to managerial behavior. *Journal of Cross-Cultural Psychology, 33*(2), 188–208.

Smith, P. K., Cowie, H., Olafsson, R. F., Liefooghe, A. P. D., Almeida, A. Araki, H., … Wenxin, Z. (2002). Definitions of bullying: A comparison of terms used, and age and gender differences, in a fourteen-country international comparison. *Child Development, 73*(4), 1119–1133.

Smith, P. K., Mahdavi, J., Carvalho, M., Fisher, S., Russell, S., & Tippett, N. (2008). Cyberbullying: Its nature and impact in secondary school pupils. *Journal of Child Psychology and Psychiatry, 49*(4), 376–385.

Smith, P. K., Morita, Y., Junger-Tas, J., Olweus, D., Catalano, R., & Slee, P. (1999). *The nature of school bullying. A cross-national perspective*. London: Routledge.

Smith, S. M., Stinson, F. S., & Dawson, D. A. (2006). Race/ethnic differences in the prevalence and co-occurrence of substance use disorders and independent mood and anxiety disorders: Results from the National Epidemiologic Survey on Alcohol and Related Conditions. *Psychological Medicine, 36*(7), 987–998.

Snarey, J. R. (1985). Cross-cultural universality of social-moral development: A critical review of Kohlbergian research. *Psychological Bulletin, 97*(2), 202–232.

Snibbe, A. C., Kitayama, S., Markus, H. R., & Suzuki, T. (2003). They saw a game: A Japanese and American (football) field study. *Journal of Cross-Cultural Psychology, 34*, 581–595.

Snowden L. R. (2001). Barriers to effective mental health services for African Americans. *Mental Health Services Research, 3*, 181–187.

Snowden, L. R., Masland, M., Ma, Y., & Ciemens, E. (2006). Strategies to improve minority access to public mental health services in California: Description and preliminary evaluation. *Journal of Community Psychology, 34*(2), Special Issue: Addressing mental health disparities through culturally competent research and community-based practice, 225–235.

Snowden, L. R., Masland, M. C., Peng, C. J., Lou, C. W.-M., & Wallace, N. T. (2011). Limited English proficient Asian Americans: Threshold language policy and access to mental health treatment. *Social Science & Medicine, 72*(2), 230–237.

Snowden, L. R., & Yamada, A.-M. (2005). Cultural differences in access to care. *Annual Review of Clinical Psychology, 1*(1), 143–166.

Snowdon, C. T. (2003). Expression of emotion in nonhuman animals. In R. J. Davidson, K. Scherer, & H. H. Goldsmith (Eds.), *Handbook of affective sciences* (pp. 457–480). New York: Oxford University Press.

Song, M.-J., Smetana, J. G., & Kim, S. Y. (1987). Korean children's conceptions of moral and conventional transgressions. *Developmental Psychology, 23*, 577–582.

Sorkhabi, N. (2005). Applicability of Baumrind's parent typology to collective cultures: Analysis of cultural explanations of parent socialization effects. *International Journal of Behavioral Development, 29*(6), 552–563.

Sorokowski, P., Szmajke, A., Sorokowska, A., Bog Cunen, M., Fabrykant, M., Zarafshani, K., … Fang, T. (2011). Attractiveness of leg length: Report from 27 nations. *Journal of Cross-Cultural Psychology, 42*, 131–139.

Sow, I. (1980). *Anthropological structures of madness in Africa*. New York: International Universities Press.

Spearman, C. E. (1927). *The abilities of man*. New York: Macmillan.

Spencer-Rodgers, J., Peng, K., & Wang, L. (2010). Dialecticism and the co-occurrence of positive and negative emotions across cultures. *Journal of Cross-Cultural Psychology, 41*(1), 109–115.

Spencer-Rodgers, J., Williams, M. J., & Peng, K. (2010). Cultural differences in expectations of change and tolerance for contradiction: A decade of empirical research. *Personality and Social Psychology Review, 14*(3), 296–312.

Spiro, M. E. (1993). Is the western concept of the self 'peculiar' within the context of the world cultures? *Ethos, 21*(2), 107–153.

Sponsel, L. E. (1998). Yanomami: An arena of conflict and aggression in the Amazon. *Aggressive Behavior, 24*(2), 97–122.

Sprecher, S., & Chandak, R. (1992). Attitudes about arranged marriage and dating among men and women from India. *Journal of Sex Research, 32*, 3–15.

Stankov, L., & Lee, J. (2014). Overconfidence across world regions. *Journal of Cross-Cultural Psychology, 45*, 821–837.

Stauffacher, K., & DeHart, G. B. (2006). Crossing social contexts: Relational aggression between siblings and friends during early and middle childhood. *Journal of Applied Developmental Psychology, 27*(3), 228–240.

Steele, C. (1998). How stereotypes shape intellectual identity and performance. *American Psychologist, 52*(6), 613–629.

Steele, C., & Aronson, J. (1995). Stereotype threat and the intellectual test performance of African Americans. *Journal of Personality and Social Psychology, 69*, 797–811.

Steinberg, L., Dornbusch, S. M., & Brown, B. B. (1992). Ethnic differences in adolescent achievement: An ecological perspective. *American Psychologist, 47*, 723–729.

Steinberg, L., Lamborn, S., Dornbusch, S., & Darling, N. (1992). Impact of parenting practices on adolescent achievement: Authoritative parenting, school involvement, and encouragement to succeed. *Child Development, 63*, 1266–1281.

Steptoe, A., Dockray, S., & Wardle, J. (2009). Positive affect and psychobiological processes relevant to health. *Journal of Personality, 77*(6), 1747–1775.

Steptoe, A., Hamer, M., & Chida, Y. (2007). The effects of acute psychological stress on circulating inflammatory factors in humans: A review and meta-analysis. *Brain, Behavior, and Immunity, 21*(7), 901–912.

Steptoe, A., & Kivimäki, M. (2013). Stress and cardiovascular disease: An update on current knowledge. *Annual Review of Public Health 34,* 337–354.

Steptoe, A., Sutcliffe, I., Allen, B., & Coombes, C. (1991). Satisfaction with communication, medical knowledge, and coping styles in patients with metastatic cancer. *Social Science and Medicine, 32*(6), 627–632.

Steptoe, A., & Wardle, J. (Eds.). (1994). *Psychosocial processes and health: A reader.* Cambridge: Cambridge University Press.

Sternberg, R. J. (1986). *Intelligence applied: Understanding and increasing your intellectual skills.* New York: Harcourt Brace Jovanovich.

Sternberg, R. J. (1988). Triangulating love. In R. J. Sternberg & M. L. Barnes (Eds.), *The psychology of love* (pp. 119–138). New Haven, CT: Yale University Press.

Sternberg, R. J. (2004). Culture and intelligence. *American Psychologist, 59*(5), 325–338.

Sternberg, R. J., & Lubart, T. I. (1995). *Defying the crowd: Cultivating creativity in a culture of conformity.* New York: Free Press.

Sternberg, R. J., & Lubart, T. I. (1999). The concept of creativity: Prospects and paradigms. In R. J. Sternberg (Ed.), *Handbook of creativity* (pp. 3–15). New York: Cambridge University Press.

Stevenson, H. W., & Zusho, A. (2002). Adolescence in China and Japan: Adapting to a changing environment. In B. Brown, R. Larson, & T. Saraswathi (Eds.), *The world's youth: Adolescence in eight regions of the globe* (pp. 141–170). New York: Cambridge University Press.

Stewart, V. (1973). Tests of the "carpentered world" hypothesis by race and environment in American and Zambia. *International Journal of Psychology, 8,* 83–94.

Stice, E. (2002). Risk and maintenance factors for eating pathology: A meta-analytic review. *Psychological Bulletin, 128,* 825–848.

Stigler, J. W., & Baranes, R. (1988). Culture and mathematics learning. In E. Rothkpof (Ed.), *Review of research in education* (Vol. 15, pp. 253–306). Washington, DC: American Educational Research Association.

Stiles, D. A., Gibbons, J. L., & Schnellman, J. D. (1990). The smiling sunbather and the chivalrous football player: Young adolescents' images of the ideal women and men. *Journal of Early Adolescence, 7,* 411–427.

Stone, L. (1990). *Road to divorce: England 1530–1987.* New York: Oxford University Press.

Streltzer, J. (1997). Pain. In W. Tseng & J. Streltzer (Eds.), *Culture and psychopathology: A guide to clinical assessment* (pp. 87–100). New York: Brunner/Mazel.

Strodtbeck, F. L. (1964). Considerations of meta-method in cross-cultural studies. *American Anthropologist, 66*(3), 223–229.

Stryker, S. (1986). Identity theory: Developments and extensions. In K. Tardley & T. Honess (Eds.), *Self and identity* (pp. 89–107). New York: Wiley.

Suárez-Orozco, C., Rhodes, J., & Milburn, M. (2009). Unraveling the immigrant paradox: Academic engagement and disengagement among recently arrived immigrant youth. *Youth & Society, 41*(2), 151–185.

Substance Abuse and Mental Health Services Administration. (2003). *Summary of findings from the 2000 National Household Survey on Drug Abuse* (DHHS Publication No. SMA 01–3549, NHSDA Series H-13). Rockville, MD: Author.

Suchman, R. G. (1966). Cultural differences in children's color and form perception. *Journal of Social Psychology, 70,* 3–10.

Sue, D. (1998). The interplay of sociocultural factors in the psychological development of Asians in America. In D. R. Atkinson & G. Morten (Eds.), *Counseling American minorities* (5th ed., pp. 205–213). New York: McGraw-Hill.

Sue, D. W. (2003). *Multicultural social work practice.* Hoboken, NJ: John Wiley and Sons.

Sue, D. W., Capodilupo, C. M., Torino, G. C., Bucceri, J. M., Holder, A. M. B., Nadal, K. L., & Esquilin, M. (2007). Racial microaggressions in everyday life: Implications for clinical practice. *American Psychologist, 62*(4), 271–286.

Sue, D. W., Lin, A. I., Torino, G. C., Capodilupo, C. M., & Rivera, D. P. (2009). Racial microaggressions and difficult dialogues on race in the classroom. *Cultural Diversity & Ethnic Minority Psychology, 15*(2), 183–190.

Sue, D. W., & Sue, D. (2003). *Counseling the culturally diverse* (4th ed.). New York: John Wiley and Sons.

Sue, D. W., & Sue, D. (2007). *Counseling the culturally diverse: Theory and practice (5th ed.).* New York: John Wiley & Sons.

Sue, D. W., & Sue, D. (2013). *Counseling the culturally diverse: Theory and practice* (6th ed.). Hoboken, NJ: John Wiley & Sons.

Sue, S. (1977). Community mental health services to minority groups: Some optimism, some pessimism. *American Psychologist, 32,* 616–624.

Sue, S., Fujino, D. C., Hu, L. T., Takeuchi, D. T., & Zane, N. W. S. (1991). Community mental health services for ethnic minority groups: A test of the cultural responsiveness hypothesis. *Journal of Counseling Psychology, 59,* 533–540.

Sue, S., Zane, N., Hall, G. C. N., & Berger, L. K. (2009). The case for cultural competency in psychotherapeutic interventions. *Annual Review of Psychology, 60,* 525–548.

Sue, S., Zane, N., & Young, K. (1994). Research on psychotherapy with culturally diverse populations. In A. E. Bergin & S. L. Garfield (Eds.), *Handbook of psychotherapy and behavior change* (4th ed., pp. 428–466). New York: Wiley.

Suhail, K., & Nisa, Z. (2002). Prevalence of eating disorders in Pakistan: Relationship with depression and body shape. *Eating and Weight Disorders, 7*(2), 131–138.

Sui, J., Zhu, Y., & Chiu, C.-Y. (2007). Bicultural mind, self-construal, and self- and mother-reference effects: Consequences of cultural priming on recognition memory. *Journal of Experimental Social Psychology, 43*(5), 818–824.

Super, C. M., & Harkness, S. (1986). The developmental niche: A conceptualization at the interface of child and culture. *International Journal of Behavioral Development, 9,* 545–569.

Super, C. M., & Harkness, S. (1994). The developmental niche. In W. Lonner & R. Malpass (Eds.), *Psychology and culture* (pp. 95–99). Boston: Allyn & Bacon.

Super, C. M., & Harkness, S. (2002). Culture structures the environment for development. *Human Development, 45*(4), 270–274.

Supple, A. J., Ghazarian, S. R., Peterson, G. W., & Bush, K. R. (2009). Assessing the cross-cultural validity of a parental autonomy granting measure: Comparing adolescents in the United States, China, Mexico, and India. *Journal of Cross-Cultural Psychology, 40*(5), 816–833

Sussman, L. K., Robins, L. N., & Earls, F. (1987). Treatment seeking for depression by black and white Americans. *Social Science and Medicine, 24*, 187–196.

Sussman, N. M., & Rosenfeld, H. M. (1978). Touch, justification, and sex: Influences on the aversiveness of spatial violations. *Journal of Social Psychology, 106*, 215–225.

Sussman, N. M., & Rosenfeld, H. M. (1982). Influence of culture, language, and sex on conversational distance. *Journal of Personality and Social Psychology, 42*(1), 66–74.

Swami, V., Frederick, D. A., Aavik, T., Alcalay, L., Allik, J., Anderson, D., … Zivcic-Becirevic, I. (2010). The attractive female body weight and female body dissatisfaction in 26 countries across 10 world regions: Results of the international body project I. *Personality and Social Psychology Bulletin, 36*(3), 309–325.

Szapocznik, J., Amaro, H., Gonzalez, G., Schwartz, S. J., Castro, F. G., & Bernal, G., Mora, J. & Navarro, A. (2003). Drug abuse treatment for Hispanics. In H. Amaro & D. E. Cortés (Eds.), *National strategic plan on Hispanic drug abuse research: From the molecule to the community* (pp. 91–117). Boston: National Hispanic Science Network on Drug Abuse, Northeastern University Institute on Urban Health Research.

Ta, V. M., Juon, H.-S., Gielen, A. C., Steinwachs, D., & Duggan, A. (2008). Disparities in use of mental health and substance abuse services by Asian and Native Hawaiian/other Pacific Islander women. *The Journal of Behavioral Health Services & Research, 35*(1), 20–36.

Tadmor, C. T., Galinsky, A. D., & Maddux, W. W. (2012). Getting the most out of living abroad: Biculturalism and integrative complexity as key drivers of creative and professional success. *Journal of Personality and Social Psychology, 103*, 520–542. doi: 10.1037/a0029360

Tadmor, C. T., Hong, Y.-Y., Chao, M. M., Wiruchnipawan, F., & Wang, W. (2012). Multicultural experiences reduce intergroup bias through epistemic unfreezing. *Journal of Personality and Social Psychology, 103*, 750–772. doi: 10.1037/a0029719

Tafarodi, R. W., & Swann, W. B., Jr. (1996). Individualism-collectivism and global self-esteem: Evidence for a cultural trade-off. *Journal of Cross-Cultural Psychology, 27*(6), 651–672.

Tajfel, H. (1982). Social psychology of intergroup relations. *Annual Review of Psychology, 33*, 1–39.

Tajfel, H., & Turner, J. C. (1986). The social identity theory of intergroup behavior. In S. Worchel & W. G. Austin (Eds.), *Psychology of intergroup relationships* (pp. 7–24). Chicago: Nelson-Hall.

Takahashi, K. (1990). Are the key assumptions of the 'Strange Situation' procedure universal? A view from Japanese research. *Human Development, 33*(1), 23–30.

Takahashi, K., & Takeuchi, K. (2006). Japan. In J. J. Arnett, R. Ahmed, B. Nsamenang, T. S. Saraswathi, & R. K. Silbereisen (Eds.), *Routledge International Encyclopedia of Adolescence.* New York: Routledge.

Takaki, R. (1998). *Strangers from a different shore: A history of Asian Americans* (rev. ed.). Boston: Back Bay Books.

Takano, Y. (1989). Methodological problems in cross-cultural studies of linguist relativity. *Cognition, 31*, 141–162.

Takano, Y., & Noda, A. (1993). A temporary decline of thinking ability during foreign language processing. *Journal of Cross-Cultural Psychology, 24*(4), 445–462.

Takano, Y., & Noda, A. (1995). Interlanguage dissimilarity enhances the decline of thinking ability during foreign language processing. *Language Learning, 45*(40), 657–681.

Takano, Y., & Sogon, S. (2008). Are Japanese more collectivistic than Americans? Examining conformity in in-groups and the reference-group effect. *Journal of Cross-Cultural Psychology, 39*(3), 237–250.

Takeuchi, D. T., Zane, N., Hong, S., Chae, D. H., Gong, F., Gee, G. C., Walton, E., Sue, S., & Alegría, M. (2007). Immigration-related factors and mental disorders among Asian Americans. *American Journal of Public Health, 97*(1), 84–90.

Talge, N., Neal, C., & Glover, V. (2007). Antenatal maternal stress and long-term effects on child neurodevelopment: How and why? The Early Stress, Translational Research and Prevention Science Network: Fetal and neonatal experience on child and adolescent mental health. *Journal of Child Psychology and Psychiatry, 48*(3–4), 245–261.

Talhelm, T., Zhang, X., Oishi, S., Shimin, C., Duan, D., Lan, X., & KItayama, S. (2014). Large-scale psychological differences within China explained by rice versus wheat agriculture. *Science, 344*, 603–608.

Tareen, A., Hodes, M., & Rangel, L. (2005). Non-fat-phobic anorexia nervosa in British South Asian adolescents. *International Journal of Eating Disorders, 37*(2), 161–165.

Tedlock, B. (1992). The role of dreams and visionary narratives in Mayan cultural survival. *Ethos, 20*(4), 453–476.

Terracciano, A., Abdel-Khalek, A. M., Adam, N., Adamovova, L., Ahn, C.-K., Ahn, H.-N., … McCrae, Robert R. (2005). National character does not reflect mean personality trait levels in 49 cultures. *Science, 310*, 96–100.

Teti, D. (2002). Retrospect and prospect in the psychological study of sibling relationships. In J. McHale & W. Grolmck (Eds.), *Retrospect and prospect in the psychological study of families* (pp. 193–224). Mahwah, NJ: Erlbaum.

Tetsuro, T, Murakami, K, Washizuka, T, Ikuta, N., Nishizono, A., & Miyake, Y. (2005). Application of the eating disorder examination (EDE) to Japanese patients with eating disorders: Reliability and validity of the Japanese version of EDE. *Japan Journal of Psychosomatic Medicine, 10*, 785–792.

Thomas, A., & Chess, S. (1977). *Temperament and development.* New York: Brunner/Mazel.

Thompson, J. (1941). Development of facial expression of emotion in blind and seeing children. *Archives of Psychology, 37*, 1–47.

Thompson, M. A., & Gray, J. J. (1995). Development and validation of a new body-image assessment scale. *Journal of Personality Assessment, 64*(2), 258–269.

Thomsen, L., Frankenhuis, W. E., Ingold-Smith, M., & Carey, S. (2011). Big and mighty: Preverbal infants mentally represent social dominance. *Science, 331*(28), 477–480.

Thurstone, L. L. (1938). *Primary mental abilities.* Chicago: University of Chicago Press.

Timimi, S. (2004). A critique of the international consensus statement on ADHD. *Clinical Child and Family Psychology Review, 7*(1), 59–63.

Ting-Toomey, S. (1991). Intimacy expressions in three cultures: France, Japan, and the United States. *International Journal of Intercultural Relations, 15,* 29–46.

Ting-Toomey, S. (Ed.). (1994). *The challenge of facework.* New York: SUNY Press.

Ting-Toomey, S. (1996). Managing intercultural conflicts effectively. In L. A. Samovar & R. E. Porter (Eds.), *Intercultural communication: A reader* (8th ed., pp. 392–404). Belmont, CA: Wadsworth.

Todorov, A., Mandisodza, A. N., Goren, A., & Hall, C. C. (2005). Inferences of competence from faces predict election outcomes. *Science, 308*(10), 1623–1626.

Tolson, T. F., & Wilson, M. N. (1990). The impact of two- and three-generational Black family structure on perceived family climate. *Child Development, 61*(2), 416–428.

Tomasello, M. (1999). *The cultural originals of human cognition.* Cambridge, MA: Harvard University Press.

Tomasello, M., & Herrmann, E. (2010). Ape and human cognition: What's the difference? *Current Directions in Psychological Science, 19*(1), 3–8.

Tomasello, M., Kruger, A. C., & Ratner, H. H. (1993). Cultural learning. *Behavioural and Brain Sciences, 16,* 495–552.

Tomkins, S. S. (1962). *Affect, imagery, and consciousness: Vol. 1. The positive affects.* New York: Springer.

Tomkins, S. S. (1963). *Affect, imagery, and consciousness: Vol. 2: The negative affects.* New York: Springer.

Tomkins, S. S., & McCarter, R. (1964). What and where are the primary affects? Some evidence for a theory. *Perceptual and Motor Skills, 18*(1), 119–158.

Tong, J., Shi, J., Wang, J., Zhang, H., Zhang, S. F., Wu, X. Y., & Hsu, L. K. G. (2011). Validity and reliability of the Chinese language version of the Eating Disorder Examination (CEDE) in Mainland China: Implications for the identity and nosology of the eating disorders. *International Journal of Eating Disorders, 44*(1), 76–80.

Tooby, J., & Cosmides, L. (2008). The evolutionary psychology of the emotions and their relationship to internal regulatory variables. In M. Lewis, J. M. Haviland-Jones, & L. F. ldman Barrett (Eds.), *Handbook of Emotions* (3rd ed., pp. 114–137). New York: The Guilford Press.

Torelli, C. J., & Shavitt, S. (2010). Culture and concepts of power. *Journal of Personality and Social Psychology, 99*(4), 703–723.

Torres, K. (2009). 'Culture shock': Black students account for their distinctiveness at an elite college. *Ethnic and Racial Studies, 32,* 883–905.

Trafimow, D., Silverman, E. S., Fan, R. M.-T., & Law, J. S. F. (1997). The effects of language and priming on the relative accessibility of the private self and collective self. *Journal of Cross-Cultural Psychology, 28*(1), 107–123.

Trafimow, D., Triandis, H. C., & Goto, S. G. (1991). Some tests of the distinction between the private self and the collective self. *Journal of Personality and Social Psychology, 60,* 649–655.

Trends in the International Mathematics and Science Study. (2007). Retrieved http://www.iea.nl/timss_2007.html

Triandis, H. C., Bontempo, R., Betancourt, H., Bond, M., Leung, K., Brenes, A., ... de Montonollm, G. (1986). The measurement aspects of individualism and collectivism across cultures. *Australian Journal of Psychology, 38,* 257–267.

Triandis, H. C., Bontempo, R., Villareal, M. J., Asai, M., & Lucca, N. (1988). Individualism and collectivism: Cross-cultural perspectives on self-ingroup relationships. *Journal of Personality & Social Psychology, 4,* 323–338.

Triandis, H. C., & Lambert, W. W. (1958). A restatement and test of Schlosberg's theory of emotion with two kinds of subjects from Greece. *Journal of Abnormal and Social Psychology, 56,* 321–328.

Triandis, H. C., Leung, K., Villareal, M. J., & Clack, F. (1985). Allocentric versus idiocentric tendencies: Convergent and discriminate validation. *Journal of Research in Personality, 19,* 395–415.

Triandis, H. C., McCusker, C., & Hui, C. H. (1990). Multimethod probes of individualism and collectivism. *Journal of Personality and Social Psychology, 59,* 1006–1020.

Triandis, H. C. (1972). *The analysis of subjective culture.* New York: Wiley.

Triandis, H. C. (1989). The self and social behavior in differing cultural contexts. *Psychological Review, 96,* 506–520.

Triandis, H. C. (1994). *Culture and social behavior.* New York: McGraw-Hill.

Triandis, H. C. (1995). *New directions in social psychology: Individualism and collectivism.* Boulder, CO: Westview Press.

Triandis, H. C. (1996). The psychologist measurement of cultural syndromes. *American Psychologist, 52*(4), 407–415.

Triandis, H. C. (2001). Individualism and collectivism: Past, present, and future. In D. Matsumoto (Ed.), *Handbook of culture and psychology* (pp. 35–50). New York: Oxford University Press.

Triandis, H. C., Marin, G., Lisansky, J., & Betancourt, H. (1984). Simpatia as a cultural script of Hispanics. *Journal of Personality and Social Psychology, 47,* 1363–1375.

Trickett, E. (2009). Community psychology: Individuals and interventions in community context. *Annual Review of Psychology, 60,* 395–419.

Tripp, G., & Wickens, J. R. (2009). Neurobiology of ADHD. *Neuropharmacology, 57*(7–8), 579–589.

Trompenaars, F. (1993). *Riding the waves of culture.* London: Brealey.

Tropp, L. R., & Pettigrew, T. F. (2005). Relationships between intergroup contact and prejudice among minority and majority status groups. *Psychological Science, 16*(12), 951–957.

True, M., Pisani, L., & Oumar, F. (2001). Infant-mother attachment among the Dogon of Mali. *Child Development, 72*(5), 1451–1466.

Tsai, J. L. (2007). Ideal affect: Cultural causes and behavioral consequences. Perspectives on *Psychological Science, 2*(3), 242–259.

Tsai, J. L., Knutson, B., & Fung, H. H. (2006). Cultural variation in affect valuation. *Journal of Personality and Social Psychology, 90*(2), 288–307.

Tsai, J. L., & Levenson, R. W. (1997). Cultural influences of emotional responding: Chinese American and European American dating couples during interpersonal conflict. *Journal of Cross-Cultural Psychology, 28,* 600–625.

Tseng, W., McDonnell, D. D., Takahashi, L., Ho, W., Lee, C., & Wong, S. (2010). *Ethnic health assessment for Asian Americans, Native Hawaiians, and Pacific Islanders in California.* San Francisco, CA: The California Endowment.

Tucker, C. J., Updegraff, K. A., McHale, S. M., & Crouter, A. C. (1999). Older siblings as socializes of younger siblings' empathy. *Journal of Early Adolescence, 19*(2), Special Issue: Prosocial and moral development in early adolescence, Part II, 176–198.

Tulviste, P. (1978). On the origins of the theoretic syllogistic reasoning in culture and in the child. *Acta et commentationes Universitatis Tortuensis, 4*, 3–22.

Turiel, E. (1983). *The development of social knowledge: Morality and convention.* Cambridge: Cambridge University Press.

Turiel, E. (1998). The development of morality. In W. Damon (Series Ed.) & N. Eisenberg (Vol. Ed.), Handbook of child psychology: Vol. 3. *Social, emotional, and personality development* (5th ed., pp. 863–932). New York: Wiley.

Turiel, E., Killen, M., & Helwig, C. C. (1987). Morality: Its structure, functions, and vagaries. In J. Kagan & S. Lamb (Eds.), *The emergence of morality in young children* (pp. 155–243). Chicago, IL: University of Chicago Press.

Twenge, J. M., Campbell, W. K., & Gentile, B. (2012). Changes in pronoun use in American books and the rise of individualism, 1960–2008. *Journal of Cross-Cultural Psychology, 44*, 406–415. doi: 10.1177/0022022112455100

Tylor, E. B. (1865). *Researches into the early history of mankind and development of civilisation.* London: John Murray.

U.S. Census Bureau. (2013). Income and poverty in the United States: 2013. Retrieved http://www.census.gov/content/dam/Census/library/publications/2014/demo/p60-249.pdf

U.S. Census Bureau. (2014). *State and County QuickFacts.* Retrieved http://quickfacts.census.gov/qfd/states/00000.html

U.S. Department of Health and Human Services. (2001). *Mental health: Culture, race, and ethnicity—A supplement to mental health: A report of the surgeon general.* Rockville, MD: U.S. Department of Health and Human Services, Substance Abuse and Mental Health Services Administration, Center for Mental Health Services.

Ueno, A., Ueno, Y., & Tomonaga, M. (2004). Facial responses to four basic tastes in newborn rhesus macaques (Macaca mulatta) and chimpanzees (pan troglodytes). *Behavioural Brain Research, 154*, 261–271.

Uleman, J. S., Rhee, E., Bardoliwalla, N., Semin, G., & Toyama, M. (2000). The relational self: Closeness to ingroups depends on who they are, culture, and the type of closeness. *Asian Journal of Social Psychology, 3*, 1–17.

United Nations, Department of Economic and Social Affairs, Population Division. (2009). World Population Prospects: The 2008 Revision, Highlights, Working Paper No. ESA/P/WP.210.

United Nations High Commissioner for Refugee. (2015). Worldwide displacement hits all-time high as war and persecution increase. Retrieved http://www.unhcr.org/558193896.html

Updegraff, J. A., Silver, R. C., & Holman, E. A. (2008). Searching for and finding meaning in collective trauma: Results from a national longitudinal study of the 9/11 terrorist attacks. *Journal of Personality and Social Psychology, 95*(3), 702–722.

Urton, G., & Brezine, C. J. (2005). Khipu accounting in ancient Peru. *Science, 309*, 1065–1067.

Usborne, E., & Taylor, D. M. (2010). The role of cultural identity, clarity for self-concept clarity, self-esteem, and subjective well-being. *Personality and Social Psychology Bulletin, 36*, 883–897.

Valenzuela, A., Mellers, B., & Strebel, J. (2009). Pleasurable surprises: A cross-cultural study of consumer responses to unexpected incentives. *Journal of Consumer Research, 36*(5), 792–805.

van de Vliert, E. (2003). Thermoclimate, culture, and poverty as country-level roots of workers' wages. *Journal of International Business Studies, 34*, 40–52.

van de Vliert, E. (2006). Autocratic leadership around the globe: Do climate and wealth drive leadership culture? *Journal of Cross-Cultural Psychology, 37*, 42–59.

van de Vliert, E. (2009). *Climate, affluence, and culture.* New York: Cambridge University Press.

Van de Vliert, E. (2011). Climato-economic origins of variation in ingroup-favoritism. *Journal of Cross-Cultural Psychology, 42*, 494–515. doi: 10.1177/0022022110381120.

van de Vliert, E., Huang, X., & Levine, R. V. (2004). National wealth and thermal climate as predictors of motives for volunteer work. *Journal of Cross-Cultural Psychology, 35*, 62–73.

van de Vliert, E., Huang, X., & Parker, P. M. (2004). Do colder and hotter climates make richer societies more but poorer societies less happy and altruistic? *Journal of Environmental Psychology, 24*, 17–30.

van de Vliert, E., Schwartz, S. H., Huismans, S. E., Hofstede, G. H., & Daan, S. (1999). Temperature, cultural masculinity, and domestic political violence: A cross-national study. *Journal of Cross-Cultural Psychology, 30*, 291–314.

van de Vliert, E., & Smith, P. B. (2004). Leader reliance on subordinates across nations that differ in development and climate. *The Leadership Quarterly, 15*, 381–403.

van den Bos, K., Brockner, J., Stein, J., Steiner, D. D., Van Yperen, N. W., & Dekker, D. M. (2010). The psychology of voice and performance capabilities in masculine and feminine cultures and contexts. *Journal of Personality and Social Psychology, 99*(4), 638–648

van Herk, H., Poortinga, Y. H., & Verhallen, T. M. M. (2004). Response styles in rating scales: Evidence of methods bias in data from six EU countries. *Journal of Cross-Cultural Psychology, 35*, 346–360.

Van Hoof, J. A. R. A. M. (1972). A comparative approach to the phylogeny of laughing and smiling. In R. A. Hinde (Ed.), *Nonverbal communication* (pp. 209–241). Cambridge, England: Cambridge University Press.

van IJzendoorn, M. H., & Sagi, A. (1999). Cross-cultural patterns of attachment: Universal and contextual dimensions. In J. Cassidy & P. R. Shaver (Eds.), *Handbook of attachment: Theory, research, and clinical applications* (pp. 713–734). New York: Guilford Press.

van Ommeren, M., Sharma, B., Sharma, G. K., Komproe, K., Cardena, E., & de Jong, J. T. V. N. (2002). The relationship between somatic and PTSD symptoms among Bhutanese refugee torture survivors: Examination of comorbidity with anxiety and depression. *Journal of Traumatic Stress, 15*(5), 415–421.

van Os, J., & Kapur, S. (2009). Schizophrenia. *The Lancet, 374*(9690), 635–645.

van Os, J., Rutten, B. P. F., & Poulton, R. (2008). Gene-environmental interactions in schizophrenia: Review of epidemiological findings and future directions. *Schizophrenia Bulletin, 34*(6), 1066–1082.

Van Oudenhoven, J. P., Selenko, E., & Otten, S. (2009). Effects of country size and language similarity on international attitudes: A six-nation study. *International Journal of Psychology, 45*(1), 48–55

Vandello, J. A., & Cohen, D. (2003). Male honor and female fidelity: Implicit cultural scripts that perpetuate domestic violence. *Journal of Personality and Social Psychology, 84*, 997–1010.

Vandello, J. A., Cohen, D., Grandon, R., & Franiuk, R. (2009). Stand by your man: Indirect prescriptions for honorable violence and feminine loyalty in Canada, Chile, and the United States. *Journal of Cross-Cultural Psychology, 40*(1), 81–104.

Vandello, J. A., Cohen, D., & Ransom, S. (2008). U.S. Southern and Northern differences in perceptions of norms about aggression. Journal of *Cross-Cultural Psychology, 39*(2), 162–177.

VandenBerghe. P. L. (1981). *The ethnic phenomenon*. New York: Elsevier.

Varnum, M., Grossman, I., Kitayama, S., & Nisbett, R. E. (2010). The origin of cultural differences in cognition: The social orientation hypothesis. *Current Directions in Psychological Science, 19*(1), 9–13.

Verkuyten, M., & Hagendoorn, L. (1998). Prejudice and self-categorization: The variable role of authoritarianism and in-group stereotypes. Personality and *Social Psychology Bulletin, 24*(1), 99–110.

Verkuyten, M., & Pouliasi, K. (2002). Biculturalism among older children: Cultural frame switching, attributions, self-identification, and attitudes. *Journal of Cross-Cultural Psychology, 33*(6), 596–609.

Vinacke, W. E. (1949). The judgment of facial expressions by three national-racial groups in Hawaii: I. Caucasian faces. *Journal of Personality, 17*, 407–429.

Vinacke, W. E., & Fong, R. W. (1955). The judgment of facial expressions by three national-racial groups in Hawaii: II. Oriental faces. *Journal of Social Psychology, 41*, 184–195.

Volbrecht, M., & Goldsmith, H. (2010). Early temperamental and family

predictors of shyness and anxiety. *Developmental Psychology, 46*(5), 1192–1205.

Vontress, C. E. (1991). Traditional healing in Africa: Implications for cross-cultural counseling. *Counseling and Development, 70*, 242–249.

Vygotsky, L. S. (1978). *Mind in society*. Boston: Harvard College.

Wagner, D. A. (1977). Ontogeny of the Ponzo illusion: Effects of age, schooling and environment. *International Journal of Psychology, 12*, 161–176.

Wagner, D. A. (1980). Culture and memory development. In H. C. Triandis & A. Heron (Eds.), *Handbook of cross-cultural psychology: Vol. 4. Developmental psychology* (pp. 187–232). Boston: Allyn & Bacon.

Wagner, J. A., III. (1995). Studies of individualism-collectivism: Effects on cooperation in groups. *Academy of Management Journal, 38*(1), 152–172.

Walder, D. J., Faraone, S. V., Glatt, S. J., Tsuang, M. T., & Seidman, L. J. (2014). Genetic liability, prenatal health, stress and family environment: Risk factors in the Harvard adolescent family high risk for Schizophrenia study. *Schizophrenia Research, 157*(1–3), 142–148. doi: 10.1016/j.schres.2014.04.015

Walker, L. J. (1984). Sex differences in the development of moral reasoning: A critical review. Child Development, 55, 677–691.

Walker, L. J. (2006). Gender and morality. In M. Killen & J. G. Smetana (Eds.), *Handbook of moral development* (pp. 93–115). Mahwah, NJ: Lawrence Erlbaum Associates Publishers.

Walkey, H. F., & Chung, C. R. (1996). An examination of stereotypes of Chinese and Europeans held by some New Zealand secondary school pupils. *Journal of Cross-Cultural Psychology, 27*(3), 283–292.

Walsh Escarce, M. E. (1989). A cross-cultural study of Nepalese neonatal behavior. In J. K. Nugent, B. M. Lester, & T. Brazelton (Eds.), *The cultural context of infancy, Vol 1: Biology, culture, and infant development* (pp. 65–86). Westport, CT: Ablex Publishing.

Wang, C., & Mallinckrodt, B. (2006). Acculturation, attachment, and psychosocial adjustment of Chinese/Taiwanese international students. *Journal of Counseling Psychology, 53*, 422–433.

Wang, H., Masuda, T., Ito, K., & Rashid, M. (2012). How much information? East Asian and North American cultural products and information search performance. *Personality and Social Psychology Bulletin, 38*, 1539–1551. doi: 10.1177/0146167212455828

Wang, J., Leu, J., & Shoda, Y. (2011). When the seemingly innocuous "stings": Racial microaggressions and their emotional consequences. *Personality and Social Psychology Bulletin, 37*, 1666–1678. doi: 10.1177/0146167211416130

Wang, P. S., Aguilar-Gaxiola, S., Alonso, J., Angermeyer, M. C., Borges, G., Bromet, E. J., … Wells, J. E. (2007). Worldwide use of mental health services for anxiety, mood, and substance disorders: Results from 17 countries in the WHO World Mental Health (WMH) surveys. *Lancet, 370*(9590), 841–850. doi: 10.1016/s0140-6736(07)61414-7

Wang, Q. (2001). Cultural effects on adults' earliest childhood recollection and self-description: Implications for the relation between memory and the self. *Journal of Personality and Social Psychology, 81*, 220–233.

Wang, Q. (2004). The emergence of cultural self-constructs: Autobiographical memory and self-description in European American and Chinese children. *Developmental Psychology, 40*, 3–15.

Wang, Q. (2006). Culture and the development of self-knowledge. *Current Directions in Psychological Science, 15*(4), 182–187.

Wang, Q., & Ross, M. (2005). What we remember and what we tell: The effects of culture and self-priming on memory representations and narratives. *Memory, 13*, 594–606.

Wang, Q., & Ross, M. (2007). Culture and memory. In S. Kitayama & D. Cohen (Eds.), *Handbook of cultural psychology* (pp. 645–667). New York: Guilford.

Wang, Z.-Q., Yang, S.-J., & Zhang, Y.-P. (2008). Use of a structured questionnaire to assess the concordance of the diagnosis of depression based on DSM-IV and the Chinese Classification of Mental Disorders (CCMD-3). *Chinese Mental Health Journal, 22*(7), 497–500.

Ward, C., Bochner, S., & Furnham, A. (2001). *The psychology of culture shock*. New York: Routledge.

Ward, C., & Chang, W. C. (1997). "Cultural fit": A new perspective on personality and sojourner adjustment. *International Journal of Intercultural Relations, 21*, 525–533.

Wasti, S. A., Bergman, M. E., Glomb, T. M., & Drasgow, F. (2000). Test of the cross-cultural generalizability of a model of sexual harassment. *Journal of Applied Psychology, 85*, 766–778.

Wasti, S. A., & Cortina, L. M. (2002). Coping in context: Sociocultural determinants of responses to sexual harassment. *Journal of Personality and Social Psychology, 83*, 394–405.

Watson, O. M. (1970). *Proxemic behavior: A cross-cultural study.* The Hague, Nederlands: Mouton.

Watson, O. M., & Graves, T. D. (1966). Quantitative research in proxemic behavior. *American Anthropologist, 68*, 971–985.

Watson-Gegeo, K. A. (1992). Thick explanation in the ethnographic study of child socialization: A longitudinal study of the problem of schooling for Kwara'ae (Solomon Islands) children. In W. A. Corsaro & P. Miller (Eds.), *New directions for child development: Interpretive approaches to children's socialization* (pp. 51–66). San Francisco: Jossey-Bass.

Watters, C. (2002). Migration and mental health care in Europe: Report of a preliminary mapping exercise. *Journal of Ethnic and Migration Studies, 28*(1), 153–172.

Way, N., Okazaki, S., Zhao, J., Kim, J. J., Chen, X., Yoshikawa, H., . . . Deng, H. (2013). Social and emotional parenting: Mothering in a changing Chinese society. *Asian American Journal of Psychology, 4*, 61–70.

Weisbuch, M., & Ambady, N. (2009). Unspoken cultural influence: Exposure to and influence of nonverbal bias. *Journal of Personality and Social Psychology, 96*(6), 1104–1119.

Weisbuch, M., Pauker, K., & Ambady, N. (2009). The subtle transmission of race bias via televised nonverbal behavior. *Science, 326*, 1711–1714.

Weisman, A. (2005). Integrating culturally based approaches with existing interventions for Hispanic/ Latino families coping with schizophrenia. *Psychotherapy: Theory, Research, Practice, Training, 42*(2), 178–197.

Weisner, T. S., & Gallimore, R. (1977). My brother's keeper: Child and sibling caretaking. *Current Anthropology, 18*(2), 169–190.

Weiss, A., King, J. E., & Enns, R. M. (2002). Subjective well-being is heritable and genetically correlated with dominance in chimpanzees (Pan troglodytes). *Journal of Personality and Social Psychology, 83*, 1141–1149.

Weiss, A., King, J. E., & Figueredo, A. J. (2000). The heritability of personality factors in chimpanzees (Pan troglodytes). *Behavior Genetics, 30*, 213–221.

Weisz, J. R., Weiss, B., Suwanlert, S., & Chaiyasit, W. (2006). Culture and youth psychopathology: Testing the syndromal sensitivity model in Thai and American adolescents. *Journal of Counseling and Clinical Psychology, 74*, 1098–1107.

Weldon, E., & Gargano, G. M. (1988). Cognitive loafing: The effects of accountability and shared responsibility on cognitive effort. *Personality and Social Psychology Bulletin, 14*, 159–171.

Weller, S. C., Baer, R. D., de Alba Garcia, J. G., & Rocha, A. L. S. (2008). Susto and nervios: Expressions for stress and depression. *Culture, Medicine and Psychiatry, 32*(3), 406–420. doi: 10.1007/s11013-008-9101-7

Wertheim, E. H., Paxton, S. J., & Blaney, S. (2009). Body image in girls. In L. Smolak & J. K. Thomspon (Eds.), *Body image, eating disorders, and obesity in youth: Assessment, prevention, and treatment,* (pp. 47–76). Washington, DC: American Psychological Association.

West, T., Shelton, J. N., & Trail, T. E. (2009). Relational anxiety in interracial interactions. *Psychological Science, 20*(3), 289–292.

Westaby, J. D. (1995). Presence of others and task performance in Japan and the United States: A laboratory investigation. *International Journal of Psychology, 30*(4), 451–460.

Wheeler, L., & Kim, Y. (1997). What is beautiful is culturally good: The physical attractiveness stereotype has different content in collectivistic cultures. *Personality and Social Psychology Bulletin, 23*(8), 795–800.

White, G. M. (1980). Conceptual universals in interpersonal language. *American Anthropologist, 88*, 759–781.

Whitehorn, J., Ayonrinde, O., & Maingay, S. (2002). Female genital mutilation: Cultural and psychological implications. *Sexual and Relationship Therapy, 17*(2), 161–173.

Whiten, A., Horner, V., & De Waal, F. B. M. (2005). Conformity to cultural norms of tool use in chimpanzees. *Nature, 437*, 737–740.

Whiting, B. B., & Edwards, C. P. (1988). *Children of different worlds.* Cambridge, MA: Harvard University Press.

Whiting, B. B., & Whiting, J. M. (1975). *Children of six cultures.* Cambridge, MA: Harvard University Press.

Widmer, E. D., Treas, J., & Newcomb, R. (1998). Attitudes toward nonmarital sex in 24 countries. *The Journal of Sex Research, 35*, 349.

Williams, J., & Best, D. (1982). *Measuring sex stereotypes: A thirty nation study.* Beverly Hills, CA: Sage.

Williams, J. E., & Best, D. L. (1990). *Measuring sex stereotypes: A multination study.* Beverly Hills, CA: Sage.

Williams, J. E., & Best, D. L. (1994). Cross-cultural views of women and men. In W. Lonner & R. Malpass (Eds.), *Psychology and culture.* Boston: Allyn & Bacon.

Williams, J. E., Satterwhite, R. C., & Best, D. L. (1999). Pancultural gender stereotypes revisited: The five factor model. *Sex Roles, 40*(7–8), 513–525.

Willinger, M., Ko, C. W., Hoffman, H. J., Kessler, R. C., & Corwin, M. J. (2003). Trends in infant bed sharing in the United States, 1993–2000: The National Infant Sleep Position study. *Archives of Pediatrics and Adolescent Medicine, 157*(1), 43–49.

Wittenbrink, B., Judd, C. M., & Park, B. (1997). Evidence for racial prejudice at the implicit level and its relationship with questionnaire measures. *Journal of Personality and Social Psychology, 72*, 262–274.

Wittgenstein, L. (1953). *Philosophical investigations.* New York: Macmillan.

Wober, M. (1974). Toward an understanding of the Kiganda concept of intelligence. In J. W. Berry & P. R. Dasen (Eds.), *Culture and cognition* (pp. 261–280). London: Methuen.

Wolf, R. M. (1965). The measurement of environments. In C. W. Harris (Ed.), *Proceedings of the 1964 Invited Conference on Testing Problems.* Princeton, NJ: Educational Testing Service.

Wolff, B. B., & Langley, S. (1968). Cultural factors and the response to pain: A review. *American Anthropologist, 70*(3), 494–501.

Wolpoff, M., & Caspari, R. (1997). *Race and human evolution: A fatal attraction.* New York: Simon & Schuster.

Wong, F., & Halgin, R. (2006). The "model minority": Bane or blessing for Asian Americans? *Journal of Multicultural Counseling and Development, 34,* 38–49.

Wong, P., Lai, C. F., Nagasawa, R., & Lin, T. (1998). Asian Americans as a model minority: Self-perceptions and perceptiosn by other racial groups. *Sociological Perspectives, 41,* 95–118.

Wood, D., & Roberts, B. W. (2006). Cross-sectional and longitudinal tests of the personality and role identity structural model (PRISM). *Journal of Personality, 74*(3), 779–809.

Wood, W., & Eagly, A. H. (2002). A cross-cultural analysis of the behavior of women and men: Implications for the origins of sex differences. *Psychological Bulletin, 128*(5), 699–727.

Woodzicka, J., & LaFrance, M. (2001). Real versus imagined gender harassment. *Journal of Social Issues, 57*(1), 15–30.

Woolley, A. W., Chabris, C. F., Pentland, A., Hashmi, N., & Malone, T. W. (2010). Evidence for a collective intelligence factor in the performance of human groups. *Science, 330,* 686–688.

World Health Organization. (1948). *Constitution of the World Health Organization.* Geneva: Author.

World Health Organization. (1973). Report of the International Pilot Study of Schizophrenia (Vol. 1). Geneva: Author.

World Health Organization. (1979). *Schizophrenia: An international follow-up study.* New York: Wiley.

World Health Organization. (1981). *Current state of diagnosis and classification in the mental health field.* Geneva: Author.

World Health Organization. (1983). *Depressive disorders in different cultures: Report of the WHO collaborative study of standardized assessment of depressive disorders.* Geneva: Author.

World Health Organization. (1991). *World health statistics quarterly.* Geneva: Author.

World Health Organization. (1992). *The ICD-10 Classification of mental and behavioural disorders.* Geneva: World Health Organization.

World Health Organization. (1997). *World Health Assembly.* Geneva: World Health Organization.

World Health Organization. (2013). *WHO traditional medicine strategy 2014–2023.* Retrieved http://apps.who.int/iris/handle/10665/92455

World Health Organization. (2014). Health for the world's adolescents: A second chance in the second decade. Retrieved http://apps.who.int/adolescent/second-decade/

World Health Organization. (2015). Depression: Fact sheet No 369. Retrieved http://www.who.int/mediacentre/factsheets/fs369/en/

Wright, D. B., Boyd, C. E., & Tredoux, C. G. (2001). A field study of own-race bias in South Africa and England. Psychology, Public Policy, and Law, 7(1), 119–133.

Wylie, R. C. (1979). *The self concept: Theory and research on selected topics* (Vol. 2). Lincoln: University of Nebraska Press.

Wynn, K. (1992). Addition and subtraction in human infants. *Nature, 358,* 749–750.

Yamagishi, T. (1986). The provision of a sanctioning system as a public good. *Journal of Personality and Social Psychology, 51,* 110–116.

Yamagishi, T. (1988). The provision of a sanctioning system in the United States and Japan. *Social Psychology Quarterly, 51,* 265–271.

Yamagishi, T., Hashimoto, H., Li, Y., & Schug, J. (2012). Stadtluft Macht Frei (city air brings freedom). *Journal of Cross-Cultural Psychology, 43,* 38–45.

Yamagishi, T., Hashimoto, H., & Schug, J. (2008). Preferences versus strategies as explanations for culture-specific behavior. *Psychological Science, 19*(6), 579–584.

Yamagishi, T., Makimura, Y., Foddy, M., Matsuda, M., Kiyonari, T., & Platow, M. J. (2005). Comparisons of Australians and Japanese on group-based cooperation. *Asian Journal of Social Psychology, 8,* 173–190.

Yamaguchi, S. (2001). Culture and control orientations. In D. Matsumoto (Ed.), *The handbook of culture and psychology* (pp. 223–243). New York: Oxford University Press.

Yamaguchi, S., Lin, C., Morio, H., & Okumura, T. (2008). Motivated expression of self-esteem across cultures. In R. M. Sorrentino & S. Yamaguchi (Eds.), *Handbook of motivation and cognition across cultures* (pp. 369–392). San Diego, CA: Elsevier.

Yamaguchi, S., Okamoto, K., & Oka, T. (1985). Effects of cofactor's presence: Social loafing and social facilitation. *Japanese Psychological Research, 27,* 215–222.

Yan, W., & Gaier, L. E. (1994). Causal attributions for college success and failure: An Asian-American comparison. *Journal of Cross-Cultural Psychology, 25,* 146–158.

Yang, J. (2013). Fake happiness: Counseling, potentiality, and psycho-politics in China. *Ethos, 41,* 292–312.

Yang, Y., Liu, X.-X., Fang, Y., & Hong, Y.-Y. (2014). Unresolved World War II animosity dampens empathy toward 2011 Japanese earthquake and tsunami. *Journal of Cross-Cultural Psychology, 45,* 171–191. doi: 10.1177/0022022113509118

Ybarra, O., & Trafimow, D. (1988). How priming the private self or collective self affects the relative weights of attitudes and subjective norms. *Personality and Social Psychology Bulletin, 24,* 362–370.

Yee, H. A., Fairchild, H. H., Weizmann, F., & Wyatt, E. G. (1993). Addressing psychology's problems with race. *American Psychologist, 48*(11), 1132–1140.

Yeh, C., Hunter, C. D., Madan-Bahel, A., Chiang, L., & Arora, A. K. (2004). Indigenous and interdependent perspectives of healing: Implications for counseling and research. *Journal of Counseling & Development, 82*(4), 410–419.

Yip, K. (2005). Chinese concepts of mental health: Cultural implications for social work practice. *International Social Work, Special Issue: China, 48*(4), 391–407.

Yodanis, C. (2005). Divorce culture and marital gender equality: A cross-national study. *Gender and Society, 19*(5), 644–659.

Yoshida, T., Matsumoto, D., Akiyama, T., Moriyoshi, N., Furuiye, A., Ishii, C., & Franklin, B. (2002). The Japanese returnee experience: Factors that affect reentry. *International Journal of Intercultural Relations, 26,* 429–445.

Yurkovich, E. E., & Lattergrass, I. (2008). Defining health and unhealthiness: Perceptions held by Native American Indians with persistent mental illness. *Mental Health, Religion & Culture, 11*(5), 437–459.

Zaccaro, S. J. (1984). The role of task attractiveness. *Personality and Social Psychology Bulletin, 10,* 99–106.

Zane, N., Sue, S., Chang, J., Huang, L., Huang, J., Lowe, S., … Lee, E. (2005). Beyond ethnic match: Effects of client-therapist cognitive match in problem perception, coping orientation, and therapy goals on treatment outcomes. *Journal of Community Psychology, 33*(5), 569–585.

Zayas, L. H. (2011). *Latinas attempting suicide: When cultures, families, and daughters collide*. New York: Oxford University Press.

Zayas, L. H., Hausmann-Stabile, C., & De Luca, S. M. (2015). Suicidal behaviors and U.S. Hispanic youth: Social, psychological, and cultural factors and challenges for interventions. In D. A. Lamis, N. J. Kaslow, D. A. Lamis, & N. J. Kaslow (Eds.), *Advancing the science of suicidal behavior: Understanding and intervention* (pp. 269–282). Hauppauge, NY: Nova Science Publishers.

Zayas, L. H., Lester, R. J., Cabassa, L. J., & Fortuna, L. R. (2005). Why do so many Latina teens attempt suicide? A conceptual model for research. *American Journal of Orthopsychiatry, 75*(2), 275–287.

Zebrowitz, L. A. (1997). *Reading faces: Window to the soul?* Boulder, CO: Westview.

Zhang, L. (2014). Bentuhua: Culturing psychotherapy in postsocialist China. *Culture, Medicine, and Psychiatry, 38,* 283–305.

Zhang, Y., Young, D., & Lee, S. (2002). Chinese Taoist cognitive psychotherapy in the treatment of generalized anxiety disorder in contemporary China. *Transcultural Psychiatry, 39*(1), 115–129.

Zhao, X., & Dawson, J. (2014). The new Chinese mental health law. *Psychiatry, Psychology and Law, 21*(5), 669–686. doi: 10.1080/13218719.2014.882248

Zhu, Y., Zhang, L., Fan, J., & Han, S. (2007). Neural basis of cultural influence on self representation. *Neuroimage, 34,* 1310–1317.

Ziller, E. C., Anderson, N. J., & Coburn, A. F. (2010). Access to rural mental health services: Service use and out-of-pocket costs. *Journal of Rural Health, 26,* 214–224.

Zimmermann, J., & Neyer, F. J. (2013). Do we become a different person when hitting the road? Personality development of sojourners. *Journal of Personality and Social Psychology, 105,* 515–530. doi: 10.1037/a0033019

Zuckerman, M. (1990). Some dubious premises in research and theory on racial differences: Scientific, social, and ethical issues. *American Psychologist, 45*(12), 1297–1303.

Zukow-Goldring, P. (1995). *Sibling interaction across cultures*. New York: Springer-Verlag.

NAME INDEX

SUBJECT INDEX

Note: Locators followed by 'f' and 't' refer to figures and tables respectively.